SYNTAX and SEMANTICS

VOLUME 12

EDITORIAL BOARD

A complete list of the contents of previous volumes appears at the end of this book.

SYNTAX and SEMANTICS

VOLUME 12
Discourse and Syntax

Edited by

Talmy Givón

Department of Linguistics
University of California, Los Angeles
Los Angeles, California
and
Ute Language Program
Southern Ute Tribe
Ignacio, Colorado

ACADEMIC PRESS

A Subsidiary of Harcourt Brace Jovanovich, Publishers

New York London Toronto Sydney San Francisco

ACADEMIC PRESS, INC.
111 Fifth Avenue, New York, New York 10003

United Kingdom Edition published by
ACADEMIC PRESS, INC. (LONDON) LTD.
24/28 Oval Road, London NW1 7DX

LIBRARY OF CONGRESS CATALOG CARD NUMBER: 72–9423

ISBN 0–12–613512–6

PRINTED IN THE UNITED STATES OF AMERICA
82   9 8 7 6 5 4 3 2

CONTENTS

PART I BETWEEN DISCOURSE AND SYNTAX

○ The Flow of Thought and the Flow of Language 159

WALLACE L. CHAFE

Communicative Goals and Strategies: Between Discourse and Syntax 183

DAVID M. LEVY

PART III THE FLOW OF DISCOURSE

Aspect and Foregrounding in Discourse 213

PAUL J. HOPPER

LIST OF CONTRIBUTORS

Numbers in parentheses indicate the pages on which the authors' contributions begin.

A. L. BECKER (243), *Linguistics Department, University of Michigan, Ann Arbor, Michigan 48104*

DWIGHT BOLINGER (289), *Professor Emeritus of Romance Languages and Literatures, Harvard University, Cambridge, Massachusetts 02938*

WALLACE L. CHAFE (159), *Department of Linguistics, University of California, Berkeley, Berkeley, California 94720*

CHET A. CREIDER (3), *Department of Anthropology, University of Western Ontario, London, Ontario, Canada*

ALESSANDRO DURANTI (377), *Linguistics Department, University of Southern California, Los Angeles, California 90007*

NOMI ERTESCHIK-SHIR (441), *Department of English as a Foreign Language, Ben Gurion University of the Negev, Beer Sheva, Israel*

ERICA C. GARCÍA (23), *Linguistics Program, Herbert Lehman College, City University of New York, New York, New York 10025*

TALMY GIVÓN (81), *Department of Linguistics, University of California, Los Angeles, Los Angeles, California 90024 and Ute Language Program, Southern Ute Tribe, Ignacio, Colorado 81137*

JOHN HINDS (135), *Department of East Asian Languages, University of Hawaii at Manoa, Honolulu, Hawaii*

PAUL J. HOPPER (213), *Linguistics Department, University of Michigan, Ann Arbor, Michigan 48104*

ROBERT S. KIRSNER (355), *Department of Germanic Languages, University of California, Los Angeles, Los Angeles, California 90024*

xi

SUZANNE LABERGE (419), *Department of Anthropology, University of Montreal, Montreal, Quebec, Canada*

DAVID M. LEVY (183), *Stanford University and Xerox Palo Alto Research Center, Palo Alto, California 94304*

CHARLES N. LI (311), *Linguistics Department, University of California, Santa Barbara, Santa Barbara, California*

CHARLOTTE LINDE (337), *Structural Semantics, P.O. Box 5612, Santa Monica, California 90405*

R. E. LONGACRE (115), *The University of Texas at Arlington, Summer Institute in Linguistics, Dallas, Texas*

ELINOR OCHS (51, 377), *Department of Linguistics, University of Southern California, Los Angeles, California 90007*

GILLIAN SANKOFF (419), *Anthropology Department, University of Montreal, Montreal, Quebec, Canada*

EMANUEL A. SCHEGLOFF (261), *Department of Sociology, University of California, Los Angeles, Los Angeles, California 90024*

SANDRA A. THOMPSON (311), *Linguistics Department, University of California, Los Angeles, Los Angeles, California 90024*

BENJI WALD (505), *Linguistics Department, University of California, Los Angeles, Los Angeles, California 90024*

DAVID A. ZUBIN (469), *Department of Linguistics, State University of New York at Buffalo, Buffalo, New York 14261*

PREFACE

In the past decade or so, it has become obvious to a growing number of linguists that the study of the syntax of isolated sentences, extracted, without natural context from the purposeful constructions of speakers is a methodology that has outlived its usefulness. First, isolated sentences and their syntax are often at great variance with the syntax of sentences or clauses in natural, unsolicited speech, so much so that serious doubts may be cast over their legitimacy and ultimate reality except as curious artifacts of a particular method of elicitation. Furthermore, the study of syntax, when limited to the sentence–clause level and deprived of its communicative–functional context, tends to bypass and even to obscure the immense role that communicative considerations affecting the structure of discourse play in determining so-called syntactic rules. Finally, the dogma of autonomous syntax also precludes asking the most interesting questions about the grammar of human language, namely, why it is the way it is; how it got to be that way; what function it serves, and how it relates to the use of human language as an instrument of information processing, storage, retrieval, and—above all—communication.

The reaction to the barrenness of studying syntax and grammar in isolation from discourse has been slow and halting, arising over a quarter of a century from a number of independent research foci of divergent points of departure and motivation. One of the earliest may be traced to Bolinger (1952, 1954) and his pioneering work on the pragmatics of word order. Another approach was followed within the Praguean school (Fibras 1966a,b), picked up by the Firthians (Halliday 1967, 1970, 1974), and later elaborated by Kuno (1972a,b). Work on text grammar and paragraph structure evolved within the Tagmemics framework at SIL (Grimes 1975, Longacre 1971, 1976); it probed the structural regularities obtaining beyond the sentence–clause level. Other investigators pursued similar approaches to the study of narrative, story flow, and coherence (Chafe 1976,

1977, Halliday and Hassan 1976, Hinds 1976, 1977, van Dijk 1972). In another vein, studies into the structure of several narrative types were conducted by Labov and his students, (Labov 1973, 1975, Labov and Waletzky 1967, Linde 1974, Linde and Labov 1975). In yet another approach, Sacks, Schegloff, and their associates investigated conversational structure and its interaction with grammar (Sacks and Schegloff 1974, Sacks *et al.* 1974, Schegloff and Sacks 1973). From a different point of departure, psycholinguists began to probe into discourse pragmatics (Clark and Haviland 1976, Haviland and Clark 1974), and a growing group of researchers in child language acquisition turned their attention to the acquisition of communicative skills (Antinucci and Miller 1976, Bates 1974, Bloom 1973, Carter 1974, Ervin-Tripp 1973, Greenfield and Smith 1976, Keenan 1974, 1975, Keenan and Schieffelin 1976, Sconlon 1974). Furthermore, a number of ethnographers were also at that time studying the structure of traditional narratives (Colby 1973, Foster 1974, Rumelhart 1975).

Closer to home, within the narrower confines of syntax proper, a number of works appeared that investigated pragmatic aspects of grammatical structure (Creider 1975, Foley 1976, Givón 1974, Hooper and Thompson 1973, Hawkinson and Hyman 1974, Sadock 1974, Sadock and Zwicky 1976). The relationship between the discourse notion *topic* and the syntactic notion *subject* was investigated in some detail in a volume edited by Li (1976). And a number of investigations focused on the seminal role of discourse pragmatics in determining diachronic change (Bickerton and Givón 1976, Givón 1976a,b, 1977, Hyman 1975, Sankoff 1976, Sankoff and Brown 1976, Venneman 1973). Finally, a number of functionally oriented text studies were undertaken within the form–content paradigm (García 1975, Kirsner 1973, Zubin 1972).

Given such a multifocused groundswell in the study of discourse, it is only natural to wonder whether some overall coherence is about to emerge and whether all these divergent lines of investigation could yield an overall cohesion. That is, one wonders whether our understanding of the structure, function, and use of human language has advanced far enough so that a coherent whole may emerge, one in which structure and function may be described, in terms of their mutual interaction and interdependency, as one complex entity. The Symposium on Discourse and Syntax, held at UCLA in November, 1977, was convened with such wonderings in mind. It was assumed from the very start that the study of discourse and, particularly, of the relationship between discourse and syntax was not yet at the stage where a coherent unifying statement was possible or even desirable. We felt that both the facts and the task were too vast and complex, and, thus, that a premature integration would be ill-conceived. Rather, we chose to bring together representatives of some of the major lines of research responsible for the recent groundswell in discourse studies so that we could all benefit from the interaction and exchange.

The present volume, *Discourse and Syntax,* arose out of that 1977 symposium and includes all but three of the papers presented there, as well as three papers that were added later on. The participants—in both the symposium and this volume—cannot be easily identified in terms of ideological affiliation or methodological preference, a diversity that we were happy to accommodate. Still, one suspects that in one way or another each participant tends to subscribe to at least one of the following principles:

1. A conviction that the structure of language cannot be fruitfully studied, described, understood, or explained without reference to communicative function.
2. A strong sense that the methodology of studying artificially contrived sentences isolated from their communicative context has outlived its usefulness in linguistics, and that the preliminary methodological distinction between "performance" and "competence" has, over years of being treated as a theoretical prime, become destructive to the empirical integrity of the field.
3. A correspondingly strong fondness for live, diachronic, psycho-linguistic, or developmental data as most relevant for the study of human language.
4. A growing disdain for the orgy of "formalism for formalism's sake," arbitrated solely by criteria of "simplicity" and masquerading as both theory and explanation.

In structuring this volume, we have been bound to acknowledge that striving for an overall coherence of the field is premature but that, nevertheless, a number of underlying unifying themes have indeed emerged. Each one of them was given a part in this volume.

Part I, "Between Discourse and Syntax," presents a number of overviews of the subject. Chet Creider's chapter deals with the discourse-function definition of so-called movement transformations. Erica García's chapter is an attempt to stretch the argument against the existence of an independent structural level called *syntax* as far as it can go, suggesting that all syntactic behavior within a given range of data (certain word-order phenomena in Old English) can be predicted from functional considerations. Elinor Ochs's chapter deals with the register dichotomy of planned versus unplanned speech; it shows that the pair exhibits isomorphism with another pair, adult versus child language, respectively, and goes on to point out that early modes of child communication survive in the adult's unplanned register. Talmy Givón's paper pursues the same theme in a wider context, beginning with the diachronic process of syntacticization by which discourse structure converts, over time, into syntactic structure. A similar process is traced in the development of child-to-adult and Pidgin-to-Creole, as well as in the informal versus formal register in adults. Syntax is then viewed as a mode of the automatic processing of speech, arising out of discourse under specific sociocultural, informational, and interactional conditions.

Part II, "The Organization of Discourse," brings together works dealing with the structural organization obtaining in narratives, going from clause to sentence to paragraph to story. Both Robert Longacre and John Hinds deal in their chapters with the subunits of narrative structure, and Wallace Chafe deals with the same units as a flow model, that is, in the dynamics of narrative delivery. David Levy's contribution, given from the perspective of earlier work on artificial intelligence, deals with the integration of the speaker's goals with communicative strategies in the structure and flow of personal narrative.

Part III, "The Flow of Discourse," focuses upon the subject from a more dynamic point of view. Paul Hopper's chapter is a detailed cross-language study of the use of the tense–aspect modalities of verbs in the flow-control of narrative, in terms of foreground ("main line of the action") and background ("side trips") information. A. L. Becker's chapter is a detailed study of narrative structure in Classical Malay in terms of foreground–background interplay and the embedding of narrative style within both the informational and the cultural contexts. Emanuel Schegloff's article is a tour de force of conversational analysis, the only piece in the collection taking the multiparticipant conversation—rather than the single-participant narrative—to be the more fundamental discourse type. The structural level of sentential syntax is shown to be functionally related not only to the information-processing aspect of language but also to the participants' interaction and the flow-control of conversation.

Part IV, "Pronouns and Topic Recoverability," introduces a number of studies dealing with devices used to identify topic referents in discourse, most particularly anaphora, pronominalization, and topicalization. Dwight Bolinger discusses discourse-pragmatics control over the choice of pronouns versus full noun phrases in anaphoric/definite contexts in English. Charles Li and Sandra Thompson probe into the discourse factors controlling the choice of zero anaphora versus marked pronouns in Mandarin Chinese texts. Charlotte Linde discusses in her chapter the contrast between the anaphoric *it* and the more stressed *that* in English narrative, in terms of "degree of being in focus of attention" and thus, ultimately, ease of topic recoverability. Robert Kirsner's contribution deals with a similar topic in Dutch narratives, where the deictic contrast of *this–that* is used in subtle ways to identify discourse referents. Allessandro Duranti and Elinor Ochs report on the use of left dislocation and other topic-identifying devices in spoken Italian, relating syntactic devices to both discourse function and conversational interaction. The leitmotif of this part is the gradation of degree-of-obviousness of referent-topics and, thus, the differential use of syntactic devices to affect their recoverability.

Part V, "Discourse Control of Syntactic Processes," presents a number of chapters identifying discourse-pragmatic governance of so-called "syntactic" phenomena. Suzanne Laberge and Gillian Sankoff have contributed a detailed diachronic study of the evolution of the personal-pronoun system in spoken Quebec French. Nomi Erteschik-Shir's contribution demonstrates pragmatic constraints on the rule of dative-shifting in English. David Zubin's paper deals with the discourse control over the distribution of Nominative morphology in German texts. And Benji Wald discusses the discourse constraints on the distribution of the clitic object pronoun in Swahili.

It was noted by Erica García, not without a certain irony, that our 1977 symposium took place on the twentieth anniversary of Chomsky's *Syntactic Structures,* in which the independence of syntax from language was celebrated. It is perhaps more appropriate to note, following Emanuel Schlegloff, that the same year also marked the twenty-fifth anniversary of Dwight Bolinger's *Linear Modification* where, in the midst of rampant structuralism in linguistics, the fundamental unity of language structure and language function was reaffirmed.

REFERENCES

Antinucci, F. and R. Miller (1976) "How children talk about what happened," *Journal of Child Language* 3.

Bates, E. (1974) *Language in Context: Studies in the Acquisition of Pragmatics,* Doctoral dissertation, University of Chicago, Chicago, Illinois.

Bickerton, D. and T. Givón (1976) "Pidginization and syntactic change: From SOV and VSO to SVO," *Papers from the Parasession on Diachronic Syntax,* Chicago Linguistic Society, Chicago, Illinois.

Bloom, L. (1973) *One Word at a Time: The Use of Single-Word Utterances Before Syntax,* Mouton, The Hague.

Bolinger, D. (1952) "Linear Modification," in D. Bolinger, *Forms of English* (1965), Harvard University Press, Cambridge.

Bolinger, D. (1954) "Meaningful word order in Spanish," *Boletín de Filología,* Universidad de Chile, tomo 8.

Carter, A. (1974) *Communication in the Sensory-Motor Period,* Doctoral dissertation, University of California, Berkeley, California.

Chafe, W. (1976) "Creativity in verbalization and its implications for the nature of stored knowledge," in R. Freedle, ed., *Discourse Production and Comprehension,* Erlbaum, Hillsdale, New Jersey.

Chafe, W. (1977) "The recall and verbalization of past experience," in R. Cole, ed., *1975 Linguistic Institute Visiting Lecture Series.* Indiana University Press, Bloomington, Indiana.

Clark, H. and S. Haviland (1976) "Comprehension and the given–new contract," in R. Freedle, ed., *Discourse Production and Comprehension,* Erlbaum, Hillsdale, New Jersey.

Colby, B. N. (1973) "A partial grammar of Eskimo folk-tales," *American Anthropologist 75.*

Creider, C. (1975) "Thematization and word-order," manuscript from Winter Meeting Linguistic Society of America.

Ervin-Tripp, S. (1973) "Discourse agreement: How children answer questions," in J. Hayes, ed., *Cognition and the Development of Language,* Wiley, New York.

Fibras, J. (1966a) "Non-thematic subjects in contemporary English," *Travaux Linguistique de Prague 2.*

Fibras, J. (1966b) "On defining the theme in functional sentence perspective," *Travaux Linguistique de Prague 1.*

Foley, W. (1976) *Comparative Syntax in Austronesian,* Doctoral dissertation, University of California, Berkeley, California.

Foster, M. K. (1974) "From the earth to beyond the sky: An ethnographic approach to four Longhouse Iroquois speech events," *Mercury Series 20,* National Museum of Man, Ottawa.

García, E. (1975) *The Role of Theory in Linguistic Analysis: The Spanish Pronoun System,* North Holland, Amsterdam.

Givón T. (1974) "Toward a discourse definition of syntax," manuscript, University of California, Los Angeles, California (revised as Chapter 2 of *On Understanding Grammar,* Academic Press, New York, 1979).

Givón, T. (1976a) "On the VS word-order in Israeli Hebrew: Pragmatics and typological change," in P. Cole, ed., *Studies in Modern Hebrew Syntax and Semantics,* North Holland, Amsterdam.

Givón, T. (1976b) "Topic, pronoun and grammatical agreement," in C. Li, ed., *Subject and Topic,* Academic Press, New York.

Givón, T. (1977) "The drift from VSO to SVO in Biblical Hebrew: The pragmatics of tense-aspect," in C. Li, ed., *Mechanisms for Syntactic Change,* University of Texas Press, Austin, Texas.

Greenfield, P. and J. H. Smith (1976) *The Structure of Communication in Early Language Development,* Academic Press, New York.

Grimes, J. (1975) *The Thread of Discourse,* Mouton, The Hague.

Halliday, M. A. K. (1967) "Notes on transitivity and theme in English, II," *Journal of Linguistics 3.*

Halliday, M. A. K. (1970) "Language structure and language function," in J. Lyons, ed., *New Horizons in Linguistics,* Penguin Books, New York.

Halliday, M. A. K. (1974) *Explorations in the Function of Language,* Arnold, London.

Halliday, M. A. K. and R. Hassan (1976) *Cohesion in English, English Language Series 9,* R. Quirk, ed., Longman, London.

Haviland, S. and H. Clark (1974) "What's new? Acquiring new information as a process of comprehension," *Journal of Verbal Learning and Verbal Behavior 13.*

Hawkinson, A. and L. Hyman (1974) "Natural topic hierarchies in Shona," *Studies in African Linguistics 5.*

Hinds, J. (1976) *Aspects of Japanese Discourse Structure,* Kaitakusha, Tokyo.

Hinds, J. (1977) "Conversational structure," in J. Hinds, ed., *Proceedings of the 2nd Annual Meeting of the University of Hawaii–Hawaii Association of Teachers of Japanese,* University of Hawaii Press, Honolulu, Hawaii.

Hooper, J. and S. Thompson (1973) "On the application of root transformations," *Linguistic Inquiry* 4.

Hyman, L. (1975) "The change from SOV to SVO: Evidence from Niger-Congo," in C. Li, ed., *Word Order and Word Order Change,* University of Texas Press, Austin, Texas.

Keenan, E. (1974) "Conversational competence in children," *Journal of Child Language,* 1.

Keenan, E. (1975) "Making it last: Uses of repetition in children's discourse," *Papers from the First Annual Meeting Berkeley Linguistics Society,* University of California, Berkeley, California.

Keenan, E. and B. Schieffelin (1976) "Topic as a discourse notion: A study of topic in the conversation of children and adults," in C. Li, ed., *Subject and Topic,* Acadamic Press, New York.

Kirsner, R. (1973) "Natural focus and agentive interpretation: On the semantics of in Dutch expletive *er,*" *Standford Occasional Papers in Linguistic, 3,* Stanford University, Stanford, California.

Kuno, S. (1972a) "Pronominalization, reflexivization and direct discourse," *Linguistic Inquiry* 3.

Kuno, S. (1972b) "Functional sentence perspective: A case study from Japanese and English," *Linguistic Inquiry* 3.

Labov, W. (1973) *Language in the Inner City,* University of Pennsylvania Press, Philadelphia, Pennsylvania.

Labov, W. (1975) "On the pragmatics of everyday speech," paper read at State University of New York, Binghamton, New York.

Labov, W. and J. Waletzky (1967) "Narrative analysis: Oral versions of personal experience," in J. Helm, ed., *Essays on the Verbal and Visual Arts,* University of Washington Press, Seattle, Washington.

Li, C. (ed., 1976) *Subject and Topic,* Academic Press, New York.

Linde, C. (1974) *The Linguistic Encoding of Spatial Information,* Doctoral dissertation, Columbia University, New York.

Linde, C. and W. Labov (1975) "Spatial networks as the site for the study of language and thought," *Language* 51.

Longacre, R. (ed.) (1971) *Philippine Discourse and Paragraph Studies in Memory of Betty McLachlin, Pacific Linguistics, 22,* Australian National University, Canberra.

Longacre, R. (1976) *An Anatomy of Speech Notions,* The Peter de Ridder Press, Lisse.

Rumelhart, D. (1975) "Notes on a schema for stories," in D. Bobrow and A. Collins, (eds.), *Representation and Understanding: Studies in Cognitive Science,* Academic Press, New York.

Sacks, H. and E. Schegloff (1974) "Two preferences in the organization of reference to persons in conversation and their interaction," in N. H. Avison and R. J. Wilson, eds., *Ethnomethodology: Labeling Theory and Deviant Behavior,* Routledge and Kegan Paul, London.

Sacks, H., E. Schegloff, and G. Jefferson (1974) "A simplest systematics for the organization of turn-taking for conversation," *Language* 50.

Sadock, J. (1974) *Toward a Linguistic Theory of Speech Acts,* Academic Press, New York.

Sadock, J. and A. Zwicky (1976) "The soft pragmatic underbelly of Generative Semantics," in P. Cole and J. Morgan, eds., *Syntax and Semantics,* vol. 3, Academic Press, New York.

Sankoff, G. (1976) "Grammaticalization processes in New-Guinea Tok Pisin," paper read at the Symposium on Mechanisms for Syntactic Change, University of California, Santa Barbara, California.

Sankoff, G. and P. Brown (1976) "On the origins of syntax in discourse: A case study of Tok Pisin relatives," *Language* 52.

Schegloff, E. and H. Sacks (1973) "Opening up closings," *Semiotica* 8.

Sconlon, R. (1974) *One Child's Language from One to Two: The Origins of Structure,* doctoral dissertation, University of Hawaii, Honolulu, Hawaii.

van Dijk, T. (1972) *Some Aspects of Text Grammars,* Mouton, The Hague.

Vennemann, T. (1973) "Topic, subject and word-order: From SXV to SVX via TXV," in J. Anderson, ed., *Proceedings of the 1st International Conference on Historical Linguistics,* Cambridge University Press, Cambridge.

Zubin, D. (1972) *The German Case System: Exploitation of the Dative-Accusative Opposition for Comment,* unpublished Master's thesis, Columbia University, New York.

PART I   BETWEEN DISCOURSE AND SYNTAX

ON THE EXPLANATION OF TRANSFORMATIONS

CHET A. CREIDER
University of Western Ontario

1. INTRODUCTION

This chapter consists of three parts. The first part is a discussion of a representative sample of movement rules in English. Consideration of the extrasentential contexts in which sentences derived with these rules are appropriate leads to the conclusion that discourse factors are probably the major force responsible for the existence and shape of the rules. This is so both on the basis of appropriateness contexts for the individual rules and also on the basis of the collective similarities in appropriateness contexts shared by large numbers of rules. The second part is a discussion of parts of the English stress–intonational system and its interaction with the movement rule system outlined in part one. The final section is a brief discussion of the

Syntax and Semantics, Volume 12:
Discourse and Syntax

variety of discourse organizing systems found across languages and of the place of English in this variety of system types.[1]

2. TOPICALIZING RULES

Topicalization

Topicalization (Ross 1967), also called Y-Movement (Postal 1971), is exemplified in (1b):

(1)   a.   *I can eat English muffins every morning.*
            b.   *English muffins I can eat every morning.*

That the fronted constituent is **not** being asserted in (1b) is clear from the inappropriateness of (1b) as an answer to the question in (2) and the perfect appropriateness of (1a).

(2)   *What kind of breakfast food can you eat every morning?*

That *English muffins* is a topic in (1b) is also clear. Note that if (1b) follows (3), further talk is NOT possible about waffles but IS about English muffins, whereas if (1b) does not follow (3) further talk IS possible about waffles, as

---

[1] There should be no problems with the terminology used here, but there are important differences between that provided in Chafe's excellent 1975 article and that used here. Chafe treats the initial constituents of sentences such as (i)–(iii) as functionally identical: "The so-called topic [in (i) and (ii)] is simply a focus of contrast that has for some reason or other been placed near the beginning of the sentence [1975:49]."

(i)   *The pláy, John saw yésterday.*
(ii)   *As for the pláy, John saw it yesterday.*
(iii)   *Rónald made the hamburgers.*

Examples (i) and (ii), and (iii), are, however, not of the same functional type. Note that it is difficult or impossible to include the initial constituent of (i) or (ii) in the scope of a negation:

(iv)   ?? *It is not the case that the pláy, John saw yésterday.*
(v)   ?? *It is not the case that as for the pláy, John saw yésterday.*

However, (vi) below is perfectly good.

(vi)   *As for the pláy, it is not the case that John saw it yésterday.*

In addition, (iii) (and any cleft or pseudo-cleft equivalent) can be negated with Ronald under the negation:

(vii)   *It is not the case that Rónald made the hamburgers.*

The point here is that *Ronald* is being asserted in (iii), but *the play* is not in (i) or (ii). Chafe is correct in pointing out that the initial element in all sentences is contrastive. In addition, it should be noted that these elements are new information. They are, nonetheless, fundamentally different in function, (i) and (ii) having initial topics and (iii) having an initial focus. Every one of the dozen or so languages that I have studied in this regard carefully distinguishes topic from focus, and I would be very surprised to find a language that did not do so. We need to do the same ourselves (again, as Chafe notes, the term EMPHASIS is the worst offender, since it can serve to designate topic, focus, and contrastive topic or focus).

in, for example, (4).[2]

(3)   *I don't like to have waffles very often in the morning.*

(4)   *They're too filling.*

Left-Dislocation

Left-dislocation (Ross 1967) is illustrated in (5).

(5)   a.   *I hope to meet Griselda's husband someday.*
            b.   *Griselda, I hope to meet her husband someday.*
                  topic

That *Griselda* is not being asserted in (5b) is shown by the inappropriateness of (5b) as an answer to the question in (6) and by the appropriateness of (5a).

(6)   a.   A: *Whose husband do you hope to meet?*
        b.   B: # *Griselda, I hope to meet her husband someday.*[3]
        c.   B: *I hope to meet Griselda's husband someday.*

That *Griselda* is the topic in (5b) is shown in (7), where (5b) = (7b) is appropriate as an answer to the question, but (5a) = (7c) as well as (7d) are terrible.

> want to
> know about G?

(7)   a.   A: *What do you find exciting about Griselda?*
        b.   B: *Griselda, I hope to meet her husband someday.*
        c.   B: # *I hope to meet Griselda's husband someday.*
        d.   B: # *Griselda's husband, I hope to meet him someday.*

Note that Left-dislocation differs in an interesting way from Topicalization: A constituent topicalized by Topicalization can serve as the topic of a succeeding utterance as well, as is shown in (8).

(8)   *English muffins I can eat every morning. They're just the right thing.*

[2] For many speakers of English, a sentence derived with Topicalization is grammatical only with contrastive topics. Both contrasted elements are available as topics, and this provides an interesting argument for the topicality of the constituent fronted by Topicalization. If the other contrasted element is explicitly given, as in (i) below, then the talk reverts to this other topic. However, if a pronoun is used, as in (ii), the antecedent may only be the fronted and newly established topic.

(i)   *I don't like to have waffles very often in the morning.*
        English muffins I can eat every morning.
        Waffles're too filling.
(ii)   *I don't like to have waffles very often in the morning.*
        English muffins I can eat every morning.
        They're not too filling.

(Contrast #*They're too filling* as the final sentence in (ii) above. Here, where the antecedent is intended to be waffles, the sentence is inappropriate.)

[3] The double cross is employed here to indicate that the sentence so marked is inappropriate in the given discourse context.

It is often <u>not</u> possible for a constituent thematized by Left-dislocation to serve as a topic in this way:

(9)   a.   *Griselda, I hope to meet her husband someday.*
            b.   # *She's a very interesting person.*
            c.   *He's a very interesting person.*

As the appropriateness of (9c) suggests, the function of the topicalized constituent in (5b) is to serve as a "bridging topic." This is not the sole function of Left-dislocation, but it is one of the more interesting ones.

Passive

Passive is a rule that has long been understood as having a topicalizing function (Mathesius 1915). Sentence (10) below is from Williams (1977).[4]

(10)   a.   *What did John do?*
            b.   # *The artwork was done by John.*
            c.   *John did the artwork.*

Note also:

(11)   a.   *Who was the artwork done by?*
            b.   *The artwork was done by John.*
            c.   # *John did the artwork.*

Dative Movement

Dative movement (Ross 1967) is shown in (13) and (14).

(12)   a.   *What did you do with the pennywhistle?*
            b.   *I gave the pennywhistle to George.*
            c.   # *I gave George the pennywhistle.*

(13)   a.   *What did you give to George?*
            b.   *I gave George the pennywhistle.*
            c.   # *I gave the pennywhistle to George.*

Example (12c), derived with Dative Movement, shows that Dative Movement is inappropriate when the indirect object is not a topic. In (13), however, where (13a) establishes *George* as topic, (13b), derived with Dative Move-

---

[4] Williams uses these data in a discussion in which he points out that Passive is not a rule of discourse grammar. Although the argument is formally correct within Williams' framework of definitions (rules of sentence grammar refer to terms contained in single sentences, and rules of discourse grammar utilize terms derived from more than one sentence), these data clearly show (as Williams points out) that the conditions on the application of Passive must refer to more than one sentence. Any restriction of the term DISCOURSE to exclude consideration of these conditions seems to me to miss the main sense of the term.

ment, is appropriate. (It is important to read these sentences with normal, i.e., breath group final, stress. I will deal in Section 4 with the complexities introduced by movable stress.)[5]

Note that Dative Movement is topicalizing and not focusing in function: A sentence derived with Dative Movement can never have the indirect object as part of the assertion it makes (unless it is stressed).

How about
I gave him a
haircut,
etc. ?

about-**Movement**

The rule of *about*-Movement (Postal 1971) is very much like Dative Movement. The sentences of (14) illustrate the rule, and those of (15) provide proper contexts for its application and nonapplication.

(14) a. *Mord talked to the Njalssons about Hoskuld.*
     b. *Mord talked about Hoskuld to the Njalssons.* — *Can't (14b) answer*
                                              (15a) ?

(15) a. *What did Mord talk about to the Njalssons?*
     b. *Who did Mord talk about Hoskuld to?*

Note that (14a) goes with (15a), and (14b) goes with (15b). The pairing of (15a) with (14b), and (15b) with (14a) gives very bad results. Again, one must be careful to read these sentences with normal, phrase-final stress. Moving the stress does alter the acceptability pattern, but this has nothing to do with *about*-Movement, as will be shown later.

Note that, as with Dative Movement, a constituent moved by *about*-Movement can never be asserted.

Adverb Fronting

The sentences of (16) are related by Adverb Fronting.

when will you return home?

(16) a. *I hope to return home the day after tomorrow.*
     b. *The day after tomorrow I hope to return home.*

what will you do the d a.t.?   *asserted*

Sentence (16a) is appropriate when the adverbial phrase is being asserted, as in (17a); sentence (16b) is appropriate when the complement of *hope* or

---

[5] The decision to separate stress and intonation from purely syntactic processes and to analyze the two systems separately is defensible on a number of grounds. First, many languages have no regularized stress patterning (e.g., Nandi, Eskimo); others have nonmovable stress in that the position of stress is fixed within the breath group (e.g., Luo). All languages, however, have syntactic processes, and all languages appear to use these for discourse-structuring purposes. Second, this kind of separation of subsystems is basic to linguistic analysis. For example, we analyse demonstratives without reference to nonverbal resources that may be utilized systematically. Similarly, our discussions of verbal tense-systems normally omit consideration of the numerous other ways in which time reference may be established in discourse (here, both verbally and extraverbally). These procedures are entirely justified (as initial steps in an analysis) by the distinctness of the structural domains in which the different subsystems exist.

the whole sentence minus the adverbial is being asserted, as in (17b). Once again, the cross-pairings [(16a) with (17b), (16b) with (17a)] are horribly infelicitous.

(17)   a.   *When will you return home?*
               b.   *What will you do the day after tomorrow?*

Particle Movement (Postal 1974)

The sentence (18a) is appropriate in a context such as that provided by (19a), and the sentence (18b), derived with Particle Movement, is appropriate with a context such as that in (19b). The cross-pairings are very bad.

(18)   a.   *He wore out the valve.*
          b.   *He wore the valve out.*

(19)   a.   *What did he wear out?*
          b.   *And then what happened?* (e.g., in a story about a valve)

Clearly, (18b) is an assertion about a valve, and Particle Movement has been utilized to topicalize *valve*, which is the assertion in (18a).

Subject–Subject Raising

Subject-subject raising relates (20a) to (20b) and (22a) to (22b).

(20)   a.   *That the interface between the interactional software will go down while we are on line is virtually certain.*
          b.   *The interface between the interactional software is virtually certain to go down while we are on line.*

(21)   a.   *Will the interface between the interactional software go down while we are on line?*
          b.   *When will the interface between the interactional software go down?*

(22)   a.   *That John will foot the bill is certain.*
          b.   *John is certain to foot the bill.*

(23)   a.   *Is it true that John will foot the bill?*
          b.   *What will John do?*

The pattern of acceptabilities here (the a's together and the b's together, but no a and b pair together) shows that when the entire embedded proposition is the topic then Raising is inappropriate, but when the subject of the embedded sentence is the topic then Raising is mandatory.

tough-Movement

(24)   a.   *What's it like to fluff up a foam rubber pillow?*
           b.   *What is it about foam rubber pillows that you don't like?*

(25)   a.   *To fluff up foam rubber pillows is tough.*
           b.   *Foam rubber pillows are tough to fluff up.*

The same pattern of acceptable response obtains here: (24a) and (25a), (24b) and (25a). In addition, note the following example of an inappropriate application of *tough*-Movement. There is no basis for the topicality of *I*, and the sentence is awkward. In (27) the constituent *I* does reference the topic, and the sentence is good.

(26)   *You advise that the quartz grains have wavy extinction and that both it and the pyrite are fractured and crumbled. These certainly are indicative that the schistosity came after quartz and pyrite. Now the quartz eyes may have formed as an alteration (i.e., as porphyroblasts), but I would be difficult to convince that the abundant pyrite was emplaced along with or after the schistosity.*

(27)   *You might be able to convince me that quartz eyes formed as an alteration (i.e., as porphyroblasts), but I would be difficult to convince that the abundant pyrite was emplaced along with or after the schistosity.*

3. FOCUSING RULES

Extraposition (*it*-Insertion)

(28)   a.   *That the interface between the interactional software will go down while we are on line is virtually certain.*
           b. *It is virtually certain that the interface between the interactional software will go down while we are on line.*

The rule of Extraposition moves a sentential constituent out of subject position and to the end of the sentence of which it was formerly a constituent. In context, this rule is applicable just when the former sentential subject is being asserted. Thus, (28a) is not appropriate to (29b), whereas (28b) is. Sentence (28a) is not appropriate because its assertion is about the truth of a proposition, whereas the question of (29a) elicits an event (not a likelihood).

(29)   a.   *Is there anything we can count on with these machines?*
           b.   *What will happen when we go on line?*

there-Insertion

(30)   a. *An Irish Rover is in the garden.*
        b. *There is an Irish Rover in the garden.*

(31)   a. *Where is an Irish Rover to be found?*
        b. *Who is in the garden?*

Here, (30a) is appropriate only in answer to (31a); as an answer to (31b), it is appropriate only if the subject NP is stressed. Sentence (30b) is appropriate in answer to both (31a) and (31b). If it is in answer to (31a), the ex-subject NP must not be stressed. In answer to (31b), it must be stressed.

Extraposition from NP (Relative Clause Extraposition)

(32)   a. *The man who had pitched a no-hit, no-run game was praised by the press.*
        b. *The man was praised by the press who had pitched a no-hit, no-run game.*

(33)   a. *Who praised the man who pitched a no-hit, no-run game?*
        b. *Which man was praised by the press?*

Here, (32a) goes only with (33a), and (32b) goes only with (33b). It is clear that the constituent that is moved by Extraposition from NP is the asserted constituent.

(34)   a. *The press praised the man who had pitched a no-hit, no-run game yesterday in this morning's edition of the Chronicle.*
        b. *The press praised the man in this morning's edition of the Chronicle who had pitched a no-hit, no-run game yesterday.*

(35)   a. *When did the press praise the man who pitched the no-hit, no-run game yesterday?*
        b. *Who did the press praise in this morning's edition of the Chronicle?*

In (34) Extraposition from NP applies to a relative clause embedded in an NP functioning as a direct object. An analogous pattern of acceptabilities holds for the sentences of (35) paired with those of (34) [(34a)–(35a), etc.]. Again, the moved constituent is nontopical and is asserted.

Complex NP Shift (Heavy NP Shift)

(36)   a. *I consider the problem of keeping the house warm in the winter unsolvable.*

> a. *I consider the problem of ~ unsolvable,*
>
> b. *I consider unsolvable the problem of keeping the house warm in the winter.*   asserted

(37)   a.   *How will we keep our house warm in the winter?*

       b.   *That will take care of getting the food in; is there anything that looks like it can't be done?*

As with previous examples, (37a) may only be answered by (36a), etc. What this means is that when the NP is shifted to the right it is for purposes of assertion.

Quantifier Postposing

(38)   a.   *All the linguists in this room know at least one language.*

       b.   *The linguists in this room all know at least one language.*

(39)   a.   *What do all the linguists in this room have in common?*

       b.   *How many linguists in this room know at least one language?*

Sentence (38a) may be an answer to either (39a) or (39b), but (39b) may only be answered by (38b), showing that, in a context where the quantifier is to be part of the assertion, quantifier postposing must apply. When the quantifier is not part of the assertion, quantifier-postposing may or may not apply.

An examination of similarities in appropriateness contexts for the rules just discussed may now be undertaken. First notice that, without exception, those rules that move constituents to the left are topicalizing (the major exception to this generalization that I know of, clefting, is discussed later, in 4). Second, note that all focusing rules move constituents to the right (toward the end of a sentence). The major exception to this generalization, the putative rule of Right-dislocation (Ross 1967), is, in fact, the exception that proves the rule, for Right-dislocation is primarily a rule for "after-thought" topics. Referent-identificational work may be done in this location if the speaker judges that such work is still needed. This amounts to the conclusion that such topic identifying should have been done earlier; if it had been done earlier, some means other than Right-dislocation would have been employed, and that means would fall under our generalization above.

The two "conspiracies" just uncovered clearly involve the majority of movement rules in English and allow us to speak of the discourse functions of topicalization and focusing as major forces behind the development of movement rules. If we are to seek for the explanation of transformations

(Jackendoff 1972), discourse function must clearly play an important explanatory role.[6]

4. STRESS AND INTONATION

Stress as a Separate System

I have imposed heavily on the reader's kindness in insisting that all of the above sentences be read with neutral, phrase-final stress without even demonstrating that there is such a thing. English is unusual in its grammar in two ways (and there can be no doubt but that these facts are related): It has one of the most rigid word orders among the languages of the world (which means among other things that, in general, to move a constituent the grammatical relation of the constituent must change); and it not only allows free placement of stress within the breath group (this itself is relatively uncommon), but it makes extensive use of this potential. I suspect that there are many reasons for why this is so, and one of them, in particular, is the peculiar interruptability of English discourses—movable stress allows speakers to fit important pieces of information into "holes" in the stream of speech. A further reason is given in the following subsection.

Let us begin with the examples of the section on Passive. We add some further sentences and transcribe all sentences in the system of Halliday (1967). Breath groups are enclosed in double slash lines. The accentual center of the breath group (the period of greatest pitch movement) is in bold italic, and the two types of intonational contour we will be concerned with, the falling and the (rising)-falling-rising, are indicated by the numbers 1 and 4, respectively.

(40)   a.   //1 *Who did the **artwork**?//*
         b.   //1 *The artwork was done by **John**.//*
         c.   # //1 *John did the **artwork**.//*
         d.   //1 ***John** did the artwork.//*
         e.   //4 ***John** did the artwork.//*

---

[6] I have used the device of appropriateness contexts here as the closest analog to the conventional starring of sentences. This is partly done to emphasize that the kinds of constraints on rule application determined here could have been discovered long ago if generative linguists had not determined so blindly to keep the single sentence as the sole frame of reference. Problems with the starring convention (the assessment of grammaticality) are well-known (see Labov 1972 for extensive discussion), and I hope that the conclusions made here will be subjected to critical assessment in the light of instances of actual usage. As the following section makes clear, it will be necessary to consider stress and intonation together with movement of constituents. This renders text counts less than wholly useful, since sentences in written text are read with stress and intonation supplied by the reader but not indicated by the writer.

pron.?

f. # //4 John did the **artwork**.

g. //4 The artwork was done by **John**.//

Note first that the bad sentence type (c) becomes good when the stress is moved, as in (d). Note second that there is no contrast in meaning between (d) and (e) but that both of these contrast subtly with (b). Sentences (d) and (e) both contrast John with other individuals who either were actual possibilities for doing the artwork or were in some way in the air (e.g., as individuals who should have been possible candidates). Sentence (b) has no such contrast. Now note that (g) and (b), which pattern like (d) and (e), are not equivalent in meaning. Sentence (g) has exactly the same implication that (d) and (e) have.

I believe we may conclude from this example two important things about English stress. First, on the ground that that position that displays the least neutralization of potential contrast is the more basic (an argument often applied to declarative versus interrogative, activepassive, etc., clause differentiation—see, for example, Givón 1978), we may take final position as the basic position of stress in English. Halliday (1967) gives additional arguments for this conclusion. Second, we may conclude that, in general, sentences with contrastive stress are semantically different from sentences without it (i.e., that contrast and simple focus must be separated—cf. footnote 1). Again, this is not a new conclusion but an important piece in the justification of my claim that the stress system and the movement rule system must be considered separately (at least initially) in order to understand the functions of movement rules.

Stress and Intonation as an Alternative to Movement

Now consider the following, where boldface italics indicate the intonational center of the utterance and a constituent placed in parentheses indicates that it is pronounced with low-level intonation.

(41)
    a. I gave (Max) **the long-nosed gogols**.
    b. I gave **Max** (the long-nosed gogols).
    c. I gave (the long-nosed gogols) **to Max**.
    d. I gave **the long-nosed gogols** (to Max).

who did you give ...?

In answer to

(42) What did you give to Max?

both (41a) and (41d) are appropriate, whereas (41b) and (41c) are not.

It is evident that an alternative to Dative Movement here is to move the accentual center. Now note that in answer to

(43) What did you do with the long-nosed gogols?

only (41c) is appropriate, but with

(44)   *Who did you give the long-nosed gogols to?*

both (41b) and (41c) are OK.

Clearly, here the stress is emphatic or focusing. To state the generalization: A constituent affected by a transformation may only receive "exhaustive listing" stress (Kuno 1972) or contrastive stress, whereas a constituent in an untransformed S may receive simple focus stress as well.[7]

Let us now consider why English has this functional alternative to movement transformations. The key, I believe, is that there is a conversational convention in English not to delay the main thrust of a sentence. This rule clearly runs counter to the focus-to-the-right principle. It is responsible for the shifting accent alternative and, in addition, is responsible for a large variety of deletion processes in English. For example:

(45)   A: *What is your name?*
                        B: *Peter Lawrence*
                        C: * *My name is Peter Lawrence.*

This is a highly language-specific convention. An amusing example was provided on the Voice of Kenya radio when a European coffee farmer was being interviewed in Swahili. The Swahili pattern of acceptable replies is exactly the reverse of the English, the Swahili interviewer was completely thrown off stride by the farmer's answer, and a long and awkward silence followed:

(46)   A: *Haya bwana, jina lako hasa ni nani?*
                        'Now then, what is your name?'
                        B: *Peter Lawrence*

the response should have been

                        B: *Jina langu ni Peter Lawrence.*
                        'My name is Peter Lawrence.'

---

[7] Note that cleft sentences, which are the major exception to the generalization stated before in the conclusion to Section 3 that constituents moved to the left are topical, are type cases where the stressed constituent is focused. It is impossible to read (i) below without stressing the underlined constituent:

(i)   *It is **John** who likes "An Goirtin Eornan"* (*The Little Field of Barley*).

The only situation in which *John* would not be stressed would be one where a correction was being made with respect to *John*, as in (ii) (with focusing stress on the portion in boldface italics):

(ii)   *It is John who likes "**An Goirtin Eornan**.*"

It is inherent to metacontexts such as this that normal values be reversed.

5. THE PLACE OF ENGLISH IN TYPES OF DISCOURSE ORGANIZING SYSTEMS

We may initially divide languages into those that exploit linear order for discourse purposes and those that do not. English is clearly one of the former. Examples of the latter appear to be quite rare. An example that is one of the clearest that I know of is Eskimo (Central or Canadian), where, in general, any linear ordering is appropriate in any discourse context. Tests that distinguish discourse appropriateness very clearly for other languages simply fail with Eskimo speakers (this, incidentally, is an important test of the validity of these tests for the other languages). In place of linear ordering, Eskimo uses rules that change grammatical relations of constituents and, possibly, simply makes less use of focusing and backgrounding information, highlighting, etc.

Eskimo is an ergative language, and there is a strong association between absolutive NPs and topicality and ergative NPs and focus.

(47)   a.   *Inuk   suna-mik   tautuk-pa?*
            man-(ABS) what-ACC look at-INTERR + he
            'What is the man looking at?'

       b.   *Inuk   tuktu-mik   tautuk-puq.*
            man-(ABS) caribou-ACC look at-IND + he
            'The man is looking at a caribou.'

(48)   a.   *Kia   tuktu   tautuk-pauk?*
            who + Erg. caribou-(ABS) look at-INTERR + he + it
            'Who is looking at the caribou?'

       b.   *Inu-up   tuktu   tautuk-paa.*
            man-Erg. caribou-(ABS) look at-IND + he + it
            'A man is looking at the caribou.'

Sentence (48b) is not an appropriate answer to (47a), nor is (47b) an appropriate answer to (48a), but the constituents in (47b) and (48b) may occur in a variety of orders and still be appropriate as answers to their respective questions; for example, the orders ERG-ABS-V and ABS-ERG-V are both appropriate in (48b).[8]

---

[8] A fuller investigation of the possibility that Eskimo does not utilize word order for pragmatic purposes will require examples of actual usage. The claim made here is that, with reference to appropriateness context tests, Eskimo speakers do not feel that constituent ordering differences are correlated with different contexts, whereas speakers of the other languages cited most definitely do. Sentences (47) and (48) are in the Rankin Inlet dialect (West coast of Hudson Bay).

To the best of my present knowledge, all languages utilize at least some changes in grammatical relations (Perlmutter and Postal 1977) to effect topic–focus changes, and all term-changing rules are associated with changes in topic–focus. An additional example illustrating a rule not found in English is the "Alienable Possessive Rule," which raises a possessor NP from within a prepositional phrase to become a direct object in Kinyarwanda (Kimenyi 1977, personal communication).

(49)   a. *w-ii-kw-iicar-a*   *kuu ntebe yaa njye.*
                 you-NEG-to-sit-ASP on   chair of   me
                 'Don't sit on my chair.'

             b. *w-ii-ny-iicar-ir-a*   *kuu ntebe.*
                 you-NEG-me-sit-BEN-ASP on   chair
                 'Don't sit on my chair.'

The version in (49a) may be used in a situation where the focus is on whose chair it is; the version in (49b) is inappropriate in this context.

(50)   *w-ii-mu-gayi-ir-a*   *ubugiiza*
             you-NEG-her-criticize-BEN-ASP beauty
             u-ra-mu-gayi-ir-e   *umutima*
             you-PRES-her-criticize-BEN-ASP heart
             'Don't criticize her beauty criticize her heart.'

Sentence (50) (with raised possessor NP) may be used in a situation where the daughter of one is being talked about as a suitable spouse for the son of the other.

Languages such as Eskimo, which use only changes in grammatical relations to effect changes in topic and focus, are extremely rare, and the majority of so-called free word-order languages are languages that exploit word order principally for the signalling of topic and focus. As a result of the work of Prague School linguists, Czech and Russian are the best-known of these languages. Czech and Russian have systems in which initial position is topical and final position is focusing (e.g., Daneš 1964, 1967). Hungarian is another "free word-order" language, and it is of particular interest because it shows that languages can differ in where they send their topicalized and focused constituents. In Hungarian initial position is used for topic, but the focus position is immediately preceding the (finite) verb (Karoly 1972, Kiss 1977).

Quechua, like Hungarian, is basically an SOV language with relatively free word-order in elicitation contexts. In texts, the orders SV and SOV are by far the most frequent. Quechua differs from Hungarian in having a topic-marking suffix *-qa* and a suffix *-m(i)* that marks the focused constituent (the latter is part of a system of three morphemes indicating degree of conjecture of the assertion; *-mi* is the most frequent in occurrence and indicates the highest level of conviction). In the following text[9] all occurrences of *-qa* and *-mi* are printed in ***boldface italics***. Note the following generalizations: There is a strong tendency for the constituent marked with *-qa* to occur initially, even when it is a direct object; the constituent marked with *-m(i)* occurs in preverbal or postinitial position (as does the focused constituent in Hungarian).

M: *Ima-nuy-la   kay-anki Pedro?*
    how-like-just are-you
    'How are you Pedro?'

P: *Nuqa ali-**m**   kay-á i   qam-**qa**   ima-nuy-la-**m**   kay-anki?*
    I   fine-FOC am-I and you-TOP how-like-just-FOC are-you
    'I'm fine and how are you?'

M: *Nuqa-**qa** ali-**m**   kay-á*
    I-TOP   fine-FOC am-I
    'I'm fine.'
    *Familyay-kuna-**qa** ima-nuy-la   ka-rka-ya-n?*
    family   pl-TOP how-like-just are-pl-ing-3rd
    'How are the members of your family?'

P: *Pay-kuna-s ali-**m**   ka-rka-ya-n.*
    he-pl-also   fine-FOC are-pl-ing-3rd
    'They're also fine.'

M: *Qay Pedro may-ču-**mi**   urya-ra-yki   kanan-kama?*
    listen   where-at-FOC work-ing-you now-until
    'Listen Pedro, where have you been working up to now?'

P: *Nuqa-**qa** uryay-á Uruya-ču.*
    I-TOP   work-I La Oroya-at
    'I'm working in La Oroya.'
    *Qam-**qa**   may-ču-**mi**   kay-anki?*
    you-TOP where-at-FOC are-you
    'Where are you working?'

---

[9] QUECHUA is a term that covers a very large number of dialects. These dialects are divided into two major groups, termed Quechua A and Quechua B by Parker (1969). The dialect reported on here is a Quechua B dialect spoken in and around the city of Tarma in the Department of Junín, Peru. The text is an acted-out conversation dictated by Z. Helario. There is considerable variation in the various dialects with respect to rigidity of word order and with respect to frequency of use and, possibly, function of topic and comment markers. In the absence of detailed information on other dialects, the conclusions presented here should not be generalized.

M: *Nuqa-qa Limaq-ču-mi uryay-á fruta-kuna-ta ranti-ku-ya-r.*
    I-TOP   Lima-at-FOC work-I fruit-pl-ACC buy-MID-ing-while
    'I'm working in Lima selling fruit.'

P: *Ali-č   čay nigusiyu aywa-šu-nki?*
    well-INTERR that work   (Sp. negocio) go-it-you
    'Does that work go very well with you?'

M: *Aw purke   čay-ču-qa   alitaran gan-á.*
    yes because that-at-TOP well   earn-I
    'Yes because I still earn well at it.'

P: *Qam-ta-qa ayka-ta-m   paka-sŭ-nki   čay kumpaña.*
    you-ACC how much-ACC-FOC pay-they+you that company
    'How much do they pay you in that company?'

M: *Nuqa-ta paka-paka-ma-n sesenta solis-la-ta.*
    I-ACC pay- pay-me-it sixty   soles-just-ACC
    'They only pay me 60 soles.'

P: *Kanan-qa may-ta-m   aywa-ya-nki apuradu?*
    now   where-ACC-FOC go-ing-you   hurried
    'Where are you going now in such a hurry?'

M: *Nuqa-qa wayi-ta-m   ayway-á čuri-kuna šuya-rka-ya-ma-n.*
    I-TOP   house-ACC-FOC go-I   child-pl wait-pl-ing-me-3rd
    'I'm going to my house for my children are waiting.'

P: *Čawraq nuqa-s aywa-ku-šaq   wayi-ta.*
    well   I-also go-REFL-fut+I house-ACC
    'Well then I'll go home too.'

A similar tendency for a topic that is explicitly marked to occur in a fixed position is found in Tagalog, where a topic NP is marked with *ang*. According to Naylor (1975), the *ang* NP is normally final in a sentence. This is the neutral position for topics in verb initial languages, that is, topics that are not new information. It thus appears to be the case that even those languages that have specialized morphemes for marking topic and/or focus also specialize positions for this purpose.

Languages such as English differ from the preceding languages in utilizing word order to signal basic grammatical relations (Thompson 1978). As we have seen, however, English also makes positional specializations, and they are like those of Czech and Russian: Initial position is topical, and final position is for focus (with the exception of "afterthought" topics). Malagasy, a VOS language that, like English, utilizes word order to signal grammatical relations, has final position as its topical position (E. L. Keenan, personal communication). In these relatively strict word-order languages, in the cases of the basic grammatical relations of subject, direct and indirect objects, and some oblique objects, processes involving the change of grammatical relations effect changes of topic and focus, but these changes also of necessity involve changes in word order as well. The use of the passive in English as an analog to simple reordering of subject and object in Czech was pointed out long ago by Mathesius (1915). As we saw in Sections 2 and 3, however, English has numerous other constituent reordering processes that do not involve changing grammatical relations, and these processes collectively justify the indication of initial and final positions as targets for topic and focus.

We may summarize the current state of knowledge of the association of linear ordering and discourse factors across languages in terms of three major strategies, each correlated with a major syntactic order type. Languages that treat initial position as topical and final position as focusing are SVO (English, Spanish, Czech, Russian). Languages that treat initial position as topical and preverbal position as focusing are verb-final (Hungarian, Quechua).[10] Finally, languages that treat initial position as focusing and final position as topical are verb-initial (Nandi, Tagalog, Malagasy). These latter languages always have a means of reversing this order to produce sentences that have initial topics. This reversed order is found in discourse contexts where the topic is not known or predictable from the preceding context (see Creider 1975, 1977).

The preceding associations indicate that a very close relationship exists between a language's basic syntactic order and its positional strategy for locating topic and focus constituents. Givón (1978) has presented data indicating that in English there is a very high correlation between topic and subject, and the Quechua text given before indicates the same for that language. Givón (1978) has also noted that, in sentences with a direct object, that constituent is usually the least presupposed, that is, the constituent most central to the focus. The positional strategies for both SVO and SOV languages then involve setting up the location of the subject as the location for the topic such that nonsubject topics are moved into this position and setting up the location of the direct object as the location for the focus such that non-direct-object focused constituents can be moved into this position. In the case of languages such as Czech, Quechua, and Hungarian, these movements are made without changing the grammatical status of the constituents, whereas, in the case of English topical position, the moved constituent acquires the grammatical status of subject if it is a direct object (i.e., with passivization).

---

[10] This possibility was first suggested to me by William Kemp.

VSO languages have a syntax that presents conflicting suggestions for the locating of topic and focus: VS suggesting focus first and topic second and VSO suggesting focus final. [VOS languages do not have this dilemma, and Givón (personal communication) has suggested that as a reason why a rigid VOS order, as in Malagasy, might develop in a verb-initial language.] This is undoubtedly a major factor contributing to the instability of VSO order (where the shift to SVO occurs spontaneously, e.g., in Arabic and in numerous Nilotic languages). In Nandi, where the verb-initial order appears stable, the words orders VOS and VSO are correlated with subject–topic and object–topic, respectively. That is, the final position is reserved for topics only.

In the case of SVO, SOV, and VOS orders, the use of subject and direct object as targets for topic and focus points to another close relationship between the use of language and features of language. The reasons subjects are topical are that subjects are primarily agents and agents are typically topical (Givón 1978). The reasons direct objects are typically focus elements are that the direct object is much less likely than the subject to be human or animate (Givón 1978) and that the direct object is affected by and frequently is a result of the process of which it is a part (i.e., there is a partially iconic relationship between the initial giveness of the agent and subsequent existence or state of existence of the object and topic and focus).

ACKNOWLEDGMENTS

I would like to thank Margaret Seguin for a careful critical reading of this preliminary draft. Most of the errors that remain are due to my failure to follow her advice. The capitalization of the names of TRANSFORMATIONS is intended only to reflect the consensus in the literature of the recent past that the processes so labeled are transformational.

REFERENCES

Chafe, W. L. (1975) "Givenness, Contrastiveness, Definiteness, Subjects, Topics, and Points of View," in C. Li, ed., *Subject and Topic*, Academic Press, New York.

Creider, C. (1975) "Thematization and Word Order," presented at the Annual Meeting of the Linguistic Society of America, San Francisco.

Creider, C. (1977) "Functional Sentence Perspective in a Verb Initial Language," in P. F. A. Kotey and H. Der-Houssikian, eds., *Language and Linguistic Problems in Africa*, Hornbeam Press, Columbia, S.C., 330–343.

Daneš, F. (1964) "A Three-Level Approach to Syntax," *Travaux Linguistiques de Prague* 1, 225–240.

Daneš, F. (1967) "Order of Elements and Sentences Intonation," in *To Honour Roman Jakobson; Essays on the Occasion of his Seventieth Birthday*, Mouton, The Hague, 499–512.

Givón, T. (1979) *On Understanding Grammar*, Academic Press, New York.

Halliday, M. A. K. (1967) *Intonation and Grammar in British English*, Mouton, The Hague.

Jackendoff, R. S. (1972) *Semantic Interpretation in Generative Grammar*, MIT Press, Cambridge, Massachusetts.

Karoly, S. (1972) "The Grammatical System of Hungarian" in L. Berko and S. Imre, eds., *The Hungarian Language*, Mouton, The Hague.

Kimenyi, A. (1977) "Possessor Objectivization in Kinyarwanda," in P. F. A. Kotey and H. Der-Houssikian, eds., *Language and Linguistic Problems in Africa*, Hornbeam Press, Columbia, South Carolina, pp. 303–329.

Kiss, K. E. (1977) "Topic and Focus in Hungarian Syntax," *Montreal Working Papers in Linguistics* 8, 1–42.

Kuno, S. (1972) "Functional Sentence Perspective: A Case Study from Japanese and English," *Linguistic Inquiry* 3, 166–195.

Labov, W. (1972) *The Study of Language in Its Social Context. Sociolinguistic Patterns.* University of Pennsylvania Press, Philadelphia, 183–259.

Mathesius, V. (1915) "O passivu v modern anglictine," *Sbornik filologicky* 5, 198–220.

Naylor, P. B. (1975) "Topic, Focus, and Emphasis in the Tagalog Verbal Clause," *Oceanic Linguistics* 14, 12–79.

Parker, G. J. (1969) "Comparative Quechua Phonology and Grammar I: Classification," *University of Hawaii Working Papers in Linguistics* 1, 65–87.

Perlmutter, D. M. and P. M. Postal (1977) "Toward a Universal Characterization of Passivization," in *Proceedings of the Third Annual Meeting of the Berkeley Linguistics Society*, 394–417.

Postal, P. (1971) *Crossover Phenomena*, Holt, Rinehart, and Winston, New York.

Postal, P. M. (1974) *On Raising*, M.I.T. Press, Cambridge, Massachusetts.

Ross, J. R. (1967) *Constraints on Variables in Syntax*, unpublished Doctoral dissertation, Massachusetts Institute of Technology, Cambridge, Massachusetts.

Thompson, S. A. (1978) "Modern English from a Typological Point of View: Some Implications of the Function of Word Order," *Linguistische Berichte* 54, 19–35.

Williams, E. S. (1977) "Discourse and Logical Form," *Linguistic Inquiry* 8, 101–139.

DISCOURSE WITHOUT SYNTAX[1]

ERICA C. GARCIA
Herbert H. Lehman College, CUNY

1. INTRODUCTION

It is both appropriate and significant that a conference on "Discourse and Syntax" should be held on the twentieth anniversary of Noam Chomsky's *Syntactic Structures*. The title of this conference at once pays tribute to the deep influence of generative thought on syntactic studies throughout the world and unmistakably signals in what direction that approach has been found wanting.

Indeed, much of the recent interest in discourse clearly arises from the desire to avoid the problems that inevitably beset transformational grammar

[1] This is a much shortened version of the paper presented at the Conference on Discourse and Syntax; the presentation of the data and the argumentation underlying the analytic procedure, in particular, have been severely curtailed. The present version was prepared during the author's residence at the Netherlands Institute for Advanced Study in the Humanities and Social Sciences. It is hoped that it will eventually prove possible to publish the original paper in its entirety.

Syntax and Semantics, Volume 12:
Discourse and Syntax

Copyright © 1979 by Academic Press, Inc.
All rights of reproduction in any form reserved.
ISBN 0-12-613512-6

(Linde and Labov 1975:924). One obvious reason for these problems is generative grammar's restriction of syntax to the SENTENCE. This restriction is not unreasonable if we make the following assumptions:

1. Syntax is autonomous; that is, it studies those aspects of language organization that are independent of communicative content.
2. A sentence is the expression of a complete (coherent) thought.

It follows from these assumptions that the sentence will prove to be the best unit in terms of which to discover the principles of language structure. Transformational grammar thus discounts the possibility that certain characterestics of a sentence may simply be consequences of the larger discourse of which it is a part. Now, if a certain aspect of a "sentence" is the CONSEQUENCE of something else from which it can be understood, there is no point in setting up that aspect of a sentence as an autonomous syntactic phenomenon. It is thus by no means trivial to ask what facts of so-called "sentence structure" properly belong "within" the sentence (i.e., are arbitrary characteristics of SENTENCE structure and require description by the "syntax" of the sentence) and which are merely the result of general facts of discourse. Experience shows, in any case, that the "sentence" has proven a most unsatisfactory unit of analysis for anybody interested in the distribution of grammatical units, even WITHIN the "sentence." The position seems to be more and more widespread (e.g., Juhasz 1973, Kuno 1972, Williams 1977) that restriction of linguistic analysis to sentences in isolation, with total disregard of the larger context in which they occur (both linguistic and extralinguistic), can only lead to failure in the search for the structure of language.[2]

However, both "autonomous syntax" (i.e., sentence-based grammar) and "discourse studies" appear to share the basic assumption that there exist certain facts of structure that are independent of the content of particular sentences or texts. These facts are assumed not to be contingent upon the individual characteristics of particular sentences or texts and, thus, need to be stated inasmuch as they do not follow (i.e., are not explicable) from anything else, in particular, NOT from the communicative intent of the speaker. In short, most linguists appear to agree that there are, in language, certain regularities that must be stated. To these regularities a speaker must adhere in communicating (whether his output be "isolated" sentences or "connected" discourse, Grimes 1975:21); they CONSTRAIN a speaker's use of language: They are rules that GOVERN a speaker's behavior, and the job of a linguist would consist of describing (i.e., "formalizing") these regularities.

---

[2] It may be not inappropriate here to voice our admiration for those scholars who were clear-sighted and strong-backboned enough to make this very point in the heyday of Chomskian syntax—among others, Bolinger (1968, *et passim*) and Uhlenbeck (1963, 1967).

Now, the one thing that is fundamental to transformational grammar, even more than its commitment to the "sentence," is the position that the search for the arbitrary regularities of language is to be carried out independently of communicative intent: Grammaticality is NOT the same as "making communicative sense" (Chomsky 1957:93, 100–103); it is a separate, independent property of sentences.[3] It is indeed self-evident that if the regularities are to constitute bona fide linguistic constraints on speakers' behavior they must perforce be ARBITRARY, that is, they cannot follow from anything else. If the regularities did follow from something else (e.g., what the speaker wished to say), they would not deserve independent description. It cannot be stressed too much that something cannot simultaneously be "independent" and "the result of larger considerations." However, if it should turn out that communicative considerations DO play a role in explaining certain facts of distribution, and we ignore them, then we clearly will run the risk of postulating as independent, arbitrary facts of language structure to which a speaker must conform merely the consequences of other facts (of a communicative nature) that we have not bothered to explore.

It is, unfortunately, far from clear what the position of "discourse studies" is on this point, and that makes a contribution to this conference by no means easy. We will therefore attempt to start from a position we may count on as being universally acceptable, namely, that the job of the linguist is indeed to record and to state the arbitrary facts of language to which a speaker must conform. In seeking to establish these, however, we see no point in ignoring obvious characteristics of language, such as that it is a device of communication and that it is used by human beings. Our position is that of Form–Content analysis (Diver 1975, García 1975), and starting from that position we will attempt to establish whether certain aspects of Old English word-order that have been regarded as "arbitrary facts" of that language can indeed be elucidated by appeal to communicative considerations. In doing so we shall have occasion to deal with both "sentence internal" and "discourse" facts; to the extent that our attempt is successful, the aspects of Old English word-order we will discuss can be ruled out as of

---

[3] Syntax, in Chomsky's view, should deal exclusively with the structure of the tool, regardless of the use to which the tool might be put. This emphasis on the autonomy of syntax—on the independence of syntax from actual meaning or even from potential communication—is quite understandable if we recall that Chomsky's primary concern is NOT with the nature and role of language as a communicative device but rather with the nature of the human mind. Considerations of space preclude any detailed elaboration of this point, which has been discussed elsewhere (Derwing 1973, García 1976, 1977). Suffice it to say that—given Chomsky's interest and assumptions—it makes complete sense that generative grammar should have seen syntax as the study of FORMAL structures for which no use or motivation in actual communication is either necessary or desirable (Chomsky 1971:44, 46, 19).

interest to anybody intent on describing the "structure" or listing the "constraints" of either Old English sentences or Old English texts. Once the facts have been communicatively explained, there will obviously remain nothing to LIST as an "arbitrary regularity."

2. THE PROBLEM

The question we will examine is the relative order of Nominative and a second case construed with the verb in Old English.[4] We wish to ascertain the following: Can the order of Nominative versus a second case be understood on the basis of communicative considerations, or must it be described as an arbitrary fact of Old English grammar (reflecting either sentence or discourse "constraints")?

Most studies of Old English word order have concentrated chiefly on the position of the Nominative vis-à-vis the verb (Barrett 1953, Rothstein 1922, Smith 1893), a preoccupation that is at least consistent with (if not derived from) the traditional parsing of sentences into subject and predicate. Our work on the diachronic evolution of Old English word-order (García, forthcoming), however, has led us to view the relative position of Nominative versus other cases as a much more promising point of attack.

So far as the facts of Old English word order are concerned, two approaches are found in the literature:

1. The facts are merely listed: All observed orders are described, illustrated, and counted (e.g., Shannon 1964). No position is taken on the linguistic status or value of any particular order.
2. An attempt is made to establish a basic, fundamental order, departures from which are significant precisely as being DEVIATIONS from a linguistic (not necessarily merely statistical) norm (Bacquet 1962:585; Reszkiewicz 1966:8, 105, 110).

What answer is given to the question "Why is the basic order what it is?" depends on how the basic order has been set up. Thus, Reszkiewicz (1966:114) operates with a hybrid formula based partly on "grammatical" categories (Subject and Predicate) and partly on "ordering classes" defined in terms of "relative weight," which depends on a combination of phono-

---

[4] We shall NOT discuss the position of a Genitive in construction with a noun. The reason for this is that the opposition of FOCUS, which sets the Nominative apart from the oblique cases, involves participation in the event named by the verb, but the meaning of the Genitive (most probably INDEFINITE or PERIPHERAL) makes this case appropriate for "adnominal" usage, that is, to convey messages that do not involve participation in the event and, hence, are irrelevant to the opposition of FOCUS.

logical, morphological, and syntactic criteria (1966:10–13). The two grammatical categories occur basically in the order Subject–Verb, but no reason is given why THIS should be the "basic" order other than that it is semantically more neutral (1966:110), that is, it conveys a "straightforward, unmarked, unemphatic statement." This, however, is not demonstrated, nor is it shown why this semantic "unmarkedness" should be evidence of syntactic "basicness." One suspects that the ultimate motivation is the statistical frequency of SAADs.

The basic order in which the "weight" classes occur (which is, to increase in weight through time) is again not motivated: No reason is given as to why "heavier" items should plausibly follow "lighter" ones, though a semblance of reason is lent to the formula by Reszkiewicz's practice of numbering his classes in ascending order (1966:9–13). The linguistic implications of either the numerical notation or the "increasing weight" pattern are nowhere developed. Indeed, Reszkiewicz (1966:116) explicitly states that "a detailed discussion of the forces that may influence the ordering of elements *in the* FUNDAMENTAL PATTERN [emphasis mine] as well as of the resulting deviating, non fundamental ordering patterns, has been outside the scope of the present piece of research." We may conclude, then, that:

1. Reszkiewicz makes no explicit statement as to the order of Nominative versus a second case.
2. Reszkiewicz's description of Old English word-order consists of the postulating of an ARBITRARY NORM describable only, in his opinion, in terms of communication-independent (1966:13) formal weight-categories.
3. This basic norm (which is arbitrary inasmuch as it is not shown to follow from any other consideration) is nonetheless assumed to be linguistically significant, as providing the base-point from which deviations may be defined (1966:110, 116).

It is important to stress that the significance of the "fundamental ordering pattern" lies in its opposition to departures therefrom. To fulfill this end, however, clearly ANY order will do provided it is frequent enough to be recognizable as the norm.

Bacquet differs from Reszkiewicz both in setting up his basic order in terms of traditional categories such as Subject, Verb, Direct Object, Indirect Object, "noun" versus "pronoun," etc. and in occasionally seeking to motivate the facts he describes. Thus (1962:67, 70), he attempts to explain the preverbal position of pronominal objects (as opposed to the POST-verbal position of nominal objects) from their phonological "weight" and "givenness." Similarly (1962:691), he attempts to "motivate" the temporal sequence in the basic order as reflecting the syntactic ties of determination that organize the group.[5] However, this "natural ordering" (assumed to be characteristic of earlier stages of Germanic, cf. pp. 691, 693) is no longer the norm for Old English. In the vast majority of cases, then, Bacquet confines himself to stating what the (inherently arbitrary) basic order is. The value of establishing this order is (as with Reszkiewicz) that it allows us to determine what the "marked" departures are (1962:585–742, especially pp. 729–742).[6]

The positions taken by Bacquet and Reszkiewicz do not differ in principle from the one stated much earlier by Smith (1893:213), who said:

> The syntactic norm must be clearly established before a rhetorical norm can be thought of, for the latter is largely a simple inversion of the former. If it be established, for example, that the usual position of pronominal objects is before the verbs that govern them, it follows that any other position MUST BY ITS VERY NOVELTY [emphasis mine] arrest attention and make for emphasis, whatever Goodell may say of the logical or psychological aspects of the question.[7]

3. THE ANALYSIS

One might take a position very different from that of Smith, Bacquet, and Reszkiewicz. It might be argued that the statistical norm is just that, a STATISTICAL norm, but that it has no further claim to "linguistic" significance.

[5] This is basically the position taken in Vennemann (1975:288).

[6] On the matter of Nominative–second-case order, Bacquet does not take an explicit stand: His basic ordering (1962:66–70) involves the verb, which he characterizes (1962:67) as "*noyau de phrase.*" The subject–predicate break thus dominates both Reszkiewicz's and Bacquet's analyses.

[7] It is worth pointing out that in Smith (1893) we have an early unifier of "syntax" and "discourse" rules:

> The reason why pronouns prefer the initial positions in a sentence is to be sought, I think, in the very nature of pronouns. They are substitutes not merely for nouns, but for nouns that have preceded them in the paragraph or sentence. All pronouns are, thus, essentially relative; and just as relative pronouns proper follow as closely as possible their antecedents, so personal pronouns, partaking of the relative nature, partake also of the relative sequence [p. 221].

Note that Smith does not appeal to the communicative nature of pronouns (whether relative or personal) or to the psychological properties of "earlier positions in the sentence," nor does he explain why relative pronouns should follow their antecedents as closely as possible. He simply establishes a larger generalization than had previously been entertained, one whereby the relative pronoun–antecedent relation, which holds within the sentence, is extended to (and thus becomes a particular instance of) the personal pronoun–antecedent relation that holds among sentences in discourse. If the equation is correct, it will enable him to describe in the same way the "early position" of both relative and personal pronouns.

Thus, an inquiry as to WHY SAADs should be so frequent in the Anglo-Saxon Chronicle or in the Cura Pastoralis would be answered by pointing to the subject matter of those works; their authors were NOT trying to convey messages for which "question" or "command" forms would be appropriate. This, of course, entails a very different status for "deviations": These would not be departures from a basic order, but merely different orderings. Finally, both the majority and the minority types would be equally NON-arbitrary, as being motivated by the same forces.

Such a position places two responsibilities on the analyst:

1. He must show that the forces motivating both "norm" and "departure" are indeed the same.
2. He must state what the forces are, that is, demonstrate that "word order," being explicable from other known facts, need not be independently described as an "arbitrary rule" or "constraint" of the language.

We shall attempt to show here, then, that the relative position of Nominative and a second case need NOT be seen as reflecting the (arbitrary) "structure" of either sentence or discourse in Old English.

We begin by stating the facts: In the majority of cases, the Nominative (N) PRECEDES a second case (which we shall call X) (Passek 1955:472–474). Now, from our communication-oriented point of view, there might be two explanations for this fact:

1. The order NX could be the signal of one meaning, the order XN being the signal of another meaning.[8] The greater frequency of the order NX would then be due to the fact that the meaning (whatever it might be) signaled by NX would be demonstrably more useful to the messages the Anglo-Saxons wished to write down than the meaning of XN (whatever THAT might be). This possibility has never been suggested by any Old English scholar, and we have found nothing in the texts we have studied to suggest, even remotely, that the orders NX and XN might be the SIGNIFIANTS of specific SIGNIFIÉS.

2. There is something about TEMPORAL SEQUENCE that makes earlier position more congruent with the nature (i.e., meaning) of the Nominative than with the nature of X.

To make good our promise we will thus have to specify: (a) the nature of the Nominative; (b) the nature of X; (c) the nature of temporal sequence. that one particular ordering (i.e., NX) should be more congruent (and hence more frequent) than another (XN). Furthermore, and very important, we

---

[8] Word order, being recognizable, can serve as the signifiant of a signifié (cf. English *John hit Bill* versus *Bill hit John*; Spanish *blanca oveja* versus *oveja blanca*).

must demonstrate (paradoxically!) that when XN does occur it occurs FOR THE SAME REASON (i.e., congruence of temporal sequence with the nature of X) as NX occurs. In other words: What looks like an exception (i.e., XN) really proves the "rule" (NX)!

We shall begin with the least controversial item, the Nominative. There is good reason to believe that the meaning of the Nominative in Old English was FOCUS, that is, that it marked the one participant of the event most worthy of the speaker's interest. Indeed, the traditional characterization of the Nominative as "the case of the subject" and the definition of "subject" as "that about which something is said" would seem, if anything, to support such an analysis. We shall not undertake a validation of this analysis here; suffice it to say that

1. Extensive research on the Anglo-Saxon Chronicle (García, forth-coming) and other Old English texts has produced both qualitative and quantitative evidence for it.
2. The compelling arguments used by Zubin (1979) to support his analysis of the German Nominative as meaning FOCUS would apply equally to Old English texts.

We turn, then, to X. By X we mean one of two things:

1.   An oblique case (Dative, Accusative, Instrumental, Genitive) in construction with the verb (see Footnote 4). These cases are opposed to the Nominative in a complex interlock of at least three semantic substances (FOCUS, PARTICIPATION, and DEFINITENESS, for want of a better term), and all LACK the meaning FOCUS; in fact, there is reason to believe that the Accusative, the Dative and the Instrumental actually mean NONFOCUS.

2.   A "descriptive" Nominative (rather than a "naming" or "identifying" one) in copulative sentences, as in

> *Twegen hi   waeron*   'They were two'
> Nom.   Nom.
>   X   X

A brief discussion is required to motivate our grouping "descriptive Nominatives" with oblique cases, despite the fact that the Nominative means FOCUS. In so-called "copulative," "descriptive," or "characterizing" sentences we find, basically, two references to the same entity, as against the two references to two different entities typical of all other constructions. Since the number of entities involved in an event characteristically influences the inference of the message in a drastic way, it is essential that the hearer not be misled as to the number of entities referred to. However, all the speaker has at his disposal is the morphology of the language, which establishes a distinction between the Nominative ($=$FOCUS) and the oblique cases (NOT FOCUS).

There are, then, in principle, three ways in which the problem of referring to a SINGLE entity in TWO DIFFERENT WAYS could be solved:

1.   Supplement the morphology of the language by adding a special form that would be reserved to signal a second characterization of the same entity. That is, Accusative, Dative, Instrumental, etc. would be kept for referring to a participant different from the Nominative, and a special "predicative" case would be developed to convey messages like 'Alfred was a good king,' that is, *Aelfred waes god-Z cyning-Z*, where 'Z' is a special, nonexisting predicative case.

It need hardly be pointed out that Old English did not follow this route, desirable as it might appear in terms of "clarity of parsing"—perhaps because extra morphology does represent a burden on the memory and attention of the users of the language. Now, if the morphology already available is to be made use of, there are two routes that may be followed:

2.   Make use of the oblique morphology for one of the two references and leave the hearer to figure out which instances of Nominative–oblique refer to different entities, which to the same. The obvious source for this inference is, of course, the lexical meaning of the verb: Copulas would suggest only one participant, other (action) verbs would suggest two. Since, however, we do find in Old English instances of Nominative + *beon* 'be' + Dative, as in

Him sy wuldor
'Glory be to him'

where the Nominative and the oblique (Dative) do refer, as they normally do, to different participants, it would be necessary to press only the Accusative into this special service, which would yield

Aelfred ofsloh godne cyning
'Alfred killed a good king'
Aelfred waes godne cyning
'Alfred was a good king'

in "pseudo" Old English.

3.   Alternatively, the oblique cases (all of them, including the Accusative) might be reserved for reference to a participant different from the one in the Nominative, and RE-USE of the meaning FOCUS would be the device resorted to in order to suggest that only one participant is involved (after all, it is impossible to focus equally on two distinct things). The hearer would thus be left to figure out only which of the two FOCUS references was to be taken

as more basic, "naming" the entity, and which as secondary, "characterizing" it, since the whole point of referring TWICE to the same entity is to present it from two DIFFERENT points of view.

It is this third alternative that Old English adopted, and, although both Nominatives mean FOCUS (indeed, they MUST, if the maneuver of conveying "same entity" is to work), it is nonetheless the case that the LEXICAL material to which the two Nominative endings are attached allows us to infer (in context) which reference is to be interpreted as basic and which as secondary. Thus, in the following examples we have printed the Nominative "naming" the entity in **boldface roman**, and the Nominative "characterizing" the entity in *boldface italic*:

> **He** *is ordfruma and ende*
> '**He** is *beginning and end*'
> **He** *is ealra cyninga* **Cyning**
> '**He** is *King* of all kings'
> **Ðeos þrynnys** *is an God*
> '**This Trinity** is *one God*'
> *Ydel biþ* **se laecedom** *þe ne maeg þone untruman gehaelan*
> '*Vain* is **the medicine** that cannot heal the sick'

Now, it is the case that, if we examine sentences with two Nominatives and ask which of the two is the naming, which the describing (X) Nominative, it turns out that the order N–N(X) is again much more frequent than the order N(X)–N. It further appears that "characterizing" Nominatives share with oblique cases the semantic trait of LESSER PRIMACY vis-à-vis the (basic) Nominative, a characterization being "secondary" in the sense that it presupposes prior naming or identification of the entity being characterized. Oblique cases owe their "lower status" to their grammatical meaning (NOT FOCUS); "second" Nominatives owe it to the LEXICAL meaning of the roots, which suggest characterization rather than naming. In both cases, then, the status of being an X (i.e., a second case, recognizably different from the basic, "naming" Nominative) flows from a meaning, either directly (grammatical meaning, oblique cases) or indirectly (lexical meaning, "characterizing" Nominatives).

We turn now to TEMPORAL SEQUENCE and inquire what is known about it that may help us explain why NX is used most of the time and why XN is used where it is.[9] In inquiring about the difference between earlier and later positions, it will be important to consider the implications of placing some-

---

[9] Recall that XN may not be an exception to, or departure from, NX but must, rather, confirm the reason why NX is natural.

thing at the very beginning of a communicative unit, since the "very beginning" is the limiting case or "earlier." Furthermore, nothing that we know about human nature requires us to expect that a difference in kind must necessarily be made between first and all non-first items; indeed, the reverse is rather the case. Memory studies have characteristically found a bowed serial-position curve for errors (Aaronson 1968:133 and references there cited), with fewest errors for first and last positions, increasing smoothly from these to the midpoint of the sequence.

As long, then, as N and X occur roughly in the first half of the unit containing them,[10] we must seek an explanation for the "normal" precedence of Nominative over X in the nature of FIRST POSITION. That is, we shall assume (and our assumption can be shown to be erroneous if disconfirmed by the facts) that whatever is true of absolute initial position will hold (to a lesser degree) of NON-absolute initial position (i.e., of simple precedence) and that if we wish to understand why the Nominative did so very often precede other cases we should inquire into the properties of the ABSOLUTE BEGINNING of communicative units, as being the "ideal" place in which a Nominative would be put.

Now, one thing is indisputably true of the beginning of communications and (in our opinion) of great importance if we are to understand WHY speakers place certain particular items in that spot: IT IS AT THE BEGINNING OF COMMUNICATIONS THAT THE ADDRESSEE KNOWS LEAST, that is, IS MOST IGNORANT.[11] Therefore, if the speaker wishes his communication to be effective, he must take this fact into account: He will build on it and will order his words accordingly.

That the addressee is (relatively speaking) maximally ignorant at the BEGINNING of utterances has an extremely important consequence: It is there (if anywhere) that the speaker may expect him to be attentive, since his very ignorance will force him to depend on the speaker's words.[12] The speaker will, consequently, do well if he places at the beginning of his communications those items that (for any of a variety of reasons) he may wish to bring to the hearer's attention.

---

[10] Either N or X (and generally both) do in fact always occur extremely close to the beginning of the unit ("sentence") containing them.

[11] For the relevance of this fact to apparent "arbitrariness" in phonotactics, cf. Diver (1979); to speech phenomena, cf. Liebermann (1963).

[12] One need hardly appeal to the very common experience of "losing one's audience": This expression (rather than "winning one's audience") would hardly be the norm if it were not likewise the norm for people to be curious (and therefore attentive) when ignorant (i.e., in expectation of novelty), and for familiarity to breed contempt. Why people are so, why, like the Gauls, we bore quickly and are fond of new things, is for the psychologist (or biologist) to find out. It is sufficient for the linguist to know that people ARE SO.

Now, what is in fact placed at the beginning of Old English communicative units[13] can easily be understood in terms of what has just been pointed out. Beginning Old English "sentences," one finds one of four things:

1. An item that is familiar from the context
2. An item that is important, that is, on which the speaker wishes to concentrate the hearer's attention
3. An item that is indispensable for the understanding of other material
4. An item that provides "background" information for the event

That items referring to familiar information occur earlier than those introducing new information has long been observed (cf. such terms as "given–new," "functional sentence perspective," "communicative dynamism," etc.) and is easily understandable. After all, the first rule of good teaching is that one should build on familiar knowledge. The most common and pervasive reflection of this principle in Old English texts is the high frequency with which pronouns occur early in the sentence (Bacquet 1962:712, Smith 1893:221).

It is, likewise, understandable that, if the speaker wishes to call attention to an item, he should place it where attention is (because of maximum ignorance) at its highest, namely, at the beginning. Note in this connection the equation between "attention" and "prior perception" reported by Stone (1926): Subjects presented with two stimuli (one auditory, one tactual) were instructed to attend to one modality and to report whether that stimulus came before or after the other (unattended) one. They characteristically reported the ATTENDED stimulus as occurring FIRST, regardless of the real order of presentation. Similarly, both item and order errors in recall are the lowest for the first item in a series (Aaronson, Markowitz, and Shapiro 1971:339). We may thus conclude that initial position is a position of communicative prominence, one where we may expect to find those items that the speaker has reason to emphasize.

It is equally understandable that, if a form conveys a meaning necessary for the understanding and interpretation of other forms, the "instruction" or "pointer" should be placed early, BEFORE the material to which it is pertinent, so that the hearer knows how to take the information. The most striking instance of this principle in Old English texts is the regularity with which *hw* forms occur at the very beginning of sentences.

---

[13] It will be apparent that no objective FORMAL definition can be given of a communicative unit, since what or how much is a unit depends on the context of the communications. We consequently will make use of the familiar term "sentence" only as a terminological convenience, NOT as a theoretical unit, it being understood that what we refer to by it is, in fact, a communicative unit not definable except by approximation, any attempt at whose formal delimitation inevitably entails arbitrariness.

Finally, "background" or "setting" information resembles familiar information in that it provides a perspective from which further information is to be interpreted.

It follows from the preceding that conflicts might arise whenever a communication contained more than one item worthy (for whatever reason) of initial position. An analysis of the resolution of this conflict requires a discussion, far beyond the scope of this paper, of Old English word-order; we will therefore limit ourselves to an attempt at explaining (i.e., motivating) the actual placement of N and X.

Our argument at present stands as follows:

1. The beginning of a unit is the position of maximum ignorance.
2. It is extremely likely that the hearer will be most attentive at this point and will retain best the item placed there.
3. Considerations of communicative economy make it appropriate, therefore, to place in initial position
   (a) a familiar item or
   (b) an important item.

Now, on both counts a Nominative is a "natural" candidate for initial position (*a*) because the Nominative MEANS FOCUS, that is, it marks the item the speaker views as important and wishes the hearer to concentrate on; (*b*) because, being the item the speaker views as important, the Nominative is likely to be mentioned more than once throughout the discourse and, thus, to be a familiar item (cf. Zubin, this volume; statistical skewings in the Anglo-Saxon Chronicle bear out the "familiar" character of the Nominative).

It should not surprise us in the least, then, that N should precede X: IF temporal sequence has the perceptual properties we have ascribed to it (and it is hard to see how they could be denied), then the Nominative (meaning FOCUS!) is indeed THE entity that should precede items that are less important than it (X) and, therefore, less likely to be familiar. And, indeed, most of the time N does precede X.

The problem is now: Why does it not ALWAYS precede? If word order is as "natural" as we argue, what could override the claims to precedence of the Nominative?

Answer: What Nature has done for the Nominative, Art can do for X.

If an Old English speaker placed a Nominative "first" BECAUSE that was the item he was emphasizing (by making it Nominative), he would naturally place an X "first" in order to emphasize it. Similarly, if an Old English speaker placed a Nominative "first" because the Nominative was (generally) the most familiar item, we would expect an X to be placed "first" if it happened to be even MORE familiar than the Nominative. That is, the reasons why the Nominative GENERALLY ("by rights") went first should be the reasons why an X OCCASIONALLY went first: because the particular communicative circumstances were such as to make X familiar or important.

Indeed, these must be the reasons why something other than a Nominative goes front, if we are to show that the reasons for the "norm" are the same as the reasons for "departures" therefrom. Note that we are not saying that ONLY the reasons that make it "natural" for the Nominative to be first can put anything else there: As argued before, there are at least four different reasons, all plausibly related to "maximum initial ignorance," for which something can go first, and only two of these apply to the Nominative. Things may and do go first in Old English (e.g., hw- words, þa, etc.) for reasons that do not apply to the Nominative. But we DO say that the reasons that explain the Nominative's precedence must also hold for some non-Nominatives.

And, indeed, no question has ever been raised as to the fronting of "familiar Xs," that is, it has been generally recognized that familiar, "given" items "naturally" occur first. We will, therefore, not belabor that point, merely stressing

1. that the EARLY position of familiar items has a communicative–psychological explanation.
2. that the FOCUS meaning of the Nominative makes it likely that the item in the Nominative will be generally more familiar than non-Nominative items and that this is (at least partly) the reason why N generally precedes X.

The situation is not so clear as far as "emphatic" fronting of X is concerned. Though it is widely admitted that placing items at the beginning was an emphasizing device in Old English (Mitchell 1971:62, §147, Quirk and Wrenn 1957:93 §146), any attempt at a psychological explanation of this fact in terms of the "natural prominence" of initial position is often viewed with grave suspicion (cf. Smith 1893:213). One reason why the emphatic value of initial position should not be unquestioningly accepted may be the following: Although the emphasis is easy to perceive for fronted non-Nominatives, it is not perceived at all for Nominatives; that is, there is no "emphasis" on Alfred in

> Aelfred ofsloh þone cyning
> Nom.   Acc.
> 'Alfred slew the king'

It thus appears that though Accusatives (say) WERE fronted for the sake of emphasis, this is not true of Nominatives, because the order NX is "communicatively neutral" and "contains no emphasis."

Such an objection, of course, misses the fundamental point that the Nominative does mean FOCUS. There is no reason to believe that NONFOCUS + prominence through earlier mention (i.e., XN) should achieve the same communicative effect as FOCUS + prominence through earlier mention (i.e., NX). In fact, if it did, what would be the point of having the meanings FOCUS and NONFOCUS in the language at all? Finally, it should be noted that when a GRAMMATICAL indication of primacy (FOCUS) and a TEMPORAL indication of primacy (first position) coincide, it is very difficult to parcel out in the message the contribution of each.

We are arguing, then, that the frequent early position of Nominatives is not a matter of "arbitrary rule" but is rather a consequence of the MEANING of the Nominative (=FOCUS) and of the psychological properties of initial position (i.e., maximum attention) as they are relevant to communication: "(hierarchically) first things (temporally) first." It is, therefore, incumbent upon us to show that "emphasis" on fronted Xs is not a matter of subjective appreciation on the part of the reader but that there is objective evidence that when Xs occur before Nominatives for which the familiarity of the Xs canNOT be blamed the reason for the fronting must be sought in the speaker's desire to concentrate attention on X.

We will therefore attempt to show

1. That examination of the context in which instances of XN occur allows us to understand why the speaker regarded the X as so important as to warrant his preposing it to the Nominative.
2. That those instances of XN order that canNOT be explained by the "familiarity" of X are nonrandomly distributed in discourse and that their frequent occurrence in certain parts of the discourse (but not in others) can plausibly be explained by the speaker's desire to make the X prominent.

The corpus from which we have drawn our data comprises ten of Aelfric's Catholic Homilies (see the Appendix for the list of Homilies). We have analyzed every instance of X-fronting in this corpus and have tried to establish, by examination of the context and of the message conveyed, what prompted Aelfric to use the order XN rather than NX.

By "X fronting" we mean the placing of a non-Nominative or of a "descriptive" (rather than of an identifying) Nominative earlier than the ("naming") Nominative, as in

> *He dyde þa swa **him** God bebead*
> 'He did as God bade **him**'
> ***Twegen** hi waeron*
> 'They were **two**'

> *Swa micel* he haefde swa he rohte
> 'He had **as much** as he recked of'
> *Ðas þing* we ne magon don butan earfoþnyssum
> '**These things** we cannot do without difficulties'

It should be noted that we are concerned with instances in which X precedes the Nominative and do not require that X occupy absolute initial position. As indicated earlier, we are leaving undiscussed "familiar" frontings; these are recognized only for purposes of contrast with those for which the familiarity of X CANNOT be the only reason.

We shall begin by examining in detail one example of X-fronting that we judge to be emphatic; The Modern English translation for all our citations is always Thorpe's. We shall indicate the fronted X by means of boldface italics, the Nominative by boldface roman. In Homily I, *On the Beginning of Creation* (p. 10), we find:

> *Maran cyþþe habbaþ* **englas** *to Gode þonne men, and þeahhweþere hi ne magon fulfremedlice understandan ymbe God.*
> '*Greater affinity* have **angels** to God than men, and yet they may not perfectly understand concerning God.'

Here we have an Accusative *maran cyþþe* preceding the Nominative *englas*. Why the Accusative is being made prominent becomes apparent when we consider the preceding context, which we quote only in Modern English:

> There is one origin of all things, that is God Almighty. He is beginning and end; he is beginning, because he was ever; he is end without any ending, because he is ever unended. He is King of all kings, and Lord of all lords. He holdeth with his might heavens, and earth, and all creatures, without toil, and beholdeth the depths which are under this earth. He weigheth all hills with one hand, and no thing may withstand his will.

It is clear that this passage dwells on the unspeakable and awe-inspiring power of God, which makes him completely inaccessible to man. This is especially brought out by the clause preceding the one which concerns us:

> No creature may perfectly search out nor understand concerning God: greater affinity have angels to God than men, and yet they may not perfectly understand concerning God.

Together, the two clauses are designed to convey the message: God is unknowable.

To achieve this end, it is highly appropriate that the greater affinity that angels have to God should be stressed, since not even that (*þeahhweþere* 'and yet') allows them to understand about God.[14] We can see, then, why emphasis on the favored position of angels should contribute to the message that God is really unknowable. We may inquire, however, why (this being the case) Aelfric did not put "greater affinity" in the Nominative but chose instead to put the angels in the Nominative. The only way of achieving that end would have been to make use of some periphrastic "passive-like" device that would have removed the angels from the scene entirely; that is, they would have ceased to be direct participants in the event of "having affinity." But, this is clearly undesirable: It is important that the angels not be lost sight of, since their superiority to men is unquestioned. If then angels, who are known to be higher and better than we and to have greater affinity to God than we mortals have, do NOT understand about Him, what amount of knowledge or understanding of God can WE claim to have? Clearly, practically none. Q.E.D., God cannot be known. The implication for people, then, demands that the angels remain on the scene as powerful possessors of the (unavailing) greater affinity to God. To ensure this implication, the angels are put into the Nominative, which assures them FOCUS (and, consequently, the higher participant role) in the event of "having": But their greater affinity (precisely because unavailing) is made prominent by fronting.

The point of this detailed discussion is to demonstrate that a judgment of "emphasis" is NOT inevitably subjective, arbitrary, or circular: The context does allow us to appreciate whether a particular item (i.e., *maran cyþþe* in our example) is highly important or not. Indeed, if we are in ignorance of the general message communicated, it will be impossible to do any kind of grammatical analysis whatsoever (Diver 1975, García 1975:45, Hockett 1961). In this particular case, our control of the message is threefold:

1. We know what the Homily is saying from our general knowledge of Old English and through the internal redundancy (i.e., coherence) of the text.

2. We know enough of Christian doctrine to appreciate Aelfric's theological points.

3. We have the independent evidence of Thorpe's translation. It should be stressed that Thorpe was NOT directly concerned, as we are, with Old English word-order and that his translation can be trusted as that of a nineteenth century Christian gentleman and scholar who did not have a linguistic axe to grind.

[14] Note in this connection the use of a preposition (*ymbe* 'about') to characterize the understanding of God—that any creature should understand God "straight" (i.e., "in the Accusative") is ruled out by definition: What is under discussion as the only possibility is that someone might *understandan ymbe God*, and this is not the case even for those beings that have the most affinity for God, that is, angels.

Now, rather than undertake an argumentation similar to the one just presented for all nonfamiliar X-frontings in the corpus (though such a validation is certainly possible), we will attempt to argue our case by taking advantage of the fact that Aelfric's homilies were coherent discourse.[15]

It becomes very quickly apparent to the reader that most of Aelfric's Homilies are built on the following scheme:

A. Reading of the biblical passage
B. Narrative (i.e., Aelfric retells the story contained in the reading in his own words.)
C. Explication of the reading (i.e., Aelfric interprets the story in terms of its spiritual significance.)
D. Application of the reading (i.e., Aelfric draws the moral of the story, in terms of its practical significance for his audience's behavior.)

These four parts need not be physically separate, though often they are. In particular, part A is missing entirely in many Homilies (e.g., I, II, III), no doubt because it is easily supplied; sometimes parts B and C are disjoint (as in Homilies II and III), whereas other times they are intermixed, so that after one or more incidents in the story the spiritual interpretation is immediately given (e.g., Homilies V, VII); finally, there is not always the same balance between explication and application: They are about equally important in Homily III; the former overrides the latter in Homily II; the latter predominates in Homily VI; and they are intimately interwoven in Homilies X and XIV.

Nonetheless, although rules cannot be written as to the structure of the discourse, a decision may be made with very little difficulty as to whether a particular paragraph is of a chiefly expository or a chiefly exegetical nature. This distinction leads now to a double prediction:

> *We would expect that those frontings motivated by emphasis will show a greater concentration in the exegetical than in the expository portions in comparison to the "familiar" frontings and also that the exegetical portions of the Homilies will contain comparatively more frontings for the sake of emphasis than the expository ones.*

That is, if we compare those XN due to the familiarity of X to those XN where X is NOT familiar (and where according to us EMPHASIS was the reason for the fronting), we would expect the "emphatic" frontings to be more frequent in the exegetical portions (i.e., most of the emphatic frontings will

---

[15] It will be appreciated that it is precisely the coherence of the discourse that makes possible an explanation of why a particular X was fronted on a particular occasion, as in the example just discussed.

occur in exegesis, and most of the frontings in the exegetical portions will be emphatic, rather than familiar, in nature). The reason for this prediction is the COMMUNICATIVE COHERENCE between concentrated attention on the fronted item ("emphatic fronting") and the purpose of exegesis, that is, to enlighten and edify the congregation, as opposed to exposition, that is, to provide factual information.[16]

Note that we are departing here from the realm of "sentence grammar" and are entering that of "discourse." In particular, we are making a prediction concerning the distribution of a linguistic phenomenon (i.e., the order XN, where X is not familiar) within certain "discourse units" (i.e., paragraphs) and asserting that a skewing will be observed depending on the nature (i.e., exegetical versus expository) of the "discourse units." If this skewing should indeed be observed, it might be seen in two lights:

1. As FOLLOWING NATURALLY from the coherence between the communicative natures of exegesis and emphatic fronting
2. As reflecting an arbitrary constraint of discourse structure upon sentence structure (i.e., the speaker's competence contains information to the effect that he must front for emphasis more often in exegetical than in expository paragraphs)

The first viewpoint would provide an EXPLANATION of the skewing; the second would merely formalize it but regard it as essentially arbitrary. We will attempt to show that there is reason to take the first viewpoint, which renders the second unnecessary.

We have proceeded to test our prediction as follows: The ten homilies selected were analyzed in detail, each paragraph being classified as to whether it was fundamentally expository or fundamentally exegetical in nature. The result of the analysis is shown in the Appendix. A paragraph was judged to be expository when it narrated events (e.g., Hom. IV §3, 4, 5) or described customs or beliefs (Hom. VI §10, 11, 15). A paragraph was judged to be exegetical when it clarified points of doctrine (e.g., Hom. VII §10, 11, 12), explained the symbolic significance of events (e.g., Hom. VII §4, 6, 7, cf. Clemoes 1966:188), or exhorted the faithful to upright living (Hom. VI §12, 13, 14).

Within each paragraph, all instances of fronting were noted in which an oblique case or a predicative Nominative preceded the (naming) Nominative. These instances of fronting were classified (in the light of the context and of the nature of the preposed item) as being fundamentally attention-attracting,

---

[16] It is clear that familiar Xs may ALSO be fronted for the purpose of emphasis. It is impossible within the confines of this paper to do justice to this aspect of the problem: We will, therefore, confine ourselve to those X frontings where the motivation was clearly either emphasis or familiarity.

familiar, or both familiar and attention-attracting. These last, which constitute 20% of all frontings, will be left out of consideration.

The question may be raised as to how reliable our estimate of "exegesis" is. Would it not be possible to "improve" our figures by judging those paragraphs to be exegetical where emphatic fronting is particularly frequent? Undoubtedly, but our judgment as to character of the paragraphs (cf. Appendix) is based on the CONTENTS of the paragraphs and is open to challenge on these grounds. Now, though there exists no "objective," "formal" (i.e., communicative content-independent) proof that a particular paragraph IS predominantly exegetical or expository, corroboration of our judgment can be found.

There is in Aelfric's homilies a rhetorical device that is extremely obvious and fairly leaps at the reader, that is, parallelism, as in Homily III, *The Passion of St. Stephen*, p. 50:

> *Done deaþ soþlice þe se Haelend gemedemode for mannum prowian,*
> *þone ageaf Stephanus fyrmest manna þaem Haelende.*
> 'That death verily which Jesus vouchsafed to suffer for men,
> Stephen gave first of men to Jesus.'

and again:

> *Swiþor he besorgade þa heora synna þonne his agene wunda;*
> *swiþor heora arleasnysse þonne his sylfes deaþ;*
> *and rihtliche swiþor,*
> *forþan þe heora arleasnysse fyligde se eca deaþ,*
> *and þaet ece lif fyligde his deaþe.*
> 'He was more afflicted on account of their sins than of his own wounds,
> more for their wickedness than his own death,
> and rightly more,
> seeing that eternal death followed their wickedness,
> and eternal life followed his death.'

The attention-getting effect of parallelism is obvious: It has been recognized (with fronting) as an extremely important technique in Aelfric's prose (Clemoes 1966:197–200). We would expect, then, that parallelism too would be skewed towards occurrence in those paragraphs (i.e., the exegetical ones) for which a greater impact on the audience was desirable. To this end, all instances of parallelism were noted as occurring in expository versus exegetical paragraphs, in order to establish whether there was indeed the expected skewing.

Notice the significance of this skewing—should it exist—on the "structure of discourse" position on emphatic fronting. We are arguing that the coincidence of emphatic fronting and parallelism in exegetical paragraphs is due to the coherence between the communicative effect of both "devices" (i.e., the seizing of attention) and the type of message conveyed in that type of paragraph. A "formalist," on the other hand, would presumably argue that the "structure" of the discourse (i.e., the division into exegetical and expository paragraphs) variably "constrains" the speaker to use a greater proportion of both parallelism and emphatic fronting in a certain environment (i.e., in exegetical paragraphs) but that there is no connection between the two phenomena, that is, it is a pure coincidence that exegetical paragraphs should favor a greater proportion of BOTH these devices. Furthermore, no causal connection of any sort would be established between the environment and the effect of the "rule": The skewing might just as well go the other way; that is, parallelism and emphatic fronting could be more frequent in EXPOSITORY paragraphs—the rule would formalize THAT fact just as easily. Of course, if a connection could be established (which is exactly what we attempt to do by appealing to the need for coherence in communication), there would be no point in writing the rule at all: One does not need to list as an arbitrary fact of language structure something that can be otherwise explained.

We turn now to the data. In Table 1 we show the distribution, by type of paragraph, of "emphatic" versus "familiar" fronting.

TABLE 1

RELATIVE CONCENTRATION OF TYPE OF FRONTING DEPENDING ON TYPE OF PARAGRAPH

	Homily										
	I	II	III	IV	V	VI	VII	X	XIII	XIV	Total
Emphatic											
Expository	9	1	0	10	3	1	0	0	1	0	25
Exegetical	0	5	7	3	5	3	7	6	7	9	52
Total	9	6	7	13	8	4	7	6	8	9	77
Percentage exegesis	0	83	100	23	63	75	100	100	87	100	74
Familiar											
Expository	2	2	3	2	0	3	0	0	1	0	13
Exegetical	0	1	0	0	0	2	3	0	3	1	10
Total	2	3	3	2	0	5	3	0	4	1	23
Percentage exegesis	0	33	0	0	—	40	100	—	75	100	43

We see that in no homily is it the case that, in comparison to familiar frontings, emphatic frontings are more frequent in expository than in exegetical portions. To be sure, there are two Homilies (I and IV) in which the percentage of emphatic frontings occurring in exegesis is very low

(0% and 23%, respectively). But that is not because FAMILIAR frontings are more common in exegesis: These are 0% in both instances. What must be explained, rather, is why there should be so few emphatic frontings in exegesis in these particular homilies, which deviate from the pattern that emerges clearly in the remaining ones.

The explanation can be found in the fact that these two Homilies are basically expository rather than exegetical in nature. This can be seen from Table 2, where we show the proportion of emphatic fronting concentrated in exegesis versus the general proportion of homily lines (a rough measure of "discourse material") invested in exegesis. We see that, for the homilies as a whole, as well as for 9 of the 10 taken individually (Homily I is the exception), the percentage of fronting motivated by concentration of attention occurring in exegetical passages is GREATER than the share of text (measured by number of lines) falling to those passages.

TABLE 2
PROPORTION OF EMPHATIC FRONTING VERSUS PROPORTION OF LINES IN EXEGESIS

	Homily										
	I	II	III	IV	V	VI	VII	X	XIII	XIV	Total
Percentage emphatic fronting	0	83	100	23	63	75	100	100	87	100	74
Percentage lines	8	69	71	12	28	55	81	90	65	87	54

It appears, then, that emphatic fronting is concentrated in exegesis above and beyond the norm, that is, general amount of lines (roughly, time) given to exegesis by the speaker, and that the more the entire Homily is fundamentally exegetical in character, the more is emphatic fronting concentrated in exegesis.

In Table 3 we look at the data from the point of view of the paragraphs and show what percentage of the total number of frontings observed in the different types of discourse is motivated by familiarity versus emphasis. We find that a true comparison is possible only for 6 of the 10 Homilies and that in none of the 6 is it the case that the exegetical portions show a SMALLER proportion of emphatic frontings than do the expository ones. In Homilies VII, X, and XIV the expository paragraphs have no fronting at all: These are the homilies that are more than 80% exegesis, as can be seen from Table 2. That is, we have the reverse phenomenon from that in Homily I, where exegesis so rare altogether (8% of the total) that no fronting of either sort occur in it.

TABLE 3

PROPORTION OF FRONTING DUE TO EMPHASIS IN DIFFERENT TYPES OF PARAGRAPH

					Homily						
	I	II	III	IV	V	VI	VII	X	XIII	XIV	Total
Expository paragraphs											
Emphatic frontings	9	1	0	10	3	1	0	0	1	0	25
Familiar frontings	2	2	3	2	0	3	0	0	1	0	13
Total	11	3	3	12	3	4	0	0	2	0	38
Percentage emphatic	81	33	0	83	100	25	—	—	50	—	66
Exegetical paragraphs											
Emphatic frontings	0	5	7	3	5	3	7	6	7	9	52
Familiar frontings	0	1	0	0	0	2	3	0	3	1	10
Total	0	6	7	3	5	5	10	6	10	10	62
Percentage emphatic	—	83	100	100	100	60	70	100	70	90	84

We will now show that our judgment as to which paragraphs are exegetical and which expository is borne out by our second prediction, the one concerning the distribution of parallelism. The data appear in Table 4.

TABLE 4

DISTRIBUTION OF PARALLELISM IN EXEGESIS VERSUS EXPOSITION

					Homily						
	I	II	III	IV	V	VI	VII	X	XIII	XIV	Total
Percentage parallelism in exegesis	33	100	100	50	100	81	92	100	83	86	84
Percentage lines	8	69	71	12	28	55	81	90	65	87	54

We note that, in the 10 Homilies as a whole, and in all but one individually (and there by a negligible margin), the percentage of parallelism occurring in the exegetical paragraphs is considerably greater than the percentage of exegetical text as a whole (measured by number of lines). The paragraphs we have labeled as exegetical, then, are of such a nature as to exhibit a concentration of parallelism: Their "selection" by emphatic fronting is thus not ad hoc or coincidental. We would argue, rather, that BOTH parallelism and emphatic fronting are skewed toward occurrence in exegetical passages because it is the CONTENT of these that motivates the recourse to attention-getting devices of different types (lexical, prominent placing). The bearing-out of a communication-based prediction thus makes it unnecessary to view these facts as arbitrary marks of "discourse structure."

4. CONCLUSIONS

In one favorite area of "arbitrary syntax" (i.e., "word-order facts"), BOTH the so-called "departures from the syntactic norm and the "syntactic norm" itself can be seen to dissolve into intelligibility when we consider such things as:

1. What did Aelfric want to say?
2. What is the meaning of the Nominative as opposed to that of oblique cases; that is, what are the resources of the language?
3. What is true at different times in a communication?

It will be noted that in our study we have explained a "fact of sentence grammar" (the occurrence of fronting) partly by appeal to discourse considerations, that is, the context in which the sentences occur. In that sense, one might conclude that "text considerations affect sentence grammar." But the reverse also holds: We have been able to understand the unequal distribution of both fronting and parallelism in different kinds of paragraphs from the nature of the devices: Here, an understanding of what fronting (a "sentence-grammar phenomenon") entails has shed light on a skewing that characterizes LARGER units.

Should we therefore conclude that Aelfric followed "rules of discourse" or that his discourse had "structure" or was marked by "constraints" or that his usage of Old English morphology can be accounted for only by a variable syntactic rule that includes discourse features as a relevant environment?

None of these. Throughout his Homily, in the smaller as in the larger communicative chunks, Aelfric was always doing one and the same thing: getting his message across by using his tools (the meanings of the signals of the language) in the most effective way possible.

To appeal to "autonomous syntactic rules" implies that a speaker does something because he MUST and for no other reason. If we can show that language usage is EXPLICABLE by appeal to the meanings of the language and to known, independently establishable properties of language users, to that extent rules are unnecessary, unmotivated, and worse than useless. Why have them?

Once the communicative intent is clear (i.e., once we know what Aelfric wished to communicate) and its connection to the observed phenomena is demonstrated by showing how such and such a communicative need, given such and such known linguistic resources (i.e., the meanings of the language) and such and such known properties of human beings, results in the actually observed ordering of the morphology, WHAT DOES THERE REMAIN TO BE DONE?

It is, admittedly, very hard to prove a negative, namely, that language contains no "arbitrary constraints" save for THE one recognized as *l'arbitraire du signe*. It can only be done by elimination, as we have tried to do here, by showing that there is NO need for "autonomous syntax," "discourse structure," "rules," or "constraints" once one takes seriously the proposition that language is a device of communication manipulated by human beings.

APPENDIX. THE CORPUS

HOMILY I. *On the Beginning of Creation*
Expository paragraphs: 1, 2, 3, 4, 6, 8–14
Exegetical paragraphs: 5, 7.

HOMILY II. *On the Nativity of Our Lord*
Expository paragraphs: 1, 2, 8
Exegetical paragraphs: 3–7, 9.

HOMILY III. *The Passion of the Blessed Stephen Protomartyr*
Expository paragraph: 1
Exegetical paragraphs: 2–7.

HOMILY IV. *The Assumption of St. John the Apostle*
Expository paragraphs: 1–5, 7–13
Exegetical paragraph: 6.

HOMILY V. *The Nativity of the Innocents*
Expository paragraphs: 1–4, 9–11
Exegetical paragraphs: 6–8, 12.

HOMILY VI. *The Octaves and Circumcision of Our Lord*
Expository paragraphs: 1, 2, 6, 10, 11, 15
Exegetical paragraphs: 3–5, 7–9, 12–14, 16

HOMILY VII. *The Epiphany of the Lord*
Expository paragraphs: 1–3, 5, 8, 16
Exegetical paragraphs: 4, 6, 7, 9–15, 17–19.

HOMILY X.   *Shrove Sunday*
Expository paragraph: 1
Exegetical paragraphs: 2–11.

HOMILY XIII.   *The Annunciation of St. Mary*
Expository paragraphs: 1, 2, 10
Exegetical paragraphs: 3–9, 11–13.

HOMILY XIV.   *For Palm Sunday*
Expository paragraphs: 1–3, 16
Exegetical paragraphs: 4–15, 17–20.

REFERENCES

Aaronson, D. (1968) Temporal course of perception in an immediate recall task, *Journal of Experimental Psychology*, 76, 129–140.

Aaronson, D., N. Markowitz, and H. Shapiro (1971) Perception and immediate recall of normal and compressed auditory sequences, *Perception and Psychophysics*, 9, 338–344.

Bacquet, P. (1962) *La structure de la phrase verbale à l'époque alfrédienne*. Paris: Société d'Editions 'Les Belles Lettres.'

Barrett, C. R. (1953) *Studies in the Word Order of Aelfric's Catholic Homilies and Lives of the Saints*. University of Cambridge, Museum of Archaeology and Ethnology. Department of Anglo-Saxon Occasional Papers No. 3.

Bolinger, D. (1968) "Judgments of grammaticality," *Lingua* 21, 34–40.

Chomsky, N. (1957) *Syntactic Structures*, Mouton, The Hague.

Chomsky, N. (1971) *Problems of knowledge and freedom*, Vintage Press, New York.

Clemoes, P. (1966). Aelfric, in E. G. Stanley ed., *Continuation and beginnings. Studies in Old English Literature*, Nelson, London, pp. 176–209.

Derwing, B. (1973) *Transformational Grammar as a Theory of Language Acquisition*. Cambridge University Press, Cambridge.

Diver, W. (1975) Introduction, *Columbia University Working Papers in Linguistics*, II. New York, pp. 1–25.

Diver, W. (1929) "Phonology as human behavior," in J. Rieber and D. Aaronson, eds., *Psycholinguistics: Research Implications and Practical Applications*, Erlbaum, Hillsdale, New Jersey.

García, E. (1975) *The Role of Theory in Linguistic Analysis*, North Holland, Amsterdam.

García, E. (1976) "The Generative Approach to the Spanish Reflexive," *Romance Philology* XXX, 361–389.

García, E. (1977) "On the Practical Consequences of Theoretical Principles," *Lingua* 43, 129–170.

García, E. (forthcoming) "Old English word-order strategies and the loss of case morphology."

Grimes, J. (1975) *The Thread of Discourse*, Mouton, The Hague.

Hockett, C. F. (1961) "Linguistic Elements and their Relations," *Language* 37, 29–53.

Juhász, J. (1973) "Sprachliche Einheiten—Linguistische Begriffe," in H. Sitta and K. Brinker, eds., *Studien zur Texttheorie und zur deutschen Grammatik*, Pädagogischer Verlag Schwann, Düsseldorf, pp. 192–198.

Kuno, S. (1972) "Pronominalization, Reflexivization and Direct Discourse," *Linguistic Inquiry* 3, 161–196.

Lieberman, P. (1963) "Some Effects of Semantic and Grammatical Context on the Production and Perception of Speech," *Language and Speech* 6, 172–187.

Linde, C. and W. Labov (1975) "Spatial networks as a site for the study of language and thought," *Language* 51, 924–939.

Mitchell, B. (1971) *A Guide to Old English*, Oxford University Press, London.

Passek, V. V. (1955) "K Voprosu o sootnošenij meždu reduktsiej okončanij i vydviženiem sintaksičeskich sredstv v anglijskom jazyke," in *Voprosy grammatičeskogo stroja*, Akademia Nauk SSSR, Moscow, pp. 461–480.

Quirk, R. and C. L. Wrenn (1957) *An Old English Grammar*, Holt, Rinehart, and Winston, New York.

Reszkiewicz, A. (1966) *Ordering of Elements in Late Old English Prose in terms of their Size and Structural Complexity*, Zakład Narodowy Imienia Ossolińskich. Wydawnictwo Polskiej Akademii Nauk, Warsaw.

Rothstein, E. (1922) "*Die Wortstellung in der Peterborough Chronik*," *Studien zur Englischen Philologie*, LXIV, Halle.

Shannon, A. (1964) *A Descriptive Syntax of the Parker Manuscript of the Anglo-Saxon Chronicle from 734 to 891*, Mouton, The Hague.

Smith, C. A. (1893) "The order of words in Anglo-Saxon Prose," *Publications of the Modern Modern Language Association of America*, 8, 210–244.

Stone, S. A. (1926) "Prior entry in the auditory-tactual complication," *American Journal of Psychiatry* 37, 284–287.

Thorpe, B. (1844) *The Homilies of the Anglo-Saxon Church*, vol. I, London.

Uhlenbeck, E. M. (1963) "An appraisal of transformational theory," *Lingua* 12, 1–18.

Uhlenbeck, E. M. (1967) "Language in Action," in *To honor Roman Jakobson*, Mouton, The Hague, pp. 2060–2066.

Venneman, T. (1975) "An Explanation of Drift," in C. N. Li, ed., *Word Order and Word Order Change*, Univ. of Texas Press, Austin, Texas, pp. 271–305.

Williams, E. S. (1977) "Discourse and Logical Form," *Linguistic Inquiry* 8, 101–139.

PLANNED AND UNPLANNED DISCOURSE

ELINOR OCHS
University of Southern California, Los Angeles

1. INTRODUCTION

In studies of child language, there is an implicit assumption that the child produces an imperfect version of the adult code. The adult code represents the target toward which the child's language is developing. In this perspective, the child moves through a series of "stages" (Brown 1973) until he[1] achieves "competence" (Chomsky 1965) in the language of the adult speech community. For example, recent literature on the "single word stage" suggests that the child at first deletes certain highly predictable information, then, at some later stage, the child expresses that information in the utterance itself (Bates 1976, Greenfield and Smith 1976). Another development noted during this period is the movement away from the sequential expression of a proposition toward the syntactic expression of a proposition (Atkinson 1974, Bloom 1973, Keenan and Klein 1976, Scollon 1976). The

---

[1] In English the unmarked pronoun is *he*. However, the reader should bear in mind that the pronoun refers to both males AND females.

Syntax and Semantics, Volume 12:
Discourse and Syntax

child points out some referent in one utterance and predicates something of that referent in a subsequent utterance. The child uses discourse to convey the proposition, producing what Scollon calls "vertical constructions." Over time, the child comes to encode argument and predicate in the space of a single utterance, utilizing syntactic rather than a discourse means. The literature on multiword utterances suggests again that the child moves through a series of stages in which not only utterance length but also syntactic complexity of the child's speech corpus is increased (Bloom 1970, Brown 1973, Brown, Cazden, and Bellugi 1969, Slobin 1973).

This paradigm may lead one to assume that stages are transitory phenomena. As the child moves from one stage to the next, he does not "go back" to utilize strategies developed at an earlier developmental period. Rather, strategies emerging at a later period are seen as replacing earlier strategies. The present chapter examines this assumption. It suggests that language development be viewed alternatively as the development of certain linguistic POTENTIALITIES. Becoming more competent in one's language involves increasing one's knowledge of the potential range of structures (e.g. morphosyntactic, discourse) available for use and increasing one's ability to use them. In this view, communicative strategies characteristic of any one stage are not replaced. Rather, they are retained, to be relied upon under certain communicative conditions. The retention of emerging communicative strategies goes on not only during language acquisition but also throughout adult life.

The difference in the two perspectives on language development is represented visually in Figure 1. The replacement model sees language development as stepwise in nature; each step takes the child closer to the adult norm. Hence, auxiliaries at some point are permuted in interrogatives; agreement is marked; plural suffixes emerge (Brown 1973); and so on. With the exception of severe physical damage or extreme environmental interference, these processes do not reverse themselves. The view of language development as a broadening of knowledge of the language's potential expressive power is better visualized as a series of textures in which developmentally prior communicative patterns coexist with more recently developed patterns (retention model). The extent to which earlier patterns continue to remain prominent (i.e., are used) depend upon the linguistic structures under consideration and the developmental period observed.

We present an alternative model for language development as a vehicle for understanding not only child language but adult language as well. It is not only in the course of becoming competent that developmentally earlier communicative strategies are retained. We also rely on a number of these same strategies as adult communicators, as well under certain contextual conditions.

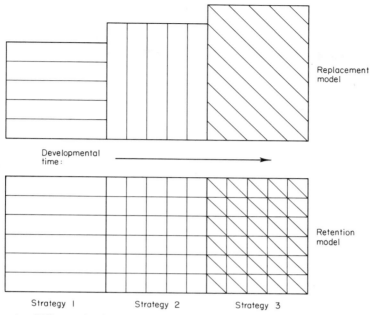

Figure 1. Difference in the two perspectives on language development. Horizontal lines indicate Strategy 1; vertical lines indicate Strategy 2; diagonal lines indicate Strategy 3.

A major condition affecting adult reliance on early communicative patterns is the extent to which the communication has been PLANNED prior to its delivery. We find that adult speech behavior takes on many of the characteristics of child language, where the communication is spontaneous and relatively unpredictable. For example, spontaneous dialogues and multi-party conversations among adults evidence greater reliance on developmentally early communicative strategies. Similarly, stream-of-consciousness writing, casual letter-writing, and so on display this reliance. On the other hand, more planned communicative behavior makes greater use of more complex structures and of strategies developed later in the child's life. Formal expository writing, for example, or presidential addresses to the nation display this kind of speech behavior.

This claim has interest for those oriented toward integrating psychological and sociological dimensions of language behavior. Traditionally, notions such as "spontaneous," "casual," and "planned" have been the concern of sociologists of language. Here we suggest that they may have a psychological basis as well. That is, we suggest that, when speakers have not planned the form of their discourse, they rely more heavily on morphosyntactic and discourse skills acquired in the first 3–4 years of life.

What about non-natives ?? (handwritten margin note)

The counterpart of this suggestion is that more planned language use draws on knowledge that is acquired or learned (cf. Krashen 1976, 1977) later in life. In the case of our own society, the suggestion is that more planned uses of language draw upon knowledge transmitted through formal education. This knowledge includes use of complex syntactic structures (e.g., complementation, cleft constructions, certain types of relative clauses, passives) and more formal discourse devices (e.g., use of textual cohesion and transitional terms such as *for example, that is, furthermore, on the other hand*, and the use of topic sentences to open paragraphs in written discourse).

We make this claim on the basis of speech behavior characteristic of middle-class American adults (Anglo). It may be the case that unplanned and planned discourse can be so characterized only for this population. In this case, we would be offering a culture-specific description of American English varieties. We may find, on the other hand, that, if we looked at unplanned discourse across a number of societies, it would be characterized by a greater reliance on structures acquired early in language development. To the extent that these early-acquired structures transcend particular languages, we may find certain features of unplanned discourse that are common to diverse speech communities.

2.   DATA BASE

In the present chapter, we present our research to date concerning planned and unplanned discourse. Generalizations drawn in this paper are based on analyses of several types of communicative situations: child–child (Keenan 1974, Keenan and Klein 1975, Keenan and Schieffelin 1976), child–adult (Bloom 1973), and adult–adult (Jefferson, transcriptions, Schegloff, transcriptions, Shimanoff, transcriptions). We have examined relatively informal conversations among adult speakers of English, both native speakers and second-language learners (Brunak, transcriptions). Additionally, we have looked at personal narratives delivered under two conditions by the same speakers. In the first instance, the speaker related the narrative without preparation, orally, within a classroom setting. Second, the speaker wrote the narrative and turned it in as a class assignment (2 days later). The first context displayed relatively unplanned discourse, the second relatively planned discourse. The narratives obtained in this manner were transcribed and analysed as a joint project by the 1976–1977 discourse seminar of the Department of Linguistics at the University of Southern California. Members of the seminar included T. Bennett, J. Brunak, P. Giunchi, B. Kroll,

C. Lehman, S. Peck, S. Shimanoff, S. Staron, S. Tenenbaum, and J. Walcutt (with E. Ochs as director).

Our data reflect a variety of speaker–hearer relationships, topics, genres, and modalities (speaking–writing). We have not, however, covered all the relevant contexts for understanding planned and unplanned communication. In particular, we lack material to date on unplanned written discourse and planned spoken discourse. Our generalizations are, then, necessarily preliminary.

3. DIMENSIONS OF PLANNED AND UNPLANNED DISCOURSE

Definition

Before proceeding, let us establish a working definition of UNPLANNED and PLANNED and set out contexts relevant to these concepts.

At the heart of our notion of planning is the idea of FORETHOUGHT. Unplanned discourse is talk that has not been thought out prior to its expression. In this sense, it is spontaneous. Second, our notion of planning involves the idea of a DESIGN or ORGANIZATION. In unplanned discourse, the communicator has not organized how an idea or set of ideas is going to be expressed or how some speech act (Searle 1969) or event (Hymes 1972) is going to be performed prior to the time of communication.

We have arrived at two working definitions:

1. UNPLANNED DISCOURSE *is discourse that lacks forethought and organizational preparation.*
2. PLANNED DISCOURSE *is discourse that has been thought out and organized (designed) prior to its expression.*

Clearly, these definitions characterize extremes of the concept of planning. At the one extreme, we have unplanned discourse that evidences not a shred of preparation or an attempt to structure in an effective and appropriate manner the verbal act. The result is a string of nonsensical, haphazard sounds. At the other extreme, we have planned verbal behavior in which every idea and every lexical item and every structure in which the idea is to be expressed is considered and designed in advance.

Most of the discourse we encounter in the course of day-to-day communications falls at neither extreme. We usually find ourselves producing and listening to language that is relatively unplanned or relatively planned. We shall address ourselves primarily to these less extreme expressions of discourse planning in the discussion at hand, since they more accurately represent the data we have examined. We do not wish to give the impression, however, that the extremes are never observed. Anyone who has worked on a transcript of young children's speech can find numerous instances of speech in which predications are not thought out in advance, in which the informational needs of the intended addressee are not taken into consideration at the time of utterance production, and so on (cf. Atkinson 1974, Keenan and Schieffelin 1976, Scollon 1976). On the other hand, we can find extreme examples of total discourse planning when we deliver or listen to a speech that has been written down in advance and has been read aloud.

Referential and Nonreferential Dimensions of Planning

Nearly every endeavor that addresses itself to pragmatic considerations of language recognizes that language serves a variety of ends (Austin 1962, Grice 1967, Hymes 1962, 1972, Jakobson 1960, Searle 1969, Silverstein 1976). Language is used not only to articulate propositions (arguments and predicates) but also to display deference, to control the interaction at hand, and to persuade, comfort, antagonize, intimidate, impress, and so on. We have adopted Silverstein's view that all of these uses are social in the sense that "they get some socially constituted 'work' done; they accomplish or 'perform' something [1976:18]." Indeed, earlier work on the expression of propositions among young children and caretakers indicates that reference itself is subject to negotiation, checking, confirmation, and the like (Atkinson 1974, Keenan and Klein 1975, Keenan and Schieffelin 1976, Keenan, Schieffelin, and Platt 1978). Reference in these contexts is characteristically INTERACTIONALLY ACCOMPLISHED.

In our discussion of discourse planning, we need to address this multiplicity of social uses of language as well. To characterize a discourse simply as planned or unplanned underrates the social behavior carried out and the breadth of planning demanded in particular situations. For the purposes of this analysis, we have divided the social uses of language into the two categories suggested by Silverstein (1976). The first category includes the use of language to refer and to predicate, that is, to express propositions. Silverstein calls this use the REFERENTIAL FUNCTION of language. The second category includes all the other uses of language; these uses are referred to collectively as the NONREFERENTIAL FUNCTIONS of language.

A discourse may be planned with respect to all the social functions carried out. On the other hand, it may be planned with respect to certain of these functions but unplanned with respect to others. For example, a speaker may have planned his discourse with respect to referring and predicating but have not planned his utterance with respect to the level of politeness appropriate to the communicative situation. Similarly, a speaker (communicator) may have designed his utterance to meet the politeness norms of the situation but may have failed to take into account the fact that his addressee may not be able to identify a referent specified in the utterance expressed. In this case, the discourse was unplanned with respect to its referential dimension but planned with respect to its nonreferential dimension.

Within and across Social Acts

A second important context for assessing discourse planning is the verbal unit under consideration. We can discuss planning with respect to individual social acts and with respect to sequences of social acts. We consider a sequence of two or more social acts to constitute a DISCOURSE. Hence, a discourse may consist of two or more descriptions or adjacency pairs (Sacks and Schegloff 1974), for example, summons–response, invitation-acceptance–decline, greeting–greeting, and so on.

As in our discussion of social functions, we may find that a communication may be planned to varying extents. We can find individual social acts that are well-designed, but the sequence of social acts, the discourse in which they are couched, is unplanned. For example, a speaker may produce a well-thought-out, well-designed predication, but the predication may unintentionally contradict a previous or subsequent predication in the discourse. Similarly, a speaker may have thought out the first part of a riddle sequence but may forget the appropriate response to the riddle. Children are famous for this behavior.

We do not wish to suggest that planning ends at the level of individual social acts. Planning also takes place WITHIN individual acts, in the course of their production. Goodwin (1975) has demonstrated that, in multi-party conversations, speakers alter the content of individual utterances according to shifting contextual factors. For example, the speaker may alter what he is saying according to who gives the speaker positive nonverbal feedback. The speaker may start out directing an utterance to one recipient but may fail to get satisfactory eye contact and may move on to another potential recipient.

We can talk about planning, then, on a number of levels. Discourses may vary in the degree to which they are planned. Discourses in which the form of every social act is worked out in advance are the most planned. Discourses in which only certain acts are attended to in advance are somewhat less planned. And discourses in which acts are thought out in the course of their production are even less planned, and so on.

Discourses vary not only in the extent to which they are planned but also in the extent to which they are PLANNABLE. For example, truly spontaneous conversation is, by definition, relatively unplannable well in advance. Unlike other forms of discourse, in spontaneous conversation it is difficult to predict the form in which entire sequences will be expressed. The content may be even less predictable. Rather, what will be said, the form in which it will be said, and who will say it can be anticipated for limited sequences only (e.g., certain adjacency pairs for certain speaker–hearer relationships). In terms of conversational analysis (Sacks, Schegloff, and Jefferson, 1974), spontaneous conversation is "locally managed." It tends to be designed on a turn-by-turn basis. Other forms of discourse are more plannable. For example, ritualized speech events tend to have more predictable sequential ordering of social acts and more predictable message content. Communicators can anticipate more what will be said and what their verbal contribution should be. Furthermore, written discourse may be more plannable than spontaneous spoken discourse. In writing, the communicator has more time to think out what he is going to say and how it will be said. Additionally, the writer can rewrite and reorganize the discourse a number of times before it is eventually communicated.

In the discussion of unplanned and planned discourse presented later, we shall consider planning in terms of whether or not the discourse has been planned and in terms of whether or not the discourse is plannable. For example, the spoken narratives in the data base are not planned, in the sense that the speakers did not know in advance that they would perform this task. The spontaneous conversations in the data base constitute relatively unplannable discourse, in the sense previously described.

4. FEATURES OF CHILDREN'S DISCOURSE

In turning to the features of discourse planning, I would like to bring our attention back to the original motivation for this concern. I began this discussion with the remark that relatively spontaneous discourse between adult native speakers of English shared certain properties with the discourse of children. I posited the hypothesis that, in these situations, speakers may rely on certain communicative strategies that emerge in the early stages of language development. I would like now to state more specifically what these strategies and features are.

In pursuing this exercise, let us examine a continuous stretch of discourse produced by two children, aged 35 months, in the course of interacting with one another:

(1)   Toby and David (both 2:11), bedroom, early morning
             (An alarm clock rings in the next room.)

DAVID	TOBY
bell/	*bell/*
bell/	
its mommys/	*(?) it/*
was mommys alarm clock/	*'larm clock/*
	yeah/
	goes dindong ding dong/
no/	
no/	
goes fip fip/fip fip/	

This passage exhibits a number of communicative features generally characteristic of young children's discourse:

1. On the ideational level, a proposition is conveyed over a series of utterances. Objects and entities noticed in one utterance are subsequently used as major arguments of one or more predications. Here, *bell/* is noticed in one utterance, and subsequently *bell* becomes the major argument for the predications *its mommys/* and *was mommy's alarm clock/*. Similarly, Toby uses the referent of *'larm clock/* as the argument for his subsequent predication *goes ding dong ding dong*, and so on.

The sequential character of expressed propositions is by now a fairly widely observed phenomenon. For reports of this feature in adult–child discourse, see Bloom (1973), Keenan and Schieffelin (1976), Keenan, Schieffelin, and Platt (1978), Ochs, Schieffelin, and Platt (1979), Scollon (1976), and Atkinson (1974).

2. A corollary of the sequential expression of propositions is that arguments and their predicates are often tied through their position in the discourse rather than through syntactic means. We relate the two parts of the proposition because they appear in sequentially adjacent positions. We use some pragmatic principle in making the connection. For example, we connect *'larm clock* with *goes ding dong ding dong* because they are in close proximity of one another and because we expect utterances in close proximity to be relevant to one another (unless otherwise signaled) (cf. Grice, 1967, Sacks and Schegloff 1974) and because it makes sense to relate the utterances to one another given our knowledge of the world.

At 35 months, it is obviously not the case that all propositions have this status. We get a mixture of syntactically bound propositions and sequentially bound propositions. At the single word stage, however, the sequential connection predominates. Bloom (1973) calls such constructions "holistic" and Scollon (1976) calls them "vertical." The development of language is seen as a gradual progression away from pragmatic devices toward greater reliance on syntax ("horizontal constructions"). A point I would like to stress here is that the sequential strategy does not eventually disappear altogether. Adult discourse as well evidences this feature under certain conditions.

3.   Notice as well in this passage that there is a great deal of repetition. The repetition is of two sorts: self-repetition and other-repetition. In other-repetition, the speaker repeats what someone else previously uttered. Self- and other-repetition carry out a variety of communicative functions, only a few of which are displayed in this example. Self-repetition may be used to draw the hearer's attention to something the speaker has noticed, as in example (2):

(2)   Toby and David (both 2:11), bedroom, early morning
         (D. holding a truck, picks up rabbit. T. whistles on pretend flute
             continuously while facing D.)

DAVID   TOBY
rabbit/rabbit/
I find truck/rabbit/
(?) like rabbit/
truck/rabbit/
rabbit/rabbit/
truck truck rabbit/
truck/rabbit/
(showing truck and rabbit to T.)
truck/rabbit/rabbit/
rabbit/   *truck/rabbit/*
let me blow?/

Self-repetition may also be used to emphasize a point. Example (2) displays both of these uses. Furthermore, self-repetition may be used to clarify or to correct a previous utterance, as in example (1), where David says *its mommys/was mommys alarm clock/*. In the second utterance, the tense is changed and utterance is expanded to include the noun phrase *alarm clock*. It is a fuller and more accurate expression of what has happened.

The use of other-repetition has been analyzed in some detail in previous papers (Keenan 1974, 1975, Keenan and Klein 1975, Keenan and Schieffelin 1976). Other-repetition is one of the most widely used devices among language-acquiring children. Among other uses, it serves to let the speaker know that the addressee is attending to some object under consideration. For example, in (1) Toby's utterance *bell/* lets David know that he too has noticed/is attending to the bell. In example (2), Toby finally lets David know he has noticed the truck and rabbit David is holding up. He does this by eventually repeating *truck/rabbit/*. Similarly, the repetition of propositions or parts of propositions may serve to acknowledge, agree with, disagree with, or challenge or question, depending on the nature of the prior communicative act (a request for information, an announcement, an assessment, etc.) and the manner in which the repetition is produced (e.g., the intonation contour).

4. There is a tendency to use lexical items having similar phonological features across a series of adjacent utterances (Keenan 1974, 1975, Keenan and Klein 1975, Weir 1970). In the discourse of young children, we find recurrent use of certain sounds and clusters of sounds. For example, in (2) we see that both *truck* and *rabbit* contain the sounds /t/, /k/, /b/. These sounds all share the features of being STOPS, varying only in place of articulation. On many occasions, the sound patterns themselves become a major focus of attention rather than the literal meaning of the lexical item. This could account in part for why David repeats *truck/rabbit* in an apparently tireless fashion. We of course have observed cases in which the focus of the child was exclusively on the sound patterns, where the resulting combinations have no referential meaning whatsoever. Example (3) illustrates such an orientation:

(3)   Toby and David (both 33 months), bedroom, early morning

DAVID	TOBY
apple kings/apple keys/	
apple kings/	
	apples/apples/apples/apples . . .
gi:naug/ ginɔːg/ ginɔː/	
	ginɔːg/ginɔːg/ginɔːg/ginɔːg/
(laughs)	
ki:tan/ki:tan/	
kakadu/kakadu/	*no/ kakadu/*
kakadu/	
	no kakadu/wʌps koːsʌps koːz/
zʌp koːz ka/	

5. In addition to the aforementioned properties, it is, of course, the case that children use relatively simple morphosyntactic structures. We find reliance on simple, active sentences, or unmarked SVO word order for declaratives. We find reliance on deictic items (*this, that, there, here,* etc.) rather than on definite articles and relative clauses. We find deletion of major terms of reference as well as deletion of functor words (articles, prepositions, etc.). In short, we find the kind of morphosyntactic form that characterizes early child language (cf. Bloom 1970, Brown 1973, Slobin 1973, etc.). Much

of the deleted information is, alternatively, conveyed through nonverbal means, such as pointing, touching, reaching toward, gaze direction, and the like (Keenan and Schieffelin 1976).

5. FEATURES OF RELATIVELY UNPLANNED AND PLANNED DISCOURSE

I present here a number of features that characterize and distinguish relatively unplanned and planned discourse of English speakers. The principles are by no means exhaustive. They are presented as initial generalizations to be refined and extended over the course of future research. I will relate these features to the strategies of young children. However, my order of discussion will not necessarily follow the ordering of child language features presented before.

FEATURE 1 : *In relatively unplanned discourse more than in planned discourse, speakers rely on the immediate context to express propositions.*

This principle claims that, in spontaneous communication, speakers (communicators) rely less heavily on syntax to articulate semantic relations obtaining between referents or between whole propositions. That is, along a continuum of use, reliance on context to communicate information falls toward the unplanned pole, and reliance on syntax falls towards the planned pole.

Context is used to link referents (logical arguments) to their relevant predications, and it is used to link whole propositions to one another. Let us consider first the reliance on context to link arguments and predicates.

Argument–Predicate Relations

REFERENT DELETION

One of the observations on child language previously presented above is that children frequently do not articulate the semantic relation of an argument to its predicate through syntactic means. On the one hand, we find reliance on nonverbal means to supply the missing information, for example, the use of pointing, reaching, holding up, eye gaze, etc. Second, we find reliance on the verbal environment to supply the necessary information. In particular, we observed a pattern whereby the listener has to turn to the previous discourse to locate exactly what the child is referring to. It is the "nextness" of the referent and the predication that creates the link between the two pieces of information. The link is not made through syntactic means.

We find a similar pattern in the spontaneous discourse of certain speakers. In particular, we find predications in which the major argument is deleted in the current utterance. To locate the relevant referent, the listener must turn back to the discourse history or to the situation at hand. With respect to the situation at hand, it is primarily reference to the speaker and to the hearer that is deletable, as in (4) below:

(4)   Two Girls (Schegloff, transcript)

       B: *Uh how's school goin.*
       A: *Oh: same old shit.*
       B: *Hhhh//(really?)*
→ A: *'have a lotta tough courses.*

With respect to the discourse history, speakers will rely on the listener's acquaintance with any referent, regardless of person (third person referents are as likely to be deleted as are first person referents) and number (singular, plural). Examples (5), (6), and (7) illustrate predications that rely on previously specified referents:

(5)   Two Girls

       B: *Y'have any cla- y'have a class with **Billy** this term/*
       A: *Yeah he's in my Abnormal class*
       B: *Oh yeah//how*
       A: *Abnormal Psych.*
→ B: *Still not married*
       A: *((loud)) Oh no definitely not// (no)*

(6)   A Jewish Grandfather (Shimanoff, transcription)
      (G. has been talking about the fact that his grandson is difficult to please. He gives one example—oatmeal cereal)

       G: *And **its** uh **got ta good taste**, its **good**. And the **cereal**-grandma e don't like **cereal** but she **finished** to the last (**dish**) and I enjoy— I like it too. It's tasty! And I uh (1.2) He didn't want the **cereal**,*
→   **doesn't** *eat. I said, "**Todd** it wouldn't **kill ya**, **taste** it!" . . . .*

(7)   Subways in London (Brunak, transcript) (unplanned version)
      (G. has been telling story of how she had to grab hold of a woman to keep from falling off a subway platform. The woman started to fall back as well but was stopped by a nearby man.)

       G: *and it seemed like a long time when it happened but when I look back at it it happened just like that ((snaps his fingers)) this man-this guy there almost **casually** looked over at 'er and just **grabbed** '**er arm** (.7) and pulled '**er** back up and then I just kind*
→   *'a grabbed her ((laugh)) and **looked** at me like I had **the nerve** to assault 'er. it was like **how dare you** ((high-pitched))*

Notice in these examples that it does not seem to matter what grammatical status the previous NP holds. Prior objects of prepositions (5), subjects (6), direct objects (7), and so on may in turn be employed as deleted subjects of subsequent predications. Deletions such as these do not appear in more planned, more formal discourse. For example, (7) is part of the USC seminar project on unplanned and planned narrative form. In the planned version, the episode was expressed as in (8) below:

(8)   Subways in London (planned).

> *The train sped nearer as we were both ready to fall off the edge. A friend with whom she had been talking, clutched her other arm and steadied her as I pulled on the purse's shoulder strap moving closer to her arm. My balance was finally steadied and it wasn't until after some exchanges of looks did I move on with a quick "Excuse me."*

We can see here how in the more planned version, the narrator does not delete any of the referents.

REFERENT AND PROPOSITION

Thus far we have looked at cases in which there is no syntactic relation between a referent and its predication because the referent is, in fact, missing. There are, however, other cases in which a referent is specified initially, and, subsequently, an entire proposition relevant to the referent is expressed. These contributions have been treated in two earlier papers (Duranti and Keenan 1976, Keenan and Schieffelin 1976). We refer to them as "Referent + Proposition" (Ref + Prop) constructions. They differ from the previously illustrated sequences in that no referent is deleted. In certain of these Ref + Prop constructions, it is rather that the semantic relation between the referent and the subsequent predication is not expressed. In a certain sense, these initial referents serve as topics (Li and Thompson 1976) for the subsequent propositions and imply an *as for* or *concerning* relation. This is illustrated in (9) below:

(9)   Two Girls (Schegloff, manuscript)
        (Discussing classes at the local university)

                              Ref
→B: *Ohh I g'ta tell ya **one** course*
A: (*incred-*)
                              Ref   Prop
→B: *The mo- the modern art   the twentieth century art, there's about eight books*

Here, there is a reference to B's twentieth century art course, and the reference is followed immediately by an entire proposition, that is, *there's about eight books.* We might paraphrase the sequence *As for one course, the modern art, the twentieth century art, there's about eight books.* However, as it stands, there is no explicit *as for* or its equivalent, and the semantic relation obtaining between the initial three noun phrases and the subsequent sentence is inferred only from the positioning of these two structures. It is not syntactically expressed. We use the principle of NEXTNESS to make the link and associate the referent and the proposition.

As with the argument–predicate constructions discussed earlier, these Ref + Prop constructions as well rarely appear in more formal, prearranged Standard English discourse. Work carried out by Duranti and Keenan (1976) evidences that this difference is characteristic of Italian discourse as well. Ref + Prop constructions appear in spontaneous conversation between intimates but rarely appear in newspaper articles and magazines, scholarly papers, and so on (Duranti and Keenan 1976).

There is a particular type of Referent + Proposition construction that is more commonly discussed in the linguistics literature. This is the construction linguists have called left-dislocation (Ross 1967, Gundel 1975). According to Ross, left-dislocation is a transformation that moves an NP out of and to the left of a clause, leaving in its place a co-referential pronoun. A series of these constructions are illustrated in examples (10), (11), and (12) below:

(10)   GTS 4:1 (Jefferson, manuscript)
         (K has been talking about the fact that his car radio was taken
         from his car)

         K: *They cleaned me out. And my father oh he's//he's fit to be tied.*

(11)   GTS 4:15

         K: *Uh Pat McGee. I don't know if you know him, he- he lives
         in//Palisades.*

(12)   GTS 5:35
         (Discussing students falling asleep in class)

    → K: *Uh::this guy, you could yell "Hey John, Hey Joh-" 'n you c'd
         go over an' tap him on the shoulder*
      R: *So he's gotta//good imagination*
      K: *That's the only way you c'd snap him out of it.*

In these examples, the left-dislocated NPs are *my father, Pat McGee,* and *this guy,* respectively.

The left-dislocations differ from both of the previously discussed constructions in that there is a reference to the relevant referent within the subsequent predication. This reference is through the coreferential pronoun in the predication. The constructions are of interest to us because they otherwise appear to share many of the properties of sequentially expressed propositions. The initial referent appears to be part of a separate utterance, a separate speech act, if you will, in much the same way as the other referents we have considered are. We can not say that the principle of NEXTNESS alone encourages the listener to link the initial referent to the subsequent proposition, the copy pronoun does this as well. These constructions, then, stand somewhere between single subject–predicate constructions and discourse. They share properties of both.

A second reason why left-dislocations are of interest to this discussion is that they too rarely appear in highly planned discourse. We rarely find left-dislocations in written prose, for example. On the other hand, we do find left-dislocations or rather constructions like left-dislocations abundantly in the speech of young children producing multi word utterances. For example, in (1) David's two utterances *bell/its mommys/* could be considered as a left-dislocation (see also Gruber 1967). These constructions may as well be transitional structures anticipating more syntactically coherent sentences. They are not transitional in the sense that they disappear altogether. We have just witnessed that adult speakers produce these constructions when they are speaking under casual, spontaneous circumstances. They may be transitional in the sense that the child may first use this type of construction exclusively to express certain semantic relations. At a later point, the child comes to utilize both the subject–predicate and the left-dislocation construction to express those relations.

Proposition–Proposition Relations

Context may link whole propositions as well as constituents within a single proposition to one another. We may link one proposition to another because they appear next to one another and because we expect sequentially expressed propositions to be relevant to one another. In using context, the communicator does not make the semantic relation obtaining between the propositions explicit. For example, if the communicator produces the sequence *I don't like that house. It looks strange.*, he does not specify explicitly the link between these assessments. As recipients of this communication, we use our knowledge of the world and our expectations concerning the sequencing of talk to relate the two propositions. We treat the second utterance not only as relevant but also as relevant in a particular sense, for example, as providing an explanation or basis for the initial assessment.

Our observations of discourse indicate that context is an alternative to syntax and that planned and unplanned discourse differ in their utilization of the two alternatives. Syntax makes the semantic link explicit, for example, *I don't like that house, **because** it looks strange.* It is relied upon more heavily in planned versus relatively unplanned discourse. This association may be due to the possibility that it takes more planning to express a specific semantic relation (using a syntactic term) than to imply only that some semantic relation obtains. In the former case, the speaker's encoding task is greater and may demand greater planning.

The spontaneous conversations and unplanned versions of personal narratives in the data base were laced with contextually linked propositions. An analysis of subordinate and coordinate constructions done by Kroll (1977) indicated that, in the unplanned narratives, only 7.1% of the clauses were subordinate constructions, whereas in the planned narratives 20% were subordinate.

To see these two types of propositional links, compare (13) with (14) below. Example (13) presents a portion of a spontaneous narrative. Example (14) presents the same event described in the planned version of the same narrative.

(13)   Driving Home (Kroll, transcription) (Unplanned Version)
        [M describes to class (C) how his father nearly crashed into a truck]

        M: *so he decides that he's gonna pass these cars (?) and uh (.4) he*
            pulls out in the other lane and starts passin' 'em (.5) and all of
            a sudden we see this big truck, you know
        C: (laughter)
        M: *This truck comin' for us and uh (.5) this guy was going pretty*
            fast and (.5) and we had passed one car and there's no way we
            can get (in or out) and uhm this trucker's comin' and he's just
            sort of bearing down on us and honkin' his horn. He wasn't
            slowing down
        C: (laughter)

(14)   Driving Home (Planned Version)

        After some five minutes of tailing these cars, my father decided it
        was time to pass the cars.

        He pulled into the other lane and accelerated. As we passed the first
        car we noticed a large Mack truck coming our way.

Examples of the immediate context alone linking propositions are provided in (15) and (16):

(15)   Two Girls

        A: *I'm so.... tired I played basketball today ( ) the first time since*
            I was a freshman in high school
        B: *Bask(hh)etb(hhall) heh heh/heh*
        (versus *I am so tired, **because** I played basketball for the first time*
        since I was a freshman in high school)

(16)   Jewish Grandfather

> G: *Alright, he moved **out**, he's- in fact, **Ruthie**: wro:te to me e*
> *Joseph (hey Pa:) is not good for him to **stay** here. let him stay*
> *here jist **one** week**end** to let him get uh (   ) **dormotory** and*
> *(for what)- he's earning the **money**. Let him **spend it**. He'll be*
> ***too much** for **you**.*
>
> (versus *It is not good for him to stay here, **therefore**. . . . . Let him*
> *stay here just one weekend. . . . . **because**. . . . , etc.)*

FEATURE 2: *In relatively unplanned discourse more than in planned*
discourse, speakers rely on morphosyntactic structures acquired in the
early stages of language development. Relatively planned discourse makes
greater use of morphosyntactic structures that are relatively late to
emerge in language.

As suggested in the preceding section, in relatively unplanned discourse
speakers tend to avoid using grammatical structures that are late to emerge
in language development. For example, Limber (1973) indicates that the
use of subordinate conjunctions appears later in the child's speech than does
the use of coordinate conjunctions. In fact, "The earliest suggestion of conjunction is the grouping of two sentences together without a distinguishable
conjoining morpheme. Very often, in listening to tapes made between 2:0
and 2:4, one is apt to perceive a *so, and,* or *if,* when, in fact, upon replay
there is not any direct basis for this percept [p. 182]."

In addition to the above structures, we find the following morphosyntactic preferences in relatively unplanned discourse:

Modes of Reference

We find a greater reliance on earlier emergent forms of reference in
spontaneous discourse. For example, we find frequent use of demonstrative
modifiers where definite articles are used in planned discourse. Compare,
for example, the unplanned version of a narrative, as in (17), with the
planned version, as in (18):

(17)   Subways in London (Unplanned)

> G: *I'd done this many times before so I didn't think twice about it*
> →   *(I was walk-) I tried to walk between the edge of this platform*
> *(.7) A:nd this group of people*

(18)   Subways in London (Planned)

> *Squeezing through narrow spaces and finding my way between people*
> →   *I continued in my pursuit of an emptier spot on the train platform*

and a woman whose back was turned toward me as she wildly conversed with some friends.

Similarly, in reference, there is a reliance on simpler, determiner (demonstrative, definite article, etc.) plus noun constructions in situations in which, in planned discourse, the communicator would use a RELATIVE CLAUSE CONSTRUCTION. Compare, for example, the unplanned and planned versions of the narrative "Subways in London." In the unplanned version illustrated in example (7), a character is referred to as *this man-this guy*. The same individual is referred to as *a friend with whom she had been talking* in the planned version, illustrated in (8). Similarly, in the same narrative, the major female character is referred to as *this woman lady* in the unplanned version. This is illustrated in (19):

(19)   Subways in London (Brunak, manuscript) (Unplanned)

      G: *So I was walkin' along the edge and uh as I said there were these*
  →   *people talkin' and this woman **lady** was describin' somethin'. . .*

In the planned version, the same woman is referred to as *a woman whose back was turned*. This is illustrated in (18).

Other alternatives to relative clause constructions found in relatively unplanned discourse include referent + proposition constructions (see FEATURE 1) and noun + prepositional phrase constructions.

Schachter (1974) has discussed the avoidance of relative clauses as a strategy of certain speakers learning English as a second language. Here we can see that native speakers as well often rely on syntactically simpler alternative forms of reference. Indeed, in many cases, we can see the avoidance explicitly in unplanned discourse. The speaker starts to use the relative clause construction but cuts the construction off before its completion and reformulates the reference in an alternative fashion. In the example below, the speaker reformulates the relative clause as an independent construction:

(20)   Two Girls

      B: *That is s- y'know this 'the Indian class an' they stuck us in this*
  →   *crazy building- that they j- they're not even finished with it.*

Verb Voice

Another area in which relatively planned and unplanned discourse differ concerns the use of active and passive voice. Developmentally, the passive voice is acquired much later than the active voice among English-speaking children (Bever 1970). We find that the passive voice is rare in both planned and unplanned discourse. However, relative to unplanned discourse, it appears with much greater frequency in planned discourse. Bennett (1977) examined verb voice in the unplanned and planned personal narratives. In the unplanned narratives, the passive accounted for .9% of the total verbs. In the planned versions, the passive accounted for 7.05% of the total verbs. The contrastive use of these two voices is illustrated in examples (7) and (8).

Verb Tense

An additional point of contrast between relatively planned and unplanned communication concerns the use of verb tense. Developmentally, the use of the present tense anticipates past and future tenses (Antinucci and Miller 1976, Brown 1973). That is, even when the past or future is referred to, children will initially use the present tense. The narratives in our data base all concern past events in the experience of the narrator. In referring to these events, the speaker did not always use the past tense in the unplanned versions. In contrast to the planned versions, the speaker frequently used the present tense in relating past events. Examples (13) and (14) illustrate the different use of tense to relate the same events. Typically, the past is used in the initial part of the narrative, to orient the addressee to the temporal and spatial context of the event related. Once the context is specified, the speaker moves toward greater use of the present tense (Walcutt 1977). Notice here that this way of marking temporal ordering is similar to that described for certain pidgin–creole languages (Sankoff and Kay 1974).

> FEATURE 3: *In relatively unplanned discourse more than in relatively planned discourse, speakers tend to repeat and replace lexical items in the expression of a proposition* (Shimanoff and Brunak 1977).

In most cases, repetition and word replacement within a speech act reflect trouble spots in the communication. Repetition of a lexical item may be part of the speaker's search for a particular word (Schegloff, Jefferson, and Sacks 1977) or predication. The search may be motivated by the speaker's desire to select a term or construction that is appropriate to the addressee or clear to the addressee. Or the speaker may repeat a term (set of terms) because the speaker feels that the initial term has not been decoded by the addressee. For example, in (13) the speaker repeats *this truck* following the occurrence of laughter simultaneous with the first mention of *this truck*. Schegloff *et al.* (1977) treat these repetitions as "repairs" on the occurrence of overlap in conversation. Repetition may also be simply part of the speaker's attempt to think out an idea.

Repetition is a highly versatile device, and it is among the earliest behaviors emergent in the speech of the language-acquiring child (Keenan 1975, Scollon 1976).

Word replacement is another example of what Schegloff, Jefferson, and Sacks (1977) call "repair" or error-correction. As with the use of repetition, the motivations for the replacement are diverse. The speaker may replace one term with another because the initial term is inappropriate:

(21)   Two Girls

> B: *This fella I have uh "**fella**" This **man**, he had uh f- who I have for linguistics is*
> A: *Hm hm*
> B: *really too **much***

Or the term (set of terms) initially used may not accurately express what the speaker wishes to convey:

(22)   Skiing over a Cliff (Shimanoff, transcription) (Unplanned)

> M: *So: I sor:ta rushed myself. And I uh went down (1.1) this this uh (cliff) not really a cliff but it was a very sharp incline of the mountain.*

Word replacement is part of a more general phenomena characteristic of relatively unplanned discourse—afterthought (Hyman 1975). The communicator remembers after the relevant point in the discourse that certain information is missing. In many cases, the personal narratives in our corpus contained whole propositions as afterthoughts. The narrator would remember that relevant background information had not been provided. Example (23) below illustrates the appearance of afterthoughts in the unplanned version of a narrative. Example (24) illustrates the omission of such afterthoughts in the planned version of the same narrative.

(23)   People Scare Me (Staron, transcription) (Unplanned)

> F: *Well (.2) we ( ) came um we stayed across the street from our house.⌊I used ta live in Florida an' we stayed across the street cuz my mom was in the hospital an' we were really small. ⌋ ?*

(24)   People Scare Me (Planned)

> *When I was ten years old my sister, brother, and I stayed with the neighbors across the street while my mother was in the hospital.*

The use of repetition and word replacement for the purpose of improving or correcting some dimension of the communication indicates that planning is going on in the course of the speech act itself. When we speak of these features as characteristic of relatively unplanned discourse, we mean that either the communicator has not planned his communication prior to the individual speech act or the communication was unplannable prior to the individual speech act (e.g., shifting addressees, speaker–hearer roles, etc.).

The use of repetition and other hesitation phenomena, word replacement, and other forms of afterthought and repair lead to lengthy formulations of particular social acts. We find that, in relatively unplanned discourse, the expression of social acts tend to take up more discourse "space" (cf. Keenan and Schieffelin 1976) than in planned discourse. That is, the same social act verbalized in planned discourse will be more compact than the unplanned version. For example, compare the unplanned and planned versions of "People Scare Me" illustrated in (23) and (24). Other features mentioned in previous sections also contribute to this characteristic of unplanned discourse. The use of referent + proposition constructions rather than subject–predicate constructions and the use of coordinate constructions in place of subordinate constructions lead as well to more "spacious" renditions of descriptions, requests, announcements, and the like. Differences in discourse space created by these alternative constructions are demonstrated in (13) and (14).

> FEATURE 4: *In relatively unplanned discourse, the form and content of sequentially arranged social acts tend to be more similar than in relatively planned discourse.*

In our discussion of FEATURE 3, we mentioned that unplanned discourse contained repetition within social acts. Here we treat another form of repetition in which parts of previously expressed social acts are incorporated in subsequent acts. The features incorporated may be morphological, syntactic, or phonological. For example, a LEXICAL ITEM appearing in one utterance in an unplanned discourse may be repeated in one or more subsequent utterances:

(25)   Two Girls (Schegloff ms.)

        A: (*You sounded so// far*)
→ B: *Right/*
        A: *Yeah*
→ B: *See/ I- I'm doin' something right t'day finally*
        A: *Mm*
→ B: *I finally said something right. You are home hh.*

In many cases, the lexical item repeated serves the same grammatical function in the series of utterances in which it appears. We sometimes find the repetition of two or more lexical items, both occupying the same grammatical roles in the sequence in which they appear. Example (26) illustrates such a case.

(26)   Jewish Grandfather (Shimanoff, manuscript)

→ G: *So sometimes you know you can lose the letter you can-something can happen in Beverly Hills.*

This example as well as example (6) illustrates how a speaker may become locked into a subject or subject–verb frame. Shifts in perspective are sometimes accomplished only by cutting off an existing frame and recyclying (Schegloff 1974) the speech act using a novel frame, for example, the *you can* frame is replaced by *something can* in (26).

The repetition of prior utterances or parts of prior utterances is a basic characteristic of early child discourse. Scollon (1976) for single-word and Keenan (1974, 1975) and Weir (1970) for multiword utterances show that cross-utterance repetition dominates the earliest discourses of children. An earlier study by the author (Keenan 1974, 1975, Keenan and Klein 1975) showed that, over time, reliance on repetition gives way to substitution (*Mommys silly/Daddys silly/, not sketis/ makaronis, not shoes/ slippers*) and to formally novel means of maintaining continuity across utterances. In the initial period, form and content are maintained across utterances. In the subsequent period, form is maintained, but content changes; and, in the final period, both form and content change. (That is, in each subsequent period an alternative means of maintaining coherence is available; options are increased over time.) It may be the case that it requires more forethought and planning to alter both the form and the content of a message than to alter the content alone. Language development may be linked to an increased capacity of the child to attend to both the form and the content of the propositions they express.

Similarly, in the adult corpus, it may be the case that, when speakers have not previously organized their discourse, they may retain the same morphosyntactic format to express novel content. Hence, stream-of-consciousness writing and on-the-spot working-out of a difficult concept may exhibit repeated use of a formal frame.

The similarity in form across utterances in relatively unplanned discourse is not limited to morphological and syntactic form. We find as well similarities in the PHONOLOGICAL shape of sequentially placed speech acts. For example, in (27)

(27)   Two Girls

A: *Ripped about **four** nails, and oh::ch*
B: *Fantastic*
A: *But it was **fun**. Y'sound very far away*

we have repetition of the phone /f/. Furthermore, we have repetition of the phone sequence /f/ + /r/ (*four, far*) and the phone sequence /f/ + /n/ (*fantastic, fun*).

As noted in Section 4, phonological repetition is a very early feature of children's discourse (Jakobson 1968, Keenan 1974, Weir 1970). Children at times seem to select lexical items on the basis of their phonological similarity rather than on the basis of their appropriateness to the message conveyed. Previous reports of this phenomenon describe the behavior as "language play" or "sound play." It has been exclusively associated with the speech behavior of very young children. In terms of the "replacement" model, this behavior apparently disappears in the course of language development. We see here that this kind of behavior does not in fact disappear. Adults as well appear to select their words at least in part on phonological grounds (i.e., phonological similarity).

Schegloff (personal communication) refers to this phenomenon as "sound touch offs" in adult speech. That is, the sound of one item in the discourse may "touch-off" the articulation of other items sharing those sound patters. These sound touch-offs represent one type of touched-off behavior. For example, Schegloff has discussed the phenomenon of lexical touch-offs as well. In certain cases, one lexical item may touch-off another lexical item having a complementary or opposite meaning. We have found, in our spontaneous data, discourse of this character. The speaker mentions a particular lexical item in one utterance, and, in subsequent utterances, its opposite appears. Example (28) illustrates this behavior:

(28)   Skiing over a Cliff (Unplanned)

> M: *And we were caught **up** in a snow: storm (1.5) An:d we were skiing **down** the mountain. An:d he was in **front** of me with some other **friend** an:d **I** had **stopped** at a corner, cuz one of my **bindings** were **broken**, and was trying to git my ski boot back up to the **skii:es**. (1.0) So I **wasn** uh: very **sharp**, and I'd say about **six** people i:n front of **me**. . . . .*

Here we find *up* followed by *down* in the subsequent clause and then *up* reappearing four clauses later. Similarly, *front* is followed by *back* three clauses later with *front* reappearing two clauses after that.

From our point of view, we cannot tell if it is always the case that sounds or meanings of lexical items "touch off" subsequent items. It may not be the case that the initial item triggered the production of subsequent items. Rather, it could be the case that the speaker (writer) is thinking ahead, projecting what he is going to say next in the course of the current utterance or just before the current utterance. This projection may lead him to produce the initial lexical item in the first place (see Fromkin 1973).

(29)   Jewish Grandfather
            G: *So **we** had a **couple** of **skirmishes**. Not only **this** with the **food**,
            but the you know he's he's hon- you know his he **doesn't trust**
            people.*

For example, in (29), it does not appear that the initial item *honest* touches
off *doesn't trust*. Rather, it appears as if the speaker was thinking about
doesn't trust but unconsciously articulated a term having its opposite
meaning. That is, it is the FUTURE CONCEPT that touches off the initial lexical
item.

6. CONSTRAINTS ON DISCOURSE PLANNING

In this section I ask the question "What conditions create relatively
unplanned discourse?" In previous sections, I have mentioned that planning
must be discussed for both referential and nonreferential functions of language. I suggest here that, if one or the other of these functions place heavy
demands on the communicator, that relatively unplanned discourse will be
produced. That is, in many cases it is because the communicator is attending
to ideational or situational demands that he is unable to attend to all dimensions of the message form. Let us consider each of these demands in turn.

Situational Demands

In some cases, a communicator cannot plan the form of his communication because the situation in which he is participating requires more or less
continuous monitoring. For example, in spontaneous conversation, who
will assume the floor, when the floor will be assumed, and what will be
communicated is negotiated on a turn-by-turn basis. The participant in such
a situation must attend closely to each turn in order to deal with each of
these questions. If he wishes to take hold of the floor, he must listen for the
first possible moment in which he can appropriately do so (i.e., the first
possible "transition relevance space"—see Sacks, Schegloff, and Jefferson
1974). In previous studies (Duranti and Keenan 1976, Keenan and Schieffelin
1976), we found that referent + proposition constructions (or left-dislocations) appear in the context of such behavior. In an effort to take hold of
the floor, the speaker makes reference to some entity ("referent") initially
and only subsequently formulates the predication relevant to the referent.
The initial NP acts as a place-holder allowing the speaker to maintain the
floor. Where turn-taking is locally managed in this sense, it may take priority
over the expression of well-formed propositions for the communicator. The

more predictable the sequential ordering of talk, the freer the communicator is to attend to the propositions he wishes to express and the form in which they are to be expressed.

Conceptual Demands

Just as situational demands may interfere with the planning of propositions, so the demands of expressing a proposition may interfere with the organization of other social acts. Conceptual demands may be of various sorts. For example, a concept may demand the speaker's (writer's) concentration because it is cognitively complex for that individual. The communicator may need to focus primarily on working out the idea and on articulating it. With this priority at hand, the communicator may fail to plan his discourse on other social levels. For example, he may fail to attend to social norms constraining how long a turn at talk should be, how much information should be conveyed, and the appropriate form of expression for that addressee.

This kind of conceptual demand is the basis of EGOCENTRIC speech in young children. Braunwald (forthcoming) observes that young children stop attending to the needs of their conversational partners when they talk about some topic that slightly exceeds their cognitive capacity. So, for example, when children start talking about the remote past, they may not attend to the needs of the intended recipient of the talk. On the other hand, when children talk about topics with which they are familiar and that are within their cognitive capacity, they are much more sociocentric. This study is consistent with the observations of the author of children's discourse. The most highly social behavior of the children observed involved songs, rhymes, sound play, and topical talk linked to the here-and-now (Keenan 1974).

As with other dimensions of language development, we do not see egocentric speech as ultimately replaced by social speech. Rather, egocentric speech persists throughout adult life, appearing under much the same conditions as in child language. When an adult is thinking through a difficult idea, he may "tune out" the behavior of others present. Often, for example, the speaker will avoid eye contact. Here, the speaker appears unwilling to establish intersubjectivity and to register additional social demands.[2]

In our discussion of sources of unplanned discourse, we do not wish to suggest that situational demands take their toll only on the planning of propositions and that conceptual demands take their toll only on non-

---

[2] We have mentioned only one source of egocentric speech, but there exist other sources as well. For example, the speaker may be concentrating on what he is doing or thinking because it is interesting or is of some importance to him.

referential planning. The demands may affect every dimension of discourse planning. Thus, for example, conceptual demands may lead a communicator not to take into consideration critical informational needs of his listeners (readers) prior to its expression. Similarly, situational demands on the level of turn-taking may lead a speaker to ignore displays of politeness appropriate to that situation.

7. PLANNED UNPLANNED DISCOURSE

This chapter would not be complete without some discussion of the self-conscious expression of unplanned discourse features. There are cases in which a speaker or writer will intentionally produce discourse that appears unplanned. For example, a novelist trying to recreate a casual situational context will use many of the features (e.g., left-dislocation, deletion, hesitations) of unplanned discourse in his story. In fact, we regard a novelist highly if she or he is able successfully to reproduce such verbal spontaneity.

Second, we can find planned unplanned discourse in many speeches and lectures of skilled rhetoricians. Journalists, politicians, even academics at times have planned their discourse to appear as if it were being planned in the course of its delivery when, in fact, it has been worked out well in advance.

Third, in the anthropological literature there are accounts of cultures in which lower-status individuals are expected to speak as if they had not or *cf. 593* could not organize what they have to say. Albert's study of the Burundi makes this point effectively:

> It would be an unforgivable blunder for a peasant-farmer, no matter how wealthy or able, to produce a truly elegant, eloquent, rapid-fire defense before a herder or other superior. However, the same peasant who stammers or shouts or forces a smile from a superior by making a rhetorical fool out of himself when his adversary is a prince or herder may (elsewhere) . . . show himself an able speaker, a dignified man who speaks as slowly and as intelligently as ever a highborn herder could [1972:83].

We do not have to venture to distant cultures to witness this behavior. Accounts of lower socioeconomic status groups within our own society describe the same expectations (cf. Abrahams 1964).

In all of these situations, features of unplanned discourse are exploited for specific ends, for example, to get something. We offer here a framework for describing the distinguishing characteristics of this communicative behavior, one that is potentially productive for cross-cultural studies of communicative strategies. Future research is needed to assess not only the extent to which features of unplanned discourse are common across languages and cultures but also the extent to which these features match more self-conscious attempts to produce unplanned discourse. Do the screen play writer, novelist, politician, and Burundi peasant in fact utilize the actual features of unplanned discourse? To what extent have certain features become conventionalized? Are there features of unplanned discourse that have become stereotyped or stigmatized across a number of speech communities?

It is important to distinguish this use of unplanned discourse features from truly unplanned discourse. Simply displaying certain features is not sufficient for a discourse to be unplanned. The discourse must lack forethought and prior organization on the part of the communicator. (See Section 3 for this definition of unplanned discourse.) We can draw an analogy here between this behavior and that of the sober man pretending to be drunk. He may stagger from pillar to post, roll back his eyes, and slur his speech, but we would not want to say "This man is drunk." Similarly, when a communicator self-consciously adopts features of unplanned discourse, we do not want to say "This discourse is unplanned."

REFERENCES

Abrahams, R. (1964) *Deep Down in the Jungle*, Hatboro, P., Folklore Associates.
Albert, E. (1972) "Cultural Patterning of Speech Behavior in Burundi," in J. Gumperz and D. Hymes, eds., *Directions in Sociolinguistics* Holt, Rinehart, and Winston, New York.
Antinucci, F. and R. Miller "How Children Talk about What Happened," *Journal of Child Language* 3, 167–189.
Atkinson, M. (1974) "Prerequisites for Reference," paper read at B.A.A.L. Annual Meetings (to appear in E. Ochs and B. Schieffelin, eds., *Developmental Pragmatics*, Academic Press, New York, 1979).
√ Austin, J. L. (1962) *How to Do Things with Words*, Oxford University Press, Oxford.
Bates, E. (1976) *Language and Context: The Acquisition of Pragmatics*, Academic Press, New York.
Bennett, T. (1977) "Verb Voice in Unplanned and Planned Narratives," in E. O. Keenan and T. Bennett, eds., *Discourse across Time and Space*, S.C.O.P.I.L., 5, University of Southern California, Los Angeles, California.
Bever, T. (1970) "The Cognitive Basis for Linguistic Structures," in J. R. Hayes, ed., *Cognition and the Development of Language*, Wiley, New York, pp. 279–362.
Bloom, L. (1970) *Language Development*, M.I.T. Press, Cambridge, Massachusetts.
Bloom, L. (1973) *One Word at a Time: The Use of Single Word Utterances before Syntax*, Mouton, The Hague.
Braunwald, S. (forthcoming) "Forms of Children's Speech, Private, Social and Egocentric," in K. Nelson, ed., *Children's Language*, vol. II, Halstead Press, New York.
Brown, R. (1973) *A First Language*, Harvard University Press, Cambridge, Massachusetts.
Brown, R., C. Cazden, and U. Bellugi (1969) "The Child's Grammar from I to III," in J. P. Hill (ed), *Minnesota Symposia on Child Psychology*, vol. 2, University of Minnesota Press, Minneapolis, pp. 28–73.
Chafe, W. (1976) "Givenness, Contrastiveness, Definiteness, Subjects, Topics and Point of View," in C. Li, ed., *Subject and Topic*, Academic Press, New York.

Chomsky, N. (1965) *Aspects of the Theory of Syntax*, M.I.T. Press, Cambridge, Massachusetts.

Duranti, A. and E. Ochs Keenan (1976) "The Organization of Reference in Italian Discourse," paper presented at the Winter Meeting Linguistics Society of America.

Fromkin, V. (1973) *Speech Errors as Linguistic Evidence*, Mouton, The Hague.

Goodwin, C. (1975) "The Interactional Construction of a Turn," paper presented at the American Anthropological Association Annual Meetings, San Francisco, California.

Greenfield, P. and J. Smith (1976) *The Structure of Communication in Early Language Development*, Academic Press, New York.

Grice, H. P. (1967) "Logic and Conversation," William James Lectures, Harvard University. (Also in P. Cole and J. L. Morgan, eds. 1975, *Syntax and Semantics*, vol. 3: *Speect Acts*, Seminar Press, New York, pp. 41–58.)

Gruber, J. (1967) "Topicalization in Child Language," *Foundations of Language*, No. 1, pp. 37–65.

Gundel, J. (1975) "Left-Dislocation and the Role of Topic–Comment Structure in Linguistic Theory," *Ohio State Working Papers in Linguistics* 18, 72–132.

Hyman, L. (1975) "On the Change from SOV to SVO: Evidence from Niger-Congo," in C. Li, ed., *Word Order and Word Order Change*, University of Texas Press, Austin, Texas.

Hymes, D. (1962) "The Ethnography of Speaking," in T. Gladwin and W. C. Sturtwant, eds., *Anthropology and Human Behavior*, Anthropology Society of Washington, Washington, D.C., pp. 13–53.

Hymes, D. (1972) "Models of the Interaction of Language and Social Life," in John J. Gumperz and D. Hymes (eds.), *Directions in Sociolinguistics*, Holt, New York, pp. 35–71.

Jakobson, R. (1960) "Linguistics and Poetics," in T. Sebeok, ed., *Style In Language*, M.I.T. Press, Cambridge, Massachusetts, pp. 350–377.

Jakobson, R. (1968) *Child Language, Aphasia and Phonological Universals*, Mouton, The Hague.

Keenan, E. Ochs (1974) "Conversational Competence in Children," *Journal of Child Language*, 163–185.

Keenan, E. Ochs (1975) "Making It Last: Uses of Repetition in Children's Discourse," in *Proceedings of First Annual Meeting of the Berkeley Linguistics Society*, University of California, Berkeley, California.

Keenan, E. Ochs and E. Klein (1975) "Coherency in Children's Discourse," *Journal of Psycholinguistic Research* 4, 365–378.

Keenan, E. Ochs and B. Schieffelin (1976) "Topic as a Discourse Notion: A Study of Topic in the Conversations of Children and Adults," in C. Li, ed., *Subject and Topic*, Academic Press, New York, pp. 337–385.

Keenan, E. Ochs, B. Schieffelin, and M. Platt (1978) "Questions of Immediate Concern," in E. Goody, ed., *Questions and Politeness*, Cambridge University Press, Cambridge.

Krashen, S. (1976) "Linguistic Puberty," paper presented at NAFSA Conference, San Diego, California, May 7, 1976.

Krashen, S. 1977. "The Monitor Model For Adult Second Language Performance," in M. Burt, H. Dulay, and M. Finocchiaro, eds., *Viewpoints on English as a Second Language*, Regents, New York.

Kroll, B. (1977) "Ways Communicators Encode Propositions in Spoken and Written English: A Look at Subordination and Co-ordination, in E. O. Keenan and T. Bennett, eds., *Discourse Across Time and Space*, SCOPIL, University of Southern California, Los Angeles, California.

Li, C. and S. Thompson (1976) "Subject and Topic: A New Typology of Language," in C. Li, ed., *Subject and Topic*, Academic Press, New York.

Limber, J. (1973) "The Genesis of Complex Sentences," in J. Moore, ed., *Cognitive Development and the Acquisition of Language*, Academic Press, New York.

Ochs, E., B. Schieffelin, and M. Platt (1979) "Propositions across Utterances and Speakers," E. Ochs and B. Schieffelin (eds)., *Development Pragmatics*, Academic Press, New York.

Ross, J. (1967) *Constraints on Variables in Syntax*, Doctoral Dissertation, M.I.T. Press, Cambridge, Massachusetts.

Sacks, H., E. Schegloff, and G. Jefferson (1974) "A Simplest Systematics for the Organization of Turn-Taking for Conversation," *Language* 50, 696–735.

Sankoff, G. and P. Kay (1974) "A Language—Universal Approach to Pidgins and Creoles," in D. DeCamp and I. Hancock, eds., *Pidgins and Creoles*, Georgetown University Press, Washington, D.C.

Schachter, J. (1974) "An Error in Error Analysis," *Language Learning*, 24, 205–215.

Schegloff, E. (1973) *Recycled Turn Beginning: A precise repair mechanism in conversation's turn-taking organization*, unpublished manuscript.

Schegloff, E., G. Jefferson, and H. Sacks (1977) "The Preference for Self-Correction in the Organization of Repair in Conversation," *Language* 53, 361–383.

Scollon, R. (1976) *Conversations with a One Year Old*, University of Hawaii Press, Honolulu, Hawaii.

Searle, J. R. (1969) *Speech Acts*, Cambridge University Press, Cambridge.

Shimanoff, S. and J. Brunak (1977) "Repairs in Planned and Unplanned Discourse," in E. O. Keenan and T. Bennett, eds., *Discourse Across Time and Space*, SCOPIL, no. 5, University of Southern California, Los Angeles, California.

Silverstein, M. (1976) "Shifters, Linguistic Categories and Cultural Description," in K. Basso and H. Selby, eds., *Meaning in Anthropology*, University of New Mexico Press, Albuquerque, New Mexico.

Slobin, D. (1973) "Cognitive Prerequisites for the Acquisition of Grammar," in C. A. Ferguson and D. Slobin, eds., *Studies of Child Language Development*, Holt, Rinehard, and Winston, New York, pp. 175–208.

Walcutt, J. (1977) "The Topology of Narrative Boundedness," In E. O. Keenan and T. Bennett, eds., *Discourse Across Time and Space*, S.C.O.P.I.L. no. 5, University of Southern California, Los Angeles, California.

Weir, R. (1970) *Language in the Crib*. Mouton, The Hague.

FROM DISCOURSE TO SYNTAX: GRAMMAR AS A PROCESSING STRATEGY

TALMY GIVÓN

University of California, Los Angeles
and Ute Language Program, Ignacio, Colorado

1. INTRODUCTION[1]

In an earlier study (Givón 1979:Chapter 2) I investigated the relation between discourse and syntax, concluding that <u>discourse-pragmatics played a decisive role in explaining the syntax of human language</u>. Put another way, syntax was there to perform a function, rather than because it was "innate." Given such an approach, one is prompted to ask whether syntax has any independent axistence apart from discourse structure. As I have suggested elsewhere (Givón 1979:Chapter 1), the orthodox transformational generative approach to "Independent Syntax" was untenable on two grounds:

1. It arose out of artificially restricted, presanitized data.
2. It did nothing to further our understanding of why the grammar of human languages is the way it is.

[1] The title of the chapter owes much to Sankoff and Brown's (1976) "The Origins of Syntax in Discourse."

Syntax and Semantics, Volume 12:
Discourse and Syntax

On the other end of the ideological scale, we have suggestions, such as that of García (in this volume), that syntax per se does not exist at all and that human language can be described exhaustively by reference to the COM-MUNICATIVE PRINCIPLES that underlie the structure of discourse. While pursuing research into discourse-pragmatic constraints on syntax (Givón 1979: Chapters 2, 3, and 4), I found myself slowly gravitating toward a position as extreme as García's, that is, toward rejecting the existence of syntax altogether and viewing it as a complex ARTIFACT arising from the interaction of various communicative principles and processing strategies. The artifact itself seemed STABLE enough, I thought, because the underlying principles and strategies—as well as their interactions—were themselves stable.

What I propose to do in this study is in a sense a TACTICAL RETREAT from that extreme position. I hope to illustrate that (*a*) there are many facts supporting the existence of some "structural" level called syntax; but (*b*), in order to explain the formal properties of that "structural" level, one must make reference once again to a number of SUBSTANTIVE explanatory param-eters of language. Rather than wind up with a formal and AUTONOMOUS level of structural organization in language, we do indeed find syntax to be a DEPENDENT, functionally motivated entity whose formal properties reflect—perhaps not completely, but nearly so—the properties of the explanatory parameters that motivate its rise.

The range of data upon which I will build the argument involves four sources whose underlying unity is not hard to perceive. For reasons that will be made apparent later on, it is easy to interpret all four as processes:

(1)   a.   DIACHRONIC: *loose parataxis → tight syntax*
         b.   ONTOGENETIC: *early pragmatic mode → later syntactic mode*
         c.   PIDGINS–CREOLES: *nongrammar → grammar*
         d.   REGISTER LEVEL: *unplanned–informal speech → planned–formal speech*

Per se, several of the processes just listed have been dealt with in the recent literature. Thus, (1c) was discussed in Sankoff and Brown (1976), the paral-lels between (1b) and (1d) were discussed by Elinor Ochs (in this volume), and the parallels among (1a), (1b), and (1c) were discussed in Slobin (1977). This chapter is thus intended as a synthesis.

2. THE DIACHRONIC PROCESS OF SYNTACTICIZATION

In this section I will describe a number of recurring themes in diachronic syntax. I would like to suggest that all of them represent processes by which loose, paratactic, PRAGMATIC discourse structures develop—over time—into tight, GRAMMATICALIZED syntactic structures. For each one of these processes one could prepare a balance sheet of communicative GAINS and communicative LOSSES. The principles that control the balance of gain and loss here are, presumably, what we are investigating.

If language constantly "takes discourse structure and condenses it—via syntacticization—into syntactic structure," one would presumably expect human languages to become increasingly syntacticized over time. In fact, this is not the case. Rather, syntactic structure in time ERODES via processes of MORPHOLOGIZATION and LEXICALIZATION. I have dealt with this end of the cycle elsewhere,[2] and the principles motivating the erosion of syntax are not necessarily identical to those that motivate its rise. Nevertheless, one must keep in mind that we are dealing here with cyclic WAVES that may be characterized roughly as:

(2)   *discourse → syntax → morphology → morphophonemics → zero*

The last two steps are motivated largely by phonological attrition and will not be discussed further here. The first two steps, which are often COUPLED (i.e., occur simultaneously), are motivated by various COMMUNICATIVE NEEDS and will form the bulk of the cases discussed below.

From Topic to Subject

Quite a few recent works have dealt with the relation between the discourse-functional notion TOPIC and the syntactic–grammatical notion SUBJECT.[3] Thus Edward Keenan (1976) has shown that most of the properties of subjects can be understood in terms of topic properties.[4] Li and Thompson (1976) and Schachter (1976, 1977) illustrated the considerable difficulties involved in deciding whether in a particular language one deals with subject or topic. Following Li and Thompson (1976), the possibility is still open that some languages may have more grammaticalized subjects whereas others may have more discourse-pragmatic topics, although only a serious distributional study of texts—of both formal and informal registers—can settle this issue conclusively.

In Givón (1976a), I pointed out that one of the most acclaimed properties of subjects, that of GRAMMATICAL AGREEMENT on the verb, is fundamentally a topic property and that it arises diachronically via the reanalysis of topic

---

[2] See Givón (1971, 1975a, 1976a).
[3] See various papers in Li (1976).
[4] And a small residue of AGENT properties.

into subject and—simultaneously—of an anaphoric pronoun into a (normally verb-bound) agreement morpheme. As an illustration, consider the following example from noneducated American English, where this process is currently endemic:[5]

(3)   *My ol' man, **he** rides with the Angles* $\implies$
        TOPIC   PRO   V

> *My ol' man **he**-rides with the Angels*
> SUBJECT AG-V

One must remember, however, that English has both SUBJECT and TOPIC constructions and that they serve normally different discourse functions (see Givón, 1979, Chapter 2). The grammaticalization of topics into subjects, thus, does not mean that the language has lost the topic construction but only that it has gained grammatical agreement as an added morphological CODING PROPERTY for its "grammatical" subject.[6] As we shall see later, there are reasons to believe that every language has a wide range of DISCOURSE REGISTERS, from the loose–informal–pragmatic to the tight–formal–syntactic.

As I have also shown in Givón (1976a), unrelated and typologically diverse languages undergo the development schematized in (3) in very much the same fashion, leaving the same indelible marks in terms of grammatical agreement. In one case, Sankoff (1976) showed three consecutive cycles of the same process occurring in one language (Tok Pisin, a Pidgin language in the New Guinea Highlands) within a hundred years. The communicative balance sheet for such a process may be divided as follows:

1. TIME OF DELIVERY: *Subject constructions are delivered faster and without an intonational break, whereas topic construction typically take more time.*
2. CODING: *Subject constructions are typically* BETTER CODED *morphologically than are topic constructions (see Edward Keenan 1976), with verb agreement being one typical instance of such coding, but case marking possibly another one and rigidity in word-order another.*
3. RESOLUTION: *In terms of identifying the topic of discourse, topic constructions obviously exhibit 100% correlation between form and function. Although it is true that subjects in discourse are* MOST COMMONLY *also*

---

[5] This example was heard in a waiting room of County General Hospital, Los Angeles, by Jean Tremaine. Only the grammaticalized form on the right was attested, though its source on the left is transparent.

[6] As Pete Becker (personal communication) points out, the diachronic process is really from topic + subject to subject + agreement.

the topic, there is probably a residue of between 10–20% in which the topic does not coincide with the grammatical subject.[7]

Whether the communicative loss (3) is real remains problematic, since the pragmatic and lexical redundancies present in the discourse context presumably could offset such a loss. Furthermore, since most languages retain both topic and subject constructions, a certain division of labor between the two is normally observed (see Givón 1978:Chapter 2). Thus, subject constructions are typically used when the topic maintained is the SAME, that is, when it is reasonably easy to identify, and topic constructions are typically used when the discourse topic is CHANGED, that is, when it is harder to identify.[8] Thus, one may conceive of the SUBJECT strategy as that of AUTOMATIC PROCESSING to be used when the going is easy, when one maintains the same subject over a chain of clauses, and when time-saving is thus possible and is further facilitated by the enhanced coding properties of SUBJECT. Finally, we shall see later, the coupling of syntacticization with the rise of morphology (coding) is a recurring theme in diachronic change and exhibits many parallels in other areas of the data base, specifically in the development of child language toward the adult mode of communication.

From Topicalization to Passivization

In Givón 1976a, I cited two examples of this diachronic process, one from Kimbundu, the other from Indonesian. It is obviously a process closely related to the one just discussed. However, here an OBJECT TOPIC ("left-dislocated" object) becomes grammaticalized into the SUBJECT-OF-PASSIVE, with certain coding consequences arising simultaneously. As an illustration, consider this process in Kimbundu, a Bantu language:

(4)

OBJECT-TOPIC CONSTRUCTION   PASSIVE CONSTRUCTION

    Nzua, a-mu-mono $\Longrightarrow$ *Nzua a-mu-mono*   (*kwa meme*)
    John they-him-saw   John they-him-saw (by me)
    'John, they saw him'   'John was seen (by me)'

---

[7] The 10–20% figure is based on a rough estimate derived from the fact that, in general, in connected human narrative, equi-subject chains are about 5–10 verbs long. In some languages (New Guinea), these chains tend to be much longer (up to 50 verbs per chain, ending with a finite verb). Thus, human discourse tends to be multipropositional and topic-maintaining. This makes the strategy of using well-coded and faster-processed subjects a viable means to render equi-topic chains. See further discussion here as well as in Chapter 7.

[8] For further detail, see Keenan and Scheffelin (1977) and Duranti and Ochs (in this volume).

The balance sheet of communicative gain and loss is very much the same as in the previous subsection. The morphological adjustment in the agreement system is more complex, however. The left-dislocated topic construction on the left in (4) has a third-person-plural subject agreement that may be totally viable (though it may be also "impersonal"), a fact that may be demonstrated from inserting a fully specified subject:

(5)   *Nzua, a-ana   a-mu-mono*
                         John   children they-him saw
                         'John, the children saw him'

In the passive construction on the right, on the other hand, the *a-* morpheme in the subject-agreement position is frozen and agrees neither with the new subject–patient nor with the agent, a fact that is obvious from the ungrammaticality (indeed the absurdity) of:

(6)   **Nzua a-ana   a-mu-mono   kwa meme*
                         John children they-him-saw by   me

Furthermore, the erstwhile object agreement (*-mu-* 'him') of the neutral pattern has, in fact, become the subject-of-passive agreement, thus contributing to special morphological coding of the new passive construction.

From Topic Sentences to Relative Clauses

Many languages[9] have or used to have what is often referred to as unembedded–unreduced relative clauses.[10] Those are basically TOPIC sentences roughly arranged before or after the main clause, much like adverbial clauses. I will illustrate this pattern schematically by paraphrasing the Hittite examples given in Justus (1976a, 1976b):

(7)   a. *If we see **any** man, we'll report **him** to the king*   (OBJ REL)
         b. *If **a** man comes, we'll report **him** to the king*   (SUBJ REL)

Now, Justus (1976b) has suggested that a certain relative-clause type in Germanic, Romance, and Indic, where a RELATIVE MARKER precede the head noun but the clause itself follows, is diachronically derived from the Hittite-type topic-sentence construction as paraphrased in (7) above. For subject relative clauses—the most common type cross-linguistically and the

---

[9] This has been reported in Hittite (Indo-European), Bambara (Mendeic, Niger-Congo), Hindi-Urdu (Indo-European), Wappo, Navajo (Athabascan), Diegeño (Yuman), and Japanese, among others, and is probably quite extensive elsewhere.

[10] This pattern has been discussed in Givón (1979:Chapter 4) as one of the available patterns of relativization.

least-complex psycholinguistically[11]—such a development may be schematically outlined as:

(8)   ***a man comes, we'll report him** to the king* ⟹
        INDEF   **PRO**

                                *a man **comes** we'll report   to the king*
                         whatever NP REL
                         'Whatever man comes we'll report to the king'

In Hittite, an SOV language, such reanalysis will involve no dislocation
whatever in the neutral syntactic pattern. In later Germanic and Romance
dialects, a reanalysis as in (8) would place the object NP at a topicalized
position, a relatively mild dislocation.[12] In subject relativization, where the
head noun is also the subject of the MAIN clause, no disruption of the neutral
pattern occurs at all:[13]

(9)   ***a man comes, he'll visit the palace*** ⟹

                         ***Whatever** man comes will visit the palace*

Finally, Justus (1976a, 1976b) points out that the prenominal 'relative'
marker in Hittite (*ku-*), Romance (*qu-*), and Germanic (*wh-*) is etymologically
a CATAPHORIC element related to INDEFINITE pronouns. This supports the
paraphrases given on the left in (8) and (9).

   A reanalysis of this type is also reported for Yuman (Langdon 1977), for
Tok Pisin (a Pidgin–Creole; see Sankoff and Brown 1976), and for Wappo
(Li and Thompson, private communication). The actual morphological
consequences (or "coding gains") of the reanalysis may vary. In Bambara,
for example, the topic sentence may be either left-dislocated or embedded.
When it is left-dislocated, an anaphoric pronoun appears in the main clause.
When it is fully embedded, no anaphoric pronoun appears. But in both
cases the coreferent noun within the topic-sentence/relative-clause is marked
by a special suffix (reminiscent of the *ku-* element in Hittite):[14]

(10)   *cę **min** ye mùru sàn, n ye **o** ye*   (UNEMBEDDED)
        man **REL** past knife buy, I past **him** see
        'The man who bought the knife, I saw him'

---

[11] See discussion in Keenan and Comrie (1975).

[12] See comments in Givón, (1979:Chapter 4) concerning the fact that head nouns modified
by relative clauses tend to be "more topical."

[13] Hawkins and Keenan (1974) also cite evidence that subject relative clauses are psycholinguistically easier to process, but the evidence is not altogether conclusive.

[14] For the Bambara data, I am indebted to Ibrahima Coulibali (personal communication).

(11)   *n ye cè **min** ye mùru sàn ye*   (EMBEDDED)
        I past man **REL** past knife buy see
        'I saw the man who bought the knife'

With the exception of the *min* morpheme, the pattern in (10) is a loose, paratactic pattern indistinguishable from sentence concatenation. Although this cannot be documented for all languages, it is still possible that ALL embedded, "syntactic" relative clauses in language arose diachronically from loose, paratactic concatenations.

The communicative balance sheet is here again rather obvious: One gains automatic, fast, morphologically-coded processing, while the loss presumably involves the effects of deletion under coreference and the rise of the recoverability problem (see Givón 1979:Chapter 4). Again, lexical, contextual, and general pragmatic redundancies are likely to pick up the communicative slack, especially since restrictive relative clauses are over-whelmingly background–presupposed information.

From Conjunction to Subordination in the Verb Phrase

The first type of case to be discussed here involves the infinitival comple-ments of verbs imposing an equi-NP condition, either those with an equi-subject condition (*want, try, begin*) or those with an equi-object condition (*order, force, ask*). The complement verb in many languages is NONFINITE, as in English, and this involves a marked reduction in the tense-aspect morphology, lack of subject agreement, and, often, some special infinitival–nominal morphology. In many other languages, however, the complement verb is either FINITE or, at least, exhibits subject pronominal agreement on the verb. This may be seen in Arabic, Greek, some Slavic languages, and Icelandic,[15] among others. Thus consider the following, from Palestinian Arabic:

(12)   *ʔana bɨddi ʔɨ-mshi*
                              I   I-want I-go
                              'I want to go'

Now, since the subject agreement pronoun marking the complement verb is the very same type used in simple subject ANAPHORA in equi-subject con-catenations, it is most likely that the current subordinate, "syntactic" construction in those languages in fact arose from a loose, paratactic con-catenation via syntacticization. In fact, the possibility is still open that ALL

---

[15] For the latter, see Andrews (1976), where the presence of pronominal traces on the com-plement verb is used as an argument for a SYNCHRONIC derivation. As in many synchronically oriented transformational arguments, I think the real import of the data is DIACHRONIC.

equi-NP verb complements in language arose via such a process, which may be thus schematized as:

(13)   a.   For equi-subject verbs:

          *I want **I**-go* $\Longrightarrow$ *I want **to**-go*
             SUBJ-FINITE   SUBORD-INFINITIVE

    b.   For equi-object verbs:

          *I tell you **you**-go* $\Longrightarrow$ *I tell you **to**-go*
           OBJ SUBJ-FINITE   OBJ SUBORD-INFINITIVE

Another type of condensation from a looser paratactic to a tighter, subordinate pattern in the verb phrase was described, for Mandarin Chinese, in Thompson (1973). It involves resultative verb compounds, as in:

(14)   *tā lā-kāi   le   mén*
                   he pull-open ASP door
                   'He pulled the door open'

(15)   *tā lā-de-kāi   mén*
                   he pull-can-open door
                   'He can pull the door open'

Although Thompson (1973) points out that a synchronic-transformation derivation of sentences such as (14) and (15) from looser conjunctions is untenable, it is most likely that, in fact, that very derivation happened diachronically, roughly along the schematic pattern[16]

(16)   *He pulled the door, and (it) opened* → *He pulled the door open*

Lexicalized and semilexicalized verb compounds of this and other types are highly prevalent in the Sino-Tibetan, Southeast Asian, and Niger-Congo linguistic areas. The most likely source of such condensations is looser, concatenated structures.

Similar cases are common elsewhere. Thus, for example, Akiba (1978) suggested that the tightly-bound constructions of auxiliary verb plus verb in Japanese developed historically from looser, CONJOINED structures.[17] Hyman (1971) suggested that the tightly-bound serial verb constructions in Niger-Congo (specifically in Kwa) arose historically from loose consecutive conjunctions.[18]

[16] In Chinese, the anaphoric pattern in such a close concatenation (i.e., where the coreferent argument is both syntactically and pragmatically rather transparent) is deletion ("zero pronoun"). See Li and Thompson (in this volume).
[17] For the condensation involved in the development of auxiliary verbs into tense–aspect–modal markers, see later discussion.
[18] For the condensation of serial-verb constructions and its role in the rise of case-making, see later discussion.

Causativization and the Rise of Complex Verbs

Another common process by which looser, sentential constructions get condensed into tighter, "syntacticized" verb phrases and, as a result, more simple predicates become more complex,[19] is the process of lexical causativization. This process involves, diachronically, PREDICATE RAISING, by which two verb phrases ("clauses") carrying their own case-marked arguments become condensed into a single verb phrase. The two verbs become a single lexical-causative verb, and the subject of the lower clause gets accommodated as an OBJECT of the resulting compound verb.[20] This process may be represented schematically as:

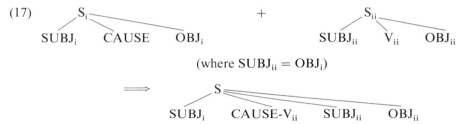

(17)

$$
\begin{array}{ccccccc}
& S_i & & + & & S_{ii} & \\
\text{SUBJ}_i & \text{CAUSE} & \text{OBJ}_i & & \text{SUBJ}_{ii} & V_{ii} & \text{OBJ}_{ii}
\end{array}
$$

(where $\text{SUBJ}_{ii} = \text{OBJ}_i$)

$$
\Longrightarrow \qquad
\begin{array}{cccc}
& S & & \\
\text{SUBJ}_i & \text{CAUSE-}V_{ii} & \text{SUBJ}_{ii} & \text{OBJ}_{ii}
\end{array}
$$

This type of condensation, as well as the one arising from the reanalysis of serial verb constructions (see later discussion), are both major contributors to the diachronic rise of syntacticized, complex verb phrases. They both increase the number of nominal arguments per lexical verb in a clause. They both, in a sense, create the real problem of case marking, that is, the fact that an increasing number of nominal arguments are present per verb so that the verb itself cannot serve as indicating the function of the noun. The language then must resort to case-marking morphology on the nouns themselves (see later discussion). This general phenomenon is an illustration of how the loose, paratactic mode–level of language is one that is transparent enough and, therefore, requires relatively little morphological coding. The rise of the grammatical morphology in language may thus be seen as COUPLED TO the rise of the syntactic mode.

The Rise of Some Complex Genitive Construction

In a number of languages, there exists a seemingly complex genitive construction that must have arisen via syntacticization from a looser paratactic

---

[19] Complexity can be measured here in terms of the number of nominal arguments per verb. For an extensive discussion of synchronic semantic and pragmatic aspects of causativization, see Shibatani (ed., 1976) and Givón (1975b). For more diachronic aspects, see Givón (1971, 1976b).

[20] For the principles governing such an accommodation cross-linguistically, see Comrie (1976) and Cole (1976).

construction. As an illustration, consider the normal possessive construction of Krio, a Creole language:[21]

(18)   *Jón*   **hin-ós**
                            John his-house
                            'John's house'

Since the history of Krio, a relatively recent English-lexicon-based Creole, is rather transparent, the syntacticized construction in (18), in which the normal anaphoric genitive pronoun is used obligatorily (and the intonation contour is unified), must have arisen from a looser, topicalized (left-dislocated) construction, that is, from

(19)   *John, his house*

A parallel situation may be shown in the more literary level of Modern Hebrew, except that here the order is different:[22]

(20)   *bet-o*   **shel**   *Yoav*
                        house-**his** that-to Yoav
                        'Yoav's house'

The genitive particle *shel* is a composite of the relative subordinator *she-* (full–older form *asher*) plus the dative preposition *l-*. Here the paratactic source was more likely either an after-thought topic (right dislocation) or an emphatic construction of the type:

(21)   *bet-i*   *she-l-i*
                        house-**my** that-to-**me**
                        'my own house'

If the after-thought topic construction was the source, then (20) may be viewed as the condensation–syntacticization of the looser construction in:

(22)   *bet-o*,   *shel*   *Yoav*
                        house-**his** that-to Yoav
                        'His house, the one belonging to Yoav'

The naturalness of this process is not difficult to discern: In possessive constructions, the possessor—normally human—is MORE TOPICAL than the possessed, and, therefore, quite often it winds up being topicalized if the construction to begin with has it at a less-topical position.[23]

---

[21] For the data, I am indebted to Sori Yilla (personal communication).

[22] I could find no attestation of this construction in Biblical Hebrew, and I tend to suspect that it may have arisen during the Mishnaic or Talmudic period. In Modern Hebrew, it is not used at the most colloquial register.

[23] For a general discussion as well as more examples of similarly motivated reanalyses of existential and possessive expressions, see Givón (1976a).

The Rise of Cleft and WH-Question Constructions

One of the most puzzling universals of word order is that of the left-attraction of the focus-assertional-emphatic constituents in cleft and WH-questions. It is particularly puzzling to find it in many subject-first languages, where it is reasonably clear that the general pragmatic principle governing word-order is that more topical material precedes and more assertional material follows. In the past, I have attempted to explain this glaring discrepancy by pointing out that in cleft sentences the focus constituent is at the same time both topical and assertional.[24] It seems to me, however, that a much more simple and straightforward explanation can be constructed, one that makes reference to the DIACHRONIC rise of these constructions via the syntacticization of a looser, paratactic construction.

It is well-known that in both cleft and WH-question constructions one element—most commonly a nominal—is in the assertion (or interrogation) FOCUS, whereas the rest—the material that often resembles the syntax of a RELATIVE CLAUSE—is presupposed. Thus:

(23)   *It's John who left*
                               FOCUS:PRESUPPOSED

(24)   *Who   left?*
                               FOCUS:PRESUPPOSED

Now, in actual discourse contexts in the informal conversational register, most often there is no need to pronounce the entire construction in (23) or (24), since the presupposed portion is not only known to both participant but also quite often has been mentioned in the directly preceding discourse. The more prevalent conversational strategy is, thus, much more likely to be:

(25)   A: *Mary did it.*
                               B: *No, **it was John**.*

(26)   A: *.... did it*
                               B: ***Who?***

If that is a reasonable argument, then one may view the rise of the syntactic patterns in (23) and (24) as coming as a result of the tacking onto the focus constituent (25), (26) the presupposed portion as an AFTERTHOUGHT, paratactic construction, as in (27) and (28), respectively:

(27)   ***It was John**, (the one) who did it.*

---

[24] See Givón (1979: Chapter 2). This is another example in which a diachronic explanation of the details of synchronic syntactic properties turns out, I think, to be more insightful. See discussion of this general phenomenon in Givón (1979: Chapter 6).

(28)   ***Who (was it)**, (the one) who did it?*

The correlation to relative clauses observed by Schachter (1973) and Takizala (1972) thus finds a diachronic—that is, a solid—motivation. But, furthermore, the relative clause phenomenon associated with focus/WH constructions in many languages is pragmatically of the NONRESTRICTIVE kind. That is fully compatible with the parenthetic, afterthought nature of those presupposed clauses.[25]

The Biblical Hebrew Sentential Complements

In Givón (1974), I have shown that the verb-complement constructions in Late Biblical Hebrew that use the erstwhile relative-clause subordinator *she-/asher* must have arisen via the reanalysis of a more paratactic "blend" construction. What was apparently involved is the fact that verbs such as *see*, *think*, or *know* can—in language in general—take both direct-object nominal complements as well as a sentential complement. In Early Biblical Hebrew, one already finds the following kinds of blends, in which such a verb takes both a nominal and a sentential complement. The sentential complement, in turn, may be of the normal V-comp type in Early Biblical Hebrew, that is, with the subordinators *ki* or *vehine*, as in:

(29)   *va-yar? ?elohim ?et   ha-?or   **ki**   tov*   (Gen. 1:4)
        and-saw God   ACC the-light **that** good
        'And God saw the light, that it was good'

But the blend pattern can also exhibit the sentential complement in a relative-clause form. And that form may be "headless," as in:

(30)
*shama'nu ?et **?asher** hovish Jhwh   ?et   may   yam   suf*   (Josh. 2:10)
we-heard ACC **that**   dried JHWH ACC water-of sea-of Suf
'We heard it, that God dried up the water of the Red Sea'

But it can also be a 'headed' form, as in:

(31)   *?al   tir ?u-**ni**   she-?ani shxaxoret*   (Song of Solomon 1:6)
        don't you-see-**me** that-I   swarthy
        {'Don't see me, who is dark-skinned'}
        {'Don't see that I am dark-skinned' }

---

[25] That is, there is no way in which one could conceive of them synchronically as "narrowing the domain of the head NP," or "functioning to establish definite description," which is the normal function of restrictive relative clauses.

The data strongly suggests that the later V-comp constructions, fully syntacticized as in:

(32)   yada'ti **she**-gam hu? r'ut   ruax   (Eccl. 1:17)
            I-knew **that**-also it   folly-of spirit
            'I knew that it too was folly'

in fact arose from the looser, paratactic blends just described. In those, the speaker in fact HEDGES: He first expresses the nominal object; then, on realizing that it is not that nominal per se but rather a proposition about that nominal (i.e., in which that nominal is an argument) that he intended to express, he adds that preposition as an AFTERTHOUGHT. And one of the most natural patterns to be used in such an afterthought is, naturally, a nonrestrictive relative clause, since one argument of the proposition has already been mentioned and can thus be deleted under coreference.

It is likely that the type of reanalysis described here is much more widespread. For example, in Aramaic the subordinator for both relative clauses and verb complements is the same demonstrative *di*, and it may well be that it spread into the V-comp paradigm via a similar "blend" pattern. A similar situation is observed in Germanic, and Vennemann (personal communication) has suggested that the reanalysis proceeded along similar lines, schematically:

(33)   *I know **that**, (i.e.) it is true* $\Longrightarrow$ *I know **that** it is true*
            OBJ   SUBORD

The Rise of Grammatical ("Inflectional") Morphology

In the preceding sections, I have shown that in almost every case where loose, paratactic structure is condensed historically into tight, syntactic structure, the condensation involves the simultaneous rise of grammatical morphology to better code the emergent syntax. In this section, I would like to pursue this theme further. By way of illustration, I will cite two major subsystems of inflectional morphology, one usually arising as noun inflection, the other as verb inflection. Though in the past[26] I have looked at these processes in a narrower context, dealing with the rise of morphology per se, it seems to me now that it may be more revealing to treat syntacticization and the rise of grammatical morphology as two mutually dependent parts of the same process. Via syntacticization, the language loses message transparency while gaining processing speed. The concomitant rise of morphology offsets the losses by adding CODING to the construction, thus facilitating the emergent mode of AUTOMATIC PROCESSING.

---

[26] As in Givón (1971, 1973, 1975a).

FROM SERIAL VERBS TO CASE MARKERS

This subject has been surveyed in great detail in the past few years. Some works dealt with the synchronic status of serial verbs.[27] Others dealt with several diachronic aspects.[28] In Givón (1975a), I surveyed the subject from the perspective of the rise of case-marking morphology via the de-verbal channel of serial verbs. What is involved diachronically is a slow process of reanalysis by which the description of an event—that is, proposition—is first assembled as a concatenation of small propositions in which, roughly, a one-to-one correlation is maintained between verbs an nominal arguments so that, in essence, the function of each nominal argument is marked by the verb that precedes or follows it.[29] In the course of time, however, a slow and gradual reanalysis occurs, by which the verbs EXCEPT FOR ONE become grammaticalized as case markers, eventually becoming bound to their respective nominal arguments. The loosely concatenated, paratactic expression then becomes a single sentence falling under a single intonational contour, with ONE complex verb. As an illustration, consider the following examples:[30]

(34)   *ū lá dùkũ là*   (ACCUSATIVE, Nupe)
       he **take** pot   **break**
       'He broke the pot'

(35)   *íywi awá òtsi ikù utsí*   (INSTRUMENTAL,
       boy **took** stick **shut** door   Yatye)
       'The boy shut the door with a stick'

(36)   *ū bícī lō dzūká*   (LOCATIVE, Nupe)
       he **ran** **go** market
       'He ran to the market'

(37)   *íywi awá ínyahwè awa ítywi*   (LOCATIVE, Yatye)
       boy **took** book   **went** house
       'The boy brought the book home'

(38)   *mo mú íwé wá fún o*   (DATIVE-BENEFAC-
       I   **took** book **come give** you   TIVE, Yoruba)
       'I brought a book for you'

---

[27] Stahlke (1970), Li and Thompson (1973b, 1973c), Hyman (1971).

[28] Lord (1973), Li and Thompson (1973a).

[29] The subject-agent argument is normally the only one to break this generalization, and one may argue that it is marked POSITIONALLY. All known serial-verb languages are subject-first languages (SVO or SOV).

[30] These examples are cited from Givón (1975a), where the original sources are acknowledged.

(39)   *Zhāng-sān bèi   Lǐ-sí pīping   le*   (AGENT-OF-PASSIVE,
       Zhang-san **submit** Li-si **criticize** ASP   Mandarin)[31]
       'Zhang-san was criticized by Li-si'

The type of verb eventually giving rise to a particular case marker is amazingly consistent over wide areas of Africa and Southeast Asia, where this phenomenon is recorded at its most elaborate. Furthermore, it illustrates in the clearest fashion the intimate connection between syntacticization and the rise of grammatical morphology. The original, paratactic, loosely concatenated expression has no need for case marking, since each nominal argument is sufficiently identified in terms of its case-function by the verb to which it is paired in a small atomic clause. When the serial chain is re-analyzed as a single sentence with one complex verb, the problem of case marking then arises. This is so because the verb can mark only two arguments—topic-agent and object—positionally. But the syntacticization added more object arguments, and they need to be marked with respect to their case-function. Hence the "extra" verbs, which, in a sense, already had been functioning, in part to mark the case-role of their paired arguments, and now assume this case-marking function as their major *raison d'être*. The development of grammatical morphology thus becomes necessary when the language shifts from the paratactic to the syntactic mode.

FROM AUXILIARY VERBS TO TENSE–ASPECT–MODALITY MARKERS

There is a small group of "auxiliary" verbs that, in an amazingly uniform fashion cross-language, develop into highly specific tense-aspect modality markers, with the latter most commonly becoming—sooner or later—bound to the verb. The most common changes, cross-linguistically, are:[32]

(40)   *want* → FUTURE
       go → IRREALIS → FUTURE
       come → PERFECTIVE → PAST
       finish → PERFECTIVE → PAST
       have → PERFECTIVE → PAST
       be → PROGRESSIVE/HABITUAL → FUTURE
       start → FUTURE
       know → 'can' → HABITUAL/POSSIBLE/PERMISSIBLE
       lack/fail/refuse → NEGATION
       done → PERFECTIVE → PAST

---

[31] This example is from Li and Thompson (1973a).
[32] For further discussion, see Givón (1973).

In most cases, the construction in which such changes take place is the equi-subject construction discussed previously. Diachronically, the process thus involves the condensation–syntacticization of two loosely concatenated clauses, with the second one exhibiting subject anaphora under corefer-ence—by either ZERO, an anaphoric pronoun, or subject-agreement pronoun on the verb—into a single clause under a single intonation contour. In-variably, the "main" verb becomes morphologized, most commonly as a tense-aspect–modal marker, whereas the second verb—semantically much more specific or "weighty"—remains the sole verb of the syntacticized construction. Once again, then, syntacticization and the rise of grammatical morphology seem to go hand in hand.[33]

3. AN INTERIM SUMMARY

In the preceding sections, we have covered virtually all the major syn-tactic, tightly-bound, "subordinated" constructions in language. In each instance, I have shown that many languages present evidence that such constructions arose diachronically, via the process of SYNTACTICIZATION, from looser, conjoined, paratactic constructions. Thus, the entire process labeled by transformationalists as EMBEDDING TRANSFORMATIONS turns out to be a mere recapitulation of attested diachronic changes. I would like to suggest now that these diachronic processes should be properly viewed in the context of THE GENESIS OF SYNTAX EX-DISCOURSE. Furthermore, I would like to posit two extreme poles of COMMUNICATIVE MODE, the PRAGMATIC mode and the SYNTACTIC mode. In the cases surveyed above, we have, then, been dealing with the rise of the latter out of the former. That every human lan-guage known to us has BOTH extremes—as well as any intermediate in between—will become rapidly obvious from the further discussion given below. The extreme poles can, nevertheless, be characterized as such, in terms of their structural properties. This characterization is an INTERIM one and will be further elaborated later. In particular, I will attempt in the following sections to probe into the FUNCTIONAL PARAMETERS that constrain the use of these two communicative modes.

---

[33] It is most likely that the main–auxiliary verb already carried—as one of its functions—the signal for some tense–aspect–modal notion. The amazing universality of this process and the high semantic specificity of the verbs contributing to it point in that direction. But, in the syntacticized construction, the erstwhile verb has shed its other (earlier) functions and has become specialized.

(41)

Pragmatic Mode	Syntactic Mode
(a) *topic–comment structure*	*subject–predicate structure*
(b) *loose conjunction*	*tight subordination*
(c) *slow rate of delivery (under several intonation contours)*	*fast rate of delivery (under a single intonational contour)*
(d) *word-order is governed mostly by one* PRAGMATIC *principle: old information goes first, new information follows*	*word-order is used to signal* SEMANTIC *case-functions (though it may also be used to indicate pragmatic–topicality relations)*
(e) *roughly one-to-one ratio of verbs-to-nouns in discourse, with the verbs being semantically simple*	*a larger ratio of nouns-over-verbs in discourse, with the verbs being semantically complex*
(f) *no use of grammatical morphology*	*elaborate use of grammatical morphology*
(g) *prominent intonation–stress marks the focus of new information; topic intonation is less prominent*	*very much the same, but perhaps not exhibiting as high a functional load, and at least in some languages totally absent*

In the following sections, I will attempt to show that to quite an extent this dichotomy also characterizes three other contrastive pairs of human communication: Pidgin versus Creole, child versus adult and informal versus formal language.

4. PIDGINS AND CREOLES

It is appropriate to discuss this topic next, since in a way it involves similar DIACHRONIC developments as the ones shown above, although in this case they are much more rapid. The difference between Pidgin and Creole languages has often been obscured in earlier studies. More recently, it has been shown[34] that the two types of language contrast sharply in some rather fundamental ways. Briefly, it seems that Pidgin languages (or, at least, the most prevalent type of Plantation Pidgins) exhibit an enormous amount of internal variation and inconsistency, both within the output of the same speaker as well as across the speech community. The variation is so massive that one is indeed justified in asserting that the Pidgin mode has NO STABLE SYNTAX. No consistent "grammatical" word-order can be shown in a Pidgin, and little or no use of grammatical morphology. The rate of delivery is excruciatingly slow and halting, with many pauses. Verbal clauses are small, normally exhibiting a one-to-one ratio of nouns to verbs.

[34] Bickerton (1975, 1977), Bickerton and Odo (1976, 1977), Bickerton and Givón (1976).

Whereas the subject–predicate structure is virtually undeterminable, the topic–comment structure is transparent. Virtually no syntactic subordination can be found, and verbal clauses are loosely concatenated, usually separated by considerable pauses. In other words, the Pidgin speech exhibits almost an extreme case of the PRAGMATIC mode of communication.

In contrast, the Creole—apparently a synthesis *di novo* by the first generation of native speakers who received the Pidgin as their data input and proceeded to "create the grammer"—is very much like normal languages in that it possesses a syntactic mode with all the trimmings, as described in (41).[35] The amount of variation in Creole speech is much smaller than in the Pidgin, indistinguishable from the normal level found in "normal" language communities. And, although Creoles exhibit certain uniform and highly universal characteristics that distinguish them, in degree though not in kind, from other "normal" languages,[36] they certainly possess the entire range of grammatical signals used in the syntax of natural languages, such as fixed word-order, grammatical morphology, intonation, embedding, and various constraints.

The most fascinating feature of Pidgin speech is the fact that although it seems "not to have any syntax," its pragmatics at the discourse level is virtually intact. Thus, although identifying subject and predicate is a tantalizingly difficult task, identifying the message—and, in particular, the topic and comment—is much easier. Let me illustrate this peculiar quality of the Pidgin by an example taken out of transcripts collected by D. Bickerton from a Japanese Pidgin-English speaker in Hawaii.[37]

(42)   *Oh me? . . .*
       Oh me over there . . .
       nineteen-twenty over there say come . . .
       store me stop begin open . . .

       me sixty year . . .
       little more sixty year . . .
       now me ninty . . .
       na ehm . . .

[35] Bickerton and Odo (1977) claim that Hawaiin Creole has a higher frequency of topicalized (as against "grammatical") subjects than does "normal" natural languages. However, they compare an extremely INFORMAL register of Hawaiian Creole with Standard Educated American English. See later discussion in Section 6.

[36] See Bickerton (1975), Givón (1975c), Kay and Sankoff (1974), Traugott (1977), and Slobin (1977).

[37] The speaker was a Japanese male, age 90, recorded in the island of Hawaii, where he had lived since 1907, that is, close to 70 years. The data is courtesy of Derek Bickerton and his tape collection. I have marked with [. . .] interclausal intonation breaks and with wider spacing more major breaks. The spelling has been adjusted to be closer to standard English.

little more . . .

this man ninety-two . . .

yeah, this month over . . .
me Hawaii come [desu] . . .
ninteen-seven come . . .
me number first here . . .
me-[wa] tell . . .
You sabe guruméru? . . .
You no sabe guruméru? . . .

yeah, this place come . . .
this place been two-four-five year . . .
stop, ey . . .
then me go home . . .
Japan . . .
by-m-by wife hapái ('carry') . . .
by-m-by . . . little boy . . . come . . .
by-m-by he been come here . . . ey . . .
by-m-by come . . .
by-m-by me before Hui-Hui stop . . .
Hui-Hui this . . .
eh . . . he . . . this a . . . Manuel . . . you sabe [ka]? . . .

The creation of a Creole language out of the Pidgin thus represents another instance of syntacticization. The Pidgin mode of communication is essentially our pragmatic mode (41). The Creole went on to develop the syntactic mode out of it. The important question to raise at this point is: What are the conditions that, in the Pidgin, govern the exclusive use of the pragmatic mode only? At this point I would like to suggest three of those:

(43)   a.   COMMUNICATIVE STRESS: *The Pidgin-speaking community is thrown together without a common language but has urgent tasks to perform.*

         b.   LACK OF COMMON PRAGMATIC BACKGROUND: *Members of the Pidgin community come from different cultural and racial communities, they share relatively* LITTLE *of the general, pragmatic presuppositional background that forms the general context for human communication.*[38]

[38] As suggested in Givón (1979: Chapters 2 and 3), communication takes place on the vast background of a shared ("presupposed") universe of knowledge, including real-world knowledge, cultural conventions, social structure, the likely motivation of one's interlocutor(s), etc. Knowledge of the preceding discourse is a subset of this background.

c. IMMEDIATELY OBVIOUS CONTEXT: *The tasks or topics of communication in the Pidgin-using society are* IMMEDIATE, OBVIOUS *and* NONREMOTE. *They are* RIGHT THERE *in both time and space, involving various—largely physical—tasks to be performed on the plantation.*

The communicative stress and the lack of common pragmatic background are the chief contributors to the SLOW RATE of communication. But, to some extent, the obviousness of the *immediate context* and *tasks* is what makes this mode of communication possible at all.

The Creole society, on the other hand, grew slowly out of the Pidgin situation. Children took the normal 5–7 years to create a grammar; the range of subjects, contexts, and tasks to be dealt with has expanded to the normal social range. Years of living together have created an increasing body of common pragmatic background and common cultural assumptions, as well as a growing knowledge of members of the community, of their personality and motivation. On this facilitating background, the syntactic mode of communication, with its condensation and its time-saving and structuralized, automated coding procedures, can evolve.

5. CHILD VERSUS ADULT LANGUAGE

Hints suggesting that early child language is basically of the pragmatic mode come as early as Gruber (1967), with his now-forgotten observation that early child language seems to abound with TOPICS at the expense of subjects. For a while, this pioneering insight was buried under a veritable avalanche of purely syntactic studies purporting to document the acquisition of STRUCTURE without reference to communicative skills. By now, the pendulum has swung the other way, and a growing number of studies show that children first acquire a COMMUNICATIVE SYSTEM and that in all fundamental ways this early communicative system exhibits the characteristics of our PRAGMATIC mode (41).[39] Its rate of delivery is slow, it is concatenated rather than embedded, it lacks grammatical morphology, the noun-to-verb ratio approaches one-to-one, topics prevail over subjects, word-order is mostly pragmatic, and one of the earliest discernible principles is that of assigning higher intonation contours to the focus of new information.

---

[39] Some of the studies in this rapidly growing field are by Elinor Keenan (1974a, 1974b, 1975a, 1975b, 1977), Keenan and Schieffelin (1976), Bates (1974, 1976), Sconlon (1974, 1976), Greenfield and Smith (1976), Bloom (1973).

In terms of the characteristics of the communicative situation prevailing at the early stages of child language, we find a striking parallel with what was earlier described for Pidgins (43):

(44)   a.   COMMUNICATIVE STRESS: *The child is thrown into the world with urgent functions to be taken care of and no mode of communication to be shared with the surrounding human community.*

        b.   LACK OF COMMON PRAGMATIC BACKGROUND: *The child obviously lacks the shared common background of knowing the world, the culture, the social structure and the probable motivation of his interlocutors.*

        c.   IMMEDIATELY OBVIOUS CONTEXT: *Early child communication involves immediately obvious topics, tasks, and contexts of the here-and-now, the most immediate and obvious of which is, of course, the child himself.*

As Elinor Ochs (in this volume) pointed out, what follows in the subsequent development of adult linguistic skills from the child's mode is a gradual change in the parameters that govern the communicative situation (44). The communicative stress slowly elevates as the child acquires language skills. Larger and larger portions of the common pragmatic background are acquired. The range of topics, tasks, and contexts slowly enlarges itself from the immediate to the less immediate, from the obvious to the less obvious, from the concrete to the more abstract. And this is paralleled by the shift in communicative mode from the child's early, totally PRAGMATIC mode toward the gradual acquisition of the SYNTACTIC mode. The child never loses the early mode, and as an adult he controls an entire SCALE going from the extreme pragmatic to the extreme syntactic. The epitome of the latter is the formal, WRITTEN mode (see the previous discussion). But the adult may always, under the appropriate communicative situation, revert back to a largely PRAGMATIC mode. The type of communication used by adults learning a SECOND LANGUAGE is largely of the pragmatic mode, as is the PIDGIN register. This earliest-acquired type of communication, then, remains with us through life. In some fundamental ways, it must be considered our EMBRIONIC, RUDIMENTARY form of communication.[40] Furthermore, although the study of the universals of language has confined itself, under both transformational and nontransformational schools, almost exclusively to the syntactic mode, it is quite likely that the pragmatic mode is actually the MOST universal component of our communicative skills, the bottom-line register shared by all humans.

[40] The obvious phylogenetic implications of this, in terms of the evolution of human language, is discussed in Givón (1979: Chapter 7).

To sum up, then, in the development of the adult linguistic mode out of the child's, one observes a striking parallel to the diachronic processes previously discussed as well as to the development of the Creole mode out of the Pidgin. In each case, the syntactic mode evolved over time out of the pragmatic mode. The process of syntacticization is strikingly similar in those three. In the following section, I will discuss the consequences of such development in the adult, non-Pidgin speaker, that is, the coexistence of a RANGE of registers or communicative modes, with the extremes being our syntactic and pragmatic modes.

6. INFORMAL VERSUS FORMAL SPEECH

One of the greatest shocks administered to the psyche of a devout generative linguist is likely to come on that rare day when he makes the unfortunate move toward tackling natural, live, informal and unsolicited speech. Such an experience may result in the total collapse of the intricate frame of "grammaticality" and "competence," an edifice that was initially erected in order to insulate the generative linguist from precisely such a discouraging confrontation with the real world of language data. If a linguist is honest about his empirical responsibilities, then at some point in his career he has to face the profound—and disturbingly SCALAR—difference between the formal and informal registers of adult language. The first, the formal register, has been the traditional stock-in-trade of the linguist and almost his sole data input. In this sense, the transformationalist and the traditional grammarian share a common prejudice, though the traditionalist tends to ignore the informal register because of deep-seated PRESCRIPTIVE prejudices and the transformationalist dismisses the data as chaotic, degenerate, and reflecting "performance" factors. The seemingly chaotic, nongrammatical nature of unplanned,[41] informal speech tends to parallel the situation found in early child language, and studies dealing with the structural properties and communicative constraints on informal speech are relatively recent. Earlier studies tended to dwell upon the social-interactional aspects of the transaction, thus paying less attention to the information transaction and to the grammatical structure.[42] More recently, a number of related studies focused on the difference between the informal and formal registers.[43] These

---

[41] The terms PLANNED and UNPLANNED discourse were introduced by Elinor Keenan (1977). They overlap with my FORMAL versus INFORMAL distinction.

[42] See Sacks, Schegloff, and Jefferson (1974), Schegloff (1973), Schegloff, Jefferson, and Sacks (1976).

[43] In a collection edited by Keenan and Bennett (1977), with the relevant papers being by Elinor Keenan (1977), Bennett (1977), Kroll (1977), and Shimanoff and Brunak (1977).

studies have been summarized by Elinor Ochs (this volume), as she comments on the amazing parallelism between the child versus adult and the planned versus unplanned discourse registers.[44] In summary, informal–unplanned discourse tends to:

1. show more topicalized (left-dislocated) constructions; those are almost entirely absent in the formal–planned register.
2. favor loose coordination over tight subordination, that is, less embedding.
3. involve more repetition, pauses, and, in general, an increased time of delivery.
4. involve a considerable reduction and simplification of the grammatical morphology, that is, reduced tense-aspect systems and less complex case-morphology, thus dispensing with subordinating morphemes for both verb complements and relative clauses, and an increased use of zero anaphora over anaphoric pronouns.
5. exhibit shorter verbal clauses with fewer nominal arguments per verb.
6. exhibit a much more prominent topic–comment structure, as against the more prominent use of grammatical subjects in the planned–formal register.

As Elinor Ochs points out in her summary, the adult has never forgotten his first-acquired communicative skill, the PRAGMATIC mode. He simply added onto it, via the gradual rise of the SYNTACTIC mode. And, although it is unlikely that an adult, in relaxed informal conversation among people sharing his cultural and linguistic code, will revert ALL the way to the EXTREME pragmatic mode, the similarities are, nevertheless, quite striking. Furthermore, under situations of extreme communicative stress, such as those prevailing in the Pidgin situation or under a pressing need to communicate in a foreign language, the adult does, in fact, revert almost all the way[45] to the extreme pragmatic register on the scale.

When one turns to consider the communicative situation under which informal–unplanned discourse is used, a much more complex picture is found, one with many parameters interacting with each other in a complex fashion. At the moment, it seems to me that at least the following may be said:

[44] Apparently, the research underlying this article and Elinor Och's work was carried on independently, along similar lines. I am more than delighted to acknowledge this fruitful convergence.

[45] Given that the adult is already a mature speaker of SOME language, with a vast lexicon, an organized and coded world view, and many presuppositions about the universe, society, human motivation, and interaction, it is unlikely that he will revert ALL the way to the child's mode of communication.

1. COMMUNICATIVE STRESS: One very common type of informal communication is under relaxed conditions without time pressure, where planning is simply NOT NECESSARY. On the other hand, under extreme emergency conditions in which there is no time for planning at all, pragmatic (unplanned) rather than syntactic speech is also used.[46]

2. TIME PRESSURE: Thus, whereas the most common pragmatic mode seems to involve NO time pressure, emergency situations—including, perhaps to a lesser degree, the Pidgin and foreign-language situations—also seem to precipitate the use of the pragmatic mode.

3. DEGREE OF PLANNING: Here Elinor Ochs's characterization is quite apt. The pragmatic mode is, for whatever reason (too much time or no time at all), an unplanned mode, that is, when you PLAN AS YOU GO;[47] and the ultimate example of the planned mode is tight, educated written language.

4. FACE-TO-FACE MONITORING: As Manny Schegloff (personal communication) has pointed out, face-to-face communication can afford to be less planned, less tightly organized, more repetitious, and, seemingly, more slapdash PRECISELY because of the constant monitoring of the interlocutor, his following the topic, his degree of comprehension, and his reaction to the presuppositions upon which the communication float. This affords the speaker the opportunity for instant repair, for repetition, for slowing down, for simplification and clarification as he follows the facial, gestural, and interjectional clues emitted by the hearer. Such repetition, repair, and slowdown are part of the characteristics of pragmatic speech.

5. SHARED GENERAL PRAGMATIC BACKGROUND: Here, again we find a complex interaction with another factor, that is, the DEGREE OF IMMEDIATELY OBVIOUS CONTEXT. In general, informal speech is found first among FAMILIARS who share a large background of their pragmatic presuppositions about the universe and themselves. Under such conditions, the topic, context, or task for the communication may be less immediately obvious. On the other hand, this mode is also found among STRANGERS, in superficial encounters. But there the topic, task, or context tends to be much more immediately obvious. These two factors tend, thus, to form an aggregate of shared background. The child's case and that of the Pidgin speaker fall at the same extreme here. That is, though the general pragmatic background is minimal, the communication is strictly face-to-face and involves mostly the immediately obvious, the here-and-now, the interlocutors themselves, thus tending to PRECLUDE third persons, past–future time, and nonvisible space.

---

[46] For this suggestion I am indebted to Patricia Greenfield (personal communication).

[47] In terms of the overall time spent on planning AND delivery, one may suspect that a certain balance prevails, so that the more time one spends on PRE-planning, the less one spends on actual delivery. The extreme emergency situations (*Fire!*) correspond to neither extreme here, since there is little time for either preplanning or delivery.

The extreme instance of the formal–planned pole is educated, book-written language, and it is, therefore, of great interest to assess the communicative parameters under which it is used. Those may be summarized as:

1. There is extremely careful planning, with corrections, rewriting, and reformulation.
2. Considerable time-pressure is, on the one hand, obvious in terms of space-saving and saving in printing costs. On the other hand, a much longer time is spent on preplanning.
3. There is an almost total lack of communicative stress, since the message usually is written for delayed reading.[48]
4. There is a total absence of face-to-face monitoring.
5. There is a relatively small body of assumed presuppositional background at the very onset, since one is, then, in fact writing FOR STRANGERS.[49] However, the presuppositional background is then built up gradually, in a carefully planned manner, with each new line increasing it, to the point where the expository portion gives way to the main body of the narrative.
6. There is virtually no immediately obvious context, topic, or task. Typically, one writes about other times, other places, and nonpresent people.

The written register, much like the formal public-address register, is, thus, the utmost mode of communication in the MASS SOCIETY OF STRANGERS. It is a product of need; it is there for a purpose. Conversely, since language evolved as an oral tool, initially in immediately obvious contexts and dealing with immediately obvious topics and tasks involving face-to-face communication among small groups of intimates who shared much of the pragmatic presuppositions about their universe and the social and motivational structure, an inescapable conclusion is that in the evolution of language, the pragmatic mode was the EARLIER type of human communication, whereas the syntactic mode is a later outgrowth from it.[50]

---

[48] In writing under time-pressure, the characteristics of the register veer sharply toward the pragmatic mode, as may be seen in Janda (1976).

[49] Obviously, the reduction could not be complete here, since, as the context, task, and topic are not immediately obvious; communication could not proceed unless there was SOME shared background.

[50] There are no linguistic communities known to me in which ONLY the pragmatic mode is used. So, obviously, the human species wherever it be has evolved to the point where nonimmediately obvious contexts, topics, and tasks can be dealt with and where one may communicate with strangers as well as—sometimes overwhelmingly—with familiars. To the extent that written language represents the apex of the syntactic mode, the majority of societies (and speakers) do not exhibit that extreme [see the discussion in Givón (1979: Chapter 7)].

7. DISCUSSION

Diachrony and Child Development

There seems to be an inescapable connection between the two, in the sense that processes that seem to occur as the child modifies its early communicative mode via syntacticization are identical to processes that generate syntactic structures in language over time. This probably involves an active, creative interaction between the corrective, instructive adult input and the evolving needs of the communicative situation. But the causal relation is far from clear, and it may well be that language evolves diachronically the way it does PRECISELY because children indulge in syntacticization under specific communicative constraints, needs, and requirements.

The Diachronic Cycle

Although pragmatics gives rise to syntax, syntax in turn gives rise to grammatical morphology, which then decays via phonological attrition.[51] At least at their present stage, it seems, human languages keep renovating their syntax via the grammaticalization of discourse.

Universality and Evolution

It seems rather clear that the pragmatic mode of human communication, as defined in (41) above, is ontogenetically earlier, phylogenetically earlier, and, in terms of cross-language attestation, more universal than the syntactic mode. At the latter level, languages tend to diverge enormously. At the former, they tend to be amazingly similar. The fact that this mode is always used under the stressful conditions of no common language—as in Pidgins or foreign-talk—simply underscores its status as the UNIVERSAL COMMON DENOMINATOR.

Coexisting Registers

A mature speaker has not lost his earlier mode but, rather, has slowly acquired progressively-more-syntacticized registers. Although the extremes on this scale are attested in early child speech and in formal, educated written language, a complex interaction of communicative parameters—as

---

[51] Here, the SEMANTIC BLEACHING of lexical words into grammatical morphemes goes hand in hand with the phonological bleaching ("reduction") that is, destressing, cliticization, and assimilatory erosion.

discussed earlier—determines the choice (or necessity) of the appropriate point on the register scale.

Coding Modalities in Syntax

Out of the four major coding modalities used in the syntactic mode—rigid word-order, grammatical morphology, constraints,[52] and intonation—the first three arise together via the process of syntacticization and should be viewed as necessary correlates for it. Intonation, on the other hand, remains largely pragmatic and may or may not be used in the syntactic mode.[53]

On Explaining Synchronic Syntax

Quite often it turns out that the structure of synchronic syntax cannot be understood without reference to either dianchronic or developmental processes. And in either case, the process of syntacticization, which brings syntax into being, cannot be understood without reference to its initial departure point, the pragmatic mode, as well as to the communicative parameters that govern its evolution ontogenetically and diachronically.

Grammar as an Automatic Processing Strategy

One may view the rise of rigid word-order, condensed—tight, subordinate—syntactic constructions, rich grammatical morphology, and tight syntactic constraints–rules as the rise of the AUTOMATIC PROCESSING of speech. The pragmatic mode is analytic and slow; it has a high degree—for all practical purposes, 100%—of communicative fidelity, a one-to-one correlation between code and message. But it is also a cumbersome mode requiring a high degree of face-to-face interaction and is often limited to topics, tasks, and contexts that are not too far removed from here, now, and us. In the syntactic mode, one may view the more-evolved coding devices as the TOOLS of automatic processing. But, while one gains speed, one loses resolution, since in syntax typically the correlation between form and meaning is somewhere BELOW 100%. The syntactic mode is thus used

---

[52] By "constraints" I mean conditions such as coreference, case-identity, parallel structure, etc., which are normally associated with so-called syntactic transformations.

[53] Most typically, languages with a highly productive lexical tone, as well as those with a highly productive use of the pragmatic word-order principle of topic–comment, tend to make less use of intonation as a signal for topic–focus relations. Mandarin Chinese and Yoruba are examples of the first type, and current Spanish of the second. English, on the other hand, is one of the most extreme examples of rigid word-order and the highly evolved use of pragmatic intonation. For more details, see Bolinger (1958, 1972, 1977a, 1977b, 1977c).

only when other parameters that govern the communicative situation make it possible to OFFSET such a loss. Does syntax exist, then? Yes and no. It does exist as a mode of linguistic communication, and it does have highly specific structural properties. Therefore, the extreme position as represented by García (in this volume) seems rather untenable. On the other hand, syntax cannot be understood or explained without reference to BOTH its evolution ex-discourse and the communicative parameters and principles that govern both its rise out of the pragmatic mode and its selective use along the register scale of human communication. Therefore, the other extreme position, that of the transformational-generative orthodoxy, seems even more untenable.

ACKNOWLEDGMENTS

I have benefited enormously from comments and suggestions made by the symposium's participants and would like to record my indebtedness here. In particular, I would like to thank Elinor Ochs, Manny Schegloff, Patricia Greenfield, Edward Keenan, David Zubin, Bob Longacre, and Pete Becker for their many helpful suggestions.

REFERENCES

Akiba, K. (1978) *Topics in Japanese Historical Syntax*, Doctoral dissertation, University of California, Los Angeles, California.

Andrews, A. (1976) The VP complement analysis in Modern Icelandian,'' manuscript, Australian National University, Canberra.

Bates, E. (1974) *Language in Context: Studies in the acquisition of Pragmatics*, PhD dissertation, University of Chicago, Chicago, Illinois.

Bates, E. (1976) *Language and Context: The Acquisition of Pragmatics*, Academic Press, New York.

Bennett, T. (1977) "An extended view of written and spoken personal narratives," in E. Keenan and T. Bennett, eds., *Discourse Across Time and Space*, S.C.O.P.I.L., 5, University of Southern California, Los Angeles, California.

Bickerton, D. (1975) "Creolization, linguistic universals, natural semantax and the brain," manuscript, University of Hawaii, Honolulu, Hawaii.

Bickerton, D. (1977) "Creoles and language universals," manuscript, University of Hawaii, Honolulu, Hawaii.

Bickerton, D. and T. Givón (1976) "Pidginization and syntactic change: From SOV and VSO to SVO," in S. S. Mufwene, C. A. Walker, and S. B. Steever, eds., *Papers from the Parasession on Diachronic Syntax*, Chicago Linguistic Society, Chicago, Illinois.

Bickerton, D. and C. Odo (1976) *Change and Variation in Hawaiian English*, vol. 1, NSF Report, Social Science and Linguistics Institute, University of Hawaii, Honolulu, Hawaii.

Bickerton, D. and C. Odo (1977) *Change and Variation in Hawaiian English*, vol. 2, NSF report, Social Science and Linguistics Institute, University of Hawaii, Honolulu, Hawaii.

Bloom, L. (1973) *One Word at a Time*, Mouton, The Hague.

Bolinger, D. (1958) "A theory of pitch-accent in English," *Word* 14, 109–149.

Bolinger, D. (1972) "Accent is predictable (if you are a mind reader)," *Language* 48, 633–644.

Bolinger, D. (1977a) "Another glance at main-clause phenomena," *Language* 53.

Bolinger, D. (1977b) "Intonation across languages," in J. Greenberg, ed., *Universals of Human Language*, Stanford University Press, Stanford.

Bolinger, D. (1977c) "Accent that determines stress," in M. Kay and J. Fishman, eds., *Verbal and Non Verbal Communication*, The Hague, Mouton (in press).

Cole, P. (1976) "The grammatical role of the causee in universal grammar," manuscript, University of Illinois, Urbana, Illinois.

Comrie, B. (1976) "The syntax of causative constructions: Cross-language similarities and divergences," in M. Shibatani, ed., *Syntax and Semantics*, vol. 6, Academic Press, New York.

Givón, T. (1971) "Historical syntax and synchronic morphology: An archaeologist's field trip," in *Papers from the Seventh Regional Meeting of the Chicago Linguistic Society*, Chicago Linguistic Society, Chicago, Illinois.

Givón, T. (1973) "The time-axis phenomenon," *Language* 49.

Givón, T. (1974) "Verb complements and relative clauses in Biblical Hebrew: A diachronic case study," *Afro-Asiatic Linguistics* 4.

Givón, T. (1975a) "Serial verbs and syntactic change: Niger-Congo," in C. Li, ed., *Word Order and Word Order Change*, University of Texas Press, Austin, Texas.

Givón, T. (1975b) "Cause and control: On the semantics of interpersonal manipulation," in J. Kimball, ed., *Syntax and Semantics*, vol. 4, Academic Press, New York.

Givón, T. (1975c) "Prolegomena to any Creology," in E. Polome, M. Goodman, B. Heinz, and I. Hancock, (eds.), *Readings in Pidgins and Creoles* slory-scientia, Ghent (in press).

Givón, T. (1976a) "Topic, pronoun, and grammatical agreement," in C. Li, ed., *Subject and Topic*, Academic Press, New York.

Givón, T. (1976b) "Some constraints on Bantu causativization," in M. Shibatani, ed., *Syntax and Semantics*, vol. 6, Academic Press, New York.

Givón, T. (1979) *On Understanding Grammar*, Academic Press, New York.

Greenfield, P. and J. H. Smith (1976) *The Structure of Communication in Early Language Development*, Academic Press, New York.

Gruber, J. (1967) "Topicalization in child language," *Foundations of Language* 3.

Hawkins, J. and E. Keenan (1974) "On the psychological validity of the accessibility hierarchy," manuscript, Linguistic Society of America Summer Meeting.

Hyman, L. (1971) "Consecutivization in Fe'fe'," *Journal of African Languages* 10.

Janda, R. (1976) "The language of note-taking as a simplified register," manuscript, Stanford University, Stanford, California.

Justus, C. (1976a) "Topicalization and relativization in Hittite," in C. Li, ed., *Subject and Topic*, Academic Press, New York.

Justus, C. (1976b) "Syntactic change: Evidence for restructuring among coexistant variants," manuscript, State University of New York at Oswego.

Kay, P. and G. Sankoff (1974) "A language-universal approach to Pidgins and Creoles," in D. Decamp and I. Hancock, eds., *Pidgins and Creoles: Current trends and prospects*, Georgetown University Press, Washington DC.

Keenan, Edward (1976) "Toward a universal definition of 'subject'," in C. Li, ed., *Subject and Topic*, Academic Press, New York.

Keenan, Edward and B. Comrie (1975) "The Noun Phrase accessibility hierarchy and Universal Grammar," *Linguistic Inquiry*.

Keenan, Elinor (1974a) "Conversational competence in children," *Journal of Child Language*.

Keenan, Elinor (1974b) "Again and again: The pragmatics of imitation in child language," manuscript, University of Southern California, Los Angeles.

Keenan, Elinor (1975a) "Making it last: Uses of repetition in children's discourse," *Papers for the First Annual Meeting of the Berkeley Linguistic Society*, Berkeley Linguistic Society, Berkeley, California.

Keenan, Elinor (1975b) "Evolving discourse: The next step," manuscript.

Keenan, Elinor (1977) "Why look at planned and unplanned discourse?" in E. Keenan and T. Bennett, eds., *Discourse Across Time and Space*, SCOPIL, University of Southern California, Los Angeles, California.

Keenan, Elinor and T. Bennett, eds., (1977) *Discourse Across Time and Space*, Los Angeles: University of So. California, SCOPIL, University of Southern California, Los Angeles, California.

Keenan, Elinor and B. Schieffelin (1976) "Topic as a discourse notion: A study of 'topic' in conservations of children and adults," in C. Li, ed., *Subject and Topic*, Academic Press, New York.

Keenan, Elinor and B. Schieffelin (1977) "Foregrounding referents: A re-consideration of left-dislocation in discourse," manuscript, University of Southern California, Los Angeles.

Kroll, B. (1977) "Ways communicators encode propositions in spoken and written English: A look at subordination and coordination," in E. Keenan and T. Bennett, eds., *Discourse Across Space and Time*, SCOPIL, University of Southern California, Los Angeles, California.

Langdon, M. (1977) "Syntactic change and SOV structure: The Yuman case," in C. Li, ed., *Mechanisms for Syntactic Change*, University of Texas Press, Austin, Texas.

Li, C., ed., (1976) *Subject and Topic*, Academic Press, New York.

Li, C. and S. Thompson (1973a) "Historical change in word-order: A case study in Chinese and its implications," in J. Anderson, ed., *Proceedings of the First International Conference on Historical Linguistics*, Cambridge: Cambridge University Press, Edinburgh.

Li, C. and S. Thompson (1973b) "Serial verb constructions in Mandarin Chinese: Subordination or coordination?," in C. Corum, T. Smith-Stark, and A. Weiser, eds., Papers from the Comparative Syntax Festival, Chicago Linguistic Society, Chicago, Illinois.

Li, C. and S. Thompson (1973c) "Coverbs in Mandarin Chinese: Verbs or prepositions?," manuscript, University of California, Los Angeles, California.

Li, C. and S. Thompson (1976) "Subject and topic: A new typology for language," in C. Li, ed., *Subject and Topic*, Academic Press, New York.

Lord, C. (1973) "Serial verbs in transition," *Studies in African Linguistics*, 4.

Sacks, H., E. Schegloff, and G. Jefferson (1974) "A simplest systematics for the organization of turn-taking for conversation," *Language* 50.

Sankoff, G. (1976) "Grammaticalization process in New-Guinea Tok-Pisin," manuscript.

Sankoff, G. and P. Brown (1976) "The origins of syntax in discourse," *Language* 52.

Schachter, P. (1973) "Focus and relativization," *Language* 49.

Schachter, P. (1976) "The subject in Philippine languages: Topic, actor, actor-topic or none of the above?," in C. Li, ed., *Subject and Topic*, Academic Press, New York.

Schachter, P. (1977) "Reference related and role-related properties of subjects," in P. Cole and J. Morgan, eds., *Syntax and Semantics*, vol. 8, Academic Press, New York.

Schegloff, E. (1973) "Recycle turn beginning: A precise repair mechanism in conversation's turn-taking," manuscript, University of California, Los Angeles

Schegloff, E., G. Jefferson, and H. Sacks (1976) "The preference for self-correction in the organization of repair in conversation," manuscript, University of California, Los Angeles.

Sconlon, R. (1974) *One child's language from one to two: The Origins of Structure*, Doctoral dissertation, University of Hawaii, Honolulu, Hawaii.

Sconlon, R. (1976) *Conversations with a One-Year Old Child*, University of Hawaii Press, Honolulu, Hawaii.

Shibatani, M., (1976) *Syntax and Semantics, The Grammar of Causative Constructions*, vol. 6, Academic Press, New York.

Shimanoff, J. and S. Brunak (1977) "Repairs in planned and unplanned discourse," in E. Keenan and T. Bennett, eds., *Discourse Across Time and Space*, SCOPIL, University of Southern California, Los Angeles, California.

Slobin, D. (1977) "Language change in childhood and history," in J. MacNamara, ed., *Language Learning and Thought*, Academic Press, New York.

Stahlke, H. (1970) "Serial verbs," *Studies in African Linguistics* 1.

Takizala, A. (1972) "Focus and relativization: The case of Kihung'an," *Studies in African Linguistics* 3.

Thompson, S. (1973) "Resultative verb compounds in Mandarin Chinese: A case for lexical rules," *Language* 49.

Traugott, E. (1977) "Pidginization, Creolization and language change," in A. Valdman, ed., *Pidgin and Creole Linguistics*, Indiana University Press, Bloomington, Indiana.

PART II THE ORGANIZATION OF DISCOURSE

THE PARAGRAPH AS A GRAMMATICAL UNIT

R. E. LONGACRE
The University of Texas at Arlington
and the
Summer Institute of Linguistics

1. INTRODUCTION

In this paper, it is assumed (*a*) that discourse has GRAMMATICAL STRUC-
TURE; and (*b*) that this structure is partially expressed in the hierarchical
breakdown of discourses into constituent embedded discourses and paragraphs and in the breakdown of paragraphs into constituent embedded
paragraphs and sentences—not to speak of further hierarchical parcelling
out into clauses, phrases, and word structures. It is a special thrust of this
paper to marshal whatever arguments may be marshaled for the grammatical
structure of the paragraph.[1]

"Paragraph" is taken here to designate a structural rather than an orthographic unit. The paragraph indentations of a given writer are often partially

---

[1] I acknowledge here my indebtedness to an unpublished paper (1970) of Alan Healey: "Are
there grammatical paragraphs in English?" An abbreviated version of his paper was used over
a 5-year period in grammar classes at the University of Texas at Arlington and in classes of the
Dallas Summer Institute of Linguistics. The general stimulus of this paper and its many specific
germinal thoughts have so entered into the present paper that detailed acknowledgment is
quite impossible.

Syntax and Semantics, Volume 12:
Discourse and Syntax

dictated by eye appeal; that is, it may be deemed inelegant or heavy to go along too far on a page or a series of pages without an indentation or section break. A writer may, therefore, indent at the beginning of a subparagraph to provide such a break. Conversely, a writer may put together several paragraphs as an indentation unit in order to show the unity of a comparatively short embedded discourse. Finally, the orthographic rule in English composition that we must indent for each change of speaker in a dialogue obscures the unity of dialogue paragraphs (where, e.g., assuredly a question and its answer constitute a unit).

As far as the status of the paragraph at the present time in linguistic thinking is concerned, van Dijk (1972:125–126), although scarcely using the term PARAGRAPH as such, tells us emphatically that we cannot consider that a discourse is composed directly of a concatenation of sentences; rather, we must consider it to be composed of sequences of sentences. I do not see why the traditional term PARAGRAPH should not be applied to at least some of the sequences of sentences that van Dijk finds essential to the analysis of a discourse. Furthermore, explicit research on the structure of the paragraph is currently being carried out by Hinds (this volume) and Winter (1977).

I argue in this paper that we have good evidence in many languages of the world for paragraph closure (i.e., features of beginning and end) and paragraph unity and that we are able to construct a system of paragraphs that does not compare unfavorably with constructing, for example, a system of clauses in a given language.

Some assumptions of this paper are:

1.   Monologue discourse in any language has a hierarchical constituent structure that runs somewhat as follows (the scheme can vary a bit from language area to language area): morpheme, stem, word, phrase, clause, sentence, paragraph, discourse.

2.   In this scheme, since paragraph is spaced between sentence and discourse, it resembles in certain ways the two contiguous levels. Thus, in certain respects, a paragraph resembles a long sentence on the one hand and a short discourse on the other hand.

3.   The best way to describe this constituent structure is to distinguish the functional slot from the set of items that may fill the slot. In particular, a functional slot within a paragraph (e.g., its setting, or its culmination) need not be expressed by just a sentence but can be expressed by a group of sentences that constitute an embedded paragraph. This assumption is very important throughout this chapter in that, although many of the examples involve only one sentence per functional slot, they are, in principle, recursively expandable to examples in which a group of sentences (embedded paragraphs) fill one or more such slots.

4. The functional parts of a paragraph (whether consisting of a sentence or of an embedded paragraph) are often marked by overt sequence signals (conjunctions, sentence adverbs, back reference to a previous sentence, or deictics). But, even when unmarked (in a given example in a given language), the notional parallelism with marked structures justifies grammatical analysis. Thus, in languages such as Mandarin, Vietnamese, Cambodian, and Laotian, we still find "subject" (or topic), "object," and "verb" even when formal marking is almost nonexistent.

2. ARGUMENTS FOR THE GRAMMAR OF THE PARAGRAPH

Closure

Many languages have particles that indicate either the beginning or the end of a paragraph.[2] Thus, "paragraph introducers" in Huichol (Mexico) include *mérikʌ* 'well' and *hiikʌ́ʌ* 'then'—which occur on the first or second word of a main or of a dependent clause (Grimes 1964:73–74). In Shipibo (Peru), *jainoasr* and *jainsron*, both roughly translatable as 'thereupon', serve a similar function. In fact, we are told that these words occur only as the first word of a paragraph (Loriot and Hollenbach 1970). In Capanahua, a form of the verb *ha-* 'do, be, have' serves a similar function as in: *ha-ska-ʔi-ya* 'and so then . . .' and *ha-ska-ska-há-ʔi-ya* 'So that is the way it was when . . .' (Loos 1973:701–702).

Another similar (and often interlocked) feature is back reference between paragraphs. Back reference occurs in many languages in various distributions between successive sentences of a discourse. It is not, as such, limited to the onset of a new paragraph. Thus, we can have such sequences as *Jim went downtown to see the parade. After watching it go by, he jumped in his car and came home*, where *after watching it go by* is a back reference to *to see the parade* in the preceding sentence.

Schulze and Bieri (1973:390), however, describe for Sunwar some peculiar kinds of back reference that are characteristic of paragraph initial. One, which consists of "chaining with identical verb phrases," apparently has no temporal or sequential function but functions merely to mark the end of one paragraph and the beginning of another. Thus, we may have at the end of the paragraph *I will buy a cow*, and the next paragraph will begin *I will buy a cow and . . . .* Paragraph onset can also be marked by chaining with temporal reference of the sort illustrated in my own example of back reference given above.

[2] Gary Singleton marshaled these data for me in a term paper at the University of Texas at Arlington.

In other languages (e.g., Gurung of Nepal and Sanio-Hiowe of New Guinea) we find back reference exclusively within the paragraph and not between paragraphs. Lack of back reference is indicative, therefore, of a paragraph boundary.

Another feature that often serves to mark off paragraphs from each other is the occurrence of characteristic constituents either at the beginning or at the end of such a unit. I have become accustomed to refer to sentences that introduce a paragraph as either SETTING or INTRODUCTION (depending on the discourse genre involved), whereas those that close a paragraph I refer to as TERMINUS. In regard to setting (with narrative) and introduction (with explanatory or hortatory material), I think we are faced with the psychological need for an "ice breaker." There is a certain reluctance on the part of the speaker to plunge immediately into a topic. He wants to spend a sentence orienting himself and the audience to what he is going to talk about. I do not mean here something as explicit as a topic sentence. I mean, rather, something that indicates time, place, or circumstances or gives a broad hint of what is to come in the body of the paragraph. Such a unit may be followed by a topic sentence proper in the explanatory paragraph or by the first sentence with the onset of action in a narrative paragraph.

Whereas in narrative discourse the setting is often used to reset the time or the place of a new paragraph, the terminus is often used to take one main participant off the stage or to indicate a lapse of time. The terminus often contains verbs of motion such as *he went away* or *he went off and slept* or *he waited until the next day* or something on that order.

Thematic Unity

Possibly of considerably more importance than the incidental occurrence of particles, back reference, setting, terminus, and other surface structure features to mark the onset or end of a paragraph is the fact of the thematic unity of a paragraph. Again, we do not simply allege thematic unity; rather, we find it reflected in the surface structure features of the paragraph itself. In narrative discourse, a narrative paragraph is built around a thematic participant, occasionally a small set of thematic participants. In other types of discourse, we find the paragraph built around a theme that is not different in kind from a thematic participant. I illustrate briefly.

In Paez (Colombia), Gerdel posits a paragraph topic that, presumably, would include both the thematic participant of a narrative paragraph and the theme of a non-narrative paragraph. She describes it as follows:

> Paragraph Topic is a paragraph-level feature which gives cohesion to a paragraph by indicating what topic is being developed in the paragraph as a whole. Paragraph topic may consist of a noun or locative phrase, or include a clause, or a certain type of

sentence. It is marked in the same way as Sentence Topic, i.e., by a clitic -a'/-' occurring phrase-final or clause-final. It differs from Sentence Topic in the following respects: 1) Paragraph Topic must be referred to at least twice in the paragraph, as marked topic at least once; re-referal may be by a lexical surrogate occurring one or more times within the paragraph; 2) paragraph topic occurs initially in the paragraph and often finally in the paragraph, thus indicating the beginning and end of a topic and incidentally indicating the bounds of a paragraph; 3) paragraph topic occurs initially in linear order in the sentence and is grammatically independent of the rest of the sentence, although it may be cross referenced to by some other word in the sentence such as a demonstrative pronoun or verb; 4) a whole sentence, occurring initially in the paragraph, may function as paragraph topic [Gerdel and Slocum 1976:275].

In the following example of a Paez paragraph, *mestlu cyã'* 'that shaman' is the paragraph topic. The paragraph topic is cross-referred to by *cyã* in the same sentence. He is also referred to again as *mestlu* 'shaman' in the last sentence. All the activities reported in the paragraph are, moreover, activities of the shaman (SS-"same subject marker").

Mestlu cyã'   "yu'tse'j ya'vatj"   jĩrra',   **cyã'** wallinde
Shaman that-one   cure   I-am-going-to saying-SS, **he**   liquor
(Paragraph Topic)   (cross-ref.)

wẽjy   ẽsh   cyã'wẽ uty pẽyi.   Vite   yu'   "cyã' cytũus
tobacco coca thus   they demand. Others (theme)   that rainbow

yafyte acjwa'j" jĩna   viyu   pẽjyna   ẽsh   ya'ja cshavyte ãshna
eyes-in to-put   saying money demanding coca bag   into   putting

uty yũ'. Cjĩrra cyajũ' ãtsã'saty cusa'   eca   cutyi'jrra'
they do. Doing then   sick-ones at-night outside making-go-SS

yu'cjte   caachi'jrra'   "ipy-cjũch uweya' spayuutstja'u"   jĩna
woods-in making-set-SS   firefly   to-catch we-are-looking saying

ipy-cjũch teerráava   uwerra'   wala-yuj wechana neeyũ'uty.
firefly   even-just-one catching-SS very   happy   they-remain.

"Na' aca ũssa's uwetja'u" jĩna   "na' ptjãawesa   caajnita'"
This pain giver we-caught saying   this harmful-one sent-by

jĩna ẽjya etste jyũtj   yacj yaprra'   uty cjicje'. Manz
saying bush leaf-in with   with wrapping-SS they place. Many

cus   **mestlurráa** e'su-yã'ja' case'je'uc ipy-cjũch yupya'
nights **shaman-only** afterwards he-goes-out firefly   to-intercept
(cross-ref.)

sa'   cuj   uwerra'   "ãtsã'a' catyjina"   jĩ'c.
and-SS several catching-SS   sick-one will-recover he-says.

The shaman demands liquor, tobacco, and *coca*, saying: "I am going to perform a cure." Others, saying: "that is for throwing in the eyes of the rainbow," demanding money, they put it into the *coca*-bags. They, taking the sick persons outside at night and making them sit in the woods, they say: "we are going to watch for fireflies to catch," and catching even one firefly, they are very happy, saying: "we have caught this one that gave the sickness; this was sent by someone as a curse" and, wrapping them in a leaf with the remedy, they put them there. Afterwards, the shaman alone goes out several nights to intercept fireflies and, catching several, he says: "the sick person will recover."

For Ica (Colombia), the identification of the thematic participant is of peculiar importance. Thus, a colleague of mine who has studied Ica for several years was puzzled for some time as to the formal means to distinguish subject from object within an Ica clause in connected discourse. He had to go mainly by such lexical probabilities as the fact that it is more probable that *the dog bit the man* than that *the man bit the dog*. Otherwise, he simply had no clue as to who was meant to be subject of a given clause. A study of paragraph structure, however, resolved the difficulty in the following manner. Ica paragraphs have a thematic participant who is referred to in the first sentence or two and is marked by the suffix *-ri*. He is assumed to be the subject of all clauses in the paragraph unless something is marked to the contrary. The latter is accomplished by adding the suffix *-se?* to any noun that is indicated as subject of a clause when that noun is not the thematic participant of the paragraph. There is even a means of switching the thematic participant of the paragraph halfway through it (so as to yield a compound paragraph with one thematic participant in the first part and another in the second part). To accomplish this, the noun that comes on not only as subject but also as new thematic participant is suffixed by both suffixes, namely, *-se?ri*. Here, an understanding of the paragraph is crucial to an understanding of the constituent structure of individual clauses within it, so that we are inevitably carried to the grammar of the paragraph from the grammar of the clause (Tracy and Levinsohn 1977).

To these examples could be added illustrative material from the Philippines, Southeast Asia, and Biblical Hebrew—to cite only a few possibilities.

3. A SYSTEM OF PARAGRAPHS WITH STRUCTURAL PARAMETERS

In the preceding section, I have argued that a paragraph unit exists, that with various degrees of clarity its boundaries are indicated in the languages of the world—both in spoken and written discourse—and that such a unit has thematic unity. There are, however, other considerations that are possibly more conclusive.

Thus, from the standpoint of Halliday and Hasan (1976:10), the sine qua non of grammatical structure in regard to such a unit as the paragraph is the ability to demonstrate system, that is, systematic parameters and choice among them. It is to this task that I address myself in this section. In outlining a system of paragraph types, I posit in the first subsection three basic parameters. I suggest, then, in the next subsection, how paragraph types produced by the intersection of these parameters are in turn realized as genre-conditioned variants. Thus, we may have, for example, a sequence paragraph that must occur either as a narrative paragraph in narrative genre or as a procedural paragraph in procedural genre. Genre imposes on the paragraph certain characteristics of itself. In the third subsection, I posit further context-conditioned variants of the sort frequently called STYLISTIC. Finally, this whole main section is followed by another section in which I claim that such a system of basic uncomplex paragraph types as are here described is sufficient to account for the wild and woolly variety of paragraphs in the real world of discourse. This is demonstrable by showing that paragraph structure is recursive, that is, that paragraphs may occur within paragraphs in an open-ended way that is sufficient to account for whatever variety of paragraph structure is encountered anywhere.

Because of limitations of space, the system of paragraph types here suggested will have to be presented in summary form, with only partial illustration.

The Basic Parameters

I posit here as basic parameters to a system of paragraphs in any language the following: (a) binary versus n-ary constructions; (b) movement along a parameter with the following values: conjoining, temporal relations, logical relations, elaborative devices, reportative devices; and (c) weighting considerations. The first parameter is essentially a matter of division of all possible paragraphs into closed versus open structures. Closed structures are typically binary; that is, the paragraph has two constituents. Occasionally, claims are made that we encounter trinary paragraphs. Although these are somewhat doubtful, if such structures exist they are also essentially closed structures—versus the open structures, which have n-ary constituents.

The second parameter is essentially a parameter involved with notional relations. These relations are not semantic in the referential sense of *dog* versus *cow* or *hit* versus *slap* but, rather, have to do with the underlying notions whereby clauses or sentences combine into larger units (Longacre 1972, 1976).

As for the third parameter, it is a matter somewhat similar to the metrical distinction between spondaic, iambic, and trochaic meters. In reference to binary paragraphs, we find that the two constituents may have equal weight or that the second may outweigh the first or that the first may outweigh the second. We can then proceed to marshal *n*-ary paragraphs under essentially the same heads. *N*-ary paragraphs may likewise consist of nuclear constituents all of which are of the same weight or of constituents with greater weight on the last (nuclear) constituent or of constituents with greater weight on the first (nuclear) constituent. Positing weighted variants brings together as essentially the same some paragraphs that at first blush appear to be different.

THE BINARY VERSUS *n*-ARY AND NOTIONAL STRUCTURE PARAMETERS

I handle here together the first two parameters by taking the second as basic to my argument and dividing it according to the binary versus n-ary parameter. In regard to the notional structure, we progress along a parameter consisting of the following values: conjoining, temporal relations, logical relations, elaborative devices, reportative devices. Conjoining has to do with grouping considerations; that is, items are grouped, contrasted, or given as a field of choice. In temporal relations, items are ordered temporally. In logical relations, they are ordered logically. In the elaborative devices, detail of various sorts is added. In reportative devices, detail is also added, but more from the standpoint of the discourse as a whole; that is, quotations are introduced into the discourse; introduction and identification paragraphs are used to bring on to stage new participants or props; and comment paragraphs are used to make possible evaluative observations by the composer of the discourse. Reportative devices are found only among binary paragraphs, and temporal relations are found only among open-ended paragraphs.

As for the conjoined binary structures, we find contrast, exception, and frustration encoded under the antithetical paragraph, as well as alternative paragraphs with only two logically possible alternatives. I use here conjoining in a more loose and inclusive sense than I have used it in former editions of my notional apparatus (such as is found in Longacre 1976: Chapter 3).

The antithetical paragraph exists, I assume, primarily to encode contrast, as in the following example: *I got on a bus, traveled around an hour or two, got off, went through the museum, and altogether had a delightful time. Tom, on the contrary, stayed home and felt sorry for himself.* Here *I* and *Tom* are contrasted as to differing courses of activity.

I handle exception as a variety of contrast in which one member of a set is contrasted with all the other members of the set. This is seen in such an example as the following: *Everybody got drowsy and eventually fell sound asleep. Only grandfather kept awake and watched for his chance.*

The antithetical paragraph also has come (in many languages) to include frustration, which is not, properly speaking, a conjoining notion but is subsumed here because it typically encodes in the same surface structure or in a very similar surface structure to those used to express contrast and exception. Thus: *He drives down crowded streets where there are children at play and adults wandering leisurely over the pavements. He never, however, seems to be on the lookout for pedestrians.* This illustrates frustrated overlap, that is, we do not get in the second sentence the expected concomitant activity indicated by the first sentence, but quite the contrary. Note also the following paragraph: *They started out for Paris promptly at seven o'clock, as planned. They never, however, got there.* Notice that it is not appropriate to these sentences to use a sequence signal such as *on the contrary*, which would be appropriate to an antithetical paragraph of the contrast variety. *But, however,* or some such conjunction is the appropriate sequence signal for a frustration paragraph. This paragraph just given is an example of frustrated succession; that is, we do not get the anticipated sequel indicated by the first sentence.

A further type of conjoined binary structure, one that encodes two alternative choices or possibilities, can fittingly be termed the ALTERNATIVE PARAGRAPH. An example follows of such a paragraph in which only two possibilities are envisioned: *John was possibly the one who turned the air conditioner on over the weekend. If he didn't, then it must have been Titus.*

Still other types of binary paragraphs encode logical relations. Exemplification of certain types of implicational paragraphs follows. Take, for example: *It may be that he'll come and call for me between six o'clock and seven o'clock tonight. If he comes, I'll be glad to spend the evening with him in whatever place he chooses.* Notice that in this paragraph the *if he comes* in sentence two is a recapitulation, contraction, and back reference to the first sentence. Or, viewed somewhat differently, the first sentence may be thought of as the full statement of the antecedent, whereas the initial stretch of the second sentence constitutes an abbreviated statement of that antecedent. At any rate, we can see that the conditional paragraph that expresses hypotheticality is essentially an expansion of a one-sentence unit that expresses the condition within itself. The following paragraph is not dissimilar; it illustrates a conditional paragraph with a universal quantifier: *First we sent Bill, then James, then Arthur, then Meredith. Whomever we sent got lost every time.* Here we see that the first sentence is essentially an expansion and elaboration of the abbreviated structure *whomever we sent* that occurs in the second sentence. Again, the conditional paragraph with universal quantifier is a rather obvious elaboration of the corresponding sentence type. Note, finally, the contrafactual paragraph that follows: *He almost came over to get me last night. Had he come, I would have gone out with him.*

Notice again that *had he come* is an echo and summary of the first sentence. So, the contrafactual paragraph, like the preceding types just mentioned, is essentially an extrapolation from the corresponding sentence type by virtue of expansion of the first member of the conditional sentence.

Result and reason paragraphs will have to be discussed more at length in that they present a more varied picture. Result and reason paragraphs may both use recapitulation via sentence margins to show the relationship of the two parts of the paragraph. Thus, a result paragraph such as the following is translated from a language of the Philippines (Dibabawon): *It's really a beautiful place there at Nasuli. That's why they choose to live there, because it's really beautiful there at Nasuli.* We note in this paragraph that the cause margin of the second sentence is a recapitulation of the entire first sentence. Again, notice that the whole relation, result and reason, is given in the second sentence, so that we can think of the first sentence as an extrapolation and prior statement of the cause margin of the second sentence. This is one way to mark the result. Notice also how easily the cause margin can be omitted: *It's really a beautiful place there at Nasuli. That's why they choose to live there.* Here, *that's why* acts as a sequence signal expressing result without further reinforcement.

Similarly, in a reason paragraph we have such examples as the following: *He came because his boss forced him to come. McDougal simply told him that he was to go to the party.* Here note that there is a cause margin in the first sentence that is expanded and stated more fully in the paraphrase element that composes the entire second sentence. This is the inverse of the function of the cause margin in the result paragraph.

Rather than a cause margin in sentence one of such a paragraph, we could have a purpose margin. *Jim dropped in on us to get another free meal. He hoped that we would continue to be generous.* Note that *to get another free meal* is somewhat freely paraphrased as *he hoped that we would continue to be generous*, that is, defining generosity as giving another free meal, in which *free meal* is the specific and *generosity* is the generic term. Again, the purpose margin of the first sentence is brought down and expanded and paraphrased in the second sentence, and we are in the structure of a reason paragraph.

Further varieties of both result and reason paragraph involve either other explicit sequence signals or juxtaposition. Space forbids their exemplification here.

I now turn to illustrations of elaborative devices of binary structure. Two varieties of binary paraphrase remain to be illustrated: *He's one of the most reliable men that we have ever had on the job. He's not always trying to evade responsibility, like so many of our employees.* This paragraph is really a roundabout way of saying *He's one of the most reliable; he's not unreliable.*

and thus is clearly seen to be negated antonym paraphrase. For an example of contraction paraphrase, take the following: *All I know is that he has taken off for the fresh air, the fields, the open country where he can feel like himself again. All I know is that he has taken off.*

A further elaborative device is illustration. The illustration paragraph (simile) is also an expansion of a one sentence unit. Thus, we could have a sentence like *Getting money out of that old miser was like a dentist extracting a wisdom tooth.* But this can be expressed as a two-sentence unit in such a paragraph as follows: *It was like watching a dentist extract a wisdom tooth. That's how it was getting some money out of the old miser.* Here *that's how* is the crucial sequence signal in the second half of the paragraph.

As elaborative devices, both introduction and identification paragraphs have important discourse functions in terms of introducing new characters. For introduction paragraph, note the following: *There was a man who lived on our street 25 years ago. Soon after my Dad opened the grocery store, he came to ask for employment and was hired on the spot.* In such a paragraph as that just given, there is no overt sequence signal. Very commonly, however, such paragraphs have a deictic element in the second sentence. Thus, we could have *There was a man who lived on our street 25 years ago. That man was one of the first men ever employed by my father in his new business.* For identification paragraph, note the following: *They found an old house with weeds growing around it, a leaking roof, and a treacherous floor. That's what they eventually made into their home.* This could, of course, have been expressed without the deictic element in the second part, in such a paragraph as the following: *They found an old house with weeds growing around it, a leaking roof, and a treacherous floor. They eventually made it into their home.* So close are illustration and identification paragraphs in surface structure that they are often taxonomically grouped together (as deictic paragraphs) with other paragraphs that involve a deictic element in the second part.

There are also reportative devices of binary structure. One such structure, the quote paragraph, exists in English (alongside the more usual quotation sentence; see Longacre 1978). This structure is the standard device of quotation in certain languages, such as Guanano and other South American languages. An English example might run something as follows: *"I saw her downstairs at two o'clock a.m. reading a book." Those were his words the next morning.* Note, however, the deictic element in the second clause of this example, which probably means that this and the two preceding examples could all be grouped together in a common deictic paragraph in English.

Another reportative device is the comment paragraph. For a comment paragraph, note the following: *She began to pick her way through the mud. That road was always pretty muddy, I recall.* We have here a comment by the narrator in the second part of the paragraph. Note, however, the deictic element. Again, this might lead us to combine this paragraph in English with others as a deictic paragraph. In Guanano, however, there is a very important difference in tense forms in such paragraphs as that just given. The verb *began to pick her way* would be in the regular uninvolved narrative tense, but the comment by the narrator would be in the involved tense. It is his own comment that involves him as an observer. This difference in tense forms would not characterize other paragraphs that are called deictic in Guanano. Therefore, in Guanano the comment paragraph is clearly distinct from the deictic paragraph. This distinction may run through quite a few South American languages, in that the involved–uninvolved or witnessed–unwitnessed distinction is very common through a large area of South America (cf. Waltz 1976)

I now turn my attention to *n*-ary paragraphs. Conjoining paragraphs of *n*-ary structure include the coordinate paragraph and alternative paragraphs that express more than two alternatives and are, presumably, open in structure.

For the coordinate paragraph, consider the following (in which, however, the first sentence is introductory): *Here is a bit about our family. My brother John is a sculptor. My sister Jane is a portrait painter. I myself do pen sketching.* This paragraph is essentially a list with one sentence each devoted to *John, Jane,* and *I.*

An alternative paragraph of *n*-ary structure follows: *A passing motorist might have seen and reported the accident. Alternatively, it could have been someone who lived nearby. It might even have been noticed by a traffic helicopter.* Further possibilities could be listed and probably exist in the reported situation.

Temporal relations that are, I believe, in principle always *n*-ary and never binary—whatever the stringencies of surface structure in a given language—are of two main varieties: overlap and succession.

Temporal overlap is illustrated in the following paragraph, where it is marked by the presence of *meanwhile*: *My wife did the town that morning—especially the tourist market and the popular bazaar. Meanwhile, I spent the time in a leisurely inspection of the municipal museum.* Notice, however, that temporal overlap need not be exclusively of the coterminous activities variety illustrated above. We can have a period of time indicated during which something happens, as in the following paragraph: *She was nursing the baby in a drowsy, contented sort of way. She fell asleep, and the baby nursed on.* This paragraph could be recast as *She was nursing the baby in a drowsy, contented sort of way. As she was nursing, she fell asleep.* In the first instance, the second part of the coordinate sentence is a back reference to the first sentence. In the second recasting of the paragraph, we find an adverbial clause initial in the second sentence, which is a back reference to the first sentence.

The following example of temporal overlap involves punctiliar–punctiliar; that is, the two actions represented are not time spans but are simple events that are conceived of as simultaneous. *Standing there, I brought my head up to steal a look at her. As I brought my head up, she threw the knife in one deft, sweeping motion.*

To show that paragraphs expressing various varieties of temporal overlap are not necessarily binary, note the following example, which is an expansion of a paragraph already given: *My wife did the town that morning—especially the tourist market and the popular bazaar. Meanwhile, I spent the time in a leisurely inspection of the municipal museum. At the same time, my daughter, escorted by a Mexican friend, attended a bullfight. As for my teenage boys, they slept through the whole morning.*

Temporal sequence of the event–event variety is illustrated in the following: *John was at no loss as to how to proceed. He went back quickly to get an ax. Returning to the fallen tree, he lopped off all the branches. Cutting them up, he threw them on to the sled and set off. On getting to the cabin, he carefully stored away his hoard of firewood.* We can just as easily have temporal sequences that involve spans rather than events, as in: *They played tennis for 2 hours under the vertical tropical sun. After that, they swam for another 2 hours in the warm ocean by the coral reef. Then they stretched out on the sand and slept the rest of the day.*

Induction, attestation, and syllogism paragraphs are all types of logical relations of the argumentative variety. They are as open-ended as the necessary links in the argument or the necessary bolstering evidence requires. In the induction paragraph, the conclusion is given at the end, as in: *She looked haunted and tired, and her voice was absolutely colorless. I saw immediately that something was wrong.* Here, *I saw that* is a sequence signal that marks the conclusion of the paragraph. This paragraph could have run through several sentences before the conclusion was stated at the end. For an example of attestation paragraph, I use the preceding paragraph, invert the order of conclusion and evidence, and add on a few more bolstering arguments: *I saw right off that something was wrong. She looked haunted, tired, and old. Her voice came out devoid of any inflection and absolutely colorless. There was a big purple bruise on the side of her face.* The similarity of these two paragraphs is such that they probably prove to be weighted variants (cf. below) of each other, much like the variants of the antithetical or alternative paragraphs.

An example of a syllogism paragraph follows: *Socrates is a man. All men are mortal. Therefore, Socrates is mortal.*

Elaborative *n*-ary structures exist as well. Equivalence paraphrase is, I believe, not essentially a binary structure—although it often emerges as binary due to the paucity of near synonyms. Note the following example: *I've never met such a prejudiced man. I've never known such a complete bigot.* Amplification paraphrase can be described as a circling-in-on-the-target sort of structure. This is evident in such a paragraph as the following: *He took off yesterday. He took off for the country. He took off for the open fields, the woods, the mountainsides, where he could feel like himself again.* Here the third sentence embodies the most adequate and full expression of the content of the paragraph.

As for the other elaborative devices, two other varieties of paraphrase, generic–specific and specific–generic, have been mentioned as encoding into paragraphs. Note the following example of generic–specific: *They took care of his needs. They sobered him up, fed him, clothed him, and gave him a place to stay.* This is a two-sentence paragraph in which a generic expression *took care of* occurs in the first sentence and details are given in the second sentence. Obviously, this could be expanded into a paragraph in which there is a series of sentences rather than just one describing what they did for him or how they took care of him. With no difficulty at all, this paragraph could be permuted as follows: *They sobered him up, fed him, clothed him, and gave him a place to stay. They took care of his needs.* Now the paragraph is specific–generic, and the last sentence comes across as some kind of summary.

For exemplification, a further elaborative device, note the following: *There is a lot that could be done to ease the situation. For example, you could try taking her problems as real instead of as imaginary. You might also try listening to her once in a while.* Notice that the sequence signal *for example* occurs in sentence two. The further example in sentence three is indicated by the sequence signal *also* in that sentence.

WEIGHTING CONSIDERATIONS

Because of space limitations, nothing like a complete treatment of this parameter is possible. I give only a few examples of how attention to weighting considerations can (*a*) bring together similar but differing types; and (*b*) explain certain variations within a given type.

In English, the result paragraph has efficient cause in the first member and result in the second member, whereas the reason paragraph has efficient cause in the second member and the event or happening in the first member. I therefore classify the result paragraph as IAMBIC and the reason paragraph as TROCHAIC. The two are seen, therefore, to be related as weighted variants.

Induction and attestation paragraphs are types of argumentation. In the induction paragraph there is a final conclusion, and in the attestation paragraph there is an initial thesis. In both cases, other sentences in the paragraph support the conclusion or the thesis. I call the induction paragraph IAMBIC and the attestation paragraph TROCHAIC. On this basis, the two paragraph types are seen to be related (as illustrated). Finally, generic–specific paraphrase and specific–generic paraphrase paragraphs likewise emerge as weighted variants (see above).

As far as the consideration of *n*-ary paragraphs, it would seem at first blush that coordinate paragraphs of all descriptions would be essentially SPONDIAC because they are a list. Take again the following paragraph (in which the first sentence is part of the periphery of the paragraph): *Here is a bit about our family. My brother John is a sculptor, My sister Jane is a portrait painter, I myself do pen sketching.* It appears that no part of this paragraph is meant to be more prominent than the other but that the three nuclear sentences simply deal with three different members of a family and with their artistic interests. What about, however, such a paragraph as the following: *Here is a bit about our family. My brother John is a sculptor. My sister Jane is a portrait painter. I myself do pen sketching. Best of all, my youngest brother Charles is a capable young pastor–counselor—whose artistry is human lives.* Here, it appears that the paragraph is definitely weighted toward the last sentence, as is seen in the use of the introductory sequence signal *best of all.* I therefore consider that this is an iambic paragraph—and use the term IAMBIC here to indicate a structure that is not strictly iambic in the sense of unweighted plus weighted but consists of a sequence of three unweighted followed by a weighted.

With sequence paragraphs, wherein we express a series of spans or events or a mixture of spans and events in the same series, we can likewise expect to find weighted variants. If there is no climax to the paragraph, it is spondaic. If there is a climax, the paragraph is iambic in that, presumably, the climax comes at the end of the paragraph and the rest of the paragraph builds up to that climax. Take, for instance, the difference between the following two paragraphs (again, the first sentence of the paragraph is setting): *John was at no loss as to how to proceed. He went back quickly to get an ax. Returning to the fallen tree, he lopped off all the branches. Cutting them up, he threw them on to the sled and set off. On getting to the cabin, he carefully stored away his hoard of firewood.* Expressed in this fashion, the paragraph simply records a series of events, although no doubt getting to the cabin and storing away the wood is what the action is all about. Still, there is no surface structure marking of climax, and very probably we are in a spondaic paragraph. It is possible, however, to reinforce the final sentence in various ways so as to make clear that this is the climax of the whole paragraph. A frequent marker of such climax is simply the addition of the term *finally*, as in *Finally on getting to the cabin, he carefully stored away his hoard of firewood.*

Further Parameters

It is important to note here that each of the preceding examples of paragraphs has inevitably been of a basic paragraph type in a genre-conditioned variant. It now remains to show how the genre choice conditions variants and to show something of the range and variety of genre conditioning.

I will attempt to show for one of the paragraph types already given how genre choice necessarily influences the structure of the paragraph. Thus, the antithetical paragraph can occur in any discourse genre. The examples given were those of the antithetical paragraph in narrative discourse. In accordance with the fact that it was narrative discourse, the main-line verbs were past tense and, obviously, here we seemed to be dealing with a segment of a continued story. But the antithetical paragraph need not be narrative. We can, for example, have a procedural antithetical paragraph. The following has to do with burial customs among the Tboli, where at one stage of the rites the pallbearers engage in a tug-of-war with the family of the deceased: *Here, the ones who are trying to bear the coffin off to burial take it up and try to get out of the front yard of the house with it. The relatives of the dead one try, however, to hold it back and keep it from going to the burial place.* Notice that we do not deal here with past-tense verbs but with the present-tense forms that are typical of procedural discourse. Furthermore, we do not deal here with specific agents, as in a narrative, but rather with the activities of typical people involved in such a situation. We are here in a discourse that is essentially activity-oriented instead of agent-oriented. Again, the antithetical paragraph may occur in a behavioral discourse, such as the following: *Concerned citizens of Dallas, get out and vote in the next election and choose responsible men for county commissioners. Those of you, however, who are unconcerned with the quality of county government can stay home (for all I care)—and complain about how things go.* Here, we are still in an antithetical paragraph of the contrast variety. The contrast is between getting out to vote and staying home and not voting, between the concerned and the unconcerned. As befits a hortatory discourse, the main verbs are imperative. Finally, we can have within expository discourse an antithetical paragraph of the contrast variety. *We submit, with varying degrees of passivity, to a great burden of federal, state, and local taxes. Our forebears of 200 years ago rose up, however, in active resistance to throw off a tax levy that was not even a tithe of our present burden.* Let's assume that the preceding is from an essay on taxation past and present. The contrast here is between *we* and *our forebears*, between *passivity* and *resistance*, between *a great tax burden* and *a relatively small tax burden*.

OTHER CONTEXT-CONDITIONED VARIANTS

Here we get into the realm of things that are often referred to as *stylistic*. We can consider the parameters described here as multipliers of the basic system that consists of Basic Parameters × Discourse Genre Specifications.

Many, if not all, paragraph types can be made cyclic by repeating at the end an element found at their beginning. In some paragraph types, the cyclic element must be done through a setting or introductory element that is not part of the nucleus proper. In other cases, an element of the nucleus may be reechoed at the end in order to give cyclic structure. In a few cases, the cyclic structure is expounded to a full-blown chaismus. We get, for example, paragraphs structured a,b,c,c′,b′,a′ as the paragraph winds itself up and then unwinds itself in reverse order.

It is also possible to give a paragraph a rhetorical question-and-answer structure, which gives it special poignancy as a teaching device or, perhaps, as effective scolding.

Then, a whole paragraph may be quoted, not in the sense that we say *John said . . .* and then give a whole paragraph, but with multiple indication of quotation all through it. This interrupts the sequence of the paragraph so that sometimes one has to ignore the interspersed quotation formulas if he is to get at the structure of the paragraph itself. Then he finds that it conforms to one of the Basic Types + Genre Specifications as already described.

It must also be mentioned that in some parts of the world there is a special predilection for some of these devices or for a special avoidance of some of them. Thus, cyclic paragraphs are extremely common in Australian Aborigines languages, but rhetorical question-and-answer paragraphs are extremely rare in the typical Mesoamerican language.

4. THE STRUCTURE OF UNRESTRICTED PARAGRAPHS

The great majority of the examples given in the previous sections of this paper have been simple examples with no layers of embedding, that is, have not contained two or more sentences that constitute a paragraph within a paragraph. Actually, of course, in the world of real discourse such examples are comparatively rare—although they have illustrative value in a paper of this sort. Actually, here we must face the fact that a theory of a finite number of paragraph types must have as its corollary the proviso that there is recursive embedding of paragraph within paragraph. We can have a theory of a finite number of paragraph types for language in general or for one language in particular if and only if we admit the possibility of recursion within the paragraph unit. Otherwise, every new embedding situation we encounter would be a new paragraph type, and, ultimately, the number of paragraph types would be infinite. It is the purpose of this section to give an analyzed example of such unrestricted paragraph structure.

The following example is from a travelogue book concerning Mexico (Castillo 1939). The paragraph here reproduced conforms to the general structure of the discourse, which is procedural. That is, the whole discourse may be paraphrased as *If you were to come to Mexico, these are some things which you would see in a typical itinerary.*

(1) *By the light of the electric bulbs which have been placed inside the caves, you look about in amazement.* (2) *Turning your eyes upward, you get a wonderful view of the great, long stalactites that hang from the ceiling.* (3) *These, as you know, have been formed by the limestone-containing water that has seeped down through the roof of the caves.* (4) *Then, looking down, you see the enormous stalagmites that seem to grow upward out of the floor, where they have been formed by the water that has dripped from the ceiling.* (5) *As you look at these strange formations, you get the idea that each is reaching for the other, that the two are trying to meet.* (6) *Then, on going farther, you see that some of them have succeeded, for here and there you find a huge, glistening column which has been formed by the meeting of a stalactite and a stalagmite* [p. 175].

In looking at the above example, I think it may be rationally held that sentence (1) is an introduction to the whole unit. It has preview value in that it says *you look about in amazement* and that the rest of the paragraph tells what you see as you look about. Whatever the notional structure of this unit, I think that the function of the sentence in the surface structure is clearly simply to break the ice and to get the paragraph going by providing a preview of what is going to happen. The body of the paragraph is a sequence paragraph in which sentences 2–5 form an embedded simultaneous paragraph that expounds the antecedent, and sentence 6 is a single sentence that expounds the consequent. Within the embedded simultaneous paragraph (sentences 2–5), Simul$_1$ is expounded by a sequence paragraph (sentences 2–4) and Simul$_2$ is expounded by sentence 5. The embedded sequence paragraph has as its antecedent an embedded deictic paragraph (sentences 2 and 3) whose topic is sentence 2 and whose comment is sentence 3, and the consequent of the embedded sequence paragraph is sentence 4. For the formal justification of this structure, note that sentence 6 is marked as consequent by the phrase *then, on going farther*, which is a typical sequence marker and describes the trajectory of the trip within the cave. Sentence 5 is marked as Simul$_2$ versus sentences 2, 3, and 4 by virtue of the initial stretch *as you look at these strange formations* in sentence 5. Sentence 4 is marked as a consequent in reference to sentences 2 and 3 by the initial conjunction *then*. Sentence 3 is marked as a comment in reference to sentence 2 by virtue of the occurrence of the word *these* (cross-reference to *stalactites* in sentence 2). See the accompanying indented analysis diagram.

Sequence ℙ
PREVIEW (S_1)
ANTECEDENT: SIMULTANEOUS ℙ
SIMUL$_1$: SEQUENCE ℙ
ANTECEDENT: DEICTIC ℙ
TOPIC: S_2
COMMENT: S_3
CONSEQUENT: S_4
SIMUL$_2$: S_5
CONSEQUENT: S_6

Space forbids presenting the analysis of more examples of unrestricted paragraphs. There seems to be good reason to believe, however, that the system of basic types in genre variants, with further possible stylistic variants, is able in principle to describe the wild and woolly world of "real" paragraphs—provided we admit recursive embedding of type within type.

REFERENCES

Castillo, C. (1939) *Mexico* (ed. by Burton Holmes), Wheeler Publishing Co., Chicago.

Gerdel, F. and M. C. Slocum, (1976) "Paez Discourse, Paragraph and Sentence Structure," in R. E. Longacre ed., *Discourse Grammar, Part I*, The Summer Institute of Linguistics, Dallas.

Grimes, J. E. (1964) "Huichol Syntax," *Janua Linguarum, Series practica* 11. The Hague: Mouton.

Grimes, Joseph E. (1975) "The Thread of Discourse," *Janua Linguarum 207*. The Hague: Mouton.

Halliday, M. A. K. and Ruqaiya Hasan. (1976) "Cohesion in English," in R. Quirk, ed., *English Language Series, No. 9.*, Longman, London.

Healey, A. (1970) "Are there grammatical paragraphs in English?," unpublished paper.

Longacre, Robert E. (1972) Hierarchy and Universality of Discourse Constituents in New Guinea languages: discussion. Washington: Georgetown University Press.

Longacre, Robert E. (1976) *An Anatomy of Speech Notions*, The Peter de Ridder Press, Lisse.

Longacre, Robert E. and F. Woods, eds. (1976–77) "Discourse Grammar: Studies in Indigenous Languages of Colombia, Panama, and Ecuador, Parts I–III," *Summer Institute of Linguistics Publications in Linguistics and Related Fields*, No. 52, The Summer Institute of Linguistics, Dallas.

Longacre, Robert E. (1977) "Discourse Genre," paper read at the XII International Congress of Linguists in Vienna.

Longacre, Robert E. (1978) "Sentences as Combinations of Clauses," paper to appear in Stephen Anderson *et al.*, eds., *Language Typology and Linguistic Field Work*, Center for Applied Linguistics, Washington.

Loos, E. (1963) "Capanahua Narrative Structure," *Texas Studies in Literature and Language* 4 (supplement), 697–742.

Loriot, J. and B. Hollenbach. (1970) "Shipibo Paragraph Structure," *Foundations of Language* 6(1), 43–66.

Schulze, M. and D. Bieri. (1973) "Chaining and Spotlighting: Two Types of Paragraph boundaries in Sunwar," in A. Hale, ed., *Clause, Sentence and Discourse Patterns in Selected Languages of Nepal, Part I*, The Summer Institute of Linguistics of the University of Oklahoma, Norman.

Tracy, H. P. and S. H. Levinsohn. (1977) "Participant Reference in Ica Expository Discourse," in R. E. Longacre, ed., *Discourse Grammar, Part III*, The Summer Institute of Linguistics, Dallas.

van Dijk, Teun A. (1972) *Some Aspects of Text Grammars*, The Hague: Mouton.

Waltz, N. E. (1976) "Discourse Functions of Guanano Sentence and Paragraph," in R. E. Longacre, ed., *Discourse Grammar, Part I*, The Summer Institute of Linguistics, Dallas.

Winter, E. (1977) *Replacement as a Function of Repetition; A Study of Some of Its Principal Features in the Clause Relations of Contemporary English*, University Microfilms International, London.

ORGANIZATIONAL PATTERNS IN DISCOURSE

JOHN HINDS
University of Hawaii

1. INTRODUCTION

This chapter founds itself on the premise that there are organizing principles in language that exist in extended speech and in writing beyond the single sentence in isolation. I intend to show that some of these organizing principles can be elucidated at even this rudimentary stage in our understanding of discourse processes. There are two basic types of organization in discourse, both of which influence speech behavior. One type concerns the linear organization of language, a topic discussed primarily in terms of turn-taking behavior by Duncan (1972), Hinds (1976a), Sacks, Schegloff, and Jefferson (1974), and others. In Hinds (1977b), Longacre (1976), and elsewhere, it is argued that linear organization has a strong influence in monologue as well as in dialogue. The second type of organization is hierarchical. This type of structure has been documented meticulously for narrative discourse [for example, Longacre (1976), Meyer (1975), and Thorndyke (1977)], where plot structures, without significant distortion, can be represented by branching tree diagrams. The existence of hierarchical organization in other types of discourse is not as widely documented, and

Syntax and Semantics, Volume 12:
Discourse and Syntax

one of the purposes of this chapter is to demonstrate that hierarchical organization does exist in discourse types other than narrative.

The basic position that I will advance here is that discourses of all types are organized in terms of paragraphs, a paragraph being defined as a unit of speech or writing that maintains a uniform orientation.[1] I further intend to demonstrate that paragraphs are themselves optionally composed of successively smaller units of uniform orientation larger than the sentence and that this hierarchical organization imposes severe constraints on the form conversations may take.

I start with the assumption that conversation is the most basic language type. If the definition of conversation is extended to include language that occurs in any interactional situation (as I believe it should be), it is difficult to imagine any piece of language, with the exception of linguistic examples, that does not constitute conversational data. The novelist writes to an addressee, as do the physicist, the advice columnist, the writer of recipes, and the writer of instructions for putting together bicycles.

The language that occurs in a conversation is by no means monolithic. It varies depending on the goals of the speaker–writer and of the addressee. The understanding of this variation owes a considerable debt to Longacre's (1968, 1971, 1972, 1976) work on discourse taxonomies. Longacre has recognized four major discourse types: NARRATIVE, or "story"; PROCEDURAL, or "how-to-do-it"; EXPOSITORY, or "essay"; and HORTATORY, or "sermon." His summary of these discourse types (1976:200), with relevant grammatical characteristics of each, is presented in (1).

(1)

	− Projected	+ Projected
	Narrative	Procedural
+ Succession	1. First/Third person 2. Agent oriented 3. Accomplished time 4. Chronological linkage	1. Nonspecific person 2. Patient oriented 3. Projected time 4. Chronological linkage
	Expository	Hortatory
− Succession	1. No necessary reference 2. Subject matter oriented 3. Time not focal 4. Logical linkage	1. Second person 2. Addressee oriented 3. Mode, not time 4. Logical linkage

[1] Grimes (1975:102ff) suggests four specific ways texts can be segmented, each segmentation corresponding roughly to a paragraph. Each of these segmentation techniques relies on the notion of uniform orientation. The partitioning principles involve uniform spatial orientation, uniform temporal orientation, uniform thematic orientation, and uniform participant orientation.

A conversation may consist primarily of one of these types, or it may have other functions, such as eliciting or exchanging information, passing time pleasantly, duelling verbally, etc. The point I wish to emphasize is that, in Longacre's sense of the term, each discourse type occurs with a speaker–writer and an addressee. It is quite possible, then, that a given conversation will have embedded within it a narrative, a procedural statement, etc. Longacre himself admits this possibility when he states (1976:209), "A discourse of a given surface structure genre may embed within a discourse of the same or different genre."[2]

The significance of discourse taxonomies for this paper is that different discourse types have different organizing principles. This should be no more surprising than the fact that declarative sentences, for instance, have different properties than do interrogative or imperative sentences.

In order to discuss most effectively the organizational properties of discourse, this paper has been arranged in a series of loops, each loop dealing with a number of discourse types. Within each loop, properties of each discourse type are presented, and these properties are essential to the understanding of the more detailed analysis of the discourse types in the succeeding loop. The initial loop discusses characteristics of all discourse types inasmuch as these discourse types involve two or more participants. The second loop focuses on three major discourse types (procedural, expository, and information-exchanging conversation), giving more information about their respective characteristics. The next loop discusses specific structural characteristics of each of these discourse types, with particular reference to the facts that each paragraph is made up of SEGMENTS and that segments have clearly defined functions. The final loop covers the structural properties of segments by explicating a general distinction between dialogue and monologue, dialogue being represented by information-exchanging conversation and monologue being represented by procedural and expository discourses.

2. SEGMENTATION OF DISCOURSE

To the extent that all language involves a speaker–writer and an addressee, all types of discourse must be investigated from the perspective of the interaction between the speaker and the addressee. Seen in this light, discourse progresses along three parallel planes. One plane involves the linear progression of sentences and clauses that establish antecedent–postcedent relationships [roughly "adjacency pairs" in the sense of Schegloff and Sacks (1973)]. Another plane involves the progression of paragraphs, and this imposes a hierarchical structure on the linear progression of sentences. The

---

[2] Longacre discusses this in a different context, but the principle holds in the current context as well.

third plane involves the relationship between the speaker and the addressee as those roles interact with one another in the course of a conversation.

The following slightly edited excerpt from an informal interview between two Japanese females will illustrate the nature of these characteristics. In the portion of interview immediately preceding this excerpt, the interviewer (A) has been eliciting background information from the interviewee (B).[3]

(2)   A-1:   *sore de, urawa de umareta **wake**?*
                'So, it's that you were born in Urawa?'

       B-2:   *soko de umareta **wake**.*
                'I was born there.'

       A-3:   *soko de umarete, soko de sodatta **wake**?*
                You were born there, and you grew up there?

       B-4:   *sodatta **wake**.*
                I grew up there.

       A-5:   *zya, hawai ni wa itu kita **wake**?*
                Well, when did you come to Hawaii?

       B-6:   *NN, nanazyuunineN da kara, yoneN mae?*
                Hmm, it was '72, so four years ago?

       A-7:   *yoneN mae.*
                Four years ago.

       A-8:   *sosite, sore kara, zutto hawai ni ippanasi?*
                Then, you've been in Hawaii ever since?

       B-9:   *N, soo zya nakute.*
                No, that's not right.

      B-10:   *itido kotti ni kite, mata mukoo e modotta **wake**.*
                I came here once, and then returned there again.

      A-11:   *nihoN ni ne.*
                To Japan, right?

      A-12:   *tte iu koto wa hawai ni itibaN hazime ni kita no wa naNde*
                Given all of that, the first time you came to Hawaii, what did
                *kita **wake**?*
                you come for?

Beyond the obvious fact that answers follow questions rather than vice versa, there is a second feature of interest that arises because the sentences occur sequentially, and this feature does not relate to hierarchical organization. There is a general tendency in Japanese conversation to repeat the words, phrases, or grammatical patterns of the other participant in an attempt to achieve solidarity [see Hinds (1978a) for a justification of this

---

[3] This videotape recording was planned and transcribed by Mark Thorpe at the University of Hawaii in 1976.

statement]. Quite obviously, repetition is an antecedent–postcedent relationship. In this example, the interviewer ends her first two questions, (2A-1) and (2A-3), with the nominal *wake* 'is it that . . .'.

She might have asked a more neutral question instead of (2A-1), such as *urawa de umareta no*? 'Were you born in Urawa?' However, the fact that she chose to ask her question in the form that she did influenced the interviewee to answer as she did in (2B-2), using the same grammatical structure as the interviewer. The use of *wake* by the interviewee is recognized as an attempt to achieve solidarity with the interviewer. If the interviewer had not used *wake* first, the interviewee's use of the form would be considered very strange.

The second type of progression concerns the paragraph topic. The paragraph topic throughout (2) is the interviewee B. This, too, has its grammatical consequences, since it is not necessary for either A or B to use any overt linguistic form to refer to B as long as the paragraph topic remains constant [see Hinds (forthcoming) for details]. Note that the English translations of B's utterances have three occurrences of the personal pronoun *I* that refer to her and that the translations of A's utterances have seven occurrences of the personal pronoun *you* that refer to B. The Japanese original has no forms that correspond to either *I* or *you*.

The diagram in (3) is termed a RETICULUM, a diagrammatic format introduced originally in Taber (1966) and modified in Hinds (1976a) to represent the information of relevance in conversations.[4]

(3)

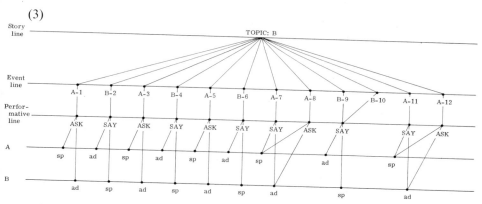

The reticulum diagrams the three major simultaneous progressions. Paragraph progression develops along the STORY LINE, the topmost line in this diagram. As the paragraph topic changes, which it invariably does in a conversation of any length, the change is indicated along the story line through the addition of appropriate nodes. The development of paragraph topics is discussed in Hinds (1976a, 1977a, 1978a).

[4] The revised format for the reticulum is due to observations by Momoi (1977).

Sentential, or clausal, progression is indicated along the EVENT LINE, the next lower solid horizontal line in the diagram. Each sentence or clause is marked as a node on this line. Each line connects upward to the paragraph topic of which it is a part. The node also connects downward to an appropriate performative verb. The directions upward and downward are artifacts of two-dimensional representations and have no theoretical implications.

The PERFORMATIVE LINE, the next lower solid horizontal line, describes what type of sentence is being uttered. I assume that there are a relatively small number of abstract performative verbs, including ASK, SAY, IMP, and SUG, that underlie INTERROGATIVE, DECLARATIVE, IMPERATIVE, and HORTATIVE sentences, respectively. The situation is clearly more complex than this, but these abstract performative verbs provide a first approximation for indicating sentence types. Extending downward from the performative verbs are lines that connect to PARTICIPANT NODES; in this case, A and B. Under each participant node is a set of features that specifies whether the participant is currently a speaker (sp) or an addressee (ad), as well as any other information that may be relevant to the sentence currently being uttered. A complete discussion of what other types of information may be found in this set of features is presented in Hinds (1976a).

The participant nodes indicate that both A and B alternate their roles as speaker and addressee. Whenever the performative verb does not change, as in (3B-9) and (3B-10), there is no reason to rewrite the verb on the performative line. Lines thus extend from the same performative verb to both of these sentences. If the speaker does not alternate, even though the performative verb changes, as in (3A-7) and (3A-8), only the verb must be rewritten. This completes the first loop.

3. THE SECOND LOOP

The second loop begins with an indication that the reticulum in (3) is incomplete in one major respect: It does not indicate how paragraphs are organized internally. This internal organization defines relations among parts of the paragraph. At present, I have determined three major paragraph-internal sets of relationships. One set is associated with procedural discourse, another with expository, and the third with spontaneous conversation, a subtype of narrative [see Longacre (1971)]. In all three types, paragraphs may consist of constituents termed SEGMENTS.[5] Each segment contains an

---

[5] Longacre (1976, personal communication) prefers to use the term EMBEDDED PARAGRAPH to refer to this phenomenon. Longacre (1976) also uses this term to refer to the embedding of one discourse genre in another. For this reason, I prefer to maintain a separate term, SEGMENT, for this level within the paragraph.

indeterminate number of sentences or clauses, all of which maintain a unified orientation. This unified orientation is further constrained in that it forms a subcategory of the paragraph topic.

Procedural Discourse

In procedural discourse, segments are related to one another as discrete steps to be followed. Often, as will be seen in the case of recipes, these steps follow a rigid chronological order. However, as in the following example taken from the ordering instructions for the Indiana University Linguistics Club Papers (January, 1977), the steps may simply consist of a number of alternative suggestions.

(4) a. *Please pay in U.S. funds.*
     b. *Do not pay with stamps or postal coupons.*
     c. *Postal money orders, however, **are** acceptable.*
     d. *Because of a recent change in policy at our bank, we are now charged $2.50 for each check which is not drawn on or payable through a U.S. bank.*
     e. *We are sorry to require this extra charge, but, if it is impossible for you to pay through a U.S. bank, $2.50 must be added to the price of your order.*
     f. *We suggest that you use a foreign draft drawn on a bank with an affiliation in the U.S.*
     g. *Please identify your order with your payment.*
     h. *If this is not possible, please send a separate letter indicating the precise nature of your payment, and from whom it will be received.*

This paragraph has three segments, each of which contains a number of sentences. This example of procedural discourse may be tentatively diagrammed as in (5). Notice for the present that the subject matter of each segment maintains a uniform orientation with respect to the paragraph

(5)

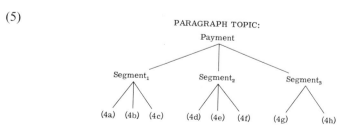

topic: Sentences (4a), (4b), and (4c) explain how to make payments; (4d), (4e), and (4f) concern the reason a $2.50 charge might be levied; and (4g) and (4h) explain what to do if payment does not accompany the order.

Expository Discourse

Expository discourse is discussed from the perspective of hierarchical organization in Hinds (1977b) and Kimura (1977). These works show that an expository paragraph consists of segments that are in four possible relationships to the paragraph topic. The initial segment is always INTRODUCTORY. Subsequent segments offer a MOTIVATION, HIGHLIGHT, or UNEXPECTED TWIST. The following article from *Time Magazine* (4/23/73), analyzed in Hinds (1977b), illustrates each type of segment.

(6)   OUT OF THE SHADOWS

   a.   *Pale and unsmiling, the diminutive Mao-suited official walked into the grand banquet hall of Peking's Great Hall of the People one day last week.*

   b.   *He paused uncertainly at the door, but protocol officials hustled him over to stand in line with Premier Chou En-lai and great guests at a dinner honoring Cambodia's exiled Prince Norodom Sihanouk.*

   c.   *In this low-key style, Vice Premier Teng Hsiao-ping, now 69, returned from the shadows that have enveloped him since 1966, when he was purged along with Chief of State Liu Shao-chi as "one of a handful of party leaders who took the capitalist road."*

   d.   *Teng had once ranked fourth in the party hierarchy (behind Mao, Liu, and Chou, and just ahead of the now-dead Defense Minister Lin Piao).*

   e.   *He was party General Secretary and a member of the Politburo.*

   f.   *Accused in the early months of the Great Proletarian Cultural Revolution, Teng confessed immediately, admitting that "my thought and attitude were incompatible with Mao's thought."*

   g.   *He now seems to rank about 20th in the hierarchy, though he has not regained his party posts.*

   h.   *His return to at least a degree of prominence is another indication of Mao's continuing effort to reunite the leadership.*

   i.   *But Teng's duties are modest.*

   j.   *He is believed to have been put to work reorganizing the youth corps.*

(7)

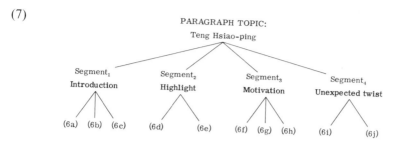

Segment$_1$ introduces this article and announces that Teng has reemerged into the communist hierarchy. Segment$_2$ gives some relevant background material on Teng's life. Segment$_3$ gives the motivation for the problem Teng has. Segment$_4$ brings the reader up to date and lets him know that, despite previous statements to the contrary, Teng is not quite in the position of power that he should be.

Conversation

Conversation also consists of paragraphs structured into segments. In relatively spontaneous conversation, these segments consist of perspectives on the paragraph topic. Although it is never possible to predict with any certainty which perspective will be introduced into a conversation [however, see Creider (forthcoming) for some intriguing suggestions], it is possible to specify what types of perspectives will be introduced. When a paragraph is introduced into a conversation and is agreed upon by the participants, a number of related concepts automatically accompany this topic. Following Grimes (1975:43ff), these related concepts may be termed PARTICIPANTS and PROPS.[6] That is, topics in conversation are not isolated entities. They have connotations and associations that participants in the conversation are aware of and utilize. Of course, the number and quality of such associations will differ depending on the specific conversational participants and their relationship to one another. A conversation of considerable length analyzed in Hinds (1976a:56ff) will serve as an illustration. Two friends were talking about a mutual female acquaintance who gave birth to an illegitimate child. The topic of conversation was quite clearly the girl. However, the establishment of this topic brought with it a number of associations that the participants in the conversation could react to. Some of

---

[6] More recent research, reported in Hinds (1978b), suggests that these related concepts are more properly ANIMATE, INANIMATE, and EMOTIONAL perspectives. Similar concepts are discussed by Schank and Abelson (1977).

these associations were human—the alleged father, the girl herself, the child; some were inanimate or conceptual—court proceedings, responsibility (or blame), finances. These associations correspond to Grimes's participants and props, respectively.

Segments in spontaneous conversation are constrained such that the topic, for the duration of time it remains the topic, will be discussed from the perspectives it has associated with it. These perspectives correspond to the list of participants and props. Quite obviously, no conversation will ever approach a topic from every conceivable perspective. Equally obvious is the fact that perspectives are not completely predictable to observers or even to the conversational participants themselves.

The concept of "repair mechanisms" discussed in Schegloff, Jefferson, and Sacks (1977) has relevance to the notion of topic perspectives. Schegloff *et al.* (1977) do not generally talk about the triggers for such repair mechanisms,[7] so here I would like to suggest that one situation in which "other-initiated repair" occurs frequently is that in which the speaker introduces a perspective that the addressee is not able to associate with the topic. In the following slightly edited conversation, two Japanese males are talking about a newspaper article that appears in the newspaper that A is holding.[8]

(8)   A-1:   *a, anoo, are, sitte ru?*
              Oh, do you know about that?

       A-2:   *anoo, oosaka, oosaka.*
              You know, in Osaka.

       B-3:   *doo sita no?*
              What happened?

       A-4:   *nanazyuu naNniN siNda.*
              Seventy-some people died.

       B-5:   *huN* [pointing to newspaper in A's lap], *sore eigo na no?*
              Oh, is that in English?

       A-6:   *kyaroru da moN, kyaroru.*
              [Yes,] because Carol [brought it], Carol.

       B-7:   *a, nyuusu ne.*
              Ah, the news, huh?

[7] However, Schegloff (this volume) suggests that self-repair occurs regularly in first-sentences in topic-initial turns or in first sentences in topic-shift position. In Hinds (1978b), both self- and other-repair are discussed in terms of their occurrences in these positions.

[8] This audiotape recording was made at the State University of New York at Buffalo in 1971 and was transcribed by Wako Hinds.

B-8: *zuibuN kaNkei nai no ni siNpai site kurete ru wake?*
Even though it has nothing to do with her [being an outsider],
you mean she's worried about it?

A-9: *nanazyuu naNniN siNde, hyakuniNizyoo keganiN,*
Seventy-some people died, and over a hundred were hurt.

A-10: *sugoi yo, hora.*
It's awful, see?

B-11: *kore, naNka, koozigeNba ka naNka de?*
Where did it happen, at some place like a construction site?

A-12: *are na N da tte.*
That's what it says.

A-13: *gasu ga tamatte te, sore ga.*
The gas built up.

B-14: *doo iu imi?*
What do you mean?

A-15: *a, tosigasu da yo.*
Oh, it's city gas.

B-16: *tosigasu? a, morete ta wake?*
City gas? Oh, you mean it was leaking?

A-17: *uN, morete ta N da yo.*
Yeah, it was leaking.

A, as a result of having read the newspaper article, knew that leaking gas caused the accident. Thus, in (8A-13), when he attempts to talk about the accident from the perspective of one of the props he is aware of—the leaking gas—B must ask him (8B-14) what he is talking about, since B has not yet read the article and is not able to associate this perspective with the topic of an explosion in Osaka. In (8A-15), A misunderstands B's question and mistakenly tells him what kind of gas was involved. B, in (8B-16), is once more confused as he repeats the answer with questioning intonation. B is finally able to make the correct association—that the gas had been leaking and that the gas caused the explosion. A then confirms this in (8A-17).

4. PARAGRAPH STRUCTURE

So far, I have attempted to show that paragraphs of all discourse types consist of segments, although these segments are related to one another differently depending on discourse type. I now wish to claim that these segments are the structural building blocks of the paragraph. A body is structured if its parts are formally or functionally identifiable. Thus, there is a long tradition associated with the notion that a sentence is structured. A sentence is structured because it consists of, among other elements, noun phrases and verbs. Noun phrases are often formally identifiable, although, for Japanese at least, there has been considerable controversy over the precise formal definition of the noun phrase [see, for instance, Nakau (1973) and Tonoike (1976)]. Verbs are also formally identifiable in most languages, but, in some, Indonesian for example, there is no distinction between nouns and verbs. Functionally, noun phrases are identifiable by the roles they play: subject, object, etc. But here too there is controversy [see, among others, Kuroda (1976) and Shibatani (1977)]. Even though there is not complete agreement on the identifying characteristics of sentential elements, linguists still wish to consider the sentence to be structured. Paragraphs, I maintain, consist of parts that are equally well-identifiable both formally and functionally.

Procedural Discourse

In procedural discourse, a paragraph consists of an indeterminate number of segments, each of which is a step in the procedure. In English, it is difficult to determine formal parameters for the segmentation of steps, although I suspect a better understanding of intonation will provide some of the formal criteria for this type of segmentation.[9] In Japanese, procedural discourse steps are clearly segmented formally, in that a sentence boundary separates one step from the next.

Japanese conjoins sentences by using either the gerundive *-te* form of a verbal or the infinitive form to separate two clauses. Thus, the two sentences in (9a) may be conjoined as in (9b) or (9c).

(9)   a.   *tookyoo ni ikimasita. mata hawai ni modotte kimasita.*
             I went to Tokyo.   I came back again to Hawaii.

         b.   *tookyoo ni itte, mata hawai ni modotte kimasita.*
             I went to Tokyo and came back to Hawaii.

         c.   *tookyoo ni iki, mata hawai ni modotte kimasita.*
             I went to Tokyo and came back to Hawaii.

The differences between these types of conjunction are discussed in detail in Hinds (1976b) and Kuno (1973). Essentially, conjoining with the infinitive, as in (9c), indicates a more formal or prepared expression than does con-

---

[9] For instance, the sentence final intonation used to conclude a specific news item by TV newsmen drops considerably lower than normal sentence final intonation. See also the discussion in Section 4.

joining with the gerundive, as in (9b). As a result, conjunction with the infinitive occurs more frequently in planned discourse than in unplanned discourse (see Ochs, this volume).

The discourse shown in (10), a commercial shown on KIKU-TV (Channel 13: Honolulu), illustrates a number of conjunction types, as well as the formal segmentation of steps.

(10) a. *mamuzu no osusume suru oryoori wa harumaki no kurisupii kureepusu desu.*
         The food that Mum's recommends is their Crispy Crepes spring rolls.

      b. *mamuzu no siitake to hosiebi o mizu ni modosimasu.*
         Return Mum's dried mushrooms and dried shrimp to water.

      c. *yoNbuN no itipoNdo no pooku wa hosoku **kiri**; sio to osake o syoosyoo hurikakemasu.*
         Cut $\frac{1}{4}$ pound of pork thinly and sprinkle a little salt and sake on it.

      d. *siitake, takenoko, tamanegi o hosoku **kiri**; ebi wa miziNgiri ni simasu.*
         Cut the dried mushrooms, the bamboo shoots, and the onions thinly; mince the shrimp.

      e. *huraipaN ni abura o **ire**; ebi, pooku, tugi ni moyasi to kitta yasai o **ire**; satto itamemasu.*
         Put some oil in a pan; put in the shrimp, the pork, and then the bean sprouts and the cut-up vegetables; fry quickly.

      f. *syooyu, miriN, kooNsutaati o **kuwae**; hi kara **orosi**; gomaabura o kakete mazemasu.*
         Add soy sauce, mirin, and corn starch; take from the flame; add sesame oil and mix.

      g. *kono gu o mamuzu no harumaki no kawa de **tutumu no desu ga**; huraua to mizu o mazeta mono de **siiru simasu to**; kuzure-maseN.*
         Wrap these ingredients in Mum's spring roll skins, and, if you seal them with a mixture of flour and water, they won't break open.

      h. *zyukko no harumaki ga **dekiagarimasitara**; abura de koNgari to **age**; dekitate o mesiagatte kudasai.*
         When ten spring rolls are prepared, fry them until brown in oil; now, eat the finished product.

      i. *kuwasii resipi wa mamuzu no syokuhiNtoriatukaiteN de ouketori kudasai.*
         Get the detailed recipe at Mum's specialty stores.

The decision for how a procedural discourse should be organized is largely an individual matter. There are often a number of different ways a process could be completed successfully, so there may be several extremely different "correct" organizational patterns. It is, therefore, impossible to predict with any degree of certainty how an individual (even a corporate individual, in the case of commercials) will segment a recipe; but, once the individual has constructed the discourse, it is possible to determine what he considers to be the discrete steps.

Many steps consist of more than one EVENT, an event being, roughly, a simple sentence or clause. Events may lead up to a natural culmination, or they may be semantically parallel in that they describe the same type of procedure. In this commercial, both of these event sequences appear.

Nine separate steps in the process of making spring rolls are presented. Each step is marked formally by a polite finite verbal with sentence final intonation.

The first step is actually an introduction to the commercial. In procedural course of this type, such lead-ins are quite common but are not obligatory.

The second step, (10b), consists of a single event, whereas the third, (10c), consists of two events. The two events are connected formally by the verb stem *kiri* 'cut'. Functionally, the first event is necessary to the completion of the second.

The fourth step, (10d), also consists of two events formally connected by the verb stem *kiri* 'cut'. The connection here, however, is that both events describe the same type of procedure—cutting up ingredients.

The fifth step, (10e), consists of three events connected by two occurrences of the verb stem *ire* 'put in'. The connection is that the first two events culminate in the third.

The sixth step, (10f), also consists of three events connected by the verb stems *kuwae* 'add to' and *orosi* 'take from'. These first two events also culminate in the third.

The seventh step, (10g), consists of three steps connected with *tutumu no desu ga* 'wrap (them) and' and *siiru simasu to* 'if you seal (them)'. In this case as well, the two preliminary events are necessary for the successful completion of this step.

The eighth step, (10h), consists of three steps connected with *dekiagari-masitara* 'when (they) are prepared' and the verb stem *age* 'fry'. A common method of ending a written or prepared recipe in Japanese is to encourage the addressee to eat the finished product after putting on the final touches.

The ninth step, (10i), is a concluding statement that is quite common, perhaps even necessary, for commercials but that does not occur at all in normal conversational procedural discourse.

The tree in (11) diagrams the structure of this example of procedural discourse.

(11)

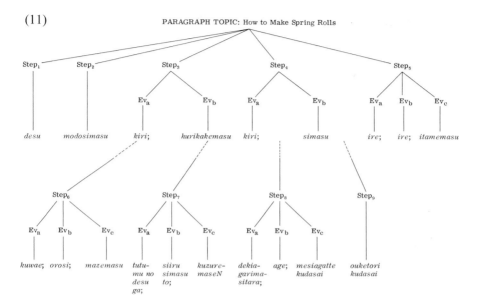

Expository Discourse

In expository discourse, a paragraph consists of an indeterminate number of segments, all of which are in one of four functionally defined relationships to one another. They are either INTRODUCTORY, HIGHLIGHT, MOTIVATION, or UNEXPECTED TWIST [see the discussion of (6) above for details].

Conversation

In spontaneous conversation, a paragraph consists of an indeterminate number of segments, each of which discusses the paragraph from a different PERSPECTIVE [see the discussion of (8) for details].

Internal Organization

In each type of discourse examined, a level of organization termed the SEGMENT has been illustrated, and these segments have been defined in either formal or functional terms, or both. If we compare this type of organization with the organization of sentences, we find that there are strong parallels. Halliday and Hasan (1976:10) state that

> within the sentence, or any similar unit, we can specify a limited number of structures, such as types of modification or subordination, transitivity or modal structure and the like. . . .

The internal organization of the paragraph can be defined in a similar manner.

> *Within the paragraph, there are a limited number of structures, termed segments, which are in a limited number of possible relationships to the paragraph topic—these relationships are termed steps, perspectives, highlights, etc. depending on the discourse type.*

The claim I wish to advance, therefore, is that paragraphs are structured internally but that, contrary to van Dijk (1972), the elements of structure within the paragraph are not classes of sentences, but segments.

5. SEGMENT STRUCTURE

Segments also have internal structure. In most cases, the constituents of segments are sentences in specified relationships to one another. In the investigation of conversation, I have found that an essential structural feature of the segment is the SWITCHING MECHANISM,[10] that set of conventions that allows participants to alternate their roles as speaker and addressee. I find that it is easiest and most correct to define two basic types of switching mechanisms: QUESTION–ANSWER (Q–A) and REMARK–REPLY (RM–RP) [see Hinds (1976a:98ff) for details].[11] In the case of MONOLOGUE, the essential structural feature of the segment is that it contains one functionally determined and often syntactically marked sentence termed the PEAK. Often, sentences within a segment are semantically subordinate to the peak.

[10] This mechanism has to be recognized by everyone who has examined conversational data at all seriously. It is subsumed under the term ADJACENCY PAIR by Sacks *et al.* (1974), whereas Longacre (1976:165) distinguishes among three types of REPARTEE: question–answer, proposal–response, and remark–evaluation. Duncan (1972, 1974a, 1974b) has discussed turn-taking behavior from the perspectives of verbal and nonverbal clues necessary to signal when turns may occur.

[11] As with everything else, the situation is in fact much more complex than this. Both of these patterns are often followed by a confirmatory statement [discussed in Hinds (1976a)] whose function is generally to evaluate the second member of the pair in some way. Creider (forthcoming) cites numerous cases of repetitions in Kipsigis the function of which appears to be phatic yet structurally important. Embedded segments are also a commonplace.

The major segment types for conversation and monologue are dia-grammed in (12).

(12)

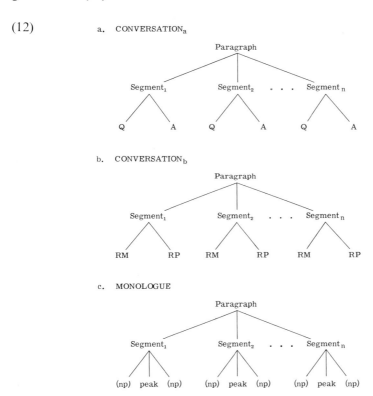

( ) indicates optional items; np indicates a "nonpeak."

There are a number of complexities involving these basic structures, of which only one will be discussed (see also Footnote 11). For conversations, the sentences that correspond to Q–A and RM–RP are in a paratactic relationship with one another. Each is roughly the semantic equal of its partner. However, not all segments in conversation consist of two and only two sentences or clauses. Any other sentences or clauses in a segment beyond the Q–A or RM–RP sequence will form a hypotactic relationship with one of the major sentences. The two permissible types of hypotactic relationships are ELABORATIONS and EXPLANATIONS. That is, a given question may also contain an elaboration or explanation, as may an answer, a remark, or a reply. The following examples taken from Schegloff *et al.* (1977:363) illus-trate both types of hypotactic relationships.

(13)   a.   *And for ninety-nine cents uh especially in, Rapture, and the Au*
               Coeur which is the newest fragrances,
        b.   *uh that is a **very** good value.*

(14)   PARAGRAPH TOPIC:
                                    Avon Products

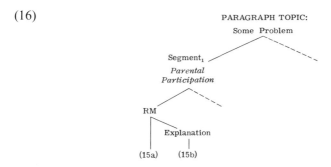

(15)   a.   *en I think if more parents of kids these age c'd participate in this*
               *kind of an **at**mosphere, 'hhh it would certainly help develop a*
               lot of understanding.
        b.   *A:n' Mister Warden said that was certainly one of the things*
               thet he hed been considering . . .

(16)   PARAGRAPH TOPIC:
                                    Some Problem

        Segment₁
       Parental
    Participation

    RM

            Explanation

    (15a)   (15b)

Sentence (13b) is subordinate to (13a) because it elaborates the virtues of
the perfumes the Avon lady is trying to sell by editorializing on the price.
Sentence (15b) is subordinate to (15a) since it explains why Bernice believes
the participation of the parents of the kids would help develop understanding by appealing to the authority of Mister Warden.

Monologue Discourse

If we return now to the ordering instructions from the Indiana University
Linguistics Club discussed first in (4) as an example of monologue discourse, we find that diagram (17) more accurately reflects the structure of

(17)

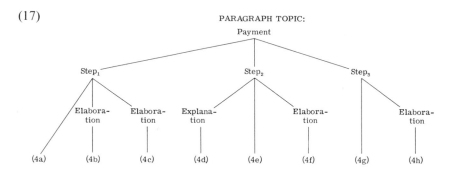

this text than does (5). Sentence (4a) gives the major instruction in Step$_1$ and (4b) and (4c) elaborate this instruction. The major instruction in Step$_2$ is (4e); (4d) explains why this instruction is necessary, and (4f) elaborates it. In Step$_3$, the major instruction is given in (4f), and this is elaborated in (4g).

While there are no obligatory syntactic manifestations of the paratactic and hypotactic relationships in English discourse of this type, this example does contain a grammatical reflex of the functional separation of steps. Step$_1$ contains primarily imperative sentences [(4c) contains, of course, a nonspecific person]. Step$_2$ is separated from Step$_1$ by virtue of using *we* forms. Step$_3$ then returns to the unmarked use of imperative forms which we expect in English procedural discourse [see Longacre (1976), Hinds (1975, 1976b)].

Expository Discourse

The example of expository discourse presented in (6) exhibits an obligatory manifestation of paratactic and hypotactic relationships. The diagram in (18) is a revised diagram of (7), incorporating the relevant information introduced since the original discussion. The major innovation in (18) over (7) concerns

(18)

the relationship of individual sentences to the segments. As illustrated in (13c), nonpeak sentences may either precede or follow peaks. What is at issue is the semantic subordination of nonpeak sentences to peak sentences, not the linear ordering of these sentences.

In (6), both pronouns and full noun phrases are used to refer to Teng Hsiao-ping. Rather than an arbitrary alternation of noun phrases and pronouns in texts of this sort, the choice of noun phrase over pronoun is strictly governed by the structure of the text. Within peak sentences, full noun phrases occur, and within nonpeak sentences, pronouns occur to refer to the topic of the paragraph. Although, the situation is sometimes more complex than this, it is a clear instance of a syntactic manifestation of segment structure.

This type of conditioned alternation is not limited to English, as is shown in Kimura (1977). The functional equivalent of English pronouns in Japanese is ellipsis [see Kuroda (1965), Hinds and Shibatani (1977)]. Within a Japanese expository text, full noun phrases, as in English, occur in peak sentences of a segment, and ellipsis occurs in nonpeak sentences. One interesting aspect of the Japanese case is the lexical item *doosi* 'the aforementioned person,' which appears to be intermediate in status between a full noun phrase and ellipsis. The function of this form is primarily to indicate that there has been a shift in orientation, and, as a result, it occurs in either peak or nonpeak sentences.

Conversation

If we return to diagram (3), the relevant details concerning the structure of the conversation presented in (2) can be added. (19) illustrates all of the relevant information that should be included between the STORY LINE and the EVENT LINE.

(19)

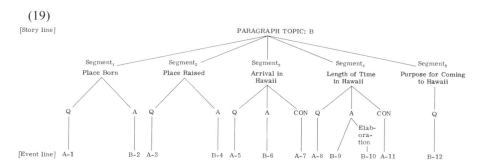

Three comments are necessary. First, segment$_5$ is quite obviously interrupted. In the actual videotaped interview, question (2A-12) was answered. Second, a new node, CON, has been introduced (see Footnote 11). CON stands for CONFIRMATION, or FEEDBACK. The existence of this optional constituent has been discussed by Sinclair and Coulthard (1975) and Hinds (1976a, 1978a). The function of this constituent is to bind together a segment, often for the purpose of clarification or evaluation. Third, the segments approach the paragraph topic B from a variety of perspectives, in the same way that the segments of the story about the girl who gave birth to an illegitimate child approach that topic.

6. CONCLUSION

In this chapter I have attempted to demonstrate that conversational discourse is affected by both linear and hierarchical organization. Three specific types of discourse were examined—procedural, expository, and information-exchanging conversation—and it was shown that the level of paragraph constitutes a significant unit of organization in each. The paragraph itself is composed of subunits of uniform orientation, termed *segments*, whose function and form are defined vis-à-vis specific discourse types.

Segments for procedural discourse specify the discrete steps involved in achieving the goal. For English procedural discourse, there are no obligatory grammatical markers to separate steps, but steps in Japanese procedural discourse constitute a single sentence. If a step in Japanese procedural discourse consists of more than one EVENT, these events are connected with sentence-internal conjunctions.

Segments in expository discourse specify the purpose of a given unified section of the paragraph. There are four types: INTRODUCTORY, MOTIVATION, HIGHLIGHT, and UNEXPECTED TWIST. Within each segment, there will be one sentence of particular semantic importance, termed the PEAK. In both Japanese and English expository discourse, there are grammatical reflexes of this phenomenon. With reference to the individual under discussion in the paragraph, full noun phrases are used within the peak sentence of a segment. Within nonpeak sentences, English pronouns and Japanese ellipsis occur to refer to the individual under discussion.

Conversational discourse also consists of segments. In discourse of this type, the segments reflect a perspective on the discourse type. Perspectives correspond to the necessary accompaniments, both animate and inanimate, of a paragraph topic. Moreover, the segment in conversation consists of one of two types of switching mechanisms: QUESTION–ANSWER or REMARK–REPLY. Both of these patterns allow an optional confirmation component. These patterns constitute paratactic relationships. Within a given segment, there will be one, and only one, paratactic relationship. Other sentences or clauses within the segment form hypotactic relationships. These hypotactic relationships have one of two possible functions: EXPLANATION or ELABORATION. Other possible functions are discussed in Hinds (1977b, 1978a).

The elucidation of these organizational principles provides a framework for the further investigation of extended speech and writing beyond the single sentence in isolation. The fact that such principles operate in languages as fundamentally different as English and Japanese suggests that both linear and hierarchical organizing principles exist universally.

ACKNOWLEDGMENTS

I wish to thank Wako Hinds, Bart Mathias, Kazu Nagatomo, Matt Shibatani, and Don Smith for specific suggestions on earlier versions of this paper. I would also like to express my appreciation to Talmy Givón for organizing the conference at which this paper was presented. The three days of interaction with the participants in that conference opened up to me a number of new perspectives on discourse analysis and helped clarify my thinking in a number of areas. Full responsibility for errors of fact or judgment remains mine. My participation in the symposium was made possible by a travel grant from the University of Hawaii Asian Studies Program. The research reported in this paper was supported in part by a grant from the University of Hawaii Japan Studies Endowment, funded by a grant from the Japanese Government.

REFERENCES

Creider, C. (forthcoming) "Anaphora in Nandi-Kipsigis Conversation," in J. Hinds, ed., *Anaphora in Discourse*, Linguistic Research, Alberta.

Duncan, S. (1972) "Some Signals and Rules for Taking Speaking Turns in Conversations," *Journal of Personality and Social Psychology* 23, 283–292.

Duncan, S. (1973) "Toward a Grammar for Dyadic Conversations," *Semiotica* 9, 29–46.

Duncan, S. (1974a) "Language, Paralanguage, and Body Motion in the Structure of Conversations," in W. McCormak and S. Wurm, eds., *Language and Thought*, The Hague, Mouton.

Duncan, S. (1974b) "On the Structure of Speaker–Auditor Interaction during Speaking Turns," *Language in Society* 3, 161–180.

Grimes, J. (1975) *The Thread of Discourse*, Mouton, The Hague.

Halliday, M. and R. Hasan. (1976) *Cohesion in English*, Longmans, London.

Hinds, J. (1975) "Korean Discourse Types," in H. M. Sohn, ed., *The Korean Language: Its Structure and Social Projection*. Center for Korean Studies, University of Hawaii, Honolulu, 81–90.

Hinds, J. (1976a) *Aspects of Japanese Discourse Structure*, Kaitakusha, Tokyo.

Hinds, J. (1976b) "A Taxonomy of Japanese Discourse Types," *Linguistics* 184, 45–54.

Hinds, J. (1977a) "Conversational Structure," in J. Hinds, ed., *Proceedings of the Second Annual Meeting of the University of Hawaii-Hawaii Association of Teachers of Japanese*, University of Hawaii, Honolulu, Hawaii.

Hinds, J. (1977b) "Paragraph Structure and Pronominalization," *Papers in Linguistics* 10, 77–99.

Hinds, J. (1978a) "Conversational Structure: An Investigation Based on Japanese Interview Discourse," in J. Hinds and I. Howard, eds., *Problems in Japanese Syntax and Semantics*," Kaitakusha, Tokyo, 79–121.

Hinds, J. (1978b) "Levels of Structure within the Paragraph," *Berkeley Linguistic Society* 4, 598–609.

Hinds, J. (forthcoming) "Anaphora in Japanese Conversation," in J. Hinds. ed., *Anaphora in Discourse*, Linguistic Research, Alberta.

Hinds, J. and M. Shibatani (1977) "Towards a Unified Theory of Anaphora in Japanese Discourse," Unpublished paper, University of Hawaii, Honolulu, Hawaii.

Kimura, S. (1977) "Paragraph Structure and Zero Anaphora in Japanese Obituaries," Unpublished paper, University of Hawaii, Honolulu, Hawaii.

Kuno, S. (1973) *The Structure of the Japanese Language*, M.I.T. Press, Cambridge.

Kuroda, S.-Y. (1965) *Generative Grammatical Studies in the Japanese Language*, Unpublished Doctoral dissertation, Massachusetts Institute of Technology, Cambridge, Massachusetts.

Kuroda, S.-Y. (1976) "Subject," in M. Shibatani, ed., *Syntax and Semantics 5, Generative Grammar*, Academic Press, New York.

Longacre, R. (1968) *Discourse, Paragraph, and Sentence Structure in Selected Philippine Languages*, Summer Institute of Linguistics, Santa Ana.

Longacre, R. (1971) "Narrative versus Other Discourse Genre," in D. Hays and D. Lance, eds., *From Soundstream to Discourse*, University of Missouri Press, Columbus, pp. 167–186.

Longacre, R. (1972) *Hierarchy and Universality of Discourse Constituents in New Guinea Languages*, Georgetown University Press, Washington, D.C.

Longacre, R. (1976) *An Anatomy of Speech Notions*, Peter de Ridder Press, Lisse.

Meyer, B. (1975) *The Organization of Prose and Its Effect on Recall*, North-Holland, New York.

Momoi, K. (1977) "Review Article of Hinds: '*Aspects of Japanese Discourse Structure*,'" *Journal of the Association of Teachers of Japanese* 12, 41–53.

Nakau, H. (1973) *Sentential Complementation in Japanese*, Kaitakusha, Tokyo.

Ochs, E. (this volume) "Planned and Unplanned Discourse."

Sacks, H., E. Schegloff, and G. Jefferson (1974) "A Simplest Systematics for the Organization of Turn-Taking in Conversation," *Language* 50, 696–735.

Schank, R. and R. Abelson (1977) *Scripts, Plans, Goals, and Understanding*, L. Erlbaum Associates, New York.

Schegloff, E. (this volume) "The Relevance of Repair for Syntax-for-Conversation."

Schegloff, E. and H. Sacks (1973) "Opening up Closings," *Semiotica* 8, 289–327.

Schegloff, E., G. Jefferson, and H. Sacks (1977) "The Preference for Self-Correction in the Organization of Repair in Conversation," *Language* 53, 361–382.

Shibatani, M. (1977) "Grammatical Relations and Surface Cases," *Language* 53, 789–809.

Sinclair, J. and R. Coulthard (1975) *Towards an Analysis of Discourse: The English Used by Teachers and Pupils*, Oxford University Press, London.

Taber, C. (1966) *The Structure of Sango Narrative*, Hartford Seminary Foundation, Hartford.

Thorndyke, P. (1977) "Cognitive Structures in Comprehension and Memory of Narrative Discourse," *Cognitive Psychology* 9, 77–110.

Tonoike, S. (1976) "The Case Ordering Hypothesis," *Papers in Japanese Linguistics* 4, 191–208.

van Dijk, T. (1972) *Some Aspects of Text Grammars*, Mouton, The Hague.

THE FLOW OF THOUGHT AND THE FLOW OF LANGUAGE

WALLACE L. CHAFE
University of California, Berkeley

1. INTRODUCTION

A couple of the worthwhile questions that can be asked about language pertain to how it follows and at the same time influences a speaker's stream of thought and how—as it moves forward itself—it provides clues as to the nature of the thought processes that lie behind it. "Thought," of course, covers a broad range of mental activities. What I am going to discuss here is restricted to only one aspect of it: the remembering of past experience. I am not downplaying the importance of other kinds of thought, such as problem solving (see, for example, Mayer 1977), though I do suspect that the contribution of the latter to normal, everyday thinking has been exaggerated. In any case, I see no reason to doubt that a significant portion of our mental activity involves the remembering of things we have experienced in the past. I ask you to keep in mind throughout this discussion a situation that begins with some experience and ends with some discourse that is used to communicate the speaker's memory of the experience. What lies between the experience and the language is hidden from direct view. Psychological experiments can provide us with occasional glimpses of it through small windows. But it is also true that various aspects of language use, in addition to the content of what is said, can provide some important evidence. I have been especially interested in looking from this point of view at what might once have been called linguistic "performance."[1]

Most of the data I will mention come from a situation in which a group of us at Berkeley tried to control the initial experience in such a way that we would have a reasonably large sample of verbalizations of the same material by different people. To accomplish this, we produced a 7-minute 16-mm color film; it had sound but no language, since we wanted, among other things, to show the film to speakers of a variety of different languages. Our procedure was to show it to groups of about five people at a time and then to interview them one by one, asking them to tell what happened in the film. We have more than 60 tape-recorded narratives of this kind in English and at least 20 in each of nine other languages, including Greek, Persian, German, Malay, Thai, Chinese, Japanese, Sacapultec (a Mayan language), and Haitian Creole. I will discuss here only the English narratives and, in fact, only those that we have so far analyzed in some detail: 20 that were obtained within 5–25 min after the speaker had seen the film, plus an additional 5 from some of the same speakers who came back 6 weeks later and told about the film a second time. Although they will not be included in the discussion here, there also exist 3 narratives produced by three of the last mentioned five speakers, who came back a third time after a year had passed. I need to emphasize that this research is still very much in progress. To understand these things better, it is going to be necessary not only to carry further our analyses of the English data and the data from other languages but also to extend the range of data to include verbalizations of real experiences in more natural settings. In addition, there are plans to conduct various experimental studies related to hypotheses generated by this material.

What I am going to do here is to present first a model for the verbalization of recalled experience that I used to find reasonably satisfactory (Chafe 1977a,b, both written in 1975). I will then discuss a somewhat different way of looking at things, one that I think takes care of certain inadequacies in

[1] The work reported here was supported by Grant MH-25592 from the National Institute of Mental Health. I owe a great deal to the efforts and ideas of my co-workers on that project: Robert Bernardo, Patricia Clancy, Pamela Downing, John DuBois, and Deborah Tannen. I have also profited considerably from conversations with Kristina Hooper on the matters discussed here. Talmy Givón made a number of useful suggestions for the improvement of the original manuscript.

the earlier model. I will refer to the earlier one as the HIERARCHICAL MODEL and the later one as the FLOW MODEL.

2.   THE HIERARCHICAL MODEL

As its name suggests, the chief property of the earlier model was that it was hierarchical. It posited four levels of integration of cognitive material—of larger cognitive units containing smaller ones. I will call these four kinds of units, from largest to smallest, MEMORIES, EPISODES, THOUGHTS, and FOCI. It will be easy to relate to these units if you imagine that a memory is expressed in language by a story, an episode by a paragraph, a thought by a sentence, and a focus by a phrase. These are, of course, four rather well-established linguistic units, but I must admit having been somewhat surprised to find in our material that they emerge rather clearly from spontaneous speech and that there do appear to be just these four kinds of units—no more, no less. There also appear to be some independent kinds of psychological evidence supporting certain aspects of this hierarchy.

The largest cognitive unit—that is, the notion that experience is recalled in terms of isolated "memories"—actually has received minimal attention from the psychological profession, though it seems to have strong intuitive support. I know it to be true for myself, and I believe it to be true for other people, that we do not recall experience as a continuous record that we can replay in our consciousness in a steady stream. Rather, to the extent that we can be said to reexperience the past at all, we apparently are able to do so only in terms of islands: disjointed chunks, highly selective, with large gaps between them that are much larger than the chunks themselves. Autobiographical accounts confirm this picture, though published autobiographies tend to rely on research that gives the illusion that the author has been able to remember much more than he or she could have recalled spontaneously. Completely honest literary explorations of recall (e.g., Salaman 1970) make the island like nature of it quite clear, and what little psychological research there has been on autobiographical memory (e.g., Robinson 1976) leads to the same conclusion. Such an island, then, is what I am calling a MEMORY. I should point out that a large linguistic production, such as an autobiography or a novel, and even usually a chapter in such a work, does not express a single coherent unit of recall but, rather, a collection of such units. Neither "book" nor "chapter" bears any direct relationship to a chunk of memory.

When we move down to the next level in the hierarchy—to what I am calling the EPISODE—we find linguistic evidence that is fairly strong, though some important qualifications will have to be made when I come to discuss the "flow model." To begin with, of course, there is the very existence of paragraphs in written language. There is a tradition of concern in literary studies for what makes a paragraph (e.g., Christensen 1965), and many of us have been exposed to a certain amount of schooling on this subject. I have been especially interested to see in our material that paragraphs also emerge from spontaneous spoken language, most obviously through the occurrence of major hesitations at those places in a narrative where paragraph boundaries seem to belong. For example, look at the following portion of one of our film narratives, in which the speaker finishes telling about a boy's theft of some pears and begins telling about some other things that happen subsequently (Speaker 22):

> *And as he's holding onto the handlebars he takes off with them.* (1.1)
> *Um*—(.7) *then* (.4) *uh*—(2.1) *a girl*— *on a bicycle,* (1.15) *comes riding towards him, . . . in the opposite direction.*

The figures in parentheses give the time in seconds occupied by pauses at the points indicated. *Um*— and *uh*— are lengthened pronunciations of those "pause fillers." The total amount of time spent hesitating between the end of the first sentence and the beginning of *a girl on a bicycle* was 6.25 sec. We have here clear evidence of some important and time-consuming mental processing. Many such boundaries are conspicuously present in our data, and they typically occur at points where it would be natural to imagine a paragraph boundary if the narrative were written. I will confirm this intuition with some further evidence below.

To proceed now with our hierarchy: If we suppose that a memory contains episodes, we can go on to suppose that an episode contains what I will call THOUGHTS. My terminology may seem pretentious. Have I finally found a way of making precise the nature of a thought? But it does have the advantage of enabling us to say that a sentence (typically) expresses a complete thought, which is certainly a nice thing to be able to say.

Our data show the sentence to be one of the most obvious, most strongly signaled of linguistic units. In the written form of many languages, of course, it is given special treatment with its initial capital letter and its final punctuation mark. In spontaneous speech, as everyone who has transcribed it is sure to be aware, sentence boundaries are not always clearcut; often, one finds distortions and fragments of sentencehood. Examples like the following are present in our material (Speaker 20):

> *There's no spoken communication at all. Going on. Throughout the whole movie, and they just pick up his basket.*

Such cases are better handled within the flow model. Just now we can sweep them under the rug by interpreting them as deviations from prototypical sentencehood.

Two manifestations of sentencehood are quite obvious in spoken language. One is what we have been calling SYNTACTIC CLOSURE: the kind of well-formed grammatical structure that grammarians have always told us sentences should have. The other is intonation: There are certain intonation contours, most commonly a distinctive kind of falling pitch, that are regularly associated with sentence endings. Usually, though certainly not always, these two indications coincide.

We have noticed several other manifestations of sentencehood in these data. There is, for example, a tendency for a sentence to be pronounced more vigorously at its beginning than at its end. Often there are one or more words with heightened amplitude and/or pitch near the beginning of a sentence, and sometimes there is a decrescendo and/or a ritardando as the sentence approaches its end. This observation may seem to run counter to the notion that accented elements carrying so-called new information are likely to come toward the end of a sentence, but, in fact, in spontaneous speech, that notion may apply more appropriately to the phrase (to be discussed). There are also conspicuous cases in which a significant increase or decrease in total loudness and/or pitch level extends over the domain of an entire sentence. And there is another intonational phenomenon that we have noticed repeatedly in these data. There are a number of examples of sentences containing a series of phrases each of which ends in the same intonation contour, until the final phrase signals the end of the sentence with a falling pitch. We have labeled this phenomenon "intonational rhyme," since the phrases in such a sequence can be regarded as rhyming with respect to pitch.

Finally, it may be noted that sentences are typically separated by pauses and, often, by hesitational phenomena of other kinds: pause fillers, lengthenings, false starts, and repetitions. This is not to say that hesitations occur only between sentences; certainly, many of them are sentence-internal. But, whereas one cannot predict a sentence boundary from the presence of a hesitation, the presence of a sentence boundary makes a hesitation highly likely. In these data, such hesitations average about 1 sec in length if an episode boundary is not also present. And 88% of the occurences of sentence-final intonation are followed by hesitations of some kind.

Thus, language makes sentences appear to be especially crucial ways of organizing cognitive material, and it is no wonder that a well-known school of linguistics has made S its "initial symbol." It would be good also to have some wholly nonlinguistic evidence that people perceive, store, and recall experience in terms of conceptual units of the type that are expressed in sentences. One promising line of research in this direction is suggested by the experiments of Darren Newtson (surveyed in Newtson 1976). His method is to show people a videotape or film, asking them to press a button whenever they judge one meaningful action to have ended and a different one to have begun, that is, "when the [actor in the film] stops doing one thing and begins to do something discriminably different [p. 224]." People are able without difficulty to mark in this way what Newtson calls "break points" in the flow of actions; there is considerable agreement as to where the break points occur; and the same person will repeat something close to the same pattern of break points after a period of time. Furthermore, people are able to segment the flow of actions into units of different size according to whether they are instructed to mark "the smallest actions that seem natural and meaningful" or the largest. "For example, one might see a person get up from a chair, walk over to a door, close it, turn, and walk back to his chair, and mark off each segment as a discrete, meaningful action, or one might see the whole sequence as just one action—closing the door [Newtson 1976:225]." Our interest at this point lies in the fact that Newtson's so-called "gross units" seem suggestively close to the kinds of thoughts expressed in sentences. The correspondence now needs to be tested further by systematically comparing the button-pushing units with verbalizations of the same material. We hope to do this.

In summary, we find what seems to be a universal tendency for people to express their thoughts in linguistic segments with highly distinctive phonological and syntactic properties, with a mean length in our data of about 16 words and a mean temporal length of about 6 sec if we include hesitational phenomena. There seems to be some independent evidence that people process experience in terms of units of a similar kind. Ultimately, we would like to know what gives the thoughts that underlie sentences their coherence. I will return to some speculations on this score when we come to the flow model below.

If, then, in the hierarchical model memories contain episodes and episodes thoughts, we can go one step further and say that thoughts contain FOCI, expressed linguistically in PHRASES (usually "clauses," but not always). Just as it is readily apparent that our narratives exhibit sentences, it is equally apparent that they segment themselves into these smaller units. This segmentation is evident above all from intonation. Between the sentence-final intonation boundaries, there are numerous "phrase-final" intonations, not all of the same contour, but all easily identifiable as signaling some kind of unit boundary. The segments so defined have a mean length of about 5 words, a mean duration of slightly less than 2 sec. In terms of syntactic structure, about two-thirds of them consist of single case frames (a verb with its associated nouns), and a full three-fourths fall into the single-case-frame category if we extend it to include verbs with complement case frames as their arguments, phrases containing identificatory restrictive relative clauses, double verb constructions (such as "came leading"), and the like. Most of the remaining 25% of the phrases consist of adverbs, interjections, or topic like noun phrases. Only about 4% consist of what are clearly two independent case frames, and, intuitively, one has the impression that these few instances were places where the speaker made a "mistake," running together two things when the normal use of language would have required separation, using a phrase-final intonation boundary in the middle. The notion that case frames correspond to a single basic unit of information has been suggested by Givón (1975:202), and the preeminent role of the clause in spontaneous speech has been stated as the "one-clause-at-a-time hypothesis" by Pawley and Syder (forthcoming).

Another obvious property of phrases is the frequency with which they begin with one of a small list of conjunctions, by far the most common of which is *and*. About 40% of the phrases in this material begin with *and*, and many of the remainder with *but*, *so*, *then*, or a combination of these. Although beginning with a conjunction is a somewhat less consistent property of phrases than is expressing a single case frame, it is a reliable index of phrasehood in the many places where it does appear.

The Newtson-type button-pushing data provide again some independent evidence for the existence of cognitive units of the "focus" variety, specifically in the fine units, as opposed to the gross units that we earlier identified with "thoughts." When people are instructed to mark "the smallest actions that seem natural and meaningful," it is these focuslike units into which they evidently segment their experience. Another kind of evidence that I think is going to repay further investigation is eye-movement data. As is widely known, the eyes are continually moving restlessly from one fixation to another, each fixation lasting only a fraction of a second. These fixations, however, typically occur in clusters, called in one early work "centers of interest" (Buswell 1935). As yet, we have no clear data that would enable us to answer such basic questions as the mean length of a fixation cluster, how much variability there is in this length, or, especially, how closely fixation clusters correspond to phrases in a verbalization of the knowledge acquired from a scene for which eye movements have been monitored. There is a small amount of evidence, however, that such a correspondence does exist and that we pick up information from a visual scene under the guidance of an overall executive system that also controls the manner in which we recall and verbalize information.

The hierarchical model, then, was a vertical one that posited the existence of units of thought and corresponding units of language organized in terms of larger units containing smaller ones. It assumed that the units at each level are stored in memory and that recall involves the activation of such units as they are called for, probably under the influence of schemas that provide established patterns for moving from one cognitive unit to the next. Memories, episodes, thoughts, and foci were viewed as being expressed linguistically by stories, paragraphs, sentences, and phrases (cf. Longacre 1976, and in this volume). This hierarchical cognitive organization was seen to be reflected in this hierarchical linguistic organization, manifested in the stream of speech, especially in syntactic boundaries, intonation contours, hesitations, and the use of conjunctions. In terms of ongoing processing, the major hesitations separating episodes could be seen as caused by the speaker's need to recall and organize a new episode, presumably a more difficult, time-consuming task than recalling and organizing a new thought or focus. And a new thought, in turn, could be seen to take more time than a focus. In our data, relatively few of the non-sentence-final phrases are followed by any hesitation at all. Thus, speech could be seen as the production of a series of phrases, proceeding with relatively little difficulty so long as they lay within a single thought, with a certain amount of difficulty if a new thought had to be retrieved (or created) and with considerable difficulty if a switch to a new episode was necessary (cf. the correspondence between hesitations and "semantic planning" reported in Butterworth 1975).

But, in fact, by describing the hierarchical model in such terms I have provided a good introduction for the FLOW MODEL, in which the vertical, hierarchical organization of thought and language is supplemented and enriched through more attention to the horizontal aspect. In the rest of this paper, I want to emphasize the role of the speaker as someone who is engaged in a real-time process of focusing on a sequence of ideas and converting these ideas, one after another, into language. The metaphors of thoughts flowing through time and of language flowing, also—in a way that follows or expresses the thought flow but also influences it significantly—are a useful starting point. The general idea that is captured by the metaphor would seem to be incontrovertible. Introspection tells us clearly enough that we are thinking different things at different times. And it is obvious that language moves along in parallel, often helping to shape the thoughts themselves. I am trying to look more carefully at the flow, hoping to find more about what constitutes and controls it, what it is that is flowing, and the valves, dams, and locks that affect its course.

3.   THE FLOW MODEL

Suppose we begin by thinking of this process as the activation and verbalization of a series of what I have been calling FOCI. For that is, up to a point, what one of our narratives looks like: a series of brief phrases. We cannot go very far in examining this sequencing, however, without observing the effect of larger cognitive elements: thoughts, episodes, and memories. For example, we notice that every so often there is a phrase that ends with falling pitch intonation and that, on other grounds as well, can be identified as sentence-final. And we notice that there are major hesitational phenomena signaling the boundaries of episodes. But we also notice that the speaker engages in a great deal of backing and filling, trying out phrases and discarding them often before they have been completed, revising and expanding phrases already uttered, adding phrases as afterthoughts to sentences already completed, and so on. The general picture is of a speaker who not only has things to say, partly at least things recalled from memory, but who is also at the same time constantly concerned with how well what is being said is getting these things across—how well the decisions regarding verbalization are communicating to another mind what is in the speaker's mind.

Look, for example, at the following beginning of one narrative (Speaker 37):

(1)   (4.25) *Um . . it starts out . . there's a (3.3) well,* hedge

(2)   (1.45) *the—landscape is like uh—a f— (2.35) sort of peasant landscape*

(3)   *but it isn't really farmland,*   lengthening

(4)   *it's like an orchard.*

(5)   (.6) *It's a small orchard,*

(6)   (.65) *and— uh— (.55) it's green.*

(Two periods indicate a break in timing too brief to be measured as a pause; a dash indicates lengthening.) Before this person began talking, the interviewer had asked her to "tell what happened in the movie." There followed the 4.25-sec hesitation shown at the beginning of (1) before the speaker said anything. It is a good guess that during this interval the speaker was engaged in some time-consuming mental processing that, in fact, she had not completed by the time she began talking. (One might suppose that she finally felt obligated to say something, 4 sec of silence being close to the limit of endurance in our society.) Judging from what she started out saying, evidently at least one of the things that was occupying her was the need to choose, from all the foci available in her memory, that focus with which it was best to begin her narrative.

In making this choice, she was evidently guided by an awareness of what is expected in such a narrative and by a concern for conforming to such expectations. Specifically, she must have been guided at this point by the knowledge that a narrative is expected to mirror in its own chronology the chronology of the experience being related; in other words, she felt called upon to relate the events of the film in chronological order (cf. Labov 1972:359–362). Thus, her very first words were *it starts out*, making quite explicit this concern. Her next words, *there's a*, suggest that at this point her conscious attention was focused on a character in the film I will call the "pear picker," the first character one sees. This supposition is strengthened by the fact that she returned to this focus, temporarily abandoned in phrase 1, in what she said immediately after the portion quoted:

(7)   *And there's this sort of* (1.75) *Latin . . looking . . middle-aged man*

Her response to the interviewer's request, in other words, involved initially a search of salient foci available from her memory with the goal of finding which focus would provide a starting point most in conformity with expectations as to how one tells something of this kind. However many foci may have occurred to her during the initial 4.25 sec, she must have been guided in part—as she herself makes explicit—by the chronological expectation and in part by the salience of her recall of the human being who appeared first in the film. The cognitive salience of humans to other humans is reflected in language in a variety of ways, and I need not dwell on that point.

But then, having started to verbalize this detail of the pear picker with the words *there's a*, she realized that that was not the best place to start after all—that something else should be verbalized first. So she paused for 3.3 sec more, said *well*, and paused for another 1.45 sec. Eventually, her first successful verbalization dealt not with the first character but with what we may call the "setting." We can imagine two influences on this choice. One may have been the speaker's realization that there is a schema for story-telling that includes the notion that one should begin with the setting. It is expected that a narrative should begin with some kind of spatial–temporal orientation that allows the hearer to get his or her bearings. The other influence may have been the speaker's realization that the movie did, in fact, begin with a shot of the setting before it cut to the pear picker. Thus, she was simply following here the chronology of the film itself. These two possibilities are not incompatible. Certainly, the filmmaker was influenced by the "setting first" expectation, and we may suppose that the viewers of the film, including our present speaker, found it congenial. Thus, this speaker, in eventually settling on the setting as the focus with which to begin her narrative, was in all probability combining her recall of the film itself with a more general knowledge of schematic expectations.

We may suppose that now, by the time she arrived at the lengthened *the*— at the beginning of (2), she had clearly focused her attention on the setting. Her problems in (2), which still seem to have been considerable, no longer had to do with what focus to verbalize but, rather, with how to verbalize the one she had. It would carry us too far afield to explore in detail here the processes involved in categorizing and finding the right words for one's recall of a particular object or scene (cf. especially the work of Rosch, e.g., Rosch and Mervis 1975). But those processes do seem to be the ones operative here, where the speaker had a scene in mind that was not especially codable— not able to be verbalized immediately and obviously. Thus, the choice of the word *landscape* was difficult enough to cause a lengthening of the word the—. Her attempt, then, to find an analogy for the landscape floundered considerably—her first choice, evidently *farm*, being abandoned after the initial consonant, with her second choice, *peasant landscape*, being neatly hedged by *sort of*, and then immediately the explicit denial in (3), *but it isn't really farmland*. Having not as yet succeeded in communicating anything very clear about setting, she finally was able in (4) to say with a little more assurance *it's like an orchard*. Thus, the linguistic phrases in (2)–(4) did not really express three different cognitive foci but constituted three stabs at expressing one and the same focus. Phrases and foci are not necessarily in a one-to-one relation.

At the end of (4), we have a sentence boundary. This example would lead us to believe that speakers signal sentence boundaries when they judge that a focus has been successfully verbalized. That conclusion is, I think, correct as far as it goes; that is, it does identify one among several reasons for sentence boundaries. Other evidence will suggest other reasons.

But we have not yet exhausted the lessons to be learned from this example. Phrase (4) was evidently still not a verbalization of the setting with which the speaker could be completely happy. She indicated as much in that phrase itself, with the qualification *like*. If she had been wholly satisfied with her categorization, presumably she would have said triumphantly, *It's an orchard!* With objects that are of low codability, one recourse a speaker has is to modify the chosen categorization, making use of such linguistic devices as adjectives and relative clauses. Without the modification in this case, the hearer would be expected to understand that the setting was something resembling a prototypical orchard. But that was clearly wrong; in the movie, in fact, there was only one pear tree. However the speaker may have re-membered the setting, she knew that it deviated significantly in size from prototypical orchardhood. In monitoring the likely effect on the hearer of what she had just said, she found it necessary to qualify the orchard categorization by adding, after a pause of .6 sec, the phrase in (5)—*It's a small orchard.*

She must have judged, however, that the setting deviated from proto-typicality in more ways than size. After a more significant hesitation, one lasting a total of 2 sec, she added the second qualifier, *it's green.* There may be more involved here than just the speaker's awareness that the setting she had in mind differed from a prototypical orchard with respect to its greenness. The greenness of the film was something commented on by several other speakers. For example (Speaker 24), with hesitations omitted:

> *Something that I noticed about the movie particularly unique was that the colors were just very strange. Like the green was an inordinately bright green, for the pears, and these colors just seemed a little kind of bold, almost to the point of being artificial.*

This speaker, then, judged the film as a whole to have deviated from the prototypical film with respect to greenness. It is possible that the speaker we have been discussing made a similar judgment but that when she found herself in difficulty categorizing the setting she picked on the ambient greenness as one way of coping with that difficulty. In other words, if pressed she might have been willing to admit that it was not just that this orchard was greener than other orchards but that this film was greener than other films. There is in addition a tendency, exhibited in a variety of materials I have seen, for categorizations, when they are qualified at all, to be qualified in terms of color. Color is one of the first properties of an object people will mention. When a speaker is trying to deal linguistically with his or her memory for an object of low codability, he or she may follow the strategy "qualify it" in fairly diffuse terms, mentioning not necessarily or only a property in which the object deviates from prototypicality but also a property that has general salience in human experience, color being in many cases the prime candidate. Thus, when our speaker felt the need to qualify *orchard* she used not only the relevant qualification *small* but also the globally salient *green.*

4. THOUGHTS IN THE FLOW MODEL

The quoted portion of Speaker 37's narrative expressed what was conceptually a single thought, though in terms of both syntax and intonation it can be divided into two sentences. What was filling the speaker's consciousness during this portion of her narrative [after the fumbling in (1)] was the setting (I would like very much to say "a mental image of the setting"). That is what gave unity to this portion of the narrative. If she had had more time to think about her verbalization—if she had been writing it, for example—she might have said something like *The movie begins in a small orchard.* But, certainly, the spoken version provides us with far richer evidence for her ongoing mental processing. We can see it as containing a single focus, expressed most directly in (4), *it's like an orchard,* the climax of this thought. The other phrases led up to or away from this one. In (1), there was an effort to find the right focus to settle on, in (2) and (3) attempts to find the right categorization for the chosen focus, and in (5) and (6) efforts to qualify the categorization provided in (4). This example suggests, then, that a thought may contain a central focus, with others within the same thought being ancillary. It suggests, too, that thoughts and sentences do not always coincide or that some sentences express what can quite appropriately here be called "after-thoughts." Finally, the example suggests that at least one of the factors that can bring unity to a thought is a single coherent referent, in this case the setting. But we need now to look at other examples to see that this is not the only principle of coherence, that foci may be unified within a thought in various other ways.

Speaker 22 began her narrative as follows:

(8)   *Okay.*

(9)   *Well—,*

(10)   (.75) *let me see.*

(11)   (1.5) *It opens with um—* (.4) *I guess a farm worker,*

(12)   (1.2) *picking pears,*

(13)   (.75) *in a tree.*

In (8) we find a very brief sentence expressing the speaker's acquiescence to the interviewer's request, followed immediately by a brief two-phrase sentence that communicates explicitly her difficulty in getting started. Finally, in (11), like our previous speaker, she expresses her adherence to chronology by saying *It opens with,* and then, after more hesitation and unlike the previous speaker, she is content to begin focusing on the film's first character. (Note the hedge *I guess* in her categorization of him.) Our data show that, when people first direct their attention to the idea of a person, they typically have a concern for how that person can be categorized (*farm worker*), whatever ongoing activity he or she is engaged in (*picking pears*), and where he or she is located (*in a tree*). This same speaker a little later introduced another character by saying:

(14)   (.95) *Then um—* (1.5) *a little boy on a bicycle,*

(15)   (1.15) *comes riding past the tree,*

where she coalesced what he was doing and its location into a single focus (15), perhaps because the already-known presence of the tree made it unnecessary to introduce it in a separate phrase. Or, still later:

(16)   (1.1) *Um*— (.7) *then* (.4) *uh*— (2.1) *a . . girl on a bicycle,*

(17)   (1.15) *comes riding towards him,*

(18)   *. . in the opposite direction.*

I will refer to this pattern as the character–action–location schema.

Let us return to the sentence expressed in (11)–(13). Here we have something a little different from our earlier example of sentencehood, in which separate phrases were necessitated by the difficulty in categorizing the setting. A parallel case to the earlier one would be one in which several phrases were devoted to an adequate categorization of the speaker's memory for the pear picker, as, for example (Speaker 25):

(19)   (1.1) *Uh*— *he looks* (.95) *like your uh* (.2) *typical . . farmer,*

(20)   *or* (.3) *whatever,*

(21)   *kind of plump,*

(22)   *and* (.7) *moustache,*

which shows processing much like that exhibited by Speaker 37 in talking about the setting. But our present subject, in (11)–(13), has been content to call the man a *farm worker* and has followed the character–action–location schema in focusing first on his farm worker status, second on his picking pears, and third on his location in a tree. Adherence to a single schema thus seems to be another kind of unity that a thought can exhibit.

Speaker 22's narrative continued as follows:

(23)   (1.0) *And*— *um*— (2.6) *you see him taking . . picking the pears off the leaves,*

(24)   *and putting them in a . . white apron,*

(25)   (.5) *and he walks down the* (.75) *ladder,*

(26)   *and dumps the pears into a basket.*

The focus expressed earlier in (12), *picking pears*, was a general notion that we now find expanded in the focus expressed in (23): a cognitive "zooming in" on the picking operation. But (23) now provides the taking-off point for a series of foci, each of which involves a temporally separate action. The coherence of this entire sentence may come principally from the speaker's conception of these separate actions as constituting a coherent chain that leads to the realization of the picker's goal: to arrive at a state where the pears that were formerly in the tree are now in baskets on the ground. The contribution of each of the actions to this goal is clear. Thus, thoughts can achieve coherence in various ways: through their involvement with a single referent, with a single schema, or with a single goal. Undoubtedly, there are other integrating principles, and I will return to some other possibilities later.

The alert reader may have noticed that the last quoted sentence from Speaker 22 neatly divides itself into two parts, with phrases (23) and (24) as one and phrases (25) and (26) as the other. Among other things, this is a matter of what is usually called SUBJECT DELETION: Phrases (24) and (26) have no overt subjects. It is also a matter of aspect shift (cf. Hopper's paper in this volume): the -ing forms in (23) and (24) versus the historical presents of (25) and (26). And there appear to be two cognitive factors behind these overt differences. One is the spatial shift: Phrases (23) and (24) take place in one location at the top of the ladder, (25) and (26) follow a path away from that location. The other is a shift from repeated actions to particular single actions. The picking as well as the putting in the apron were repetitive, nonunique events. The walking and dumping, on the other hand, although they might have been (and were by many speakers) supposed to have occurred repeatedly, belonged at least to a longer repetition cycle than the other actions and were treated by the speaker at this point as unique events. Thus, the two aspects in this sentence directly reflect this difference in what was being talked about. The lesson is that thoughts may contain more in the way of structure than just a sequence of foci. We saw earlier that there may be a central focus that others lead up to or away from. We see now that the foci within a thought may form clusters of their own, as determined by spatial, aspectual, and, undoubtedly, other factors.

Imagine now that one of our speakers is recalling a sequence of foci from her memory and that from time to time she reaches the end of what she judges to be an integrated thought, making that fact known by closing off the sentence syntactically and by dropping her pitch. An important question about memory is whether the thought units that surface as sentences are already formed in the mind prior to verbalization or whether the material that goes into a sentence is decided on as the speaker is talking. There is, in fact, a certain amount of evidence that the latter is true. It comes from repeated narratives obtained from the same person. As mentioned earlier, we obtained from a few subjects second versions of their story about 6 weeks after the first version had been given. We have found that the distribution of foci among thoughts can differ significantly from one version to another, with apparently different principles of integration being used to give coherence to sentences at different times.

For example, we might compare corresponding portions of Speaker 37's narratives given 6 weeks apart. It is useful to line them up as follows [phrases (27)–(39) are from the earlier narrative; phrases (40)–(46) are from the later one]:

(27)   . . *And then* (5.2) *tsk so*— . .
        then we switch to the boy
        riding on the bicycle,

(28)   *and he's riding down the*
        gravel . . path.

(29)   (1.4) (*clears throat*) *And*—
        (1.0) *we see it,*

(30)   . . *the gravel path,*

(31)   *from his point of view,*

(32)   (.8) *and then we see . . a girl*
        riding a bike,

(33)   *coming the opposite direc-*
        tion.

(34)   (.9) *And then . . the camera's*
        backed up

(35)   *and you see them going like*
        this.

(36)   . . *And then you see it from*
        his point of view again.

(37)   . . *And* (.3) *his hat blows off,*

(38)   (.55) *when they cross,*

(39)   (.25) *and* (.65) *his bike hits*
        into a rock.

(40)   (.8) *And* (.8) *tsk* (.65) *ri*—*des*
        down the path.

(41)   (2.9) *And a camera follows*
        him,

(42)   *and um* (2.95) *tsk sudden*
        there's a (.15) *girl riding*
        a bicycle,

(43)   *coming the opposite direc-*
        tion,

(44)   (.5) *and as they cross each*
        (.25) *each other,*

(45)   (1.25) *the boy's cap* (.35) *flies*
        off his head.

(46)   (.85) *And*— (.5) *he*— (.2)
        hits something,

In her first version (on the left), this speaker began what was not only a new thought but even a new episode. The thought in (27) and (28) evidently follows the character–action–location schema, in which (28) repeats the action but adds location to it. The corresponding portion of the second version was phrase (40). That focus was, however, an afterthought tacked onto the thought that had just ended, which consisted of a long sequence of foci of which I will quote only the last two, repeating (40):

(47)   *and he takes a whole box,*

(48)   *and puts it on the handlebars of his bicycle.*

(40)   (.8) *And* (.8) *tsk* (.65) *ri—des down the path.*

That (40) belongs to the preceding thought is obvious enough from the subject deletion, which is not normally found at the beginning of a new thought. To be sure, there is evidence in (40) that the speaker was at an important boundary point, that her mind was already in part occupied with what was to follow. Her expression of this focus is full of hesitations. But the point here is that, whereas the first time around the speaker included this focus of the boy riding down the path in what was clearly the beginning of something new, the second time she appended it to the end of something old. Certainly, the thoughts were organized differently with respect to this focus.

It might be supposed that this was an exceptional case, attributable perhaps to the transitional nature of the boy's riding down the path, which could be interpreted either as the end of one thing or as the beginning of another. But this is by no means an isolated example; our repeated narratives show numerous instances of differently organized thoughts. Let us proceed further with the present example. Foci (29)–(33) of version one line up pretty well with (41)–(43) of version two. Except that (29)–(31) regarding the camera angle were compressed into the single focus (41) after 6 weeks, the foci here are parallel. But we can notice that this sequence of foci completed a sentence the first time, whereas they did not do so later. Why they might complete a sentence is evident: Phrases (32)–(33) conform to the character– action–location schema. The question is why this speaker did not signal a sentence boundary after *coming the opposite direction* in her second version, as she had after exactly the same words in her first. The answer, I believe, is that she chose in her second version a different principle of thought coherence, one that led to a different alignment of foci. Rather than break after the introduction of the girl, she added the foci of their crossing and the loss of the hat, all of this together evidently comprising the entire set of events that led up to the following climax: the bike hitting a rock and falling over. Foci (41)–(45) are coherent as the set of events preparatory to the fall.

But in version one the speaker had no such coherence in mind. Having introduced the girl in the sentence ending with (33), she inserted two sentences missing from the second version, expressing thoughts that had to do with other changes of camera position. The presence of (34)–(36) marked a clear boundary between the girl's approach and the loss of the hat. There was no question in version one of those events' being included in the same thought, as they were in version two.

It thus seems to be the case that the organization of foci into thoughts is sometimes accomplished only at the time a person is talking, since it may differ from one version to the next. So far as the structure of memory is concerned, that means at the very least that a hierarchical arrangement in which each thought contains a certain fixed inventory of foci is ruled out. My guess at the moment is that people have in memory a large number of foci involving knowledge of particular objects, events, and so on plus a relatively small number of principles of coherence by which these foci can be organized into the larger units that appear in language as sentences. These principles of coherence have to do with unity in terms of images, schemas, goals, and the like. To some extent, foci are already sorted out in memory according to such principles, but to some extent the sorting takes place only when the foci are being verbalized. Bernardo (forthcoming) has performed some experiments that tend to substantiate this view, particularly by demonstrating lesser degrees of coherence at sentence boundaries.

5.   EPISODES IN THE FLOW MODEL

As a speaker moves from focus to focus, forming thought clusters as she goes, from time to time she arrives at places where the transition is particularly difficult, as is evidenced especially by an unusual amount of hesitating and stumbling. It is these places that we identified earlier as episode boundaries or, in written language, as the boundaries of paragraphs. Aside from our intuitions on this score, we have some corroboration that the location of major hesitations tends to be correlated with paragraph boundaries. A written version of Speaker 37's first narrative, minus the hesitations, was given to over a hundred subjects who were asked to put a mark wherever they thought a paragraph boundary belonged. I will refer to their responses as PARAGRAPH JUDGMENTS. If we limit our interest to those points in the narrative where at least 10% of the judges placed a boundary, we find a close correspondence with those points in the spoken narrative where the speaker hesitated for at least 2 sec.

But that is not all. It is possible to rank the paragraph judgments according to the number of people marking a boundary at the point in question. With some boundaries, there was considerable agreement, with others less, and, in fact, there was a continuum of degrees of agreement. It is also possible to rank the boundaries in the narrative according to the length of the hesitation; here, again, there is a continuum. The rank order correlation between the paragraph judgments and the hesitation lengths was .8 ($p < .05$). One is led to conclude that there is a continuum of episode boundary strengths ranging downward from those places in the narrative where there was extensive hesitating and near unanimity in paragraph judgment to those places where both measures were relatively weak.

There are various reasons for episode boundaries. A particularly strong reason is likely to be a <u>shift from one "world" to another</u>. Our speakers had been exposed to and were still thinking in terms of two distinct worlds of experience. One was the "real" world, which contained among other things a room, in which the speaker had recently sat, with a projector and screen, as well as the room in which she was presently sitting with the interviewer who had just asked her to tell what had happened in the film. The other world to which she had been exposed was the "imaginary" film world, a world in which there was a man picking pears, a boy on a bicycle who took some of the pears, and so on. Most of the time, our speakers talked about the film world, but now and then they digressed into the real one—sometimes, for example, to make a critical comment about the film, as in the following example (Subject 37):

(49) (1.15) *There's like three baskets sitting there*

(50) *and he's already got two baskets full.*

(51) *. . He does this a couple of times.*

(52) (2.55) *Um* (4.05) *the thing I noticed all the way through is that . . there's* (.5) *there's no—. . dialogue in the film,*

(53) *but there . . is* (1.0) *a lot of sound effects.*

At the beginning of (52), there was a total of 7.05 sec of hesitating, longer than at any point except the beginning of the narrative. And 97% of our judges placed a paragraph boundary at this point. It can be seen that the speaker was shifting worlds in order to comment on the sound track. Evidently, it takes a significant amount of time to make such a shift, and evidently the shift is recognized by almost everyone as a major break in the content of the narrative.

The next most striking boundary in Speaker 37's narrative occurred during the following sequence:

(54) *And all this time the guy's up in the* (.6) *tree,*

(55) *. . and he doesn't notice it.*

(56) (.9) *However the sounds are extremely loud.*

(57) (*cough*) (1.3) *So . . it's kind of funny.*

(58) *. . And then* (5.2) *tsk so—. . then we switch to the boy riding on the bicycle,*

(59) *and he's riding down the gravel . . path.*

At the beginning of (58), there was a total of 6.1 sec of hesitating and a paragraph boundary assigned by 71% of the judges. There are several reasons worth considering as to why this should be a strong boundary. Space

and time both suggest themselves as contributing factors. Spatially, this is
the point in the movie at which there was the most radical change of scene.
Unit now, everything was centered around the pear tree: The first protagonist
was seen picking in the tree, the theft of pears took place below it, and so
on. With (58) we leave the pear tree scene and follow the boy to a new
location somewhere on the path. As for time, we find a quality at the beginning of (58) that might be called TEMPORAL ELASTICITY. The boy's ride
down the gravel path may take a greater or lesser period of time—it makes
no difference. Whether he rides for a few seconds, a few minutes, or longer
is irrelevant to the telling of the story. Before this point, event followed
event in quick, inexorable succession, as will shortly be the case again.
But, at this boundary, time is stretchable and vague. Marked breaks in both
spatial and temporal coherence thus seem to produce the need for time-
consuming mental processing of the kind we are considering.

Another change observable at (58) has to do with configurations of
characters. It is here that we leave the pear picker, who will take no further
part in the action until we return to him near the end of the narrative. The
girl is shortly to appear, herself then to be replaced by three other characters
central to the interaction. Although the continued presence of the boy
provides some continuity across this boundary, we are clearly leaving one
major character alignment and entering another.

Finally, we can consider the nature and relationships of the events themselves. What happened prior to this point was centered on the theft of pears.
We are now about to enter a sequence of events centered on the accident
on the path, with details leading up to it and a number of events involved
in its aftermath. Thus, the boundary at (58) is a trough between two peaks
of event salience: the theft and the accident. Event structure, then, seems
to be another factor contributing to this type of boundary. The events
within a coherent episode are enabling or causing events for a climactic
central event that forms the episode's peak or else are aftermath events
leading away from such a peak. An episode boundary is the point of transition between such clusters of events.

Thus, the beginning of (58) represents a strong conjunction of change in
all the main factors that lead to episode coherence: spatial change, temporal
elasticity, character change, and orientation toward a new central event.
To the extent that other people interpreted the film in the same terms, we
might expect that they, too, would exhibit strong episode boundaries at
this point. And, in fact, if we exempt those long hesitations associated with
other factors, such as shifts into a different world, we find that 12 out of
20 narratives show their longest hesitations at just this point, with a mean
length of hesitating of 4.13 sec. (It is interesting also to note the different
way in which Speaker 37 handled this same boundary in her second narra-

tive, as shown particularly in phrases 40–41, where hesitation and sentence boundary did not completely coincide.)

The following can be cited as an episode boundary of intermediate strength:

(60)   . . *And he pulls the (.8) tsk goat by the guy who's up in the tree,*

(61)   *(.9) and disappears.*

(62)   *(.9) And— (2.9) the next people . . who come by,*

(63)   *(.9) and there's a little boy on a bicycle*

(64)   . . *who comes by from the other direction.*

The total hesitating at the beginning of (62) is 4.35 sec, and 53% of our judges placed a paragraph boundary at that point. The rank order is 5 (out of 11) on both scales. Spatially, it should be noted, there is little change at this point, except that the boy approached the tree from a different direction. There was something of a temporal break as the boy approached. And there was something of a change in event structure as new details were to be aimed at the theft of the pears, although preceding events to some extent were also preparatory to the theft. The strongest factor at this boundary was, undoubtedly, the introduction of a new and important character. I doubt that these various factors are quantifiable in any completely objective way, but we can see informally that, whereas character change is particularly strong at this point, other factors influencing such boundaries are weaker than in the previous example. Spatial change, evidently a factor of special importance, was the weakest of all. Hence, the midway ranking on both scales.

I will not cite here other examples of episode boundaries with decreasing strength but will rest my case by repeating that the strength of such boundaries does clearly vary with the strength of the several factors I have mentioned. Our data, then, do not support the hypothesis that a narrative can be unambiguously divided into a fixed number of episodes or paragraphs. They instead suggest that as a speaker moves from focus to focus (or from thought to thought) there are certain points at which there may be a more or less radical change in space, time, character configuration, event structure, or, even, world. Each of these factors may contribute to a processing difficulty at such a point, and each may contribute more or less. The processing difficulty appears in speech as hesitation and is recognized in writing as a paragraph division. Rather than think of an experience as being stored in memory in terms of distinct episodes, it seems preferable to think of a more complex storage in terms of coherent spaces, coherent temporal continuities, coherent configurations of characters, coherent event sequences, and coherent worlds. At points where all of these change in a maximal way, an episode boundary is strongly present. But often one or another will change considerably while others will change less radically, and all kinds of varied interactions between these several factors are possible.

6.   CONCLUSION

Let me summarize the points I have tried to make. There seem to be certain units of information storage in the mind of the sort that I have called FOCI. They are, in a sense, the basic units of memory in that they represent the amount of information to which a person can devote his central attention at any one time. During the verbalization of something recalled, the speaker's focus of attention moves from one focus to the next, although it is capable of abandoning a focus before it has been completely verbalized, of dwelling on the same focus for several phrases, or of returning to a focus already but perhaps not satisfactorily communicated. Foci are expressed linguistically in units, phrases, that are usually characterized by a case frame syntax and by a phrase final intonation contour. Many of them in English begin with *and* or other similar conjunctions.

A speaker clusters foci into thoughts, which appear in language as sentences, syntactically closed, with a characteristic sentence-final intonation contour. There are various principles that bring coherence to the foci within a sentence. Those exemplified above were unity with respect to a certain object or setting, unity of schema, such as the character–action–location schema, and the unity that comes from events being aimed at a single goal. Doubtless, there are a number of other principles of thought coherence. The fact that there do exist various principles of this sort allows a speaker to integrate foci in different ways when he or she is talking about the same thing at different times.

As one moves from focus to focus or from thought to thought, there are at certain points significant breaks in the coherence of space, time, characters, events, and worlds. Such breaks lead to conspicuous hesitations and are identified as paragraph boundaries in written language. People seem not to store episodes as such, however, but rather to store coherent scenes, temporal sequences, character configurations, event sequences, and worlds, all of which interact with each other to produce greater or lesser boundaries when some or all of them change more or less radically.

That, at least, is how it looks at present. Further work will undoubtedly lead to revisions, extensions, and elaborations of these ideas. There is, above all, a pressing need to corroborate them through similar studies of more natural verbalizations of real experiences; for example, of narratives embedded in actual conversations. And the cross-cultural aspect of our work was omitted here; it remains to be discussed in other works at other times.

REFERENCES

Bernardo, Robert (forthcoming) "The Coherence Theory of Sentence Use."

Buswell, Guy Thomas (1935) How People Look at Pictures, University of Chicago Press, Chicago.

Butterworth, Brian (1975) "Hesitation and Semantic Planning in Speech," Journal of Psycholinguistic Research 4, 75–87.

Chafe, Wallace L. (1977a) "Creativity in Verbalization and its Implications for the Nature of Stored Knowledge," in Roy O. Freedle, ed., Discourse Production and Comprehension, Ablex, Norwood, New Jersey.

Chafe, Wallace L. (1977b) "The Recall and Verbalization of Past Experience," in Roger W. Cole, ed., Current Issues in Linguistic Theory, Indiana University Press, Bloomington, Indiana.

Christensen, Francis (1965) "A Generative Rhetoric of the Paragraph," College Composition and Communication 16, 144–156.

Givón Talmy (1975) "Focus and the Scope of Assertion: Some Bantu Evidence," Studies in African Linguistics 6, 185–205.

Hopper, Paul (this volume) "Aspect and Foregrounding in Discourse."

Labov, William (1972) Language in the Inner City: Studies in the Black English Vernacular, University of Pennsylvania Press, Philadelphia, Pennsylvania.

Longacre, Robert E. (1976) An Anatomy of Speech Notions, Peter de Ridder Press, Lisse.

Longacre, Robert E. (this volume) "The Paragraph as a Grammatical Unit."

Mayer, Richard E. (1977) Thinking and Problem Solving: An Introduction to Human Cognition and Learning, Scott, Foresman, Glenview, Illinois.

Newtson, Darren (1976) "Foundations of Attribution: The Perception of Ongoing Behavior," in J. H. Harvey, W. J. Ickes, and R. F. Kidd, eds., New Directions in Attribution Research, Erlbaum, Hillsdale, New Jersey.

Pawley, Anthony and Frances Syder (forthcoming) "English Conversational Structures."

Robinson, John A. (1976) "Sampling Autobiographical Memory," Cognitive Psychology 8, 578–595.

Rosch, Eleanor and Carolyn B. Mervis (1975) "Family Resemblances: Studies in the Internal Structure of Categories," Cognitive Psychology 7, 573–605.

Salaman, Esther A. (1970) "A Collection of Moments: A Study of Involuntary Memories," St. Martin's Press, New York.

COMMUNICATIVE GOALS AND STRATEGIES: BETWEEN DISCOURSE AND SYNTAX

DAVID M. LEVY

Stanford University and Xerox Palo Alto Research Center

> *When thinking attempts to pursue something that has claimed its attention, it may happen that on the way it undergoes a change. It is advisable, therefore, in what follows to pay attention to the path of thought rather than to its content.*
>
> —MARTIN HEIDEGGER (1969:23)

1. INTRODUCTION

In the introduction to their recent book, *Cohesion in English* (Halliday and Hasan 1976), Halliday and Hasan make the point that cohesion, which they describe as "the set of semantic resources for linking a sentence with what has gone before," is not a structural property of texts. Their argument is sound and careful. (I will return to it briefly in Section 5.) I agree with their basic analysis but not with some of the presuppositions and implications

Syntax and Semantics, Volume 12:
Discourse and Syntax

of their approach; for, although denying the centrality of a particular kind of structure, they are still committed to (or focused on) the TEXT AS SUCH. One might say that they are TEXT-BASED. "Cohesion," they say, "is part of the system of language. The potential for cohesion lies in the systematic resources of reference, ellipsis and so on that are built into language itself [p. 5]." But the text is only one-third of the communicative trinity, the other two-thirds consisting of the speaker (or writer) and hearer (or reader), both of whom participate by virtue of certain mental capacities. Cohesion, I will argue, is most certainly REALIZED THROUGH the speaker's language resources, but its ultimate reference point must be found in the structure of the linguistic content and in the flow of the speaker's thought processes. In this chapter I will initially adopt a MIND-BASED stance in order to see what discourse looks like from the perspective of the producing and comprehending mind rather than from the structured text. I intend to examine the importance of characterizing and understanding the speaker's mental states and processes in relation to discourse and syntax.

As a researcher in the field of artificial intelligence, I am currently attempting to formulate a process model of language comprehension. Although I do not intend to describe this model here, I do plan to bring certain of its principles to bear on the issue of the coherence and comprehensibility of discourse. The work on natural language in artificial intelligence can be roughly distinguished from that in linguistics by its preference for a mind-based rather than a text-based approach. Such an approach deemphasizes the study of the text as an object of study in itself and stresses the study of mental representations in relation to the PROCESS of communication.

The central thesis of this chapter is that the study of discourse must come to terms with the mental activity of the speaker, that it must make reference to the processes in which he is engaged while speaking. I will attempt to show that the speaker encodes important components of his thought processes in his utterance (the very thought processes that lead to the production of that utterance). I will explore the form that this encoding takes as well as the role that the recognition of these processes plays in the hearer's process of comprehension. I will argue that much of the cohesive properties of discourse[1] are best captured by reference to the speaker's mental states

---

[1] In English we have two adjectives that are closely related etymologically, "cohesive" and "coherent," both of which can be applied to discourse; we can say that a discourse is cohesive or coherent, and, in either case, we communicate that the discourse "hangs together." But for me, at least, there is a shade of connotative difference in this choice. "Cohesive" suggests only structural binding, whereas "coherent" borders on "comprehensible" and suggests, in addition to cohesion, the mental processes whereby the discourse is understood. If this naive analysis is right, we have, built right into our lexicon, a folk linguistics and psychology that instructs us in the relationship between the structure of discourse and the process of comprehension.

and processes and that the current research on text grammars is not only mistaken (as Halliday and Hasan imply) by imputing structure where there is none but also that it is working at the wrong level of description to capture the salient generalizations. I will propose an alternative formulation in terms of COMMUNICATIVE GOALS and COMMUNICATIVE STRATEGIES framed in a larger model of language production as a planning process.

The argument of this chapter will proceed from intuitive, pretheoretical observations of some data to the search for a theoretical formalism and the questions that the search raises. I will start, in Section 2, by presenting and examining several examples from the data I have collected that strongly suggest the need for the representation of mental processes. In Section 3 I will pursue one of these examples far enough to sketch the outline, if not the details, of such a process representation. In Section 4 I will consider what the larger framework must look like, what issues must be dealt with, and which directions are most likely to bear fruit. Finally, in Section 5 I will compare this fledgling approach to speech act theory and to the research on text grammars.

2. RECONSTRUCTING THE SPEAKER'S MENTAL PROCESSES

During the 2-day period of course registration preceding the Fall 1976 quarter at Stanford, I collected a set of oral discourses. Standing with a tape recorder outside the hall within which registration was taking place, I approached students as they completed the registration process and made the request (more or less): "Please tell me your course schedule and explain how you ended up with it, what made you to decide to organize it in the way you did." The following is typical of the responses I got to my request, this one from a female undergraduate:

> *OK, well, I'm taking French, it's either two or three . . . . I signed up for both and I'm going to one or the other, and then Poly Sci one and American Economic History, because I want to major in Econ and I use my French for Humanities, 'cause otherwise I had to take some drama thing, and didn't want that. And like it's nine, ten, eleven, I hope, and that's perfect, because then I, it's not too early but then I've got the whole afternoon. And, I don't know, there were a lot of ones that I wanted to take at ten, but there were too many at ten so that ruled out a bunch of choices, just from the time conflict. And then, like my adviser told me to take American Economic History this quarter because Elementary Econ is next quarter, and it's a better teacher. So that's sort of what I did, I think.*

This discourse reveals the rambly, discursive[2] style of an oral, unplanned response. It is, in some sense, more loosely structured than carefully prepared and edited text, but, in exchange for its less elegant design, it offers some fascinating insights into the speaker's thought processes while she was producing it. In this section I want to propose a particular kind of "explanation," a reconstruction of what the speaker's thought processes were likely to have been while she was in the process of producing the text. This will be an informal characterization of what the speaker was "thinking," couched not in the theoretical terms of psychology or linguistics but in the ordinary, phenomenal language of goals and intentions. I will look at three examples taken from the above discourse, each of which focuses on a different aspect of the reconstruction process.

Example 1: The Flow of Thought

In this first example, I want to examine the initial segment of the above discourse.

> *OK, well, I'm taking French, **it's either two or three** .... **I signed up for both and I'm going to one or the other**, and then Poly Sci one and American Economic History*

What I find particularly striking about this segment is the fact that an entire parenthetical remark (indicated in bold) has been inserted into what would have otherwise been a simple listing; that is, the speaker has said the above rather than *I'm taking French, Poly Sci one, and American Economic History*. Why did this happen? The simplest and most intuitively satisfying answer can be found by reconstructing what must have been going on in the speaker's mind as she framed and produced these utterances. I therefore propose the following steps:

STEP 1

My request of the speaker presented her with three initial goals:

1. to specify the courses in her course schedule;
2. to specify the times of her courses;
3. to present some motivation, justification, or explanation for each of her selections.[3]

---

[2] Note the common etymology of "discourse" and "discursive." They derive from the Latin meaning "the act of running about," thereby suggesting the origin of discourse in the FLOW, the PROCESS of speech.

[3] Of course, it was not necessary that she propose a separate explanation for each course and course time. She could also have provided explanations couched in terms of an overall PATTERN of choices. She did so, in fact, as we will see below, when she said *that's perfect, because then I, it's not too early, but then I've got the whole afternoon.*

The speaker initiated her response with the intention of satisfying the first of these goals, that of specifying her courses. One of the strategies available to her for achieving this goal[4] was to LIST her courses one by one. So, she first said *I'm taking French*, this statement being the expression of one of the activities in her course schedule.[5] On tape, in fact, you can hear the speaker's voice rise at the end of her pronunciation of *French*, this being a characteristic "listing" intonation contour.

STEP 2

In the process of producing this first utterance, it was necessary for the speaker to describe the course to her hearer, and she chose the surface expression *French*. But, realizing that this was a less informative description than the situation probably warranted,[6] she established the goal of FURTHER SPECIFYING the referent. To satisfy this goal, she then said *it's either two or three* (meaning, most likely, that she was taking French 2 or French 3).

STEP 3

The use of *or* is typically ambiguous. An expression of the form "x or y" can be the result of (at least) indecision or the inability to recall the right description of some object. Here, the speaker probably meant to express the fact that either she had NOT YET DECIDED between French 2 and French 3 or she COULD NOT REMEMBER whether the description of the course she had enrolled in was French 2 or French 3. She "realized" this potential ambiguity, established a subsidiary goal of reducing it, and satisfied this new goal by saying *I signed up for both*.

STEP 4

This last statement would, in itself, have been sufficient to disambiguate, but she chose to ELABORATE this statement with the comment *and I'm going to one or the other*. This elaboration shed further light on her indecision and her response to it by referring to a particular registration strategy known to

---

[4] To see that LISTING her courses was possibly only one of several strategies available to her for specifying them, consider the following discourse:

> *Okay. It's not gonna help you a whole lot, from the standpoint that I'm a business student. First-year business students, they have a core of required courses. If a person exempts some of the core or required courses, then they're at liberty to take other courses, but for the fall, the autumn quarter, you're . . . they have assigned courses. And since I wasn't able to exempt any courses, then I had to take the assigned courses for the fall quarter.*

We see the speaker here employing a very general communicative strategy that might be called INSTANCE-OF-CLASS. Its use permitted him to characterize his courses without listing them by establishing that he was an instance of the class of first-year business students. His courses were deducible from this fact.

[5] Note also that, because of the context in which this statement was uttered, it was a description of a choice made, its having been necessary for her to choose which courses she would take.

[6] See the maxim of quantity in Grice's (1967) cooperative principle: Be as informative as required but not more informative than is required.

all students: If you can't decide between several course alternatives, postpone your decision by enrolling in all of them, attending them all for a while, and making your eventual decision based on what you observe while attending them.

STEP 5

Finally, having cascaded through this series of goals, each utterance triggered by a need established by the previous one, she returned to her listing of courses and said *and then Poly Sci one. . . .*

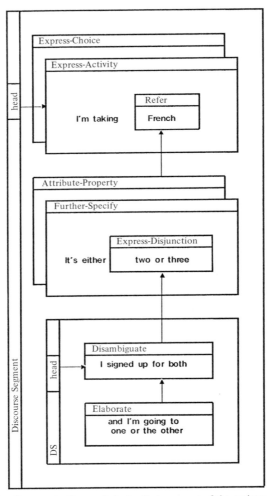

Figure 1   Communicative goals in the first segment of the registration text.

Figure 1 summarizes these observations in terms of the speaker's communicative goals. A box surrounding an English phrase should be interpreted as meaning that this phrase was uttered in order to satisfy the goal printed at the top of the box. Overlapping boxes mean that the speaker was trying to satisfy more than one goal by producing that utterance. So, for example, the boxes labeled "Express-activity" and "Express-choice" are a shorthand for the conjecture that by saying *I'm taking French* the speaker was trying to satisfy the goals of expressing an activity (in her course schedule) and expressing a choice made. And the overlapping boxes marked "Attribute-property" and "Further-specifiy" indicate that the speaker, by saying *It's either two or three*, was trying to further specify *French* by attributing the property *two or three* to it. Vertical arrows indicate dependencies between goals, like the arrow from "Further-specify" to "Refer," which indicates that *it's either two or three* is a further specification of *French*. Finally, the boxes vertically labeled "Discourse-segment" are intended to provide bracketing for the goal boxes. In each of these, an arrow points from the label *"Head"* to the box that functions as the organizing goal for the entire segment. Thus, the discourse segment whose head points to "Disambiguate" should be interpreted as saying that the function of the discourse segment *I signed up for both and I'm going to one or the other* as a whole was to resolve the ambiguity of *it's either two or three*.

So why didn't the speaker just say *I'm taking French, Poly Sci one, and American Economic History?* The answer seems to be that, in attempting to characterize her French course, she was led to specify it in slightly ambiguous terms that led her to a disambiguating statement and a natural (follow-through) elaboration. The cohesiveness of this portion of the discourse, its comprehensibility, derives from the functional links between the utterances provided by the communicative goals like Further-specify and Disambiguate. (Such goals, called TEXTUAL goals, will be discussed in Sections 3 and 4.) But these links derive their meaning from an understanding of the speaker's mental processes: why and how she was carried along by a set of embedded subgoals. The FLOW of this portion of the discourse can be understood and explained only with reference to the flow of the speaker's thought processes.

Example 2:   Manipulating the Mental Representation of an Object

Let us now turn to a second example from the same discourse:

And like it's nine, ten, eleven.

First of all, what does it mean? On my own reading (upheld by all native "informants" whose opinion I have asked), the speaker is saying that her three courses—French, Poly Sci one, and American Economic History—are at nine, ten, and eleven o'clock. These are almost certainly morning clock times. Less certain, although likely, is the fact that the French course is at nine o'clock, Poly Sci one at ten, and American Economic History at eleven. Also likely is that all three courses meet on the same days. Under this interpretation, then, *it* is some sort of reference to the speaker's course schedule, and *nine, ten,* and *eleven* are elliptical references to or descriptions of clock times.

This is a fascinating clause, not just from the point of view of the speaker's underlying goals, but also in terms of its syntactic complexity. I have used this clause elsewhere to make the point that language comprehension cannot (always) proceed linearly from syntactic parsing to semantic interpretation. This clause presents numerous syntactic ambiguities, especially in its oral form—Is *like* a preposition? Is *its* a contraction or a possessive? Where is the clause boundary? After *nine*? After *ten*?—which cannot be resolved without reference to its meaning, without understanding that *it* is a reference to the speaker's course schedule.

Before attempting the reconstruction of this clause, we will need to examine several kinds of mental structures that appear to play an important role in the speaker's production of the clause: a conceptual structure, two communicative goals, and two surface syntactic structures. The conceptual structure is the notion of course schedule, the elusive referent of *it* in our target clause. What exactly is a course schedule? In sparsest logical terms, a course schedule is really quite simple: a pairing or one-to-one mapping between activities called "courses" and entities called "time slots." This simple characterization is inadequate, however, for a course schedule really has quite a bit more

	Monday	Tuesday	Wednesday	Thursday	Friday
9AM					
	French		French		French
10AM					
	Poly Sci one		Poly Sci one		Poly Sci one
11AM					
	Amer. Econ. History		Amer. Econ. History		Amer. Econ. History
noon					
1PM					
2PM					

Figure 2   A typical representation of a course schedule.

"structure." A hint of this can be gotten by considering a typical representation of a course schedule as depicted in Figure 2, a two-dimensional grid with days along one axis and clock hours along the other, into which the student fills the names or descriptions of his/her courses. Hidden in this diagram is a great deal of culturally and institutionally determined knowledge of time. This includes the knowledge that:

1.   A university week stretches from Monday to Friday and from about eight in the morning to five in the evening.

2.   There is a cyclical repetition to university weeks. A certain number of them strung together constitute a semester or quarter.

3.   There is also a pattern of repetitions to course meeting times within and across weeks. Two examples of typical Stanford time-slots are: Monday, Wednesday, and Friday from 9:10 a.m. to 10 a.m. (repeated over 8 to 10 weeks) and Tuesday and Thursday from 9:10 a.m. to 10:30 a.m.

The point here, then, is that a course schedule is actually a tremendously complex mental and cultural object with many "dimensions." The notion of time-slot (as that of a course or of taking a course[7]) has quite a lot of structure derived from various cultural, physical, mental, and institutional "facts."

Let us now turn to the two communicative goals, Attribute-property and Express-set, the first of which was introduced briefly as one of the goals satisfied by the utterance *it's either two or three*. (See Figure 1.) Property attribution is a goal in which an ATTRIBUTER intends to associate some PROPERTY with an OBJECT. So, if I say *The bread knife is under the cookie sheet*, I am trying to satisfy the goal of attributing the property of being *under the cookie sheet* to the bread knife. (Actually, of course, the communicative goal is to get the hearer to associate the location *under the cookie sheet* with his knowledge of the knife.) Or, more simply, by saying *Andy is*

---

[7] As a hint of the complexity inherent in the notion of taking a course, consider the fact that it has at least two facets. Taking a course is a kind of contract between student and university, with the professor functioning as the university's agent. The student agrees to perform certain services—paying tuition, gaining the professor's approval as indicated by grades—in return for which the university grants the student credit that he can apply toward a degree. In this sense, taking a course is some kind of abstract, atemporal relation. But this contract is also realized by certain "physical" actions—attending classes, taking exams, writing papers. Combined with the resources provided by tense and aspect in English, these different perspectives on course-taking result in some very interesting utterances in the registration texts. Exercise for the reader: Why, in the following fragment, did the speaker REPAIR (see Schegloff in this volume on "repairs") his utterance, changing *I'll take* to *I took*?

> And then the last class I'm taking is Chemistry 31. The nine o'clock class was closed, the ten o'clock will probably already be filled up, so **I'll take**, **I took** the eight o'clock class."

five years old I intend to attribute a certain age to a particular person.[8]
Express-set is the speaker's goal of naming or describing some set of objects
he has in mind, as when the student in our discourse says *I'm taking
French . . . and then Poly Sci one, and American Economic History.*

Finally, we need to consider the two syntactic structures that will play
a role in the reconstruction. The first of these, which I will call *it-be-*
complement, consists of the word *it* followed by some form of the verb *be*
followed by a complement construct. The discourse given earlier contains
three instances: *it's either two or three, it's nine, ten, eleven, it's not too early*,
and *it's a better teacher.* The second structure, called Surface-listing, consists
of a sequence of surface syntactic entities separated by commas.[9] Examples
include: *I came, I saw, I conquered* and *two pounds of coffee, three dozen
eggs, and a jar of mustard.* These two structures are important, it should be
obvious, because of their functional relationship to the two communicative
goals immediately above. A clause having the structure of *it-be-*complement
is often used to attribute some property to the referent of *it*, and a phrase
with the structure of Surface-listing is often used to satisfy or achieve the
goal Express-set.[10]

Now, how does the clause *And like it's nine, ten, eleven* mean what it
means? Why did the specification of the speaker's course times come to
expression in this particular form? At this point in the discourse, the speaker
wanted to specify the times of her courses. She was focusing on her course
schedule. But a course schedule, as we have already seen, is not by any means
inherently a linear object. At this moment, however, the speaker was
THINKING OF her schedule as a linear sequence of courses (probably because
she had just completed a listing of them: *French, Poly Sci one, American
Economic History*). She needed to express the set of course time-slots (the
Express-set goal), and, since she might have been "picturing" a typical
day in her schedule (see, for example, the Monday morning portion of
Figure 2), it was natural for her to choose a Surface-listing structure. She

[8] It is common in linguistics to distinguish between ATTRIBUTIVE and EQUATIVE clauses. An
attributive clause, for example, *The grass is green*, assigns the property green to grass, whereas
an equative clause, for example, *John is the guy I told you about yesterday*, merges two referents
(the idea being that the hearer was previously aware of John and the guy mentioned yesterday
as two separate entities. My use of property attribution here subsumes these two categories,
for an equative clause still implies directionality of association. So, for example, by saying
John is the guy I told you about yesterday I am focusing on John and am assigning to him the
identity of the guy mentioned yesterday.

[9] For the limited purposes of this example, I am concentrating on written rather than on
spoken language. The description of Surface-listing adequate for spoken language would have
to take prosody rather than punctuation into account.

[10] To see that these surface structures do not ALWAYS function to satisfy these two communicative goals, consider clauses like *It is John who came in* and *my friend, the baker, who
lives next door.*

was then able to specify the course times by (*a*) setting up a syntactic parallel, *nine, ten, eleven*; and (*b*) selecting a syntactic device, the *it-be*-complement pattern, which could communicate that some property was being attributed to an object. What made such a strategy reasonable was a reliance on the hearer's ability to figure out what must have been meant by attributing the PROPERTY *nine, ten, eleven* to the OBJECT *French, Poly Sci one, American Economic History*.

This example focuses on a different aspect of mental processes than does the first one. The first example emphasized the flow of the speaker's thought processes. This example, however, suggests the need for a more complex notion of the way words and phrases refer to mental objects. Reference has sometimes been viewed as a link between phrases. As others have observed that phrases can refer to constructs that are not even explicit in the text, this view has been amended to say that phrases refer to concepts. But the example given argues for yet another modification. The referent of *it* is neither the phrase *course schedule* nor a single, unified concept of course schedule. Course schedule, as we have seen, is a vast tapestry woven from many strands of physical, mental, and cultural knowledge. In uttering *it* in this context, the speaker adopts a particular PERSPECTIVE ON, a particular way of viewing the mass of relations that constitute the course schedule—in this case, as a sequence of courses. (In fact, we see the speaker adopting a different perspective on her course schedule several clauses later in the discourse. When she says *it's not too early*, she appears to be thinking of a "typical day" in her school week and viewing the three courses as a coherent "chunk" that can be slid along the day's time axis.) Hence, reference must be viewed as a strategic process whereby the speaker does not simply IDENTIFY a particular, clearly bounded object but even CONSTRUCTS that object by selecting from a field of relations those properties that are momentarily relevant. On this alternative view, then, the speaker confers object status; he does not simply point.

A second point that emerges concerns the relationship between the structures of the speaker's thought and language. The adoption of a particular strategy for talking about her courses (the listing *I'm taking French . . . and then Poly Sci one, and American Economic History*) appears to have led her to think about her course schedule in a particular way, one that then influenced her later choice of words for asserting her course times.

Finally, we also see through this example that the notion of syntactic parallelism—in this case, between *French, Poly Sci one, American Economic History* and *nine, ten, eleven*—needs to be understood with reference to the flow and structure of the speaker's thought processes. This is not to say that the parallelism is not THERE IN THE TEXT, only that its roots are deeper than its surface manifestation.

Example 3:   Discourse Structure

As a final example of the method of reconstruction, let us look at the overall shape of our sample discourse. How can we understand or explain it? I propose answering this question with reference to (*a*) the communicative goals that the discourse satisfies; and (*b*) the language structures that were used to satisfy them.

Introduction	Open discourse
	Okay, well
Movement 1: Focus on courses	Specify courses
	I'm taking French, it's either two or three . . ..I signed up for both, and I'm going to one or the other, and then Poly Sci one and American Economic History.
	Explain course choices
	because I want to major in Econ, and I use my French for Humanities, 'cause otherwise I had to take some drama thing, and didn't want that.
Movement 2: Focus on times	Specify times
	And like it's nine, ten, eleven, I hope.
	Explain times
	and that's perfect, because then I, it's not too early, but then I've got the whole afternoon.
Movement 3: (Coda) Focus on explanation	Further explain one time slot
	And, I don't know, there were a lot of ones that I wanted to take at ten, but there were too many at ten, so that ruled out a bunch of choices, just from the time conflict.
	Further explain one course slot
	And then, like my adviser told me to take American Economic History this quarter, because Elementary Econ is next quarter, and it's a better teacher.
Conclusion	Close discourse
	So that's sort of what I did, I think.

Figure 3   The structure of the discourse.

Figure 3 presents, in outline, the structure of the discourse. We see that it decomposes into three major "movements." In the first movement, the speaker focuses on the courses in her schedule. (We might say that she PLAYS ON THE THEME of her courses.) Choosing a listing strategy, she enumerates her courses, followed by which she expresses some of the motivations for these choices (i.e., she explains her choices). The first segment of this movement, then, the course listing, can stand alone as an independent structure—a "free-standing structure," one might say—but the second segment is clearly dependent. This can be seen in part just because the second segment begins with a dependent clause (. . . *because I want to major in Econ . . .*) but also because it refers back to the courses presented in the first segment. In other words, there is a structural dependence in the latter segment that can be understood with reference to its dependence on the goals of the first segment.

In the second movement, the speaker focuses on the times of her courses. This movement also breaks down into two segments. In the first, she specifies her course times, and in the second she further motivates or evaluates her choice of schedule. Whereas the motivational segment in part two of the first movement was based on individual course choices (i.e., the speaker explains her choice of French with reference to the Humanities requirement and her choice of American Economic History and Poly Sci one with reference to her major), this new explanation is based on the overall shape of her schedule (i.e., it starts not too early in the morning and ends not too late in the afternoon).

In the first two movements, then, courses and times are the dominant themes with explanation or motivation as subthemes. This is reversed in the third movement, where, in a kind of coda, the speaker focuses on explanation and relegates courses and times to the status of subthemes. She first focuses on the 10 o'clock time slot to further specify some of the constraints on it. Then she returns to the subject of one of her courses to further elaborate the reasons for choosing it.

We see, then, that the form of the discourse is well-motivated and comprehensible, if not extremely regular. (It does not reduce to a single, elegant structure.[11]) To understand it, we need to realize that my initial request of the speaker presented her with three initial IDEATIONAL goals[12]:

1. to specify her course choices
2. to specify the times of her courses
3. to explain or motivate these choices

[11] In Footnote 4, we saw a more "elegant" design. By using the instance-of-class strategy, the speaker was able to package all three major communicative goals into a simpler structure.

[12] Ideational goals, along with the textual goals mentioned in Example 1, and a third class, interpersonal goals, will be discussed in Sections 3 and 4.

Viewed from the perspective of these goals, her discourse has a clearly identifiable shape, which might be summarized as follows.

Express courses
Explain courses

Express times
Explain times

Explain one time
Explain one course

Viewed at a more surface level of structuring, it also has a clearly identifiable shape, but of a different kind. If we just attend to the clausal structure, we can see that there is a great deal of syntactic parallelism across movements:

MOVEMENT 1:   *Okay . . . because*

MOVEMENT 2:   *And . . . because*

MOVEMENT 3:   *And . . . but*

MOVEMENT 4:   *And . . . because*

There is, of course, a great deal more that can be—and needs to be—said about the regularities that structure this discourse. The point of this third example is a simple one: What we call the discourse structure of this text is a complex function of the structure of the speaker's schedule, the structure of her thought processes, and the structure of her language.[13]

These three examples highlight different aspects of the method of reconstructing the speaker's mental processes. The first example focused on the flow of the speaker's thought processes (the structure of THOUGHT), the second on the representation of the ideas beings expressed (the structure of CONTENT), and the third on the structure of the discourse as realized by the speaker's language resources (the structure of LANGUAGE). These three kinds of structure are in no sense independent, as should be obvious from the fact that each example was forced to make reference to all three. These examples, while oriented toward understanding and explaining language production, also suggest that the reconstruction of the speaker's mental processes is an important component of the comprehension process itself.

This concludes the informal discussion of reconstruction. In the next two sections I turn to the question of formalizing the notions of communicative goals and strategies.

---

[13] See Grosz's (1977) examination of "task-oriented" dialogues (between an expert and a novice assembling an air compressor). She discovered that their structure arose from the structure of the task itself and the structure of language and explored the ways in which the structure of the task helped a comprehender "focus" on the most salient portions of the dialogues.

3. COMMUNICATIVE GOALS AND STRATEGIES

> Revealing semantic descriptions will stop being so elusive when linguists and phi-
> losophers start to recognize that the complex semantic structure of natural languages
> cannot be described by the simple apparatus devised for the limited vocabulary of
> logical words [Jerrold J. Katz 1977:583].

The model to be proposed here is very much a functional one. A speaker has a number of ideas he wants to express and a corresponding set of communicative goals. Some of these goals (called IDEATIONAL goals) are concerned directly with the communication of these ideas or propositions; some (called TEXTUAL goals) are concerned with the weaving of these ideas into a coherent text; and still others (called INTERPERSONAL goals) deal with presentation of self in relation to the hearer, with matters of status and attitude.[14] The speaker's language provides him with a set of resources for expressing these goals: with words and phrases that express concepts, with conjunctions that interrelate utterances, with intonation patterns that express attitudes, and so on. But this still leaves one gaping hole: between goals and expressions (or, metaphorically, between discourse and syntax). How is this gap to be bridged? I propose the term COMMUNICATIVE STRATEGY (or COMMUNICATIVE PROCESS) for the mental process whereby the speaker realizes a particular communicative goal as a linguistic expression. In this section, I will explore the nature of these strategies by way of an example suggested by the registration text, the use of *or*.

As mentioned in the previous section, the use of *or* in the clause *it's either two or three* is potentially ambiguous; the speaker is saying either that she can't recall the name of the course she has selected (and is therefore listing the two candidate descriptions that come to mind) or that she hasn't been able to decide between two candidate courses. What these two possibilities have in common is the "logical meaning" of *or*, namely, the presentation of a set of logical alternatives, only one of which is "true." What is missing from this description, however, yet is clearly necessary for the comprehension of the text, is some reference to mental processes, the process of recollection (retrieval from memory) in the first instance, and the process of choosing in the second. How might we capture these insights?

Consider the communicative goal called Refer the goal of referring by linguistic means to some physical or mental object. Imagine that there is a communicative strategy that realizes this goal, that allows the speaker to formulate and utter a linguistic expression that will allow the hearer to identify this object. (I will label this strategy or process with the name of the goal it realizes and call it Refer as well.) What might this strategy look

---

[14] The terms IDEATIONAL, TEXTUAL, and INTERPERSONAL are borrowed from Halliday (1970). He uses them to describe the three functions of language.

like? A major portion of it would be concerned with categorizing the object in such a way that the hearer could uniquely identify it and could understand the speaker's attitude toward it. But there would be certain instances in which a unique characterization could not be achieved, two of these cases being those just mentioned above. In the first case, that in which the attempt to recollect yielded an incomplete description that could characterize more than one object, this strategy would specify satisfying the more specific goal of expressing an incompletely retrieved description; in the latter case, it would call for the satisfaction of the communicative goal of expressing an unresolved choice. Figure 4 presents a partial description of this Refer strategy, written, on the analogy of a computer program, as a sequence of steps with conditional branches. Adopting the conventions of computer programs, a parenthesized expression following the name of a strategy is the ARGUMENT to that strategy. Hence, *Express-incompletely-retrieved-description (candidate descriptions)* in this figure means: Execute the Express-incompletely-retrieved-description strategy, giving it the candidate descriptions as initial inputs.

Refer (object)

.
.

Formulate a description of object

.
.

If there is more than one description, then
  If this is due to a memory retrieval problem, then
    Express-incompletely-retrieved-description (candidate descriptions)
  else, If this is because a choice has not yet been made, then
    Express-unresolved-choice (candidate descriptions)

Figure 4   A partial description of the "Refer" strategy.

Let us pursue this exercise a bit further and examine the constructs called Express-incompletely-retrieved-description and Express-unresolved-choice. These are the names of communicative goals that must be satisfied, but (continuing the convention of naming communicative strategies by the goals they are intended to realize) they can also be considered the names of communicative strategies. In keeping with the computer program analogy, we can view the mention of these constructs in Figure 4 as subroutine calls to communicative SUBstrategies. What would they look like internally? Express-incompletely-retrieved-description would include the possibility of expressing the candidate descriptions by invoking a recursive call to the Refer strategy and by stringing together the resulting linguistic expressions with *or*. The communicative strategy called Express-unresolved-choice would include such options as expressing the choice candidates again as a disjunct or making explicit reference to the decision-making process by saying, for example, *I haven't decided yet.* But Express-unresolved-choice would itself also be a substrategy of a communicative strategy called Express-choice, which is depicted in Figure 5.

```
Express choice


Recall the Choose strategy associated with this situation
If a single choice has been identified by the Choose process,
    then Refer (choice)
else, if Choose has identified a set of candidates, then
    Express-unresolved-choice (candidates)
```

Figure 5 A partial description of the "Express choice" strategy.

This communicative strategy differs from those already mentioned in that it requires (or presupposes) a nonlinguistic process, that of choosing or of making a choice. So, if the Choose strategy has already yielded a choice, the communicative strategy specifies that this choice should be expressed; otherwise, some linguistic expression must be found for communicating to the hearer the speaker's state of indecision.

The point of this exercise, although certainly incomplete, has been to illustrate the amount of knowledge about mental processes and strategies, both linguistic (or communicative) and nonlinguistic, that is "hidden" in the use of the word *or* and to suggest the value of exploring the representation of communicative strategies for "explaining" discourse production and comprehension. Notice, in particular, how these strategies (e.g., Refer, Express-choice, Express-unresolved-choice) are deeply intertwined and can refer to nonlinguistic processes (e.g., Choose) as well.

4. LANGUAGE PRODUCTION AS A PLANNING PROCESS

Planning, in the sense in which it is used here, is a formal notion that has grown out of the attempt in artificial intelligence to program computers to solve problems.[15] Planning, in this sense, is conceived of as a process where-by an agent devises a course of action to satisfy or achieve one or more goals. The planner's knowledge consists of a set of GOALS that can be broken down into a set of subgoals and a set of operations or ACTIONS for achieving some subset of these goals. The planning process consists in breaking down

---

[15] Early, if controversial, "successes" include Newell and Simon's General Problem Solver (see Newell and Simon 1963) and SRI's Shakey, a robot that formed and executed simple plans (see Fikes and Nilsson 1971). Fairly early on, psychologists also began exploring the applicability of the metaphor to human performance, as can be seen in Miller, Galanter, and Pribram's *Plans and the Structure of Behavior* (1960).

the initial goal or goals into a set of subgoals for each of which there exists an action for achieving it. The resulting plan is then considered to be either the sequence of subgoals or their corresponding actions.

By viewing the act of speaking itself as the result of a planning process like that just described, we arrive at the larger framework into which the notion of communicative goals and strategies must fit. Viewing language production as a planning process (I will henceforth refer to this notion as the PLANNING METAPHOR) is certainly not a new idea, but it is one that has been gaining popularity in the last few years. Recently, for example, in artificial intelligence Winograd has described speaking as a "design process" (Winograd 1977), and Cohen has been studying speech acts from the point of view of their use as planning objects (Cohen 1977). In linguistics, Chafe has used schemata and the notion of planning to study hesitations and false starts (Chafe 1977, and his article in this volume).

The planning metaphor can be roughly elaborated as follows:

The speaker initiates his discourse with certain ideas "in mind." Corresponding to these ideas are an initial set of communicative goals to express these ideas. His task is then to choose from among his linguistic resources in such a way that he SATISFIES his initial goals (where their successful realization includes some notion of the hearer's comprehension). And this process of goal satisfaction can consist either in the direct mapping of a goal onto a resource (as when the speaker in the sample text given utters *American Economic History* to satisfy the goal of "expressing a choice," in this case a course selection) or in breaking the goal down into one or more subgoals, each of which is satisfied in turn (as when the speaker fragments the goal of expressing her course schedule into a sequence of subgoals, each being the expression of one of her courses).

It should be noted that the metaphor can be (and has been) applied both on the macro- and on the microlevel. Macrolevel planning includes deciding which "chunks" of the discourse to say when, and how they are to be organized. This corresponds to the notion of discourse structure. Microlevel planning includes the choices to be made in deciding how to order the constituents of a sentence, corresponding to such notions as focus, theme, given–new, etc. Of course, sometimes a given plan can have application on both macro- and micro-levels. We saw earlier how the Express-set goal could give rise to the (micro) listing structure *nine, ten, eleven*. But the macrostructure of the following discourse can be seen to be that of a listing as well. (Each element of the listing is of the form *I'm taking x because y*.)

> *Okay. I'm taking Math 2A and I'm taking it because I need to fulfill my science requirement here at Stanford, and it's three-fifteen in the*

afternoon . . . Monday through Thursday. And then I'm also taking Spanish-American literature . . . and that meets at one-fifteen in the afternoon Monday, Wednesday, and Friday. And I'm also taking English 101, which is a section of English language, and that meets at two-fifteen . . . Mondays, Wednesdays, and Fridays, and an extra hour on Monday. And I'm taking that because my major is Spanish and English literature. I had to kind of compromise myself. I wanted to take a physics class but it conflicted with my math class, so I had to take the math class instead.

The planning metaphor can be viewed as a process-oriented analogue of (and therefore complementary to) functional approaches to the study of language. Linguistic theories like Lamb's stratificational linguistics (Lamb 1966) and Halliday's systemic grammar (Halliday 1970) factor the space of linguistic descriptions into a number of levels (e.g., phonological, morphological, lexical, syntactic, etc.) that are then related by a "logical" relation called REALIZATION. So, returning to an earlier example, we could say that Express-set is (sometimes) realized by Surface-listing and that Attribute-property is (sometimes) realized by *It-be*-complement. With this terminology, it can be seen that what I have called communicative goals can be viewed as a higher, intentional level of linguistic description realized by lower (e.g. syntactic) linguistic descriptions.

These two perspectives, then—functional and planning—are really duals along a structure–process scale. From the functional point of view, the speaker's linguistic resources consist of static linguistic descriptions that are connected by the realization relation, whereas, from the process-oriented perspective of the planning metaphor, his resources consist of communicative goals that can be realized by certain active communicative strategies. So, for example, from the static–functional point of view, there is a realization relationship between Express-set and Surface-listing. From the process–planning perspective, there is a strategy for realizing Express-set that consists in constructing a Surface-listing.

However, the two approaches differ in emphasis. The planning metaphor, as does any metaphor, biases one's view of language, emphasizing some issues at the expense of others and making some observations easier to handle than others. One of its obvious strengths is the ease with which notions of planning and goal satisfaction carry over to language production. Just as our nonlinguistic plans are obviously the result of the attempt to satisfy many goals and constraints, so are our linguistic plans or utterances. This allows us to talk about the real-time activity of the speaker, which is necessary, for example, if one wants to study false starts, hesitations, and the like.

In the remainder of this section, I would like to consider several important issues. In general, what research must be done, what answers provided, if notions of planning and communicative goals and strategies are to prove useful?

The first question concerns the nature and the number of communicative goals. How many of them are there all together? What does it mean to postulate a goal with a complex (and apparently ad hoc) name like Express-incompletely-retrieved-description? In order to answer this question, it is necessary to resort to one of the more important insights of twentieth century linguistics. In his *Course in General Linguistics*, Ferdinand de Saussure stressed that language was a system of relations: "In a language-state everything is based on relations [p. 122]." The idea was that any individual linguistic element (a phoneme, for example) was meaningless independent of its relationship to the other elements in its system (in this example, the entire set of phonemes), that its identity was based on its participation in a CLOSED SYSTEM of elements, each of which was defined in relation to the other elements in the system.

Applying this insight to communicative goals, we arrive at the notion of a CLOSED NETWORK OF COMMUNICATIVE GOALS. Each of the goals in this network is defined in terms of its relation to the other goals in the network. Each receives its "meaning," in effect, by virtue of its position in the network. It is easy to see this in the case of Express-choice, which is clearly meaningless independent of Choose, but it is equally, and perhaps more importantly, true of a goal like Express-incompletely-retrieved-description. In the latter case, its meaning is its use: how and when (i.e., in what contexts) it is activated. This is an important property of the network, for, if it can be made to work, it solves the problem of introducing goals with apparently ad hoc names like Express-incompletely-retrieved-description. Under this interpretation, a name like Express-incompletely-retrieved-description is just a convenient shorthand[16] for a piece of process description that is activated in certain contexts and performs a certain function: namely, that which takes a poorly specified description of an object and produces an

---

[16] A similar statement is made by Lockwood in discussing the names assigned to linguistic entities in stratificational grammar:

> [T]he entities discussed here are points in the total network of relationships, and their labels are assigned as a matter of convenience, having no status in the theory what-soever. In the stratificational system of relationships . . . these labels are simply added at various points in the total network of relationships as reference points to aid the linguist in discussing this system. When all necessary relationships are properly represented, the internal structure of the language will be resolved into these relationships, as only they have a status in the theory. . . . Labels placed within such a system make no contribution to its content, but they do contribute to its readability, and this is their primary justification [Lockwood, 1972, p. 26]."

utterance that, as best as possible, describes that object. (Hence, to say that the hearer recognizes Express-incompletely-retrieved-description as being one of the speaker's communicative goals is shorthand for his recognition of the production of the utterance in response to certain mental conditions—in this case, to certain problems with memory retrieval.)

But what does this network look like? What is its "shape"? A good starting point in the search for an answer would seem to be a taxonomy of communicative goals based on the categories proposed in Section 3: ideational goals, like Express-choice, which express ideas or propositions; textual goals, like Further-specify and Elaborate (see Figure 1), which relate an utterance to other utterances in the text; and interpersonal goals, which convey status and attitude. Of these, it is surely the textual goals that are the most relevant for the study of cohesion. One of the major "tasks" in the process of comprehension is the determination of the ways in which an utterance relates to what has already been said. In fact, what we often mean when we say that we fail to understand a piece of text is that we fail to see how it connects. (Of course, this task cannot be accomplished without reference to the goals in the other two categories.) Although the proponents of functional linguistics have made this point rather well, I know of no one who has attempted to devise a taxonomy of textual functions and goals. (My use of terms like Elaborate and Further-specify are intended to be suggestive, surely not definitive.) For anyone interested in such an endeavor, there are many hints to be found in A Grammar of Contemporary English (Quirk *et al.* 1972).

Thus far I have spoken of communicative goals in the network, but what of communicative strategies? In Section 3 I defined communicative strategies as the mental processes that realize communicative goals, and I adopted the convention of naming strategies by the goals they realize. This suggests that there is a one-to-one correspondence between goals and strategies, but surely this cannot be right, no more so than can be the notion that every syntactic form is the realization of a single communicative goal. Not only that, but if the act of producing an utterance is the attempt to satisfy many communicative goals, then many communicative strategies must be called into play. How are they orchestrated and "bound together"? A partial answer to these questions can be found by realizing that goals and their corresponding strategies are really duals along the description–process dimension. Either one thinks of a communicative goal as DECOMPOSING into simpler subgoals (and so on, recursively, until only the most primitive goals, which can be trivially satisfied, remain), or one thinks of a communicative strategy CALLING simpler substrategies (and so on, recursively). So, for example, one might think either of the goal Refer as decomposing to one particular subgoal, Express-incompletely-retrieved-description, or one might think of the Refer strategy calling the substrategy, Express-incompletely-retrieved-description, the difference being whether one was observing certain structures (goals) or was executing them (strategies).

This goal–strategy or description–process duality, if it is workable, might also shed some light on the relationship between language production and language comprehension. According to the framework thus far laid out, the hearer comprehends by reconstructing the speaker's thought processes, working backward from the linguistic expressions and using a network of communicative goals and strategies that is similar to the speaker's. Whereas the speaker is EXECUTING the strategies to achieve certain goals, the hearer is OBSERVING the linguistic expressions left in the wake of the speaker's processes and is using them to postulate the speaker's goals. The image is very much one of the speaker dropping linguistic clues to mark his path and of the hearer following close upon his heels, doing a kind of retracing or SIMULATION. For this to work, however, it seems important that the hearer also be a speaker. But this raises an interesting question: Does the hearer use the same knowledge of goals and of their relation to linguistic expressions for comprehension that the speaker uses for production? Is it in the same form? Is it as detailed? It is possible, for example, that a hearer needs a weaker formulation of this network than does a speaker? (Here, the data on second language acquisition may prove illuminating.) In short, how much of our competence as speakers is essential to our competence as hearers?

Having come this far, we need to consider the ontological status of these communicative goals and mental processes. Do they really exist in the mind of the speaker and hearer? For the limited purposes of this paper, I think it is sufficient to say that it does not matter. Whether or not such conditions as inadequate memory retrieval "really" exist, they do have a place in our phenomenology, in the folk psychology that we as native speakers and hearers bring to bear in our comprehension of utterances, and they therefore can help elucidate our understanding of the coherence of discourse.[17] Nonetheless, this is an important question to address, with ties to the issues of descriptive and explanatory adequacy.

In summary: Regarding language production as a planning process seems to be a useful metaphor. It suggests new ways to approach the issues of cohesion and of the relationship between comprehension and production. But, to make it "respectable," if this can be done, it will be necessary to

[17] A similar remark could be made about nonlinguistic strategies like Choose. If I were to sketch this process as I have sketched Refer, it would include steps like: (a) identifying a set of candidates; (b) selecting one from among them; and (c) postponing the choice for lack of sufficient evidence. The actual act of choosing is, of course, never linear or discrete in these ways, but, when we SPEAK of such processes, we make simplifications, and it is these simplifications that such a process description can capture. We speak AS IF the process is discrete and linear.

map the topology of the network of communicative goals and strategies, to explore the internal structure of individual goals and strategies, and to understand the ontological claims that such an approach makes.

5. RELATION TO OTHER APPROACHES: SPEECH ACTS AND TEXT GRAMMARS

The reader will undoubtedly have noticed that the concept of communicative strategies bears a striking ressemblance to the concept of SPEECH ACTS (Searle 1969). In earlier formulations of these ideas, I have in fact called them speech acts. The difference between the two is one of emphasis. Speech acts (actually, illocutionary acts), with their notions of illocutionary force and propositional content, have grown out of the philosophical interest in language games and have been largely oriented toward specifying the necessary and sufficient conditions for the successful execution of a move in one of these games. (Have I successfully promised, a typical question in this framework asks, if I knew that I did not intend to execute the action promised?) Speech act theoreticians have not, in general, been interested in the detailed mapping relationship between speech acts and the surface forms of language. Coming to the study of language from the vantage point of artificial intelligence, with its emphasis on processes and mental representations, however, I have been interested not so much in the rules that constitute the successful performance of one of these acts as in the processes, the regularities that allow a speaker to realize his communicative goals as linguistic expressions and that allow the hearer to reconstruct the speaker's mental state from these utterances.

What I am proposing, then, is an alternative, orthogonal classification of communicative goals and intentions, with an emphasis on the strategic aspects of the *process* of production and comprehension. (There is, of course, a great deal of overlap. Indirect speech acts—executing one "literal" speech act, for example, asking a question, in order to execute a second, primary speech act, for example, making a request—are just one class of communicative strategies.) Its value must ultimately derive from the light that it can shed on the structures of language in relation to the mental processes that realize them. And, as Figure 1 demonstrates, it seems at least to offer some descriptive tools for examining the FLOW of discourse.

I now turn to the issue of text grammars. In recent years, there have been a number of attempts to capture the regularities of discourse (often referred to as DISCOURSE STRUCTURE) by writing grammars that generate strings of sentences. Such efforts have not been confined to a single field but have been manifested in linguistics, psychology, and artificial intelligence. (For

Story → Setting + Episode
Setting → (State)*
Episode → Event + Reaction
Event → (Episode | Change-of-state | Action | Event + Event)
Reaction → Internal Response + Overt Response
Internal Response → (Emotion | Desire)
Overt Response → (Action | (Attempt)*)
Attempt → Plan + Application
Application → (Preaction)* + Action + Consequence
Preaction → Subgoal + (Attempt)*
Consequence → (Reaction | Event)

Figure 6 Rumelhart's "Story" Grammar. (The symbol '+' is used to form two items in a sequence; the symbol '|' is used to separate mutually exclusive alternatives. A '*' following a structure name indicates one or more of those units; for example, A* is one or more As.)

example: Rumelhart 1975, Thorndyke 1975, Van Dijk 1972). Based on the model of sentential generative grammars, these TEXT grammars have been intended to produce all and only the discourses in some limited domain. Figure 6 provides an example of one such grammar, this one written by Rumelhart.

These efforts are plagued by several major problems. First, by their adoption of the generative grammatical formalism, they suggest—whether intentionally or unintentionally (and it is often difficult to determine whether a particular researcher has intentionally or unintentionally fallen into this trap)—that discourse exhibits THE SAME KIND OF STRUCTURE as the structure of the sentence, that is, constituent structure. But this is simply not so. Halliday and Hasan address this issue rather well:

> A text is a unit of language in use. It is not a grammatical unit, like a clause or a sentence; and it is not defined by its size. A text is sometimes envisaged to be some kind of super-sentence, a grammatical unit that is larger than a sentence but is related to a sentence in the same way that a sentence is related to a clause, a clause to a group and so on: by *constituency*, the composition of larger units out of smaller ones. But this is misleading. A text is not something that is like a sentence, only bigger; it is something that differs from a sentence in kind. . . . A text does not *consist of sentences*; it is *realized by*, or encoded in, sentences. If we understand it in this way, we shall not expect to find the same kind of *structural* integration among the parts of a text as we find among the parts of a sentence or clause. The unity of a text is a unity of a different kind [Halliday and Hasan 1976:1–2].

A second problem concerns the applicability of "grammaticality judgments" in the study of discourse. Attention to the grammaticality of discourse (and judgments of grammaticality by native speakers) fails to acknowledge the central issues in the study of discourse. It is based on the mistaken analogy with sentential grammaticality (which has itself come under attack in recent years). Really, to what extent can we assess the grammaticality, to what extent is it relevant to assess the grammaticality, of speeches, fairy tales, short stories, novels, etc? And what role would such an assessment play in our processes of production and comprehension? In response to this, it might be said that text grammarians do not play the same games as sentential grammarians, that they do not star texts or extract judgments of grammaticality from subjects. My point is, in part, that analogies often allow unwanted or unnecessary properties to sneak in. Discussions couched in terms of grammaticality force subtle shifts of emphasis on one's approach to the study of text. So, for example, in his psychology doctoral thesis, Thorndyke scrambled the sentences of a text and measured the decrease in comprehension. Would the idea of such a manipulation have occurred outside of the framework of text grammars?

Finally, text grammars speak in a language that misses the "significant generalizations." Texts convey meaning, and what is called DISCOURSE STRUCTURE is best "explained" with reference to the speaker's mental processes. Some aspects of the structure of texts could be captured equally well with a grammar, but there are aspects, for example, the ambiguity of *or*, that cannot be treated at all.

It is important to realize that my quibble with grammars is relative to their use. In linguistics, especially, they have come to be associated with particular styles and methodologies that are not intrinsic to their essence.[18] As a general descriptive device, they are a powerful and important tool for capturing the regularities of any system. In this sense, they might be used to capture the shape of my network of communicative goals. I am not arguing with this use but, instead, with their treatment as an ingredient of a "theory of language" that would account for language production and comprehension in a manner that makes mistaken, if unintentional, claims about structure and ignores the mental processes that shape the text.

6. CONCLUSIONS

I have tried to suggest in this chapter that notions of communicative goals, of mental processes and strategies, are necessary for capturing some important components of the coherence or cohesion of discourse. Cohesion, after all, is not a property of text per se. It is an assessment by the hearer or reader of the extent to which some marks on paper or acoustic waves give him access to the speaker's ideas, ideas that are mediated by the mental

---

[18] Text grammars have been applied in fields like folklore to the task of labeling texts. Here, they are intended only as descriptive or classificatory aids.

activity of the speaker. Mental ACTIVITY is the key here, for the speaker is not merely communicating ideas or propositions, but thought PROCESSES. A coherent text is one that allows the hearer to connect each of its pieces with what has come before; it is a text that leads the hearer down a strategic trail of mental operations.

Underlying these ideas, then, is a conception of language production as a planning process whereby the speaker chooses linguistic expressions from the options provided by his language in order to satisfy a number of (possibly simultaneous) communicative goals. And his aim in selecting expressions is not only to convey those goals to his hearer but also to convey the mental processes that led to the establishment of those goals. My earlier statement that the speaker's mental processes are ENCODED in his utterance now needs to be amended. These processes are not encoded in the same sense that information about laundry detergent is encoded by the sequence of thick and thin black lines on the box. Rather, the speaker's linguistic expressions serve as clues that allow the hearer, by virtue of his similar knowledge of communicative goals and strategies, to (partially) reconstruct the speaker's mental states and thought processes.

I also declared initially that my approach was MIND-BASED, opposing it to the TEXT-BASED approach. This statement, too, now needs to be amended. Although my orientation does indeed take mind rather than text per se as its focus, it cannot—and, as the examples presented here should indicate, it does not—ignore the structures in the text. Discourse, I would claim, should be viewed as the convergence or intersection of four kinds of "structure" (the last of which has not been considered in this chapter):

1. the structure of the ideas expressed in the text
2. the structure of the speaker's thought processes
3. the structures of the speaker's language
4. the structure of the speech situation (the relations between speaker and hearer)

I have based my presentation on one small piece of an unplanned, oral discourse. Of course, there can be no "proof" based on such meager evidence. It might be argued, for example, that what I have seen is an artifact of unplanned discourse only. For the moment, I will have to leave it as an article of faith, to be empirically verified, that the cohesion and comprehensibility of carefully planned text is amenable to and elucidated by reference to mental processes.

I have tried to suggest that the appropriate language for the study of discourse is, in part, a language of mental processes, that this language is an intermediary between syntax and discourse. This should not be taken as a suggestion that syntax be ignored, rather that syntactic patterns be studied in relation to the mental processes, the meanings that they convey. We all seem to agree with Chomsky that a language user is one who "has internalized a system of rules that relate sound in meaning in a particular way [Chomsky 1972:26]." If we are to make a go of establishing this, I believe we will have to determine the links between syntax and meaning, where meaning is described not in terms of features or of logical propositions, but of mental processes.

ACKNOWLEDGMENTS

I would like to thank Wally Chafe, Barbara Grosz, Henry Thompson, and Terry Winograd for reading and commenting on various drafts of this paper.

REFERENCES

Chafe, W. (1977) "Creativity in Verbalization and Its Implications for the Nature of Stored Knowledge," in R. O. Freedle, ed. (1977), *Discourse Production and Comprehension*, Erlbaum, Hillsdale, New Jersey.

Chomsky, N. (1972) *Language and Mind*, Harcourt, Brace, Jovanovich, New York.

Cohen, P. (1977) *A Framework for a Computer Model of Conversation*, unpublished Doctoral dissertation, University of Toronto, Toronto.

Fikes, R. E., and N. J. Nilsson (1971) "STRIPS: A New Approach to the Application of Theorem Proving in Problem Solving," *Artificial Intelligence* 2, 189–208.

Grice, H. P. (1967) William James Lectures, Harvard University, Cambridge, Massachusetts, (published, in parts, as "Logic and Conversation," in P. Cole and J. L. Morgan eds., *Syntax and Semantics 3: Speech Acts*, Academic Press, New York.

Grosz, B. J. (1977) "The Representation and Use of Focus in Dialogue Understanding," Stanford Research Institute, Technical Note 151, Stanford, California.

Halliday, M. A. K. (1970) "Language Structure and Language Function," in J. Lyons ed., *New Horizons in Linguistics*, Penguin, New York.

Halliday, M. A. K. and R. Hasan (1976) *Cohesion in English*, Longmans, New York.

Heidegger, M. (1969) *Identity and Difference* (trans. Joan Stambaugh), Harper and Row, New York.

Katz, J. J. (1977) "The Real Status of Semantic Representations," *Linguistic Inquiry* 8, 559–584.

Lamb, S. M. (1966) *Outline of Stratificational Grammar*, Georgetown University Press, Washington, D.C.

Lockwood, D. G. (1972) *Introduction to Stratificational Linguistics*, Harcourt, Brace, and Jovanovich, New York.

Miller, G. A., E. Galanter, and K. H. Pribram (1960) *Plans and the Structure of Behavior*, Holt, Rinehart, and Winston, New York.

Newell, A. and H. A. Simon (1963) "GPS, A Program That Simulates Human Thought," in E. A. Feigenbaum and J. Feldman eds., *Computers and Thought*, McGraw-Hill, New York.

Quirk, R., S. Greenbaum, G. Leech, and J. Svartvik (1972) *A Grammar of Contemporary English*, Longmans, New York.

Rumelhart, D. E. (1975) "Notes on a Schema for Stories," in D. G. Bobrow and A. Collins eds., *Representation and Understanding*, Academic Press, New York.

Saussure, F. (1959) *Course in General Linguistics* (translated by Wade Baskin), Philosophical Library, New York.

Searle, J. (1969) *Speech Acts*, Cambridge University Press, Cambridge.

Thorndyke, P. W. (1975) *Cognitive Structures in Human Story Comprehension and Memory*, unpublished Doctoral dissertation, Stanford University, Stanford, California.

Van Dijk, T. A. (1972) *Some Aspects of Text Grammars*, Mouton, The Hague.

Winograd, T. (1977) "A Framework for Understanding Discourse," Stanford Artificial Intelligence Laboratory Memo AIM-297, Stanford, California.

PART III **THE FLOW OF DISCOURSE**

ASPECT AND FOREGROUNDING IN DISCOURSE

PAUL J. HOPPER
SUNY—Binghamton

1. GENERAL PROPERTIES OF FOREGROUNDING

It is evidently a universal of narrative discourse that in any extended text an overt distinction is made between the language of the actual story line and the language of supportive material which does not itself narrate the main events. I refer to the former—the parts of the narrative which relate events belonging to the skeletal structure of the discourse—as FOREGROUND and the latter as BACKGROUND. Swahili provides a typical and relatively uncomplicated example of the distinction. We find that each narrative episode begins with a verb having an explicit tense marker, usually the preterite prefix *li-*. Subsequently, verbs denoting those events which are on the main story line, that is, foregrounded events, are marked with the prefix *ka-* (replacing *li-*). Events marked as subsidiary or supportive, that is,

Syntax and Semantics, Volume 12:
Discourse and Syntax

backgrounded events, receive the prefix *ki-*. The example which follows is taken from a nineteenth century traveler's tale (Selemani 1965:119):

> *Tu-ka-enda kambi -ni, hata usiku tu-ka-toroka, tu-ka-safiri   siku*
> we   went camp to and night we   ran off we   traveled days
>
> *kadha, tu-ki-pitia   miji   fulani, na   humo mwote hamna   mahongo*
> several we   passed villages several, and them all   was-not tribute

'We returned to the camp, and ran away during the night, and we traveled for several days, we passed through several villages, and in all of them we did not have to pay tribute.'

The "meaning" of the prefixes *ka-* and *ki-* is not one of temporal deixis, since they have no tense value apart from the one established at the outset by the tense prefix (here, *li-*) on the initial verb. Nor are they "aspectual" in the usual sense of the word, that is, having an inherent value of completed or noncompleted view of the action; the action denoted by the verb *tukipitia* 'we passed' is just as much "completed" as that of *tukatoroka* 'we ran away'. There is, however, a real and very concrete distinction between the *ki-* verb and the *ka-* verbs in this passage. This distinction becomes clear if we arrange the events in the form of a flowchart, with the chronology of the events running from top to bottom, and events not on the main route indicated by a "shunt" or subroutine to the side:

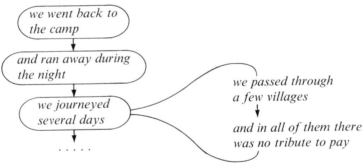

The difference between the sentences in the foreground (the "main line" events) and the ones in the background (the "shunted" events) has to do with sequentiality. The foregrounded events succeed one another in the narrative in the same order as their succession in the real world; it is in other words an iconic order. The backgrounded events, on the other hand, are not in sequence to the foregrounded events, but are concurrent with them. Because of this feature of simultaneity, backgrounded events usually amplify or comment on the events of the main narrative. The statement *We passed through a few villages* is not an occurrence separate from *We*

journeyed several days, but it serves to expand the latter. Significantly, it could be rendered in English with a nonfinite verb form:

We journeyed for several days, passing through a few villages.

Furthermore, the two backgrounded clauses are not sequenced with respect to one another. This is another typical feature of backgrounding: Because the sequentiality constraint is lifted, backgrounded clauses may be located at any point along the time axis or indeed may not be located on the time axis at all. Consequently, the relationships among backgrounded clauses are often quite loose.

Because of the less strict connection between backgrounded clauses, one frequently, in fact typically, finds the following further characteristic, that the focus structure of the backgrounded clause is different from that of the foregrounded clause. In backgrounded clauses, there is a greater likelihood of topic changes and of new information being introduced in the preverbal position (i.e., indefinite subjects). In foregrounded clauses, on the other hand, it is unusual for completely new information to be introduced in the subject; more often, subjects are highly presuppositional, and the new material in the story is introduced in the predicate, either in the verb or in the combination of verb plus complement.

Because foregrounded clauses denote the discrete, measured events of the narrative, it is usually the case that the verbs are punctual rather than durative or iterative. This correlation can be stated as a correlation between the lexical, intrinsic AKTIONSART of the verb and the discourse-conditioned ASPECT. One finds, in other words, a tendency for punctual verbs to have perfective aspect (i.e., to occur in foregrounded sentences) and conversely for verbs of the durative/stative/iterative types to occur in imperfective, i.e. backgrounded, clauses. In the Swahili passage cited, two of the three *ka-* verbs are punctual (*went back*, *ran away*), and one is durative (*journeyed*). In the background part, ·one verb is iterative (*passed through*), while *hamna* 'there is not', insofar as it can be considered a verb, must be stative. Foregrounded clauses generally refer to events which are dynamic and active. Furthermore, the sequencing of these clauses usually imposes the constraint that a foregrounded event is contingent on the completion of a prior event. The tendency for foregrounded events to have punctual verbs follows as a probability from these two factors, but it is by no means a requirement.

I shall mention in this introduction one more property of foregrounded clauses. Strictly speaking, only foregrounded clauses are actually NARRATED. Backgrounded clauses do not themselves narrate, but instead they support, amplify, or COMMENT ON the narration. In a narration, the author is asserting the occurrence of events. Commentary, however, does not constitute the assertion of events in the story line but makes statements which are CON-TINGENT and dependent on the story-line events. Typically, therefore, one finds in backgrounding those forms associated with a lower degree of assertiveness, and even forms designated as irrealis: subjunctives, optatives, other "modal" verb forms (including those expressed as modal auxiliaries), and negation. In the Swahili passage, for example, one of the background clauses is negated (*hamna* 'there was not').

The following table, adapted from my earlier paper (Hopper 1977), sums up the chief properties of the foreground–background distinction and forms the basis of the remainder of the chapter:

PERFECTIVE	IMPERFECTIVE
chronological sequencing	*Simultaneity or chronological overlapping of situation C with event A and/or B*
View of event as a whole, whose completion is a necessary prerequisite to a subsequent event	*View of a situation or happening whose completion is not a necessary prerequisite to a subsequent happening*
Identity of subject within each discrete episode	*Frequent changes of subject*
Unmarked distribution of focus in clause, with presupposition of subject and assertion in verb and its immediate complements (or other unmarked focus)	*Marked distribution of focus, e.g., subject focus, instrument focus, focus on sentence adverbial*
Human topics	*Variety of topics, including natural phenomena*
Dynamic, kinetic events	*Statis, descriptive situations*
Foregrounding. Event indispensible to narrative	*Backgrounding. State or situation necessary for understanding motives, attitudes, etc.*
Realis	*Irrealis*

2. FOREGROUNDING THROUGH TENSE-ASPECT MORPHOLOGY

It is quite common for languages to realize the foreground–background distinction through a specialized verb morphology. Two well-known groups in which this strategy is found are Romance and Slavic. French provides a particularly convenient example, since it has been investigated from a point of view which corresponds quite closely to that adopted here. For example,

W. Reid's (1976) paper "The Quantitative Validation of a Grammatical System" presents detailed statistical information concerning the environments of the imperfect and past historic tenses. For Russian, we have the sophisticated treatment of aspect by J. Forsyth (1970).

French

The study by Reid (1976) shows that the past historic (passé simple, preterite), which is the foregrounding form of the verb in my framework, favors the following environments:

1. Actions as opposed to states
2. Affirmative as opposed to negative verbs
3. Human subjects as opposed to nonhuman subjects
4. First person subjects as opposed to third person (definite animate pronominal) subjects
5. Singular subjects as opposed to plural subjects
6. Main character of discourse as subject as opposed to secondary character as subject
7. Main clause as opposed to subordinate clause
8. Proper name subject as opposed to pronominal subject

Reid's statistics provide a picture of a distinction between what he calls HIGH FOCUS and LOW FOCUS of the verb. The terminology which I use here instead reflects my view that the foreground–background distinction is a universal of some kind, one that may be realized formally in a number of different ways, depending on the language concerned; in other words, I view aspectual distinctions such as that of French as DERIVING FROM discourse, rather than as ready-made devices "deployed" in discourse because they happen already to exist. Nonetheless, at one level of discussion the data which Reid has collected are equally relevant to the notion of discourse foregrounding. For example, actions (1) which are asserted (2), have human agents (3), who are singular persons (5), and are performed by the central character of the discourse (6) are more likely to figure in story-line episodes. The subjects of main-line verbs are, furthermore, higher on the agency hierarchy than subjects of backgrounded verbs; hence the preference for proper names and first person pronouns.

A further generalization which may be made is that in foregrounded clauses the subject of the verb is topical and highly presupposed. This assumption follows from the animate–definite property of such subjects and from the greater continuity of topic–subject in ongoing narration. Conversely, we may expect that the new actions which are predicated of these subjects will be expressed in the finite verbal predicate, that is, the main verb and its complements. This observation takes on especial significance in Russian, where according to the discussion in Forsyth's *A Grammar of*

Aspect the selection of perfective versus imperfective verb forms is conditioned not only by the discourse functions of foreground and background but also by the distribution of focus (i.e., new and old information) in the sentence.

Russian

It is clear that Russian aspect shares at least one important function with the French past tense systems. In the Russian past tense, the perfective aspect appears in contexts which closely parallel those of the past historic, and the imperfective aspect functions like the French imperfect. Forsyth's monograph (1970:9–10) contains an extensive example of this parallel. He illustrates the use of perfective verb forms for single, sequential events and the imperfective in clauses containing backgrounded material: descriptions of scenery and natural phenomena, subordinate events which are repeated (i.e., iteratives), and activities which are viewed as occurring simultaneously with the main events.

ASPECT AND SENTENCE FOCUS IN RUSSIAN

An especially striking correlation which exists in Russian is that between the aspect of the verb and the distribution of information in the sentence (focus structure). The perfective aspect is associated with an informational structure such that there is a high degree of topicality in the subject and the predicate of the verb is the focus of the sentence.

We have noted that the subject of the verb in foregrounded clauses in French has a tendency to be definite, human, and pronominal and to have the hallmarks of the oldest, most presupposed part of the sentence. In Russian it seems that imperfective aspect is elicited whenever this distribution is disrupted, that is, when the verb and its complements do NOT together represent the newly imparted information. Forsyth gives numerous examples of this phenomenon, for example:[1]

1. Subject focus:

    Kto pisal[i] "Voinu i mir" ?
    'Who wrote "War and Peace"?'

    -Tolstoi pisal[i] "Voinu i mir"
    -Tolstoy wrote "War and Peace".'

    Ya ubiral[i] komnatu vchera, a kto ubiral[i] segodnya ne znayu.
    'I cleaned the room yesterday, but who cleaned it today I don't know.'

[1] The superscript *i* indicates that the verb is in the imperfective form.

2. Focus on adverbial:

> *V etoy porternoy ya obdumyval svoyu dissertatsiyu i napisal[p] pervoe lyubovnoe pis'mo k Vere. Pisal[i] karandashom.*
>
> 'In this tavern I pondered my thesis and wrote my first love letter to Vera. I wrote it in pencil.'
>
> *Spuskayas' po lestntse, on muchitel'no pytalsya vspomnit', gde zhe on vstrechal[i] etogo cheloveka.*
>
> 'As he went downstairs he racked his brains trying to remember where on earth he had met that man.'

3. Other marked focus: Under this heading come several disparate phenomena which have in common the presupposition of the action itself and an assertion only that the action itself did (as opposed to "did not") take place. Among the examples of this found in Forsyth (1970:82–84) are common expressions like:

> *Vy uzhe zakazyvali[i] ?*
>
> 'Have you already ordered?'

Two more examples (again from Forsyth) of the same thing:

> *Vy chitali[i] "Voynu i Mir"?—Chital[i].*
>
> 'Have you read "War and Peace"?'—'I have.'
>
> *Chtoby ekhat' vdvoyom, nuzhny sredstva: k tomu zhe mne ne dadut prodolzhitel'nogo otpuska. V etom godu ya uzhe bral[i] raz otpusk.*
>
> 'We need funds to travel together; and besides, they won't give me a long holiday. Because I've already had leave this year.'

At the lexical or sentence level, this distribution is difficult to understand, but it perhaps becomes clear when discourse contexts are taken into consideration. The crucial difference between perfective and imperfective which leads to the choice of imperfective in these examples is surely that no new event is signaled; instead an old event (one that is presupposed) is as it were resurrected and commented on. Consequently, the examples discussed under (3) are of exactly the same type as those in (1) and (2).

3. FOREGROUNDING THROUGH WORD ORDER

The relationship between focus and aspect is a particularly important one from a cross-linguistic viewpoint, and it is therefore appropriate before continuing, to sum up some of the main ideas about the connection between the two. Aspect considered from a discourse perspective is a device or set of devices which exists in order to guide the language user through a text. Consequently aspect may take on one of a number of morphosyntactic forms, and the examples which I have been considering from Swahili,

French, and Russian show aspect in its morphological form, as a set of inflections or stem-forms on the verb. The aspects pick out the main route through the text and allow the listener (reader) to store the actual events of the discourse as a linear group while simultaneously processing accumulations of commentary and supportive information which add texture but not substance to the discourse itself. Aspect can therefore be likened to a "flow-control mechanism";[2] as such, it surely has significant psycholinguistic correlates.

Foregrounded sentences have a strong tendency to have an unmarked pragmatic structure; new events in the discourse tend to be introduced in the predicate, and the subject of the verb tends to be the central character or characters in the discourse and, hence, to be presupposed. In commentary, on the other hand (that is, in background), new events are not introduced so often as old already-related events are retold and amplified in some way. Frequently, therefore, what is asserted in a background clause is not the verb and its immediate complements but something else—the subject, an instrumental adverb, the tense of the verb, or even the direct object alone.

A common, indeed practically universal strategy for realizing focus is word order, and, since the perfective–imperfective distinction in Russian is evidently closely tied to the focus structure of the sentence, it seems that the possibility exists of a word-order strategy for foregrounding (perfective aspect). R. Hetzron has, in fact, brought to my attention (personal communication) the instance of certain African languages in which word order—specifically the order of verb and object—is crucially involved in the tense-aspect paradigms. Unfortunately no textual data are available; I shall therefore illustrate this strategy with Early Germanic materials, concentrating here on Old English.[3]

Old English[4]

Foregrounded Clauses in Old English

To illustrate first the structure of foregrounded clauses in (early) Old English, a typical passage from the Parker Chronicle for 870 A.D. is given:

[2] I owe this insightful metaphor to Talmy Givón.

[3] It should be stressed that the phenomenon is not restricted to Old English but is found, with some modifications, in other older Germanic dialects also, for example, Old Norse and Old High German. Cf. Hopper, 1977.

[4] Old English narrative prose will be illustrated with extracts from the Parker Manuscript of the *Chronicle*. This manuscript represents the best source for indigenous archaic prose with a minimum of contamination by Latin; for example, the Cynewulf story (755 A.D.) is probably almost contemporary with the actual events. I use only the earlier parts, up to the year 891 A.D., the last entry written by the "A" scribe.

The text used is the edition of Earle and Plummer, of which the Parker Manuscript has been transferred onto computer tape. A concordance and word-count were generated from this (Lehmann and Hopper 1966).

> *Her rad se here ofer Mierce innan East Engle ond winter setl namon æt*
> *Þeodforda, ond Þy wintre Eadmund cyning him wiÞ feaht, ond Þa*
> *Deniscan sige namon, ond Þone cyning ofslogon, ond Þæt lond all ge*
> *eodon.*

'In this year (her) the army rode (rad) across Mercia into East Anglia, and took up (namon) winter quarters at Thedford, and that winter King Edmund fought (feaht) against them, and the Danes took (namon) the victory and slew (ofslogon) the king, and overran (ge eodon) all the land.'

The significant parameter here is the position of the verb with respect to the other constituents of the clause. In foregrounded patterns, the principle is that the verb is PERIPHERAL. This means that the verb either precedes the subject (VS) or follows its immediate complements (OV). The alternation VS/OV is itself governed by further discourse considerations: The OV pattern is found when a chain of events in the same episodic series follows a sequence-initial VS clause. In the entry for 870 A.D. quoted above, for example, we have:

1.	*her rad se here ofer Mierce innan East Engle*	VS
2.	*ond winter setl namon æt Þeodforda*	OV
3.	*ond Þy wintre Eadmund cyning him wiÞ feaht*	OV
4.	*ond Þa Deniscan sige namon*	OV
5.	*ond Þone cyning ofslogon*	OV
6.	*ond Þæt lond all ge eodon*	OV

The choice of VS rather than OV sometimes depends on factors which appear quite arbitrary. It is common for a lengthy narrative sequence to be broken up into a series of internal episodes, each of which is initiated by a VS clause. In the Cynewulf story, for example, we find basically OV syntax with a new minor episode beginning every three or four clauses—that is, a pattern:

VS–OV–OV–OV; VS–OV–OV–OV; VS–OV–OV . . . etc.

Sometimes there is a clear motivation for the break, that is, a distinct thematic shift of some kind. Just as often, however, the break seems to come as a sort of breathpause or, perhaps, an aesthetic effect: Possibly it was considered trite to maintain an unbroken series of OV clauses.[5]

---

[5] It should be noted at this point that in discourse work explanations and hypotheses are not obviously validated with every example. Apparent inconsistencies and irregularities often mean that a certain proportion of the data contradict the general hypothesis. As a rule of thumb, I take this proportion to be about 20%; that is, I expect my explanations to account for an obviously large majority of the data. The remainder are then assumed not to be contradictory or arbitrary but to REFLECT A SPECIFIC INTENTION OF THE AUTHOR. The exegesis of this remainder may be quite convincing, or it may be guesswork.

BACKGROUNDING IN OLD ENGLISH

The other basic syntactic type in Old English is the clause in which the verb immediately follows the subject—that is, the SV type. This type of clause is backgrounded in the same sense as I have described for the Russian imperfective aspect. SV clauses in Old English are found whenever the narrative material is part of the supporting or amplifying discourse rather than of the main story line. They are, therefore, found when preliminary actions, explanations, or lasting states are being presented. In the Cynewulf story (755 A.D.), SV syntax is confined to the introduction, which presents the prior history of the relationship between Cynewulf and Cyneheard:

> Her Cynewulf benam Sigebryht his rices ond West Seaxna wiotan for unryhtum dædum, butan Ham tun scire; ond he hæfde þa oþ he ofslog þone aldor mon þe him lengest wunode; ond hiene þa Cynewulf on Andred adræfde, ond he þær wunade oþ þæt hiene an swan ofstang æt Pryfetes flodan; ond he wræc þone aldor mon Cumbran; ond se Cynewulf oft miclum gefeohtum feaht wiþ Bretwalum; ond ymb .xxxi. wint. þæs þe he rice hæfde, he wolde adræfan anne æþeling se was Cyneheard haten, ond se Cyneheard wæs þæs Sigebryhtes broþur;
>   ond þa geascode he þone cyning lytle werode on wifcuþþe on Merantune, ond hine þær berad, ond þone bur utan be eode. . . .

In this year Cynewulf and the West Saxon elders deprived Sigebryht of his kingdom for unrighteous deeds, except Hampshire; and he held that until he slew the alderman who stayed with him the longest. And then Cynewulf exiled him to the Weald, and he remained there until a herdsman stabbed him to death at Priffet's Flood, and he was avenging the alderman, Cumbra. And this Cynewulf often, in mighty battles, fought against the Cornishmen. And 31 winters after he took the kingdom, he resolved to exile a nobleman who was called Cyneheard, and this Cyneheard was Sigebryht's brother.

And he [Cyneheard] found the king with a small band of men visiting a mistress at Merton, and surprised him there, and surrounded the hut outside. . . .

The onset of VS/OV syntax coincides with the start of the actual events of the narrative (ond þa geascode he 'And he found. . . .'), and the verb-peripheral sentence type is used consistently until the Ausleitung (coda), when we are told what happened AFTER the main events:

> Ond se Cynewulf ricsode .xxxi. wint. ond his lic liþ æt Wintan ceastre, ond þæs æþelinges æt Ascan mynster, ond hiera ryht fæder cyn gæþ to

Cerdice; ond þy ilcan geare mon ofslog Æþelbald Miercna cyning on Seccan dune, ond his lic liþ on Hreopa dune; ond Beornrǽd feng to rice, ond lytle hwile heold ond ungefealice; ond þy ilcan geare Offa feng to rice, ond heold .xxxviiii. wint. ond his sunu Egfer (þ) heold .xli. daga ond .c. daga. Se Offa was þincgferþing, þincgferþ Ean wulfing. . . .

'And this Cynewulf reigned 31 winters, and his body lies at Winchester, and that of the nobleman at Ashminster, and their paternal line goes back to Cerdic. And the same year was slain (lit.: one slew) Ethelbald, king of the Mercians, at Sedgedown, and his body lies at Reepdown. And Beornred came to the throne, and held it for a short while unsuccessfully. And the same year Offa came to the throne, and held it for 39 winters. Then his son Edgferth held it for 141 days. This Offa was a son of Thingferth, and Thingferth (was) the son of Eanwulf. . . .'

The Einleitung (introductory, scene-setting part) and the Ausleitung between them contain 23 finite verbs, of which 17 are found in SV clauses. The types of backgrounding functions associated with this word order are the following:

1.   There is a tendency for the subjects of the verbs to be relatively new and "unexpected," that is, nontopical. In the Einleitung, the subjects are composed in part of pronouns, but the full NP subjects are frequently either stressed (*se Cynewulf, se Cyneheard*) or are marked as being nontopical by complexity (*Cynewulf . . . ond West Seaxna wiotan*) or by the indefinite article (*an swan*). In the Ausleitung, we also find stressed subjects (*se Cynewulf, se Offa*); furthermore, some of the subjects are inanimate (and hence automatically of reduced intrinsic topicality): *his lic, hiera ryht fæder cyn*, while others are completely new names introduced for the first (and sometimes the last) time in the text: *Beornrǽd, his sunu Egferþ*. Now although new characters can be, and often are, introduced in foregrounded narrative, it is usually with a view to a role of some kind in the narrative, which is then related immediately; the casual presentation of new personages is characteristic rather of backgrounded material.

2.   Another facet of backgrounding that emerges in these examples is the distortion of the "normal" time-frame. The events of a typical foregrounded narrative occur in a regular, measured succession. Generally, in fact, the foregrounded events follow on one another's heels, with E_2 occurring immediately upon the completion of E_1. But stage-setting sequences require the ability of ranging over large time-spans. Whereas the foregrounded narration is bound by the sequentiality constraint, there is in backgrounding

the necessity for ACCESS to any point on the temporal line. The possibility of "wandering" up and down the temporal-deictic axis might be reflected linguistically in the use of compound tenses, including modal auxiliaries. In fact, Old English narrative as exemplified in the Parker Chronicle makes rather little use of such tenses, perhaps because the word-order difference between foreground and background adequately compensates for the lack of a more specific range of "past tense"; at any rate, the use of compound tenses seems to increase as SV word order becomes syntactically established.

3. There is a tendency to have verbs denoting states, processes, and descriptions rather than single dynamic events. It should be emphasized that this is a tendency, not a requirement. Punctual events can and do occur in background, just as verbs denoting some inherently drawn-out process can occur in foregrounding. But durative and iterative verbs are, statistically, associated with backgrounding. (It should be recalled that in Russian a punctual verb in the imperfective aspect of the past is ordinarily interpreted as an iterative.)

FOREGROUNDING IN OLD ENGLISH

The salient features of foregrounding are the converse of the features of backgrounding. In addition to the word-order properties I have discussed, we find:

1. High topicality of the subject, which is almost always either an anaphoric pronoun or a definite noun without focus. The characteristic "oldness" of the subject in foregrounding is, of course, a natural consequence of the tendency for narratives to be concerned principally with a small number of participants and, hence, to have continuity of topic–subject in the main story-line. In background, on the other hand, a variety of other topics can be introduced to support and amplify the story line.

2. The time frame is measured and unidirectional. There is no back-tracking or summarizing, no glances forward, no unasserted suppositions; the events are stated in immediate succession to one another.

3. Verbs show some tendency to be active and punctual.

In order to test the validity of the correlation between punctuality and foregrounding, I have made a count of the syntactic environments of presumed punctual verbs (e.g., *gefliemde* 'put to flight,' *ofslog* 'slew') and of presumed durative verbs (e.g., *ricsode* 'reigned,' *sæt* 'remained'). If the hypothesis that there is a correlation between the Aktionsart of the verb and the aspect of the sentence is correct, then we should find that durative verbs favor SV clauses and punctual verbs favor VS/OV clauses.

The first of these correlations is overwhelming, as Table 1 shows:

TABLE 1
COUNT OF DURATIVE VERBS IN THE THREE CLAUSE TYPES

Verb	Gloss	VS	OV	SV	Subtotal
ricsode	'reigned'	1	2	19	22
heold	'held (the throne)'	1	6	37	44
sæt	'remained'	1	2	9	12
liþ	'lies'	0	0	10	10
resteþ	'rests'	0	0	2	2
Total		3	10	77	90

Expressed as percentages, this means that 85% of durative verbs are in SV clauses.

A positive correlation of the opposite phenomenon, that is, of punctual verbs with VS/OV word order, is not so clear. Table 2 shows that even for punctual verbs there is still a high incidence of SV syntax:

TABLE 2
COUNT OF PUNCTUAL VERBS IN THE THREE CLAUSE TYPES

Verb	Gloss	VS	OV	SV	Subtotal
forþferde	'died'	6	0	32	38
ofslog	'slew'	1	23	16	40
feng	'came (to the throne)'	36	1	34	71
nam	'took'	4	20	5	29
onfeng	'received'	2	5	16	23
for	'went'	25	2	10	37
com	'came'	18	6	6	30
gefliemde	'put to flight'	3	14	0	17
sende	'sent'	6	1	3	10
Total		101	72	122	295

The proportion of punctual verbs in SV sentences, however, is only 41.4% of the number of punctual verbs overall; that is, durative verbs are more than twice as likely to occur in SV clauses as punctual verbs.

It should also be observed that very many of the punctual SV clauses occur in environments which are strictly speaking not truly narrative. For example, the verb *forþferde* 'died' occurs mainly (32 out of 38 times) in postsubject position; yet, often sentences of the form *X died* are not part of a narrative but are a means of marking a particular year by the formula *This was the*

year when X died. The same is true of the other principal TRANSITIONAL
verb *feng (to rice)* 'came (to the throne).' Many of the calendrical entries
in the Chronicle, in fact, consist solely (or almost so) of these verbs (and
their arguments); for example:

> 640 A.D. *Her Edbald Cantwara cyning forþferde, ond he ricsode .xxv.
> wintr.*
> 'In this year Edbald king of the Kentishmen died, and he had reigned
> for 25 winters.'

> 616 A.D. *Her Æþelbryht Cont wara cyning forþferde, ond Edbald his
> sunu feng to rice.*
> 'In this year Ethelbriht king of the Kentishmen died, and his son Edbald
> came to the throne.'

The focus in such phrases is, inevitably, not on the event itself but on the
personage involved. Consequently, there is subject focus, and such sentences
are instances of backgrounding. Examples of this kind point up clearly the
necessity to distinguish between lexical (sentence-level) AKTIONSART, and
the discourse-level phenomena of ASPECT.

4. FOREGROUNDING THROUGH "VOICE"

I have thus far examined two types of foregrounding: (*a*) that represented
by French and Russian, in which foregrounding is marked in the tense-
aspect systems of the verb; and (*b*) the Germanic type (represented by Old
English), in which aspectual distinctions are indicated by word order
(verb-peripheral for foreground, SV for background).

There are several other strategies available for realizing aspect; for
example, the use of sentence particles to mark either foregrounded or
backgrounded clauses is quite common and may also be used as an ancillary
device secondary to some other marker. The remainder of this chapter will
be devoted to just one further strategy, the use of the "voice" system—the
active–passive distinction—to distinguish foreground and background. The
languages which I will be discussing here are Malay and Tagalog.

Malay

TEXTS

The Malay narrative texts which will be discussed here are written in a
style modeled quite closely on the classical form of the language, which
persisted as a literary language until the end of the nineteenth century. They
are taken from the writings of Abdullah bin Abdul-Kadir Munshi, a Ma-

laccan writer of Arab descent who can be described as a conscious stylist and a conservative rhetorician. Abdullah's writings concern modern subjects (the consolidation of British hegemony in Malaysia), but his language has more in common with the traditional Hikayat ('sagas') than to, say, the modern Malay novel. In addition to its historical interest, Abdullah's work provides examples of both lively narrative and reflective didactic commentary which illustrate with especial clarity the contrast between foregrounded and backgrounded discourse.

FOREGROUNDING IN MALAY

The morphosyntax of foregrounding in Malay involves two components. One is the use of the narrative particle *-lah*, which is attached enclitically to the verb. This particle is in essence a focus particle; it is used to denote contrastive emphasis on the word or constituent to which it is attached, for example (Abdullah 1932:82):

> *karna   di-antara jurutulis itu semua-nya **aku-lah** sa-orang yang terkechil*
> because among   the clerks all   I   the one who smallest
> 'because **I** was the youngest of all the clerks'

When the particle *-lah* is affixed to the verb, it denotes that the action or event of the clause is one of the main points of the narrative. Such verbs are almost always perfective; they denote completed actions, the beginning of which is contingent on the prior event and whose completion, in turn, is anterior to the following event. *-Lah* on the verb highlights and foregrounds the event, gives it especial prominence in the narrative, and announces it as one of a series of actions. Almost always the verb denotes a kinetic activity:

> *Maka ada pun lama-nya ia duduk di-darat itu ada enam tujuh hari.*
> and   was now time   he stay on shore   was six   seven days.
>
> *Kemudian turun-lah ia ka-laut. Serta ia sampai, maka*
> Then   went   he to sea. When he arrive   then
>
> *di-surohkan-nya   bongkar sauh, lalu belayar. Maka*
> was ordered by him to raise anchor then sail.   And
>
> *di-layarkan-nya-lah kechi itu sampai kapada anak-anak sungai itu*
> was sailed by him   the ketch as far as   inlets   river the,
>
> *lalu di-suroh-nya   berlaboh. Maka tinggal-lah di-sana*
> then was ordered by him shelter.   And   remained   there
>
> *pula sampai enam tujoh hari. Maka ada-lah   datang sa-buah top*
> again up to six   seven days. And   it happened came   a schooner
>
> *hendak   lalu dari situ   maka di-tembak-nya   lalu*
> intending to pass through there and   was fired by him and

di-balas   *oleh orang top   itu, maka mati-lah dua*
(the fire) was returned by crew   schooner the and dead   two

orang dalam kechi. Se-telah   berperang-lah sampai masok matahari,
men in the ketch. After that was fought   until   set   sun

maka angin pun turun-lah, maka top   itu berlayar-lah, entah
and   wind   died   and schooner the sailed away not know

ka-mana-kah ia pergi,   tiada lagi   kelihatan.
whither   they went not   again was seen

'He remained on shore for six or seven days, and then came back on board. And when he arrived, he ordered the anchor to be weighed, and we sailed. He sailed the ketch into the inlets of the river, and then ordered us to anchor, and we remained there another six or seven days. A schooner came and wished to pass through, and he fired at it, but the men in the schooner returned our fire, and two men in the ketch were killed. We continued to fight until the sun went down, and then the wind fell, and that vessel sailed away, and where it went we could not see any more.'

A second and more consistent marker of foregrounding is the use of the so-called "passive" verb. Transitive sentences in Malay can be expressed in at least two ways, illustrated as follows:

ACTIVE: *ia mem-bawa barang-barang ka-darat*
        he brought   the goods   ashore

In this type of sentence, which is commonly called "active" in Malay grammars, the stem of the verb (here: *bawa* 'bring') is prefixed with *meng-*, the nasal *-ng* being homorganic to the stem-initial consonant. An alternative form of the same sentence is

PASSIVE: *di-   bawa- nya   barang-barang ka-darat*
         PASS bring he (AGT) the goods   ashore

It is customary to translate such sentences as 'The goods were brought ashore by him.' In actual fact, however, the Malay "passive" as it is used in the classical narrative rarely corresponds to the English passive. Rather, the Malay "passive" form is used for events that are perfective, active, foregrounded, and realis (as opposed to irrealis).[6]

---

[6] In the spoken Malay of Jakarta, the nasal prefix which corresponds to the *meng-* of Standard Malay carries somewhat similar meanings of irrealis, continuous, nonsegmented events. Stephen Wallace's data from this dialect (Wallace 1976) are revealing for the way in which considerations of focus, aspect, and the idiosyncracies of individual lexical items condition the selection of an affix.

With intransitive verbs, and also with transitive verbs which idiosyn-
cratically do not take the prefix *meng-*, foregrounding is indicated by the
obligatory use of *-lah*; for example, in Abdullah (1932:69) we have:

> *maka se-bentar itu   juga   datang-lah ia*
> and   at that   very moment came   he
> 'and at that very moment he came'

> *maka ia pun   kembali-lah*
> and   he TOPIC returned
> 'and he returned'

THE AGENT IN FOREGROUNDED CLAUSES

In foregrounded clauses, the agent of the transitive verb is marked
differently from the object and from the agent of the intransitive verb. The
third person pronoun has the forms *-nya* (transitive agent) and *ia* (intransitive
agent/transitive object). In the first person, the transitive agent is proclitic
ku-, and the other two functions are *aku*, for example (from Abdullah 1932,
pages 44, 44, and 101, respectively):

> *maka aku pun   berlari-lah*
> and   I   TOPIC ran
> 'and I ran'

> *maka ku-dapati budak Basir itu*
> and   I   found boy   the
> 'and I found the boy Basir'

> *maka di-suroh-nya   aku menulis demikian*
> and   was told by him I   to write thus
> 'and he told me to write thus'

With full nouns, an agentive preposition *oleh* is used for agents of transitive
verbs (Abdullah, 1932:115)

> *maka oleh tuan   itu di-suroh   aku berdua*
> and   by master the were told we two
> 'and the master told us both'

The distribution of these forms can thus be summed up as follows:

	A_{tr}	A_{itr}	0_{tr}
1st Person	*ku-*	*aku*	*aku*
3rd Person	*-nya*	*ia*	(*ia*)
Full Noun	*oleh*	$\emptyset$	$\emptyset$

Here, the object of the transitive verb *ia* is placed in parentheses because this pronoun normally has zero representation, and clear examples of exceptions to this are difficult to find; it has been put in here by analogy with the first person.

This distribution is, of course, typical of passives. The discourse function of the Malay "passive," however, is quite different from that associated with passives in Western languages, where passive is primarily a way of suppressing the agent of the transitive verb and secondarily denotes some kind of topic shift (e.g., object-thematization)—the details are, of course, controversial. In Malay classical narrative, the "passive" contrasts with the "active" as foregrounding to backgrounding.

Backgrounding in Malay

As an illustration of this backgrounding function of the "active" verb, I will present two parts of an episode in which Abdullah criticizes the behavior of a British officer. He introduces the episode with a general account of the British sailors in the early period of contact. This introduction to the main episode has continuing or repeated actions; the transitive verbs have the prefix *meng-*; and the intransitive verbs lack the foregrounding suffix *-lah*:

Shahadan ada   pun pada zaman itu   dalam negeri Malaka belum-lah
Now   there was at   time   that in   state   Malacca not yet

ada   banyak Inggeris. Maka orang   melihat Inggerispun seperti melihat
were many   English. And   people saw   the English like   seeing

harimau sebab   nakal-nya   dan garang-nya. Maka jikalau datang
tiger   because viciousness and fierceness. And   when   came

sa-buah dua buah kapal Inggeris singgah di-Malaka, maka orang-orang
one   two   ships English arrive   in Malacca then   people

Malaka   semua-nya menutup pintu rumah-nya.   Maka ada-lah
Malacca all   lock   doors their houses. And

berkeliling lorong itu beberapa matrus itu mabok,   ada yang
around   streets   numerous sailors   got drunk some

memechahkan pintu-pintu rumah orang, dan ada yang mengajar
broke down   doors   houses people and some   chased

perempuan-perempuan berjalan, dan ada yang berkelahi sama
women   walking and some   fought   with

sendiri-nya, pechah belah muka-nya, menjadi huru-hara   besar-lah
themselves break split faces their became disturbance great

'Now there were at that time not many English in the State of
Malacca, and the population looked upon the English as one looks
upon a tiger, as being vicious and fierce. And whenever one or two
English ships would come and stop in Malacca, the population of
Malacca would lock the doors of their houses. And everywhere in the
streets there would be sailors getting drunk, some breaking down
people's doors, some chasing the women as they walked, and some
fighting among themselves and breaking one another's heads, and
great was the uproar.'

The introductory passage is followed by the story of the scandalous behavior
of the British officer. This story consists, for the most part, of single events
happening in succession. It thus contrasts with the Einleitung, which consists largely of simultaneous or repeated events. The verbs in the actual
narrative are, therefore, in the foregrounded function, i.e. they are "passive":

Se-telah itu   dalam sedikit hari lagi maka di-beli-nya pula
after   that within a few days more   he bought again

burong punai berkurongan, maka ada-lah ia berdiri dengan senapang,
pigeons   in cages   and   he stood with   rifle

maka di-lepaskan oleh orang-nya sa'ekursa'ekur, lalu
and   were freed by   his servant one by one   then

di-tembak-nya. . . . Kemudian di-beli-nya pula   beberapa ekur monyet,
he shot (them)   After that he bought again several   monkeys

maka di-lepaskan ka'atas pohon sena   di-hadapan rumah-nya,
and   released   up in   tree angsana in front of his house

kemudian di-tembak-nya jatoh mati.
then   he shot   fall dead

'After that a few days later he bought some pigeons in cages, and
while he stood by with his rifle his servant freed them one after
another, and he shot at them. . . . After that he bought a number of
monkeys and set them free in the angsana tree in front of his house,
and shot at them until they fell dead.'

Since "active" and "passive" constructions are assigned different but
equal discourse functions, it can, I believe, be argued that it is wrong to
attribute primary or secondary status to either one of them. From a morphological point of view they are equally complex, both "active" and
"passive" being derived from simple stems. I shall therefore refer to the
so-called passive as the ERGATIVE SYSTEM.

The "Discourse Passive" and Ergativity

The introduction of the term ERGATIVE into this context raises some interesting questions concerning the origins of ergativity in discourse. These questions are also very complex, and it would not be appropriate to discuss them at great length here. At the same time, ergativity is linked to tense and aspect in a number of languages. In Malay, where tense is not overtly marked, the "voice" system serves the same function in narrative—to assert the respective anteriority of events and to indicate which events actually advance the narrative and which events are ancillary. Because this sequence-marking function of tense-aspect (and voice) is in turn bound up with focus marking, it is not surprising that syntax is also affected by the voice system.

Languages which are ergative in case marking tend to be either SOV or VSO in basic word order, while conversely SVO languages are accusative in case-marking.

This pattern is followed in Malay also, since the narrative ergative is characterized by VSO word order and the accusative system (i.e., the backgrounding form) is generally SVO, as is illustrated in the following clause-types:

ACCUSATIVE: *ia*   *membawa barang-barang ka-darat*
           'they brought   the goods   ashore'

ERGATIVE: *Maka di-bawa-**nya** barang-barang ka-darat*
           'and   they brought the goods   ashore'

The backgrounded sentence in Malay typically has a "thematized" subject; that is, in the transitive sentence the subject is placed before the verb. Although SVO syntax in backgrounded clauses was presumably once a matter of pragmatics—the greater likelihood of having a "new" subject in background—the situation in the Malay narratives is virtually grammaticized to the point where the verb prefixed with *meng-* MUST be preceded by the subject. On the other hand, the *di-* form of the verb is almost invariably followed by the subject. With the third person pronoun *-nya*, this distribution is fixed, whereas, with full-noun agents having the agentive preposition *oleh*, the preverbal position is rare.

The relationship between verb position and the ergative in Malay appears to be that FOREGROUNDED NARRATIVE CONTEXTS REQUIRE FRONTING OF THE VERB. The verb is the locus of actions and events and is therefore the newest part of a narrative clause. We have seen that foregrounding, whether it is carried out by morphology, syntax, or both, is invariably indicated by reference to the verb and not by some other constituent of the clause. In backgrounding, on the other hand, new information is likely to be located anywhere in the clause, including the subject. Backgrounding is therefore more disposed to "thematized" word orders, with the subject preceding the verb. In Malay, these word orders are associated with the voice of the verb: VSO for "passive" (predicate focus), SVO for "active" (subject or other focus).

The preceding account, of course, still begs several questions, the most important being the origin of the morphological passive itself. This question is the more intriguing in that the *di-* prefix, which is said to be a passive marker, is itself probably a frozen form of a third person pronoun dia. It is interesting that in older Malay prose one finds occasional examples of the *di*-prefix with INTRANSITIVE verbs, for example, *di-tangis-nya* 'they wept', suggesting perhaps that the restriction of the *di-* form to transitives (i.e., the ergative distribution) is a relatively recent phenomenon. If this is so, then *di-* may at one time have been an unspecified subject marker (derived, of course, from a third person pronoun) for ALL verbs, which would for rather obvious pragmatic reasons become restricted to transitive verbs and eventually was reanalyzed as an agreement marker with third person agents. The pragmatic causes of this restriction would have been (*a*) the greater usefulness of the unspecified subject construction with transitive verbs; and (*b*) the greater frequency of truly transitive verbs in foregrounding (i.e., in VS clauses).

The point that I wish to make here is that in investigating the rise of ergative constructions it is of paramount importance to examine the discourse uses of "passive" as well as their morphosyntactic origins at the word and sentence level. Malay prose offers us an easily available example of a language which is by no means "ergative" in the sense in which this word is usually used but which cannot really be said to be simply active–passive. The Malay data may have a great deal to tell us about the development of ergativity in such languages as Samoan.

Tagalog

The Tagalog Verb

In Tagalog, which is quite closely related to Malay, a strikingly similar use of voice is found. Because of the greater complexity of the Tagalog verb system, a somewhat longer account of verbal morphology will be necessary; even so, it will be possible to give only a very general notion of structure functions; for further details, Schachter and Otanes (1972) should be consulted.[7]

---

[7] I am grateful to Paul Schachter for written comments which he sent me on the original version of this section.

The verb in Tagalog expresses two functions: (*a*) the ASPECT of the sentence; and (*b*) the CASE of the TOPIC of the sentence. The following illustrations will indicate some of the possibilities for coding the topic case into the verb:

(1)   *B-um-ili ang bata ng tinapay sa tindahan sa nanay niya.*
         bought the child bread   at store for mother his
         'The child bought bread at the store for his mother.'

Here, *bata* 'child' is topic and is therefore marked with the topic article *ang*. In addition, *bata* is the agent, and, since the agent is topic, the verb receives the agent-topic affix *-um-*, that is, *bili → bumili*. In the next example, the topic is the direct object *tinapay* 'bread':

(2)   *B-in-ili ng bata ang tinapay sa tindahan sa nanay niya.*

The verb this time has received the object-topic affix *-in-*, and the object of the verb has the topic article *ang*; the agent in this sentence, which is not the topic, has the article *ng*. In Philippine linguistics, these constructions are known as "focus" constructions; thus (1) is called agent-focus, (2) object-focus, and so on. From the point of view of normal linguistic usage, this use of the term "focus" is erroneous; it would be especially confusing in the context of the present chapter, where focus is used in the sense of "main assertion, new information," that is, the direct opposite of the Philippine sense. I shall therefore use the term TOPIC here, and will refer to sentence (1) as agent-topic, sentence (2) as object-topic, etc. Other topic constructions are represented in (3), locative-topic, and (4), benefactive-topic:

(3)   *B-in-il-han ng bata ng tinapay ang tindahan sa nanay niya.*

(4)   *I-b-in-ili ng bata ng tinapay sa tindahan ang nanay niya.*

In addition to the case of the topic, the verb also shows aspect. Aspectual morphology is engaged to topic morphology to the extent that aspectual processes are different for the various topic types. A further slight complication is that there are several morphological classes of verbs, reflected in the affixation of the perfective aspect:

1. *-um-* verbs, for example, *kain: k-um-ain* 'eat'
2. *mag-* verbs, for example, *luto: magluto* 'cook'
3. *ma-*class, for example, *ligo': ma-ligo'* 'bathe'

The agent-topic conjugation for the three classes, in the three aspects, is as follows:

	Perfective	Imperfective	Contemplated	Gloss
-um- class	*k-um-ain*	*k-um-a-kain*	*ka-kain*	'eat'
nag- class	*nag-luto*	*nag-lu-luto*	*mag-lu-luto*	'cook'
na- class	*na-ligo'*	*na-li-ligo'*	*ma-li-ligo'*	'bathe'

In object-topic constructions, aspect morphology again varies according to the morphological class of the verb, for example:

	Perfective	Imperfective	Contemplated	Gloss
in- class	*b-in-asa*	*b-in-a-basa*	*ba-basa-hin*	'read'
i- class	*i-b-in-ukas*	*i-b-in-u-bukas*	*i-bu-bukas*	'open'
an- class	*p-in-unas-an*	*p-in-u-punas-an*	*pu-punas-an*	'clean'

Similar conjugations exist for the locative- and benefactive-topic constructions; for example, for *hiram* 'borrow' there is a perfective locative-topic *h-in-iram-an*, and *bili* 'buy' has the benefactive-topic *i-b-in-ili*; there is a certain amount of homophony among the various topic forms of the same verb.

The semantic contrasts of the conjugations are, in general, as follows: (*a*) action completed (stem unreduplicated) versus action incomplete (stem reduplicated); and (*b*) realis (*-um-* infix in -um-class, prefix-initial *n-* in *mag/ma* classes) versus irrealis (zero-affix in -*um*- class, prefix-initial *m-* in *mag/ma* classes). In non-agent-topic verbs, the infix -*in-* is found in both classes.

As regards the various noun-phrase roles, the articles with full nouns are *ang* (topic), *ng* (oblique), and *sa* (locative), corresponding to which are the pronouns:

	ang	*ng*	*sa*
'I'	*ako*	*ko*	*akin*
'he/she'	*siya*	*niya*	*kaniya*
'they'	*sila*	*nila*	*kanila*

TEXTS

The texts which I have chosen are from Bloomfield's *Tagalog Texts*. These are for the most part fairly short anecdotes, some funny and some tragic, dealing with human scenes and containing both dialogue and action. They provide excellent material for studying the functions of the verb forms in narrative.

FOREGROUNDING IN TAGALOG

The formations used for foregrounding in both transitive and intransitive sentences have in common the PERFECTIVE-REALIS verb form. Clauses which actually advance the story line and narrate new events have verbs with unreduplicated stems and with either the infix or the *n-* initial on the prefix. In the following illustrative text (No. 8 in Bloomfield 1917:32–33), the foregrounded sentences in the English translation have been placed in boldface:

Nang dumating sila   sa isa ng gubat ay iniwan sila   nang kanila
when came   they to a   jungle, left   them they

ng mugulang at   pinagsabihan sila   na   hantayin sila   doon, at
parents   and told   them that wait for them there and

sila y babalik agad.   Sila y naiwan, datapwat nalalaman nila
they would return soon. They left   but   knew   they

na hindi sila   pagbabalikan nang kanila ng magulan. Nang
that not they (=to them) would return   they   parents. when

makaraan ang ila ng sandali',   ay nakarinig sila nang isa ng ingay.
had passed   short time   heard   they a   noise

Pinuntahan nila ang lugar na pinanggagalingan nang ingay. Doon ya
approached they   place   come-from   noise. there

nakita nila ang isa ng malaki ng higante na naliligo sa tabi nang isa ng
saw   they a   huge   giant   bathed   side   a

balon. Tiningnan nila ang paligid-ligid nang lugar, at sa tabi nang isa ng
well. looked   they surroundings   place   side   a

kahuy ay nakita nila ang pananamit nang higante. Ang ikapitu ng
tree   saw   they clothes   giant   seventh

bata ay pinaalis ang kanya ng manga kapatid at   sinabi niya na
child   sent away his   plur. siblings and told   he   that

magtago sila at kanya ng nanakawin ang sapatos nang higante. Ito ay
hide   they he   would steal   shoes   giant.   That

kanila ng ginawa', at   ninakaw nang bata ang sapatos.
they   did   and stole   child   shoes

'When they **came** to a jungle, their parents **left** them, **telling** them to wait for them there and that they would soon come back. They **left**, but they knew that their parents would not come back to them. When a short time had passed, they **heard** a noise. They **went** toward the place from which the noise came. There they **saw** a great giant bathing by the side of a well. They **looked** around the place, and by the side of a tree they **saw** the clothes of a giant. The seventh child **sent** his brothers and sisters away and **told** them to hide, and he would steal the giant's shoes. They **did** this, and the child **stole** the shoes.'

The verbs in clauses which advance the narrative are:

> *d-um-ating* 'come'
> *in-iwan* 'leave (transitive)'
> *p-in-ag-sabih-an* 'tell'
> *na-iwan* 'leave (intransitive)'
> *na-ka-rinig* 'hear'
> *p-in-untah-an* 'approach'
> *na-kita* 'see'
> *t-in-ingn-an* 'look'
> *na-kita* 'see'
> *p-in-a-alis* (i.e., *pa-alis*, *-in-*, and not, of course, reduplicated) 'send away'
> *s-in-abi* 'tell'
> *g-in-awa'* 'do'
> *n-in-akaw* 'steal'

The intransitives have the infix *-um-* or else the prefix *na-*, according to the verb-class. The transitives have one of the several types of topic affixes known collectively as "goal-topic" (Schachter and Otanes 1972:283–284), indicating that the topic of the clause is not identified as the agent; for example, *ninakaw* 'stole' (*nakaw* + *-in-*) has goal-topic, and *pinuntahan* 'approached' (*punta(h)* + *-in-* + *-an*) has direction-topic, namely, *ang lugar* 'the place,' of which the article *ang* identifies the noun as topic.

BACKGROUNDING IN TAGALOG

Backgrounding is indicated by a variety of formations that have in common the absence of the perfective–realis markers of foregrounding. Thus, backgrounded events and descriptions may have verbs which are:

1. Reduplicated

   > *babalik* 'would return' (i.e., irrealis)
   > *nalalaman* 'knew' (i.e., realis but imperfective)

2. Suffix *-in* instead of Infix

   > *hantayin* 'wait for' (i.e., irrealis)
   > *nanakawin* 'steal' (i.e., irrealis)

3. *Ma(g)-* Prefix instead of *Na(g)-*

   > *makaraan* 'pass, go (root: da)' (apparently pure backgrounding)
   > *magtago* 'hide' (i.e., irrealis)

Evidently this variety of formations corresponds to a variety of "semantic" functions at the sentence level. But approached from the discourse level, these semantic functions turn out to have a uniform pragmatic goal: They suggest a reduced assertion of the finite reality of the event. The devices used in backgrounding indicate events which are either contemplated or, if initiated, are not completed because they are ongoing, stative, or repeated.

AGENT AND OBJECT TOPIC

It is of course of especial interest that both in Tagalog and in Malay foregrounding is associated with voice, that is, the encoding in syntax and verbal morphology of the marked sentence topic. In Tagalog narrative, agent-topic is rather rare (cf. also Schachter 1977:279–306). It tends, in fact, to be found in sequence-initial clauses in foregrounding, the same function, it will be remembered, which elicits marked word orders in Old English; for example, in text no. 15 in Bloomfield (1971:56–57), the introduction is as follows:

> *Juan was a carpenter who had for a neighbor a Chinaman who also was a carpenter. This Chinaman was a skilled carpenter and his cleverness showed itself in his use of the plane.*
>
> *One day he bought a piece of wood forty feet in length. This he proceeded to smoothe.*

After the backgrounded scene-setting statements, the actual events of the narrative begin with the "Chinaman's' buying of the wood. This transitive sentence has the agent-topic verb:

> *Isa ng araw nakabili sya nang isa ng piraso-ng-kahoy . . . Itu y kanya ng*
> one   day   bought   he   a   piece of wood . . . this   he
> *nilinis*
> smoothed

(where *nilinis* is the object-topic form of *linis*, with *ni-* here for *-in-*). The story continues with transitive sentences in one of the goal-topic formations, as in the second of the foregrounded sentences. These goal-topic verbs are found regularly in sequential narrative-advancing clauses and thus correspond functionally in discourse to the Malay "passive" in *di-*. About all of this, obviously, very much more needs to be said.

5. CONCLUSION

One advantage which accrues from considering linguistic data in wider contexts, such as discourses and "real-world" situations, is that it begins to make sense to ask beyond the question "What morphosyntactic devices does a language possess?" the further question: "Why does this language, and languages in general, have such a mechanism?" The assumption that in a discourse the competent user of the language needs to mark out a main route through the narrative and divert in some way those parts of the narrative which are not strictly relevant to this route suggests at least a partial explanation of the existence of elaborate tense-aspect systems in some languages but not in others.

It is significant that morphological tense-aspect cannot be accounted for in the same way that we account for the famous snow vocabulary of the Eskimos, etc. Times and views of events are not imposed on cultures by external realities, at least not in any verifiable and noncircular sense. Diachronically, too, tense-aspect systems come and go within substantially the same cultures. But from a discourse viewpoint tense-aspect becomes intelligible. One finds typically an aspect marker specialized for foregrounding, or one specialized for backgrounding, or both functions indicated. Superimposed upon these markers there may be quite precise indicators of tense properly speaking, that is, the location of an action on the temporal-deictic axis. Most of these tense-markers can be expected to function in background only, for example, pluperfect, remote-past, future-perfect, future, etc. Their purpose is to gather in information and other detail scattered at arbitrary points on the axis. Because background tense markers signal happenings and states which are not "in sequence" and which by their very temporal inconsistency cannot and do not move the discourse forward, they have access to a much wider spectrum of temporal deixis. We have seen that one of the distinguishing properties of background is just such a "distortion" of the time-frame. Background is less constrained in tense than is foreground, because details of indirect relevance to the narrative do not have to be contemporaneous with the narrative but may be part of the prehistory of the narrated event (pluperfect), may provide a preview for a total perspective of the event (future or future-perfect), or may even suggest contingent but unrealized events (irrealis forms, such as conditionals and optatives). In foreground, by contrast, the only tense-indication needed is a conventional location of the successive events of the narrative in a nonreal (by which I mean "not currently being witnessed") framework. In many languages, this tense is the one known as a "preterite" or simple past; yet it is, of course, more important that a relative time-frame should be established with respect to the other events, so that, although for many languages a semantic constant "to the left of present on the time-axis" exists for this tense, the idea of speaker distance from the narrated events is paramount.

What of languages which do not possess elaborate tense-systems? Tentatively, one can say that at least the foreground–background distinction is overtly marked, and the degree of precision in tense-marking will vary from language to language, with actual morphological indicators being supplemented by adverbs and by other more lexicalized markers. The foreground–background distinction may be shown in ways other than morphology. For example, the ordinary uninterrupted flow of the narrative in foreground may elicit a different word order from the "intervening" descriptive syntax of backgrounding, with its greater possibilities for shifts of subject and points of view. In this strategy, it is the position of the verb which is crucial. The verb is the location of new, narrative-advancing information. The verb's complement may or may not contribute to the narrative, and the subject of the verb is least likely to play a significant role in the story-line. Thus we typically find the verb in one of the two most prominent positions in the clause, the beginning or the end, and the subject of the verb is likely to be highly presuppositional, in fact, usually identical with the preceding subject.

The use of focus-indicating or "voice" mechanisms as a foregrounding device is, I would speculate, ultimately quite closely related to the verb-position strategy, though I am uncertain about the exact nature of this relationship. Eventually, it might be possible to show how ergativity develops quite naturally from such specialization of passive voice in discourse. Diachronically, it seems that some kind of reanalysis of a focus-indicating system as a passive–ergative one has taken place; such a reanalysis could have come about as a result of the high frequency of definite-object constructions in contexts in which the content of the verb was consistently the most prominent discourse-advancing factor.

Finally, a syntactic foregrounding strategy may very well be reinforced by a particle or by several particles which, when attached to a particular sentence constituent, indicate the discourse status of the event. Such particles may simultaneously indicate both focus and tense-aspect. It seems a rather short step to the situation where such a particle would become a verbal clitic and would eventually be reanalyzed as an aspectual morpheme affixed to the verb. An article by James Hoskison on Gude, an African language, seems to suggest that topic–focus markers in that language are tied to aspect in such a way that each aspect selects a different focus marker (Hoskison 1975:228–229). In the absence of actual discourse data, it is hard to judge the relevance of this example. There is, however, obviously a highly interesting field of research in the diachrony of tense-aspect in discourse, which has scarcely begun to be exploited.

ACKNOWLEDGMENTS

A number of ideas in this paper result from Talmy Givón's seminar on Diachronic Syntax at the L.S.A. Institute in 1976 and from subsequent correspondence with Givón. I have also been saved from numerous errors and naivetés by the participants in the SUNY-Buffalo workshop on Focus and Aspect in Discourse (May, 1977) and by members of audiences at SUNY-Binghamton, SUNY-Stony Brook, Cornell, the University of Ottawa, and the University of North Carolina, Chapel Hill. I am especially grateful for some stimulating conversations with Sandra Thompson, Joan Hooper, Ellen Rafferty, and Stephen Wallace and am also grateful to the other members of this conference. None of these associates necessarily agrees with everything in this paper.

REFERENCES

Abdullah Munshi, bin Abdul Kadir (1932) *Hikayat Abdullah, Jalid yang Pertama.* (Malay Literature Series, Vol. 4), Malaya Publishing House, Ltd., Singapore.

Bloomfield, Leonard (1917) *Tagalog Texts with Grammatical Analysis*, University of Illinois, Urbana, Illinois.

Forsyth, J. (1970) *A Grammar of Aspect: Usage and Meaning in the Russian Verb*, University Press, Cambridge.

Hopper, P. J. (1977) "Diachronic and Typological Implications of Foregrounding Constructions," *Third International Conference on Historical Linguistics*, Hamburg.

Hopper, P. J. (1977) "Observations on the Typology of Focus and Aspect in Narrative Language," NUSA (to be reprinted in Studies in Language, 1978).

Hoskinson, James T. (1975) "Focus and Topic in Gude," in R. K. Herbert, ed., *Ohio State University Working Papers in Linguistics* 20 (*Proceedings of the 6th Conference on African Linguistics*), pp. 227–233.

Lehmann, W. P., and P. J. Hopper (1966) *Concordance to the Parker Manuscript*, Linguistics Research Center, Austin, Texas (printout).

Plummer, Charles, ed. (1929) *Two of the Saxon Chronicles* (Parallel, edited, with introduction on the basis of an edition by John Earle), Clarendon Press, Oxford.

Reid, Wallis (1976) "The Quantitative Validation of a Grammatical Hypothesis: The *passé simple* and the *imparfait*," in *Papers of the Northeastern Linguistic Society* 7.

Schachter, Paul (1977) "Reference-related and Role-related Properties of Subjects," in P. Cole and J. Sadock, eds., *Syntax and Semantics: Grammatical Relations*, Academic Press, New York.

Schachter, Paul, and Fe T. Otanes (1972) *Tagalog Reference Grammar*, University of California Press, Berkeley, California.

Selemani bin Mwenyi Chande (1965) "Safar ya Bara Afrika," in L. Harries, ed. (1965), *Swahili Prose Texts. A Selection from the Material Collected by Carl Velten from 1893–1896*, Oxford University Press, London.

Wallace, Stephen (1976) "The Semantics of Verb Nasalization in Jakarta Malay," Winter Meeting of the Linguistic Society of America, Philadelphia, Pennsylvania.

THE FIGURE A SENTENCE MAKES:
AN INTERPRETATION OF A CLASSICAL
MALAY SENTENCE

A. L. BECKER
University of Michigan

> *To understand a sentence means to understand a language. To understand a language means to be master of a technique.*
>
> —LUDWIG WITTGENSTEIN, 1958

This essay is an examination of a single sentence in Classical Malay, a sentence that I puzzled over and discussed with my friends for many months, until it began to yield its meaning and allow us, readers of Classical Malay far away in space and time, to join imaginatively in its shaping. Understanding sentences[1]—a level in the hierarchy of discourse structures—is a necessary level of competence in modern philology. Sentences have been defined by Paul Ricoeur (1971) and others (see Mukarovsky 1977)[2] as the

---

[1] It might be clearer to use the term RHETORICAL SENTENCE, a structure quite different from a clause, but the term suggests that there are nonrhetorical sentences, whereas I wish to suggest, rather, that sentences are the interface of syntactic relations and rhetorical relations, including tropes, defined separately for each language.

[2] Mukarovsky (1977:15) wrote, "The central element of narrative language is the sentence, the component mediating between the language and the theme, the lowest dynamic (realized in time) semantic unit, a miniature model of the entire semantic structuring of the discourse."

Syntax and Semantics, Volume 12:
Discourse and Syntax

basic units of discourse, the minimal unit of the text. Ricoeur makes an insightful distinction between LANGUAGE and DISCOURSE in terms of the different kinds of relations that must be taken account of to describe each. That is, discourse-internal relations [structural information] and discourse-external relations, particular relations with speaking and hearing people or reading and writing people (which are very different, since the mode of interpretation is so different for dialogue or for reading) in particular times and places. Unlike LANGUAGE (which many linguists see as their field of study), discourse (the field of modern philology) is studied in relation to a complex set of external constraints, grouped by Ricoeur into these kinds of relations: (*a*) temporality, relation to a particular time of utterance or writing; (*b*) subjectivity, relation to a particular speaker or writer; (*c*) referentiality, relations to Nature, the referential world; and (*d*) intersubjectivity, relations to hearer or reader (as a potential speaker or writer), who depends upon his experience in the other role—that is, as speaker or writer—to help him interpret the text.[3] Just as the sign can be seen as the minimal unit of LANGUAGE ("worldless" systems and structures), so sentences—described differently for different languages—can be seen as the basic, nonreducible units of discourse—that is, the least complex units that are constrained for temporality, subjectivity, referentiality, AND intersubjectivity, the discourse constraints. Structuralist linguistics (generative or nongenerative)—the description of language-internal relations—is far too reductive to describe discourse, the experiential context of language, as linguists have been learning in many different ways.[4]

The meaning of a sentence in discourse can be described as its relations to its discourse contexts (roughly, temporality, subjectivity, referentiality, and intersubjectivity) as well as its relations to its more specifically linguistic contexts (prior text or scripts and present text, the immediate linguistic context). A sentence in a written discourse can be an attempt to decontextualize the meaning of an oral discourse, at least partially, like tape-recording a conversation. Written discourse, in this sense, is more like LANGUAGE than dialogue is—that is, freer of constraints of temporality, subjectivity, referentiality, and intersubjectivity than dialogue is. The moment of reading supplies these via interpretation, and here discourse study becomes hermeneutic.[5]

Taking the perspective from sentence to context (or, in somewhat archaic terms, studying the "distribution" of sentences), one can see that the density of contextual constraints on sentences (i.e., possible distributions) varies

[3] See Ricoeur (1971:530–537), which this sentence attempts to summarize.

[4] Translators, philologists, and tagmemicists, among others, have not had to relearn this. Tagmemic grammars have for many years now included major sections on discourse constraints, see Pike (1975:17–18). For further bibliography, see Joseph Grimes (1975).

[5] For discussion of the relation of hermeneutics and linguistics, see especially Ricoeur (1976).

greatly. In terms of Givón (1977), some sentences are more marked than others, and, the more marked the sentence, the more constrained the discourse context. Sentences that evoke more detailed context also may have a kind of power[6] as metonymic representations of that context: Miltonic periodic sentences, Kennedian balanced antitheses (*ask not. . . .*), or the figure (unnamed, as far as I know) of Shakespeare's *A horse, a horse, my kingdom for a horse*. Can that figure ever be free of its context (even to someone who doesn't know it is Shakespeare's), so that we might say *A ____, A ____, my ____ for a ____* (*A theory, a theory, my tenure for a theory!*) without evoking a battlefield, near the end of the battle, on the loser's side?

Gertrude Stein (1975) made much of this power of context evocation in her dense little book, *How to Write*. She called context evocation "emotion" and observed (Stein 1975:23): "A sentence is not emotional a paragraph is." Stein did not use the same terms Ricoeur does, but she was also struck by the distinction between language and discourse. In Stein's own words [cited by Meyerowitz 1975, pp. XX and XXI, in her introduction to *How to Write*]:

> I once said in How to Write a book I wrote about Sentences and Paragraphs, that paragraphs were emotional and sentences were not. Paragraphs are emotional not because they express an emotion but because they register or limit an emotion. Compare paragraphs with sentences any paragraph or any sentence and you will see what I mean.
>
> In a book I wrote called How to Write I made a discovery which I considered fundamental, that sentences are not emotional and that paragraphs are. I found out about language that paragraphs are emotional and sentences are not and I found out something else about it. I found out that this difference was not a contradiction but a combination and that this combination causes one to think endlessly about sentences and paragraphs because the emotional paragraphs are made up of unemotional sentences.
>
> In a book called How to Write I worked a lot at this thing trying to find out just exactly what the balance the unemotional balance of a sentence is and what the emotional balance of a paragraph is and if it were possible to make even in a short sentence the two things come to be one. I think I did a few times succeed.

The following sentences (from Gass 1973) are ones in which she thinks she succeeded in making a sentence with the qualities of a paragraph—the context evoking qualities:

> *It looks like a garden but he had hurt himself by accident.*
>
> *A dog which you have never had before has sighed.*
>
> *A bay and hills hills are surrounded by their having their distance very near.*

---

[6] My thanks to Benedict Anderson for pushing me to investigate the notion of power sources in language, particularly Anderson (1976).

Gass (1973) puts these sentences next to Laurence Sterne's sentence:

> *A cow broke in tomorrow to my Uncle Toby's fortifications.*

Everyone can best describe for himself the nonstereotypic figures these sentences make when you read them and thus study that hermeneutic act of reading in her own consciousness, the growing awareness of a context for the sentence. Like poems, and like love, as Robert Frost (1979) wrote in his brief essay on poetics, they begin in delight and end in wisdom.[7]

In Classical Malay, the sentence is more like a paragraph, in Gertrude Stein's sense, and in the sense of most rhetoric books: It ESTABLISHES a topic and DEVELOPS it, CONTEXTUALIZES it. In seeking to understand more about establishing and developing a topic in Classical Malay—as potential readers—we must step back from some of our presuppositions about the figure a sentence makes. The experience of a Classical Malay sentence is different from the experiences of the sentences of Milton, Kennedy, Shakespeare, Stein, and Sterne. These are all more similar to each other than they are to Classical Malay figures, since they are all in English—which is why a foreigner has to start further back in the process of reading–interpretation. Reading Classical Malay is harder than reading Gertrude Stein: One must first clean his mental palate, like a wine taster, and stop treating Malay as deviant—usually rather bland and incomplete—English, and then try to discover the dimensions of its own world, as a reader—which is one of the two ways (there are only two, dialogue and reading) we can enter that world.

A CLASSICAL MALAY FIGURE

Sa-telah demikian maka Sang Bimanyu pun berjalan-lah sambil menchium
                            Bimanyu   walk   while sniff

bau bunga2an menghiborkan hati-nya itu, naik   bukit turun   bukit
small flowers   entertain   heart (liver) ascend hill descend hill

beberapa gunong   dan jurang dilalui.[8]
many   mountain and valley pass-over

I hope the reader who doesn't know Malay will be patient without a translation: A "good" English translation at this point would give an illusion of understanding before we know what a "good" English translation would have to include if it were to be at all close to the original Malay. Let me begin describing the untranslatable parts first.

[7] The original quotation from Frost (1949) is: "The Figure a poem makes. It begins in delight and ends in wisdom. The figure is the same as for love. . . ."

[8] This sentence, from Hussain (1964:34) begins a section, and is followed by these sentences:

> *Sa-genap batu ia berbaring, sa-genap pohon kayu ia dudok di-bawah-nya dengan leteh lesu rasa tuboh-nya. Maka bulan pun terbit-lah terlalu terang. Maka awan pun sunyi rupa-nya saperti menyuloh orang berjalan. Maka. . . .*

This Classical Malay figure, which will later be called a Classical Malay sentence, is from Hussain (1964). This text is a "translation," whatever that meant to a Moslem Malay translating a Hindu work from a middle Javanese "translation" (the Mahabharata Kawedar)[9] of a Sanskrit text. I have been trying to trace this process backward through time, to see how the text was recontextualized from Sanskrit to Javanese to Classical Malay. What did it mean to "Javanese" Sanskrit and to "Malay" Javanese? It would be premature to generalize about this larger process—the task has just begun. Suffice it to say that the kind of sentence to be discussed here has no very close Javanese or Sanskrit counterparts that I am aware of, though perhaps they will emerge under closer rhetorical examination. It seems a distinctly Malay figure—very common in classical texts but clearly archaic. That is, it does not seem to be found at all in what urban native speakers of Malay or Indonesian would call modern Malay or Indonesian (Bahasa Melayu or Bahasa Indonesia). It might be argued that it is a more Austronesian figure than many found in these modern languages and that its counterparts can be more clearly seen in Old Javanese (Kawi) or written Tagalog. In any case, the figure was chosen because it is common in Classical Malay (sentences resembling this one syntactically occur at a density of about 1–2 per page in Classical Malay texts I have studied), because it is archaic, and because it seems distinctly Malay.[10]

The sentence has three sections—to begin from a structuralist perspective (i.e., focusing on part to part relations within the text):

SECTION I. The Pre-Core: *Sa-telah demikian maka*

SECTION II. The Core: *Sang Bimanyu pun berjalan-lah*

SECTION III. The Elaboration: *sambil menchium*, etc.

These three sections are formally marked. At the core of the figure is a structure that may be called a *pun*, *-lah* structure:

SECTION II. The Core

. . . *Sang Bimanyu pun*	*berjalan-lah* . . .
topic	general event
'Bimanyu'	'walk (travel on road)'

It has been a major error, I think, to describe this structure (A + *pun*, B + *lah*) as if A were necessarily a noun phrase and B a verb phrase, or as if A were

---

[9] I am grateful for this identification of the source, and for a discussion of its contents to Bpk. Minarno of the Akademi Seni Karawitan Indonesia in Solo, Indonesia.

[10] The considerable deviance of Modern Malay (and Indonesian) from other Austronesian languages is described in Foley (1974). The notion is further developed in Becker and Wirasno (1976).

a subject and B a predicate. There are several kinds of problems with these Western grammatical labels:

1.   The distinction between "nouns" and "verbs" is not yet established for Classical Malay and is best not presupposed, particularly now that many feel Austronesian languages did/do not always distinguish grammatically between endocentric and exocentric clause relations.[11]

2.   The subject–predicate relation in English is not identical with the *pun*, *-lah* relation.[12] (Some of these differences will emerge later.) These two objections are objections to the use of a priori universal categories (noun, verb, subject, predicate) to describe Classical Malay.

However, leaving aside the difficulty of describing Classical Malay parts of speech in some Universal Grammar, there is a clear need in Classical Malay to distinguish between sentence structure and clause structure—and between sentence function and clause function; the categories subject and predicate (or the relation subject–predicate) come from a tradition (Western, Greek-based grammar) in which sentences and clauses are seldom clearly and categorically distinguished (to say nothing of their further association with logical propositions).[13] Malay and other Austroneisan languages clearly distinguished clauses and sentences, though this distinction is fading as Malay and Indonesian become more and more "Western" in system and structure.[14] Some features of sentences as distinct from clauses in Classical Malay are:

SENTENCES	CLAUSES
Topic–event structure	Subject–predicate structure
Topic initial is unmarked	Predicate initial is unmarked
Postpositional particles	Prefixes on predicates
(*pun*, *-lah*) mark topic–event	(*meng-*, *di-*) mark agentive
relations	relations (focus–nonfocus)
Referentially constrained topic	Role-focus constrained subject[15]

In Classical Malay, case relations are not relevant at sentence level, which helps to explain some of the special features of *pun*, *-lah* structures,

[11] This was a major point of discussion at the Second Eastern Conference on Austronesian Linguistics, Ann Arbor, 1974.

[12] This point is discussed thoroughly and demonstrated for Tagalog, another Austronesian language, in Foley and Van Valin (to appear).

[13] For further discussion of the Greek origins of our basic linguistic categories, see Benveniste (1973).

[14] See Foley (1974) and Becker and Wirasno (1976).

[15] The terminology in this table is chosen to indicate that sentences display rhetorical relations, clauses syntactic relations. See Footnote 2. Further details about these structures are found in Ajamiseba (1973). Ajamiseba also describes several other kinds of Malay sentences (as rhetorical figures).

particularly the observation that case-marked predicates do not in Classical Malay precede -*lah*. [This means only "verbs" with *ber*- (marking, roughly, external states and intentional motions) or *ter*- (marking nonintentional, "dative-like" involvement) or no prefixes (marking internal states and locationals) appear before -*lah* in Classical Malay, at least until quite late. The loss of this constraint appears to me central in the history of Malay.][16]

The *pun*, -*lah* structure has several variant forms, explainable, perhaps, as the result of the other sections of the sentence, which precede and follow the central *pun*, -*lah* structure, overlapping or merging with the *pun*, -*lah* structure. This overlapping will be described after these other constituents of this figure are described.

The referential relations of a *pun*, -*lah* structure are to prior text, either an earlier part of the text in which the sentence containing the *pun*, -*lah* structure occurs, or a source text. A source text can be a particular work from which a translation comes (as in the example under investigation here) or it can be a stereotypic script (i.e., a conventional or prototypical event).[17] In terms used by Longacre (1976), the sequence of *pun*, -*lah* structures forms the "backbone" or the "skeleton" of the text.[18] It indexes an event (-*lah*) and the participant (_____ *pun*) who or which will be in a single case role—in the sentence under investigation, this role is actor or agent—in the clauses that follow the *pun*, -*lah* core, clauses (SECTION III of the sentence) that fill in the details and particularize the event, IN RELATION TO THIS PARTICIPANT. Temporal order is neither regularly marked nor presupposed, either between sentences or between clauses, though it may be inherent in some scripts (i.e., stereotypic events) or in a prior text being translated.

---

[16] Written classical Malay appears to have no "standard" dialect, and texts vary widely, as one can observe by reading even short passages of the *Hikayat Pandawa Lima*, the *Hikayat Rama*, and the *Hikayat Abdullah*. One can still, I think, recognize a direction of change that includes, among other things, the loss of the *pun*, -*lah* structure and closer syntactic resemblance with Indo-European languages. One of the focal points in this history is the *Hikayat Abdullah*, an autobiography by Raffles' Malay teacher and translator, who was not a native speaker of Malay. Aspects of the language of the *Hikayat Abdullah*, including major differences from the text under consideration here, are well described in Hopper (1976), and in his excellent essay in this volume.

There is as yet no adequate "outsider's" grammar of classical or modern Malay (including *Bahasa Indonesia*). (There are several excellent works in Malay or Bahasa Indonesia.)

The meaning of these affixes remains problematic, though it is by now clear that they are not easily describable in Western grammatical terminology. Up to now grammarians have only been able to illustrate the range of their functions, which my own labels have tried to suggest.

I think that a major source of the difficulty in describing these affixes has been that discourse strategies have changed rapidly in the past few hundred years of the history of Malay—and with them the semantics of the verb affix systems. (See Footnote 10.)

[17] The notion of stereotypic scripts comes from Schank (1975). See also the notion of plot in Young, Becker, and Pike (1970).

[18] See Longacre (1976), especially Chapter 5, on plots.

Temporal sequence in Classical Malay is usually marked by a combination of the two terms *sa-telah* (roughly, 'end of one observation') and *sudah* ('finished', 'over').

Following the *pun, -lah* structure are one or more clauses (SECTION III) involving the topic (marked in SECTION III by *pun*) and within the event (marked in SECTION II by *-lah*). In this sentence, *Sang Bimanyu* (the *-pun* topic) is the agent (though not always in focus) throughout the section of the sentence following the *pun, -lah* core. He sniffs the smell of the flowers, entertains his heart, ascends hill(s), descends hill(s), and passes mountain(s) and valley(s)—except that this last act is put so that mountain(s) and valley(s) are in focus as a location:

> *beberapa gunong dan jurang dilalui.*
> many   mount and valley pass-over

Up to that point the predicates focused on the agent (the *pun* topic) or were unmarked for focus, as in the case of *naik* ('ascend') and *turun* ('descend'). The progression of the clauses is: agent focus to no marked focus to nonagent focus (*meng-* 'agent-focus' to *di-* 'nonagent focus', morphologically).

SECTION III. The Elaboration

sambil **men**chium   *bau bunga2an*
      agent-focus verb object
'while' 'sniff'   'smell of flowers'

menghiborkan   *hati-nya itu*
agent-focus verb object + article–deixis
'entertain'   'heart'   'it–that'

naik   bukit turun   bukit
no marked-focus verbs plus locations
'ascend' 'hill' 'descend' 'hill'

beberapa   gunong   dan jurang   di-lalu-i
Quantifier location   conj. location nonagent focus = verb + locative suffix
'many'   'mountain' 'and' 'valley'   'he pass-over'

This part of the sentence is like a flowering (to use a Javanese musical metaphor that seems appropriate, a *sekaran*, refering to a musical elaboration) of the script-indexing *pun, -lah* core. Because Classical Malay (and Javanese)[19] aesthetics are so closely tied to nature, this elaboration very

---

[19] Javanese aesthetic notions are described in Zoetmulder (1974), particularly pages 172–173. The word for aesthetics, *kalangwan*, can describe both art and nature. It is an inflexion of a root *langö*, which describes

> the quality by which an object appeals to the aesthetic sense. It does so not by the clarity and immediacy of its beauty, but, on the contrary, because it seems distant, half hidden and apparently inaccessible; because it is suggestive, but does not reveal itself fully; because it allures, hitting at as yet unrevealed riches, so that the seeker after beauty is consumed by longing and the desire to reach it [page 173].

frequently includes details of landscape—the physical setting, including, often, lists of names of local plants and animals found in Malaya or Java. The stereotypic act (or the translated act) is contextualized in a Malay landscape. At the end of the sentence the landscape is in focus—background becomes foreground—and in this way the limits of the domain of the *pun*, *-lah* core, the scope of the topic and event, are marked—a kind of syntactic fade-out. In the next sentence they may be reestablished or changed. The "passive" turn (the *di*-verb) at the end of the sentence gives it closure. The kinds of elaboration possible here in the final section of the sentence are constrained by the syntactic possibilities of the Classical Malay clause in playing role against focus: As readers, we experience topics moving in and out of roles and roles moving in and out of focus, the former at the sentence level, the latter at the clause level.

   The order of the verbs in the elaboration is significant here, but it is not clear to me just where to find the sources of the constraints on this order. The progression in the elaboration section from individual, agent-focused events to location-focused events (marked by the *di-* prefix and the *-i* suffix on the final verb) appears to reflect what has been called variously the Cline of Person (Becker and Oka 1977 [presented 1974]), the Referentiality Hierarchy (Foley 1976), the Natural Topic Hierarchy (Hawkinson and Hyman 1975) or the Inherent Lexical Content Hierarchy (Silverstein 1977), all of which seem to be quite similar, a continuum from self to other, marked off in strikingly similar ways from language to language. In most general terms, this cline or hierarchy can be represented as:

SPEAKER > HEARER > HUMAN PROPER > HUMAN COMMON

> ANIMATE > INANIMATE (> LOCATION)[20]

It manifests itself, both syntagmatically and paradigmatically, in such varying linguistic processes as modifier order in the English noun phrase, the structure of the Burmese classifier system, inherent topic-worthiness in Navaho, pronominal systems everywhere (which is why the label "cline of person" seems appropriate), and in the deictic inflexions of Kawi (Old Javanese), Malagassy, and many other languages.[21] If the role–referent (or role–topic, in this paper) distinction is at the heart of language, conceptually prior to metaphor and person, even, then a second order of categories grows out of the role-referent split, categories of role (cases and pronouns, for instance) and categories of referent (nominal subclassifications of various sorts, for instance CLASSIFIERS), with the principle of classification remaining

---

[20] Reverse deixis (making the hearer the reference point) is a characteristic of politeness systems of many Southeast Asian languages. It would reverse speaker and hearer in this cline. I have added *location* as the pole opposite *person*, so that the progression is from figure to ground.

[21] For Kawi, see Becker and Oka (1977). For Malagassy, see Rajaona (1971, 1972).

the same throughout both categories of role and categories of referent: I–other, and all its relatives, here–there, now–then, source–goal, observer–observed, and by extension even such linguistic metaphysics as mind–matter, slot–filler, and so forth.[22] Metaphor seems to work around the same distinction, the separability of role and referent.[23]

Whereas the elaboration section of the Classical Malay figure contextualizes the *pun*, *-lah* core in the Malay landscape (as represented in the Malay language), the first section of the sentence contextualizes that same core in the hierarchy of the prior text. We can distinguish two kinds of coherence, referential coherence (relations to a single event of a series of events in a stereotypic script) and textual coherence (marked relations between sentences, with sentences defined as discourse units). In those terms, we could say that the first section marks the textual coherence of the core, the final section the referential coherence of the core. The REFERENTIAL coherence is provided by the event (or script) of a man moving through a landscape, with perspective shifting from man to landscape. The TEXTUAL coherence is established by the first part of the figure, with the words,

SECTION I. The Pre-Core

Sa-telah demikian maka. . . .

It has taken me a long time to begin to understand these words. The first step in this gradual understanding was to experience the elaborate inflexion of deixis in Kawi, as I Gusti Ngurah Oka revealed it to me [and the very similar system in Malagassy, as described by S. Rajaona (1971, 1972)]. The widespread Austronesian deictic formative *-k-* (varying with *-t-* and *-n-* or $\emptyset$ at the center of the simplest deictic word, which has the form vowel + consonant + vowel, with inflexion appearing sometimes in all three positions), was elaborated in Kawi by prefixing, suffixing, and compounding in more than one grammatical system. That same *-k-* (meaning very generally 'to' or 'toward' or even 'shifter', to use Jespersen's term for this changing deixis as it appears in first and second person pronouns) appears in the center of Classical Malay connectives like

> *maka*
> *demikian*
> *arakian*
> *maki(a)n*
> *kalakian*

These connective terms break easily into parts, though the English equivalents for the meanings of these parts remain a problem. *Maka* can be

---

[22] This notion has also been central in the work of John Robert Ross, in many recent articles, including Cooper and Ross (1975), and in the work of Talmy Givón, particularly in Givón (1976).

[23] See Verhaar (1977).

analyzed into $ma- + (k + a)$, in which $ma-$ is a stative prefix,[24] $-k-$ is a deictic formative, and $-a$ is a third person/there/then. *Demikian* can be analyzed into $demi- + (k + i + an)$. *Demi-* is a word which can be translated by English 'in the name of' (as in a prayer or an oath), by English 'by' (as in 'one by one' *seorang demi seorang*) or by English 'for' (as in 'for the good of the people' *demi kepentigan rakyat*). *Demi-* is followed by $-k-$ is a deictic formative, $-i-$ is a first person/here/now, and $-an$ is a nominalizing" suffix. The other forms have similar etymologies.

The other word in the first section of the sentence is *sa-telah*, which dictionaries usually translate as 'after' or 'finished'. But this word, like those above, has no clear English equivalent. It frequently combines with *sudah* in Classical Malay, a word which is given an identical gloss in English, to mark temporal junctures. The *sa-* in *sa-telah* is clearly a prefix (meaning, roughly, 'one' or 'the same') and *telah* may be derivative of $te(r)- + laah$ (meaning, roughly, 'investigated', 'gone-over', 'studied').[25]

The combined form

Sa-telah demikian maka. . . .

may then "mean" something like 'having gone over, thus, then. . . .' or, in some contexts, 'after this, then,' if one remembers that the meaning is not necessarily temporal or sequential, though it may be. Clear temporal sequencing in the text from which this sentence comes is nearly always marked by *sa-telah sudah*.

Etymological explanations, fascinating though they are as a conceptual strategy, do not clearly reveal the text-building functions of these words. Part of the meaning of English connective words like *however, nevertheless, furthermore*, etc. is the sum of their semantic parts, but I don't think that when we use them we are building them out of parts: It is hard to make a joke with **hownever*, **everaless*, or **furtherless*. The main point, it seems to me, has to do with the sheer heaviness of these terms, a density in both sound and meaning that is very reminiscent of the basic principle of heaviness and lightness in Southeast Asian calendars, music, dramatic plots, and elsewhere: the coincidence of gongs at structural boundaries (the more gongs sounding together, the higher level the boundary) or—in calendric terms—the coincidence between marked (highly valued) days in simultaneously occurring "weeks" of different lengths.[26] At the level of sentences,

---

[24] See Jeffrey Dreyfuss (1977), for a more elaborate description of this "stative" prefix and its syntactic functions.

[25] The presence of the Malay form *mentelah* indicates *te-* (from *ter-* which loses -r before l-) is a prefix; if it were clearly part of the root, the form would be *menelah*. Of course, the etymology may be more complex, for example, the converging of two roots, *la'ah* and *telah*.

[26] This notion of "heaviness" came up first in a discussion of the *Hikayat Pandawa Lima* with R. Anderson Sutton. For its relevance to both calenders and music, see Judith Becker (to appear), A. L. Becker (to appear), and Geertz (1973).

the Classical Malay text uses just *maka* (or another single-word connective like *shahadan* or *hatta*, both borrowed from Indo-Persian languages) to mark separate units. At the boundary of a larger (i.e., larger in scope) unit, a cluster of sentences of some sort, heavier or denser connectives are used, two-word connectives (e.g., *arakian maka*, *demikian maka*, *hatta sa-telah*, *arakian sa-telah*, *sa-telah demikian*, and a few other combinations of these few connective words), and for larger units, three-word connectives (e.g., *maka sa-telah sudah*, *hatta sa-telah sudah*, *sa-telah itu maka*, and the form we are looking at here, *sa-telah demikian maka*). Aside from the rich meanings and significant variant orders of these words,[27] it is the "heaviness" itself that marks the figure we are observing—that Classical Malay sentence—as a MAJOR boundary in the hierarchical structure of the text, somewhat like a paragraph in English. More coinciding deictics or connectives mean a higher-level plot boundary: new place, new time, new state, new major character, etc. To put it another way, this sentence is (or for the reader, will be) the context or background for a potentially large number of lower-level sentences. Or we might say that the scope of influence of a heavier sentence is wider than that of a lighter sentence—with heaviness defined purely in terms of the number of words in the first section of the sentence.

Thus, the first part of the figure links the *pun, -lah* core to the prior text at the proper level of generalization. The figure the sentence makes is emerging. We are, I think, learning to read more and more like a reader or hearer of Classical Malay. From the ways that the sentence evokes context, we can begin to interpret—as a reader must—and reconstruct the missing context. Whether read or heard, the text is not a dialogue; it is displaced from the full discourse context and must be interpreted.

So far we have looked at the three parts of the figure, this kind of Classical Malay sentence, and something of their relations to each other:

I DEICTIC CONNECTIVES	II *PUN, -LAH* CORE	III ELABORATION
plot level relations	topic–event relations	role–focus relations
textual coherence	script indexing	referential coherence
Sa-telah demikian maka	*Sang Bimanyu pun* *berjalan-lah*	*sambil menchium . . .*

---

[27] For etymology as a strategy in Javanese theatre, see A. L. Becker (to appear). An excellent study of etymology as a strategy in linguistics is Malkiel (1975).

Notice further that the movement of the sentence is from generality to particularity, in several senses:

1. The sentence moves from nonrole and case marking "verbs" to role and case marking "verbs" (e.g., from *ber-* prefixed verbs to *meng-/di-* prefixed "verbs").

2. The sentence moves from least referential terms to most, in the sense that *maka* is less referential than *menchium* 'sniff'.

3. It moves from metacomment (about the telling) to comment (the telling), that is, from information about THE TEXT to information about THE STORY.

4. The sentence moves from language to nature.

This last is perhaps the most interesting feature of all in this particular Classical Malay sentence strategy. From language to nature. In translating the Sanskrit-Javanese text, the writer is contextualizing in the Malay world an old, old event. It is in the third section of the sentence that the distinctly Malay setting is expressed. The writer is making the text Malay, thus enriching the Malay landscape itself by association, making it historically dense.[28]

The aesthetic possibilities of the sentence seem, too, to be far richer in the third section of the sentence, the first two sections being far more constrained by prior text. In Gertrude Stein's sense, the third section is more "emotional"—more reflective of the imagination and skill of the author, into whose "subjectivity" we as readers enter in this third section.

This Malay sentence is, what might be called a PROTOTYPICAL sentence, related not by derivation but by partial resemblances in several dimensions to a great many other Classical Malay sentences with which it shares some or nearly all its meanings. In this essay I have tried to describe some of those kinds of properties, some of the nonspecific meanings the figure has. Some will be more widespread than others; that is, not all related sentences will have three sections, AND have "heavy" deictic connectives, AND have

---

[28] Density of context is a distinctive feature of Southeast Asian music, painting, and shadow puppetry. The tropical forest, as a source of generative power, is probably a model for them all; that is, all are iconic of a particular kind of Nature with multiply simultaneous seasons (e.g., trees, our stable natural calendars in the north, in a tropical forest lose their leaves at different times, in different length cycles, some years long) rather than the more nearly unified cycle of the northern forest. Without getting too reductionist about it, dominant ecosystems could not help having an influence on what we think "natural" in symbolic systems underlying wayangs, calenders, and music: in one dimension—the dimension of "naturalness"—is the perceived image of the tropical and subtropical ecology. [My thanks to Derek Brereton for his paper on this idea. See also A. L. Becker (to appear), Judith Becker (to appear), and Geertz (1973), which all imply this notion, I think.]

an agent-to-location focus progression: This figure we have been studying is the overlay of these strategies. There are less complex sentences, related to this one, with only a *pun* structure in the core and no general event marked by *lah* but, rather, an immediate movement into the clauses of the elaboration. There are less complex sentences in which a deictic connective (usually *demikian*) "enters" the core and is marked by *-lah* (e.g., *demikianlah*), indicating that the whole figure is a comment on the prior section of text. The figure or sentence we have been examining is prototypic in the sense that it shows nearly maximal complexity at the level of the sentence: It displays the possibilities of the sentence.

These steps into the landscape of Classical Malay discourse[29] are steps into a cultural past. This Malay figure is no longer alive, in the sense that a great many of the constraints that characterize it are no longer in force:

1.   The boundary between SECTIONS II and III (Core and Elaboration) is no longer clear, and the functions of the two systems (referential–topic and role–focus) no longer distinguish clauses and sentences in modern urban Malay or Indonesian. -*Pun* still can be used to topicalize (that is, it retains its referential function), whereas *-lah* appears now to mark imperative predicates (*Pergilah!* 'Go!'), and the terms used to translate the Indo-European copula (*ialah* and *adalah*) are now an obvious feature of modern, educated Malay or Indonesian. However, the two, *pun* and *-lah*, no longer are used together to mark the topic–event relationship, the core of the classical figure.[30]

2.   The other major difference is that many of the deictic connectives that established textual coherence are no longer used anymore, except in very formal situations in which an archaic flavor is important. *Maka* no longer marks sentences. Temporal and causal coherence are much more "modern" strategies than the system of deictic densities described previously.

---

[29] Many more figures—that is, sentences as rhetorical strategies—remain to be studied before we can begin to understand a TEXT, with UNDERSTANDING defined as the imagination of deep context, what Clifford Geertz calls thick description, here applied to linguistics: Sentence by sentence, text by text, a grammar emerges.

Some of the other figures are described in the works of Shelly Errington (1974, 1975, 1976), which led many of us into a deeper understanding of Malay texts—a truer reading, as she taught us to reconstruct a segment of the Classical Malay world.

[30] Hopper (1976), describes very well a later stage of Malay in the work most usually mentioned as the beginning of modern Malay, the *Hikayat Abdullah*. The date of the *Hikayat Abdullah* is mid-nineteenth century. The date of the *Hikayat Pandawa Lima* is "kira2 pada pertengahan kurun Masehi ke XV" [Syed Nasir bin Ismail, Kata Pengantar, *Hikayat Pandawa Lima*—see Hussain (1964)]: approximately in the middle of the 15th century, A.D. The great grammatico-rhetorical variety in Classical Malay texts is not only to be explained by change over time, but must also be explained by a variety of literary dialects, if not individual styles, I suspect.

Time words appear more frequently within the verb phrase now, and causal connections are marked (in modern Malay or Indonesian) in dependent clauses with rather free ordering. (The order I + II + III of the Classical Malay sentence was fixed.) And so the boundary between Section I (Deictic Connectives) and Section II (the *pun*, *-lah* Core) is lost, too.

The figure a sentence makes is a strategy of interpretation filling in subjectivity, temporality, referentiality, and intersubjectivity, which, tied to a specific cultural era, helps the people it is used by to understand and to feel coherent in their worlds. It is just as much a cultural artifact as a calendar, a genre of music, or a mode of painting.

ACKNOWLEDGMENTS

I must acknowledge the aid of several people: Danielo C. Ajamiseba, Liberty Sihombing, Ramli Salleh, Nangsari Achmad, Stephanus Djawanai, and all the advanced students of Bahasa Indonesia and Bahasa Malayu at Michigan, especially Patricia Henry and Jeffrey Dreyfuss, for imaginative commentary on these ideas. Deepest gratitude to Talmy Givón, David Levy, and Deborah Tannen for detailed commentary on the draft. I only regret that I could not make all changes you suggest, since I do not yet know enough to be able to do it. I have also drawn on extensive discussions with Fred Lupke, Aram Yengoyan, John Verhaar, William Foley, and George Lakoff, whose paper, "Linguistic Gestalts," set me to thinking about prototypical sentences. But the debt is greatest to Kenneth L. Pike, who threw me all the right challenges, including the challenge of a linguistics of particularly, a basis for modern philology.

REFERENCES

Ajamiseba, Danielo C. (1973) *A Classical Malay Text Grammar: Insights into a Non-Western Text Tradition*, Doctoral dissertation, University of Michigan.

Anderson, Benedict (1976) "A Time of Darkness and a Time of Light: Transposition in Early Indonesian Nationalist Thought," Paper presented at the Congress of Human Sciences, August, 1976.

Becker, A. L. (to appear) "Text-building, Epistemology, and Aesthetics in the Javanese Shadow Theatre," in A. Becker and A. Yengoyan, eds., *The Imagination of Reality*, Ablex, Norwood, New Jersey.

Becker, A. L. and I. G. Ng. Oka (1974) "Person in Kawi: Exploration of An Elementary Semantic Dimension," in *Proceedings of the First International Conference of Austronesian Comparative Linguistics*, Honolulu, Hawaii.

Becker, A. L. and Umar Wirasno (1976) "On the Nature of Syntactic Change in Bahasa Indonesia, "Paper presented to the Second Eastern Conference on Austronesian Languages, Ann Arbor, Michigan.

Becker, Judith O. (to appear) "Time and Tune in Java," in Becker and Yengoyan, eds., *The Imagination of Reality*.

Benveniste, Emil (1973) "Categories of Thought and Categories of Language," in *Problems in General Linguistics*, University of Miami Press, Coral Gables, Florida.

Cooper, W. and John Robert Ross (1975) "World Order," Unpublished manuscript.

Dreyfuss, Jeffrey (1977) "Verb Morphology and Semantic Case Role Information," Paper presented at the Austronesian Symposium, Honolulu, Hawaii.

Errington, Shelley (1974) "A Disengagement: Notes on the Structure of Narrative in a Classical Malay Text," in *Papers from the Conference on Indonesian and Malay Literature*, Madison, Wisconsin.

Errington, Shelley (1975) *A Study of Genre: Form and Meaning in the Malay Hikayat Hang Tuah*, Doctoral dissertation, Cornell University, Ithaca, New York.

Errington, Shelley (1976) "Some Comments on Style in the meanings of the Past," Paper presented at the Conference on Southeast Asian Perceptions of the Past, Australian National University, Canberra.

Foley, William (1974) "Whatever Happened to Malay?" Paper presented to the First International Conference on Austronesian Linguistics, Honolulu, Hawaii.

Foley, William (1976) "Inherent Referentiality and Language Typology," Unpublished manuscript.

Foley, William and Robert D. Van Valin, Jr. (to appear) "On the Viability of the Notion of 'Subject' in Universal Grammar."

Frost, Robert (1949) "The Figure a Poem Makes," in *Complete Poems of Robert Frost, 1949*, Holt, New York.

Gass, William H. (1973) Introduction to *The Geographical History of America*, by Gertrude Stein, Vintage Books, New York.

Geertz, Clifford (1973) "Person, Time and Conduct in Bali," Chapter 14 of *The Interpretation of Cultures*, Basic Books, New York.

Givón, Talmy (1978) *On Understanding Grammar*, Academic Press, New York.

Grimes, Joseph (1975) *The Thread of Discourse*, Mouton, The Hague.

Hawkinson, Ann and Larry Hyman (1974) "Hierarchies of Natural Topic in Shona," *Studies in African Linguistics* 5, 147–170.

Hopper, Paul J. (1976) "Focus and Aspect in Discourse Grammar," Unpublished manuscript.

Hussain, Khalid, ed. (1964) *Hikayat Pandawa Lima* (Siri Sastera DBP. Bil. 18), Dewan Bahasa dan Pustaka, Kuala Lumpur.

Longacre, Robert (1976) *An Anatomy of Speech Notions*, Peter de Ridder, Lisse.

Malkiel, Yakov (1975) "Etymology and Modern Linguistics," *Lingua* 36, 101–120.

Meyerowitz, Patricia (1975) Introduction to *How to Write*, Dover, New York.

Mukarovsky, Jan (1977) in *The Work and Verbal Art*, John Burbank and Peter Steiner, eds., Yale Press, New Haven, Connecticut.

Pike, Kenneth L. (1975) *On Describing Languages*, Peter de Ridder, Lisse.

Rajaona, Simeon (1971) *Problem de morphologie malagache*, Rev Perc Zucclto, Ambozontany, Fianarantsoa.

Rajaona, Simeon (1972) *Structure du malagache, etude des formes predicatives*, Ambozontany, Fianarantsoa.

Ricoeur, Paul (1971) "The Model of the Text: Meaningful Action Considered as Text," *Social Research* 38, 529–562

Ricoeur, Paul (1976) *Interpretation Theory: Discourse and the Surplus of Meaning*, The Texas Christian University Press, Fort Worth, Texas.

Shank, Roger C. (1975) "SAM—A Story Understander," Yale Artifical Intelligence Project, Research Report 43, Yale University, New Haven, Connecticut.

Silverstein, Michael (1977) "Hierarchy of Features and Ergativity," in Dixon, ed., *Grammatical Categories in Australian Languages*, Australian Institute of Aboriginal Studies, Canberra, pp. 112–171.

Stein, Gertrude (1975[1931]) *How to Write*, Dover, New York.

Verhaar, John (1977) "On Speech and Thought," in William McCormack and Stephen A. Wurm, eds., *Language and Thought, Anthropological Issues,* Mouton, The Hague.

Wittgenstein, Ludwig (1958) *Philosophical Investigations.* Macmillan, New York.

Young, Richard, Alton Becker, and Kenneth L. Pike (1970) *Rhetoric: Discovery and Change,* Harcourt, Brace, and World, New York.

Zoetmulder, P. J. (1974) *Kalangwan,* Martinus Nijhoff, The Hague.

THE RELEVANCE OF REPAIR TO
SYNTAX-FOR-CONVERSATION

EMANUEL A. SCHEGLOFF
University of California, Los Angeles

1. INTRODUCTION

The theme of this chapter is that the phenomena elsewhere treated under the rubric "repair"[1] are potentially relevant to syntax, if syntax be thought

---

[1] In Schegloff, Jefferson, and Sacks (1977), we pointed out that troubles in speaking, hearing, and understanding of "talk" are dealt with in an organized fashion in conversation, are not limited or necessarily occasioned by independently establishable "error," and are therefore referred to not as "correction" but by the more generic rubric "repair." We differentiated between repair initiation and solution, described a PREFERENCE FOR SELF-REPAIR and a PREFERENCE FOR SELF-INITIATION of repair to be operating, and showed that the organization of repair initiation operates in a restricted "repair initiation opportunity space" around the "trouble-source" or "repairable," encompassing the turn in which the trouble-source occurred ("same turn"), a next turn by some other speaker, and the turn after that. For further details, see Schegloff *et al.* (1977). For parallel findings on Thai materials, cf. Moerman (1977).

A longish segment of transcript is provided in Appendix 2 for readers who have not had occasion to examine such materials. Some notational conventions used in data citations are explained in Appendix 1.

Syntax and Semantics, Volume 12:
Discourse and Syntax

261

of as "syntax-for-conversation." In support of this theme, I will try to show:

1.   Repair operations affect the form of sentences and the ordering of elements in them, quite apart from the sheer fact of their occurrence in sentences doing so.

2.   There are structural pressures, derived from those types of discourse organization we term "turn-taking" and the "organization of sequences," that tend to concentrate repair in the same turn as contains what is being repaired and, within that turn, in the same sentence (or other "turn-constructional unit").

3.   Formal arguments are possible to show that repair is, in principle, relevant to any sentence.

4.   The phenomena of repair that occur in sentences are orderly and describable.

No decision can be reached at this time as to whether "same-turn repair" should be considered a sort of "super-syntax" that operates second-order on whatever syntax, otherwise conceived, organizes, or whether same-turn repair should be considered a part of syntax proper but a syntax reconstructed as a syntax-for-conversation, which is but one of the discourse types in which "language" is used, albeit the most common and fundamental one. Because this chapter is organized around this theme, none of the phenomena touched on in its course are explored extensively; only the minimum needed for the theme is extracted from each.

I write as one occupied with the study of the social organization—most centrally, the sequential organization—of talk in interaction. The data I work with are audio and video tapes of commonplace, everyday interaction in a variety of so-called "contexts."

The sentences in the talk that I deal with are full of the "hitches" and "disfluencies" that I have referred to. They have an incidence not limited to the environment of independently establishable "errors." They appear to be orderly. Though some are perhaps connectable to various "degeneracies" of "performance," not all of them are; and even those that are make demands on the environments of their occurrence that are accommodated in an orderly, independently organized manner. They are implicated in an organization that operates on a scope wider than that of the sentence yet appears to have decisive consequences for the organization of sentences. In this respect, they are like other aspects of sentences in conversation that are linked to types of organization operating beyond the sentences—for turns, for sequences, for conversation. What they involve, then, is not some generic "discourse organization" but the organization of a particular type of discourse, with its own organizational structures: conversation. That is why my theme potentially relates these phenomena not to "syntax" and not to "discourse" but instead to a possible "syntax-for-conversation." Other types of discourse have other types of organization, with potentially differ-ent requirements of, and consequences for, the syntax operating in them (e.g., poetry, telegraphy, philosophical debate, interviews, comedy routines, religious rituals–ceremonies, mathematical texts, etc.).

The absence of repair from the sentences with which linguists (especially syntacticians?) concern themselves (among other absences) sometimes in-clines me to share the suspicion that much of the available analysis is for written sentences or for "might-as-well-be-written" sentences. An orienta-tion to materials of this sort and the terms of analysis appropriate to them may have been inherited from such disciplinary ancestors of linguistics as philology and may have been supported by the historical and technological facts that made writing and printing the media of scholarly exchange.

Consider, however, the philologist or historical linguist of the distant or proximate future who treats as the linguistic remains of contemporary society not scrolls, books, or memoranda but film and video/audio tape of everyday, spontaneous interaction in the lives people live. Imagine as well that such a linguist is not committed to a theoretical set and to terms of analysis like those currently familiar but is prepared to derive the appro-priate terms of analysis from the materials under investigation. What under-standing of the English language might result if not only the analyses but also the very terms of analysis were formed on the basis of such materials? Perhaps what follows might be thought of as a memorandum to such a linguist.

2. ON THE EFFECTS OF REPAIR ON THE SYNTACTIC FORM OF SENTENCES

It should be noted, first of all, that the occurrence of repair in a sentence can have consequences for the shape of the sentence and for the ordering of its elements beyond the consequence embodied by sheer inclusion of the repair elements (e.g., the *uh*).

To be sure, repair may replace one word with another of the same word class, entailing no such syntactic effect, though possibly leaving an interac-tional effect, since the replacement cannot excise all traces of the word that was initially said or starting to be said (cf. Jefferson 1975). Regularly, however, syntactic changes of greater or smaller magnitude are wrought by repair. Only a small sampling of the types of changes can be suggested here. (In formulating the shifts being exemplified, I intend an essentially vernacu-lar description, so as to avoid choosing by terminology some theory or vision of syntax.)

A repair can expand a noun phrase by inserting a descriptor or "modifier" [cf. (9) to follow].

It can change the syntactic form by subsuming, under another, "frame" sentence, the whole sentence being said or starting to be said.

(1)   Gene: *. . . they're—talkin' now about goin' up tuh thirdy one* **grand**
                 ez a principal.
         Cathy: *Oh rrilly?*
         Gene: *Yeah.*
         Cathy: *Wul knowing* **you** *you'd* **have** *thirty one en, thousan' and a*
                 ni*ckel,*
         Gene: *hhh! heh-heh-heh-⌈heh*
   →Cathy: *⌊Shit y- I think y'got the*
   →   *original nickel.*
                         (Goldberg, II:1:6; also cited in Jefferson, 1975)

Or it can "unframe" such an incipiently subsumed sentence:

(2)   B: *And she didn't come* **in** *today; I haven't hy:eard or seen any-*
              thing **of** *her, I don't know what she's d(hh)oi(hh)ng heh heh*
              ⌈hah hah hah
   →A: *⌊Well I don't think she-*
   →   *eh she doesn't uh usually come in on Friday, does she*
         B: *Well, yes she does, sometimes,=*
                                                    (SBL:I:1:1:3)

It can convert what is starting to be a sentence into a subordinate clause:

(3)   →B: *Yeah, he- ez he wz handing me the book en 'e tol' me twunny*
            dolliz I almos' dro(h)pped i(h)t.
                                                    (TG:313–314)

It can convert a question into an assertion:

(4)   (J and L are husband and wife)
         J: *We saw Midnight Cowboy yesterday-*
              or ⌈Suh- Friday.
         E: *⌊Ch?*
   →L: *Didju s-* **you** *saw that, it's really good.*
                                                    (JS:II:61)

It can convert a wh-type question to a yes–no type question:

(5)   Agnes: *Chop // it.*
   →Martha: *Tell me, uh what- d'you need a hot sauce?*
                 (0.5)
         Agnes: *t'hhh a* **Ta***co sauce.*
                                                    (NB:IV:2:2)

It can reorder the elements of projected talk, inserting into a current sentence what might have been planned for a later one:[2]

(6)   A: *. . . Fridays is a funny day. mMost a' the*
→   *people in schoo:l, 'hh that's why I only*
→   *have classes on Tuesday en Fri:day 'hh*
→   *(0.3) u- one cla:ss, because most a' them*
         have o:ff those days . . .

(TG:657–660)

[2] Note here that the start of the sentence—*Most a' the people*—is not discarded by the repair but instead informs its end—*most a' them*. The same is the case in (8) below—*And uh Gene uh that Nobles . . .* to *That Gene*. It is hoped that references in the literature to "editing" (e.g., Hockett 1967, Labov 1970) will not be understood to imply that what has been "edited" is entirely "out," for this would, apparently, be incorrect. This is especially important to interaction when it is the recipient of the talk who speaks to the edited talk. Consider:

→A: *W-when's yer uh, weh- you have one.day y'only have one course, uh?*
→ B: *mMonday en Wednesday:* ⎡*s right.*⎤ *That's* ⎤*my=*
                 hhhh   ⎣ *Oh.* ⎦ *that's-*⎦
       B: = *linguistics course hh.*

(TG:121–125)

in which B answers the *when* question that had apparently been replaced. And consider as well the following:

Mark has called to complain about not being invited to a party
Bob is involved in planning. Lengthy discussion transpires.
Near the end of the conversation,
     Mark: *Okay well Bo:b? ah hhmhh Ah'll see yuh Friday.*
             (0.2)
       Bob: *t'hhh Okay Mark en uh::: yihknow, a (.) thous'n pard'ns.=*
→   *=fer yer- the oversight.*
             (0.2)
     Mark: *'t'hhhh=*
       Bob: *(Or //is it)*
→Mark: *Oh:.uh no:. Well I wasn't I didn't fee:l like I wu:z::*
→   *ah.hh wt's the wo:rd. uhm=*
→Bob: *=rebu:ffed?=*
→Mark: *='hh-'hh rebu:ffed,h*
             :
     Mark: *Uh::mhh I didn't feel rebu:ffed,*

(SF:2:24, Simplified)

Note that Bob apparently suppressed a word that he replaces with "the oversight." Mark picks it up, responds to it, and disagrees with it, even though he hasn't quite got it. When he goes into a word search for it, Bob solves the search immediately, displaying that Mark had indeed sniffed it out. All of this turns on *yer*'s not being entirely "edited out" when it is replaced by "the oversight."

It can have the consequences that a sequence of turns is inserted within the boundaries of a sentence.[3]

(7)   B: *Uh she asked me to stop by, she bought a chest of drawers from*
           uhm
           (4.0)
  →B: *what's the gal's name? Just went back to*
  →   *Michigan*
          (2.0)
  →B: *Helen uhm*
  →A: *Oh I know who you mean,*
          (1.0)
  →A: *Brady- **Brady**.*
  →B: *Yeah! Helen Brady.*
      A: *Mm hm*
      B: *And she- she says she's uh never. . . .*
                                      (SBL, SW   )

(8)   B: *No, I had the queen Clarie. And uh Gene uh that Nobles, or- no*
           their names aren't Noble. but Gene and Ruth or Roo-uhm oh
           whoever they// are
  →A: *Yeah I-I keep saying Noble- Jones.*
  →B: *Yeah, Jones*
  →A: *Uh // huh*
      B: *Uh that Gene had the ace king.*
                                        (SBL, SW   )

Repair, then, does not merely occur in sentences; it can change their shape and composition and can do so within a retained identity of "the sentence," and not only by apparently aborting one sentence in favor of another, though this, too, is a potential consequence of repair for sentences, and one with considerable frequency of occurrence.

---

[3] It is worth pointing out that the following fragments show that discourse is not necessarily external to sentences by being composed of multiples of them. Discourse can be inside sentences, just as sentences can be in discourse. Both instances in the text happen to occur as parts of "word searches," but this is not criterial to the inclusion of a sequence within a sentence; note:

    K: *That is, if the warp has sixteen greens an' two blacks an' two light blues and two blacks*
        an' sixteen greens an' sixteen blacks an' sixteen blues an' so on,=
 →K: *=y'know the warp are the long pieces*
 →F: *Mm hm*
    K: *the weft has exactly that.*
                                      (KC–4:36)

3. ON THE OCCURRENCE OF REPAIR
   IN SENTENCES

Here I want to show that the occurrence of repair within the boundaries of sentences is not incidental but is the systematic product of other sequential features of conversation.

A basic locus of organization in conversational interaction is a series of two turns-at-talk; think of them as CURRENT and NEXT. The organization of turn-taking in conversation, by which turns are allocated to the parties by the parties and have their size determined, operates by organizing successive sets of current and next, each next becoming a current as it is begun.[4]

A turn series has the potential of being a SEQUENCE or part of a sequence. That potential is realized when some next does not merely follow its predecessor temporally but is produced in some fashion by reference to it, to *it* in particular. One form this can take is that the current turn projects some range of possibilities for next turn (as a yes–no type question projects positive and negative answers as possibilities next, or an invitation projects acceptance or rejection, etc.) and, in next turn, one of these is done. We speak of this as the SEQUENTIAL IMPLICATIVENESS of a turn.[5]

Next-turn position is the organizedly systematic position for any current turn to be sequentially implicative, to have another turn produced by reference to it, and, thereby, to have its effect on the course of the conversation registered in the talk. The organization of conversation—of turn-taking and of sequences—is built for sequential implicativeness next, and participants are oriented to it: To see if some turn is/will be sequentially implicative, the structurally given place to look is next turn.

Next turn, however, is also the systematically available position for other-than-speaker of some turn that is beset by some trouble of speaking, hearing, or understanding to initiate repair on the source of the trouble.[6] When next turn is used to initiate repair on something in current turn, the sequential implicativeness of current turn is displaced from its primary home and is lost at least for that turn. Because other-initiated repair in next turn itself engenders a sequence and is itself sequentially implicative,[7] the sequential implicativeness of current turn is yet further displaced and potentially loses its organized locus of realization.[8]

[4] Cf. Sacks, Schegloff, and Jefferson (1974).

[5] Schegloff and Sacks (1973), p. 296.

[6] Schegloff, Jefferson, and Sacks (1977), p. 367, §3.12.

[7] Schegloff, Jefferson, and Sacks (1977), p. 369, §3.3; p. 377, §5.22.

[8] For some sequential units, such as the "adjacency pair" (Schegloff and Sacks, 1973, pp. 295–297), the sequential implicativeness of their first parts is almost invariably retained across the insertion of repair sequences after them. A paper on the embedding of repair sequences in adjacency pairs is planned; cf. related discussions in Jefferson (1972) on "side sequences" and Schegloff (1972) on "insertion sequences."

As between these alternative uses of next-turn position, there is a structural preference for keeping next-turn position free for sequentially implicated nexts.[9] Relative to this, other-initiated repair is DISPREFERRED in next turn. One way in which the preference for keeping next turn free is served is by the self-initiation of repair by the speaker of the trouble-source in current turn, that is, in the turn in which the trouble-source occurred, before next-turn position.

To review: A discourse feature of talk in conversation—an interest in the sequential implicativeness of current turn for next turn—structurally motivates an aspect of the conduct of a turn; there is a preference for initiating, in current turn, repair on whatever is self-repairable there, before next-turn position arrives. In fact, self-initiated, same-turn repair is, by far, the most common form of repair.

To have motivated the concentration of repair-initiation in same or current turn is not yet to have motivated its occurrence WITHIN A SENTENCE. It would be compatible with the preceding if some trouble of speaking, hearing, or understanding that arises in a sentence in a current turn were addressed in a next sentence (or other turn-constructional unit) in the same turn; that would also serve the keeping of next turn free. Repair would then be occurring in sentences, but in sentences occupied with doing the repair and not themselves intruded on by it. There ARE repairs of this sort, in which a trouble in one turn-unit is addressed just after completion of that unit, in another unit built to do the repair. These we have termed[10] TRANSITION-SPACE REPAIRS, and they do address the trouble-source while preserving the integrity of the sentence. However, by far the most common placement of repair initiation is not in the transition-space or after the sentence or other turn unit in which the trouble occurs. Most commonly the integrity of the sentence is NOT preserved, and repair occurs not in a sentence devoted to it but "intrusively" in a sentence occupied with something else (the something that can be sequentially implicative in next turn). There is a basis for this distribution.

Turns are possibly complete at the possible completion of a turn-constructional unit.[11] Possible completion of a current turn makes transition to a next turn relevant (i.e., though turn-transfer may not occur at each such point, its possibility is structurally provided for at each such point,

[9] It appears to me that this is a specification, for "sequences," of a more general preference for "progressivity," that is, for "next parts" of structured units (e.g., turns, turn-constructional units like sentences, stories, etc.) to come next; cf. the later discussion of progressivity is successive repairs on a same repairable.

[10] Schegloff, Jefferson, and Sacks (1977), p. 366, §3.11 and Footnote 12.

[11] On this and on the immediately following points, cf. Sacks, Schegloff, and Jefferson (1974), pp. 702–704 et passim.

unless otherwise provided in the talk). Sentences are turn-constructional units. Unless otherwise provided for, their possible completion can constitute possible completion of the turn in which they occur and can thereby make transition to a next turn relevant at that point; it is at such points that intending or incipient next speakers regularly begin next turns.[12] An interest in getting repair initiated in some same turn (current turn) and before next turn, in order to be methodically assured, will need to be initiated before the next possible completion of the sentence or other turn-constructional unit in which the trouble-source occurs. That means within the boundaries of the sentence. WHAT IS THOUGHT OF IN TERMS OF CURRENT SYNTAX AS THE "INTEGRITY" OF THE SENTENCE IS, THEREFORE, SYSTEMATICALLY SUBORDI- NATED TO OTHER SEQUENTIAL REQUIREMENTS.

If the preceding is correct, then it holds for any sentence (or other turn- constructional unit) in any current turn. Since any turn in conversation is at some point a current turn, it holds for any sentence in conversation. A syntax-for-conversation might be expected to incorporate provision for such systematic contingencies.

4. ON THE SYSTEMATIC RELEVANCE OF REPAIR

It is the intended conclusion of the preceding section that, if repair is relevant, there are systematic organizational pressures that concentrate its relevance within sentences in turns. But is repair systematically relevant?

Any of the systems and contingencies implicated in the production and reception of talk—articulatory, memory, sequential, syntactic, auditory, ambient noise, etc.—can fail. Aspects of the production and analysis of talk that are rule-governed can fail to integrate. In short, the exchange of talk is indigenously and exogenously vulnerable to trouble that can arise at any time. In this sense, if a peal of thunder can blot out a part of any turn at any time, thus producing a problem of hearing, then repair is potentially sys- tematically relevant to any sentence. And, although many of the sources of the relevance of repair or the "need" for it are extrinsic to syntax, the repair that is done is done in syntactic environments that, in a fashion, accommo- date it.

More formal arguments and, necessarily, more specific ones are possible for the systematic relevance of repair to sentences in conversation and, therefore, possibly to syntax-for-conversation.

[12] For this reason, "transition space repair" is not a fully reliable resource. For a discussion of a countervailing organization that helps account for the fact that transition-space repair gets done (and uninterruptedly) at all, cf. Schegloff, Jefferson, and Sacks (1977), p. 374 and Footnote 20.

Consider the question: Is there a class of sentences such that, in their actual occurrence in conversation, repair appears systematically relevant? If such a class of sentences could be described, and if what defined the class was such that any sentence of the language could on some occasion of production be a member of that class, then it would follow that repair was potentially relevant for any sentence in conversation and that provision for repair was as systematically relevant to an adequate syntax as provision for anything else.

Then consider this class: first sentences in topic-initial turns or in topic shift position.[13] For such sentences, it is the case that:

1.   They very regularly have self-repair in them, the nature of the trouble being repaired often being obscure and the positioning of the repair regularly being at the word that KEYS the new topic being initiated, as in:

(9)   B: *That's too bad* ((very quiet))
         A: *hhhh!*
            (0.5)
   → B: *(I 'unno) ˙hh Hey do* **you** *see V-* (0.3) *fat ol` Vivian anymouh?*
   →A: *No, hardly, en if we do:, y'know, I jus' say hello quick'n ˙hh*
         y'know jus' pass each othuh in the⌈*e hall(way).*⌉ *still hanging*
         B: ⌊*Is she*   ⌋
         aroun` (with) Bo:nny?

                                                                      (TG, 338–366)

Here the topic-initial turn contains a self-initiated repair of a common type, one in which a noun is cutoff at some point in its production and a descriptor or modifier is inserted before it; the repairable is *Vivian*, and the KEYNESS of its topicality is displayed in B's next turn, which continues to focus on Vivian. Or, again,

(10)   B: *˙hh But it's not too bad, ˙hh*
         A: *That's goo*⌈*d,* ((very quiet))
   →B: ⌊*Diyuh have any-cl- You have a class with Billy*
   →   *this te:rm?*
         A: *Yeh he's in my abnormal class.*
         B: *mnYeh* ⌈*how-* ⌉
         A: ⌊*Abnor*⌋*mal psy-ch*
         B: *Still not gettin married,*

---

[13] My use of the word "topic" is not related to current usages in linguistics, such as "topic-comment structure." Because nothing has yet appeared in print to describe "topic" as a sequential unit of analysis, it should be treated here as a vernacular term, roughly referring to "what is talked about" through some series of turns at talk.

Once again the topic-initial sentence gets self-initiated repair; the trouble is obscure (shift from "any classes" to "a class"), and, though B's later turn does not pursue "classes" as topically key, A focuses on it beyond a minimal turn, with a repair of her own. (In the substantial data fragment in Appendix II, the turn at lines 198–200 is topic initial, has self-initiated repair, and operates on the topical key, *the feller/man fer linguistics*.) A great many first sentences in topic-initial turns have this sort of self-initiated same-turn repair. Some, of course, do not.

2.   If first sentence in topic-initial or topic-shift position does not have self-initiated repair, then with great frequency the next-turn involves the initiation of repair by some other.

(11)   B: *Tch! I'll get some advance birthday cards, hhm hmh!*
                (0.6)
             B: *'hhh A:n:d uh,* (0.5) *Me:h,*
                (0.2)
         → B: *Oh Sibbie's sistuh hadda ba:by bo:way.*
         → A: *Who?*

(TG, 706–711)

The topic-initial turn's sentence does not have any same-turn repair, and, in next turn, one of the prototypic next-turn repair initiators is employed.[14] I might note, without citing the rest of this topical sequence, that it initially, and mostly, focuses on *Sibbi's sistuh*—the repairable located by the repair initiator (and not, for example, on the *baby boway*). Or, again,

(12)   A: *Ripped about four nai:ls, 'n okhh!*
             B: *Fantastic.*=
         → A: *=B't it wz fun-You sound very far away.*
                (0.7)
         → B: *I do?*
             A: *Nyeahm.*
             B: *mNo? I'm no:t,*

(TG, 70–76)

Here, again, there is no same-turn repair in the topic-initial turn's sentence; repair is initiated by other in the next turn.

I have tried to indicate for this class of sentences—first sentences in topic initial turns—either self-repair occurs in the sentence or other-initiated repair occurs in next turn. Repair thus appears to be generically relevant

---

[14] Schegloff, Jefferson, and Sacks (1977), p. 367.

in this sequential environment, and the by now familiar pressures tend to push the repair back into same turn.[15]

Because this class of sentences is formally characterized by its relationship to immediately preceding talk—that is, that it is in a topic-shift relationship—no sentence of the language is in principle excludable; any sentence can, in principle, occur in an environment in which it represents a topic shift from what immediately precedes. It follows, then, that repair is, in principle, potentially relevant to the construction of a sentence in conversation. In that case, it is hard to imagine that a syntax-for-conversation does not systematically provide for it.

5. ON ASPECTS OF THE ORDERLINESS OF SAME-TURN REPAIR

In preceding sections, I have tried to show that the incursion of repair into sentences can and does have substantial effects on their syntactic form; that, when relevant, repair is structurally skewed into sentences and that it is pervasively and systematically relevant. Here I want to suggest that the details of the impact of repair on the shape of sentences should be describable by showing that the components of repair are orderly in their operation. I will touch on only two areas. The first is in terms not unfamiliar to syntactic concerns; that is showing the positioning of an element to be orderly and related to its form, which I will discuss for the initiation of same-turn repair. The second concerns an area of expectable DISORDERLINESS, that is, when an initial repair fails and repeated tries are made.

The initiation of repair in same turn takes one of a limited number of forms sensitive to the most immediate sound environment of their production. One very common form is the CUT-OFF (typically a glottal or other stop), which is used for within-word (or within-sound, for *uh* also gets cut off) initiation. When repair is initiated outside the boundary of a word or

---

[15] Note that, although the repair is done to an element of a sentence and is done within a sentence, in important ways the organizational source of the repair is not the sentence but the topical sequence, for it is in sentences-in-turns characterized by their sequential status and on elements characterized by their topic-relevant status that the repair is done. A suggestion lurks here that some types of repair, of which this is one, may not be the product of a "performance frailty" in respect to the production of the sentence but may be affirmatively enjoined features of certain sequential and interactional operations. For other such types, see Jefferson (1975) and Goodwin (1977). Because anything to be done in talk will be done in a turn and, regularly, that means in a turn-constructional unit like a sentence, it appears that a syntax built for sentences in talk in interaction will make provision for the occurrence within them of whatever is needed for other orders of organization, for example, "discourse" organizations, that routinely operate.

other sound, *uh* or a pause are commonly used as initiators (they are also used AFTER the initiation of repair as components of a repair segment, and often in combination—*uh* + pause). The cut-off stops a "next sound due" from occurring when it is due; the *uh* and pause occupy the position at which a next due element of the talk would otherwise be placed.[16]

Generally, but not invariably, the cut-off initiates repair on some already-produced element of the turn; it is POSTPOSITIONED. *Uh* or a pause, standing in the place of a next-due element, is more likely to initiate repair on a next-due item; that is, it is generally PREPOSITIONED. The former is, therefore, generally disjunctive syntactically, interrupting what is syntactically projected by the sentence-so-far. The latter delays but carries forward the syntactic projection of the sentence-so-far.

The "backward" and "forward" orientations of these repair initiators, respectively, is, as indicated, not invariant. The variability is exhibited when, for example, an *uh* initiates repair, indicating a forward-oriented repair—prototypically a "search" of some kind—but the repair segment itself ends by operating on earlier elements of the turn. One basis for this type of variation lies in the capacity for REPAIR CONVERSION, that is, for a repair initiated for one type of trouble (e.g., a word is "missing") to be recast and solved by repairing another (e.g., circumlocution to avoid the need for the "missing" element). Several instances follow:

(13)   Merle: *So how's Michelle.*
              (1.0)
         Robin: *They brought her ho:me.*
              (0.7)
→ Robin: *She hadda wait up the:re fo:r- u-she:'s been there since*
              eight uh' clock this morning'n at six thirty she called me . . .
              (0.5) *Said "Please com'n get me . . .*

                                                        (PB 3–4:6)

The stretches on *the:re* and *fo:r* are common preindications of a repair, especially a search, upcoming;[17] the *u* may be beginning it. The object of the search—the next item due in the turn as built to that point—is some DURATION, that is, *n hours* with some value for *n*; it is the latter that is, apparently, being searched for. But the repair is converted. The search is not pursued; rather, the turn-so-far is reconstructed so as to eliminate the duration formulation and to provide instead for a statement of BOUNDARY TIMES, leaving it for the recipient to figure out, or not to have to figure out, how long a wait it was. What starts, then, as a repair on the next item due,

---

[16] There are other same-turn repair initiators not discussed here, for example, the sound stretch, Schegloff, Jefferson, and Sacks (1977), p. 367, §3.21.

[17] Cf. Schegloff (1978, mimeo).

a search, is converted to a different type of repair, a reorganization or reconstruction of the turn-so-far in order to achieve a solution. What gets "changed" is the turn-so-far; what was the trouble was the next element. Similarly,

(14)   A is talking about the "May Company," a department store chain with many branches.

A: *We wen'tuh the one uh- I wen'tuh the one uh-* **Thursdee** *on uh* (0.9) *up there by Knoxberry Farm.*

(NB:4 calls:1:1:7)

"A" twice comes to the point where a locational formulation of the branch referred to is "due." Each time, *uh* replaces the next element due. Each time, some alternative to the search is done, first a repair in which *we* is replaced by *I*, then the insertion of a time reference. Then, a third time, the position for the location is arrived at, but this time with a format for the location formulation exhibited—*on*, which seems to project a street name as the next element due. Again, *uh* occurs where the next element is due, and then a pause. A search is in progress for a prototypical search object—a name. But, again, the repair is converted; this time, not by reconstructing the whole turn-so-far, but by replacing the "format-exhibiting" element, the *on*. The form of location formulation is repaired from "*on* + street name" to the "near X" format,[18] and the latter format has its elements readily solved. Here, again, what starts as a repair on next element gets for its solution a repair on some prior element.[19] Some of the variability that is found in the tie between cut-off and *uh*/pause and backward and forward

[18] Cf. Schegloff (1972) on place formulations.
[19] Two more instances I leave for the reader to explicate:

(i)   District Attorney in a TV news interview concerning certain actions by his office against some nursing homes:
       DA: *Some of the nursing homes had a low bed: uh uh had a high vacancy factor in terms of the beds.*

(EAS:FN)

Talking about what will be served for dinner tomorrow.

(ii)   Grandma: *Well somebody come in here 'n said "Let's have a- we'll have ( ) steaks fer tamarra" so I was just repea:ting.*
       (0.2)
       Grandpa: *That was // last night.*
       →Dad: *Whoever said it was a- was a- was a:::::*
       Grandma: *I don't- I think it was one of the girls.*
       →Dad: *-didn't know what they was talking about.*

(Curtis:142–148)

(Can Dad's sentence be given a thorough syntactic analysis without reference to the repair in it?)

repairables, respectively, is due to such repair conversions and is, thus, orderly variation.

The generally prepositioned repair initiators appear quite restricted in their distribution (as INITIATORS, rather than as later components of a repair segment): They occur just before the "trouble-source." The post-positioned repair initiators (and, therefore, most of the postpositioned repair) are more variable in their distribution.

In fact, repair generally, and postpositioned repair in particular, can be initiated anywhere in the turn. There is no exclusion rule that I know of, even in terms that have otherwise ordered the distribution of repair, that is, relative to the repairable.[20] There are concentrations of repair initiation that can be mentioned, though I will not treat them in detail here.

1. Just-post-initiation and just-pre-completion of various unit types seem to be specially common loci of repair initiation. Thus, just after the start of a turn-constructional unit (e.g., a sentence) or just before its completion; after the first sound of a word or just before its last sound.

2. Most same-turn repairs that operate on a focused repairable, for example, a particular word or phrase in the turn-so-far, are concentrated in the proximate aftermath of the repairable, most of them within two words of the repairable. When combined with the preceding observation, this means that a great many repairs of focused items such as words are initiated just after the first sound of the word, before its last sound, or in those positions for the next several words. However, it should not be forgotten that these bunchings are within a larger distribution that excludes no particular locus of initiation in same turn.

3. There appear to be a set of subordering rules for repair initiation under particular conditions. I cite but one example. If there is a convergence between the first element of a repair and some element of the ongoing turn-in-production, the shared element is often used as the place to initiate repair. Such "pivot" elements (as they are called by several colleagues who are interested in them) can operate for the sound position in a word at which repair is initiated, as in (15):

(15)   A has had a claim of hers called an exaggeration

    A: *DON'T SAY that I'm exa-just say I'm a liar.*

                                     (Pre-Party, p. 4)

Here, the initial sound of the repair, *j*, occurs in a word in the turn-so-far (*exa*-[*ggerating*]), and at its position the repair is initiated, with the consequence that it is not apparent until a bit later that it HAS been initiated. Or,

---

[20] Cf. Schegloff, Jefferson, and Sacks (1977), pp. 365–367, §3.1; pp. 374–375, §4.3.

pivots can operate for words in sentences (and, by the way, (16) is in topic-initial position).

(16)   B: `hhh *Whad about uh*:: (0.8) *Oh yih go f*::- *you-*
        How many days? you go **five** *days a week. Ri*//*ght?*
                                                           (TG, 387–388)

Here, *How many days you go.* + (*Five days a week, right?*) (the second element is in parentheses because it is not necessarily projected by the start) is turned into *How many days- You go five days a week, right?*. The shift occurs on the pivot *you go*, which is the next element of the turn-so-far and the first element of the new version. Or, again,

(17)   M is looking at a picture of V and his family
        M: *I saw it but I never looked yihknow et did-eh-deh-deh-* **middle** *one*
        looks // *just like,*
                                                           (US, 28)

The phrase *middle one* is potentially syntactic with what precedes; it turns out to be the "subject" of a new sentence.[21]

Because nothing is excludable from the class "repairable"[22] and because repair on a repairable can be initiated any place in the turn in which it occurs

---

[21] Jörg Bergmann of the University of Konstanz has shown me the following instance in German, from a psychiatric intake interview:

Dr. F.:   *'s:**nichd** Ih:re Schdimme,*
Linda: *Nei::n 's nichd meine Schtimme*
                          . (0.4)
Linda: *'s isd Gott se:lba*
                   o   o
Dr. F.:   *mm*
                       (0.3)
              o   o
Dr. F.:   *Mm*
                       (0.7)
→Dr. F.:   *Ja:: md`hhh nu:n: gibt's ja off`nba:r*
                       (1.0)
→Dr. F.:   *is Ihr Mann nich:d ganz der gleich'n Mei:nung-g*
           wie Sie::ju⌈*nd ä:h*   ⌉
                       ⌊*Nei:n also=mein=Mann*⌋ =*ist* =
                                          = *beschtimmt* =⌈*nich' =dea=glei*⌉*ch'n* =
Dr. F.:   ⌊*f `   h   h   h*⌋
Linda: = ⌈*Meinung*   ⌉
Dr. F.:   = ⌊*die Umge:*⌋ *bung:g auch nichd g'ra:de*

The doctor's turn translates roughly as 'There are obviously (1.0) your husband is not of the same opinion as you.' In the German, it appears that, given the word order, *off`nba:r* 'obviously' is syntactically necessary to the sentence that eventuates at the end and is the pivot from the sentence with which the turn began.

[22] Schegloff, Jefferson, and Sacks (1977), p. 363, §2.13.

(not to mention the remainder of the repair initiation opportunity space), at any point in the productional course of a turn (and, therefore, of a sentence in it) there is a systematic alternative to producing next a syntactically coherent next bit of the talk. That alternative is to initiate repair, either on some prior bit of the talk or on some next bit of it. Syntax-for-conversation and repair are both sequential organizations that bear on the production of turn-constructional units like sentences. Syntax is, among other things, that sequential organization that organizes the turn-constructional unit and by reference to which the progress of that unit is exhibited by speakers and analyzed–recognized by recipients. Repair in sentences can be "intrusive" in that it regularly interrupts that progress. Syntax and repair operate in the same sequential environment; they need to be investigated together.

The preceding discussion concerning repair initiation may be said to deal with the "left" boundary of repair. I shall not discuss the right boundary extensively here. I only want to note that repair aims for success and is overwhelmingly successful at achieving it quickly. For the most part, a single repair effort deals with a trouble-source. The effect of success is, and is displayed by, the resumption of the turn-unit as projected before the repair initiation or, if the repair operation involves reconstruction of the whole turn-unit, production of the turn-unit to completion. In both cases, syntacticity and "smooth" (i.e., without hitch) production characterize and display the continuation of the talk post-repair. Successful repair is, for the most part, built to "blend back" into untroubled talk.

We have arrived at a view of talk in a turn in conversation in which some sort of syntax organizes the smooth production of sentential turn-constructional units, and, when trouble arises, an organization of repair operates with orderly components (e.g., initiators) to address it, with syntactic organization quickly reasserting itself. Sometimes, however, a single repair effort does not achieve a stable, successful solution, and almost immediately another repair is initiated on the same repairable. This repair will be no less orderly than the first—its initiator being of one of the sorts described, and with syntacticity once again being reinstituted. Although not common, two successive repairs on a same repairable, yielding (together with the repairable) three tries at that bit of talk, are not rare. (Cases with more than two repairs on a same repairable are the harder to find the more repair segments are involved.) Each repair segment taken alone is orderly along lines already described. A "repair organization" ready for syntactic or quasi-syntactic description should not, however, leave the series or succession of tries at that bit of talk unordered. Nor should a repair organization operating for natural interaction allow a speaker unregulated time to "get it right." I shall, therefore, present some evidence (far from decisive) that successive repairs on a repairable are themselves ordered as a series. Several types of ordering can be discerned that suggest an orientation to "progressivity"—to displaying that each repair has made progress toward a solution of the trouble being addressed.

1. **Each next "try" adds to the prior tries.**

(18)   Bee: *That's why they have us in this buildin-**we** finally got a' 'hhh a*
→   *roo:m tihday in-in the leh- a Iectchuh hall,.*
                                                    (TG:492–493)

(19) →T: *Yeah cause I saw- I saw s- some- dude like this jus' come*
             marchin . . .
                                                    (TH:61)

In (18), the first repair adds *the leh-* to what precedes, and the second adds *cthuh hall*. In (19), the first repair adds *s-*, and the second *some . . . .* Each try shows progress by accretion or extension.

2. **Or each next try changes an element of prior tries.**

(20)   Bee: *'hhh I said theh go, I said there's- there's **three** courses*
                  a'ready . . .
                                                    (TG:234–235)

(21)   Bonnie: *Why? Because they hg- because they have- they asked you*
                  first.
                                                    (NYI:228–229)

In (20), the first repair replaces *Theh go* with *There's* (the second adds to it). In (21), the first repair replaces *hg* with *have*; the second replaces *have* with *asked . . . .*

Note also that, in (18), the second repair replaces the prior try's *the* with *a*, yielding a series of shifts in which the first repair operates on the original try by extension and the second repair operates on the first by change or replacement. This is a not uncommon orderliness for successive repair segments; note:

(22) →Bee: *- Yihknow theyd- they **do** b-(0:2) t !'hhhh they try even **harduh***
→   *then uhr-yihknow a regular instructor.*
                                                    (TG:227–229)

(23) →Mark: *She did I think. (˙) I- (˙) don't- (˙) I was really drunk et the*
              time. .
                                                    (SN–4:7)

(24) →Mark: *She- she wa- she 'n I're gonna go out en get drunk at four*
              o'clock in the afternoon.
                                                    (SN–4:9)

3. **Each next try backs up less far than its predecessor.**   It is common for same-turn repair to repeat a bit of the talk preceding a repairable, thereby

"framing" it. Successive repair tries regularly return less far than preceding tries. Segments (18)–(21) all display this progressive return property: In (18), the first repair "goes back" to *in*, the second not so far; in (19), the first goes back to *I saw*, the second not so far; in (20), the first goes back to *I said*, the second not so far; in (21), the first goes back to *because*, the second not so far. Here, then, is a third type of ordering for a succession of repairs, one that in its own fashion displays progress.

4. **Marking time leads to overt "search."** When a try at a bit of talk is the same as the prior try (i.e., the first repair like the original, the second like the first), we may speak of MARKING TIME. This does happen, but regularly the second of these two tries adds an *uh*, marking a more overt entry into a search and converting the repair type from redoing what has preceded to a forward repair. The solution of the repair is then converted into the solution of the search. As in:

(25)   W: *An:'e took the inside out 'n found it uz full of- full of- uh:-*
→   *calcium: deposits . . .*

                                             (TH:20–21)

(26)   →Bee: *I don'know. The school- school uh, (1.0) bookstore doesn't carry*
→   *anything anymo(h)uh,*

                                            (TG:333–334)

(Note, however, that (26) is not a true case of marking time because the movement from original to first repair shows progressive return.)

5. **Regressive tries are last tries.** When a try is identical not with the preceding try but with a yet earlier one, we may speak of it as REGRESSIVE. Regularly, a regressive try turns out to be the last on a same repairable. When progress is no longer being made, the regressive try may become the one to which syntactic continuations are fitted.

(27)   →Bee: *-Eh-ye:h, ih-a,* **She** *ws rea:lly awful, she ha-duh she's the wuh-*
→   **She** *ha:duh southern accent too.*

                                            (TG:188–189)

(28)   →(   ):   *I wonder what sh- how she- what she, puts in it.*

                                            (LS:SW)

(29)   →Vic: *En* **I** *grab a pail, en I put- 'hh I see- ah-put all the glass in th'*
→   *pail,*

                                            (US:33)

Of course, the speaker may give up[23] or recipients may interrupt.[24] This last ordering is of particular importance. It suggests that a succession of

---

[23] Schegloff, Jefferson, and Sacks (1977), p. 364, instance (8).
[24] Schegloff, Jefferson, and Sacks (1977), p. 365, instance (15).

repairs is not organized only by relating any next unit to its prior but that, in its apparent sensitivity to the relationship of some try to all prior tries, the organization operates for the SERIES AS A WHOLE, an important property for a candidate syntactic organization.

In this section, I have tried to show that the materials of same-turn repair are not intractable but that there is preliminary evidence that they are orderly. Almost certainly, the types of orderliness that remain to be found are more powerful than the ones cited. It should be borne in mind that displays of progressivity will always be fashioned out of the language materials otherwise in use in the turn's sentence, and, thus, quite unintuitive forms of progressivity display should be admitted as possibilities. If the preceding sections have warranted the appropriateness of investigating repair for its possible relations to syntax, it appears that such investigations should not be frustrated by disorder in the data.

6. SYNTAX OR SUPER-SYNTAX?

In some respects, the operation of repair in sentences is like a super-syntax. In can order and reorder the arrangement of the components of the sentences as well as restructure its overall shape. It is systematically relevant to sentences and is at any point an alternative to other ordering devices for next bits of talk. One of its resources is the capacity specifically to override syntactic ordering in the production of a next bit of talk, and this resource can be used to reconstruct the syntactic ordering of the sentence-so-far. When it operates, it sometimes creates positions in the talk at which the relations between successive items in the talk are specifically not governed by syntax but instead by some other relationship (e.g., on either side of a cut-off repair initiator, or successive repair segments on a same repairable).

On the other hand, some repair operations can retain the projective import of the syntactic shape of the sentence-so-far (e.g., the *uh* repair initiator). It is not unfamiliar for some component of a syntax to operate on the product yielded by other components of the syntax. The "non-syntactic" orderings produced by repair are not unsyntactic in principle; they happen not to be components of the types of syntax of which we currently have accounts. The organization of same-turn repair might well be a natural component of a syntax-for-conversation.

What a syntax-for-conversation will look like cannot be specified before those who might describe it set about the examination of turn-constructional-units that are produced in conversation empirically. It seems to me, however, that such a syntax-for-conversation is likely to have certain characteristics.

1.   It will recognize that its sentences will be in turns and will be subject to the organization of turns and their exigencies. For example, it will recognize

(a)   that possible sentence completion implicates possible turn completion, and that can implicate next turn starts.

(b)   that there can be organizational pressures for next turns to get early starts or be deferred, and current turn, and a sentence in it, can both affect that and suffer it.

(c)   that the turn the sentence is in can have other sentences or other turn-constructional-units in it, and that can have consequences for any given sentence.

(d)   that, generically, others are present who can talk, who will talk when the turn is over, who may, under strictly regulated conditions, talk during the turn and during a sentence in it at the "invitation" of the speaker, and who may intrude on it in its course under a variety of specifiable conditions.

As a consequence, one set of terms for the description of a sentence or other turn-constructional-unit in conversation will involve its progressive development toward possible completion, so that, for example, "pre-possible-completion" could be a place in a sentence of which a syntactic account could be given. It will allow description of a succession of sentences-so-far and turns-so-far in the course of the talk.[25]

2.   It will treat the pace of talk and pauses in it as potentially deployable syntactic objects in a sentence in a turn and will admit such relationships between components of a turn as adjacency, pre- and postpositioning,[26] etc.

3.   It will recognize that the sentence may be part of a "project" (e.g., a story) pursued by the speaker through a series of turns and may be sensitive to its place in that project.

4.   It will recognize that the turn the sentence is in is regularly a turn in a sequence, a structural unit whose organizational contingencies have consequences for component turns and, consequently, for sentences in them.

5.   It will recognize that the sentence is always not only someplace in particular sequentially but is also spoken to some party or parties in particular, so that it is subject to considerations of "recipient design," which is relevant to the choice of words and syntactic forms in it.

6.   It will recognize that, whatever long-term project or "intention" the sentence's speaker has, the speaker is first and most immediately under the

[25] For example, cf. Goodwin, 1977.

[26] Some of these matters have occasionally been touched on in the past; for example, see Bolinger's "Linear Modification."

constraints of, and afforded the resources of, some sequentially local here-and-now, and

7. that all the types and orders of organization that operate in and on turns in conversation can operate on the sentence.

8. It will be grounded in the inspection of sentences actually produced in turns at talk in naturally occurring conversation.

7. CONCLUDING COMMENTS

In continually writing of a "syntax-for-conversation," I mean to treat explicitly as hypothetical what seems to me to be prematurely treated as presupposed fact, and that is the existence of A syntax. That there is a trans-discourse-type syntax may end up to be the case; it should be found, not presupposed. With that, I also mean to make explicitly hypothetical the current sense of "a language," or "language." The notion "a language" seems to be the product of an assumption about some common, stable, underlying properties of an immense range of human behavior—from talking to the family to reciting Shakespeare to cadging alms to writing memoranda to lecturing, etc.—each of which is embedded in its own combination of organizational structures, constraints, and resources. Much attention has been devoted to these supposedly common features; relatively little to their respective environments of use, which differentiate them. Accordingly, a serious weighing of the commonalities against the differentiae has yet to take place. In any environment of so-called "language use," there is a locally organized world in which it is embedded. Some of these are "speech exchange systems";[27] some do not involve talking. Until the characteristics of these locally organized settings are investigated and explicated in appropriate detail, the extraction of "language" from them is a procedure with unknown properties and consequences. A syntax-for-conversation is an attractive candidate for early treatment because conversation is the most common and, it would appear, the most fundamental condition of "language use" or "discourse."

APPENDIX 1

A full set of notational conventions used in the transcripts may be found in Sacks, Schegloff, and Jefferson (1974). The conventions most relevant to this chapter follow. The transcription system was developed by Gail Jefferson.

[27] Sacks, Schegloff, and Jefferson (1974), 729–31.

The transcript segment reproduced in Appendix 2 is a reconciliation of separate transcripts by Gail Jefferson, Richard Frankel, and myself. Most of the other data segments used in the text are the work of Jefferson.

-	The dash indicates a cut-off, usually a stop.
:	Colons indicate a stretch of the preceding sound, in rough proportion to the duration of the stretch.
[ ]	Brackets mark turns spoken in overlap: Left brackets indicate the point of onset; right brackets (not always marked) indicate the point of resolution.
//	Double slash is an alternate convention for overlap; the point of the double slash is where the next marked turn starts.
(0.5)	Numbers in parentheses indicate elapsed silence in tenths of a second (stopwatch is not used).
Boldface	Boldface italics indicate stress but do not differentiate whether pitch or amplitude is involved.

NOTE: The data fragments cited here are drawn from a collection of audio- and videotapes of naturally occurring ordinary conversation. The parties to these conversations are diverse—students, housewives, janitors, etc.—as are the "contexts"—telephone, co-present, at home, at work, etc. Sources are identified by code in the text so as to allow retrieval, should that be relevant.

APPENDIX 2

Here is a bit of transcript in which you can see a number of instances and types of instances of the phenomena I will be concerned with. I have not ensured that it is "characteristic"; it has about as much of "same-turn" repair as many other fragments, fewer than others, more than still others. It is a bit skewed, in that, for most of it, one of the parties is telling a story, so that the other says relatively little. The parties are two girls who have apparently known each other for a long time, who for a while went to the same college until B transferred to another school. They have been talking about a former mutual teacher, who is the *she* of line 179, and then B begins to tell about a current teacher of hers. I offer the fragment as a resource for those who have not examined materials from natural conversation and who might see little sense for the observation that the recurrence of the events of repair in conversation would be readily noticeable to anyone who would look. (Transcription conventions in Appendix 1.)

```
179   Ava:                              She must know somebuddy
180         because all those other teachers they got rid of .hhhh
181                (0.3)
182   Bee:  Yeh I bet they got rid of all the one:: Well one I had, t!
183         'hhhh in the firs' term there, fer the firs' term of English,
184         she die::d hhuh-uhh⌈'hhh
185   Ava:                    ⌊Oh:.
186   Bee:  She died in the middle of the 'te:rm?mhhh!=
187   Ava:  =Oh that's too ba:d hha ha!=
188   Bee:  =Eh-ye:h, ih-a, She wz rea:lly awful, she ha-duh, (('hh))
189         she's the wuh- She ha:duh southern accent too.
190   Ava:  Oh:.
191   Bee:  A:nd, she wz very difficul' tuh unduhstand.
192   Ava:  No, she ain't there anymoh,
193   Bee:  No I know I mean she, she's gone a long t(h)ime
194         (h)a'rea(h)⌈dy? hh
195   Ava:             ⌊Mm, ⌈hhmh!
196   Bee:               ⌊'hhh
197                (0.2)
198   Bee:  nYeeah, 'hh This feller I have-⁽ⁿⁿ⁾."felluh" ; this ma:n.
                                          ₍ᵢᵥ₋₎
199         (0.2) t!'hhh He ha::(s)- uff-eh-who-who I have fer
200         linguistics ⌈is    real⌉ly too much, 'hh⌈h=
201   Ava:              ⌊Mm hm?⌋            ⌊Mm⌈hm,
202   Bee:                                       ⌊=I didn' notice it
203         b't there's a woman in my class who's a nurse 'n. 'hh she
204         said to me she s'd didju notice he has a ha:ndicap en I
205         said wha:t. Youknow I said I don't see anything wrong
206         wi⌈th im, she says his ha:nds.=
207   Ava:   ⌊Mm.
208   Bee:  ='hhh So the nex' cla:ss hh! 'hh fer en hour en f'fteen
209         minutes I sat there en I watched his ha:n(h)ds hh
210         hh⌈'hhh=
211   Ava:    ⌊Why wha⌈t's the ma⌈tter ⌉ᵒwith ⁽ʰⁱˢ ʰ'ⁿᵈˢ⁾
212   Bee:            ⌊=She  ⌊meh-  ⌋     ₍ʰⁱᵐ.    ₎
213   Bee:  'hhh t!'hhh He ksh- He doesn' haff uh-full use uff hiss
214         hh-fin::gers or something en he, tch! he ho:lds the chalk
215         funny=en, 'hh=
216   Ava:  =Oh⌈:
217   Bee:     ⌊hhHe-⌈eh-his fingihs don't be:nd=en, ⌈'hhh-
218   Ava:                                          ⌊Oh⌈::      ⌉
219   Bee:                                             ⌊Yihknow⌋ she
```

```
220              really eh-so she said you know, theh-ih- she's had
221              experience. 'hh with handicap' people she said but 'hh
222              ih-yihknow ih-theh- in the fie:ld.
223                      (0.2)
224   Ava:  (Mm:.)
225   Bee:  -thet they're i:n⌈::.=
226   Ava:               ⌊(Uh⌈huh)
227   Bee:                    ⌊= Yihknow theyd- they do b- (0.2)
228              t!'hhhh they try even harduh then uhr-yihknow a regular
229              instructor.
230   Ava:  Righ⌈t.
231   Bee:      ⌊'hhhh to uh instr- yihknow do the class'n evr⌈ything.  ⌉
232   Ava:                                                     ⌊Uh huh, ⌋
232a  Bee:  An:d,
233   Bee:  She said they're usually harder markers 'n I said wo::wuhh
234              huhh! 'hhh I said theh go, I said there's- there's three
235              courses a'ready thet uh(hh)hh⌈hff
236   Ava:                                   ⌊°Yeh
237   Bee:  -I'm no(h)t gunnuh do well i(h)n,
238   Ava:  hhhh!
239   Bee:  'hhh Becaw but uh, Oh my, my north american indian class
240              's really, (0.5) tch! It's so boring.
241                      (0.3)
242   Ava:  Ye(h)e(h)ah!
243                      (0.2)
244   Bee:  I-ah- y-yihknow this gu:y has not done anything yet thet
```

ACKNOWLEDGMENTS

Much in this paper had its origin in work and conversation with my late colleague, Harvey Sacks, especially the discussion in the third section. I profited from comments on an earlier draft by Talmy Givón, Gail Jefferson, Rainier Lang, Gene Lerner, and Anita Pomerantz, but probably not enough.

REFERENCES

Bolinger, Dwight L. (1952) "Linear Modification," Reprinted in *Forms of English: Accent, Morpheme, Order*, 1965, Harvard University Press, Cambridge, Massachusetts.
Fromkin, Victoria A., ed. (1973) *Speech Errors as Linguistic Evidence*, Mouton, The Hague.
Goffman, Erving (1969) *Strategic Interaction*, University of Pennsylvania Press, Philadelphia, Pennsylvania.

Goodwin, Charles (1977) *Some Aspects of the Interaction of Speaker and Hearer in the Construction of the Turn at Talk in Natural Conversation*, Doctoral dissertation, Annenberg School of Communication, University of Pennsylvania.

Hockett, Charles F. (1967) "Where the Tongue Slips, There Slip I," in *To Honor Roman Jakobson*, Mouton, The Hague, pp. 910–936. (Reprinted in Fromkin, 93–119)

Jefferson, Gail (1972) "Side Sequences," in David N. Sudnow, ed., *Studies in Social Interaction*, Free Press, New York, pp. 294–338.

Jefferson, Gail (1975) "Error Correction as an Interactional Resource," *Language in Society* 3, 181–199.

Labov, William (1970) "The Study of Language in Its Social Context," *Studium Generale* 23, 30–87.

Moerman, Michael (1977) "The Preference for Self-Correction in a Thai Conversational Corpus" *Language* 53, 872–882.

Sacks, Harvey, Emanuel A. Schegloff, and Gail Jefferson (1974) "A Simplest Systematics for the Organization of Turn-Taking for Conversation," *Language* 50, 696–735.

Schegloff, Emanuel A. (1972) "Notes on a Conversational Practice: Formulating Place," in David N. Sudnow, ed., *Studies in Social Interaction*, Free Press, New York, pp. 75–119.

Schegloff, Emanuel A. (1978) "Some Relationships between the Temporal Organization of Hand Gesture and Aspects of the Organization of Speech Production, Deixis, and Place/Space Reference in Conversational Interaction," Mimeo.

Schegloff, Emanuel A., Gail Jefferson, and Harvey Sacks (1977) "The Preference for Self-Correction in the Organization of Repair in Conversation," *Language* 53, 361–382.

Schegloff, Emanuel A., and Harvey Sacks (1973) "Opening up Closings," *Semiotica* 8, 289–327.

Sudnow, David N., ed. (1972) *Studies in Social Interaction*, Free Press, New York.

PART IV **PRONOUNS AND TOPIC RECOVERABILITY**

PRONOUNS IN DISCOURSE[1]

DWIGHT BOLINGER
Harvard University

1. INTRODUCTION

After years of efforts at rule-making that have only led up one blind alley after another, a number of researchers have concluded that the key to "pronominalization" is not to be found in syntax, perhaps even that "the key" does not exist. Keenan (1976) says of "open coreference" (the kind of system we find in English) that it has, generally, "no structurally statable restrictions." Bílý (1977:51) says of the series of articles following Ross (1967): "These amendments have never made an integrated system of pronominalization; they are often mere ad hoc patchworks on the basic syntactic rule which does not work."[2] The starred and unstarred examples

---

[1] This is a revision and condensation of "Pronouns and Repeated Nouns," reproduced by the Indiana University Linguistics Club, 1977. The longer study should be consulted for more extensive exemplification. The main thesis here is unchanged, though some errors have been corrected.

The asterisk is used for both "unacceptable in any sense" and "unacceptable in the relevant (usually coreferential) sense."

[2] Bílý's assessment of a dozen or so papers is equally true of three additional ones I have examined, Delisle (1973), Lasnik (1976), and Hankamer (1976), though Delisle is pretty much in Bílý's own camp. See the Appendix in Bolinger (1977).

Syntax and Semantics, Volume 12:
Discourse and Syntax

used as proofs or illustrations are a jungle of distractors—many of the "ungrammatical" or "noncoreferential" examples are what they are for reasons incidental or irrelevant to the theory being expounded. One example: Lasnik (1976) cites [his example (8b)] *It surprises him that John is so well liked* to illustrate his "command" relationship. But the sentence can be modified in several ways to make it acceptable:

(1)   *It surprised him that John was so well liked.*

(2)   *It obviously surprises him that John is so well liked.*

(3)   *Does it surprise him that John is so well liked?*

His starred example is bad because it somehow pretends to read John's mind. I know what my own psychology is at the present moment as regards feeling surprise, so that *It surprises me that I am so well liked* is normal; but I do not know John's. When *obviously* is added in (2), we understand that John's surprise is being read from external evidence. The question in (3) makes no assumptions. And the past tenses in (1) are inherently external to the moment of speaking.

The perspective offered in what follows is essentially that of functional sentence perspective, though I do not try to conform to the terminology and will keep the discussion as close as possible to one central question: "At X location, what reason might the speaker have for using a word that is leaner in semantic content rather than one that is fuller, or vice versa?" Usually this means "Why use a pronoun?" or "Why repeat the noun?" What we need at this point is not more theory but a steady look at the possibilities in a variety of situations and contexts.

The motives for choice are clearest when the choices are not mixed—that is, when the speaker uses pronouns alone or nouns alone. Pronouns may be used without antecedent nouns when the referent is clear from knowledge of the world or of the circumstances:

(4)   *How's Jack? Living it up?—Yes, he's giving it all he has.*

(5)   *(Irate patient storms into office and accosts nurse.) Where is he?*

(6)   *(Football fan to favorite team.) Give 'em hell.*

The last example could be *Give the bastards hell*; epithets are like pronouns (Bolinger 1972:301–305). Not only *it* but also *they* may have a nonparticular referent:

(7)   *Why's she running?—They're after her for something, I guess.*

(8)   *What do they say about Carter's choice for Attorney General?*

There also may be coreference with a vaguely specified passive agent:

(9)   *Maxine was kidnapped but they didn't hurt her.*

I disregard deictic uses of the pronoun, as in *Who's hé?* (speaker points).
   Nouns may corefer with nouns in cases of elegant variation:

(10)   *Had Shakespeare not written **The Tempest** he would have
       deprived the world of one of the Bard's most sensitive works.*

Colloquially we find

(11)   *What do you think of our new teacher?—Oh, Mr. Jónes is all right.*

Though there are interesting correlations with pronouns, I shall have nothing
further to say about these possibilities.
   The obvious use of coreferring nouns is in identical repetition:

(12)   *What do you think of Tom?—Oh, I líke Tóm* (rise–fall–rise).

The contrast between this and *I like him* suggests that repetition when it
occurs is motivated, though the motive may not always be the same. Here
it is to highlight the topic of the sentence, the topic being marked by its
intonation (one might also have *Oh, Tóm I líke*). Elsewhere, it may be for
clarity:

(13)   **Tom turned all his friends against Tom himself.*

(14)   *Tom turned all his friends against Larry, Jerry, and Tom himself.*

Or to avoid breaking up a collocation:

(15)   *?I'm ready for bed, so I'll just go (there).*

(16)   *I'm ready for bed, so I'll just go to bed.*

(17)   **If there were sun I'd put them out in it (out there).*

(18)   *If there were sun I'd put them out in the sun.*

(*There is sun* is a weather collocation; *put something in the sun* is a collocation signifying 'to sun something.') Or to reject an alternative:

(19)   *Why don't you get limes?—She said lemons so I'll get lémons.*

(*So I'll get them* would mean 'So I'll do as she said'; *so I'll get thém* would
emphasize the choice but not repudiate the alternative.) Or, to lay emphasis
on the nature of the referent—X qua X; X has the quality suggested by the
clause in which X occurs:

(20)   *You don't need sulfur for drying apricots; sulfur ruins the flavor.*

(*It ruins the flavor* would not emphasize the inherent quality of sulfur.) This is done—banteringly—even with proper names and indefinites:

(21)   *When Joe enters a conversation, Joe expects Joe's friends to listen to Joe.*

(22)   *Somebody had better look out, or somebody is going to get in trouble with somebody's wife.*

We gather that Joe is just naturally self-centered and *somebody* is just naturally being indiscreet. A point action, which does not describe a quality, does not lend itself to repetition:

(23)   **Joe stumbled when Joe crossed the street.*

These repeated nouns seem to be underlyingly demonstrative rather than simply definite. Repeated *sulfur* refers to "that substance," repeated *Joe* to "that person." The same is true of an accented pronoun in the same context:

(24)   *When Joe walks down the street, Joe ("that guy") struts.*

(25)   *When Joe walks down the street, hé* (rise–fall–rise) *struts.*

Repetition is often divided between speakers, as in the following:

(26)   *I was sorry to hear about Tom.—Yes, the doctor warned him, but he kept on.—If he knew the danger, you'd think he would have had more sense.*

Here we have only a series of statements about a single person, minimally referred to each time by a pronoun. But either speaker is free to use the noun, so as to imply Tom's nature:

(27)   *Yes, the doctor warned him, but Tom (being Tom) kept on.*

(28)   *If he knew the danger, you'd think that Tom (being Tom) would have had more sense.*

In (27) Tom is stubborn; in (28) he is a person of normally good sense. The speaker is also free to ignore the previous identification and make a fresh start, especially after there has been a break (he muses a moment, perhaps, before going on):

(29)   *Yes, the doctor warned Tom, but he kept on.*

The characterization may be more or less explicit:

(30)   *What did John do?—He did what John always does—he complained.*

(31)   *What did John know about it?—He knew what John alone could know—that there had been a secret agreement.*

In (30), John is a complainer; in (31), he is a person in the know. Without some element to make the action characteristic (it may be just an emphatic auxiliary, as in *He did what John wóuld do*), the example fails:

(32)   *What did John do?—*He did what John does—he complained.*

The characterization may embody a sort of definition:

(33)   *How come the male is able to lord it over the female?—He takes advantage of the male's superior musculature.*

namely that *The male has superior musculature.*

Pronominal reference may occur with or without nominal coreference in the vicinity. "Vicinity" needs to be defined more broadly than within the same sentence—Hinds (1977) makes a strong case for keying the use of pronouns to the organization of the paragraph [an insight that would have benefited Delisle (1973)]. But so much interest has centered on the syntax of the sentence—particularly with the so-called "pronominalization to the left"—that I shall arrange the remaining sections accordingly.

2. NO EXPLICIT ANTECEDENT

First, there are cases with no explicit antecedent in which the pronoun and the following noun are in the same clause. The examples most often cited are with possessive pronouns, and they are commonly assumed to be ungrammatical, as Lakoff's (1976) example [(189)] obviously is:

(34)   *His mother hates John.*

unless one provides a context:

(35)   *Who hates John?—His móther hates John* (terminal rise).

But no antecedent is necessary if the noun in question is CHARACTERIZED:

(36)   *Their pride has always been the undoing of tyrants.*

This could start a discourse. Tyrants are assumed to be noted for their pride. The point needs emphasizing for those who hold that an initial pronoun requires an explicit antecedent in prior discourse. Similarly:

(37)   *His mother hates John all the time.*

(38)   *His mother hates John when he behaves that way.* (He is hateful when he behaves that way.)

(39)   *His pen is in John's pocket.*

(40)   *His pen is John's constant companion.* (Our picture of him is with pen in pocket.)

Characterization seems to presuppose prior identification. It is one aspect of a more general assumption of FAMILIARITY. Though John may not have been explicitly mentioned in the portion of the discourse preceding (40), he is present to the minds of the interlocutors as someone recently or frequently talked about.[3] This can be seen in complex sentences that are initial in discourse. Whichever clause comes first—main or subordinate—the pronoun may precede:

(41)   *Hey, Gus! Tell him to come in if you see Tom out there, will you?*

(42)   *Hey, Gus! If you see him out there tell Tom to come in, will you?*

"Pronominalization into the main clause" is no bar to (41) for the same reason that both arrangements are normal: Tom is a familiar person. Having this option enables the speaker to be relaxed and offhand—he assumes a common ground with his interlocutor. This can be contrasted with the other possibilities. Thus,

(43)   *Tell Tom to come in if you see him out there, will you?*

with de-accented *Tom* would imply an immediately prior reference to Tom, not necessarily familiarity and, accordingly, would not fit after *Hey, Gus!*. On the other hand,

(44)   *Tell Tom to come in if you see him out there, will you?*

with normally accented *Tom* is not offhand; it is almost a request to seek out Tom. As for

(45)   *If you see Tom out there, tell him to come in, will you?*,

it perhaps suggests consequences for Tom; it is not offhand. The offhand intent can be tested with a designation that is inherently offhand, the make-shift *what's-his-name*. It works well with a preceding pronoun:

(46)   *Hey, Gus! If he comes early, tell what's-his-name to wait.*

(47)   *Hey, Gus! Tell him to wait, if what's-his-name comes early.*

These are normal when the speaker does not remember the name and the situation is relaxed enough for him not to have to make the effort. But if

---

[3] Compare, for a celebrity versus a nonentity:

*In his **Memoirs**, Winston Churchill tells us. . . .*
*In his term paper, Randy Peters tells us. . . .

as sentences that might begin a discourse.

the noun comes first, the offhand intent disappears and the makeshift designation is potentially rude:

(48)   *Hey, Gus! If what's-his-name comes early, tell him to wait.*

(49)   *Hey, Gus! Tell what's-his-name to wait, if he comes early.*

The speaker may be deliberately ignoring the name: *Tell whoozis to wait.* The opposite happens with a highly formal designation:

(50)   *If the general comes back, put him to death.*

(51)   **If he comes back, put the general to death.*

(52)   *If Johnny comes back, put him to bed.*

(53)   *If he comes back, put Johnny to bed.*

Example (51) suggests that generals are executed in an offhand manner. For whatever reason, the noun in first position is more than just a reminder of someone or something already well known.

Two further tests apply here. One is with contrast—only when the noun is in first position can we have "George rather than someone else," that is, something more than mere identification:

(54)   *If Géorge asks for me, tell him I'm not in.*

(55)   *If he asks for me, tell George (*Géorge) I'm not in.*

The other is with an indefinite, which necessarily brings in new information. In the following,

(56)   *Miss Jones, if he calls for me after ten o'clock, tell Mr. Allen to get in touch with me tomorrow.*

(57)   **Miss Jones, if he calls for me after ten o'clock, tell any stranger to get in touch with me tomorrow.*

(58)   *Miss Jones, if any stranger calls for me after ten o'clock, tell him to get in touch with me tomorrow.*

Example (56) is normal because the definite noun is only for identification and (58) is normal because the indefinite noun is in the proper position for something that does more than merely identify, but (57) is unacceptable because it puts a noun that does more than identify in a position that serves only for identification.

In the preceding, I have been careful to eliminate any explicit prior context, to force the initial pronoun to take its identification from the noun to the right even though the initial position of the pronoun depends on an

informal recognition of someone or something as familiar. We come now
to an intermediate step. There is an antecedent noun that is not in strict
grammatical relationship to the pronoun but to which it nevertheless
vaguely refers. Thus, supplying (57) with a prior context we get

(59)   Secretary: *What if someone calls for you?*

        Boss: *If he calls for me after ten o'clock, tell any stranger to get in
        touch with me tomorrow.*

Semantically, *he* is sufficiently referenced by *someone* so that the main clause
(*tell any stranger*) can now introduce new information: *If he* (=someone)
*calls for me after ten o'clock, tell any such someone who is a stranger to get
in touch with me tomorrow.*

    Though the pronoun faces both ways, it agrees with the noun that follows:

(60)   *How would you feel about letting a strange teenager come in your
        house?—Listen, when they come prowling around at night I don't
        let my best friends come in.*

(61)   *You do make bosom friends out of strange people.—If he does my
        bidding, I'll embrace the dévil!*

The double reference is what makes the difference in the following:

(62)   *Jack, I called because I want you to tell me something. We've got a
        bet going here. If she asked you, would you marry Joan?*

(63)   *. . . If she asked you, would you marry a widow with five children?*

(64)   *I guess I'm enough of a pushover to take any woman who was
        reasonably willing.—If she asked you, would you marry a widow
        with five children?*

Joan is a person who is known to the interlocutors; it is possible to speak
as if she had been recently mentioned. The widow with five children needs
some kind of introduction, which is supplied by *any woman who was reasonably willing.*

    The notion of vague prior reference also applies to a much-discussed
example that is otherwise outside the scope of this section. Ross cites

(65)   *Learning that John had cancer bothered him.*

as a failure to pronominalize under identity, *learning* presumably carrying
the underlying subject *John.* But subjects of gerunds are "open," and one
can have

(66)   *Knowing that John is perfect naturally pleases him.*

The difficulty with learning that one has cancer is that it is the kind of activity or process that is not likely to result in shared knowledge. What John learns about himself is too private; there is too little hint of a vague "other" among learners. *Knowing*, on the other hand, since it has to do with what is already established, is readily shareable, and "others" are out there as a possible implied antecedent. (Compare *The knowledge that John is perfect naturally pleases him*, **The fear that John is imperfect naturally displeases him*.) There is a similar effect if the process is one that results in knowledge that can be seen from the viewpoint of "others"—this happens when the facts are CREATED by the agent:

(67)   *Deciding that the committee was the beneficiary kept it from losing substantial funds.*

The committee made the decision, but it is a published fact. Similarly,

(68)   *Arranging that John should win the prize was unfair for him to do.*

John appears in two roles: as agent, he is one with "others" who might have made the arrangement. The case is the same with knowledge that is in the nature of things:

(69)   *Realizing that the Vicar of Christ was infallible disturbed him because he was a humble man.*

Papal infallibility is a doctrine in the public domain. Another example of private intelligence:

(70)   **Wondering if John had won the prize kept him awake.*

The possibility of "impartial viewing" affects full clauses as well as *-ings*:

(71)   **John learned that John had cancer.*

(72)   **John wondered if John had won the prize.*

(73)   *The committee decided that the committee was the beneficiary.*

(74)   *John arranged that John should win the prize.*

(Another way out of the difficulty is to suggest prior context in which *John* was already subject. This can be done by adding an intensifier: *Learning that John himself had cancer bothered him*. This could occur naturally only after some mention of John's having learned of someone else who had cancer.)

The confusion on this point is partly generated by formal doctrine—in this case the notion that an *-ing* has to have a specific subject at some point in a derivation.

3.   CONNECTIONS, LOOSE AND TIGHT

Discussions of "pronominalization to the left into a main clause" have overlooked the most obvious difference between sentences like the following:

(75)   *He choked when John swallowed the bone.*

(76)   *When he swallowed the bone, John choked.*

In (75) there is no comma break and the *when* clause is in tight construction with the verb. In (76) there is a comma break and the *when* clause is in loose construction with the verb. [More on this later. Also, I will take for granted that (76) requires a previous mention of John—that is, *he* has an antecedent in prior discourse.] Suppose we hypothesize that the speaker will find it most natural to reidentify the referent—by repeating the noun—after a break of some kind. It would follow that (76) should be normal, but not (75). It would also follow that, regardless of the syntax, if a break is introduced in a sentence such as (75), repetition of the noun should become acceptable. That is what we find. If the *when* clause is turned into an explanatory parenthesis with accompanying pitch and rhythm changes, *John* can be repeated:

(77)   *He choked (when John swallowed the bone, that is).*

A break of this sort may originate in the syntax—it happens with *wh* questions that front an element and leave the rest dangling:

(78)   *When I bought it, I rented the house to John.*

(79)   **I rented it to John when I bought the house.*

(80)   *When you bought it, who did you rent the house to?*

(81)   *Who did you rent it to, when you bought the house?*

Various sorts of afterthoughts do the same:

(82)   *He lied to me—something that John was rather fond of doing.*

(83)   *He was quite a guy, if John doesn't mind my saying so.*

The tense of the verb may be a clue to connectedness:

(84)   **He shot himself before John quite knew what he was doing.*

(85)   *He had already shot himself before John quite knew what he was doing.*

Sentence (84) describes the shooting: It was reckless. Sentence (85) gives a sequence of events and contains a facultative pause: *He shot himself(,) and then realized.* The incidentalness of the reidentification can be seen in the avoidance of putting the noun in one of the positions that normally carry higher information value:

(86)   *He won't help you, unless you can convince John that you are sincere.*

(87)   *?He won't help you, unless John likes you.*

(88)   **He won't help you, unless you are on good terms with John.*

The same thing can be accomplished by downplaying—accentually—the reidentification even when it is in a prominent position. Thus, the sentence **I knew he had done me a favor and I repaid John* looks unacceptable in spite of the loose syntax, but if *John* is totally de-accented it is all right:

(89)
$$I \quad \overset{knew}{} \overset{he\ had\ done\ me\ a}{} \overset{vor\ and\ I}{} \overset{re}{} \overset{paid}{} \quad fa \quad Jo_{h_n}.$$

The extreme case—and the most natural and obvious one—of reidentification of the referent is that of a "sentence" divided between two speakers—a question and an answer. In both (90) and (91) the *him* is justified by prior context and the second of the two segments is only loosely bound to the first:

(90)   *Have you seen him?—No, John hasn't been around lately.*

(91)   *I haven't seen him because John hasn't been around lately.*

The question of tightness–looseness inevitably raises the most-discussed issue of all, that of main and subordinate clauses. Ross's original formulation read as follows (1967:358): "If one element precedes another, the second can only pronominalize the first if the first is dominated by a subordinate clause which does not dominate the second." The rule fails, as can be seen by

(92)   **He will go if Jim feels good.*

(93)   *He would have been like a son to both of us, if my wife and I could have kept Jim away from the influence of his family.*

The looseness of (93) is an invitation to reidentify the referent. Yet there is something about subordination in clauses that makes looseness much more likely in some cases than in others.

First, the connectors themselves differ, ranging from the loosest (*and, although*, etc.) to the very tight (*before, when*) to the tightest (*that*). Compare the following sentences:

(94)   *She could pass for my sister, though June wasn't related to me at all.*

(95)   ?*She could pass for my sister, before June had her facelift.*

(96)   *He didn't do as he was told, so John had to take the consequences.*

(97)   **He had promised to help me, but John refused.*

(98)   **He said that John was ready.*

Among adverb clauses, temporal are the worst, perhaps for the same reason that tense is part of the verb—this aspect of reality is seized by the verb, and more than a comma disjuncture may be required to separate it:

(99)   **He befriends everyone, when John is in the chips.*

(100)   *He befriends everyone, even the milkman and his worst enemy, when John is in the chips.*

(101)   **He looked at me, as John stood there, with a seraphic smile.*

(102)   *He looked at me, as John always did, with a seraphic smile.*

We sense that the nontemporal parenthesis in (102) is more incidental to the main verb than the temporal parenthesis in (101). The difference between a *be* passive and a *get* passive works out as the suggestion of mere time versus cause:

(103)   ?*He's going to be flunked if John cheats.*

(104)   *He's going to get flunked if John cheats.*

Sentence (104) implies 'John's cheating will get him flunked'.

But the differences among connectors only reflect the range of their meanings. *If* is looser than *when* because it more often expresses a GIVEN—in (93) it is *Given that John could have been kept away from the influence of his family*. Temporal connectors too may express a given:

(105)   **He flunked when John cheated.*

(106)   *He usually flunks when John tries to cheat.*

Given that (if) he tries to cheat, he flunks. The temporal adverb *once* embodies "given" lexically:

(107)   *He was caught, once John had betrayed himself.*

Givenness is an aspect of the thematic organization of a sentence. What is given is the theme, or part of it. The normal position of the theme is at the beginning. If it is postposed, it tends to be marked—in English—by reduced volume and/or lower pitch. Sentence (106) would be produced as

$$He \ ^{usual}{}_{l_y} \quad ^{flu}{}_{nks}, \ when \ ^{John} \ tries \ to \ ^{che}{}_{at}.$$

(Studies of adverb position speak of "adverb preposing." Where thematic adverbs are concerned, it should probably be adverb postposing.) If the content of a subordinate clause is doubtful as theme, initial position is equally doubtful:

(108)   *We stopped John before he came in.*

(109)   ?*Before he came in we stopped John.*

(110)   *Before he could come in we stopped John.*

Sentence (110) implies some previous discussion of the possibilities of his coming in.

It makes no difference which end of the sentence the theme occupies; there is the same looseness of the given and the same likelihood of re-identifying a noun:

(111)   *When I first saw him, John was just a little boy.*

(112)   *He was just a little boy(,) when I first saw John.*

(113)   **He was a little boy when I saw John.*

The presence of an ordinal (*first, last, for the second time,* etc.) suggests that "occasions of seeing" are the theme here—'Given (on the occasion of) seeing him for the first time, John was just a little boy.' The *when* clause is not captured by the main verb because it is thematic. It does not modify the main verb but provides the whole main clause with a setting.

Even an ordinarily "loose" connector may cause trouble for reidentification if the meaning of the sentence suggests that its clause is rhematic rather than thematic—for example, *although*:

(114)   **He was taken away, although John objected.* =

(115)   **He was taken away against John's wishes.*

(116)   *He was taken away, although John could hardly understand what it was all about.*

Time is of the essence in verbs of action, but other complementary notions are just as essential to certain verbs. *Live* generally requires a locative complement—and its being required makes it rhematic:

(117)   *He lives where John works.*

(118)   *Where he works John lives.*

Other verbs are less demanding, and a locative may thematize:

(119)   *He has a lot to do where John works.*

(120)   *Where he works John has a lot to do.*

[By using a compound relative, the locative in (119) can be made an after-thought, so as to justify reidentification of the noun: *He has a lot to do, there where John works.*]

Time is not so much of the essence with imperfective verbs, and it is easier to find temporal clauses in final position that are still thematic:

(121)   *When he gets one of his tantrums, Ben is impossible.*

(122)   *He's impossible, when Ben gets one of his tantrums.*

(123)   *?I caught it when the virus came along.*

(124)   *I always catch it when a virus comes along.* ("If a virus comes along, I catch it.")

But all that is necessary is some element in the subordinate clause that enhances its likelihood of being thematic:[4]

(125)   *?I don't believe him when John tells a story.*

(126)   *I don't believe him when John tells a story like that.*

(127)   *?I answered him as soon as John spoke.*

(128)   *I recognized him as soon as John spoke.* ('Given his voice, recognition followed.')

(129)   *?He was captured the instant that John showed up.*

(130)   *He'll be captured the instant that John shows up.* ('Given that John shows up, his capture is predictable.')

---

[4] Of course, what determines its being thematic is the speaker's intent. There is an element of absurdity in this interpretive style of linguistic description. As linguistic detectives, we look for signs of intentions and confuse them with the intentions.

The same principles apply to clauses other than adverb clauses. The wider prosodic break and low pitch with extraposed gerunds signals the "given" that leads to reidentification:

(131)   *?It concerns him that John is a fool.*

(132)   *?It concerns him for John to be a fool.*

(133)   *It concerns him, John's being a fool.*

An extraposed subject *that* clause is good to the extent that it carries with it the same tentativeness (suggesting something turned over in the mind) that is normal when the clause is in initial position:

(134)   *That he should have it would benefit John.*

(135)   *It would benefit him(,) that John should have it.*

(136)   **That he (actually) had it benefited John.*

(137)   **It benefited him(*,) that John had it.*

As might be expected, a *that* clause serving as direct object of a finite verb is in such tight construction with the verb that reidentifying the referent is most unlikely:

(138)   *That he was a cad John freely admitted.*

(139)   **He freely admitted that John was a cad.*

(140)   *That he was incapable of doing it I convinced John easily.*

(141)   **I convinced him easily that John was incapable of doing it.*

But other complement relations are less difficult:

(142)   *I was glad for him that John was able to do it.*

(143)   *I pity him that John can't express his feelings.*

(A strong influence here is the subject versus oblique status of the pronoun. See in the following.)

With adjective clauses, too, close a link in time destroys the likelihood that the clause is thematic. Adding some element that suggests that the matter has been brought up before makes the clause more incidental and reidentification more likely:

(144)   **I got her the mink that Mary was holding.*

(145)   *I got her the mink that Mary had picked out.*

(146)   *I got her the mink that Mary kept begging me for.*

Compare, for incidentalness:

(147)   *?I got her the mink—the one that Mary was holding.*

(148)   *I got her the mink—the one that Mary had picked out.*

(149)   *I got her the mink—the one that Mary kept begging me for.*

Though the examples up to this point have used subordinate clauses, grammatical subordination is not crucial. Provided that the other relationships are maintained, coordination gives the same results. For example, temporal "coordination" causes the same trouble as temporal subordination:

(150)   *John looks at the wall and he throws the ball at it.*

(151)   **He looks at the wall and John throws the ball at it.*

(152)   *John looks at me and he goes out of his mind.*

(153)   *He looks at me and John goes out of his mind.*

In (152)–(153) we have a given: 'If John looks at me he goes out of his mind.' Similarly, in adversative coordination:

(154)   **He lied to me and John was my friend.*

(155)   *He lied to me, and John was my friend!*

'Even given that John was my friend, he lied to me.' Similarly with disjunctive coordinations—the merely temporal ones are no good:

(156)   *Either John eats or he sleeps.*

(157)   **Either he eats or John sleeps.*

(158)   *Either John does what I say or he loses his job.*

(159)   *Either he does what I say or John loses his job.*

But temporal connections are all right if there is a separation:

(160)   **He lost the money, and John found it again.*

(161)   *He lost the money, and then John found it again.*

(162)   **He lost the money but John found it again.*

(163)   *He lost the money but naturally (eventually) John found it again.*

With *but*, the logical relation of the clauses is fixed—the given, if there is one, comes first (a reversal calls for *though* rather than *but*). Even so, the contrast between given and merely temporal is the same as before:

(164)   **He went there but John didn't stay.*

(165)   *He saw me but John didn't recognize me.*

'even given that he saw me.' The gradation of separation can be seen in the following, where "pronominal" *to* tightens things up and *nevertheless* loosens them:

(166)   *He didn't want to go but John had to.*

(167)   ??*He didn't want to go but nevertheless John had to.*

(168)   *He didn't want to go but nevertheless John had to go.*

Some coordinating conjunctions are "loose" by virtue of containing a given as part of their meaning:

(169)   *He'll do it, now that John has the money for it.*

Others are loose by being lexically nonrestrictive, as can be seen by paraphrasing with *which*:

(170)   *He was wounded badly, yet* (in spite of which) *John didn't realize it till later.*

(171)   *He's going to be late, supposing* (which depends for its truth on the fact that) *John makes it at all.*

Appositions offer the most graphic instances of the need to reidentify by using the noun. The speaker has hastily assumed a prior reference, which he then deems to be insufficient. Accordingly, he elaborates:

(172)   *He's waving at you, the fellow over there.*

(173)   *Is she a member of the committee, your sister?*

Indefinites characteristically imply "existence" and, hence, "given that"— they are readily paraphrased with *if* clauses:

(174)   *He's not going to help you, a man who acts like that.*

(175)   *He's not going to help you, if you have a man who acts like that.*

(176)   *He's lying, anybody who says that!*

(177)   *He's lying, if anybody says that!*

4. THEMES, RHEMES, AND TOPICS

Lakoff rightly observed that it is more unusual to have the combination *he . . . John* than *him . . . John* (he thought it was impossible, but that has been shown to be false). The problem involves subjects, whether nouns or pronouns, as the likeliest to serve as TOPICS. It is not that objects cannot be topics, only that they less often are and do not create the same expectation of topicality. The difficulty with objects as topic can be seen in (179), where the speaker has to work unnaturally hard at the prosodic contrasts:

(178)   *What do you think of John and Mary?—She is despicable but he is OK.*

(179)   *... I despise her but I like him.*

I hypothesize the following principle:

(180)   THE TOPIC MAY BE REIDENTIFIED EASILY IN THE THEME, BUT IN THE RHEME ONLY IF THE THEME LACKS A NORMALLY TOPICAL FORM (SUBJECT NOUN OR SUBJECT PRONOUN).

The rheme is the part of the sentence that contains new information, and a noun appearing there is most apt to seem to refer to "someone or something else," particularly if the speaker already has an expressly topical *he* (or subject noun) in the theme. But, if he passes up the opportunity to put a topical form there, in its most logical place (theme and topic have to do with what the sentence is "about"), then the topic may be reintroduced in the less appropriate place for it, the rheme. So, in a simple sentence we have

(181)   **He likes John.*,

where *he* is topic and thematic and *John* is in the rheme. *John* refers to someone else. In complex sentences we have

(182)   *Did you have any trouble telling who he was?—*He was recognizable the moment John arrived.*

(183)   *... I recognized him the moment John arrived.*[5]

(The theme is John's recognizability, the rheme is the comment on that.) In (182) and (183) *John* again appears in the less likely place, the rheme, but in (183) there has been no previous topical form to edge *John* into a nontopical role. As for

(184)   *... The moment he arrived, John was recognizable.*,

the reidentification is in the best place, the theme, where it is least likely to compel the interpretation "someone else." Add to this the prosodic break typical of a postposed theme, and there is a double reason why the sequence *he . . . John* is normal.

---

[5] What counts is SUBJECT status, not NOMINATIVE form. A predicate nominative is as acceptable as an oblique case: *I knew it was he the moment John arrived.*

The difficulty of reidentifying the referent as topic in the rheme can be seen even where the "sentence" is divided between two speakers:

(185)   *Why did he refuse the offer?—*Because John didn't need the money.*

(186)   **He refused the offer because John didn't need the money.*

(187)   *Why did you refuse him the offer?—Because John didn't need the money.*

In (187), the topic can be reintroduced in the rheme because *him* is not normally topical. There is a prior topical use of *John* somewhere, but it is widely separated from its reintroduction.

Principle (180) is a weak principle because of the ultimate effect of other factors opening the way to reidentification—separation in

(188)   *He was recognizable, I tell you, the moment John arrived.*

or the meaning "John qua John" in

(189)   *Will you have any trouble telling who he is?—He'll be recognizable the moment John steps in the room!*

John is a revelation of himself. In both (188) and (189), the reidentification is in the rheme.

5. POINT OF VIEW

Linguistic coreference has to be distinguished from objective coreference. In an exchange like

(190)   *What made you realize the man was John?—He had John's looks.*,

man, *he*, and *John* all refer to the same real object, but identification is in abeyance—*man* and *he* corefer, but *John* is still viewed as potentially someone else.

We sometimes find this same double vision on the part of the individual referred to, rather than the speaker; for example, in

(191)   *He just wouldn't believe that Mussolini could be wrong!*

Mussolini views his own identity from outside—another case of John qua John.

Alternatively, the speaker as narrator is allowed to interpolate quotations in various ways. In the pair

(192)   *His wife keeps saying that Tom is a jerk.*

(193)   *?His wife knows that Tom is a jerk.*

sentence (192) contains a suggestion of the quotation in *His wife keeps saying, "Tom is a jerk."* There is no support from quotation in (193). But in

(194)   *His wife knows perfectly well that Tom is a jerk.*

the speaker is now quoting himself, asserting *Tom is a jerk*—the collocation *X knows perfectly well* is used only for the speaker's own conviction.

6. CONCLUSION

The decision to repeat a noun or, instead, to use a pronoun depends on how necessary or desirable it is to reidentify the referent at a given point. (Or in some cases to rename or redefine, as when epithets or explanatory alternative names are used.) The majority of reidentifications probably occur after a break of some kind and serve as a justifiable but not always essential reminder. Other reidentifications respond to some implied or underlying assertion about the referent. It may be asserted as topic ("we are talking about Tom") or asserted in terms of its nature ("Tom qua Tom"), or the assertion may involve an extraneous viewpoint whereby the speaker attributes to the referent some expression that is not (or not entirely) the referent's own at the time: the referent looking at himself, some point of general information, or an opinion of the speaker—a sort of concealed quotation.

The main error of formal treatments of "pronominalization" has been to regard the presence of a pronoun rather than a noun as due to a sort of mechanical process CAUSED by the presence of a noun at this or that location rather than as a pragmatic choice between a nominal with a richer semantic content and a nominal with a leaner one.

REFERENCES

Bílý, Milan (1976) "'Pronominalization Rules' (Coreference Rules) Described in Terms of Functional Sentence Perspective (FSP)," in F. Karlsson, ed., *Papers from the Third Scandinavian Conference of Linguistics*, Hanasaari, 1–3 October 1976, Fred Karlsson, ed., Text Linguistics Research Group, Academy of Finland, Turku, pp. 51–62.

Bolinger, Dwight (1972) *Degree Words*, Mouton, The Hague.

Bolinger, Dwight (1977) "*Pronouns and Repeated Nouns*," Indiana University Linguistics Club, Bloomington, Indiana.

Delisle, Gilles S. (1973) "*Discourse and Backward Pronominalization*," Indiana University Linguistics Club, Bloomington, Indiana.

Hankamer, Jörge (1976) "The Semantic Interpretation of Anaphoric Expressions," in Clea Rameh, ed., *Semantics: Theory and Application*, Georgetown University, Washington, D.C., pp. 15–57.

Hinds, John (1977) "Paragraph Structure and Pronominalization," *Papers in Linguistics* 10, 77–99.

Keenan, Edward L. (1976) "Anaphora and Cross Referencing Systems," *Paper at Typology and Field Work Workshop*, Oswego, New York.

Lakoff, George (1976) "Pronouns and Reference," in James D. McCawley, ed., *Notes from the Linguistic Underground*, Academic Press, New York, pp. 275–336.

Lasnik, Howard (1976) "Remarks on Coreference," *Linguistic Analysis* 2, 1–22.

Ross, J. R. (1967) *Constraints on Variables in Syntax*, unpublished Doctoral dissertation, Massachusetts Institute of Technology, Cambridge, Massachusetts.

THIRD-PERSON PRONOUNS AND ZERO-ANAPHORA IN CHINESE DISCOURSE*

CHARLES N. LI
University of California,
Santa Barbara

SANDRA A. THOMPSON
University of California,
Los Angeles

1. INTRODUCTION

Since the inception of linguistics as an empirical science, a justifiably primary concern of grammarians has been the discovery of structural regularities in language. There is no doubt that statements of such regularities are vital to our understanding of the nature of language. It is equally true, of course, that not all aspects of sentence formation can be described by rules stated in terms of grammatical or even semantic properties. Rather, there are a number of facts about sentences that can only be understood in terms of speakers' and hearers' abilities to make inferences beyond what sentences actually say.[1] Furthermore, certain rules that are pragmatically based are conditioned by the perception of the speaker at the time of the

* We gratefully acknowledge the support of the Office of Education, contract G007701660, which partially supported this research.

[1] For discussion of the role of inference in interpreting utterances, see, for example, Garcia (1975) and Kirsner and Thompson (1976).

Syntax and Semantics, Volume 12:
Discourse and Syntax

utterance. The speaker's perception of the world and his interpretation of the pragmatic factors may change from instance to instance, making such rules difficult to formulate.

In this chapter we will be discussing a phenomenon that depends on the speakers' and hearers' abilities to make inferences beyond what sentences actually say, that is, the occurrence of third person "zero-pronouns" in Chinese discourse. We will also present a pragmatically based rule that interacts with a number of semantic and structural factors accounting for the occasional occurrence of third person pronouns in Chinese discourse. With regard to zero-pronouns, we will show that there are no structural properties predicting the interpretation of the referent for zero-pronouns but that the interpretation of the referent for the unrealized pronoun is inferred on the basis of pragmatic knowledge. With regard to the occasional appearance of pronouns in Chinese discourse, we will show that their occurrence is, in principle, predictable, but the principle contains variables dependent on the speaker's perception of the pragmatic situation.

The data in this part of the chapter are taken from primarily two sources: *Shuǐ-Hú Zhuàn* (translated as either "Water Margin" or "All Men Are Brothers") and *Rǔ Lín Wài Shǐ* ("Romance of Confucian Scholars"). Both are well-established works in the vernacular literature. The latter was written in the eighteenth century. The dating of *Shuǐ-Hú Zhuàn* is controversial, since many people have had a hand in editing or in changing it, but it is not earlier than the sixteenth century. The syntax of the language in these two works is basically not at variance with that of present day Mandarin Chinese. In particular, we have made sure that the discourse examples chosen for this chapter are not syntactically distinct from present day Mandarin Chinese, with the exception of certain lexical items. In other words, all the cases of zero-pronouns illustrated by the discourse texts taken from these two books could occur freely in present day Mandarin spoken or written discourse.

2. ZERO-PRONOUNS

Let us begin by examining a short excerpt of narrative from *Shuǐ-Hú Zhuàn* (p. 69) that serves as an excellent case illustrating that the occurrence of zero-pronouns in Chinese discourse is not controlled by structural factors. For the sake of convenience, zero-pronouns will be represented by the symbol $\emptyset_i$. The subscript [i] serves to identify a specific instance of a zero-pronoun in an example. The term ZERO-PRONOUN will be used to refer to the "hole" where an NP is understood and would have to be present in the fully specified version of the sentence.

(1)   a.   *Yáng-Zhì qǔ-lù*
           Yang-Zhi take-to-the-road.
           'Yang-Zhi took to the road.'

      b.   *bù shù   rì, $\emptyset_1$ lái-dào DōngJīng*
           not many day   arrive DongJing
           'In a few days, (he) arrived in DongJing.'

      c. $\emptyset_2$ *rù-de chéng-lái*
               enter city
               '(He) entered the city.'

      d. $\emptyset_3$ *xuǎn ge kè-diàn*
               find a   hotel
               '(He) found a hotel.'

      e. $\emptyset_4$ *ān-xí xià*
               settle down
               '(He) settled down.'

      f.   *zhuāng-kè jiāo-huán* $\emptyset_5$ $\emptyset_6$ *dàn-r*
           carrier   give-back   (his) luggage
           'The carrier gave back (to Yang-Zhi) (his) luggage.'

      g. $\emptyset_7$ *yù-le* $\emptyset_8$ *xie   yín-liǎng*
               give-aspect   some money
               '(Yang-Zhi) gave (the carrier) some money.'

      h. $\emptyset_9$ *zì   huí-qù-le*
               self return- aspect
               '(The carrier) went back by himself.'

The first five clauses exhibit the most frequently occurring type of zero-anaphora: The "topic chain," where the topic established in the first clause serves as the referent for the unrealized topics in the chain of clauses following it.[2] This generalization accounts in a straightforward manner for $\emptyset_1$–$\emptyset_4$ in (1a)–(1e). In (1f), however, 'the carrier gave back (to Yang-Zhi) (his) luggage', another participant is introduced, namely, *Zhuāng-kè* 'the carrier'. There are now two candidates for the referent of any unrealized pronouns. However, in (1f) itself, $\emptyset_5$ is in the object position; its interpretation follows from the semantics of the main verb *jiāo-huán* 'give back'. The meaning of this verb dictates that its agent, the subject, 'carrier', and its recipient, $\emptyset_5$, must not be coreferential. It is still necessary, though, to refer to the discourse at large to know that $\emptyset_5$ does not refer to yet some other participant mentioned earlier. And when we come to the absent genitive,

---

[2] We have taken the term TOPIC CHAIN from Dixon (1972); see also Tsao (1977) for a discussion of this notion in Chinese.

$\emptyset_6$, we can no longer appeal at all to either structural or semantic factors in accounting for its interpretation. In isolation, $\emptyset_6$ would most naturally be interpreted as co-referential with the subject of the clause, 'the carrier'. But, pragmatically, it is senseless for a carrier to give back his own luggage to someone else. Thus, we infer that *dàn-r* 'the luggage' belongs to Yang-Zhi. The next clause, (1g), involves two zero-pronouns, the subject-agent participant, $\emptyset_7$, and the dative participant, $\emptyset_8$, of the verb *yù* 'give'. Again, pragmatic but not structural information provides a natural basis for inferring the referents of these zero-pronouns. Since we have just been told that the carrier gave Yang-Zhi his luggage, it follows that Yang-Zhi should be paying the carrier for the latter's service. Hence, $\emptyset_7$ refers to Yang-Zhi, $\emptyset_8$ refers to the carrier. Structurally, there is no non-*ad hoc* way to account for the referents of $\emptyset_7$ and $\emptyset_8$. The last animate noun in the discourse preceding $\emptyset_7$ and $\emptyset_8$ is the subject of the preceding clause, 'carrier'. $\emptyset_7$ is in subject position; $\emptyset_8$ in dative position. But $\emptyset_7$ does not refer to the subject of the preceding clause. Instead, it refers to the subject of the first clause (1a) in this stretch of narrative. $\emptyset_8$, on the other hand, refers to the subject of the preceding clause. Structurally, there is no reason why $\emptyset_7$ should not be co-referential with the subject of the preceding clause, 'the carrier', for instance, or $\emptyset_8$ be co-referential with Yang-Zhi, so that the clause would read: '(The carrier) gave (Yang-Zhi) some money'. In short, no matter how one attempts to state the proper referents of $\emptyset_7$ and $\emptyset_8$, the statement does not seem to follow from any structual properties of preceding clauses. Finally, the last clause has an understood subject, $\emptyset_9$. Since we have just established that $\emptyset_7$, the understood subject of the clause preceding this last one, refers to Yang-Zhi, and since that clause does not have any human noun present in it that may serve as an antecedent for $\emptyset_9$, the most logical and natural referent of $\emptyset_9$ should also be the referent of $\emptyset_7$, Yang-Zhi. But it is NOT! $\emptyset_9$ refers to 'the carrier' instead. Again, the available pragmatic information in the narrative makes it obvious that $\emptyset_9$ should refer to the carrier. After all, Yang-Zhi has just arrived in town, found a hotel, settled down, and paid his luggage carrier. Thus, we expect that the carrier but not Yang-Zhi should leave after receiving his pay.

This example should provide an adequate initial illustration of the fact that it is not structural determinants that govern the appearance of zero-pronouns in Chinese discourse. Let us now turn to some other examples (*Shuǐ-Hú Zhuàn* p. 58). (Quotation marks in examples denotes quoted speech.)

(2)   "*fán   nǐ   yù wǒ qù yíng-lǐ   qǐng Guǎn-Yíng, Chāi-Bō liǎng-ge*
       please you for me go camp-in invite G.-Y.   C.-B.   two

       lái   shuō-huà $\emptyset_1$ wèn shí,   nǐ   zhǐ   shuō . . ."
       come   talk   ask when you only say

"Please, go into the camp for me to invite G.-Y. and C.-B. the two to come to talk. When they ask, you just say . . ."

$\emptyset_1$, the subject of the subordinate clause, *wèn shí* 'when they ask', refers to G.-Y. and C.-B., which are the objects of the pivotal verb *qǐng* 'invite' and are simultaneously the subjects of the subordinate verb *lái* 'come' in the preceding clause. Both the pivotal verb, *qǐng* 'invite' and the verb *lái* 'come' are embedded in this preceding clause, since the main verb is *qù* 'go', whose subject is *nǐ* 'you'. Thus, in this example the referent of the zero-pronoun, $\emptyset_1$, is a noun phrase buried in an embedded clause within yet another embedded clause in the preceding main clause. The pragmatic reason for inferring the proper referent of $\emptyset_1$ is again obvious. The speaker was asking the hearer to deliver an invitation on his behalf to G.-Y. and C.-B. No other person was mentioned. It follows that the only people who might ask anything would be G.-Y. and C.-B.

Example (3) is from *Shuǐ-Hú Zhuàn*, p. 39:

(3)   *Qǐng-zhǎng-lǎo jiàn Zhǐ-Shēng kěn   qù $\emptyset_1$ jiù   liú $\emptyset_2$ zài*
       abbot   see Z.-S.   willing go   then keep   at

     fāng-zhàng-li xiē-le
     chamber-in   rest-aspect

     'The abbot saw that Z.-S. was willing to go. Then, (he) kept (Z.-S.) in the chamber to rest up.'

In (3), $\emptyset_1$ refers to 'the abbot' and $\emptyset_2$ refers to Z.-S. Hence, the antecedent of a zero-pronoun (here $\emptyset_2$) in the direct object position can be the subject of an embedded clause in the preceding sentence.

Next, let us consider the following from *Rǔ Lín Wài Shǐ* (p. 25):

(4) a. *Jīn-Yǒu-Yú dào: "Xián-Dōng, wǒ   fú-zhe   tā, nǐ   qiě*
        J.-Y.-Y.   said: X.-D.,   I   support-aspect he you just

       qù-dao zuò gōng de   nà-li jiè   kǒu   kāi-shuǐ
       go-to do work rel. cl. place borrow mouthful boiled-water
                            marker

       lái guàn   tā   yī-guàn",
       force down him once

       'J.-Y.-Y. said: "X.-D., I am propping him up. You just go to the place where people work to borrow a mouthful of boiled water to force it down him",'

  b. *háng zhǔ-rén yìng-nò*
      owner   concur
      'The owner concurred.'

c. $\emptyset_1$ *qǔ-le*   *shuǐ*   *lái*
        bring-aspect water
        '(He) brought the water.'

d.   *sān* *sì-ge kè-rén yì-qǐ*   *fú-zhe* $\emptyset_2$,
        three four guest   together support-aspect
        'Three or four guests were propping (him) up, and'

e.   *guàn-le* $\emptyset_3$ *xià-qù*,
        force-aspect   down
        'forced (the water) down (him).'

f. $\emptyset_4$ *hóulong-li gē-ge de*   *xiǎng-le yi-shēng*,
           throat-in gave forth gurgling sound
        'In (his) throat, a gurgling sound came up.'

g. $\emptyset_5$ *tù-chu yī kǒu*   *chóu yán-lái*
        spit-out a mouthful thick phlegm
        '(He) spit out a mouthful of thick phlegm.'

h.   *zhòng-ren dào:* "*hǎo-le*"
        crowd   said: fine-aspect
        'The crowd said: "fine".'

i. $\emptyset_6$ *fú-zhe* $\emptyset_7$
           support-aspect
        '(They) propped (him) up.'

j. $\emptyset_8$ *lì-le*   *qǐlai*
           stand-aspect up
        '(He) stood up.'

The second zero-pronoun, $\emptyset_2$, in string (4d), is in the object position. It
has no antecedent in the two preceding clauses: 'The owner$_1$ concurred,
(He$_1$) brought the water'. Instead, its antecedent is the object of an embedded clause in a quoted speech before these two clauses, *tā* 'him' in (4a).
The third zero-pronoun, $\emptyset_3$, is the direct object of clause (4e) following the
sentence containing $\emptyset_2$. However, $\emptyset_3$ refers to 'water', which occurs in the
earlier clause (4c), '(He$_1$) brought the water'. The next two zero-pronouns
in the following clauses, $\emptyset_4$ and $\emptyset_5$, are coreferential with $\emptyset_2$ *tā* 'him'. Then,
the understood subject in (4i), $\emptyset_6$, refers to the subject of (4h) 'crowd'; but
$\emptyset_7$, which is the understood OBJECT in (4i) again refers back to the person
referred to by $\emptyset_2$, $\emptyset_4$, and $\emptyset_5$, 'him'. And it is this person, NOT the understood SUBJECT of (4i), which is the referent for the understood SUBJECT in
(4j), $\emptyset_8$.

The following schematic representation of (4) may clarify this rather complex case of zero-pronominalization. We will use superscripts for the purpose of denoting co-referentiality:

(4′)   a.   *X said* $\ulcorner$.....(...[.....he^i.....]$_s$...)$_s$...$\lrcorner$.

          b.   *owner^j* $\vee$.

          c. $\emptyset_1^j$ $\vee$ *water^k*.

          d.   ..... $\vee$ $\emptyset_2^i$.

          e.   ..... $\vee$ $\emptyset_3^k$.

          f. $\emptyset_4^i$ ....

          g. $\emptyset_5^i$ $\vee$ ....

          h.   *The crowd^n said:* $\ulcorner$.....$\lrcorner$.

          i. $\emptyset_6^n$ $\vee$ $\emptyset_7^i$.

          j. $\emptyset_8^i$ $\vee$.

There are two points to be noted about example (4). First, note that, whereas it is the SUBJECT of (4b), 'owner', that serves as the referent for the understood subject of (4c), it is the understood OBJECT of (4i), 'he', which is the referent for the understood subject of (4j).[3]

Second, we see that *he^i* in clause (4′a) serves as the antecedent of $\emptyset_2^i$ in (4′d), $\emptyset_4^i$ in (4′f), $\emptyset_5^i$ in (4′g), and $\emptyset_8^i$ in (4′j). There are, however, two intervening clauses, (4′b) and (4′c), between the occurrence of *he^i* in (4′a) and the first zero-pronoun co-referential with it in (4′d), and these two intervening clauses introduce another participant, *owner^j*.

It is clear from this somewhat lengthier example, then, that massive non-specification of arguments occurs in Chinese discourse, and that the interpretation of these unspecified arguments is neither a function of the syntactic roles of the referents nor a function of the distance of these referents from the unspecified arguments.

---

[3] This fact stands in obvious contrast with the situation in English, where a zero-pronoun is gramatically constrained to be coreferential with the subject of the preceding conjunct clause:

(i)   *Fred$_i$ spoke to George$_j$ and then* $\emptyset_i$, *$*_j$ left.*

It is important to add, however, the highly relevant fact that in English, unlike in Chinese, zero-pronouns CONTRAST WITH specified pronouns in conjunction. Thus, in English, a zero-pronoun can be used to signal a specific message because it is a member of the opposition $\emptyset$/pronoun. Our thanks to Ed Keenan for reminding us of this fact.

Consider example (5) from *Rǔ Lín Wài Shǐ* (p. 3):

(5)   a. *Wáng-Miǎn dé-le   qián, $\emptyset_1$ mǎi-le   hǎo   dōngxi, $\emptyset_2$*
           W.-M.   get-aspect money   buy-aspect good things

           xiàojing $\emptyset_3$ mǔqin
           filial   mother

           'W.-M. got some money, (he) bought some good things to be
           filial to (his) mother.

       b. *yí   chuán $\emptyset_5$ liǎng, liǎng chuán $\emptyset_6$ sān.*
           one pass-on-to   two   two pass-on-to   three
           One person told two, two people told three.

       c. *Zhū-Chàn yí   xiàn   dōu xiǎode $\emptyset_6$ shì yíge*
           Z.-C.   whole county all   know   is   a

           huà   méi-gú-huā-hùi   de   míngbǐ
           paint flower-and-plant rel. cl. famous painter

           The whole county of Zhu-Chan knew that (he) was a famous
           painter of flowers and plants.

       d. *$\emptyset_7$ zhēng-zhe   lái-mǎi $\emptyset_8$*
           fight aspect to buy
           (People from the county) were fighting to buy (his paintings).

       e. *$\emptyset_9$ dào-le   shíqi-   bā   suì*
           reach-aspect seventeen, eighteen year
           As (he) reached seventeen, eighteen,

       f. *$\emptyset_{10}$ bù   zài Qíng-jiā   le*
           not at Qing-house aspect
           (He) was no longer at the house of *Qing*.

       g. *měi   rì $\emptyset_{11}$ huà   jǐ-bǐ-huà. . . . .*
           each day   paint a little
           Each day (he) painted a little.'

The schematic representation of zero-pronominalization in (5) is as follows:

(5′)   a. *(W.-M.^{i} $\lor$ . . . . . , $\emptyset_1^i$ $\lor$ good things^j, $\emptyset_2^i$ $\lor$ $\emptyset_3^j$ N)^k*
       b. *One $\lor$ $\emptyset_4^k$ two, two $\lor$ $\emptyset_5^k$ three*
       c. *The whole county^p $\lor$ [$\emptyset_6^i$ is. . . . .]$_s$*
       d. *$\emptyset_7^m$ $\lor$ . . . . . $\emptyset_8^n$*
       e. *$\emptyset_9^i$ $\lor$ . . . . . ,*
       f. *$\emptyset_{10}^i$ $\lor$ . . . . . ,*
       g. *$\emptyset_{11}^i$ $\lor$ . . . . . .*

In this sample, three referents are explicitly introduced: These are $W.-M.^i$, *good things*^{j}, and *the whole county*^{p}. Of these, the first two pragmatically control the interpretation of zero-pronouns later in the discourse in ways similar to those we have previously discussed, again at some rather considerable distance and with intervening candidates. What is new in this sample, however, is that some of the zero-pronouns do not refer to ANY of these three referents.

Let us begin with $\emptyset_4$ and $\emptyset_5$ in clause (5b). Notice that the literal translation of (5b) is 'one pass-on-to two, two pass-on-to three.' The verb *chuán* 'pass on to' is a three-argument verb which semantically requires a subject, a direct object, and an indirect object. The referent for the missing direct objects, $\emptyset_4$ and $\emptyset_5$, is, however, neither $W.-M.^i$ nor *good things*^{j} but the entire event described in (5a), namely, that W.-M. was getting money and buying good things to offer to his mother. We have symbolized this by putting a superscript ^{k} on the entire string (5'a).

Looking now at clause (5'd), we see that both $\emptyset_7$ and $\emptyset_8$ have superscripts not found elsewhere in the discourse sample. This is, of course, because these referents can only be inferred from the discourse and are not explicitly present in it. Notice that all that clause (5d) tells us is 'were fighting to buy'. WHO was fighting and WHAT they wanted to buy have to be inferred from the earlier mention of the whole county and of the fact that W.-M. was a famous painter.

What discourse sample (5) shows us, then, is that a referent of a zero-pronoun may be a sequence of preceding clauses that does not form any grammatically identifiable unit, or it may even be something not explicitly mentioned anywhere in the discourse itself but only inferable from it. Now consider sample (6) (from *Shuǐ-Hú Zhuàn*, p. 388):

(6)   a.   *Kǒng-Liàng jiāo-fù xiǎo-lóu-luo yù-le   Lǔ-Zhī-Shēng*
            K.-L.   deliver soldiers   to-aspect L.-Z.-S.
            'K.-L. delivered the soldiers to L.-Z.-S.'

      b. $\emptyset_1$ *zhǐ dài   yí-ge bàn-dàng.*
            only bring one   companion
            (He) only brought along one companion.

      c. $\emptyset_2$ *bàn   zuò kè-shāng.*
            disguise as   a merchant
            (He) was disguised as a merchant.

      d. $\emptyset_3$ *xíng-yè tóu   Liáng-Shān-Bó lái*
            quickly came L.-S.-B.   to
            (He) quickly came to L.-S.-B.'

The schematic representation of the sentences of (6) is as follows:

(6′)   a.   *Kong-Liang^i* V . . . . . .

                       b. $\emptyset_1^i$ V . . . . . .

                       c. $\emptyset_2^i$ V . . . . . .

                       d. $\emptyset_3^i$ V . . . . . .

This example appears at first insignificant. Since $\emptyset_1$, $\emptyset_2$, and $\emptyset_3$ are all
subjects/topics of their respective clauses and they all refer to K.-L., the
subject of the first clause, one can explain the zero-pronouns here as a case
of topic chain. However, the significance of (6) lies in the fact that, in isolation, (6) is totally confusing to a native speaker of Chinese. In other words,
a native speaker cannot decide, for instance, whether $\emptyset_1$ in (6b) should refer
to K.-L. or to L.-Z.-S. in (6a) or whether $\emptyset_2$ in (6c) should refer to the
'companion' in (6b) or to the antecedent of $\emptyset_1$. This confusion on the part
of the native speaker due to the ambiguity of $\emptyset_1$ and $\emptyset_2$ indicates that the
principle of topic-chain is not an inviolable rule governing referent interpretation of zero-pronouns. In other words, it does not have any special
status among the native speaker's strategies for interpreting zero-pronouns
in Chinese discourse. As our examples have shown, zero-pronouns can
occur in any grammatical slot on the basis of coreferentiality with an antecedent that itself may be in any grammatical slot, at some distance, or not
even present. The fundamental strategy in the interpretation of zero-
pronouns in Chinese discourse, then, is inference on the basis of pragmatic
information provided by the discourse and our knowledge of the world.
Indeed, if (6) is put back into its narrative context, there will be no possibility of confusion. The narrative immediately preceding (6) is a direct
speech by L.-Z.-S. to K.-L., where L.-Z.-S. was asking K.-L. to go to L.-S.-P.
to get help. Another piece of information from the earlier narrative is that
K.-L. was a brigand wanted by the government. Since K.-L., the brigand,
had to go someplace, it follows that he was the one who took a companion,
and he, being wanted by the government, was the one who was disguised
as a merchant and went to L.-S.-P. in a hurry.

   Now let us consider another example, (7), a speech from *Shuǐ-Hú Zhuàn*
(p. 390):

(7)   "*ēn   xiàng fàng-xīn.   xiǎo-jiàng   bì-yào qíng   cǐ*
       kind sir   rest-assured humble-servant will   capture this

       bèi-yì   zhi   zéi.   zhè-jiān $\emptyset_1$ hé   tā dòu   shí,
       treasonous rel. cl. marker brigand just-now   with he fight when

$\emptyset_2$ *gùn-fǎ*   *yi-zì*   *luàn-le.*   *lái-rì* $\emptyset_3$ *jiào*
    fighting-technique already disoriented-aspect tomorrow   let

ēn   *xiàng kàn wǒ lì zhǎn*   *cǐ*   *zéi."*
kind sir   see I   decapitate this brigand

'Kind sir, rest assured. I will capture this treasonous brigand. Just now, as (I) was fighting with him, (he) was already getting disoriented in his fighting technique. Tomorrow, (I) will let you see me decapitate this brigand.'

The zero-pronoun to focus on here is $\emptyset_2$. The English translation of the clause containing $\emptyset_2$ is

(8)   *As (I) was fighting with him, (he) was already getting disoriented in his fighting technique.,*

where the pronouns in parentheses translate the zero-pronouns. What is significant about $\emptyset_2$, represented by (*he*) in (8), is that, as the subject of a main clause, it refers to the oblique object (with *him*) rather than to the subject of the preceding subordinate clause, which is $\emptyset_1$ (*I*). In fact, when we took clause (9) below in isolation and asked the judgment of four native speakers, we found that all agreed that the preferred reading was that the understood subject of the main clause should be coreferential with the SUBJECT of the preceding subordinate clause, namely, 'I'.

(9)   *wǒ hé*   *tā dòu shí,* $\emptyset$ *gùn-fǎ*   *yǐ*
    I   with he fight when,   fighting-technique already

    luàn-le
disoriented-aspect

'As I fought with him, $\begin{Bmatrix} \text{I} \\ \text{he} \end{Bmatrix}$ was already getting disoriented in his fighting technique.'

But, in the case of the narrative in (7), all four native speakers interpret $\emptyset_2$ as coreferential with the oblique object rather than with the subject of the preceding clause. The reason, again, is the pragmatic information provided by the discourse context. Since in (7) the speaker began by saying that he would capture the brigand, he was therefore hinting that the brigand was not as good a warrior as he was. It then follows that the one who became disoriented in his fighting technique in an earlier encounter should be the brigand rather than the speaker.

    The examples given should suffice to demonstrate that the interpretation of zero-pronouns cannot be explained on the basis of structural factors involving grammatical relations or grammatical functions. Instead, the referent for a zero-pronoun is inferred from the information provided by the discourse context and the knowledge shared by the speakers of the language.

3. REALIZED PRONOUNS

As the facts we have just examined make abundantly clear, zero-anaphora is widespread in Chinese discourse, so much so, in fact, that the non-occurrence of anaphoric arguments in discourse must be regarded as the normal, unmarked situation. Thus, it is the OCCURRENCE of pronouns in Chinese discourse that must be explained. The question, then, is: When does the language-user decide to use a pronoun in Chinese discourse? In what follows, we will assume that the nonoccurrence of a pronoun is the rule and that it is our task to account for the circumstances under which the rule is violated, that is, where a pronoun occurs.

Before we begin, we must mention a limitation that we have imposed on our investigation. In order to limit the scope of our undertaking, we are considering here only written narrative discourse, which means that we are dealing only with third-person anaphora. We expect, of course, that the principles that we have found to predict the occurrence of third-person pronouns in written narrative discourse will also be generalizable to conversational and non-narrative discourse.

One's initial impression in looking at Chinese narrative discourse is that, in most positions where a full pronoun appears, it could be replaced by a zero-pronoun and it could just as well have appeared in the preceding or following clause as in the clause where it does appear.

As a step toward uncovering whatever regularity might underlie this apparent randomness, we conducted an experiment to determine just what native speakers' impressions are regarding the use of pronouns. For this experiment, we took three short narratives excerpted from the literature, removed all occurrences of pronouns from these texts, and submitted them to a group of native speakers of Mandarin, all university students, who were asked to indicate, by writing the pronoun in that position, where in the texts they felt pronouns were needed. The texts were written in Chinese characters with no blanks and only commas, not periods, between clauses.[4]

In interpreting the results of this experiment, we present each text with blanks indicating the positions where an argument is unspecified, that is, where it would be structurally possible for a pronoun to occur. The blanks are filled in each case by percentages in parentheses indicating the percentage of respondents who inserted a pronoun at that point. For the first two texts, the percentages of positions in which the author had originally placed a

---

[4] We are grateful to our colleague Huang Shuan-fan of National Taiwan University for his help in administering the experiment to speakers in Taiwan and to our research assistant Li Ming-ming for her help with speakers residing in Los Angeles.

pronoun (or a full NP) are in boldface, and the author of that text is counted as a respondent.

Let us begin with an excerpt in which all the pronouns and zero-pronouns refer to the subject of the initial clause; the text is from *Rǔ Lín Wài Shǐ* (p. 4).

(10)   a.   *zhè Wáng-Miǎn tiānxíng cōngming*
            this W.-M.   nature smart
            'This W.-M. was gifted.'

       b.   (6%) *niánji bu mǎn   èrshi-suì*
            ____ age not exceed twenty-year
            '(He) was not more than twenty years of age.'

       c.   (2%) *jiù   bǎ   nà tiānwén,   dìli,   jingshǐ*
            ____ already obj. marker that astronomy, geography, classics
            shàng de dà   xuéwen   wú yī   bu guàntōng
            in   great knowledge not a bit not master
            '(He) had already mastered everything in astronomy, geography, and classics.'

       d.   *dàn   (76%) xìngqing   bu tóng*
            however   personality not similar
            'However, (he) had a different personality.'

       e.   (2%) *jì-bu   qiú guānjué*
            ____ not only-not seek officialdom
            'Not only did (he) not seek officialdom,'

       f.   (0%) *yòu bu jiāona péngyǒu*
            ____ also not make friend
            '(he) also did not make friends.'

       g.   (2%) *zhōngrì bì -hù dúshū*
            ____ all day close door study
            '(He) studied at home all day.'

       h.   (14%) *yòu zài Chǔ-Cí-Tú shang kànjian huà   de*
            ____ also at Chu-Ci-Tu in   see paint rel. cl. marker
            Qū-yuán yī-guān
            Qu-yuan attire
            '(He) also saw the attire of *Qu-yuan* painted in *Chu-Ci-Tu*.'

       i.   (8%) *biàn zì   zào yiding jǐ   gāode màozi, yijiàn jǐ*
            ____ then self make one very tall hat   one very
            kuò-de yīfu
            loose garment
            '(He) then made a very tall hat, and a very loose garment.'

j. (0%)   *yù-zhe   huā-míng-liǔ-méi-de shíjié*
              chance-upon balmy   days
    '(When he) chanced upon balmy days'

k. (12%) *bǎ   yí-chèng   niú-chē   zài-le   mǔqin*
              take a   cattle-cart bring-aspect mother
    '(He) took a cattle cart and brought his mother.'

l. **(10%)** *biàn   dài-le   gāo mào*
                than wear-aspect tall hat
    '(He) then wore a tall hat.'

m. (0%)   *chuān-le   kuò   yī*
              put on-aspect loose garment
    '(He) put on a loose garment.'

n. (0%)   *zhī-zhe   biānzi*
              hold-aspect whip
    '(He) held a whip.'

o. (0%)   *kǒu-li chàng-zhe   gēqǔ*
              month-in   sing-aspect song
    '(He) sang songs.'

p. (0%) *zài xiāngcūn zhèng-shang yǐjí   hú-biān dàochu*
              at village   town in   and lake-side everywhere

    wán-shuǎ
    cruised about
    '(He) cruised about the villages, towns, lake-side, and
    everywhere.'

q. (4%) *rě-de   xiāngxia háizi-men sān   wǔ   chéng qún*
              make country children three five from group

    gēn-zhe **(4%)** *xiào*
    follow   laugh
    '(He) made the children in the country follow him about
    and laugh in groups of three and five.'

r. **(56%)** *yě   bu   fàng-zai-yì-xia*
                even so not mind
    '(He) did not even mind.'

s. *rú-cǐ* (14%) *jiù   shēnghuǒ ānding kuàile jiànkāng*
    thus,   then live   stable happy healthy
    'Thus, (he) lived a stable, happy, and healthy life.'

In (10) the total number of respondents is 50, 39 of whom were from Taipei,
Taiwan, 10 from Los Angeles, and one is the author of the text. The per-

centage figures reveal that (*a*) the position attracting the largest percentage of inserted pronouns is in clause (10d), with 76%, still far from a unanimous judgement; (*b*) the position attracting the next highest number of pronouns supplied is in clause (10r), which gets 56%; and (*c*) the rest of the percentage figures are all very low: 14%, 12%, 10%, 8%, 6%, 4%, 2%, 0%.

Not revealed by the percentage figures, but of considerable interest, is the fact that not a single respondent inserted pronouns in just the same five positions where the author had placed them [in (10d), (10i), (10l), (10q), and (10r)]; in fact, no respondent inserted as many as five pronouns.

These results suggest very clearly the extent of the variation in judgments by Mandarin speakers on the use of pronouns. Before further discussing the significance of these facts, however, let us present the results from the other two texts in the experiment. The text in (11) is from *Rǔ Lín Wài Shǐ* (p. 14):

(11)   a.   *wàibian zǒu-jìn yige rén   lái*
               outside walk-in a   person come
               'From outside entered a man.'

         b.   (8.6%) *liǎng-zhī hóng yǎn-biān*
                    two   red eyes
               '(He) had two red eyes.'

         c.   (0%) *yìfù guōtiè liǎn*
                 a   stiff   face
               '(He) had a stiff face.'

         d.   (0%) *jǐ-gēn huáng húzi*
                 a-few yellow beard
               '(He) had a few yellow whiskers.'

         e.   (2.8%) *wāi-dài-zhe wǎléng   mào*
                    wear   tile-shaped hat
               '(He) wore a tile-shaped hat.'

         f.   (0%) *shēn-shang qīng bù   yīfu   jiù-rú yóu- lǒu yìbān*
                  body-on   blue cloth garment like   oiled basket
               '(He) had over his body a blue garment that looked like a oiled basket.'

         g.   (5.6%) *shǒu-li ná-zhe yì-gēn gǎn lǘ   de*
                    hand-in hold   a   ride donkey rel. cl. marker
            biānzi
            whip
            '(He) was holding a whip for riding donkeys.'

         h.   (2.8%) *zǒu-jìn mén lai*
                    enter   door come
               '(He) came in the door.'

    i.   <u>(0%)</u> *hé*   *zhòngrén gōng-yi-gōng shǒu*
                toward everyone salute with   hand
                '(He) saluted everyone with his hands.'

    j.   <u>(2.8%)</u> *yí-pìgu*   *jiù*   *zuò zài shàngxí*
                one-buttock then sit at seat of honor
                '(He) then immediately took the seat of honor.'

    k. **(75%)** *xìng*   *Xià*
                surname Xia
                '(He) was surnamed Xia.'

    l.   <u>(0%)</u> *nǎi Xiè-Jiā-Jí shang jiù nián xīng   cān*
                be Xie-Jia-Ji at   last year newly appointed

       de   *zǒngjiā*
       rel. cl. marker boss
       '(He) was the new boss of Xie-Jia-Ji, appointed last year.'

    m. **(19.4%)** *zuò zai shàng-xí*
                sit at the seat of honor
                '(He) sat at the seat of honor.'

    n.   <u>(5.6%)</u> *xiān fēnfù héshang dào* "-----"
                first order monk   say
                '(He) first ordered the monk by saying: say "-----"''

The total number of respondents to (11) was 36: 35 from Taipei, Taiwan, and 1 is the author of the text.

   Example (12) following is a self-contained narrative taken from a Chinese language textbook. The narrative (Wan and Johnson 1973:27) is provided by the compiler of the textbook in order to introduce the author of the text used in one of the lessons. In the textbook, it does not contain any occurrences of the pronoun.

   (12)   a. *Lı Yǎ-nóng, zhōngguó shǐxuéjiā*
                Li Y.-N.   Chinese historian
                'Li Y.-N. is a Chinese historian,'

       b. <u>(2%)</u> *chū duì*   *jiǎ-gǔ-wén   jīn*   *wén*   *yǒu*
                first toward oracle bones bronze inscription have

        xìngqu
        interest
        '(He) was first interested in oracle bones and bronze inscriptions.'

c. *kàngzhàn*   *shí,*   (14%) *cānjiā xīn-sì-jūn*
  Sino-Japanese war during   join   New-Fourth-Army
  'During the Sino-Japanese war, (he) joined the New-Fourth
  Army.'

d. (0%) *zǔzhí*   *fǎn Rì*   *yùndòng*
       organize anti Japanese movement
  '(He) organized an anti-Japanese movement.'

e. (0%) *hòu jué yánjiù gǔdài shǐ*
  (He) later then study archaic history
  'Later he did research in archaic history.'

f. (0%) *zhù-yǒu* **zhōngguó de**   *núdì*   *zhì*   *yǔ*
       write   China   possessive particle slavery system and

  fēngjiàn zhì   *děng wǔ-běn zhùzuo*
  feudal   system etc. five   work
  '(He) authored five books, such as *The Slavery and Feudal
  System of China.*'

g. *1962* (40%) *jiāng*   *cǐ*   *wǔ-běn shū*   *gǎi-yìng hé-wei*
  1962 (he)   obj. mkr. these five   books reprint   combine as

  Xīnrán Zhāishǐ Lùnjí
  Xinran Zhaishi Lunji
  'In 1962, (he) had these five books put together to become
  Xingran Zhaishi Lunji.'

The total number of respondents to (12) was 50, 39 of whom were from Taipei, Taiwan, 10 from Los Angeles, and 1 is the author of the text.

In these three texts, the total number of positions in which a pronoun could occur is 38. Of these, only three positions attracted more than half of the respondents to insert pronouns: 76% [in (10d)], 75% [in (11k)], and 56% [in (10r)]. In each of these instances, the relatively high percentage of pronoun responses occurs where the author also felt a pronoun should occur. The only other reasonably high percentage figure is 40% [in (12g)], and here the respondents are at variance with the author, who had no pronouns in this text at all. Of the 34 remaining positions, 6 show percentages between 10 and 20%; the other 28 are all below 10%. Moreover, some of these low percentages occur in positions where the author had placed a pronoun, for instance, (10l), (10i), and (11m).

These figures dramatically confirm our claims, then, that (*a*) zero-anaphora rather than pronominal anaphora is the norm in Chinese discourse; and (*b*) there is considerable variation among native speakers in their judgments as to where a pronoun should occur.

The figures also bear out to a certain extent our initial impression of arbitrariness in the distribution of pronouns. Thus, in no case did more than three-fourths of the speakers feel that a pronoun was obligatory, and in 24 cases out of 38 (63%) at least one speaker inserted a pronoun. Clearly, the occurrence of pronouns in Chinese narrative discourse does not seem to be governed by any absolute rules.

In examining the individual results, it became clear that one of the factors contributing to the variation is the sheer length of the text. What is apparent from examining individual responses, but not recoverable from the percentage figures, is that, even in a topic-chain, if it is long enough, an individual seems to need to eventually insert a pronoun. In (10), for example, the majority of respondents inserted just one or two pronouns; the noteworthy feature of these results is that not only did no individual insert pronouns in two successive positions, but, if more than one pronoun was inserted, they also tended to be placed relatively far apart. These facts suggest that there may be a reluctance to continue an unbroken string of clauses with zero-pronouns for "too long," which accounts in part for the fact that about two-thirds (63%) of the total number of positions drew a pronoun response from at least one respondent. Where speakers decide to break the string of zero-pronouns seems to be a matter of personal preference, with no governing principles discernible at present.

It is also obvious, however, that there are three positions in our samples that are attractive enough for pronoun insertion to call for an explanation. What is it about these positions that causes a majority of respondents to insert the pronoun there?

As a step toward answering this question, let us consider four invented examples by way of illustrating the conditions under which a pronoun would be predicted to occur:

(13)   a. *Zhāng-sān   jìn-le   dà   mén,*
            Zhang-san enter-aspect main door

        b. $\begin{Bmatrix} \emptyset \\ ??t\bar{a} \end{Bmatrix}$ *tuō-le*   *dà-yī,*

            $\begin{Bmatrix} \emptyset \\ he \end{Bmatrix}$ take off-aspect coat

        c. $\begin{Bmatrix} \emptyset \\ ??t\bar{a} \end{Bmatrix}$ *zuò-xiàlai*

            $\begin{Bmatrix} \emptyset \\ he \end{Bmatrix}$ sit-down

            'Zhang-san entered the main door, took off his coat, and sat down.'

(14) a. *Zhāng-sān zài dàxue   niàn-le   sān   nián*
          Zhang-san at university study-aspect three year
          'Zhang-san studied at the university for three years.'

      b. $\left\{\begin{matrix}\emptyset\\t\bar{a}\end{matrix}\right\}$ *xǐhuan hē   jiǔ*

         $\left\{\begin{matrix}\emptyset\\he\end{matrix}\right\}$ like   drink wine

         'He likes to drink wine.'

(15) a. *Zhāng-sān shì yíge huài rén*
          Zhang-san be a   bad person

      b. *wǒ bù xǐhuan* $\left\{\begin{matrix}?\emptyset\\t\bar{a}\end{matrix}\right\}$

         I   not like $\left\{\begin{matrix}\emptyset\\he\end{matrix}\right\}$

         'Zhang-san is a bad person. I don't like him.'

(16) a. *cóngqián   yǒu yíge rén   jiào Zhāng-sān*
          once upon a time exist a   person call Zhang-san
          'Once upon a time, there was a person called Zhang-san.'

      b. $\left\{\begin{matrix}???\emptyset\\t\bar{a}\end{matrix}\right\}$ *néng fēi*

         $\left\{\begin{matrix}\emptyset\\he\end{matrix}\right\}$ can fly

         'He can fly.'

The judgments expressed in these examples are those of two speakers; from what has been said so far, it should be amply clear that 100% agreement with them is not to be expected. The important point is that they serve to illustrate the principles we are about to propose as they appear to be operating for these speakers. Notice that in (13) zero-pronouns are preferred, in (14) both the zero-pronoun and the full pronoun seem equally acceptable, in (15) the zero-pronoun is somewhat less preferred, and in (16), a zero-pronoun is decidedly less appropriate. Thus, these examples present a continuum of appropriateness of zero-pronouns as compared to full pronouns.

If we examine the sequence of clauses constituting (13), we see that the verbs in all three clauses form a pragmatically natural chain of actions, connected to each other by virtue of the fact that they report a sequence of actions carried out, one directly after the other, by a single agent.

The connection between the two events named in (14a) and (14b) is somewhat less straightforward. To the extent that it exists at all, it is that going to the university correlates positively with one's liking to drink.

The two propositions in (15) are connected to each other even more tenuously: The first is about Zhang-san, whereas the second is about me, though the cause–effect relationship between his badness and my dislike of him is a naturally inferred one.

Finally, in (16) it is difficult to make any connection between the two clauses at all. They are about the same person, but the relationship between what someone is named and an ability to fly is not an easily inferred one.

It is clear from our discussion of these examples that we are claiming that the speaker's perception of the degree of "connection" between clauses in discourse has something to do with the occurrence of pronouns. Let us adopt the notion of "conjoinability" to describe this situation. Two successive clauses are "conjoinable" if the speaker/writer perceives them to share enough to warrant being presented to the hearer/reader TOGETHER AS ONE GRAMMATICAL UNIT rather than SEPARATELY AS TWO INDEPENDENT UNITS.[5,6] We may now state the basic principle governing the occurrence of pronouns in Chinese discourse:

> THE DEGREE OF PREFERENCE FOR THE OCCURRENCE OF A PRONOUN IN A CLAUSE INVERSELY CORRESPONDS TO THE DEGREE OF ITS CONJOIN-ABILITY WITH THE PRECEDING CLAUSE.

Returning to our examples (13)–(16) once again, we see that in (13) the degree of conjoinability among these three clauses will normally be perceived as very high by all speakers; (13) is, of course, an example of the "topic-chain" mentioned earlier, the most frequently occurring context for zero-anaphora in Chinese discourse. The conjoinability of the two clauses in (16), on the other hand, is very low due to the obvious reasons previously given; hence, there is a high likelihood of a pronoun occurring in (16b). Examples (14) and (15) are intermediate cases, much more open to individual judgments of conjoinability and, thus, much more likely to elicit varied responses from native speakers.

Conjoinability, then, is clearly not invariable or absolute; the degree to which a given speaker at a given time judges two clauses to be conjoinable depends on the syntactic and semantic properties of those clauses, as well as on the speaker's interpretation of events in the world and of the material in the discourse of which the clauses in question are a part. In most cases,

---

[5] We are grateful to Michael Halliday for his comments on our data, which led us to this formulation.

[6] In English, the use of *and* has been shown to correlate with conjoinability [see Lakoff (1971) for some discussion]. In Mandarin, there is no analogous neutral clause-connecting morpheme.

then, conjoinability is a matter of judgment and preference on the part of the speaker, which accounts for the wide variation we found in our experimental results.

Let us return to these results now and list some general constraints on conjoinability which predict the three positions showing relatively high percentages of pronoun responses in our samples:

1. Conjoinability appears to be greatly impaired when the clauses involved contain a switch from background information to foreground information or vice versa. Clauses (11j) and (11k) constitute a good example for illustration. Let us schematically represent clauses (11h)–(11k) in English:

> h. (2.8%) *came in the door;*
> i. (0%) *saluted everyone with his hands,*
> j. (2.8%) *then immediately took the seat of honor.*
> k. (75%) *was surnamed Xià.*

Sentences (h)–(j) provide foreground information, the action sequence of the narrative, whereas (k) provides background information. Thus, (h)–(j) constitute a topic chain. But the conjoinability between (j) and (k) is greatly impaired because (k) switches to background information. This explains the high percentage of pronoun responses in (k) and the minimal percentages of pronominal responses in clauses (h)–(j).

On the other hand, although a switch between foregrounded and backgrounded parts of the discourse impairs conjoinability, it does not always entail the occurrence of a pronoun. One of the most common situations exemplifying this phenomenon is a pair of clauses in which the first clause, the foregrounded clause, contains a verb of appearance such as *arrive, enter, appear, surface, show up,* etc. The second clause of such a pair, even though it is a descriptive backgrounded clause, will typically contain a zero-pronoun. The reason for the nonoccurrence of a pronoun in this type of situation is that a clause with a verb of appearance performs a dual function in discourse. On the one hand, it forms part of the action sequence; on the other hand, it introduces a new discourse topic. Because it introduces the topic that the following clause goes on to describe, it is highly conjoinable with that clause, hence the nonappearance of a pronoun. A good example of this phenomenon is shown by sentences (11a)–(11e), which we again render schematically in English:

> a. *From outside entered a man;*
> b. (8.6%) *had two red eyes,*
> c. (0%) *had a stiff face*
> d. (0%) *had a few yellow whiskers*
> e. (2.8%) *wore a tile-shaped hat;*

In the context of this example, we can also understand (g) and (h) of the same discourse:

> g.   (5.6%) *was holding a whip for riding donkeys;*
> h.   (2.8%) *came in the door;*

Here, (g) conveys background information [which, in fact, is a continuation of the background material in (b)–(e)], whereas with (h) the narrator has apparently switched to foreground information [and (i) and (j) following (h) also convey foreground information]. So why is the percentage of pronoun responses at the point of the switch only 2.8%? The reason is that the shift in (h) to foreground information is a RECAPITULATION of (a). The zero-pronoun in (h) signals that (h) is taken by the narrator to be VERY MUCH A PART of the sequence begun in (a), on which (b)–(g) were an elaboration and NOT a NEW GRAMMATICAL UNIT at all.

2.   Conjoinability between two clauses is greatly impaired when the second clause is marked with adverbial expressions such as time phrases or contrastive morphemes like *however, but,* etc. Such elements signal the beginning of a new sentence rather than a connected clause. Consider clauses (10a)–(10d) in English as an example.

> a.   *This Wang-mian was gifted,*
> b.   (6%) *was not more than twenty years of age,*
> c.   (2%) *had already mastered everything in astronomy, geography, and classics,*
> d.   *however,* (76%) *had a different personality*

Clause (a) introduces the topic, with (b) and (c) forming a short topic chain. Clause (d) then begins with the word *however,* which signals the end of that topic chain and the onset of a new grammatical unit. Conjoinability across a contrastive morpheme is very low, hence the 76% pronoun response. The clauses seen in (10q) and (10r) below, in English, provide another example: example:

> q.   (4%) *made the children in the country follow* (4%) *about and laugh in groups of three and five,*
> r.   (56%) *did not even mind*

Clause (10r) contains the morpheme *yě*, best understood here as 'even so'; again, its presence reduces the degree of conjoinability between (10q) and (10r), yielding a 56% pronoun response.

As a last example consider clause (12g) which contains the time phrase *1962*; here, again, the percentage is relatively high, 40%, but not as high as with the contrastive adverbs:

> g.   *1962* (40%) *had these five books put together . . .*

3. Finally, though we have not examined conversational data in depth, we observe that conjoinability appears to be impaired when the two clauses in question constitute different turns, that is, are spoken by different participants, as opposed to being part of the same turn, spoken by one participant. We submitted a pair of sentences to 39 native speakers first as (17) and then as (18), where in (17) they were presented as the speech of one person, and in (18) as being spoken by two different people:

(17) *Zhāng-sān yóu-tóu-fén-liǎn*
Z.-S.   slick-looking
Z.-S. is slick-looking.

(0%) shi yīge xiǎo-chǒu
(He) is   a   clown
He is a clown.

(18) A: *Zhāng-sān yóu-tóu-fén-liǎn*
Z.-S.   slick-looking
Z.-S. is slick-looking.
B: *(58%) shi yīge xiǎo-chǒu*
(He) is   a   clown
He is a clown.

The striking difference between 0% and 58% is a strong indication that conjoinability is related to switches of turn in conversation and suggests an obvious direction for further research.

We have analyzed the factors that affect conjoinability between clauses sharing a common referent, and we have shown that in discourse conjoinability between two clauses is correlated with the occurrence of pronouns in the second clause. But the occurrence of a pronoun can be required by the syntactic structure of a sentence. Consider a sentence containing a three-argument verb such as *quàn* 'persuade,' *qǐng* 'invite,' *mìngling* 'order' . . . etc., called "pivotal verbs" in Chao (1968).

(19) *wǒ mìngling **tā** chī-fàn*
I   order   he eat
I order him to eat.

The pivotal noun *tā* serves as the object of the verb *mìngling* 'order' as well as the subject of the complement verb *chī-fàn* 'eat.' The presence of such a pivotal noun in constructions such as (19) is obligatory. Sentence (20), for instance, is ungrammatical.

(20) **wǒ mìngling Ø chī-fàn*
I   order   eat

Thus, if the pivotal noun in (19) shares a common referent with a noun in a preceding clause in discourse, regardless of the conjoinability of the two clauses the pronoun must occur in the position of the pivotal noun. Another syntactic position that does not allow zero-pronouns is the NP position following a co-verb.[7]

(21)   wǒ gēn **tā** xué
                              I   with he learn
                              I learn from him.

(22)   *wǒ gēn Ø xué
                              I   with   learn

As with the "pivotal verbs," a clause containing a co-verb will not permit a zero-pronoun in the position immediately following that co-verb, regardless of the conjoinability of that clause with the preceding one.

4. CONCLUSIONS

In this chapter we have exemplified and illustrated the phenomenon of zero-anaphora in Chinese written discourse and have established that it is so widespread and so unconstrained that it must be considered as the normal mode of NP-anaphora in Chinese, the interpretation of referents for zero-pronouns being inferred on the basis of semantic and pragmatic knowledge and of information present in the discourse itself. We have also examined the contexts in which pronouns occur in written narratives and have found that one factor that seems to be important in determining the appearance of a pronoun is conjoinability, the extent to which a clause constitutes a single unit with the preceding clause. The lower the degree of conjoinability between two clauses, the higher is the likelihood of a pronoun occurring in the second clause. Stated this way, it should be clear that our claim is not one that is intended to predict the appearance of a pronoun at a given point in a given narrative, but rather one that predicts tendencies in the behavior of GROUPS of speakers when asked to judge the appropriateness of pronoun occurrence. Given this claim, then, the wide range of variation we found among speakers with respect to their judgments on the acceptability of pronouns is explained by the fact that conjoinability for any individual is a matter of opinion based on his perception of the relationship between events in the world, both the world he lives in and the world he is (re)creating in

---

[7] "Co-verbs" are essentially prepositions; with one exception (the demoted agent marker *bèi*), they cannot be "stranded." For discussion of co-verbs as prepositions, see Li and Thompson (1974a,b).

his narrative. Within this variation, however, there will be clusters of positive responses at various points; it is these that our hypothesis claims to account for: At just those points, conjoinability can be objectively characterized as low, and the prediction is borne out.

REFERENCES

Chao, Yuen-ren (1968) *A Grammar of Spoken Chinese*, University of California Press, Berkeley and Los Angeles.
Dixon, R. M. W. (1972) *The Dyirbal Language of North Queensland*, Cambridge University Press, Cambridge.
García, Erica (1975) *The Role of Theory in Linguistic Analysis*, North Holland, Amsterdam.
Kirsner, Robert and Sandra A. Thompson (1976) "The Role of Pragmatic Inference in Semantics," *Glossa* 10, 200–240.
Lakoff, Robin (1971). "If's and But's about Conjunction," in Charles J. Fillmore and D. T. Langendoen, eds., *Studies in Linguistic Semantics*, Holt, New York, 232–296.
Li, Charles N. and Sandra A. Thompson (1974a) "Co-verbs in Mandarin Chinese: Verbs or Prepositions?," *Journal of Chinese Linguistics* 2, 257–278.
Li, Charles N. and Sandra A. Thompson (1974b) "A Linguistic Discussion of the 'Co-verb' in Chinese Grammar," *Journal of the Chinese Language Teacher's Association* 9, 109–119.
Tsao, Feng-fu (1977) *A Functional Study of Topic in Chinese: The First Step Toward Discourse Analysis*, unpublished Doctoral dissertation, University of Southern California, Los Angeles, California.

SOURCES OF DATA

Wú Jìng-Zǐ (1973) *Rǔ Lín Wài Shǐ* 'Romance of Confucian Scholars', Huá-Zhèng Shū Jú, Taipei, Taiwan.
Yáng Jiā-lò, ed. (1966) *Shuǐ-Hǔ Zhuan* 'Water Margin', Shì-jie Shū Jú, Taipei, Taiwan.
Wan, Grace and Wallace Johnson (1973) *An Advanced Reader in Chinese History*, University of Kansas Publications, Lawrence, Kansas.

FOCUS OF ATTENTION AND THE CHOICE OF PRONOUNS IN DISCOURSE

CHARLOTTE LINDE
Structural Semantics, Santa Monica, California[1]

The general problem addressed in this chapter is the study of the conditions that control pronominal choice between sentences. Since the study of the discourse unit has only recently begun, this question has hardly been studied at all, especially since almost all of the vast literature on anaphoric reference and, specifically, on pronominalization has considered the possible kinds of reference restrictions and rule conditions operating only within the sentence, or—at the widest—between pairs of sentences presumed to be adjacent. However, if we take the question of how speakers choose pronouns within a discourse unit, a number of problems arise that could never be considered within an investigation of sentence-level pronominalization. One such issue, which is the specific topic of this chapter, is the opposition between *it* and *that*, and the factors that affect their choice.

It and *that* have not been investigated systematically as an opposition, since they have been analyzed as belonging to different types of anaphoric reference—*it* being a pronoun and *that* a deictic. Deixis is taken as involving

[1] Please address all correspondence to *Structural Semantics*, P.O. Box 5612, Santa Monica, California 90405.

Syntax and Semantics, Volume 12:
Discourse and Syntax

the orientational features of language, those features that encode information about the time, place, and participants of the speech situation (Fillmore 1975; Lyons 1968, 1977.) Pronouns, in contrast, involve reference to items within the utterance rather than outside it.

However, when we examine the choices made by speakers within a specific discourse, we find that there is a considerable overlap between *it* and *that*; reference to the same kinds of items is accomplished by both of them. This suggests that we must look not only at the type of reference accomplished but also at the particular conditions of the discourse that surrounds the reference.

Many investigators have remarked that discourse must be considered in studying pronominal reference. However, to do this precisely it is necessary to have a rigorous specification of the level of related sentences over which the investigation will be conducted. The notion of discourse has been used in a number of ways, usually very loosely. Many recent discussions of discourse effects on pronominalization use the loosest and most general definition of a discourse: any permissible sequence of two or more sentences. Such a choice of data takes no account of possible effects of the structure of the surrounding discourse, since it is concerned only with relations within the pair of sentences focused on. (Even with so imprecise a definition of discourse, a great deal more can be accomplished than if investigation is confined within the sentence. Excellent examples include Fillmore 1975, Isard 1975, and Lakoff 1974.) Another, more careful, approach is to use as data connected texts, usually written, either as a source of examples or as the basis of frequency counts (Halliday and Hasan 1976; Kirsner, this volume.) This approach avoids the dangers of using intuition to decide what is and what is not a permissible sequence in discourse. (It will become clear later in this discussion that intuition for permissible discourses is even more fragile and unreliable than is intuition for individual sentences.) In the main, however, such a procedure is also forced to ignore the question of the internal structure of the discourse and can take account only of the grossest factors, such as whether two sentences are immediate neighbors or not.

The present study requires a much more precise definition of discourse. I shall not consider ANY permissible sequence of sentences but only bounded sequences that form a unit definable both formally and interactionally. To avoid the more complex issues of literary composition and conventions, only oral units will be discussed. Units of this type that have been studied in some detail are the narrative of personal experience, the joke, planning and decision making, and the description of apartment layouts (Labov 1972a, Linde 1974 and to appear, Linde and Goguen 1978, Linde and Labov 1975, Sacks 1974, Wald 1977).

If we consider the formal structure of such units, we find that they have strong boundary properties and extremely complex and regular internal organization. Units such as jokes often have a quasi-formulaic beginning, such as *Stop me if you've heard this one*, *Then there's the one about* . . . , etc. These signal that a joke is the unit intended and that the hearers are to treat it as a joke. By marking that a joke is to follow, they also permit negotiation about whether it will be told, since, by convention, a joke is funny only to a hearer who has not heard it before (Sacks 1974).

Because of their formulaic and folkloristic character, the structure of jokes is perhaps the most immediately obvious. But it is narratives of personal experience that appear to be the most primary discourse unit, from whose structure the form of many other discourse units is derived. That is, jokes, apartment-layout descriptions, directions, etc. can be analyzed as having a pseudo-narrative structure.

Like jokes, narratives also begin with sections that, among their other functions, mark the beginning of the text. The narrative may begin with an abstract, a section that summarizes the entire story, as in (1).

(1)   *I once had to have my number changed because someone was bothering me. They were very good, they did it very quickly.*

Or the narrative may begin immediately with an orientation section, which establishes the characters, the time, the place, and the surrounding activity of the story, as in (2).

(2)   *It was last weekend on the Promenade. They had a Promenade art show.*

After establishing the initial boundary, the internal structure can be described as a sequence of narrative clauses that recount the main events of the story. These are simple past-tense main clauses whose order is taken to be the order in which the events actually happened. They form the skeleton supporting the additional evaluative clauses, which indicate what the point of the story is, how these events are to be interpreted, and how they fit into the speaker's system of values.

The narrative is often, though not always, concluded with a coda, which signals the end of the unit. A very common coda is *That was it*. This is a formal ending signal, which does nothing but indicate closing. Other codas, like (3), may give the effects of the sequence of events narrated or, like (4), may bring the speaker and hearer back to the present.

(3)   *And it worked out very well.*

(4)   *So we've been here for five years now.*

When we examine the ways in which these units function in conversation, we see that they are not only structural units but interactional units as well. That is, participants in the conversation treat them as bounded units. Specifically, they function as units in turn-taking. Once a speaker has begun a narrative or a joke and the hearers recognize that such a unit is in progress, the speaker has the right to continue until the end. More precisely, he may be interrupted by questions, comments, appreciations, side sequences, etc., but the topic will not be changed until the completion of the unit (Jefferson 1972). It can easily be observed that even when the situation is interrupted, either by an event or by the addition of a new participant to the conversation, stories and jokes are normally completed, either immediately by the speaker or after prompting by one of the other participants. The pressure for the completion of the unit is extremely powerful. I have, for example, observed a relatively unimportant story resumed at the point of rupture after an intruding event that lasted for 45 minutes.

This noninterruptability of the discourse unit is an important special case of the general rules for turn-taking. These rules provide that a new speaker may begin when the current speaker indicates that he is to do so, or he may begin by self-selection, when the current speaker has reached a point in his sentence that is syntactically a possible completion of the sentence (Sacks, Schegloff, and Jefferson 1974). That is, investigation of turn-taking in actual conversations shows that the participants are sensitive to the syntactic structure of sentences, using constituent boundaries also a boundary points for the interactional work of turn exchange. This is one very powerful piece of evidence that the sentence is indeed a unit that has social or psychological validity for the speaker. Since speakers similarly respect the structure of discourse units, using them, too, as boundaries for topic exchange, we may argue that the discourse unit also has validity for speakers.

The particular discourse unit that furnishes the data for the present study is even more tightly structured than is the narrative of personal experience. This unit is the description of apartment layouts. Speakers were asked to describe layouts of past and present apartments and, in response, produced highly coherent discourse units. Example (5) is typical of the 72 cases examined.

(5)   *That one was also a one bedroom apartment. It was a brand new building. We were the first occupants in that apartment. You walked in the front door. There was a narrow hallway. To your left, the first door you came to was a tiny bedroom. Then there was a kitchen, and then bathroom, and then the main room was in the back, living room, I guess.*

One level of structure that we can see in texts like this is a correspondence to the basic structure of the narrative. These descriptions are in the form of a tour that takes the hearer through the apartment, showing him the entrance to every room in the order that would be given by an actual tour. This strategy permits the speaker to take a spatial configuration of rooms and turn it into a temporal sequence paralleling the temporal sequence of the narrative. We may thus consider these descriptions to be pseudo-narratives, discourses that use the form of the narrative to report nonoccurring events. (Details of this and the following analysis are given in Linde 1974 and Linde and Labov 1975.)

However, we can go much further than this analysis of the apartment descriptions as pseudo-narratives because of the particular properties of the information that these units encode. In most discourse types, we have no access to the information other than that given by the discourse itself. That is, we cannot ask of a story why some events and not others were chosen, since we have no accurate information about events that occurred but were not described. (This is actually a more complex question than mere omission, since we cannot arrive at a nonlinguistic definition of an event. Something becomes an event because it is described or, at least, describable. It is possible to approach the question of what general types of happenings are amenable to narration within the discourse grammar of a particular culture (See Polanyi, to appear.) But we cannot determine what happenings could have been narrated as events but were not so treated. In contrast, the apartment layout descriptions encode objects and relations that, to a much greater extent, are given by the physical world. We can also collect information about them in another modality, by asking speakers to draw their apartments as well as describing them.[2] Thus, the apartment layout descriptions form an ideal natural experiment for investigating the principles that speakers use to go from information to discourse.

Of all the information that the speaker has about his apartment, only a very limited amount is obligatorily encoded in these descriptions. (Obligatory information is information that all the descriptions contain.) The question, of course, calls for spatial knowledge, and so generally speakers do not give information about how much the apartment costs, how it is furnished, what color it is, etc. The spatial information is given in the form of a tour through the apartment, one that indicates one way of entering each of the rooms. Information about the size or shape of the rooms or about how they fit together is usually not given. A three-dimensional structure is thus reduced to a topological structure consisting of points and the relations between them. Information in this form can most appropriately be represented as a tree structure. For example, the information in (5) is shown in such form in Figure 1.

---

[2] It is important to note that drawings of apartment layouts provide another, supporting representation of the information, not the facts themselves. Speakers found it surprisingly difficult to make these drawings, and they made many false starts and errors that they then corrected. The drawings can be used to provide support for our interpretation of the spoken texts but cannot be used to criticize or amend them.

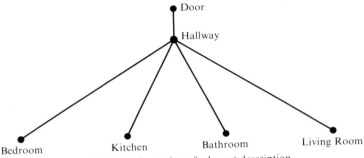

Figure 1   The information of a layout description.

It is important to note that this diagram is not a representation of the physical nature of apartments; it captures particular properties of the descriptions. This becomes clear when we examine apartments that offer the possibility of alternate routes because one or more rooms have more than one entrance. The descriptions give one route or the other; they do not take the hearer around the loop. That is, a physical structure like the one in Figure 2 is described as a structure like the ones in Figure 3. This, of course,

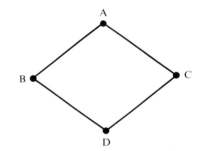

Figure 2   A layout containing a loop.

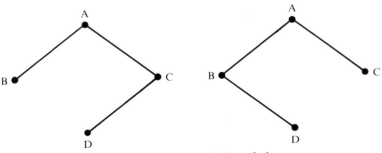

Figure 3   Alternate descriptions of a loop.

corresponds to the requirement in the formal definition of tree structure that every node but the root have one and only one parent.

It is important to clarify the nature of this hierarchically organized structure. The tree representations most familiar in linguistic use encode either the relation of set inclusion, as in semantic trees of taxonomic structure, or immediate constituency, as in trees of syntactic structure. In the trees representing the apartment descriptions, dominance encodes physical sequence. Thus, if A dominates B, A is closer to the entrance than is B.

Further points that must be discussed are the reliability of such discourse data and the types of rules that can be derived from them. The apartment descriptions are units actually produced by speakers in an interview situation that elicited discourse types also found in natural conversations. Since Chomsky's redefinition of LANGUE and PAROLE into competence and performance, respectively, it has been widely believed that speakers' actual behavior is a filtering of their ideal competence through performance factors such as memory limits, inattention, physical weakness, etc. Hence, actual speech is assumed to be too disorderly and degenerate to furnish direct information to anyone interested in linguistic regularities. This widely quoted opinion justifies the choice of data of most modern syntactic studies, but it has never been adequately established. When we examine the speech of people speaking about ordinary topics in relaxed situations (rather than in laboratory tasks or in academic seminars), we find that, in general, their speech is extremely regular and that errors are rare. The most common types of errors are simple repetition with glottal break, which can be accounted for by simple editing rules (Labov 1972), and speakers' self-corrections of lexical choice in order to prevent potential confusion on the part of the listener (Linde 1975).

This unexpected regularity of everyday speech makes it possible to use as data material that had previously been relegated to the wastebasket of performance. This is essential because studies of variation in phonology, morphology, syntax, and discourse structure have all shown that there are regular and complex linguistic patterns that are not accessible to the intuition of the analyst (Cedergren 1973, Labov 1972b, Linde 1974, Sankoff 1973). These studies also show that regularities of actual use of language are rarely categorical. To describe them, the analyst requires variable rules or some equivalent formulation for conditioned variation. In the present study, the findings have not been cast in the form of variable rules only because the number of cases of each crucial type of example is not great enough to permit numerically weighted rules. At this early stage of the study of variation in discourse, we must begin with formulations in terms of marked and unmarked choices and the conditioning factors governing them.

Using the apartment layout descriptions as an area of investigation, we can now begin to examine the way in which pronominal choice is related to and, indeed, controlled by the internal organization of the discourse. We will begin with the most obvious class of cases. Consider the boldface forms in (6).

(6)   a.   *You walk into my apartment and you walk down a long thin hall full of garbage.*
        b.   *Actually **that**'s a lie.*
        c.   *It's not full of garbage any more.*

Clearly, *it* is interpreted as referring to the hall. *That* is interpreted as referring to the previous statement taken as a statement. In this case, it is clear that the semantics of (6b) aid in interpreting the reference of *that* as the preceding statement, since we do not normally speak of a hall as being a lie. With slightly less force, the same argument holds for (6c). Metaphorically, we might say that a statement was or was not full of garbage, but this is not a condition that is likely to change over time. And, indeed, this form of reference turns out to be an extremely regular strategy. In all of the instances of reference to a preceding statement taken as a statement, the reference is accomplished with *that* rather than with *it* or any other form. Some examples of the 15 cases in this data follow.

(7)   *How would you describe your apartment?*

        *I guess an off-centered T. I shouldn't even say **that**.*

(8)   *Yeah, like a fading highway with, the living room is a little bit wider, and the bedroom less wide, and the kitchen even more narrow, and the bathroom very narrow. At the end, yeah, **that**'s the way it went.*

We may consider this type of pronominal use as an example of a logical type jump, since it moves up a logical level, thus making a metastatement about a statement.

It is worth noting that these examples of metastatement also include an element of emotional distancing from the statement being discussed. These data contain only examples like (6), (7), and (8), which involve some negative emotional tone, but there are examples like (9), which appears to be emotionally neutral.

(9)   *but it's not more than seven wide, maybe twelve wide, with windows, with two windows, one facing south and the other facing west. **That**'s how it sets up.*

However, in cases in which the speaker emphatically affirms the statement being discussed, *it* also seems possible for reference to a statement.[3] Note the following modification of example (6):

[6]   a.   *You walk into my apartment and you walk down a long thin hall full of garbage.*

        b'. *It's true! The janitor carts the stuff away only when he feels like it, which is maybe twice a month.*

In an example like (6b') we have two different scales of distance operating simultaneously: One is logical distance and the other is emotional distance. Further investigation is required on data containing examples of this type in order to determine the relative strengths of these two effects.

Reference to statements is a relatively simple problem for these data, since the rule is categorical. The more complicated cases are those in which both *it* and *that* can be used to refer to items of the same sort. In order to explicate these cases, we need the notion of FOCUS OF ATTENTION. Focus is, of course, a notion that has been widely used in linguistics, usually without being defined. [One notable exception, discussed below, is Grosz (1977), which uses a precisely defined concept of focus in the construction of a system for computer understanding of task-oriented dialogues.]

It is possible to give a precise definition of focus of attention in discourse units like the apartment description, whose structure is well-enough under-stood to be given a formal description. The focus of attention can be represented as the pairing of the underlying tree structure of the discourse with a pointer that marks a particular node of the tree. The focus of attention is on the discourse node marked by the pointer. As the discourse is con-structed, the pointer moves from node to node on the tree representing the information of the discourse. [See Linde and Goguen (1978) for a precise formal statement of these notions.] For apartment layout descriptions, pointer movement is accomplished in two ways. One is by simple addition of a new node. That is, as a new room is added to the tree representing the preceding discourse, the pointer moves to that new node. A typical example is given in (10), which repeats some of the material of (5).

(10)   *Then there was a kitchen.*

        and then bathroom

        and then the main room was in the back, living room, I guess.

---

[3] I am endebted to Dwight Bolinger for this observation and for suggesting example (6b').

Each mention of a new room creates a new node representing it. Thus, the tree shown in Figure 1 is actually the final tree, built up by the successive addition of each node. The pointer simply procedes along with the addition. The other type of pointer movement is simple pointer movement without node addition. This occurs when the speaker returns to a node previously established. We find examples of this in cases in which the apartment branches and the speaker must return to a previous point in order to traverse a second branch. A clear example is (11).

(11)   *So in other words you went to your left through a hall and you made a right and into a large bedroom.* **Now as you're coming into the front of the apartment if you go straight rather than go right or left,** *you come into a large living room area.*

The return to the point of branch can be represented by pointer movement alone, without node addition, since the node for *the front of the apartment* was previously created at the beginning of the description, when it was first mentioned.

The formulation of focus given here is sufficient only for the relatively simple trees that represent the apartment layout descriptions. These are uncomplicated, because the order of construction is heavily constrained by the interaction of the physical arrangement to be described and a general set of linearization principles for moving from a tree to a linguistic string. [Details of these principles are given in Linde (1974:Chapter 4) and Linde (1977).] Because of these strong constraints, the rules for constructing the tree include only simple node addition and pointer movement. However, more complex discourse units have been studied, specifically in the investigation of the construction of political plans by small groups (Linde and Goguen 1978). In this discourse unit, the construction of the tree may make use of all the transformational possibilities of addition, deletion, and movement of nodes and subtrees. These additional rule types obviously complicate the possibilities for pointer movement.

A related account of focus is given in Grosz (1977). The discourse type discussed here is a dialogue between an expert mechanic and an apprentice as the apprentice attempts to carry out a mechanical task. A similar tree representation is used, since the task is hierarchical, consisting of nested subtasks. As a subtask is performed, the objects and actions within it are in focus and affect the use of referring expressions, such as pronouns and definite noun phrases. When a subtask is finished, it fades from focus, although the parent task remains in focus. The formal representation used is that of partitioned semantic networks. (The representation is taken from Hendrix (1975a,b) and is extended to handle focus.) The networks contain all the objects and relations necessary to understand and describe the task, partitioned into hierarchically ordered spaces that correspond to the subtasks. Only one such space, the space corresponding to the task currently being performed, is active at a given time.

This representation bears a strong relation to the one proposed in this chapter. The most substantial difference is that Grosz's formalism reflects the underlying structure of the task directly; it reflects the task dialogue to the exent that the dialogue follows the logical structure of the task. The account of focus given in this chapter reflects the structure of the description and only indirectly the actual physical structure of the apartment. (As we have seen, p. 342, these two can differ.) However, we can expect that there will be a strong relationship between the two levels of representation, and, accordingly, we find that many of the discourse structure constraints reported by Grosz are equivalent to those reported in this chapter.

These technical formulations of focus are obviously related to notions like degree of obviousness of referent or degree of difficulty of identification of the reference. Reference within a discourse node amounts to a continuation of the current topic, whereas change of node also means change of topic and, hence, more effort required by the hearer to identify the referent. For the purposes of the present study, we will concentrate on accounts given in terms of focus, since we have a more precise definition for this, in the discourse types studied, than we do for the more intuitive concept of degree of obviousness.

We can now use this definition of focus to examine those cases in which both *it* and *that* are used to refer to items of the same sort. The first such case is reference to room, which is one of the two basic atomic units of the informational structure of the discourse. Both *it* and *that* are used to refer to rooms, but they are distinguishable by whether the room referred to is inside or outside the focus of attention. In the case of reference to a room inside the focus of attention, the pronoun chosen is *it*. This situation arises when the speaker gives information in addition to the specification of the existence and position of a room. Such information is usually evaluative material about the room just mentioned, such as the size of the room, whether the speaker liked it, whether it was pleasant or useful, etc. Evaluative material always follows the clause introducing the room or is contained within it. There are no descriptions organized in such a way as to give all the rooms and their positions followed by a sequence of evaluations of each room. Since the evaluation is always in immediate proximity to the introduction of its room, we can say that the evaluation is part of the same node as the room itself.[4] Examples of such pronominal choice within the same discourse node follow.

[4] Because the material of evaluation is so much less regular than the layout information, it is not clear how to represent it in relation to the tree structure. The work on planning discourse, however, makes it clear that this problem must be studied, since there are transformation types that require information about evaluation.

(12)   *On the right was a little kitchenette which means that **it** was just like one wall with kitchen appliances.*

(13)   *And the living room was a very very small room with two windows that wouldn't open and things like **that**. And **it** looked nice. **It** had a beautiful brick wall.*

(14)   *And then through a doorway into the living room, which sort of curves itself around so that **it**'s not really a square room. **It**'s maybe ten, twelve feet, but the width of **it** varies.*

(15)   *And the kitchen just had the kitchen appliances in **it**.*

This strategy of pronominal choice is extremely regular. In the data of this study, there are 38 cases that contain a reference within a discourse node. Of these cases, 34 use *it*, as in the preceding examples. There are 4 apparent exceptions using *that*. All of these involve contrast, the current evaluation contrasting with a previous evaluation. In such cases, the speaker has the choice of using *that* to mark the fact of contrast, although there is no condition that requires contrast to be marked. Example (16) is a complex case in which the speaker marked contrast in one of the two possible contrastive evaluations.

(16)   *And then through a little pantry to Steve's room which is very small and used to be the maid's room. It has a little bathroom in it. Then down at the end of the hall off to the left is Michael's room which is pretty big and sort of square. And at the end of the hall is Donald's room which is also the living room. And **that**'s like a really huge room with lots of windows and all, and a fire escape.*

The speaker's choice of *that* for reference to Donald's room sets up an explicit contrast with the sizes of the two rooms previously mentioned. A similar contrast would have been possible for Michael's room, and there is no evidence in the text of why the speaker did not choose to make it. Contrast is never an obligatory category, no matter what the situation being described may be like.

We now turn to the cases of reference across discourse nodes, that is, reference to an item that is not within the node in focus. The following examples are typical.

(17)   *You entered into a tiny little hallway and the kitchen was off **that**.*

(18)   *and toward the front there was a huge bedroom, much, oh I'd say, fifteen by ten, say. It was pretty big. And there was a small sleeping alcove off **that**.*

(19)   *At the end of the long hallway there's a door which is the entrance to my room, which is about seven by eleven and has a window facing the door. Next to **that** is a room which is about the same depth, about eleven feet, but about twice as wide. And next to **that** is another room which is about the same size as the one next to it.*

In each of these cases, the speaker moves from one node to the next and, in making reference to the earlier node, chooses *that*. We may regard the movement between nodes as occurring during the stage of planning the structure of the discourse rather than at the stage of the actual utterance of the sentence, since there is no effect of syntactic position of the pronoun within the sentence. Whether the reference comes after the introduction of the next room, as in (17) and (18), or before the introduction of the next room, as in (19), *that* is the pronoun chosen.

This rule, however, is not categorical. There are 25 cases of reference across nodes, and, of these, 19 use *that*, the unmarked choice. Of the remaining cases, 2 involve an apparent syntactic idiom.

(20)   *The first hall **has off it** what they call a maid's room.*

(21)   *And then through a little pantry to Steve's room which is very small and used to be the maid's room. It **has** a little bathroom **in it**.*

It is not completely clear how to represent the formal structure of the relationship of a room having another room. But it is clear that these sentences would be ill-formed with *that*.

Another case of the use of *it* for reference across nodes also involves a relation that is not yet clear.

(22)   *There's a long hall, yeah, and at right angles to **it** there's another hall.*

The situation the speaker is describing may be seen either as movement between discourse nodes or as description within a node. The same physical situation could be described as *There's a long hall and it turns right*. There are not enough cases like this in the data to determine what the differences are between the two strategies of description for halls.

Finally, there are 3 cases that clearly seem to involve reference across nodes.

(23)   *Then of course the bathroom is just around the back and then the bedroom is right next to **it**.*

(24)   *Well, when you come in there's a very large living room. And then right behind **it** is the kitchen and a hallway and a little foyer.*

(25)   *And then a kitchen and the bath across from **it**.*

This finding of the strong preference for *that* to accomplish reference to items out of the focus of attention is related to a number of issues of deictic reference discussed elsewhere. Kirsner (this volume) gives arguments for why deictics in Dutch cannot be analyzed as having a primarily spatial meaning but must instead be seen as involving high or low focus of attention. Isard (1975) discusses deictics, particularly *that*, as changing the context, that is, moving the point of reference. Although he does not have available the notion of discourse node and change of focus between discourse nodes, some of his examples, like (26) and (27), clearly involve this.

(26)   *First square 19 and then cube it.*

(27)   *First square 19 and then cube that.*

Example (27) is clearly an instruction to cube the square, whereas (26), Isard claims, is ambiguous. [For me, *it* in (26) can only refer to 19, not to the square of 19, but I am not conversant with the discourse conventions of mathematical literature.] It is clear that these examples invoke some hierarchy of actions in which (27) mandates actions represented by different nodes and (26) may mandate actions within a single node. Unfortunately, without an investigation of the structure of discourses of this type, it is impossible to confirm such an analysis, since we do not know how the two tasks fit into the larger discourse unit.

The final type of reference to be considered is reference to the entire apartment being described. The unmarked choice for this type of reference is *it*; 62 of the 65 references to the apartment use *it*. Examples (28) and (29) are typical examples, both taken from the beginning of their descriptions.

(28)   *Well, you come into, well, it's an L-shaped apartment.*

(29)   *Uh, yeah, it's a railroad apartment, converted from something larger.*

The use of *it* to refer to the entire apartment is obvious enough. What may be somewhat more surprising is that the act of reference may skip over several possible noun phrase antecedents. Examples (30) and (31) show cases in which the boldface italic *it* does not refer to an immediately preceding room but, rather, to the entire apartment.

(30)   *and it was a decent sized kitchen, it wasn't fantastic, but it was there, you know. And then **it** had a good-sized living room.*

(It is not the kitchen but the entire apartment that had the living room.)

(31)   *The last apartment was a garden apartment. It was one small bedroom, a living room which was eighteen by eighteen, maybe eighteen by twenty, a very very tiny kitchen which you stepped in and stepped out of, and a very small bathroom. But **it** did have the garden, which was mine.*

In these cases, we see that *it* is used not only for reference within the immediate node that is the focus of attention but also for reference to the basis of the entire tree, the apartment itself. This exactly parallels Grosz' finding that, in task dialogues, pronoun reference may be either to within the subtask in focus or to the entire, higher-level task. The use of the same item for accomplishing these two types of reference suggests that, in discourse, attention is actually focused on at least two levels simultaneously— the particular node of the discourse under construction and, also, the discourse as a whole. Thus, if the focus of attention indicates where we are, we are actually at two places at once. In fact, it is likely that the number is considerably greater than two, particularly in more complicated discourse types. An excellent place to investigate this would be discourse units constructed by more than one person, under norms of competition rather than cooperation.

There are three cases in which *that* rather than *it* is used to refer to the entire apartment, all of which involve a contrast with another apartment. Since the speakers were asked to describe both their present and their past apartments, they had the possibility of marking comparisons. All three descriptions using *that* for reference to an apartment are second or subsequent descriptions in the course of the interview, and all explicitly involve reference or contrast with previous apartments. Example (32), which is taken from the speaker's second description, shows this clearly.

(32)   *Tell me, how was this apartment laid out, the one you're talking about. Well, **that** also faced the street.*

This strategy is exactly parallel to the use of *that* for reference within a single node when a contrast is indicated to a room in a previous node. Here, too, contrast is a rhetorical strategy, not a grammatical category. The speaker may choose to mark contrast, but he need not do so.

We may now summarize the uses of *it* and *that* in this data in order to show the underlying principles that unite these uses.

TABLE 1

CONDITIONS ON THE CHOICE OF *it* AND *that*

It	*That*
——	Reference to a statement
Reference to the entire apartment	Reference to the entire apartment with contrast to previous apartment
Reference within the discourse node in focus	Reference within the discourse node in focus with contrast to preceding out-of-focus node
Reference across a discourse node	

The conditions above the dotted line are categorical; the condition below the dotted line is variable, with a strong preference for *that*. (As previously discussed, the number of examples of each type of case is not sufficiently great to permit numerical formulation of this rule. At present, it is only possible to state the situation in terms of a strong perference.)

The conditions summarized in Table 1 are clearly related. All of the conditions favoring the choice of *it* are cases of reference within the area of focus of attention. The conditions favoring *that* involve reference outside the focus of attention. Focus of attention operates simultaneously in a number of domains. One such domain is the structure of a hierarchically organized discourse, a factor that we see has a major influence on pronominal choice.

A further domain is the act of speaking itself—statement versus metastatement. This is a particularly interesting area, since the contrast is normally retained only on the first reference. Subsequent references to a statement as statement are within the focus of attention. Let us reexamine the first example given of this case.

[6]   a.   *You walk into my apartment and you walk down a long thin hall full of garbage.*
       b.   *Actually **that**'s a lie.*
       c.   *It's not full of garbage any more.*

The speaker first used *that* to refer to the preceding statement and then returned to the original level of discourse by making reference to a room invoked by (6a). But it would have been equally possible to continue reference to (6a) using *it*.

[6]   c'.   *It's really not true any more.*

Both *it* and *that* are possible here, although *it* seems more natural. In the case of the sequence with (6c'), it appears that the use of *that* in the preceding sentence has moved the focus of attention. This is quite different from the use of *that* for reference across nodes of the discourse, where it appears that the use of *that* does not move the focus of attention back to the node referred to. In the case of reference to statements, of course, there is the complication that the language and the metalanguage are identical. Further study is clearly required to make precise exactly what the rules are for moving the focus of attention.

A third domain for focus of attention is focus on the object of reference itself versus focus on the item with contrast to some other item of the same type. Here again, *it* is used for reference within the focus of attention, *that* implies the existence of some similar item outside the focus of attention.

Thus, we see that the diverse conditions affecting the choice of *it* and *that* are, in fact, all aspects of the same phenomenon of focus. It is not surprising to find focus of attention cited as a factor in pronominal use. What this chapter has done is to demonstrate that focus of attention can be defined precisely and that, by doing so, we can make progress on the question of how speakers actually use pronouns.

ACKNOWLEDGMENTS

I would like to thank Dwight Bolinger, Talmy Givón, Joseph Goguen, Barbara Grosz, Wolfgang Klein, George Lakoff, Jerry Morgan, Livia Polanyi, Sandra Thompson, and Veronika Ullmer-Ehrich. Their help has been invaluable in clarifying and enlarging my grasp of these problems. My original interest in discourse and any understanding I may have of it is due to William Labov, whom it is impossible to thank adequately.

REFERENCES

Cedergren, Henrietta (1973) "On the Nature of Variable Constraints," in C. J. Bailey and Roger Shuy, eds., *New Ways of Analyzing Variation in English*, Georgetown University Press, Washington D.C.

Fillmore, Charles J. (1975) "Santa Cruz Lectures on Deixis," Indiana University Linguistics Club, Bloomington, Indiana.

Grosz, Barbara J. (1977) "The Representation and Use of Focus in Dialogue Understanding," Technical Note 151, Stanford Research Institute, Stanford, California.

Hendrix, Gary G. (1975a) "Expanding the Utility of Semantic Networks through Partitioning," in *Advance Papers, International Joint Conference on Artificial Intelligence*, Tbilisi, Georgian SSR.

Hendrix, Gary G. (1975b) "Partitioned Networks for the Mathematical Modeling of Natural Language Semantics," Technical Report NL-28, Department of Computer Sciences, University of Texas, Austin.

Isard, Stephen (1975) "Changing the Context," in Edward L. Keenan, ed., *Formal Semantics of Natural Language*, Cambridge University Press, Cambridge.

Halliday, M. A. K. and Ruqaiya Hasan (1976) *Cohesion in English*, Longman, London.

Jefferson, Gail (1972) "Side Sequences," in David N. Sudnow, ed., *Studies in Social Interaction*, Free Press, New York.

Labov, William (1972a) "The Transformation of Experience in Narrative Syntax," in *Language in the Inner City*, University of Pennsylvania Press, Philadelphia, Pennsylvania.

Labov, William (1972b) *Sociolinguistic Patterns*, University of Pennsylvania Press, Philadelphia, Pennsylvania.

Lakoff, Robin (1974) "Remarks on *this* and *that*," in M. LeGaly, R. Fox, and A. Bruck, eds., *Papers from the Tenth Regional Meeting of the Chicago Linguistics Society*, Chicago Linguistic Society, Chicago, Illinois.

Linde, Charlotte (1974) *The Linguistic Encoding of Spatial Information*, unpublished Doctoral dissertation, Columbia University, New York.

Linde, Charlotte (1977) "A Production Model Based on Discourse Evidence," Research Report, Max-Planck-Gesellschaft, Nijmegen, Netherlands.

Linde, Charlotte (to appear) "The Organization of Discourse," in Tim Shope, Ann Zwicky, and Peg Griffen, eds., *The English Language in Its Social and Historical Context*.

Linde, Charlotte and J. A. Goguen (1978) "Structure of Planning Discourse," *Journal of Social and Biological Structures* 1.

Linde, Charlotte and William Labov (1975) "Spatial Networks as a Site for the Study of Language and Thought," *Language* 51, 924–939.

Lyons, John (1968) *Introduction to Theoretical Linguistics*, Cambridge University Press, Cambridge.

Lyons, John (1977) *Semantics, Vol. II*, Cambridge University Press, Cambridge.

Polanyi, Livia (to appear) "So What's the Point?," *Semiotica*.

Sacks, Harvey (1974) "An Analysis of the Course of a Joke's Telling," in Richard Bauman and Joel Sherzer, eds., *Explorations in the Ethnography of Speaking*, Cambridge University Press, Cambridge.

Sacks, Harvey, Emmanuel Schegloff, and Gail Jefferson (1974) "A Simplest Systematics for the Organization of Turn-Taking for Conversation," *Language*, 50, 696–735.

Sankoff, Gillian (1973) "Above and Beyond Phonology in Variable Rules," in C. J. Bailey and Roger Shuy, eds., *New Ways of Analyzing Variation in English*, Georgetown University Press, Washington D.C.

Wald, Benji (1977) "The Discourse Unit," unpublished manuscript, Department of Linguistics, University of California, Los Angeles, California.

DEIXIS IN DISCOURSE: AN EXPLORATORY QUANTITATIVE STUDY OF THE MODERN DUTCH DEMONSTRATIVE ADJECTIVES

ROBERT S. KIRSNER

University of California, Los Angeles

1. THE PROBLEM

Both traditional and modern grammarians describe Standard Dutch as having two types of demonstratives whose respective forms indicate gender and number, as in Table 1:

TABLE 1
THE DUTCH DEMONSTRATIVES

	Common[1] gender, singular, and common and neuter, plural	Neuter gender, singular
Proximate	*deze* 'this/these'	*dit* 'this'
Distal	*die* 'that/those'	*dat* 'that'

[1] Common gender refers to the merger of earlier masculine and feminine (cf. Modern German). The distinction between common and neuter gender also determines the choice of the definite article; *het* is used with neuter singular nouns, *de* elsewhere.

Syntax and Semantics, Volume 12:
Discourse and Syntax

Henceforth, we shall refer to the set {*deze, dit*} as *deze* and to the set {*die, dat*} as *die*. The purposes of this chapter are to show that the commonly accepted characterization of *deze* versus *die* as signaling proximate versus distal (cf. Bech 1952:7, den Hertog 1973[1903]:119–120, Rijpma and Schuringa 1962:117) does not explain the actual distribution of the forms and to validate a new, more abstract analysis using quantitative data from discourse. To keep things simple, we restrict ourselves in this exploratory study to the adjectival use of the demonstratives, where the type of referent is indicated lexically, with a following noun.[2]

2. INADEQUACIES OF PROXIMATE–DISTAL

Although the accepted analysis covers pedestrian cases such as *Deze jongen is groter dan die jongen* 'This boy [near speaker] is bigger than that boy [far from speaker]', it has long been apparent that *die* cannot be distal. In the context of the novel from which (1) (following) is taken (van het Reve 1961:69), the woman is obviously talking about the coat and hat that she herself is wearing. Hence, they are distant in neither space nor time (note that all boldfaces in such citations are mine):

(1)   *Daarna ruimde ze de tafel af en trok haar jas aan. "Staat die jas gek bij die muts?" vroeg ze.*
        'Afterwards she cleared the table and put on her coat. "Does **this** coat look crazy with **this** hat?," she asked.'

Consider also (2) from Hermans (1971:343, 1962:320)

(2)   *Nee! Verdomme, ook deze straat is recht en daar zie ik ook een brug. Al die straten lijken op elkaar!*
        No! Jesus Christ, **this** street's straight too, and there's another bridge. **These bloody** streets all look alike!

Again, *die* does not point away from the speaker but rather to the entire set of streets being examined, including the one referred to with *deze*. If *die* contrasts with *deze* (as the use of *these bloody* in the British translation surely suggests), it does so not in distance but in emotionality. Finally, consider an example (van Straten 1972:144) in which a noun introduced into discourse with *deze* is immediately repeated with *die*:

(3)   [Context: discussion of the author W. F. Hermans, who has already been mentioned by name several times] *Toch betreft het hier een*

---

[2] For discussion of the independent use of demonstratives (as pronouns), see van Haeringen (1954).

> *verhaal dat binnen het oeuvre van **deze** schrijver uitzonderlijke
> betekenis heeft, omdat **die** schrijver hierin voor het eerst . . . tot een
> formulering is gekomen van wat men gerust het centrale thema . . .
> mag noemen.* 'Yet here we are dealing with a story having excep-
> tional significance within the literary work of **this** author, because
> in it (?? **that**) **the** author for the first time . . . came to a formula-
> tion which may confidently be called the central theme. . . .'

There is no observable, testable difference between the two mentions of the
noun *schrijver* in the distance of its referent from the speaker, either in time
or in space.

Now, given such data (and we could supply many more examples), it is
clear that *die* cannot be the opposite of *deze*. Recognizing this, the Dutch
grammarian Paardekooper has suggested (1968:189) that *die* is simply an
unmarked demonstrative, unspecified for distance, whereas *deze* is marked
as PROXIMATE. Certainly, this proposal could explain why *die* can be used to
point near as well as far and why it can be exploited to repeat a noun introduced with *deze* without causing the shift in perspective found in the
English gloss with '*this* . . . *that*'. Nevertheless, two serious flaws remain.
First, the nature of "demonstrativity" remains undefined. (What would an
"unmarked demonstrative" communicate?) Second, anyone examining
actual data quickly encounters examples of *deze* not explained in any
straightforward way by PROXIMATE. Consider, indeed, *deze schrijver* 'this
author' in (3). It is apparent that, in using *deze*, the critic is concerned with
and is drawing our attention to Hermans. But it is not in any way obvious
that the critic is "near" Hermans in either time or space. Examine further
(4) from Frank (1959:7, 1966:7) and (5) from van het Reve (1961:35):

(4)   *Het is smoorheet, iedereen puft en bakt en in **die**/?**deze** hitte moet ik
        alles belopen.*
        'It is boiling hot, we are all positively melting, and in **this** heat
        I have to walk everywhere.'

(5)   *"Ha **die**/***deze** Frits!" zei de jongen, gaf hem een harde klap op de
        schouder, bleef voor hem staan en zei. . . .*
        "Aha, Frits!," the boy said, slapped him on the shoulder, remained
        standing right in front of him and said. . . .'

Even though Anne Frank is directly experiencing the heat (in the here-and-
now), informants agree that *deze* is much less likely than *die* in the sentence
cited. And even though Frits is standing next to the boy who greets him,
the boy cannot say **Ha deze Frits!* To postulate a meaning PROXIMATE
for *deze* thus creates two problems. First, *deze* turns up in association with
messages of attention and concern (not discussed in the grammers) that do

not seem to have to do with "nearness" in any testable way. Second, there
are cases in which *deze* is regarded as inappropriate, even though its alleged
meaning of proximity ("here-and-now-ness") would be literally true.

The grammarian may respond to this situation in several ways. He may
ignore it. He may actively defend Paardekooper's suggestion. Or he may
argue that NEITHER demonstrative—*die* OR *deze*—is fundamentally concerned with proximate–distal. It is this third, most radical option that we
shall defend here. In Section 6 of this chapter, we shall return to examine
Paardekooper's suggestion in the light of all the data.

3. THE SYSTEM OF DEIXIS AND ITS EXPLOITATION

We hypothesize that the meanings signaled by the Dutch demonstratives
are organized into a grammatical system (in the sense of Diver 1969:47)
that exhaustively subclassifies a semantic substance that we may call "deixis"
and define as "the force with which the hearer is instructed to find the
referent" (García 1975:65). As shown in (6), *deze* signals HIGH DEIXIS,
"greater urging that the hearer find the referent" and *die* signals LOW
DEIXIS, "lesser urging that the hearer find the referent," with neither *deze*
nor *die* explicitly mentioning proximity or distance.

(6)   DEIXIS $\begin{cases} deze = \text{HIGH} \\ die = \text{LOW} \end{cases}$

Given the definition, it is apparent that the speaker will signal deixis most
appropriately when he wants the hearer to attend to the referent—either
because (*a*) the hearer has not yet differentiated (distinguished) the referent
from all other possible ones of the noun in question; or because (*b*) the
referent—for some other reason—requires special highlighting. As an
illustration of (*a*), consider (7), where we contrast *deze* and *die* with the
definite article *de*:

(7)   a.   **De auto is niet te koop, maar de auto wel.*
               'The car$_i$ is not for sale, but the car$_j$ is.'

           b.   **De auto is niet te koop, maar **de** auto wel.*
               'The car$_i$ is not for sale, but **the** car$_j$ is.'

           c.   **Deze** *auto is niet te koop, maar **deze** auto wel.*
               'This car$_i$ is not for sale, but **this** car$_j$ is.'

           d.   **Die** *auto is niet te koop, maar **die** auto wel.*
               'That car$_i$ is not for sale, but **that** car$_j$ is.'

Unlike *de*, which signals DIFFERENTIATION REQUIRED AND MADE,[3] both *deze* and *die*, signaling deixis, urging the hearer to find the referent, communicate that the referent's identity cannot yet be taken for granted. They are thus more coherent than *de* when, as in (7), different referents of the same noun are being pointed out.

An illustration of (*b*), the use of deixis for highlighting, is (8); informants state that the choice of *die* rather than the equally possible *de* in the second mention of *wereld* 'world' provides a "tighter link" with its first mention (after Nuchelmans 1969:17):

(8)   *De logica, kennisleer en methodologie staan niet in zo'n rechtstreekse relatie tot de verschijnselen in **de wereld** maar concentreren hun belangstelling op bepaalde kanten van de manier waarop over **die wereld** wordt gedacht en gesproken.*
        'Logic, epistemology, and philosophy of science do not stand in such a direct relation to phenomena in **the world** but concentrate their interest on certain aspects of the way in which **that world** is thought about and talked about.'

The mechanism is straightforward. *Die*, insisting that the hearer search for the world, alerts him to it more, induces him to pay more attention to it than does *de*, which claims that there is no problem, that the referent is already "pinned down." The visibility of the referent is thus boosted; the hearer is led through his search to affirm that the world in question is none other than the one just mentioned with *de*.

Consider now a third aspect of deixis, namely, that the command to search for the referent favors the inference that effort is required to find it and, hence, that a specific referent exists—that is, that it is a localizable entity rather than a disembodied general concept. Observe, for example, that when industrious students have not been a prior topic of conversation, (9a), with the definite article, can be taken "generically" (as referring to a general class of students) more easily than (9b) or (9c), with demonstratives:

(9)   a.   *De vlijtige student zal slagen.*
              'The industrious student [i.e., a type of student] shall succeed.'

        b.   *Deze vlijtige student zal slagen.*
              'This industrious student [existing individual] shall succeed.'

        c.   *Die vlijtige student zal slagen.*
              'That industrious student [existing individual] shall succeed.'

---

[3] For a justification of this meaning and a detailed discussion of the Dutch article system, see Kirsner (1972:Chapter II).

The choice between *deze*, signaling HIGH DEIXIS, and *die*, signaling LOW DEIXIS is like that between either demonstrative and *de*, but with more nuance. Granted that the hearer is to be told to find the referent, what level of urging is appropriate? From common sense, we anticipate that *deze* will be used when the hearer's task is more difficult (i.e., when it is harder to select the referent in question) and that it will suggest more forcefully than *die* that a specific referent exists. More generally, three strategies suggest themselves, each of which is consistent with deixis as defined above:[4]

1. NOTEWORTHINESS. The speaker will direct attention strongest to entities that he, the speaker, is most interested in talking about.

2. GIVENNESS. The speaker will direct the hearer's attention strongest to entities that are not given, "in the hearer's consciousness" (Chafe 1974).

3. FOREGROUNDING. The speaker will use more than one means of drawing the appropriate amount of attention to the noun's referent, so that strong urging of the hearer to find it will be coupled with devices for foregrounding the noun in question and weak urging will be coupled with devices for backgrounding.

4. VALIDATION OF THE HYPOTHESIS

To show the correctness of our analytical hypothesis, namely, that *deze* signals HIGH DEIXIS and *die* LOW DEIXIS, we could continue to follow the traditional procedure of citing individual examples. Consider (10) and (11):

(10) a. *Vind je dat **die** das bij het jasje past?*
          'Do you think that **this** tie goes with the jacket?'

      b. *Vind je dat **deze** das bij het jasje past?*
          'Do you think that **this particular** tie goes with the jacket?'

(11) a. *Die/Deze student, die vlijtig is, zal slagen.*
          'That/This student, who is industrious, shall succeed.'

      b. *Die/*Deze student die vlijtig is, zal slagen.*
          'That/*This student who is industrious shall succeed.'

According to one informant, (10b) differs from (10a) in suggesting that the selection of the tie is still in progress and is being made with utmost care. Now, granted that it is harder to pick out an object when there is a choice (Posner 1973:152) and that the difficulty is obviously greater during the

---

[4] Within the framework of this exploratory paper, we must ASSUME that these strategies are psychologically real. A fuller treatment of the problem would, ideally, provide psychological evidence that they are. Obviously, only when such evidence is present can one show that the behavior of the demonstratives is a specific instance of something more general and, thereby, explain it.

choice than afterward, this contrast shows that *deze* evokes a harder task than *die* and is thus consistent with the opposition between HIGH DEIXIS and LOW DEIXIS. Sentences (11a and b), in turn, illustrate that, whereas *deze* forces a nonrestrictive interpretation upon an accompanying clause (so that *student* refers to an existing individual), *die* permits a restrictive one, defining a general class that need not have any existing members. Again, the contrast accords with our hypothesis, as discussed in Section 3. Still, there are draw-backs to this traditional procedure. First, informants do not always agree. Second, they may use language differently from the way they say they do. We therefore prefer to supplement subjective with objective data, specifi-cally statistical observations (cf. Contini-Morava 1976). We shall now provide QUANTITATIVE evidence that *deze* and *die* are used in accordance with the three strategies given above.

The frequency counts that follow are taken from two texts. Corpus H is Haasse (1972), an essay unraveling the human drama that motivated the construction, in the sixteenth century, of a strange sculpture garden at Bomarzo, Italy. Corpus N consists of the first two chapters of Nuchelmans (1969), an exceptionally lucid survey of British analytic philosophy.

In the first strategy, NOTEWORTHINESS, we assume that the speaker will call the hearer's attention most strongly to those things that he the speaker finds, noteworthy. Noteworthiness may be measured in at least two ways. First, we can consider the referents themselves and ask what kinds of entities will attract the speaker's attention. Second, we can consider linguistic evidence that the speaker is, in fact, attending to the referent.

With respect to the entities, we suggest two criteria. It is known that people tend to notice people more easily than nonpeople (Lewis 1975).[5] Second, it is apparent from everyday life that attention is selective; it is easier to attend to (keep track of) a single thing—one child (if you are a parent), one airplane (if you are an air-traffic controller)—than to a multi-plicity of things.[6] Accordingly, we predict that Dutch speakers would favor *deze*, signaling HIGH DEIXIS, to refer to more noteworthy human and singular entities and *die*, signaling LOW DEIXIS, to refer to less noteworthy nonhuman and plural entities. Consider the data shown in Table 2.

---

[5] For discussion of the impact of this factor upon another area of Dutch grammar, see Kirsner (1975, 1976). We stress to the reader that we explicitly take the controversial position that psychological studies of nonlinguistic behavior (such as Lewis 1975, on visual perception) are indeed relevant to our understanding of linguistic behavior. Though the connections do need to be worked out and though one must go beyond mere analogizing, it seems evident that language is a particular instance of human behavior in general. Hence, what is known about human behavior can help explain linguistic phenomena.

[6] See, further, Reid (1977:66), Zubin (this volume), and Posner (1973). Again, it would be desirable to have more DIRECTED psychological research EXPLICITLY supporting the plausible suggestions we make here and later. An alternative formulation is that single things stand out from their background more than pluralities, that is, are more salient perceptually.

TABLE 2
CHOICE OF DEMONSTRATIVE VERSUS HUMANNESS OF REFERENT IN CORPUS H

Demonstrative	Human NP	Other NP	Percentage	
deze	25	79	24	WR = 2.38, $p < .02$
die	18	135	12	

As predicted, human NPs attract *deze* (that is, the set of demonstratives *deze* and *dit*) significantly more than they attract *die* (the set of demonstratives *die* and *dat*): 24% of all *dezes* occur with nouns referring to people, as opposed to only 12% of *dies*. A quantitative measure of the statistical skewing is given by the weighted ratio (WR), calculated as follows. In the first column, we observe that the ratio of *deze* to *die* for human NP is 25/18 or 1.39; *deze* is used 1.39 times as frequently as *die* with nouns referring to humans. In the second column, the ratio of *deze* to *die* is 79/135 or 0.585; *deze* is used with nonhuman nouns about six-tenths as frequently as *die*. The RELATIVE FAVORING by human NP of *deze* is given by the RATIO OF THESE RATIOS or 1.39/0.585 (= 2.38), indicating that *deze* is used more than twice as frequently as *die* when the accompanying noun refers to a person rather than to a nonperson. A χ^2 test on the raw data indicates that the probability of this skewing's occurring by chance is less than 0.02. Accordingly, we may reasonably assume that chance is not a factor here and that the skewing is motivated by (*a*) the difference between human and nonhuman referents and (*b*) the difference in meaning between *deze* and *die*. Given that Dutch speakers—as humans—would notice people more readily than nonpeople and assuming (as is reasonable) that speakers would draw attention to what they regard as noteworthy, we argue that the favoring of *deze* over *die* to refer to people supports the hypothesis that *deze* signals HIGH DEIXIS and *die* LOW DEIXIS.

Look now at Table 3. In both texts, *deze* is attracted to singular NPs. Granted that speakers would point out most strongly what they themselves can concentrate on most easily, the favoring of *deze* to refer to single things supports the deictic system we have proposed.

TABLE 3
CHOICE OF DEMONSTRATIVE VERSUS NUMBER OF REFERENT

Corpus	Demonstrative	Singular NP	Plural NP	Percentage Singular NP	
H	*deze*	87	17	84	WR = 2.06, $p < .05$.
	die	109	44	71	
N	*deze*	182	70	72	WR = 1.73, $p < .05$.
	die	69	46	60	

Let us now consider linguistic evidence that the speaker is attending to a referent. Again, we suggest two criteria: names and subjecthood.

It is an undeniable fact of everyday life that one readily learns the names of "important" people (one's spouse, one's boss) and that to address someone by name indicates attention and respect (Carnegie 1963:77). We therefore suggest that, when a speaker identifies someone by name, he is probably focusing on him more than otherwise and, hence, would be more interested in pointing him out to the hearer. Accordingly, we predict that if one compares (a) proper nouns and those common nouns that refer to people who have already been named with (b) common nouns referring to unnamed people, one will find that the former attract *deze* and the latter *die*. Examine the data in Table 4:

TABLE 4

CHOICE OF DEMONSTRATIVE WITH NAMED AND UNNAMED HUMAN REFERENT IN CORPUS H

Demonstrative	Named referent			Unnamed referent	Percentage Named	
	Proper	Common	Total	Common (= Total)		
deze	7	14	21	4	84	WR = 7.49,
die	3	4	7	11	39	$p < .01.$

The prediction is confirmed. Granted that the speaker regards named persons as more noteworthy than unnamed ones and, hence, as more deserving of being brought to the hearer's attention, the use of *deze* more than seven times as frequently as *die* to refer to them clearly supports our hypothesis that *deze* signals HIGH DEIXIS and *die* LOW DEIXIS.

A second measure of the speaker's attention to the referent is subjecthood. We have suggested elsewhere (Kirsner 1975, 1976) that the number ending of the Dutch finite verb provides information about the PARTICIPANT IN FOCUS in the event the verb describes—that is, that participant (of those referred to in the sentence) that the speaker is concentrating on (García 1975:69), which is his center of interest (Zubin, this volume) and which, in consequence, is most topical (Givón 1976). We note as evidence that those NPs that are taken to be co-referential with the verb ending (traditional subjects) tend more than do non-co-referential NPs (nonsubjects) to be pronouns, characterizing their referents as fully known. Furthermore, using techniques developed by Zubin (this volume), one easily verifies that such NPs yield higher token–type ratios than nonsubjects and tend to refer to central rather than to peripheral characters in narrative—again facts suggesting that they designate FOCUS rather than NONFOCUS participants. This being so, we make the following prediction. If (a) the speaker is likely to draw attention most strongly to what he himself is concentrating on, and if (*b*) the verb ending refers to just such an entity, then the speaker should favor the HIGH DEIXIS demonstrative *deze* to corefer to that entity. Subject NPs should, then, exhibit a higher percentage of *deze*s than non-subject NPs. The data:

TABLE 5
CHOICE OF DEMONSTRATIVE VERSUS SUBJECTHOOD IN CORPUS N

Demonstrative	Subject	Nonsubject	Percentage subject	
deze	88	164	34.9	WR = 1.84, *p* < .05.
die	26	89	22.6	

Again, our prediction is confirmed. *Deze* occurs nearly twice as frequently in subject NPs than in nonsubject NPs, a skewing significant at the .05 level.

In the second strategy, GIVENNESS, we assume that the speaker will insist more strongly that the hearer find nongiven referents than given ones, which are already "in the hearer's consciousness." Here, we consider two aspects of givenness: its presence and its decay.

By and large, when a noun is used for the first time its referent is not as given as it will be upon repetition. We therefore anticipate that new nouns will attract *deze* and repeated nouns *die*. Table 6 shows that this is indeed the case:

TABLE 6
CHOICE OF DEMONSTRATIVE WITH NEW AND REPEATED NOUNS IN CORPUS N

Demonstrative	New noun	Repeated noun	Percentage new noun	
deze	191	61	75.8	WR = 2.58, *p* < .001.
die	63	52	54.8	

Observe now that givenness may "decay"; something once in the hearer's consciousness can be forgotten (Chafe 1974:127–129). The speaker who wishes to be understood when he mentions such an item again will, accordingly, have to draw the hearer's attention to it more strongly than if there were no decay. If *deze* signals higher deixis than *die*, it will be more appropriate when such forceful "reminding" is called for.

How, then, to measure decay or, rather, the speaker's estimate of it? Psychologists have shown that the less recently an item has been mentioned, the harder it is for the hearer to remember (Houston 1976:288, Klatzky

1975:19). This provides support for Chafe's proposal that, the more sentences intervening between first and subsequent mention of an item, the more reasonable will be the speaker's assumption that givenness has decayed and the more prone he will be to treat the referent as "new." Accordingly, if we reexamine the repeated nouns in corpus N, we anticipate that those mentioned furthest back in the discourse will attract *deze* upon repetition and that the others would attract *die*. The data are given in Table 7. There are three degrees of distance: prior mention of the noun (*a*) in the very same sentence as the repetition; (*b*) one sentence back within the same paragraph; (*c*) even earlier, that is, two or more sentences back within the same paragraph or in the previous paragraph:

TABLE 7
CHOICE OF DEMONSTRATIVE VERSUS DISTANCE TO PRIOR MENTION IN CORPUS N

Demonstrative	Distance to prior mention			N (Sample size)
	(a) Same S	(b) 1 S back	(c) Earlier	
deze	15	38	8	61
die	35	16	1	52
Total	50	54	9	
Percentage *deze*	30	70	89	

The prediction is confirmed; the more distant in the discourse the prior mention is, the greater the tendency to use *deze*. If one combines the figures in columns (b) and (c) to obtain the more familiar four-cell table, one finds that 75% of *deze*s but only 33% of *die*s occur with nouns whose first mention is in an earlier sentence. The relative favoring of *deze* by such nouns is given by the weighted ratio, 6.31, with $p \ll .001$ by the chi-square test.

In the third strategy, FOREGROUNDING, we anticipate that the use of *deze* versus *die* will correlate with the foregrounding of the noun (its placement in positions of "prominence"). Three measures of foregrounding suggest themselves: occurrence in (*a*) main versus subordinate clauses; (*b*) at or near the beginning of the sentence; and (*c*) in the initial sentence of paragraphs.

Intuitively, it is clear that NPs are more "prominent" or salient in main than in subordinate clauses (cf. Langacker 1974:650, 660). We may add, from a communicative viewpoint, that, since main clauses are held to express the "major" thought of a sentence (as opposed to "lesser" or "minor" thoughts; cf. Baker 1976:139), the speaker's placement of an NP in a main clause indicates that he views it as more important to his message. We expect that what the speaker shows as important by one means he will also do by another. Accordingly, we predict that *deze*, whose HIGH DEIXIS meaning would be more coherent with the foregrounding main clauses provide, would tend more than *die* to be attracted to such clauses. Consider the data in Table 8:

TABLE 8
CHOICE OF DEMONSTRATIVE IN MAIN AND SUBORDINATE CLAUSES IN CORPUS N

Demonstrative	Main clause	Subordinate clause	Percentage main clause	
deze	169	83	67.1	WR = 1.63, $p < .05$.
die	63	52	54.8	

The prediction is confirmed; *deze* occurs one and two-thirds times as frequently as *die* in main as in subordinate clauses.

Consider now that in Dutch, as in many languages, the beginning of the sentence is a point of "discourse focus" where the speaker puts those NPs whose referents he considers particularly worthy of the hearer's attention—agent-like participants, identified entities, etc. If *deze* does in fact signal greater insistence than does *die* that the hearer attend to the referent, it should be more compatible than *die* with the "spotlight" of initial position. A count was made of demonstratives occurring in and after the first three words of the sentence (an arbitrary cut-off point), and, as may be seen, the prediction is strikingly confirmed:

TABLE 9
POSITION OF DEMONSTRATIVE IN THE SENTENCE IN CORPUS N

Demonstrative	First three words	Later	Percentage first three words	
deze	76	176	30.1	WR = 5.09, $p \ll .001$.
die	9	106	7.8	

Finally, we turn to the paragraph, definable as a "group of sentences related to a central thought [Hodges 1956:327]." If (as this definition suggests) each successive paragraph is a new step in the discourse, then the first sentence of each—introducing the new thought—constitutes a naturally emphatic position (cf. Baker 1976:50; also Hinds, to appear, on "initial segments"). Granted, then, that putting a noun in the very first sentence of a paragraph would thrust it upon the hearer's consciousness and assuming that the use of *deze* would highlight its referent more than would the use of *die*, we expect the two kinds of foregrounding to cooccur and, hence, for *deze* to be attracted to paragraph-initial sentences. Consider the data in Table 10:

TABLE 10
POSITION OF DEMONSTRATIVES IN THE PARAGRAPH IN CORPUS N

Demonstrative	First S	Later Ss	Percentage first S	
deze	48	204	19.0	WR = 3.63, $p < .01$.
die	7	108	6.1	

Again, the prediction is confirmed.

To summarize, we have presented frequency counts showing that *deze* is favored over *die* when the noun refers to entities (*a*) that the speaker is likely to notice (Tables 2 through 5); and (*b*) that are not "in the hearer's consciousness" (6, 7); and when (*c*) the noun occurs in a position of prominence (8, 9, 10). If one accepts that these three strategies (NOTE WORTHINESS, GIVENNESS, and FOREGROUNDING) constitute reasonable exploitations of deixis, then these data support the hypothesis that *deze* is a "stronger" demonstrative than is *die*, signaling greater insistence that the hearer find the referent. Furthermore, when we tally the results of each of the counts on each of the two corpora (Table 11), we find that all of the skewings that attain statistical significance ($p < .05$) go in the direction predicted by the hypothesis.

TABLE 11
STATISTICAL SKEWINGS IN HAASE (1972) AND NUCHELMANS (1969)

Count	Corpus H	Corpus N	No F	No A	No nf	No na
Humanness (2)	F	nf	1	0	1	0
Number (3)	F	F	2	0	0	0
Names (4)	F	nf	1	0	1	0
Subjecthood (5)	nf	F	1	0	1	0
Givenness (6)	nf	F	1	0	1	0
Distance (7)	nf	F	1	0	1	0
Main/sub. clause (8)	na	F	1	0	0	1
Position in S (9)	na	F	1	0	0	1
Position in P (10)	nf	F	1	0	1	0
Totals			10 F	0 A	6 nf	2 na

^{a} The numbers within parentheses refer to the table containing the relevant data.

^{b} F indicates a statistically significant skewing in support of ("for") the hypothesis, A indicates a statistically significant skewing in nonsupport of ("against") the hypothesis, nf and na indicate, respectively, NONsignificant skewings in support of ("for") and in nonsupport of ("against") the hypothesis.

5. ADDITIONAL EVIDENCE: VARIATION ACROSS DISCOURSE TYPES

Additional evidence for our analysis is provided by the difference between corpus H and corpus N in the ratio of the total number of occurrences of *deze* to the total number of occurrences of *die*, shown below:

TABLE 12
TOTAL NUMBER OF OCCURRENCES OF *deze* AND *die* IN THE TWO CORPORA

Corpus	N *deze*	N *die*	Total N	Percentage *deze*	
N	252	115	367	68.6	WR = 3.22, $p \ll .001$.
H	104	153	257	40.5	

Deze is more than three times as frequent in N than in H (a skewing that could occur by chance far less than once out of a thousand times). Why?

We argue that the far greater utilization of *deze* in corpus N reflects THE GREATER COMPLEXITY OF MESSAGES IN N and, thus, strongly supports our analysis. On a purely common sense basis, it is apparent that philosophic discourse, making precise discriminations, is harder to understand than a historical narrative or an emotional outburst. The more technical the discussion, the more the speaker will have to induce the hearer to keep the various referents straight and the greater the appropriateness of HIGH DEIXIS. Certainly, nowhere in N does one find examples of pure rapture such as *dat ongelooflijk lange haar . . . die ogen als zwarte sterren*, 'that unbelievably long hair . . . those eyes like black star's (Haasse 1972:114), where *die* is chosen for emphasis. Accordingly, the favoring of *deze* in precise philosophic analysis and of *die* in the descriptive (and often emotional) historical essay is entirely consistent with the meanings we have proposed.

As support for this line of argument, we cite three skewings found in the data of a detailed computer study of Dutch word frequency (uit den Boogaart 1975). First, as one moves from novels through family magazines to popular scientific works, there is a systematic favoring of *deze* over *die*; the figures are 25.3% *deze* ($N = 722$), 46.2% *deze* ($N = 967$), and 70.6% *deze* ($N = 1,104$), respectively. Second, the overall relative frequency of *deze* is far higher in writing (56.0%, $N = 4,811$) than in speech (7.2%, $N = 1,910$). Third, as shown in Table 13 (to follow), the favoring of *deze* over *die* in writing correlates with a similar favoring of the definite article *de* over *die*.

TABLE 13

PERCENTAGES OF DEMONSTRATIVES AND DEFINITE ARTICLE IN SPOKEN AND WRITTEN DUTCH
(calculated from data in uit den Boogaart [1975])

	N *deze*	Percentage *deze*	N *die*	Percentage *die*	N *de*	Percentage *de*	Total N	Percentage
Written (a)	2,693	4.9	2,118	3.9	50,182	91.2	54,993	100
Spoken (b)	138	2.7	1,772	34.1	3,291	63.2	5,201	100
Difference (a − b)		+2.2		−30.2		+28.0		

Taking the first skewing first, we assume that novels (read for relaxation) pose less of an inferential load than does the combination of stories, recipes, gossip, and advice found in family magazines and that these, in turn, are certainly less taxing than are explanations of cyclotrons or of the genetic code. The correlation of the use of *deze* with the difficulty of the subject matter thus supports our analysis. The favoring of *deze* in writing versus speech reflects, in its turn, the greater polish and deliberateness of written discourse (Bolinger 1975:479); one can get away with imprecision in speech because the immediate context communicates so much more (Keenan 1977:16). Finally, the favoring of *de* over its de facto "emphatic allomorph" *die*[7] in writing suggests that emotional messages are, indeed, less frequent in writing than in speech. This corroborates the above characterization of writing as "deliberate" and explains why *deze* (whose meaning would lend itself to messages of discrimination rather than emphasis) is favored there.

To sum up: The relative frequencies of *deze* and *die* in different types of discourse reflect the usefulness of their respective meanings in communicating different types of messages. If it can be agreed that analytic philosophy, (corpus N), popular science, and written language in general pose greater inferential burdens than history (corpus H), novels, and spoken language in general, then the favoring of *deze* in the former supports our claim that *deze* insists more strongly than does *die* that the hearer find the referent.

6. PROXIMITY REVISITED

Having argued for an analysis in which neither demonstrative specifies the referent's physical position, we must now account for the fact that,

---

[7] See example (2) in Section 2.

when they are used to communicate distance, *deze* is always associated with proximity. Clearly, if proximity is not part of *deze*'s MEANING, this restriction must result from factors independent of that meaning that limit the inferences people make from it. We suggest here three possible factors for future research.

First, human beings are egocentric, regarding their own experiences as more interesting than those of others (Carnegie 1973:60, James 1950:289). If the speaker directs attention most vigorously to what he finds noteworthy, then he would find things near him noteworthy and would use HIGH rather than LOW DEIXIS to refer to them.[8]

Second, HIGH DEIXIS is more appropriate than LOW DEIXIS when the referent needs to be pointed out with precision. Consider now the different effectiveness of pointing near and pointing far. Imagine the speaker to be the center of a series of concentric circles. If the hearer learns that an object is in the innermost circle (near the speaker), he gains more information and can locate the object more accurately than if he learns that it is outside (far from the speaker). Accordingly, pointing near is by nature more precise than pointing far[9] and could become naturally associated with the greater precision suggested by HIGH DEIXIS.

Third, people develop behavioral routines—standard ways of solving problems (García 1977:150–151). Granted (*a*) that the strategy of correlating proximity with deictic strength is motivated from (i) egocentricity and (ii) the greater precision of near pointing; (*b*) that this strategy works; and (*c*) that no obvious communicative purpose would be served by deviating from it, it could understandably become institutionalized, abandoned no more easily than the "strategy" of driving on the right side of the road.[10] In this regard we stress that the strategy exemplifies the use of language for DESCRIPTION rather than for COMMENT (García 1975:51–52, Zubin 1972:17). If communication is to succeed, subjective comment on a situation can be indulged in only after the objective facts are known. When the speaker must

---

[8] Alternatively, it might be suggested that "egocentricity" itself will ultimately prove to be a cover term for a complex of factors, including perceptual salience. If so, one could argue that what is near the speaker will be more salient to him than what is far and that the speaker would, accordingly, want to comment on it to the hearer and to direct the hearer's attention to it more forcefully.

[9] Anecdotal evidence for congruence of precise locating with nearness is provided by the English adverb *right*, characterized by Bolinger (1972:52) as "indicating precise direction and location [in space and time]." Observe as evidence for precision that *He came right at 3:15* is more acceptable than **He came right in 1945*. Then, note such contrasts as *Please come* (*right*) *this way* / *Please go* (*right) *that way*; *He was sitting* (*right*) *next to me* / (*right) *far from me*, etc.

[10] For discussion of standard inferential strategies, in particular, of the role of habit in curtailing BUT NOT ELIMINATING inference in language use, see García (1975:49–50, 434–436).

use deixis to describe objective, physical distance, he is less free to simultaneously use it for other purposes.

Now, as noted in Section 2, an alternative to our relatively abstract analysis is Paardekooper's suggestion that *deze* is explicitly PROXIMATE and *die* unmarked. If, for the sake of the argument, we equate "unmarked demonstrativity" with deixis so that in both analyses both demonstratives instruct the hearer to find the referent, the issue becomes whether *deze* contrasts with *die* (*a*) in INSTRUCTING the hearer more forcefully (as we claim); or (*b*) in explicitly DESCRIBING the referent as near.

One way to defend (*b*) would be to demonstrate that each statistical skewing cited in Sections 4 and 5 illustrates some METAPHORIC kind of nearness. It will be obvious that, as one proceeds down the list count by count, it becomes harder to find the "right" metaphor. Because a speaker is likely to be human, named, and a single thing, he will perhaps view named, single humans as "nearer" to him (in some abstract "attribute-space") than unnamed, nonhuman pluralities (Tables 2, 3, 4). But it is not clear how referents in a discussion of cyclotrons or analytic philosophy are more explicitly closer than are those in a novel or an essay about a sculpture garden (Table 12). Neither is it clear how referents in written discourse are explicitly nearer than are those in spoken discourse (Table 13). The "metaphor" defense of Paardekooper's suggestion accordingly does not convince.

A second option is to argue essentially as we have, that is, that *deze* functions as a stronger demonstrative than does *die*, but to derive its strength from PROXIMATE rather than from HIGH DEIXIS. Now, when *deze* is used in pointing out a physical object, the meaning PROXIMATE, DESCRIBING the referent's position, could indeed direct the hearer to it more effectively than an "unmarked demonstrative." But when the referent is not physically near, PROXIMATE must be taken as comment, not as description, and its added strength must be an inference. Presumably, the speaker asserts that the referent is near in order to communicate something else about the referent that would be true if it WERE near. Now, given that the speaker can point out a near thing more precisely than a far one and can scrutinize it more intensely, the claim of nearness allows for the possibility (*a*) that the speaker has chosen to be near the referent; hence (*b*) that he is concentrating on it; hence (*c*) is involved with or interested in it; and hence (*d*) that the hearer should attend to it in order to understand the speaker. We thus move from "X is near speaker" to "speaker is involved with X" (which can be true of referents not physically near) to "hearer should concentrate on X." Accordingly, where the metaphorical approach fails, Paardekooper's defender must invoke an inferential chain that seems to us to be at least as complicated as what we have suggested, starting with HIGH and LOW DEIXIS. Is such a chain synchronically real? This depends on whether one assumes, as we do, that grammatical meanings are typically imprecise and that the detail of messages is "filled in" by inference or that meanings are typically precise and are synchronically "bleached" by incompatability. In our opinion, "The best meaning is the least meaning [Joos 1972:257]"; to start with PROXIMATE seems as unrealistic as arguing that the epistemic senses of the English modals derive SYNCHRONICALLY from the root senses, for example, that *may* in *That lump may be a tumor* still signals only PERMISSION but communicates "possibility" because (*a*) permitted states are usually thought of as possible; and (*b*) the speaker cannot literally grant permission to a lump.[11] Note, however, that the instant one moves away from a purely literal PROXIMATE to something more abstract—for example, *deze* = SPEAKER'S RESPONSIBILITY or SPEAKER'S CONCERN, etc.—then the restriction of *deze* to physical proximity is no longer AUTOMATICALLY built into its meaning and one has to invoke the same extralinguistic factors that we have in order to explain it.

Ultimately, one's analysis of *deze* and *die* must reflect his theoretical assumptions, whether overt or covert. Here, we have taken the Saussurean view that the only arbitrary aspect of language is "the sign"—the association of a particular signal with a particular meaning. From that viewpoint, the distribution of the signal (as evidenced, say, by counts) is not arbitrary but is a consequence of (*a*) its meaning, (*b*) the characteristics—interests, perceptual biases—of speakers; and (*c*) the type of message the speakers wish to convey (Reid 1977:74). Consequently, in postulating a meaning to explain a signal's distribution, one must take care not to attribute to (*a*) what really "belongs" to (*b*) or (*c*). Given that humans are generally egocentric, we have, therefore, not postulated PROXIMATE or SPEAKER'S CONCERN versus UNMARKED to explain uses of *deze* that can reasonably be held to mirror

---

[11] Precisely because permitted states (events) form a subset of possible ones, it would seem SYNCHRONICALLY more realistic to take the epistemic senses as basic and to view the root senses as inferences (cf. Diver 1964), at least if one wishes to avoid postulating homonymous modals. This requires that the grammarian recognize that what was diachronically a broader, metaphorical use of the meaning of a signal (e.g., "possibility" from PERMISSION) may become its actual meaning at a later stage and that its original, more restricted literal meaning will then, at that later stage, have to be viewed simply as an inference—a richer, more precise interpretation of the new meaning (e.g., POSSIBILITY) in a specific context. It must be noted in this regard that the issue of homonymy versus pseudo-homonymy is particularly thorny; as a form–content analyst with a decidedly Saussurean viewpoint, I probably tend to err in the direction of not recognizing homonymy where it may exist, rather than the reverse. However, whereas it might be (and usually is) argued that English modal verbs are homonymous (e.g., two *mays*, one epistemic, the other deontic), no one has even suggested that the Dutch demonstrative adjectives are. Accordingly, granted that locative meanings would be a plausible DIACHRONIC SOURCE of the present system, we argue that these meanings have been reinterpreted such that, if we postulate one and only one SYNCHRONIC meaning for *deze* and one and only one SYNCHRONIC meaning for *die*, neither is locative.

this egocentricity. A further, heuristic consideration is that grammatical systems have typically been found to subcategorize homogeneous semantic fields (for example, time; cf. Diver 1975:23–25). The meanings HIGH and LOW DEIXIS, forming a unidimensional scale, clearly have more to do with each other than PROXIMATE or SPEAKER'S CONCERN does with UNMARKED DEMONSTRATIVITY. Finally, by proposing "instructional" rather than "descriptive" meanings (cf. Diver 1975:11), we account directly for the entire range of uses of the Dutch demonstratives in centering the hearer's attention on the referent in space, time, or discourse.

7. CONCLUSION

We have argued in this chapter that the actual use of *deze* and *die*, as illustrated by examples and frequency counts, is better explained by the "instructional" meanings HIGH DEIXIS and LOW DEIXIS than by locative analyses. Though other languages exhibit some of the same skewings noted here,[12] we stress that our deictic system is proposed solely for Modern Standard Dutch. Since no one else has suggested an analysis that we think fits the synchronic Dutch facts, we would be content if ours were seen as a step in the right direction. As for the history of the Dutch demonstratives, in particular, whether our deictic meanings make sense given the diachronic evolution, we can say only that, to be able to answer, we need statistical studies of earlier texts. Despite the descriptions of the demonstratives and articles found in historical grammars (e.g., Stoet 1923, van Loey 1964), the correct analysis of Middle or even Seventeenth Century Dutch is no more obvious in advance (nor independent of one's theoretical viewpoint) than is the analysis of the modern language.[13] Clearly, much work, synchronic and diachronic, remains to be done. Perhaps this paper—an attempt to pose the problem of the Dutch demonstratives "in ways that Lord Kelvin would appreciate [Ladefoged 1976:19]"—namely, QUANTITATIVELY—will constitute a reasonable beginning.

[12] For example, the favoring of *deze* by singular NPs appears to have a parallel of sorts in Korean. Ree (1975) observes that the demonstrative *ku* (with contrastive and emotive uses) forces a singular interpretation upon unmodified nouns (interpretable elsewhere as either singular or plural), so that the otherwise optional plural affix *-tal* must be used if plural reference is intended. This suggests some sort of link between "demonstratives" (used in "picking out" referents) and "singularity," in particular, between "demonstrative STRENGTH" and "singularity," which would be worth investigating. One would want to know (a) whether such correlations occur in many languages; and (b) what CONSTITUTES "demonstrativity" in those languages (deixis? locative meanings? something else?).

[13] There is no evidence in Stoet (1923) or van Loey (1964) that the demonstratives in earlier attested Dutch were more limited to purely locative context than are the modern ones.

ACKNOWLEDGMENTS

Work on this topic was supported by Research Grant 2964 from the Academic Senate of the University of California at Los Angeles. I would like to acknowledge the helpful comments and stimulating questions of Francis Bulhof, William Diver, Erica García, Talmy Givón, Paul Hopper, Ed Keenan, Wallis Reid, Jaap de Rooij, William Shetter, Sandra Thompson, Harriet Wolf, and David Zubin. Thanks are also due my informants: Adelita Bonebakker, Seeger Bonebakker, and Marcel van den Broecke.

REFERENCES

Baker, S (1976) *The Complete Stylist and Handbook*, Thomas Y. Crowell Company, New York.
Bech, G. (1952) "Über das niederländische Adverbialpronomen ER," *Travaux du Cercle Linguistique de Copenhague 8*.
Bolinger, D. (1972) *Degree Words*, Mouton, The Hague.
Bolinger, D. (1975) *Aspects of Language*, Harcourt, Brace, and Jovanovich, New York.
Boogaart, P. C. uit den, ed. (1975) *Woordfrequenties in Geschreven en Gesproken Nederlands*, Werkgroep Frequentie-Onderzoek van het Nederlands, Oosthoek, Scheltema, and Holkema, Utrecht.
Carnegie, D. (1963) *How to Win Friends and Influence People*, Pocket Books, New York.
Chafe, W. (1974) "Language and Consciousness," *Language* 50, 111–153.
Contini-Morava, E. (1976) "Statistical Demonstration of a Meaning: The Swahili Locatives in Existential Assertions," *Studies in African Linguistics* 7, 137–156.
Diver, W. (1964) "The Modal System of the English Verb," *Word* 20, 322–352.
Diver, W. (1969) "The System of Relevance of the Homeric Verb," *Acta Linguistica Hafniensia* 12, 45–68.
Diver, W. (1975) "Introduction," *Columbia University Working Papers in Linguistics* 2, 1–25.
Frank, A. (1959) *Het Achterhuis*, Contact, Amsterdam.
Frank, A. (1966) *Diary of a Young Girl*, Pocket Books, New York.
García, E. (1975) *The Role of Theory in Linguistic Analysis: The Spanish Pronoun System*, North Holland, Amsterdam.
García, E. (1977) "On the Practical Consequences of Theoretical Principles," *Lingua* 43, 129–170.
Givón, T. (1976) "Topic, Pronoun, and Grammatical Agreement," in C. Li, ed., *Subject and Topic*, Academic Press, New York, pp. 149–188.
Haasse, H. (1972) *De Tuinen van Bomarzo*, Querido, Amsterdam.
Haeringen, C. van (1954) *Genus en Geslacht*, Meulenhoff, Amsterdam.
Hermans, W. (1962) *The Dark Room of Damocles* (R. Edwards, trans.), Heinemann, London.
Hermans, W. (1971) *De Donkere Kamer van Damocles*, Van Oorschot, Amsterdam.
Hertog, C. den (1973) *Nederlandse Spraakkunst, Derde Stuk, De Leer van de Woordsoorten, Ingeleid en bewerkt door H. Hulshof*, Versluys, Amsterdam, [Annotated reprinted of the edition of 1903].
Hinds, J. (to appear) "Paragraph Structure and Pronominalization," *Papers in Linguistics*.
Hodges, J. (1956) *The Harbrace College Handbook*, Harcourt, Brace, and Company, New York.
Houston, J. (1976) *Fundamentals of Learning*, Academic Press, New York.
James, W. (1950) *The Principles of Psychology*, vol I, Dover, New York.
Joos, M. (1972) "Semantic Axiom Number One," *Language* 48, 257–265.

Keenan, E. O. (1977) "Why Look at Unplanned and Planned Discourse?" in E. Ochs Keenan and T. Bennet, eds., *Discourse across Time and Space*, SCOPIL, University of Southern California, Los Angeles, California, pp. 1–41.

Keijzer, J. (1947) "Dit, Dat, en Nog Wat (met Naschrift van C. B. van Haeringen)," *De Nieuwe Taalgids* 40, 164–166.

Kirsner, R. (1972) *On Deixis and Degree of Differentiation in Modern Standard Dutch*, unpublished Doctoral dissertation, Columbia University, New York.

Kirsner, R. (1975) "On the Mechanism of the Restriction of the Dutch 'Pseudo-passive' to Human Actions," *Columbia University Working Papers in Linguistics* 2, 109–143.

Kirsner, R. (1976) "De Onechte Lijdende Vorm'," *Spektator: Tijdschrift voor Neerlandistiek* 6, 1–18.

Klatzky, R. (1975) *Human Memory: Structures and Processes*, W. H. Freeman, San Francisco, California.

Ladefoged, P. (1976) "The Phonetic Specification of the Languages of the World," *UCLA Working Papers in Phonetics* 31, 3–21.

Langacker, R. (1974) "Movement Rules in Functional Perspective," *Language* 50, 630–664.

Lewis, M. (1975) "Determinants of Visual Attention in Real-world Scenes," *Perceptual and Motor Skills* 41, 411–416.

Loey, A. van (1964) *Schönfelds Historic Grammatica van het Nederlands*, W. J. Thieme and Cie, Zutphen.

Nuchelmans, G. (1969) *Overzicht van de Analytische Wijsbegeerte*, Spectrum, Utrecht.

Paardekooper, P. (1968) *Beknopte ABN-Syntaksis*, Malmberg, Den Bosch.

Posner, M. (1973) *Cognition: An Introduction*, Scott, Foresman, and Company, Glenview, Illinois.

Ree, J. (1975) "Demonstratives and Number in Korean," in H. Sohn, ed., *The Korean Language: Its Structure and Social Projection*, University of Hawaii, Honolulu, Hawaii, pp. 33–46.

Reid, W. (1977) "The Quantitative Validation of a Grammatical Hypothesis: The *Passé Simple* and the *Imparfait*," *Papers from the Seventh Annual Meeting of the Northeastern Linguistic Society* 315–334. [Also in *Columbia University Working Papers in Linguistics*, 4, 59–77].

Reve, G. van het (1961) *De Avonden*, De Bezige Bij, Amsterdam.

Rijpma, E. and F. Schuringa (1962) *Nederlandse Spraakkunst, 19e druk bewerkt door J. Naarding*, J. B. Wolters, Groningen.

Stoet, F. (1923) *Middelnederlandse Spraakkunst: Syntaxis*, Martinus Nijhoff, s-Gravenhage.

Straten, H. van (1972) "Samen naar het einde," in J. Deleu *et al.*, *Kritisch Akkoord* , Manteau, Amsterdam. pp. 143–153.

Zubin, D. (1972) *The German Case System: Exploitation of the Dative–Accusative Opposition for Comment*, mimeo, Columbia University, New York.

LEFT-DISLOCATION IN ITALIAN CONVERSATION

ALESSANDRO DURANTI
ELINOR OCHS
University of Southern California, Los Angeles

1. THE SCOPE OF LEFT-DISLOCATION IN ITALIAN

In this chapter we will examine the conditions under which Italian speakers use, in spontaneous conversation, constructions such as those in (1) and (2) below:[1]

(1) (Un amico III:1)
     a Roberto l'ho fatto   aspetta' un'ora
     to Roberto$_i$ him$_i$ (I) made wait   an hour
     'Roberto$_i$, I made him$_i$ wait for an hour.'

(2) (Seminario sulla complementazione)
     "Emme" ce l'avevo io
     "em"$_i$ it$_i$ (I) had I
     '"Em"$_i$, I had it$_i$'

---

[1] All the examples of left-dislocations and any stretch of Italian conversation in this chapter are taken from transcripts of spontaneous conversation. Title, page of the transcript, and, sometimes, contextual information are presented within parentheses, next to the number of the example. Examples with no title are made up. The conventions used in transcribing the audiotapes are those of conversation analysis. We give here some of the conventions and refer the reader to the Appendix in Sacks, Schegloff, and Jefferson (1974) or to Schenkein (1978:xi–xvi) for a more detailed list. The double solidus (//) indicates the point at which the speaker's

Syntax and Semantics, Volume 12:
Discourse and Syntax

We will refer to this kind of construction as "left-dislocation," borrowing the term from Ross (1967).[2] By "left-dislocation" (hereafter "LD") we mean a construction in which a constituent (e.g., a noun, a full pronoun, etc.) that appears before/to the left of its predicate has, within the same sentence, a (nonreflexive) coreferential pronoun [e.g., *l'* in examples (1) and (2)].

---

talk is overlapped by another participant's. Sometimes this convention is accompanied by a long single bracket at the point of overlap, with the talk of the intervening speaker placed beneath:

> (Seminario sulla complementazione)
> G: *Si può dire* ⌈// *ma io non lo dire mai.*
> F: ⌊*Bruttino.*

Talk within parentheses indicates that we were not sure of the transcription. Empty parentheses indicate that no reasonable guess was possible:

> (A tavola:2)
> G: *C'è un controllo odori che è durissimo eh,*
> S: *Eh?*
> G: *C'è un controllo odori di cucina.* ('*Ndo) se fuma.*
> (Un amico II:1)
> Franco: *Sì (   ) dico "secondo me a te non ti va (. . .)*

Material within double parentheses indicates information on voice quality or other characteristics of the speech used: ((WH)) means "whispered," ((LG)) means "laughter," etc.

The equals sign (=) indicates "latching," that is, no interval between the end of a speaker's talk and the beginning of the next speaker:

> (A cena:1)
> Mother: *No.No. O in padella col pomodoro*=
> Father: =*No. Voi ce facevate le patate.*

Punctuation is not used in the traditional way. A period (.) marks a falling intonation; a comma (,) marks a slightly rising intonation; and a question mark (?) indicates a definite rising intonation. Boldfaced material indicates use of stress. Capital letters indicate very high volume.

Certain conventions have been used for the English translation of the Italian examples: In translating the examples interlinearly, a subscripted letter (*i*) is used to mark co-referentiality between different expressions (usually, between a noun or a full pronoun and a clitic pronoun). Full pronouns are glossed with capital letters (e.g., *lui* as 'HE,' *noi* as 'WE,' etc.); clitic pronouns are glossed with small letters (e.g., *gli* as 'to-him/to-her,' *li* as 'them,' etc.); subject–verb agreement is glossed with a pronoun within parentheses (e.g., *vuole* as '(he/she) wants,' *vedo* as '(I) see,' etc.). The apostrophe (') is used to mark the dropping of some segments or syllable either at the beginning or at the end of a word (e.g., *'na* for *una* 'a, 'one' (fem.),' *co'* for *con* 'with'). For the infinitive forms of the verbs, which very often lack the final *-re*, we have adopted the convention of using the apostrophe only in those cases in which, as a result of the dropping, the word acquired a final stress (e.g., *parla'* [par'la] '(to talk' versus *esse* ['ɛsse] '(to) be').

[2] In so doing, however, we are not adopting the generative view that the constituents to the left of the predicate are moved from a more "basic" position. Any proposal concerning the actual formulation of the rule responsible for so-called left-dislocations in Italian is, in fact, outside the scope of this study. (Cinque, 1977, presents some arguments for adopting a "movement" analysis of left-dislocation in Italian.)

Notice that in (1) and (2), as well as in the majority of the examples in our corpus, despite the comma we may use in the English translation there is no noticeable intonational break between the left-dislocated constituent and the rest of the sentence.

Left-dislocations have a rather exotic status as linguistic objects. They are not found in traditional grammars of Italian. Indeed, they tend not to be used in formal Italian discourse, spoken or written. They are, rather, CON-VERSATIONAL CONSTRUCTIONS: They emerge in the interactions of familiars and intimates. LDs are exotic for linguists not only in their context of use but in their construction as well. The notion of "dislocating" involves putting something out of its proper or natural place (Shorter Oxford English Dictionary). The use of this term in the description of this construction implies that the construction is somehow less proper or less natural, the norm being that the left-dislocated constituent typically belongs elsewhere in the construction.

The intention of this chapter is to turn the exotic into the familiar. LD is not a stranger to everyday talk; it appears repeatedly and without notice in informal conversational transactions. Furthermore, it carries out infor-mational and interactional work that is integral to social life. In this sense, LDs are not less or more natural than some "unmarked" counterpart. They simply respond to certain communicative and social demands that their so-called counterparts do not.

How can we gain access to these demands? To be sure, the intuitions of native speakers produce useful insights. However, the complexity of the conversational context taxes the capacity of intuition and judgment alone. To capture the role of LD in conversation, we must turn to conversation itself. Turning to spontaneous talk, we are able to consider not only the conditions under which LDs are produced but also the character of the constructions themselves. In our discussion below, we consider FORMAL PROPERTIES OF NATURALLY OCCURRING LDS. The prosodic nature of LD, the range of constituent types that appear in the left-dislocated position, the type of pronoun that refers to the left-dislocated referent, and the frequency of LD relative to other topicalization construction ("Y-movement," see Section 2) are all described on the basis of recorded and transcribed con-versational behavior.

It is by looking at actual conversation data, as shown in the following, that we are able to discover (*a*) informational similarities between LDs and Subjects; (*b*) an on-going "grammaticalization" process, that is, the rise of a new verb-agreement through the tendency to have a coreferential clitic pronoun with certain kinds of NPs; (*c*) differences between LDs and subjects at the discourse level; and (*d*) differences between subjects and LDs at the interactional level.

All the data used in this chapter are from five transcripts, representing approximately 2 hours of spontaneous conversation in informal situations (among friends, relatives, colleagues), recorded in Rome and transcribed according to the conventions of conversation analysis (see Footnote 1).

Coreferential Pronouns and Subject–Verb Agreement

In Italian, there are two types of definite personal pronouns: the so-called FULL (or TONIC) PRONOUNS (e.g., *lui, lei, noi, me*, etc.[3]) and the so-called clitic pronouns (e.g., *lo, la, gli, ci, vi*, etc.). These two kinds of pronouns behave, in many respects, very differently. Generally, we can say that full pronouns, as opposed to clitic pronouns, behave more like full nouns. For instance, full pronouns can take prepositions (e.g., *a lui* 'to him,' *da lui* 'by, from him,' *per lui* 'for him,' etc.), carry primary (or contrastive) stress, and appear in different positions in the sentence. Clitic pronouns, instead, must occur in very fixed positions, do not carry primary stress, cannot be preceded by prepositions (sometimes they are marked for "case," e.g., *lo* 'him(acc.)' versus *gli*[4] 'to him(dat.)'), and cannot be conjoined with full nouns or full pronouns.

In our data, we found only clitic pronouns used to refer to LD items. Since, in the dialect we are examining, subjects cannot be expressed by clitic pronouns (in other words, there are no subject clitic pronouns[5] in the

---

[3] In our data, as is probably typical of the informal register used in such conversations, the third-person full pronouns for inanimate definite referents are missing, and demonstrative pronouns are used instead (i.e., *questo* or *quello* instead of *esso*). Also notable is the absence of the subject full pronoun *egli* 'he,' normally found in formal (written and spoken) language. (For some interesting observations on the alternation between *egli* and *lui* through an analysis of written texts in both old and modern Italian, see Durante 1970).

[4] In the conversations reported in this chapter, *gli* is sometimes realized as [ye] or [y] (before vowels) and transcribed in the text as *je* or *j'* (on the use of the apostrophe, see Footnote 1), and it can mean not only 'to him,' but also 'to her' and 'to them.'

[5] There are, however, dialects that do have subject clitic pronouns, as is reported in Rohlfs (1968). Here are a few examples:

(i)   *icché tu fai?*   (Florentine)   (cf. Standard Italian *Che tu fai?*)
       what you do
       'what are you doing?'

(ii)   *u piöv*   (Piedmontese)   (cf. Standard It. *piove*)
       it rain
       'it rains.'

(iii) *te,   tu   se' tutto grullo*   (Florentine)
       YOU you are all   nuts
       'You are completely nuts.'

(iv)   *lü   el dorma*   (Milanese)
       HE he sleeps
       'He sleeps.'

Subject clitic forms are also found in the works of Old Italian writers, as is reported in Fornaciari (1881:56).

language), subjects never happen to be LD items. Although we might expect speakers to use, at least in this case, full (subject) pronouns, in fact, they do not (that is, we do not find constructions like *Mario$_i$(,)lui$_i$ è uscito presto stamattina* 'Mario$_i$(,) he$_i$ went out early this morning'.[6]

This fact, that is, no left-dislocated subjects, contrasts with spoken English, in which a large number of LD items are subjects (cf. Keenan and Schieffelin 1976). To understand this "gap" in the data, we must turn to the role of subject–verb agreement in Italian. We will show that many of the features of clitic pronouns are shared by subject–verb agreement, and, hence, subjects, to some extent, always have a "coreferential pro-form" in the sentence, such pro-form being the subject–verb agreement.

SUBJECT–VERB AGREEMENT AND CLITIC PRONOUNS: SHARED PROPERTIES

Grammatical Information.   Subject–verb agreement inflection conveys information about the subject, for example, person, number, and (sometimes) gender.

Consider the following verb paradigms:

(3)   *corr-o*   *corr-iamo*
         run (1st sing.)   run (1st plural)
         '(I) run.'   '(we) run.'

         corr-i   *corr-ete*
         run (2nd sing.)   run (2nd plural)
         '(you sg.) run.'   '(you pl.) run.'

         corr-e   *corr-ono*
         run (3rd sing.)   run (3rd plural)
         '(she/he/it) runs.'   '(they) run.'

(4)   *è stanc-o*   *sono   stanch-i*
         is tired (masc. sing.)   (they) are tired (masc. plural)
         '(he) is tired.'   '(They masc.) are tired.'

         è stanc-a   *sono   stanch-e*
         is tired (fem. sing.)   (they) are tired (fem. plural)
         '(she) is tired.'   '(they fem.) are tired.'

---

[6] The fact that we found no examples of such constructions does not necessarily mean that they are "impossible" or ungrammatical. However, it does say, at least, that such constructions, if used, would probably have quite different environments and/or functions from LDs. Cinque (1977) discusses some (potential) differences between sentences in which the left-dislocated noun has a co-referential full pronoun (e.g., *lui*), which he calls "hanging topics," and the constructions discussed in this paper as LD.

In (3) the suffix marks the person and the number (note that there are no identical forms). In (4) the auxiliary verb *essere* 'to be' marks the person, and the suffix on the adjective signals whether it is singular or plural and whether it is masculine or feminine. The same features are conveyed by clitic pronouns (with respect to their referents):

(5)   *mi conosc-e*   *ci conosc-e*
         me know-s   us know-s
         '(s-he) knows me.'   '(s-he) knows us.'

         ti   conosc-e   *vi   conosc-e*
         you (sing.) know-s   you (pl.) know-s
         '(s-he) knows you.'   '(s-he) knows you (pl.).'

         lo   conosc-e   *li   conosc-e*
         him/it know-s   them know-s
         '(s-he) knows him/it.'   '(s-he) knows them (masc.).'

         la   conosc-e   *le   conosc-e*
         her/it know-s   her/it know-s
         '(s-he) knows her/it.'   '(s-he) knows them (fem.).'

Referring Force.   Verb forms like those illustrated in (3) and (4) may occur by themselves in actual conversation (as well as in written texts), expressing reference with objects identifiable from the spoken or physical context.[7] Notice, in the following passage, how the only linguistic material that

---

[7] We think that this kind of agreement, which we will show to be "pronominal agreement," must be distinguished from other kinds, like, for instance, the agreement of the past participle in the past tense (*passato prossimo*) with the direct object. This is illustrated in the following examples:

(i)   *ho visto   la ragazza*   → *l'   ho   vist-a*
           (I) have seen the girl   her (I) have seen-fem. sing.
           'I have seen the girl.'   'I have seen her.'

(ii)   *ho mangiato   gli spaghetti* → *li   ho   mangiat-i*
           (I) have eaten the spaghetti   them (masc.) (I) have eaten-masc. pl.
           'I have eaten the spaghetti (pl.).'   'I have eaten them.'

This kind of agreement [illustrated in (i) and (ii)] cannot have a pronominal force, that is, cannot appear by itself. It must always co-occur with the DO; usually when the DO is a clitic pronoun, as shown above, but, for some speakers, as pointed out by Parisi (1975), sentences like (iii) are also possible:

(iii)   *ho   lavat-e   le camicie*   (instead of *ho lavato le camicie*)
           (I) have washed-fem. pl. the shirts
           'I have washed the shirts.'

clearly marks the switching of reference from the first person singular (the speaker) to the second person singular (the other character in the story) is represented by the subject–verb agreement (e.g., *arriv-o* '(I) arrive,' *sa-i* '(you) know,' *aspett-i* '(you) wait for,' etc.):

(6)   (Un amico, III:1); Franco is recalling his arrival in Torino and is telling Andrea how mad he got at Roberto for not being at home waiting for him).

Franco: *La prima cosa che faccio faccio "a   Robe' ( )*
the first   thing that (I) do (I) say hey Roberto

una volta mi avresti   trattato un po' meglio eh,"
once   me (you) would have treated a bit better

gli   ho   detto no,
to-him (I) have said y'know

Andrea: *Perché?*
why

Franco: *Eh. Inzom-* **arrivo.** *Lo* **sai** *che* **arrivo.**
well. y'know- (I) arrive it (you) know that (I) arrive.

Eh. Eh. Almeno **passa a** * * **ca**sa *aspetti   che* **arrivo**
Okay. At least (you) pass home (you) wait that (I) arrive

e   poi m-me porti   fuori no,   no che arrivo a
and then me   (you) take out okay, not that (I) arrive

casa non c'è nessuno. C'è   tua   madre . . .
home there's nobody there's your mother

'Franco: The first thing that I do I say "hey man, once you would have treated me a bit better, uhm" I told him, y'know.
Andrea: Why?
Franco: Well. I arrive, you know that I will arive, okay. At least you (could) come home and wait until I arrive and then take me out, okay. (You don't do that when) I arrive there's nobody at home. There's your mother. . . .'

Such a "pronominal" function of subject–verb agreement is not restricted to first and second person. In (7), for instance, a speaker (i.e., Mother) introduces a referent (*Alberto. L'idraulico,* 'Alberto. The plumber'). Once recognition has been obtained by the other party (i.e., Son), Mother proceeds with the story, which also involves another person (*un operaio suo* 'one of his workers'). Afterward, verb agreement is used to refer to and to differentiate between both referents together [*c'hanno aspirato* '(they) sucked for us'] and only one of them [*c'ha prestato un motorino* '(he) lent us a motor']:

(7)   [A cena: 14, the mother is telling her son about an accident that occurred on a summer vacation day (Ferragosto), when the water heater in the house broke and they were looking for a plumber].

Mother: *I*   **giorni** *di Ferragosto che* **figu**rate   *non   trovi*
they days   of Ferragosto that (you) imagine don't find

nessuno. Per fortuna abbiamo   trovato Alberto.
nobody Fortunately (we) have found   Alberto.

L'idraulico   (dell' acqua). Lo conosci   no,
The plumber of the water   him (you) know don't

┌//*quel-* (   ) *giovane che*
│   (you) that- young   who
Son: └*Mh.*
(2.0)

Mother: *Quello   è* **venu**to. *Insieme a   un operaio suo.*
that (one) is come   together with a   worker (of) his.

C'hanno-   co' 'na pompa. C'hanno   aspirato
(They) have with a   pump   to-us (they) have sucked

co- a **bo**cca *eh,*
with- mouth y'know
(1.5)

Mother: *Inzomma. C' ha   prestato un motorino nu-o-vo.*
In short. to-us (he) has lent a   motor   NEW

'Mother: In the days in the middle of the summer that you can imagine how difficult it is to find somebody. Fortunately we found Alberto. The plumber (of/for the water). You know him don't you? ┌// That young guy who-
Son: └*Mh.*
(2.0)

Mother: That one came, with an assistant. They did- with a pump. They sucked with their mouths you know.
(1.5)

Mother: In short, He lent us a NEW motor.'

A similar function is performed by clitic pronouns, as can be inferred from examples (6) and (7) [e.g., in (6), *me porti fuori* '(you) take *me* out,' and in (7), *c'ha prestato* '(he) lent *us*'].

STATISTICAL EVIDENCE FOR A SIMILAR INFORMATIONAL ENVIRONMENT OF SUBJECT–VERB AGREEMENT AND CLITIC PRONOUNS.

Both subject–verb agreement and clitic pronouns are typically used to refer to items that have been previously identified and/or established as topic.[8]

This common characteristic of subject–verb agreement and clitic pronouns can be checked by looking at the immediate preceding discourse, as shown in Table 1.

TABLE 1
INFORMATIONAL ENVIRONMENT OF SUBJECT–VERB AGREEMENT, CLITIC PRONOUN, FULL SUBJECT, AND LEFT-DISLOCATED NOUN AND PRONOUN REFERENTS

	Subject–verb agreement	Clitic pronouns	Subject full pronouns	Subject full nouns	Left-dislocated pronouns	Left-dislocated nouns
Total number	100	76	100	62	20	25
Number mentioned in immediately prior discourse	72	55	41	17	13	6
Percentage	72	72.4	41	27.4	65	24

This table indicates how often the referents are mentioned in immediately prior discourse (i.e., in the prior one or two clauses). As one can see, subject–verb agreement and clitic pronouns (with no co-occurring co-referential full nouns or pronouns) show striking similarity. Referents of subject–verb agreement are mentioned 72% of the time within the two immediately prior clauses, and referents of clitic pronouns are mentioned 72.4% of the time with respect to the same environment (i.e., two clauses back). These numbers contrast considerably with those of full nouns and full pronouns. Subject full pronouns are mentioned 41% of the time in the two prior clauses, and subject full nouns are mentioned only 27.4% of the time (we will return to these figures in a later discussion on givenness).

[8] Notice that, despite the naturally "unique" reference of first-person singular verb agreement, the speaker usually is not entitled to introduce himself into the story–conversation by simply using the subject verb agreement or the clitic pronoun. In most of the cases, a full pronoun (e.g., *io, me*) is needed, as many instances in our transcripts show.

2. CLITIC PRONOUNS AS AGREEMENT MARKERS

We have shown that sentence-initial subjects and left-dislocated constituents share several features. A major barrier, however, remains before
the total collapsing (at least from a strictly grammatical point of view) of
subjects and left-dislocated items: the obligatory nature of subject–verb
agreement on the one hand and the supposedly "optional" nature of pronominalization on the other hand.

In this section, we will show that, at least for certain kinds of NPs, this
barrier tends to disappear and the presence of a coreferential co-occurring
clitic pronoun seems more "natural" than does its absence.

LD versus Topicalization.

In addition to LD, in which, as we saw above, a coreferential copy pronoun appears in the sentence, Ross (1967) mentions another rule that can
move a constituent to the beginning of the sentence, namely, TOPICALIZA-
TION [Postal (1971) calls it "Y(iddish)-Movement"]. This kind of movement
rule does not leave any copy pronoun. Topicalization would produce
sentences like *Giovanni(,) ho visto* 'Giovanni, (I) have seen' or *la camicia(,)
ho comprato* 'the shirt, (I) bought.'

If Topicalization is, in fact, a real alternative to LD in the language, the
"optional" nature of a co-occurring coreferential pronoun in sentences in
which a non-subject constituent appears to the left of the predicate might
be used against the idea of collapsing the distinction between clitic pronouns
and subject–verb agreement. However, in our corpus we found that:

> WHEN A DEFINITE (OR GENERIC) DIRECT OBJECT (DO) OR INDIRECT
> OBJECT (IO) FULL NOUN OR PRONOUN APPEARS TO THE LEFT OF ITS
> PREDICATE, IT ALWAYS CO-OCCURS WITH A COREFERENTIAL CLITIC
> PRONOUN.[9]

That is, we did not find any instance of "topicalized" definite DO or IO.[10]
We then looked at the co-occurrence of coreferential clitic pronouns with
other types of NPs in order to see whether this is a characteristic of LDs
only or whether it could be found with other constructions as well. The
results are reported in the next section.

---

[9] The only two cases of topicalized DOs (we found no cases of topicalized IOs) in our corpus
are both indefinite. We also found two cases of topicalized (definite) obliques (cf. Footnote 10).

[10] Our sample of oblique NPs found at the beginning of sentences is too small (N=4) to
make any percentage really significant. We note, however, that they were all definite. Two of
them were left-dislocated, and two were topicalized.

Co-occurrence of a Coreferential Clitic Pronoun with DOs and IOs

Out of three transcripts we examined, we found that:

1. Of the postverbal full pronouns (DO/IOs), 77% (10) co-occur with a coreferential clitic pronoun.
2. Of the postverbal definite (full) nouns, 20.6% (13) co-occur with a coreferential clitic pronoun.
3. Only 3% (1) of the indefinite postverbal (DO/IO) NPs co-occur with a coreferential clitic pronoun.

These results are summarized in Figure 1:

$$
\begin{bmatrix} \underline{\quad}\ \text{Verb} \\ +\text{Def} \\ +\text{Pro/Noun} \end{bmatrix} > \begin{bmatrix} \text{Verb}\ \underline{\quad} \\ +\text{Def} \\ +\text{Pro} \end{bmatrix} > \begin{bmatrix} \text{Verb}\ \underline{\quad} \\ +\text{Def} \\ +\text{Noun} \end{bmatrix} > \begin{bmatrix} \text{Verb}\ \underline{\quad} \\ -\text{Def} \\ +\text{Noun} \end{bmatrix}
$$

100%	77%	20.6%	3%
(20/20 Pronouns)	(10/13)	(13/63)	(1/37)
(22/22 Nouns)			

Figure 1   Hierarchy of types of NPs (DOs and IOs only) that tend to co-occur with a co-referential clitic pronoun. The symbol "> " means "more likely to co-occur with a coreferential clitic pronoun"; "___ Verb" means "before the verb," that is, NPs (either DOs or IOs) that appear in preverbal position, and "Verb ___" indicates NPs (DO/IO) that appear in post-verbal position. "+ Def" means definite or generic. "+ Pro" means a full pronoun, for example, *lui, lei, noi*, etc., and "+ Noun" means full nouns, like *Roberto, la donna*, etc.

Figure 1 clearly shows that DEFINITENESS is a very important feature for having a coreferential clitic pronoun. It also shows that full pronouns tend almost always to co-occur with a coreferential clitic, no matter their position (i.e., either pre- or postverbally). Table 2 summarizes the results with respect to the distinction between full pronouns and full nouns:

TABLE 2
CO-OCCURRENCE OF COREFERENTIAL CLITIC PRONOUNS WITH
FULL PRONOUNS AND FULL NOUNS

	Full pronouns	Full (definite) nouns
Total number	33	85
Number coreferential clitic pronouns	29	35
Percentage	87.9	41.2

The higher co-occurrence of a coreferential clitic pronoun with a full pronoun can also be seen as a difference between the two grammatical roles of DO and IO. In fact, if we reexamine our figures with respect to this distinction, we find that most of the full pronouns are IOs and most of the full nouns are DOs. This is illustrated in Table 3:

TABLE 3
CO-OCCURRENCE OF COREFERENTIAL
CLITIC PRONOUNS WITH IOS AND DOS

	IO	DO
Total	28	90
Number coreferential		
clitic pronouns	25	40
Percentage	89.3	44.4

In the next section, we will discuss these figures with respect to Givón's hypotheses (Givón 1976) on the rise of verbal agreement in the world's languages.

The Topic Hierarchies and the Rise of Verbal Agreement

Givón (1976) has argued that pronominal verb agreement arises from so-called "grammaticalization" or ("syntacticization") of LDs and RDs (he calls the latter "afterthoughts," following Hyman, 1975). The "over-use" of those two constructions would lead, eventually, from what Givón calls "topic agreement" to subject- or DO- or IO-agreement. Givón (1976) discusses several examples from languages in which present verbal agreement is derived from pronominal sources.

We want here to point out not only that our data seem to show that Italian (at least the dialect we are concerned with in this chapter) might be undergoing the kind of process that Givón describes but also that the direction of the "spreading" of *clitic pronouns toward agreement markers* follows a route also predicted by Givón (cf. also Moravcsik, 1971). There is a series of features that seem to be characteristic of TOPICAL ELEMENTS in the discourse; more simply, features of the kinds of referents that people tend to talk about. Givón presents them in a number of hierarchical relations,[11] here reproduced in (8):

(8)   a.   human > nonhuman
         b.   definite > indefinite
         c.   more involved participant > less involved participant
         d.   Speaker > hearer > others

[11] A similar topic hierarchy has been proposed by Hawkinson and Hyman (1974) in discussing some subjectivization rules in Shona, a Bantu language. Kuno (1976) has also presented some evidence for similar hierarchical relations between different types of referents.

The hierarchical relation (8c) is also related to the following case hierarchy:

(9)   AGENT > DATIVE > ACCUSATIVE

These labels must be interpreted as "deep or abstract" (Fillmorian) kinds of cases.

The "$>$" symbol must be interpreted as "more topical than." In terms of diachronic change, the hierarchies would imply that certain kinds of referents should tend before others to trigger agreement. To a considerable extent, this is certainly true in our data. As we have shown, definite NPs always co-occur with a coreferential clitic pronoun when they are placed to the left of the predicate, and they also tend to have more often a coreferential clitic in postverbal position that indefinite NPs (cf. Figure 1). As a whole, full pronouns tend to have almost always a coreferential clitic pronoun, no matter what their position in the utterance (cf. Table 2). They are supposedly more "given" than are definite nouns (cf. also Table 1 on the immediate givenness of full pronoun subjects as opposed to nouns). All these data confirm Givón's prediction of definite nouns triggering agreement before indefinite nouns [see (8b)]. Table 3 provides some support for the precedence of dative over accusative [cf. (8c) and (9)], at least if we reinterpret them at the grammatical level as IO over DO. As shown in Table 4 (to follow), left-dislocated DOs tend to be human more often than do postverbal DOs. Some evidence, at least in terms of speaker versus others, can also be found for (8d). Out of the 20 left-dislocated full pronouns, 11 refer to the speaker (10 are first-person singular *me*, 1 is first-person plural *noi*), 3 to the hearer, and 6 to third-person referents. Out of the 10 right-dislocated pronouns (i.e., the postverbal ones), 5 were first-person (*me*), 2 were second-person (*te*), and 3 were third-person referents.

TABLE 4

Percentage of Animate–Human Referents (only nouns)
[All our animate referents are also human.]

	(V) DO	(V) IO	LD (DO Only)	LD (Total)	S (V)
Total number	100	3	20	25	62
Number animate referents	12	3	6	9	35
Percentage	12	3	6	36	56.4

The fact that coreferential clitic pronouns might start acting as agreement markers more than as independent pro-forms is also consistent with the fact that we did not find, in the majority of cases, any remarkable intonational break between the left-dislocated (or right-dislocated) constituent and the rest of the utterance. This might be a sign of the fact that they are not VERY marked constructions and that the language has a way of handling them without relying on suprasegmental features like contrastive stress or pauses—by marking the verb by means of a coreferential pro-form (i.e., the clitic pronoun).

In the next section, we will examine in much greater depth the discourse context of LD and subject–verb constructions, both from an informational and from an interactional point of view. We will point out that, even if LD and subject constituents can be distinguished in terms of their informational properties, their main differences are captured by examining their use by the speaker in controlling the conversational interaction (e.g., seeking–holding the floor, selecting next speaker, etc.).

3. THE INFORMATIONAL LEVEL

Sections 1 and 2 have focused on similarities between subject–verb agreement on the one hand and clitic pronouns in left-dislocated constructions on the other. In this section, the focus is rather on the referents themselves. In particular, the focus is on the status of left-dislocated and full-subject referents as pieces of information within a discourse. We will demonstrate that left-dislocated and full-subject referents share strikingly similar informational environments and informational functions. In this sense, subject–verb agreement in full subject (SV) constructions and clitic pronouns in left-dislocated constructions mark the same type of referent.

The Informational Status of Full Subject and LD Referents

Both subject and left-dislocated constituents have been treated as sentence topics (cf. Chafe 1976, Edward Keenan 1976, Li and Thompson 1976). That is, though differing in their syntactic properties, both tend to express what the speaker is talking about. The property of topicality, in turn, has been linked with other informational features. In particular, topics of sentences are described as typically "old" information, information assumed by the speaker to be known to the addressee (Chafe 1976, Clark and Haviland 1977, Firbas 1966, Givón 1979, Halliday 1967, Li and Thompson 1976). The breadth of the term "old information" has been discussed by Chafe (1976), Clark and Clark (1977), and Bates and MacWhinney (in press), among others. Topics can be "old information" in the sense that the speaker assumes that the hearer can identify the referent expressed (i.e., definite information). On the other hand, topics can be "old information" in the sense that the speaker assumes that the referent is currently in the consciousness of the hearer (i.e., "given" information; see Chafe 1976).

We have investigated the informational status of full-subject and left-dislocated constituents with respect to all of these purported properties. In particular, we have examined the status of these entities as (*a*) definite information; (b) given information; and (c) centers of attention. With respect to (c), we have examined not only the status of the constituent in the sentence but also the status of the constituent within the prior and subsequent discourse. That is, we have examined the place of full-subject and left-dislocated referents within the network of concerns entertained in the course of conversational interaction.

DEFINITENESS

Our results strongly support the notion that topic referents are definite information. One hundred percent of the left-dislocated and full-subject nouns and pronouns in our courpus are definite [a total of 45 LDs and 162 subjects (in preverbal position)]. With respect to left-dislocated nouns, this frequency contrasts sharply with postverbal nouns occupying similar syntactic roles. As noted within Section 2, most of the left-dislocated nouns functioned as DOs with respect to their predication. If we examine postverbal DO nouns, we find that only 54% (54) are definite. This difference in frequency suggests that items in left-dislocated positions have more in common with full subjects than with their postverbal syntactic counterparts.

GIVENNESS

In the assessment of givenness, the researcher assumes that the speaker has some basis for considering a particular item to be currently in the consciousness of the hearer. One basis would be that a speaker has JUST REFERRED TO some item in the prior discourse. In our analysis, we have used this basis as one means of determining candidates for givenness.[12]

---

[12] A second basis for givenness would be that a speaker has recently focused upon some item in the physical setting. In the analysis at hand, this selective device was inaccessible to the researchers. The interactions were not videotaped, and, thus, no record exists of eye gaze, pointing, body orientation, and so on. However, apart from references to speaker and addressee, only a small percentage of the referents under consideration [12% (3) of the left-dislocated full nouns] were locatable in the immediate environment.

With respect to speaker and addressee, the problem is rather complicated. The co-conversationalists in this study display that the mere presence of the speaker is not sufficient grounds for assuming givenness. If the speaker has NOT been attended to in recent discourse history, reference will most probably not be through use of subject–verb agreement only. Only 7.1% (8) of first-person referents expressed through subject–verb agreement were NOT located within the recent discourse history of the current utterance. Speakers refer to themselves through subject–verb agreement typically only when there has been some recent mention of themselves. On the other hand, the story differs when it comes to ADDRESSEE REFERENCE. The constraint that the referent (addressee) has to be recently selected for attention is not as strong. Speakers will often use subject–verb agreement to refer to the addressee, even when there has been no recent mention. Indeed, 41.2% (7) of the second-person subject–verb agreement referents were not located in the immediate discourse history (within two clauses back). This difference with speaker reference indicates that speakers may assume that the addressee has been attending to himself even if there has not been talk about himself. The speaker does not assume, however, that the addressee has been attending to the current speaker.

Tables 5 and 6 display the discourse histories of left-dislocated and subject referents. The appearance of the referents in the immediately prior clause, in the second clause back, and in clauses beyond the second clause back are documented:

TABLE 5
PRIOR MENTION OF FULL SUBJECT AND
LEFT-DISLOCATED NOUN REFERENTS

Noun type	Mentioned either one or two clauses back	Mentioned prior to two clauses back
LD	24%	52%
(Total $N = 25$)	($N = 6$)	($N = 13$)
LD (DO only)	30%	50%
(Total $N = 20$)	($N = 6$)	($N = 10$)
Postverbal DO		
(definite only)	18.5%	20.4%
(Total $N = 54$)	($N = 10$)	($N = 11$)
Subject in SV		
constructions	27.4%	50%
(Total $N = 62$)	($N = 17$)	($N = 31$)

TABLE 6
PRIOR MENTION OF FULL SUBJECT AND LEFT-DISLOCATED
PRONOUN REFERENTS

Pronoun type	Mentioned either one or two clauses back	Mentioned prior to two clauses back
LD	65%	30%
(Total $N = 20$)	($N = 13$)	($N = 6$)
Subject in SV		
construction	41%	58%
(Total $N = 100$)	($N = 41$)	($N = 58$)

Table 5 indicates that left-dislocated and subject nouns have remarkably similar informational histories. Their similarities set them apart from postverbal DOs on the one hand and reference through subject–verb agreement or clitic pronouns (see Table 1) on the other. For example, left-dislocated DO and preverbal subject noun referents tend to be mentioned somewhere in the prior discourse (total of 80% of LDs and 77.4% of the subjects in SV constructions); however, postverbal DO referents tend not to be mentioned in the prior discourse (total of 38.9%). Notice that we have confined ourselves to the DEFINITE postverbal DOs. These figures would be even lower if we had considered the indefinite DOs as well.

With respect to the immediate discourse history, both left-dislocated and subject nominal referents tend NOT TO BE EXPRESSED. Adding together the figures for both one and two clauses back, we see that 24% of the left-dislocated and 27.4% of full-subject nominal referents were mentioned in the recent discourse history (that is, either one or two clauses back). As noted in Section 1, these figures are significantly lower than are those for referents expressed through agreement alone (72%) or clitic pronoun alone (72.4%). Furthermore, Table 5 displays that these figures are higher than those for postverbal DO referents (18.5%).

Table 1 and Table 6 indicate that left-dislocated and full pronoun subject referents tend to appear in the recent discourse history LESS OFTEN than clitic and subject–verb agreement referents. The difference, however, is more striking between full pronoun subjects and agreement referents (41% versus 72% appearing either one or two clauses back) than between left-dislocated and clitic pronoun referents (65% versus 72.4% appearing either one or two clauses back).

Summarizing the data examined in Tables 1, 5, and 6, we can order referent types in terms of their likelihood to appear in the recent discourse history of the current utterance:

RECENTLY MENTIONED

MOST LIKELY ————————————————————————————— LEAST LIKELY

| Subject–verb agreement | Clitic pronoun | LD pronoun | Full subject pronoun | Full subject Noun | LD Noun | Post-verbal DO |

CENTER OF ATTENTION

The status of a topic as a center of attention is at once the most significant and the most difficult to assess of the topic properties. Center of attention can mean center of attention with respect to speaker, to hearer, or to both. It can mean center of attention with respect to prior, current, or immediately subsequent concerns. It can mean center of attention of a particular utterance (e.g., sentence topic) and center of attention of a particular discourse (e.g., discourse topic).

SUBSEQUENT DISCOURSE

Discussions of topic in topic-prominent languages (Li and Thompson 1976, Tsao 1977) indicate that, once introduced, topics often dominate subsequent discourse. Subsequent utterances (sentences) often predicate something of the previously expressed topic. To see if left-dislocated and subject referents share this property, we documented the extent to which such referents appear in the subsequent talk. The results are presented in Table 7:

TABLE 7
SUBSEQUENT MENTION OF FULL SUBJECT AND LEFT-DISLOCATED REFERENTS

	Nouns				Pronouns	
	Subjects in SV constructions	LD	LD (DO only)	Postverbal DO (+definite)	Subjects in SV constructions	LD
Total number	62	25	20	54	100	20
Number of subsequent mentions	54	20	17	24	99	19
Percentage	87.1	80	70	44.4	99	95

Table 7 indicates that REFERENTS EXPRESSED IN FULL SUBJECT AND LD CONSTRUCTIONS OVERWHELMINGLY RECUR IN THE SUBSEQUENT DISCOURSE. That is, they continue to receive attention beyond the utterance in which they are expressed. This property again links LD referents closer to subject referents than to their postverbal counterparts. For example Table 7 indicates that 44.4% of postverbal DO referents versus 70% of the left-dislocated DO referents can be found in the subsequent discourse.

PROMINENCE WITHIN UTTERANCE

One measure of the prominence of a referent might be the status of the clauses containing that referent. We compared referent types with respect to whether they appeared in main or in subordinate clauses. The results of this comparison are presented in Table 8:

TABLE 8
PERCENTAGE OF LD AND FULL SUBJECT REFERENTS IN MAIN CLAUSES

	Nouns				Pronouns	
	Subjects in SV constructions	LD	LD (DO only)	Postverbal DO (+definite)	Subjects in SV constructions	LD
Total number	62	25	20	54	100	20
Number of referents in main clause	45	20	16	22	68	17
Percentage	72.5	80	80	40.7	68	85

We can see from Table 8 that both LD and full subject referents typically appear in the prominent portions of utterances, that is, in main clauses. Again, this property separates LD referents from postverbal referents occupying the same grammatical role. Table 8 show that left-dislocated DO nouns appear in a main clause twice as frequently as do postverbal DO nouns.

PRIOR DISCOURSE

In some sense, we have already considered the role of LD and subject referents in prior discourse. We have already provided considerable support for the fact that both types of referent tend not to be mentioned in the immediately prior discourse but tend to be mentioned more remotely in the discourse history. Why, then, do we consider this context again?

A reconsideration is called for because frequencies of prior mention do not tell the whole story. We would not consider a biography to be adequate if it only specified if and when a particular individual existed. We expect a biography to relate something of the significance of the individual with respect to the concerns of his times. Similarly, the history of a referent needs to address the relation of that referent to the concerns expressed in the discourse up to that point.

The question of the relation of a referent to prior discourse can be adequately answered only if the ORGANIZATION OF DISCOURSE itself is considered. The informational structure of a discourse consists of one or more global concerns or themes. These concerns provide a basis for talk, a point of departure. Referents expressed in the course of a text are linked to these themes. Following Fillmore (1975) and Goffman (1974), we may consider these themes as "frames," perspectives that link referents to one another in a semantically coherent way.

When we speak of the relation of referents to one another, the frame is an important variable. Most critically, we need to know if referents are members of same or different frames. This information is not provided in assessments of givenness. An item, for example, may be new to a discourse but either a member or a nonmember of a particular frame. An item that is a new member has not itself been a center of attention but is part of a set of concerns that is currently a center of attention. An item that is a new nonmember has not been a center of attention, nor does it participate in a larger, on-going center of attention.

If we examine the referents of nouns in full subject and LD roles that have not been mentioned (either one or two clauses back), we find that the vast majority are linked to an on-going frame of reference (theme). Out of a sample of 20 noun subjects (SV), 12 (60%) are new with respect to the local discourse history. Ten of these referents are, nonetheless, linked to a semantic frame that is a center of attention in the prior clauses. In other words, the majority of these items share with items in the immediately prior discourse membership in the same semantic frame (see also Sacks 1972). Similarly, of the 25 left-dislocated nouns in our corpus, 19 (76%) are new with respect to the two prior clauses. Of these, 16 (84.2%) are linked to the semantic frame addressed in the two prior clauses. In other words, rarely is a full subject or LD referent not relevant to on-going concerns.

Having established this, let us turn now to the ways in which subject and LD referents may be linked to current frames. Basically, there are two major ways in which referents are tied to the prior discourse: (1) through REPETITION OF A PREVIOUSLY EXPRESSED REFERENT, and (2) through INTRA-FRAME REFERENT SHIFT.

1. REPETITION. With respect to (1), there are two types of repetition found in the data: (*a*) REPETITION OF A PRIOR TOPIC; and (*b*) REPETITION OF A PRIOR NONTOPIC. "Topic" here refers to a referent expressed as subject, left-dislocated, right-dislocated, or fronted constituent. If a subject or LD constituent repeats a prior topic, we refer to this move as TOPIC CONTINUITY and represent is as T → T. An example of topic continuity is provided in the following:

(10)   (Un amico III: 1)

$\overset{T}{\to}$Andrea: *E   lui   c'era,   Roberto?*
         and HE$_i$ there was, Roberto$_i$

$\overset{T}{\to}$Franco: *Sì.   Chiaro.   Ma Roberto è   arrivato **dopo**.*
         Yes. Of course, But Roberto has arrived later.

Andrea: And he was there, Roberto?
Franco: Yes. Of course. But Roberto arrived **later**.

In (10), *Roberto* is the subject of two adjacent utterances. If a subject or LD constituent repeats a nontopic, we refer to this move as a NONTOPIC-TO-TOPIC SHIFT and represent it as NT → T. Examples of nontopic-to-topic shift can be found in (12)–(14):

(12)   (A cena: 9, Father is talking about fixing up a place and the sharing of the expenses)

Father: *Bisogna   vedere se in questo preventivo è:- è compresa*
        (it) needs (to) see if in this   estimate is is included

$\overset{NT}{\underset{T}{\to}}$ *la messa in opera delle   mattonelle. Le mattonelle ve*
$\to$ the setting-up   of the tiles.   the tiles$_i$ you

le   comprate voi.   Ve le   pagate voi.
them$_i$ buy   YOU. you them pay   YOU.

Father: We must see whether in this estimate they included the setting-up of the tiles. (I think that) the tiles$_i$ **you** have to buy them$_i$. **You** have to pay for them.

(13)   (Un amico III: 13, Franco is discussing with Andrea the fact that
          their friend Roberto is into playing bowling.)

Franco: =*ma-ma intanto*   *quello po*(*tresti*) *pure esse*
          but but on the one hand that   could   even be

          bravissimo ma   se' sempre-   è sempre 'na gran
          very good but (you) are always   (he) is always a   big

          pippa. È   quello il   punto io ho voluto //   *vede' com' è*
          Klutz (it) is that   the point I   wanted   (to) see   how is

          ᴺᵀ→ *la questione. Tu   te   compri la palla no,   // prima*
          the question YOU you buy   the ball   okay,   first

          una serie di giustificazioni per di'// *una serie di*
          a   series of justifications to say a   series of

          ᵀ→ *giustificazioni a me pe' fatte   capi'   che la palla*ᵢ
          justifications to ME to let-you understand that the ball ᵢ

          gliel'   avevano quasi regalata. Poi   l'hanno
          to-him itᵢ (they) almost gave.   Then it (they) have

          pagata.
          paid.

Franco: =but-but you could even be very good at it but instead
          you are always- he is always a real Klutz. This is the
          point. I wanted// to see how the situation is. You buy
          yourself the bowling ball okay, // at first a whole series
          of justifications just to say- a whole number with me to
          let me know that the ballᵢ they practically gave itᵢ to
          him as a present. Then instead they paid for it.

(14)   (Un amico III: 1, Franco is reporting a phone call with Roberto.)

Franco: *Allora m'ha   fatto "ah. Va be' così." Dice.*
          Then me (he) has said "ah. okay like that" (he) says.

          "Allora e::   che-che-che   hai   fatto?"
          "Then and: what-what-what have (you) done?"

          M'ha   fatto. No,   "Ho parlato" dico   "un po'
          me (he) has said. y'know, "(I) talked" (I) say "a little

          ᴺᵀ→ *co' tuo padre." Perché poi   chiaramente il   padre*
          ᵀ→ with your father." Because then of course   the father

          ha detto "ah vengo   subito   (ah come?)"
          has said "ah (I) come immediately (what?)"

          dall'ufficio   no,   Allora è   venuto e   m'è
          from the office y'know, Then (he) came and me (I)

          toccato aspettarlo.
          had to wait for him.

Franco: So he said "It's okay like that." He says "Well what-
what-what have you been doing?" He said to me.
Y'know. I said "I talked a little bit with your father."
Because in the meanwhile the father of course (when he
heard that I was there) said "I'll come home right away"
from his office, y'know, So he came and I had to wait
for him.

In (12) and (13), we find two examples of LDs (*Le mattonelle$_i$ve le$_i$comprate voi* 'the tiles *you* buy them' and *la palla$_i$ gliel$_i$'avevano quasi regalata* 'the ball they almost gave it to him as a present') and, in (14), an example of subject noun (*Ho parlato* (. . .) *co' tuo padre* (. . .) *il padre ha detto* (. . .) 'I talked (. . .) with your father (. . .) his father said (. . .)').

2. INTRAFRAME REFERENT SHIFT.   As previously noted, new referents may be linked to larger themes or frames in a number of ways. We find in our data that new referents (subject/LD items) are tied to referents in the immediately previous discourse in two ways: (*a*) ITEM-TO-FRAME SHIFT ($T_i \rightarrow$ Frame$_i$ or Frame$_i \rightarrow T_i$); and (*b*) SHIFT AMONG ITEMS IN A FRAME ($T_i^n \rightarrow T_i^{n+1}$).

In the first case (*a*), the left-dislocated or subject constituent expresses a general concept that previous referents were part of ($T_i \rightarrow$ Frame$_i$) or expresses a member of a general concept referred to in the immediately prior discourse (Frame$_i \rightarrow T_i$). For example, in (15) (to follow), the left-dislocated item *le piante* 'plants' is a generic term covering the previous item *'ste piante* 'these plants.' In (16), the subject constituent *la vita sua* 'his life' refers to a global theme in which immediately previous referents participated:

(15)   (Un amico III: 17, Franco is talking about Roberto's friends, and
in particular of one of them, who is into cultivating orchids.)

Franco: *quello   lì   è il   figlio-   c'ha un   sacco di soldi*
that one there is the son (of)- (he) has lots   of money

a ( ) no,   lavora   per far   soldi.   No,
y'know, (he) works to make money. Y'know,

T_i
$\rightarrow$ *oltre   al fatto   che gli   piacciono 'ste   piante*
besides to the fact that to-him please   these plants

Frame$\rightarrow$ *no,   questo   è uno molto sensibile sai, le   piante*
y'know, this one is one very   sensitive y'know, plants$_i$

le   conosce   molto bene (è) molto bravo
them$_i$ (he) knows very   well (is) very   good

Franco: That one is the son—he's got a lot of money y'know. He works to make money, y'know. In addition to the fact that he likes these plants y'know. This one is a very sensitive (person) y'know. Plants, he knows them very well, he's very good.

(16)   (Un amico III: 7, Andrea and Franco are talking about their friend Roberto's life style, his job, and whether he is going to get a university degree. Andrea says that he asked Roberto how many exams he had taken.)

Andrea: (*be'*) *forse li farà a febbraio*=
        (well) maybe them (he) will take in February

Franco: =*be' communque il fatto che t'ha risposto "zero"*
        well anyhow   the fact that to-you (he) said "zero"

        e non t'ha risposto "no. Cinque" come aveva fatto
        and not answered   "No. Five" as (he) did

        prima (PAUSE) *è indicativo no,*
        before   is indicative isn't it,

        ?:(   )

Andrea: *Cioè quanti ne ha fatti, cinque*=
        In short how   many has (he) taken, five

$\xrightarrow{\text{Frame}}$ Franco: =((high volume)) *La vita sua si va a inserire bene in*
                 the life his goes   well in

        quella che fanno quelli capisci?
        that   that do   those (guys) (you) see?

Andrea: (Certo)
        Sure

Andrea: (Well) maybe he will take them in February=
Franco: =Well. Anyhow. The fact that he has answered "none" and not "five" as he did before (Pause) is indicative isn't it?

Andrea: So how many has he taken, five?=
Franco: =His life fits very well with the life of those other guys you see?
Andrea: (Sure)

In the second case (*b*) ($T_i^n \rightarrow T_i^{n+1}$), the discourse moves from one item to another item relevant to a global theme under discussion. For example, (17) introduces one of a set of items that make noise in the night. The talk had been centered on a barking dog and, then, on thunder. The speaker uses an LD to introduce a further item *tua madre che russa* 'your mother that snores':

(17)   (A cena: 4, At the dinner table, Father, Mother, and Son are talking about the noises they all heard the night before.)

Father: *Io c'è   una cosa de bello che (0.5) prima*
                I there's one thing   good that   before

$\xrightarrow{T_i^{n+1}}$ *d'addormentarme me dà fastidio tutto.   Tua madre*
                falling asleep   me bothers   everything. Your mother$_i$

che russa   non   me ne parla' perché   passano due ore
that snores don't me of it$_i$ talk because pass   two hours

prima che m'addormento. Però una volta che me so'
before that (I) fall asleep. But once   that (I) have

*addormentato, Perché me pijo tutte le sere   la **pillola**=*
fallen asleep, because (I) take all   nights the pill

Father: (As for) me there's one great thing. (0.5) Before falling asleep everything bothers me. Your mother$_i$ who snores, don't even mention it$_i$. Because it takes me two hours to fall asleep. But once that I have fallen asleep, Because I take a (sleeping) pill every night-

Similarly in (18) (to follow), the speaker has been talking about the family of a mutual friend (Roberto). The previous discourse centered around Roberto and his father (*il padre*). The speaker uses a subject (SV) construction to introduce the mother of the family (*la madre*):

(18)   (Un amico III: 5, Franco reports a talk he had with Roberto, in which he, Franco, tried to convince him, Roberto, to be more open with his father.)

Franco: *Secondo   me se vuoi   'n consiglio perché*
                According to ME if (you) want an advice   because

è   inutile che tu   stai così co' tuo   padre
(it) is useless that YOU stay like that with your

inzomma   è una cazz(h)ata
father y'know is a   stupid thing (Pause)

Franco: *La madre è sbottata. Davanti a me.*
                the mother exploded In front of ME

Andrea: *Ah sì?*
                Oh yeah?

> Franco: I think if you want an advice it does not make any sense that you keep this relationship with your father. That is, it's a stupid thing.
> (Pause)
> Franco: His mother exploded. In front of me.
> Andrea: Oh yeah?

After having considered the different ways in which referents are tied to prior discourse concerns, let us examine the FREQUENCY with which each discourse tie appears in the data. A comparison of LD and subject constituents discourse links is presented in Table 9. Not only the presence of specific discourse ties but also the relative absence of discourse ties (interframe shift) is noted.

The first thing to notice from this table is the remarkable similarity in frequency of discourse tie types for subject–verb (SV) and LD construction. Repetion and intraframe linkage are relied upon in roughly the same proportions. Even the proportions of frame–item subtypes are extremely close. In this sense, SV and LD constructions share similar discourse biographies.

However, although the similarities are striking, there is one important difference in the frequency of discourse ties for subject and LD. Notice that there is one type of discourse tie that has NO tokens for LD constituents, namely, that of topic continuity ($T \to T$). Left-dislocations do not appear to repeat an item that has already assumed the status of topic in the local discourse history. On the other hand, 30% of the subject constituents in the sample repeat prior topics.

What does this imply? The significance of this difference is that LD appears to be reserved exclusively for TOPIC SHIFTING FUNCTIONS. Overwhelmingly, the shift of topic remains within the discourse frame of concerns currently attended to (88%). Either a minor sentence argument appearing in the prior

TABLE 9
DISCOURSE TIES

		Subject–Verb (20)	LD (25)
I.	REPETITION:[a]	40% (8)	36% (9)
	$T \to T$	30% (6)	0% (0)
	$NT \to T$	10% (2)	36% (9)
II.	INTRAFRAME SHIFT:	50% (10)	52% (13)
	$T \to Frame_i / Frame_i \to T_i$	20% (4)	20% (5)
	$T_i^n \to T_i^{n+1}$	30% (6)	32% (8)
III.	INTERFRAME SHIFT:		
	$T_i^n \to T_j^{n+1}$	10% (2)	12% (3)

[a] Repetition covers referents expressed within 5 clauses back.

discourse shifts its status to major argument (the LD item) or thematically relevant referents are introduced or reintroduced into the discourse as LD constituents. Subject constituents can do this work, but they maintain sentence topic continuity as well. That is, they are not restricted to topic-shifting, whereas LD is.

4. INTERACTIONAL LEVEL

Margins and Starting Points

The organization and use of word order among the world's languages has been a major concern in linguistics and psychology in the past decade. The two fields draw heavily from one another in addressing this phenomenon. Psychology turns to linguistics for universal (or near universal) word order patterns (synchronic and diachronic); linguistics turns to psychology for possible cognitive and perceptual underpinnings of these patterns.

The interaction between the two fields is evident in pragmatic studies of word-order phenomena. Attempts to assess the importance of context on word order are, by and large, attempts to assess the importance of speakers' and listeners' attention to and knowledge of the propositional context of sentences or utterances. Context is a three-way relation connecting knowledge of the "world," speaker, and listener. Hence, a pragmatic account of word order typically addresses the role of old and new information, theme and rheme, topic and comment, and so on. As discussed in Section 3, in such an account the initial, subject position of the sentence is frequently seen as a locus for information that is known to or salient to speaker, listener, or both. Taking this perspective ourselves, we would say that LDs bring non-subject constituents to the initial "starting point" (MacWhinney, 1977) position to make them topics of the constructions in which they participate.

It is curious that the SOCIOLOGICAL CONTEXT of verbal exchanges has been disregarded as a potential constraint on word order. The status of a speech situation as a type of social interaction is largely ignored. Utterances (sentences) are treated as information units but not conventional, social moves. The use of language to express propositions is acknowledged, but the use of language to exert power and control in a social encounter is never integrated into explanations of word-order phenomena.

In the present section, we propose that the nature and organization of social interaction does influence the organization of word order, that word order satisfies both INFORMATIONAL and INTERACTIONAL functions.

Our concern will be primarily with the relation between conversational interaction and word order, the most prevailing context in which language is employed. In this context, utterances may or may not have propositional content, but they are always either part of or are entire conversational turns (Sacks, Schegloff, and Jefferson 1974). Similarly, in this context, the starting point or margin of a sentence (Longacre 1972; MacWhinney 1977) is a potential or actual starting point of a turn at talk.

Left-Dislocation and Turn Management

When an interlocutor has a turn at talk, he/she is also occupying the floor, in terms of the interaction as a whole. Attempts to take a turn are part of floor-seeking behavior. Seeking, occupying, and holding on to the floor are all means of controlling the direction of talk and the social situation at hand. Seeking the floor, for example, may be part of an attempt to limit the talk of a conversational partner. Holding the floor may be a means of increasing one's own influence and/or preventing another from participating, and so on.

Left-dislocation, like a variety of other constructions, is frequently used to carry out such interactional work. However, one function in particular—that of floor-seeking—distinguishes LDs from full-subject constructions.

FLOOR-SEEKING FUNCTION

One way to demonstrate that LD is widely used to bid for the floor is to show that they appear often in turn-initial position. Table 10 contrasts left-dislocation with subject constructions with respect to this position.

Table 10 indicates that, indeed, turn-initial position is a highly characteristic location for left-dislocation; furthermore, this frequency is not shared with subject constructions. For both pronominal and nominal constituents, left-dislocated constructions appear more than twice as frequently in turn-initial position as subject constructions do.

The frequent appearance of LDs in turn-initial position implies only that it very often is a bid or part of a bid to take up the floor. It, in itself, does not imply that the speaker's conversational partner is also bidding for the floor. A turn may follow a pause or another speaker's utterance. If a speaker uses an LD following a significant pause at a clause boundary, we would not say that there was competitive bidding for the floor. A necessary, but by no means sufficient, condition for alternative bids to occur is that a turn terminate (be bounded by) the turn of a conversational partner. One

TABLE 10
FREQUENCY OF NPs IN TURN-INITIAL POSITION

	Full noun		Full pronoun	
	LD	S (V)	LD	S (V)
Total number	25	62	20	100
Number in turn-initial position	14	13	10	23
Percentage	56	20	50	23

of the first considerations, then, is to assess the frequency with which left-dislocations are bounded by prior utterances versus by prior pauses. Table 11 illustrates these figures.

TABLE 11
FREQUENCY OF TURN-INITIAL LEFT-DISLOCATIONS
BOUNDED BY OTHER SPEAKERS' TURNS

	LD noun	LD pronoun
Total number	14	10
Number bounded by other speaker's turn	13	7
Percentage	85.1	70

Table 11 demonstrates that the majority of turn-initial left-dislocations border other turns rather than pauses.

Once again, we cannot be certain that these data display that left-dislocation is part of some competitive move to take over the floor. A better indication would be the relative number of turn-initial left-dislocations that OVERLAP other speakers' turns. Table 12 indicates these figures.

TABLE 12
FREQUENCY OF TURN-INITIAL LEFT-DISLOCATIONS
THAT OVERLAP WITH OTHER TURNS

	LD noun	LD pronoun
Total number	14	10
Number of overlaps	6	7
Percentage	42.9	70

These frequencies indicate that very often left-dislocations not only border prior turns, but they are also expressed concurrently with another turn. For left-dislocated nouns, roughly 40% of turn-initial utterances overlap other utterances. For pronouns, the percentage is even greater (70%). Notice that, for left-dislocated pronouns, every instance in which a turn-initial utterance bordered a prior utterance, it overlapped that utterance.

These last two tables demonstrate that, minimally, left-dislocations delimit the utterances of conversational partners. Furthermore, they suggest that such delimitation may not be "invited" by the conversational partner. This suggestion is supported by an additional count taken of locations of overlap with respect to prior utterances. An overlap that occurs at the closing portion of the prior speaker's prediction (toward end of clause) is more likely to have been invited by the current speaker than an overlap that appears earlier in the current speaker's turn. Twelve out of the 13 (92.3%) overlaps appear outside the closing portion of the prior utterance. That is, the majority appear to be interruptions that cut off the turn of a conversational partner.

We have, then, evidence that left-dislocation may be used not only to gain access to the speaking floor but also to block or to reduce the access of others participating in the social interaction. That is, left-dislocation may sometimes be a competitive move.

It is difficult to specify what factors encourage competition for the floor. In some cases, it may be the speech event itself. For example, several of our left-dislocations appear in the course of decision making, where interlocutors often disagree with one another's judgments or wish to foreground their own assessment. Additionally, competition for the floor appears greater with an increase in the numbers of conversational participants. Impressionistically, left-dislocations appear to be more frequent in our data wherever more than two interlocutors are engaging in talk. An advanced seminar in which 10 people participated is laced with left-dislocations. An example of rather elaborate competition for the floor taken from this situation is provided in the following. In this example, members of the seminar are discussing whether or not the verb *fuggire* and then *rifuggire* can take a sentence complement. Speaker V introduces the verb *rifuggire*. Once introduced, Speakers L, R, and F attempt to gain access to the floor through repetition of this lexical item.

(19)   (Seminario sulla complementazione)

    A: (. . .) *"Fuggire da:1 far   qualcosa"* *non* *mi* *sembra-*
              "escape from doing something" NEG to-me seems

        non   *mi*   ⌐// *sembra* ⌐// *un buon italiano.*
        NEG to-me | seems | a good Italian
    F: ⌐No.
    V: └(*Ce l'avresti con*)
                        (you) would have it with

        "rifuggir ⌐//*re"*
        "rifug | gire(= re-escape)"
    L: *Rifuggir* ⌐//*e*
    R: └(⌐//)
→
LD F: └*Ri-ri-*
→
    rifuggire già ⌐//   *ce l'abbiamo.*
    rifuggire$_i$ alr| eady it$_i$ (we) have
    A: └*Allora niente   "fuggire"*
          Then nothing "fuggire"

A: (. . .) "Fuggire dal far qualcosa" it doesn't seem // to me//
    good Italian.
F: No.
V: (You could do it (=complementation) with)
    "rifuggi//re"
L: rifuggi//re
R: (//)
F: "Ri-ri-
    rifuggire$_i$ we already have it$_i$.
A: Then "fuggire" should be left out.

WARRANTS FOR THE FLOOR

At this point, we might ask why LDs are effective as floor-seekers. To
understand their effectiveness, we need to consider again the informational
content of left-dislocated constituents and its relation to the informational
content of utterances in the immediately prior discourse.

Jefferson (1978) has pointed that utterances that appear (to a listener)
to be "off the point" are interrupted more often than are utterances that are
perceived as relevant to the topical talk at hand. In other words, utterances
that are not clearly tied to the current theme have a lower life expectancy
than those that address current concerns. Another way of stating this is to
say that successful turns at talk are usually "warranted" by some dimension
of the topical talk at hand. The turn is legitimized in this sense.

LDs are effective means of seeking and of occupying the floor because
they nearly always relate to some general concern under consideration.
The left-dislocated referent itself may have appeared in the prior talk and,
hence, constitute an explicit legitimizer of subsequent talk [cf. the use of
rifuggire in example (19) above]. Or, the left-dislocated referent is semantically linked to general concerns at hand (cf. Section 3). Typically, the
referent is a member of a conceptual domain under consideration [e.g., *tua
madre che russa* in (17) is one of the many things that bother the father at
night, and it does not left him fall asleep; *la stanza* in (20) is one of the things
that need to be cleaned, etc.]:

(20)   (Draft: 1)

    C: *cioè   c'hai   chi ti   fa   le pulizie   inzomma* //e:
        that is (you) got who to-you does the cleaning in   sho rt and
    A: No

        devo-   cioè per   vestiti e   cose   varie   devo   andare
        (I) must that is for clothes and things various (I) must go
        (*alla*)   *lavanderia*
        (to the)   laundry

C: *Ho   capito   ho   capito.*
(I) have understood (I) have understood

→ A: *Per la   stanza me la pulisco   da solo*
(as) For the room$_i$ me it$_i$ (I) clean myself

C: that is you got somebody that cleans up for you // and

A: No I must- I mean for clothes and various things I must go to the laundromat

C: I see I see

A: As for the room$_i$ I must clean it$_i$ up myself.

Recall that the latter environment (member of a set) is the most characteristic one for LDs in our corpus. LDs tend to draw attention to other instances of some general issue. They tend not to be "on-topic" in the sense that the center of attention of the prior turn is sustained in the current turn. As noted, left-dislocated referents appear in the prior predicate if they are to appear at all in the immediately prior context. (Recall that subject referents, in contrast, if they appeared at all, tended to function as subjects of immediately prior utterances). LDs tend to shift attention away from some immediate point of reference (immediately prior subject) to a different point of reference. In this sense, these constructions run the danger of being cut off. If Jefferson's observations are correct, topic shifting must be handled quite carefully if it is to be successful.

LDs may be successful topic-shifters in part because, while shifting focus of attention, they nonetheless are semantically relevant to the prior focus of attention. Indeed, part of the beauty of LDs is that they maintain a subject as well as a focus of attention, and the referent of that subject is often part of the immediate situation or immediate discourse history [48% (12) of subjects in full noun LDs and 37.5% (6) in full pronoun LDs].

Hence, LDs are in two ways warranted by prior consideration, through the left-dislocated referent and through the subject referent. In this sense, a left-dislocated construction is an effective means for changing the direction of talk.

Word Order and Turn Margins

We have demonstrated that there are interactional motives for placing non-subject constituents in utterance(sentence)-initial position. Such constituents may take precedence over subject constituents where the referent is warranted (legitimized) by current concerns under consideration, where the speaker is making a bid for the floor or wishes to hold the floor, and where there is competition for the floor. The referent establishes the speaker's right to talk at that point in conversational time.

The status of an NP as warranted may supercede other reasons for placing an NP in utterance-initial position. Inherent semantic properties of a referent, such as being human or animate or concrete, may assume a secondary role in assessing what will be the initial locus of attention where another type of referent is more clearly warranted by current concerns. The topic-worthiness of an NP is determined not only by inherent properties of a referent but also by its significance and relevance to the situation at hand.

5. LD AS AN ALTERNATIVE TO PASSIVE: A MULTILEVEL EXPLANATION

One striking characteristic of our data is the almost total absence of passive constructions (we found only one instance of passive out of roughly 100 pages of transcripts). This fact contrasts with the common use of passives in formal (written[13]) language.

We find numerous cases of passives in newspaper articles and scientific literature. For instance, 6 examples of passive constructions were found in only one page of a linguistics article ("Con," by Castelfranchi, Parisi, and Crisari, 1974).

At the same time, compared to passives, LDs are extremely rare in formal (written) discourse. Out of several newspaper articles that we examined, we found only one instance of LD:

(21)   (From *Il Messaggero*, Oct. 1976)

Verso   Milano va   il   furgone del   Credito Varesino incaricato
toward Milan   goes the van   of the (bank)   in charge

della   consegna dei   valori. Il   percorso lo fa   cinque volte
of the delivery   of the values. the route$_i$ it$_i$ (it) does five   times

la   settimana.
the week

'Toward Milan goes the van of the Credito Varesino in charge of the delivery of the values. The route$_i$ it does it$_i$ five times a week.'

This kind of complementary distribution of passive versus LD made us think of a possible interchangeable role of these two constructions. In this

---

[13] We will only talk here about formal WRITTEN Italian; we suspect, however, that similar characteristics can be found in formal SPOKEN Italian.

section, we investigate the extent to which LD and passive can perform the same grammatical and/or communicative function(s). We suggest several reasons why speakers prefer LD over passive in conversational interaction.[14]

Grammatical Properties

Passivization in Italian can apply (if at all) only to DOs (we are assuming here, as in other parts of the chapter, that there are such things as DOs in Italian). The rule works more or less as it does in English (mutatis mutandis): The would-be DO of the active sentence triggers subject–verb agreement, and it can occur in sentence-initial position. The would-be subject of the active sentence (if present) takes the preposition *da* 'by' and usually appears at the end of the sentence. An auxiliary verb appears (either *essere* 'be' or *venire* 'come'), and the predicate is changed into a past participle form. This is shown in the following examples (from "Con," cited previously):

(22)   *Le cinque categorie sono esemplificate dalle   sequenti   frasi*
      the five   categories are exemplified by the following sentences

      'The five categories are exemplified by the following sentences'

(23)   *tutta la seconda struttura frasale   deve venir ridotta a un*
      all   the second structure sentential must be   reduced to a

      nominale
      nominal

      'the whole second sentential structure must be reduced to a nominal'

Let us schematically summarize the effects of passivization on the (surface) structure of a sentence:

1.   WORD ORDER: The DO of the active can appear at the beginning of the sentence.
2.   REORIENTATION OF THE PREDICATE: By means of the auxiliary verb (e.g., *essere* 'be'), the predicate is reoriented toward an NP that is not the subject of the active voice. That is, it tells the hearer how to interpret the "new" subject of the sentence (or maybe how NOT to interpret it) by saying something like "the subject here is not the expected one."

---

[14] We are assuming here that our "educated" speakers have the rule of passive in their competence but do not use it in spoken informal.

3.   OPTIONAL APPEARANCE OF THE SUBJECT OF THE ACTIVE SENTENCE:
The referent expressed by the subject of the corresponding active sentence
can either not be expressed [cf. (23) above] or can be "moved" to the end of
the sentence, being marked by the preposition *da* 'by' [cf. ex. (24) above].[15]

Similar effects can be obtained by LD:

1.   By definition, in an LD a non-subject constituent (therefore also a
DO, as was illustrated) is placed at the sentence-initial position.
2.   The verb is "marked" by a pronoun-agreement (i.e., the clitic) that
specifies (some of) the characteristics of the "dislocated" NP (i.e., whether
it is a DO or an IO, e.g., *lo* 'him' versus *je, gli* 'to him').
3.   The referent of the subject can be moved to the end of the sentence,
as in (24) [cf. also examples (2) and (12)]:

(24)   (Seminario sulla complementazione)

    V: *Ma. Non so.   Io l'ho   eliminato. Però. Non*
          But NEG (I) know. I it have eliminated. But   NEG

          so.   Ci   sarebbe anche "struggersi".   Non lo
          (I) know, there would be also "consume oneself". NEG it

          so.   Ma mi   sembra di no.
          (I) know. But to-me seems   of not.
          (Pause)

    V: *"Si strugge   per diventare- per essere: "che   ne*
          (he) consumes himself to become-   to be   "what of it

          so   io ⌐// *"nominato"*
          know I | "nominated"
  → F: └*Questo lo usi   solo te.*
              this$_i$ it$_i$ (you) use only YOU.
      ((LG))

    V: Well. I don't know. I have eliminated it (from my corpus).
         Even if- I don't know. There is also (the verb) "struggersi."
         I don't know. But it doesn't seem right.
         (Pause)

    V: "Si strugge per diventare- per essere: "what can I say? //
         "nominato"

    F: This one$_i$, only you use it$_i$.)

---

[15] On the "demotional" nature of passive in the world's languages, cf. Edward Keenan
(1975). For an interesting study on one language, Dutch, see Kirsner (1976).

or it can be left unspecified by using a third-person plural verb agreement, as in (25):

(25)   (Draft: 10)

>   B: *Ma l'assegnazione del   contingente d'aviazione   la*
>   but the assignment$_i$ of the contingent of Air Force it$_i$
>
>   *fanno   a "NAME OF A PLACE" e-* (. . .)
>   (they) do at "Name   of a place"   and- (. . .)
>
>   B: But the assignment of the Air Force Contingent$_i$ they do it$_i$
>   at "Name of a place"

The only constraint on this last use is that the "unspecified" subject cannot normally be interpreted as the speaker or the hearer, whereas an agentless passive can still have that reading. Probably this means that, even if "unspecified," the third-person plural agreement still conveys the meaning of a "third referent" (i.e., not the speaker or the hearer).

GRAMMATICAL ADVANTAGES OF LD OVER PASSIVE

LD can apply to a wider range of cases than passive. As we have mentioned, passive can apply only to DOs. LD, on the other hand, can apply to almost any kind of grammatical relation–constituent, as far as that constituent can be cliticized. This means, for instance, that LD can be applied to IOs as well as to other prepositional objects, for example, genitives, as in (17); locative, as in (26); etc.:

(26)   (Un amico III: 8)

>   Franco: *In quella banca tra   l'altro   il   padre ce   l'ha*
>   in that   bank$_i$ among the other the father there$_i$ him
>
>   *portato*
>   has brought
>
>   Father: In that bank$_i$ by the way the father got him (a job) there$_i$

Furthermore, notice that, in the dialect we are dealing with in this paper, human DOs are very often marked by the preposition *a*, which is also the usual marker for IOs. It seems reasonable to assume that in those cases in which a nonsubject NP appears before the verb and is marked by *a*, the coreferential clitic (at least for third-person referents for which the clitic pronoun form is different) marks the type of grammatical role that the NP has with respect to the predicate.

Informational and Interactional Properties

Previous investigations of topic have emphasized the relationship between subjects of sentences and topics of sentences. That is, sentence subjects are said to share generally many of the properties of topics (in addition to other syntactic properties). For example, typically, subject referents are referents that appear near or at the top of suggested topic hierarchies: Relative to other constituents, they have a greater tendency to be human, to be first-person or second-person, to be agents, and so on (cf. Givón 1976, Hawkinson and Hyman 1974, Edward Keenan 1976, Kuno 1976). Sentences that contain such subjects are produced and comprehended developmentally prior to sentences with other types of subjects (Bever 1970). Furthermore, in picture-matching tasks, adults are able to verify such sentences more quickly than sentences with other types of subjects (as discussed in Clark and Clark 1977, Gough 1965, 1966, Slobin 1966). Kuno (1976) claims that sentences with such subjects display a natural empathy or identification of the speaker with the subject referent. MacWhinney (1977) indicates that a sentence that expresses an agent in subject (initial) position reflects a simpler perspective than sentences in which the agent is expressed elsewhere. All in all, there is widespread support for the idea that sentences with subject referents high on the topic hierarchy are, under most conditions, cognitively preferable to sentences with subject referents that appear low on the hierarchy.

Passive sentences very often contain such dispreferred subject referents. As would-be DOs of an active construction, they are more likely to be inanimate and/or abstract (Givón 1975, James 1972, Singer 1976). Furthermore, as such, they can never be agents and, hence, appear low on the topic hierarchy. Kuno (1976) suggests that their dispreferred nature accounts for why they appear so infrequently in spoken discourse.

In all of these discussions, there is an assumption that, by-and-large, there is one and only one topic of a sentence and that topic tends to be expressed as the subject of the sentence. Where the speaker is pictured as wanting to topicalize a referent low on the topic hierarchy, he is seen as having to make that referent the subject (producing a passive construction). But, in so doing, he has produced an utterance that is communicatively distressful. Indeed, the topicalization of such a referent in itself appears to violate natural perspectives on situations and events. It is no wonder that we found only one passive construction in our entire corpus!

But should we conclude that referents that are inanimate, third-person, etc, rarely appear as centers of attention, as starting points and initial perspectives in spontaneous, informal conversation? The data in this chapter evidence that such a conclusion should not be drawn. A speaker who wishes to use a nonhuman, nonagent as a point of departure for the rest of his utterance is not restricted to using a passive construction. The language has another option available. The referent may be expressed in sentence-initial position as a left-dislocated constituent.

LDs do not share many of the informationally distressful properties of passives. Although they may express an accusative (patient–affected object) referent in the initial, attention-locus of a sentence, that referent does not replace a referent with preferred topical properties as sentence subject. In passive sentences, the would-be subject of the active sentence is demoted to an oblique argument of the verb. In constructions with an LD, the subject remains as subject, co-occurring with the left-dislocated constituent. In this sense, LDs have two attention foci, two points of departure; that is, they have two topics. A speaker does not always have to CHOOSE between topic candidates; he may give both this status.

This is not to say that both the left-dislocated constituent and the subject constituent are topics of the same type. As discussed earlier, many left-dislocated constituents (e.g., left-dislocated DOs) gain their topic-worthiness because the context imbues them with a heightened importance. Subject referents, on the other hand, generally have inherent importance because of their semantic properties. If we consider the left-dislocated DOs (both nouns and full pronouns), 26.8% (6) were human. The subject referents co-occurring with these referents were human in 100% (23) of the cases.

Furthermore, in saying that LDs have more than one topic, we do not imply that each topic necessarily carries out the same range of pragmatic functions. Our observations indicated that the left-dislocated constituent performs interactional tasks that the co-occurring subject constituent does not. The speaker may use the left-dislocated constituent to gain access to the floor as well as to effect a topic shift (within a general discourse topic). At the same time, we suggest, the speaker wishes to maintain the perspective of the subject referent. Our examination of subjects co-occurring with left-dislocated DOs indicates that, not only are they human, they are also in the majority of cases [73.9% (17)], either as first or as second person (full pronouns or agreement). These co-occurring subjects contain highly salient, highly empathizable informational content.

LDs, then, have advantages over the passive in Italian on the grammatical, informational, and interactional level. Grammatically, as was pointed out, a wider range of non-subject constituents may appear in sentence-initial, topic position. Informationally, a referent low on the semantically based topic hierarchy may be placed in sentence-initial topic-position without replacing or usurping the status of a referent with highly topical semantic properties. Whereas the passive replaces one referent with another in this status, the LD allows both to co-occur. Thus, LDs may carry out interactional and larger topical tasks without disturbing preferred encoding strategies. The near-obligatory nature of the coreferential clitic when a DO or an IO appears in preverbal position provides further support for the existence of two topics, two perspectives in left-dislocated constructions. Like subject–verb agreement, the coreferential clitic marks the left-dislocated constituent as a basic argument of the predicate by encoding its presence and grammatical status on the verb.

ACKNOWLEDGMENTS

We wish to thank all the colleagues and friends who gave us very interesting and detailed comments on an earlier version of this paper: Prof. Marcello Durante, Talmy Givón, Larry Hyman, Robert Kirsner, Brian MacWhinney, Gillian Sankoff, Emanuel Schegloff, and Sandra Thompson. This research was in part supported by the National Endowment for the Humanities (Postdoctoral Fellowship, Grant No. 177106) and by the Consiglio Nazionale delle Ricerche in Rome.

REFERENCES

Bates, Elizabeth and Brian MacWhinney (in press) "The Functionalist Approach to the Acquisition of Grammar," in Elinor Ochs and Bambi Schieffelin, eds., *Developmental Pragmatics*, Academic Press, New York.

Bever, Thomas (1970) "The Cognitive Basis for Linguistic Structures," in J. H. Hayes, ed., *Cognition and the Development of Language*, John Wiley and Son, New York, 279–352.

Castelfranchi, Christiano, Domenico Parisi, and Maurizio Crisari (1974) "Con," *Fenomeni morfologici e sintattici nell'italiano comtemporaneo*, Bulzoni Editore, Roma, 27–45.

Chafe, Wallace (1976) "Givenness, Contrastiveness, Definiteness, Subjects, Topics, and Point of View," in C. Li, ed., *Subject and Topic*, Academic Press, New York, 25–56.

Cinque, Guglielmo (1977) "The Movement Nature of Left-dislocation," *Linguistic Inquiry* 8, 397–412.

Clark, Herbert and Eve Clark (1977) *Psychology and Language. An Introduction to Psycholinguistics*, Academic Press, New York.

Clark, Herbert and S. E. Haviland (1977) "Comprehension and the Given–New Contract," in R. O. Freedle, ed., *Explaining Linguistic Phenomena*, Hemisphere Publishing, Washington D.C., 91–124.

Durante, Marcello (1970) "I pronomi personali nell'italiano contemporaneo," *Atti del convegno di studi su lingua parlata e lingua scritta, Bollettino del Centro di Studi Filologici e Linguistici Siciliani* XI, 180–202.

Fillmore, Charles (1975) "An Alternative to Checklist Theories of Meaning," *Proceedings of the First Annual Meeting of the Berkeley Linguistics Society*, California, Berkeley, 123–131.

Firbas, Jan (1966) "On Defining the Theme in Functional Sentence Analysis," *Travaux linguistiques de Prague* 1, 267–280.

Fornaciari, Raffaello (1881) *Sintassi italiana*, Sansoni, Firenze.

Givón, Talmy (1976) "Topic, Pronoun, and Grammatical Agreement," in C. Li, ed., *Subject and Topic*, Academic Press, New York, 149–188.

Givón, Talmy (1979) *On Understanding Grammar*, Academic Press, New York.

Goffman, Erving (1974) *Frame Analysis*, Harper and Row, New York.

Gough, P. B. (1965) "Grammatical Transformations and Speed of Understanding," *Journal of Verbal Learning and Verbal Behavior* 4, 107–111.

Gough, P. B. (1966) "The Verification of Sentences: The Effect of Delay of Evidence and Sentence Length," *Journal of Verbal Learning and Verbal Behavior* 5, 492–496.

Halliday, M. A. K. (1967) "Notes on Transitivity and Theme in English, Part II," *Journal of Linguistics* 3, 177–274.

Hawkinson, Anne and Larry M. Hyman (1974) "Hierarchies of Natural Topic in Shona," *Studies in African Linguistics* 5, 147–170.

Hyman, Larry M. (1975) "On the Change from SOV to SVO: Evidence from Niger-Congo," in C. Li, ed., *Word Order and Word Order Change*, University of Texas Press, Austin.

James, C. T. (1972) "Theme and Imagery in the Recall of Active and Passive Sentences," *Journal of Verbal Learning and Verbal Behavior* 11, 205–211.

Jefferson, Gail (1978) "Sequential Aspects of Story Telling in Conversation," in Jim Schenkein, ed., *Studies in the Organization of Conversational Interaction*, Academic Press, New York, 219–248.

Keenan, Edward (1975) "Some Universals of Passive in Relational Grammar," in R. E. Grossman, L. J. San and T. J. Vance, eds., *Papers from the 11th Regional Meeting of the Chicago Linguistics Society*, Chicago Linguistic Society, Chicago, Illinois, 340–352.

Keenan, Edward (1976) "Towards a Universal Definition of 'Subject'," in C. Li, ed., *Subject and Topic*, Academic Press, New York, 303–334.

Keenan, Elinor Ochs and Bambi Schieffelin (1976) "Foregrounding Referents: A Reconsideration of Left-dislocation in Discourse," *Proceedings of the Second Annual Meeting of the Berkeley Linguistics Society*, Berkeley, California, 240–257.

Kirsner, Robert S. (1976) "On the Subjectless 'Pseudo-passive' in Standard Dutch and the Semantics of Background Agents," in C. Li, ed., *Subject and Topic*, Academic Press, New York, 385–415.

Kuno, Susumu (1976) "Subject, Theme and Speaker's Empathy: A Reexamination of Relativization Phenomena," in C. Li, ed., *Subject and Topic*, Academic Press, New York, 417–444.

Li, Charles, and Sandra Thompson (1976) "Subject and Topic: A New Typology of Language," in C. Li, ed., *Subject and Topic*, Academic Press, New York, 457–489.

Longacre, Robert (1972) *Hierarchy and Universality of Discourse Constituents in New Guinea Languages: Discussion*. Georgetown University Press, Washington D.C.

MacWhinney, Brian (1977) "Starting Point," *Language* 53, 152–168.

Parisi, Domenico (1975) "Participio passato," in D. Parisi, ed., *Studi per un modello de linguaggio*, Consiglio Nazionale delle Ricerche, Rome.

Postal, Paul (1971) *Cross-over Phenomena*, Holt, Rinehart, and Winston, New York.

Rohlfs, Gerhard (1968) *Grammatica storica della lingua italiana e dei suoi dialetti: morfologia* (translation from German by T. Franceschi and M. Cociagli Fancelli), Einaudi, Torino.

Ross, John R. (1967) *Constraints on Variables in Syntax*, unpublished Doctoral dissertation, Massachusetts Institute of Technology, Cambridge, Massachusetts.

Sacks, Harvey (1972) "On the Analyzability of Stories by Children," in J. Gumpers and D. Hymes, eds., *Directions in the Ethnography of Communication*, Holt, Rinehart, and Winston, New York, 325–345.

Sacks, Harvey, Emanuel Schegloff, and Gail Jefferson (1974) "A Simplest Systematic of the Organization of Turn-taking for Conversation," *Language* 50, 696–735.

Singer, M. (1976) "Thematic Structure and the Integration of Linguistic Information," *Journal of Verbal Learning and Verbal Behavior* 15, 549–558.

Schenkein, Jim, ed. (1978) *Studies in the Organization of Conversational Interaction*, Academic Press, New York.

Singer, M. (1976) "Thematic Structure and the Integration of Linguistic Information," *Journal of Verbal Learning and Verbal Behavior* 15, 549–558.

Slobin, Dan (1966) "Grammatical Transformations and Sentence Comprehension in Childhood and Adulthood," *Journal of Verbal Learning and Verbal Behavior* 5, 219–227.

Tsao, Feng-Fu (1977) *A Functional Study of Topic in Chinese: The First Step toward Discourse Analysis*, unpublished Doctoral dissertation, University of Southern California, Los Angeles, California.

PART V DISCOURSE CONTROL OF SYNTACTIC PROCESSES

ANYTHING *YOU* CAN DO

SUZANNE LABERGE
GILLIAN SANKOFF
Université de Montréal

1. INTRODUCTION

Discourse equivalents—even grammatical equivalents—need have nothing in common but their contemporary struggle: not history, and especially not a common "underlying" form, unless it be one in which the tortuous path to the surface is unnecessarily ad hoc and messy.

In this Chapter we will begin with the story of *on*. Before the current episode begins, plucky little *on* has shed the disyllabic baggage of its ancestor *homo* and has made it out of the content-word status of the masses into the elite corps of grammatical elements. It had done this by adhering strictly to Benveniste's dictum: *Nihil est in* **lingua** *quod non prius fuerit in* **oratione** (1966:131). From lowly beginnings as an indefinite referent, *on* has succeeded in infiltrating the personal pronouns. Not only does it take over at will from *je, tu, ils,* and the rest, but it has also virtually ousted *nous*.

In the present episode, we shall see how the personal pronouns hit back. *Tu* and *vous* have taken up the challenge and are now locked in combat with *on* in a bout for indefinite champion, a title *on* thought it had locked

Syntax and Semantics, Volume 12:
Discourse and Syntax

up. Will this battle for the hearts and minds of the speakers of French be a fight to the finish, or can the adversaries live in peaceful coexistence? (In the meantime, interested parties are advised that they needn't be overly concerned about keeping their grammars tidy.)

2. *ON*, INDEFINITE *PAR EXCELLENCE*

The versatility of the subject clitic *on* 'one' in French is legendary. Derived from Latin *homo* 'man', its original and, perhaps, still in some sense basic referent is indefinite 'anybody'. It is found, for example, in proverbial expressions such as the following, cited from our corpus of Montréal French:

(1)   *Mon père disait tout le temps, "Bien, quand* **on** *est valet* **on** *est pas roi."*   (65:6)[1]
        'My father always used to say, "Well, when one is a jack, one is not a king."'

Over time, *on* has acquired the ability to substitute for any and all of the personal pronouns, and contexts making clear its anaphoric capacity can readily be shown.

Use of *on* for *je* 'I'

Example (2) shows the substitution of *on* for *je* in a conversation recalling an automobile accident:

(2)   A: *J'ai cassé le steering avec mon genou parce que j'étais assis de côté.*
        B: *Et puis vous êtes correct?*
        A: *Ah oui,* **on** *s'en vient petit vieux, mais* **on** *est correct.*   (114:22)

        A: 'I broke the steering wheel with my knee because I was sitting on the side.'
        B: 'And you're o.k.?'
        A: 'Oh yes, the **old man**'s getting on, but **he**'s all right.'

In (2) as in other examples, we have glossed very liberally in trying to find an English expression with the same flavor. In this case, we have used the gloss 'the old man' rather than any English pronoun in order to convey the distance the speaker expresses in calling himself a *petit vieux* (coreferential with *on*).

---

[1] Examples are taken from our corpus of 120 interviews of Montréal French. The first figure in parentheses indicates the speaker's number; the second indicates the page in the transcription. This example comes from speaker 65, page 6. For further details on the methodology of the project, cf. Sankoff *et al.* (1976).

Use of *on* for *tu* ('you')

Sentence (3), said to a habitual fellow cross-puzzler, shows the use of *on* for *tu*:

(3)   *Comme ça on fait des mots croisés sans nous attendre?*
       'So **she**'s doing crossword puzzles without waiting for us?'

In this case, the speaker is using *on* to address his partner. Another possible English gloss would be: So we're doing crossword puzzles without waiting for our partner?

Use of *on* for *elle* 'she'

Example (4), said about the female interviewer and to a third party who has arrived in mid-interview, demonstrates the use of *on* for *elle*:

(4)   *Je suis en train d'être interrogé. **On** me demande si j'étais un bon petit garçon.*   (115:15)
       'I'm in the middle of being interviewed. I'm being asked if I was a good little boy. (One is asking me. . . .)'

Use of *on* for *ils* 'they' and *nous* 'we'

The specific referents of *on* substituting for *ils* 'they' and *nous* 'we' may be more difficult to identify, since these pronouns themselves often refer to incompletely defined collectivities. This is particularly the case with *ils* in sentences like (5).

(5)   *Moi je me comprends bien dans ma langue, de la manière que je te parle,—mais **ils** disent à la télévision qu'on parle cheval un peu.* (24:25)
       'I get along fine in my own language, the way I'm speaking to you, but **they** say on television that we speak **joual** (=lousy French[2]) a bit.'

Here '**they**, the people on TV' is about as specific as '**they**, the people in Luther's day' in the following example, in which *on* substitutes for *ils*.

(6)   *C'est à l'époque de Luther . . . il y avait des sorciers qu'**on** brûlait.* (73:17)
       'It was in Luther's day . . . there were witches that **they** burned.'

What these last two examples have in common is that they clearly exclude the speaker and the hearer, even though the third parties they refer to are

---

[2] "Lousy French" was the expression used to refer to Québec French in general by Prime Minister P.-E. Trudeau in a much publicized interview several years ago.

not well-defined. Indeed, one also finds nouns meaning "people" that are, semantically, rather empty, such as *les gens* and *le monde*,[3] used in very similar constructions. *Le monde* often gets plural agreement:

(7)   *Il y a des places comme à Outremont, ces affaires-là, on dirait que*
       le monde sont plus civilisés ou parce qu'ils sont plus riches.   (109:16)
       'There's places like in Outremont, and like that, it seems like **the**
       people are more civilized, or maybe because they're richer.'

On for *nous* has become the most common substitution. Indeed, it has very nearly replaced *nous* (about 98%) in current spoken French in Montréal.

(8)   *On se ramassait tous dans la salle à diner, puis la télévision, puis **on***
       écoutait le hockey.   (6:7)
       'We all got together in the dining room, with the television, and **we**
       listened to (watched) hockey.'

As such, *on* co-occurs with *nous* (*autres*) in the paradigm *moi, je*; *toi, tu*; *lui, il*; etc.

(9)   *Tu sais, ils veulent pas que **nous-autres on** reste dans la même marde*
       qu'eux-autres.   (88:21)
       'You know, they don't want us to say (that **we** stay) in the same shit
       as them.'

So great is the association of *on* with *nous* that "we" has become the un-marked, unless-otherwise-indicated reading of *on*. What, then, of the classic, indefinite *on*? We find that this *on* is, in fact, being replaced by *tu* and *vous*, as will be described in the next section.

3. *TU ~ VOUS* AS INDEFINITE: CONTEXTS OF ALTERNATION WITH *ON*

The use of *vous* or *tu* as a substitute for *on* has been noted by numerous authors, including Brunot (1922) and Sandfeld (1928). Benveniste (1966:232) has this to say on the subject:

> La définition de la deuxième personne comme étant la personne à laquelle la première s'adresse convient sans doute à son emploi le plus ordinaire. Mais ordinaire ne veut pas dire unique et constant. On peut utiliser la deuxième personne hors de l'allocution et la faire entrer dans une variété d'"impersonnel". Par exemple, "vous" fonctionne en français comme anaphorique de "on" (ex. "on ne peut se promener sans que quelqu'un *vous* aborde"). En mainte langue, *tu* (*vous*) sert de substitut à *on*. . . .

[3] *Le monde*'s semiclitic status is supported by the fact that it rarely co-occurs with another clitic, for example, *le monde, il(s)*. Most true nouns rarely occur in subject position WITHOUT a following clitic.

'The definition of the second person as the person addressed by the first doubtless corresponds to its most ordinary use. But ordinary does not mean unique and unchanging. One can use the second person outside of the address system to serve as a kind of "impersonal." For example, *vous* 'you' functions in French as anaphoric for *on* 'one' (e.g., "one cannot go walking without someone addressing you"). In a great many languages, *tu* or *vous* serve as substitutes for *on*. (translation by G. S.)

Our corpus confirms this, and a detailed study of the contexts of use of indefinite *on* shows that *tu* and *vous* can be used in virtually all of them. Perhaps the most central element unifying these various contexts is the theme of *generality* or *generalization*. The cases we have studied can be usefully grouped into three broad linguistic classes, each involving specific means of expressing generality. It is important to note that the indefinite referent here is always vague as to the possible inclusion of speaker and hearer: *Anybody* "means" just that—possibly you, possibly me, or anyone else in like circumstances. The referent here is, in this sense, "more indefinite" than the *on* equivalent to *ils*, *les gens*, or *le monde*, which is clearly [-speaker], [-hearer].

Lexical and Syntactic Indicators of Generalization

There are a great many lexical items, as well as morphological and syntactic structures, that can convey generality. Often, these markers co-occur. Many of them work to dissociate reference from specific places and times. Infinitives like *à travailler* and *à lire* in (10) are, by definition, atemporal, and adverbs like *toujours* 'always' can also contribute to the timelessness of an assertion. Other common adverbial indicators include *de nos jours*, *à c't heure*, and *aujourd'hui* (all glossed as 'nowadays').

(10)   *J'en ai peut-être regagné un peu. . . . A part ça, à travailler puis à lire **on** s'améliore toujours un petit peu.*   (30:40)
    'I've perhaps made a little progress. . . . Besides, in working and in reading **one** always improves somewhat.'

(11)   *Disons quand j'ai mis les pieds dans le vrai monde là, dans le monde où **tu** rencontres toutes sortes de gens et puis tout ça . . .*   (58:5)
    'Let's say that when I stepped into the real world, into the world where **you** meet all sorts of people and all that . . .'

The generality of the statement in (10) makes it virtually impossible to decode *on* as "we, the members of some (even vaguely defined) group." It is clear that the speaker intends *on* to refer to *anyone* who works and reads. In (11), the speaker's evocation of "the world where" sets up a general situation that "anyone" could participate in. His *tu* suddenly appearing in the middle of a first-person account can hardly be heard as "you, the person I'm talking to."

One syntactic indicator of generality is a tense change, always from a past tense (usually the *imparfait* or the *passé composé*) to the present, as illustrated in (11). Such a tense change frequently accompanies a subject change, again, as in (11), from *je* to the indefinite *on*, *tu*, or *vous*, where a speaker generalizes from his or her own experience, phrasing it as something that would apply to anybody.

There are four further morphological or syntactic structures that serve to identify generalized statements, all of which permit both *on* and *tu* or *vous*, though, for brevity's sake, only one case of each will be cited.

COREFERENTIAL *le*, *la*, *les*

(12)   ***On*** *choisit **les** amis.*   (12:16)
                       '**One** chooses **one**'s friends.'

This would contrast with *On choisit **nos** amis*, which would generally be glossed 'We choose **our** friends'.

COREFERENTIAL INDEFINITE NOUN PHRASE

(13)   *Quand **une personne** élevait une famille dans ce temps-là, **vous** étiez*
          pas capable d'avoir de luxe.   (37:16)
          'When **a person** was bringing up a family in those days, **you** couldn't
          have any luxuries.'

Though we did not study reflexives per se, the following example (one of many) confirms the identity of "second person" and indefinite forms.

(14)   ***Quelqu'un*** *qui veut travailler normalement, c'est plus facile **t'**expri-*
          *mer dans **ta** langue que d'essayer de **t'**expliquer dans une autre.*
          (6:19)
          '**Anybody** who wants to work properly, it's easier for them (you) to
          express themself in their language than to try to explain yourself
          in another.'

DEFINITIONAL STRUCTURES WITH *c'est*

(15)   *L'inconvénient c'est qu'**on** fait des réparations dans un logement, et*
          *puis quand **on** part, **on** est obligé de laisser ça là.*   (16:16)
          'The trouble is that **you** make repairs in a rented place, but when
          you leave, **you** have to leave it all there.'

CERTAIN EXISTENTIAL STRUCTURES, USUALLY WITH
THE VERBS *avoir* 'HAVE', *voir* 'SEE', AND *trouver* 'FIND'.

(16)   *Le joual, c'est une déformation, comme **tu** as des patois en France.*
          (112:34)
          '*Joual* is a deformation, like the *patois* **you** get in France.'

This structure is found in contexts where the existential *il y a* would also have been possible.

In addition to these very diverse indicators of generality, there are two specific types of utterances that deserve special mention. These are implicative constructions and constructions headed by a presentative.

Implicative Constructions

Implicative constructions are statements of cause and effect. They consist of two sentences, the first of which (the protasis) sets up a supposition and the second (the apodosis) states the implications. Conditionals with *if* are common examples of implicative constructions. The syntactic relation between the two sentences need not be one of embedding, however. Sentences may be coordinate, as in (18), or simply juxtaposed.

(17)   *Bien si **on** laisse faire les hommes c'est tout' des grosses bêtes.*
           (79:17)
           'Well if **one** lets men do what they want, they're all big brutes.'

(18)   ***Vous** allez voir deux Français de France, puis ils parleront pas tous les deux pareil*   (6:22)
           '**You** take two Frenchmen from France and they won't both speak the same.'

Propositions headed by a Presentative Construction

Presentative clauses constitute a particularly striking way of announcing the generality of the proposition that they introduce. The forms of presentatives are numerous, but they all work to put interlocutors on notice that what is coming next is a generally admitted truth or a personal opinion that speakers hope are shared, if not universally, at least by their interlocutors.

Indefinite referents in these cases occur not in the presentative clause itself but, rather, in the following sentence. Some of the presentative forms found in our corpus are:

il me semble	'it seems to me'
$\left\{\begin{array}{l} il \\ c' \end{array}\right\}$ *est vrai*	'it is true'
faut dire	'it must be said'
disons	'let's say'
je dis	'I say'
je pense	'I think'
je trouve	'I find'
d'après moi	'according to me'
il est certain	'it's certain'

The force of such presentatives in affirming the generality of the succeeding proposition is evident from the examples:

(19)   *Puis ça, moi j'ai pour mon dire,* **on** *peut pas se mettre dans la peau d'un autre.*   (42:12)
         'There's this, I would say, **one** cannot put oneself into the skin of another [another person's shoes].'

(20)   *D'après moi, c'est pas avec des guerres que* **tu** *réussis à faire un pays,* **tu** *t'assis puis* **tu** *discutes.*   (6:17)
         'As far as I'm concerned, **you** don't build a country with wars, **you** sit down and **you** discuss.'

Lexical and Syntactic Constraints on Choice among Variants

We have shown that the three major classes defined in the preceding subsection all permit both *one* and *you* as indefinite referents. Though our theoretical framework led us to seek out distributional parallels and relations of partial equivalence, it did not force us to postulate total equivalence. Specifically, we were quite prepared to consider the possibility that we might find some contexts that favor a particular form or even some contexts where one or another form was obligatory. There are only a couple of the latter. For *on*, there are a few frozen forms: structures with

$$QU + on + \left\{ \begin{array}{l} dire \\ appeler \end{array} \right\},$$

such as *comme on dit* and *qu'on appelle*, with glosses like 'as it's called'—that is, by anybody who might have occasion to call it. Here is a typical example from a word search:

(21)   *On allait manger chez Gerassimo, puis je voyais toujours euh . . .* **comment est-ce qu'on appelle** *donc, euh, Ti-Coq là.*   (57:15)
         'We used to eat at Gerassimo's, and I always used to see uh, **what's his name**, uh, Ti-Coq.'

Toward the end of our data analysis, we found that *on* is not quite categorical in these contexts. There were 8 cases (5 speakers) of *tu* or *vous* in such expressions, representing only 1.3% of the total. This may be a beginning of the invasion of *on*'s last stronghold. Here is an example, again from a word search:

(22)   *D'ailleurs les professeurs font une espèce de petite grève, comment est-ce que* **tu** *appelles ça, d'écoeurement, quelque chose du genre, enfin.*   (53:8)
         'In fact, the teachers are on a kind of little strike, what'cha macallit, a slowdown, something like that, anyway.'

(She's looking for the term *grève du zèle*, which is a work-to-rule campaign.) In addition to these expressions involving *dire* and *appeler*, there are some sequential constraints that lead to the obligatory use of *on*, as indeed there are also for *tu* and *vous*. These, however, will be explained in Section 7. The only case of categorical *tu/vous* not involving sequential matters involves co-occurrence with a past-tense verb. In such utterances, *on* would always be interpreted as meaning 'we'; to express the indefinite referent, *tu* or *vous* must be used. Thus, speaking of the Great Depression to someone who wasn't born then:

(23)   ***Vous*** *aviez pas une cenne pour vous acheter un habillement à toutes ces années-là. La femme non plus.*   (37:24)
        '**You** didn't have a cent to buy clothing for all those years. The wife neither.'

The same constraint works spatially as well as temporally. In co-occurrence with *ici* 'here', *on* would be decoded as 'we' in the following example. Instead, *vous* is used.

(24)   A : *Est-ce que vous pensez que la cuisine qui était faite avec le poêle à bois, c'était bien meilleur?*
        B : *Oui c'est pas la même chose, ça restait chaud plus longtemps aussi. C'est pas pareil. Ici* ***vous*** *chauffez là, puis le manger est froid tout de suite.*   (116:17)
        A : Do you think that food was much better, cooked on a wood stove?
        B : Yes, it's not the same, it used to stay warm longer, too. Here **you** heat, and the food gets cold right away.

Leaving these categorical contexts, which were not tabulated in the quantitative study, let us return briefly to the three major contexts of Section 3, keeping in mind decoding problems that might occur given that all three forms (*on*, *tu*, and *vous*) have readings other than indefinite. Specifically, as we saw in the discussion of (23) and (24), *on* may run into trouble by being decoded as 'we' and *tu* and *vous* by being decoded as 'you, the hearer(s)'. The hypothetical nature of implicatives, however, seems to work to diminish the possibility of ambiguity with the second-person referent when *tu* (or *vous*) is used. This would lead us to suspect that implicatives are fertile ground for the spread of *tu* and *vous*. With presentatives, on the other hand, the metalinguistic framing that these utterances accomplish often signals a distance the speaker is adopting with respect to his or her own views, thus dissociating the speaker from the referent of the subject of the sentence. The possibility of ambiguity between indefinite *on* and first person plural *on* is thereby diminished, leading us to expect the *on* variant to be numerous in this class.

Before looking at whether, and how, such considerations of speaker strategy in facilitating disambiguation may intervene to make particular syntactic categories more or less amenable to the use of particular forms, there are a few other considerations to introduce. First, what are people doing with these indefinite referents, and how might this influence the choice of form? Second, do all speakers make use of all the forms? If there are interindividual differences among speakers, what are the theoretical consequences of this for an understanding of language use and language structure? Third, once having taken into account everything we know about the properties of the indefinite *on*, *tu* and *vous* and their distribution among speakers, can we go any farther by looking at syntagmatic considerations and examining them in sequence?

4. DISCURSIVE EFFECTS: WHAT ARE INDEFINITE REFERENTS USED FOR?

In addition to examining the forms of utterances containing indefinite referents, we have also looked at their place and function within the discourse. We have arrived at two broad discursive or pragmatic categories, which we label SITUATIONAL INSERTION and THE FORMULATION OF MORALS OR TRUISMS.

Situational Insertion

The utterances we are concerned with are generalizations involving an indefinite person, and they all have the effect of locating this person in a potentially repeatable activity or context. Anyone's experience may constitute the basis for generalization, though most often it is the speaker's.

(25)   *J'aime mieux boire une bonne brosse, c'est mieux que fumer de la drogue, je trouve. Le lendemain matin **tu** as un gros mal de tête mais ça fait rien, **tu** est tout' là, tandis qu'avec la drogue **tu** sais pas si **tu** vas être là le lendemain. **Tu** peux te prendre pour Batman ou Superman puis **tu** te pitches dans les poubelles.*   (62:11)
'I prefer to drink myself stoned, it's better than smoking dope, I feel. The next morning **you** have a bad headache but that's no big deal, **you** are all in one piece, whereas with drugs **you** don't know if **you** will be there the next day. **You** might decide you're Batman or Superman and take off into a garbage can.'

(26)   *Ben **on** a qu'à prendre l'autobus puis **on** se rend compte comment les jeunes parlent; disons ça c'est le mauvais language.*   (3:30)
'Well, **one** only has to take the bus and one realizes how young people talk. Let's say it's poor language.'

At issue in (25) is the speaker's own experience with alcohol and drugs. By using *tu*, he assimilates himself to a much wider class of people, downgrading his own experience to incidental status in the discourse, phrasing it as something that could or would be anybody's.

The sentences in (26) are an example of a hypothetical activity that is open to anyone, that of "taking the bus." In this case as in many others, it is fairly clear that the "indefinite agent" serves as a rather transparent guise for the speaker's own experience and opinions. There is, clearly, more going on here than the simple avoidance of "I" due to the politeness or "refinement" that the classic French grammarians have attributed to seventeenth century nobility. Speaking of the *on* "of modesty," Brunot (1922:276) says:

> "*Le **moi** est haïssable.*" *Pour éviter de se mettre en avant, au nominal personnel, les raffinés substituaient souvent l'indéterminé **on**, qui, étant plus vague, ne choque pas.*

> '"The **me** is hateful." To avoid putting themselves forward, in the personal nominal, refined persons often substituted the indeterminate *on* which, being vaguer, is less shocking.'

In saying "you have only to take the bus to hear the bad language of the young people," the speaker is not, however, being particularly "modest." Rather, she is claiming more weight for her assertion, phrasing it as verifiable by anybody. The discursive effect of inserting an unspecified agent into a hypothetical situation seems to function to elevate her statement to the plane of conventional wisdom—thereby, perhaps, rendering it more difficult to challenge. The special status of assertions containing indefinite referents is even more evident in the class of utterances to be discussed in the next section, where "conventional wisdom" is explicitly invoked.

The Formulation of Truisms and Morals

Cases we have analyzed as the formulation of a truism or moral seem to involve a speaker in evaluating a situation. The form of this evaluation is such as to break or at least to greatly attenuate the tie with the speaker's own experience that we saw in the previous section.

(27)   *Ça sert à rien de savoir compter de nos jours; ou **tu** es bien riche puis **tu** as un comptable qui compte pour toi, ou **tu** es très pauvre puis **tu** as pas d'argent à compter.*   (6:24)
   'It's no use knowing how to count these days. Either **you**'re really rich and **you** have an accountant do your counting, or else **you** are very poor and **you** have no money to count.'

(28)   *J'ai horreur d'entendre crier, puis pourtant faut que je crie avec les
petites. Ca me déplaît beaucoup. Mais je me dis, des enfants c'est
des enfants,* **on** *peut pas les faire penser comme des adultes,* **on**
peut pas.   (9:13)
'I can't stand to hear yelling, but just the same, with the little ones,
I have to yell. I really find it unpleasant. But I say to myself,
children are children, **one** can't make them think like adults—
one just can't.'

As was the case with the general class of "situation insertion," morals
are not characterized by particular lexical or syntactic markers. They can
be formulated using any of the three construction types of Section 3. Illustrated here are an implicative in (27) and a presentative heading (*je me dis*
'I say to myself') in (28). A moral is understood as such essentially because
of its particular relation to the discourse as a whole. One thing that distinguishes morals and truisms from the category we have called "situational
insertion" is that morals constitute a kind of reflection based on conventional
wisdom, whereas "situational insertion" seems to be an attempt to elevate
particular experiences and ideas to that status. Morals, of course, inherently
involve the evocation of a situation, but they also generally possess a strong
judgmental or evaluative connotation. This is particularly clear when the
utterance is a saying or a proverb overtly borrowed from the oral tradition
of the community, as in the first example cited in this chapter. It is no
accident that a moral often appears at the beginning or at the end of a
narrative sequence or a description. Labov's CODAS (1972:365), which he
analyzes as functioning to avert the *so what* reaction, often take the form typical of morals and truisms, showing similar timelessness and indeterminacy.

Morals, then, are like situational insertion, only more so. There is a
great difference between the discursive effect of a sentence like *When I get
drunk I wake up with a headache* and that of *When one gets drunk one wakes
up with a headache.* The first is a natural for the *so what* reaction, whereas
the second seems to constitute its own *raison d'être.* Moreover, the first
can call forth a reaction of disapproval from one's interlocutor, but he or
she can do little more than disagree with the second. Morals or truisms are
even further removed from challengeability insofar as they function to
evaluate or to demonstrate the point of something else. *Children are children,
one can't make them think like adults* is in itself serving to justify the speaker's
statement that she "has to" yell at her children. Though it would be possible
for an argumentative interlocutor to respond that indeed one ought to be
able to reason with children, the evaluative role of the proverbial utterance
combines with the nonsituated quality of its reference to give it a greater
measure of protection from such a riposte.

As to the use of *on* versus *tu* and *vous* in the two pragmatic categories described here, it seems likely that morals might favor the retention of *on*, the older and more "formal" variant. Morals are at a greater remove from the running discourse, more metalinguistic in functioning as considered, "official" pronouncements.

5. SYNTACTIC AND PRAGMATIC TYPES AS CONSTRAINTS

Exempting the cases in which a particular form is mandatory, we analyzed a total of 4367 cases of the use of indefinite subject clitics. In Table 1, we present a breakdown of these cases according to the three utterance types and two pragmatic effects discussed in Sections 2 and 3.

TABLE 1
OCCURRENCE OF INDEFINITE REFERENTS ACCORDING TO LINGUISTIC AND PRAGMATIC CONTEXT

| Linguistic factors | Pragmatic factors | | | | | | Total | |
| | Situational insertion | | | Formulation of morals | | | | |
	on	*tu ~ vous*	Total	*on*	*tu ~ vous*	Total	*on*	*tu ~ vous*
Generalizations	899	951	1850 (52%)	176	78	254 (33%)	1075	1029
Implicatives	505	878	1383 (38%)	220	140	360 (46%)	725	1018
Presentative heads	233	127	360 (10%)	109	51	160 (21%)	342	178
Total	1637	1956	3593	505	269	774	2142	2225

As was to be expected, the bulk of our examples were found in the more general "situational insertion" category (3593 cases as opposed to 774 "morals"). Looking first at which utterance types are used to convey each of the two discursive effects (percentages are given at the right of each of the two major columns), we see that the two special syntactic constructions are used a higher proportion of the time in the more marked discursive category, that of the formulation of morals. The rate of use of implicatives rises from 38% in "situational insertion" to 46% in morals, and the rate of use of presentative headed constructions more than doubles, from 10% to 21%.

Scanning the marginal totals also gives us a good first impression of the effect of the linguistic and pragmatic categories on the use of *on* versus *tu* and *vous*.[4] Though the total number of each is almost identical (2142 versus 2225), they are not used equally frequently in all contexts. In particular, *on* is very much preferred in presentative-headed constructions (342 cases versus 178 of *tu* and *vous*) and dispreferred in implicatives. As for the pragmatic categories, the heavy use of *on* for formulating morals (505 cases versus 269 for *tu* and *vous*) is very striking.

In order to gauge better the interaction of the environments, however, we undertook a variable rule analysis according to the methods set forth in Rousseau and Sankoff (1978b). For the factors described so far, this analysis gave us probability weights that accord with the hypotheses formulated in the discussion of the constraints and confirmed the tendencies observed in the marginal totals. Probability weights are as follows (higher numbers indicate that *on* is favored; lower numbers indicate preference for *tu* and *vous*).

p_{syntax}:	Implicative	0.32
	Presentative	0.65
	Others	0.54
$p_{pragmatic}$:	Situational insertion	0.37
	Moral	0.63

Further details of the statistical analysis are given in Laberge 1977a and 1977b.

6. SPEAKERS' REPERTOIRES

Differences among speakers have been both a blessing and a curse in variation studies. On the one hand, the fact that in no known speech community are linguistic resources distributed equally has been a key observation in the understanding of the social underpinnings of linguistic change. On the other hand, there is always the "multiplicity of dialects" bugaboo, haunting sociolinguists with images of perfect synchronic "solutions" that will somehow do away with all the "remaining variation" after an analysis such as that reported in 5 has been carried out.

Of course, not every speaker operates according to the probabilities obtained from the group data of 120 people. Indeed, we know that the use of *tu* or *vous* to express an indefinite referent is the more recent as well as the less "proper" form. We would, therefore, be surprised to find it as

---

[4] For purposes of the statistical analysis, we have grouped *tu* and *vous* together in opposition to *on*. Further discussion of this is provided in Section 6.

popular with older and more careful speakers as it is with younger and less careful ones. We also know who the more careful speakers are likely to be: those for whom speaking "well" pays off. A detailed discussion of this issue, as well as an analysis of the degree of integration of each of the 120 speakers into the MARCHÉ LINGUISTIQUE (Bourdieu and Boltanski 1975), is available in Laberge 1977b. For present purposes, we note simply that speaking "well" is, in contemporary Québec society, likely to be characteristic of women and of those men whose socioeconomic life history has put a premium on proper, careful, normative speech.

Given all these considerations, we look at each speaker separately, attempting to find out what it is about them that might help to account for their usage preferences. The variable rule assigned each speaker a probability weight from 0 to 1.0 according to his/her preference for *tu ∼ vous* or *on* respectively.

Looking first at the 60 male speakers, we found that 7 used *tu ∼ vous* categorically, 7 used *on* categorically, and the remaining 46 showed a range of probabilities between these two extremes. There was a fairly strong age correlation with *on* use, older speakers quite clearly preferring the conservative *on* to *tu* or *vous*. Sixty-four percent of male speakers over 40 preferred *on* to *tu ∼ vous*, whereas only 28% of those 40 and younger preferred *on*.

Dividing the women into the same age groups, the older women seemed to pattern with their male counterparts, 69% of them preferring *on* to *tu* and *vous*. The younger women, however, showed a surprising difference: Even more of them (76%) favored *on*.

On, then, is the markedly female variant. Not a single woman used *tu ∼ vous* categorically, although 11 used *on* categorically (7 of whom were in the younger age group). Apart from the striking sex difference and the major age difference among men, no other social attributes of the speakers seemed to be relevant. (At least not social class, as measured by the MARCHÉ LINGUISTIQUE index. Education, as measured by years in school, was barely significant.)

These results, coupled with those of Section 5, give the following picture. Seven speakers use *tu ∼ vous* categorically; 18 use *on* categorically; and 94 alternate. (One further speaker did not use any indefinite pronouns.) These 94 are more likely to use *on* if they are women and, particularly, if they are less than 40 years of age. They are also more likely to use *on* in formulating morals or truisms, as well as in constructions headed by presentatives. We might now ask whether these likelihoods apply in more or less the same way to all 94 of the variable speakers or whether there are subgroups of these people who show very different patterns, that is, whether the weights obtained for the linguistic and pragmatic categories derive from improperly lumping speakers.

A statistical procedure developed by Rousseau (see Rousseau and Sankoff 1978a) made it possible to test the hypothesis that speakers fell into two or more distinct groups. Rousseau found two groups whose members were significantly dissimilar. The main difference between them was that, for the first group of 57 speakers, the probability weights of the linguistic factors were ordered in the same way as was reported in Section 5, except that their effects were more distinct, whereas for the remaining 37 speakers these factors seemed to level out. That is, there was one group whose members were supersensitive to the linguistic constraints and a second whose members were insensitive to them. The two groups showed almost identical behavior with respect to the pragmatic constraints.

We have not yet investigated what might be the social basis underlying these differences among speakers, particularly as concerns the last binary grouping. What does seem clear from the sex differences is that a simple "contagion" theory of dialect differences is inadequate. Differences between men's and women's speech in this case can hardly be due to any kind of "communicative segregation." The *tu* ~*vous* variant, though it is clearly the innovative form, has certainly been around long enough for everybody to catch it, if that were all that was involved.

Though in the past many studies of grammatical variation have suffered from small samples and insufficient data, we do not think this is a problem here. With 4300 tokens, each of which has been carefully studied as to its syntactic and discursive role, we feel we have an accurate idea of how each speaker uses these resources. The usage preference so clearly demonstrated by men for *tu* ~ *vous* and by women for *on* represents one instance of linguistic resources being marshaled to symbolize a social distinction—the fact that the difference is largely a question of degree bears witness to the subtlety that such processes can resort to without making much of a ripple in communicative efficacy.

One issue we have not yet dealt with may have some bearing on this point, and that is speaker preference between indeterminate *tu* and *vous*. So far, we have considered the two as equivalent and as distinct from *on*. It is, of course, the case that the distinction between *tu* and *vous* as terms of address is interactionally significant in French. And, interestingly enough, this is another area where our sample showed a great sex difference. Of the 60 women, 54 addressed the interviewer as *vous*; of the 60 men, only 25 did. (This includes 9 people who alternated between *tu* and *vous*.) Moreover, the unanswered question of the relationship between the form of address used to one's interlocutor and the form of the indefinite used is a complicated one. Certainly, there is no one-to-one relationship. Fifteen people who restricted themselves to *vous* in addressing the interviewer *never* used *vous* as an indefinite; a further 19 such speakers used both *tu* and *vous* as indefinites. One interesting fact, however, was that none of the 28 speakers who used only *tu* in addressing the interviewer used only *vous* as an indefinite (a few of them used both).

Indulging in a little speculation, we might guess that, since indefinite *tu* and *vous* have the corresponding pronouns of address as their source, there may still be a little contamination in the choice of form as between *tu* and *vous*. We would guess that for a number of reasons (including the distributions cited in the preceding paragraph) *tu* is currently the less marked of the two.

We still insist, however, that all three forms function quite equivalently in the most semantically empty contexts, where even *on* is so impersonal as to be serving more as a dummy element than as anything else. Consider the following idiomatic expressions equivalent to *everything you might imagine* or *what you will*, functioning as a kind of *et cetera* at the end of a list.

(29)   *Et puis c'était la grande fête, les cadeaux, l'excitation des cadeaux, puis les chants, puis les déclamations, puis **tout ce que vous voudrez**.* (115:435).

        'And it was always a big party, with presents, the excitement of the presents, and singing, and recitations, and **everything you might want**.'

(30)   *Le gars il peut avoir un char, une maison puis le yacht puis **tout ce que tu voudras**, mais il a le droit, hostie.*   (95:6)

        'The guy might have a car, a house and a yacht and **everything you might want**, but he has the right (to have them), for chrissake.'

(31)   *Et bien il y avait . . . le chanoine X là qui était longtemps doyen de la Faculté des Lettres et qui était en plus vice-recteur et puis en plus professeur et puis en plus doyen et puis en plus, je ne sais pas, administrateur et **tout ce qu'on veut**. Bon, il était le seul.*   (81:12)

        'And so there was . . . Canon X there who for a long time was Dean of the Arts Faculty and who was also Vice Rector and who was also a professor and also dean and also, I don't know, administrator and **everything one might want**. Well, he was the only one.'

In a further such idiomatic expression, evidence of the emptiness of the forms is given by the fact that they are in alternation with a completely clitic-less version. Three of the several possibilities are illustrated here, with *on* appearing in (32), *tu* in (33), and no clitic at all in (34):

(32)   ***Qu'on le veuille ou non**, la fille qui sort avec son jeune homme, en tout cas, elle sort, elle, sur son côté.*   (1:10)

        '**Like it or not**, the girl that goes out with a young man, in any case, she goes out on her own.'

(33)   *Tu as la chaîne d'état puis le canal 10, ben la plupart du monde c'est*
        le canal 10, tsé, **que tu le veuilles ou pas,** *tsé, le monde ils sont pas*
        interessés à voir un programme instructif.   (88:22)
        'You have the state channel as well as Channel 10, well most people
        are going to watch Channel 10, y'know, **like it or not**, y'know,
        people are not interested in seeing an educational program.'

(34)   *Je suis pas bilingue, je me débrouille disons. Mais mes soeurs, eux-*
        autres, deux langues; d'ailleurs j'ai mes deux frères qui ont marié
        des pures anglaises, fait que, **veux veux pas,** *hein, faut, faut-.*
        (29:19)
        'I'm not bilingual, let's say I sort of get along. But my sisters, two
        languages!—in fact I have my two brothers who married pure
        English girls, so, **like it or not**, eh? you have to, have to-.'

That *tu and vous* have wormed their way into these very empty, parenthetical slots, even for many vigilant but unsuspecting speakers, is, we feel,
strong evidence of their growing equivalence with impersonal *on* and of
their interchangeability with other impersonal constructions.

7. SEQUENTIAL CONSIDERATIONS

Our approach to the study of *on, tu,* and *vous* has involved syntagmatic
considerations to a greater degree than has been usual in variation studies.
Indeed, the very defining of categories like the formulation of a moral has
involved relating the utterance to other pieces of discourse. Here, we examine
specifically how the occurrence of a particular clitic may be constrained by
the sequence immediately to its left.

Sequential Constraints Leading to Categorical *on*

Indefinite *tu* or *vous* cannot be used in contexts where there is a define
"you" immediately to the left, for fear of confusion with the latter.

(35)   **Vous** [+def.] *me demandez de vous raconter une partie de ma vie là,*
        *mais il y a des choses, qu'***on** [–def.] *peut pas expliquer pourtant.*
        (9:13)
        '**You** (the interviewer) ask me to tell you a part of my life, but
        there are things that **one** just can't explain.'

        *. . . que **vous** [–def.] *pouvez pas expliquer.*

        *?. . . que **tu** [–def.] *peux pas expliquer.*

The problem of confounding an indefinite *you* with a define *you* sometimes also comes up in cases in which the ungrammaticality is one of social relations rather than due to referential confusion. Thus,

(36)   a. *Quel âge avez-vous?*
         b. *Je dis pas d'âge moi. Je parle pas des âges; **on** parle pas de ca aux femmes, des âges.*   (5:25)

         a. 'How old are you?'
         b. 'I don't say any age. I don't talk about ages. **One** doesn't talk about that to women, about ages.'

This is clearly both a refusal to reply to the question and a counterattack; the asker is reproached for asking. But saying "you don't talk" would have been, again, too clearly "you, the asker."

Obligatory *tu* and *vous* in Sequence

Recall that the "ambiguity" problem for *on* is that of being confused with "we." Thus, when there is a definite subject clitic, especially "I" or "we" in the immediate left hand context, *on* is useless as a representation of "anyone" because it would be identified with "we" [unless of course there are additional markers, such as the tense change discussed in connection with (11)]. In the following example, the speaker, a secretary, is talking about her boss' family:

(37)   *La famille, **je** les reconnais presque tous parce qu'ils viennent au bureau. **Tu** les reconnais, tsé, **tu** les vois arriver puis **tu** dis ca, ca c'est de la famille.*   (4:36)
         'The family—I recognize almost all of them because they come in to the office. **You** recognize them, y'know, **you** see them coming and **you** say, that, that's gotta be family.'

If she had said *on*, this would have immediately been decoded as 'we, the office employees', and the generalizing function would have been lost. What she wants to convey is that *anybody* would recognize these people as family, and the use of *on* would not have permitted her to do this.

Sequential Constraints with Noncategorical Consequences.

The statistical analysis described in Section 5 proceeded by first excluding all cases of categoriality (categorical speakers and all categorical environments, including sequential ones) and by then treating each instance of an indefinite as an independent binomial trial. But the fact that for this particular study we had so much data, including a fairly large number of contiguous tokens, enabled us to explore the noncategorical effects of contiguity.

Specifically, we attempted to characterize the effect of syntagmatic proximity of three types between neighboring tokens. We focused in each case on the relation a second token bears to a first. The three types are embedding-constrained tokens, sequence-constrained tokens, and unconstrained successive tokens.[5] In the case of embedding-constrained tokens, a single referent is the subject of two sentences, one of which is embedded in the other, as in (38):

(38)   *Ah! bien c'est entendu qu'on est mieux, mieux en campagne quand on est jeune.*   (116:26)
          'Well for sure you're (**one** is) better off in the country when you're young.'

Implicative structures obviously offer considerable scope for such analysis.

In sequence-constrained tokens, a single referent is the subject in two or more sentences that are conjoined or simply juxtaposed.

(39)   *L'influence de la finance, c'est ca, vous payez tout en l'utilisant, vous en êtes pas privé.*   (41:18)
          'The point about borrowing money is that **you** pay for it while **you**'re using it, so **you** don't have to go without.'

The weakest of the three relationships is that between unconstrained successive tokens. Here, two successive occurrences of a same variable are too distant to qualify for either of the above categories.

Though we noted that a switch of variants **can** occur even in the most constrained environment, that of embedding-constrained tokens, our hypothesis was that the stronger the syntagmatic relationship between the two tokens, the less likelihood there would be for a switch of variants to occur when the second token was uttered. This hypothesis was statistically validated in Sankoff and Laberge (1978). Table 2 presents data from five speakers who demonstrated at least a modicum of switching behavior in their sequence data and shows that the sequencing context is much more restrictive than simple proximity between variables.[6] Indeed, as Sankoff and Laberge (1978:126) point out, "switching rates for unconstrained pairs are not clearly different from the overall proportion of the variants." This would seem to indicate a form of text-cohesion operating between adjacent sentences that are syntactically related.

---

[5] There is a further type involving hesitation phenomena that had to be discarded due to the heterogeneity of hesitation types.

[6] Embedding-constrained tokens could not be tabulated because they were not sufficiently numerous in the data.

TABLE 2

Speaker number	Proportion of *on*	*tu ~ vous → on* Switch rate		Proportion of *tu ~ vous*	*on → tu ~ vous* Switch rate	
		Unconstrained pairs	Sequence-constrained pairs		Unconstrained pairs	Sequence-constrained pairs
5	.45	.50	.12	.55	.25	.37
6	.24	.33	.12	.76	.60	.33
13	.24	.17	.06	.76	.63	.24
44	.30	.33	.19	.70	.67	
115	.39	.50	.20	.61	.73	.05

[a] Reproduced from Sankoff and Laberge 1978:124.

[b] In almost all cases, variant proportion approximates switch rate for unconstrained pairs, whereas sequence-constrained switch rates are much lower.

8. CONCLUSIONS

We began this chapter by considering a syntactically and semantically well-defined and fairly circumscribed problem: subject clitics used for an indefinite human referent. In trying to understand the distributional facts about the three forms that are currently employed, we investigated a great range of construction types in which they occur. This led us to seek a broader understanding of the place of such constructions in discourse and forced us to realize that there was a plethora of other constructions serving somewhat similar functions, including passives, other, progressively more nouny indefinites (*quelqu'un*, *un gars*, etc.), and expressions with no clitic at all, like *veux*, *veux pas*.

The fact that *tu* and *vous* can be used even in constructions in which the indefinite is so "bleached" that it serves only as a dummy (analogous to *whatcha* [*you*] *macallit*) is clear evidence of their migration across morphological categories, from the definite to the indefinite system. This supports our view that forms with disparate grammatical origins can come to be discourse equivalents. Furthermore, we believe that such discourse equivalents sooner or later come to have an official place in the grammar as linguistic equivalents. In other words, it is through discursive practice (as Benveniste noted in our citation at the beginning) that grammar changes.

ACKNOWLEDGMENTS

The work reported in this chapter was made possible in large part by a Killam Grant from the Canada Council. Laberge (1977b) contains a full account of this research, and this chapter is grounded in that analysis. We owe much to our co-workers on the Montreal French project, especially Pascale Rousseau, David Sankoff, and Pierrette Thibault. We also thank the many participants at the Discourse and Syntax Symposium who made useful suggestions, particularly Talmy Givón for his encouragement and patience.

REFERENCES

Benveniste, E. (1966) *Problèmes de linguistique générale 1*, Gallimard, Paris.

Bourdieu, P. and L. Boltanski (1975) "Le fétichisme de la langue," *Actes de la recherche en sciences sociales* 4, 2–32.

Brunot, F. (1922) *La pensée et la langue*, Masson, Paris.

Laberge, S. (1977a) "The Changing Distribution of Indeterminate Pronouns in Discourse," presented at NWAVE VI, Georgetown University. (to appear in the *Proceedings*)

Laberge, S. (1977b) *Etude de la variation des pronoms sujets définis et indéfinis dans le français parlé à Montréal*, unpublished Doctoral dissertation, Université de Montréal, Montréal.

Labov, W. (1972) "The Transformation of Experience in Narrative Syntax," *Language in the Inner City*, University of Pennsylvania Press, Philadelphia, Pennsylvania, 354–396.

Rousseau, P. and D. Sankoff (1978a) "A Solution to the Problem of Grouping Speakers," in D. Sankoff, ed., *Linguistic Variation: Models and Methods*, Academic Press, New York, 97–117.

Rousseau, P. and D. Sankoff (1978b) "Advances in Variable Rule Methodology," in D. Sankoff, ed., *Linguistic Variation*, Academic Press, New York, 57–68.

Sandfeld, K. (1928) *Syntaxe de français contemporain, Tome I*, Champion, Paris.

Sankoff, D., and S. Laberge (1978) "Statistical Dependence among Successive Occurrences of a Variable in Discourse," in D. Sankoff, ed., *Linguistic Variation*, Academic Press, New York, 119–126.

Sankoff, D., G. Sankoff, S. Laberge, and M. Topham (1976) "Méthodes d'échantillonnage et utilisation de l'ordinateur dans l'étude de la variation grammaticale," *Cahiers de linguistique* 6, Presses de l'Université du Québec, Montréal, 85–125.

DISCOURSE CONSTRAINTS ON DATIVE MOVEMENT

NOMI ERTESCHIK-SHIR
Ben Gurion University of the Negev, Israel

> When we say two things that are different we mean two different
> things by them.—D. L. Bolinger, *Meaning and Form*

1. INTRODUCTION

In this chapter I intend to define the discourse function of Dative Movement and to show that a number of constraints on the rule that have been
regarded as mutually unrelated follow from the function defined.[1]

---

[1] I do not wish to take a stand on whether Dative Movement is a transformation that transforms (i) into (ii) or vice versa.

(i)   *John gave the book to Mary.*
(ii)   *John gave Mary the book.*

Syntax and Semantics, Volume 12:
Discourse and Syntax

The framework within which my data will be presented can best be illustrated through the following hypothetical case. A linguist discovers a coherent system similar to the one that follows:

1. X is associated with constituents in certain positions in S.
2. These constituents appear only after certain verbs.
3. Certain movement rules are restricted to apply to these constituents.
4. X interacts with the determiner system.
5. X is associated with a certain stress pattern.
6. X determines certain discourse contexts.
7. X is remembered most easily in psychological tests.
8. X is relevant to first-language acquisition.
9. X is relevant to the historical development of the language.

This list would indicate to any linguist that overwhelming evidence exists for the linguistic relevance of X. The next step—where linguists might disagree—consists in determining the basic phenomenon from which the others follow.

Linguist A might wish to say that X is defined by its position in the sentence and that the rest of its properties derive from that. Linguist B might say that its discourse function is the determining factor and that the syntactic factors and other properties follow from it. Linguist A encounters the problem that the syntactic factors vary from language to language. This is not a difficulty for linguist B, since the pragmatic notions he is using are universally relevant, even though some of the specific phenomena from the remainder of the list would be expected to differ.

The problem then becomes the definition of the discourse characteristics of X. In Erteschik-Shir (1973) it was argued that certain movement rules

---

Another possibility is the one argued for by Oehrle (1975), in which sentences such as (i) and (ii) are said to have separate deep structures. For the sake of convenience and convenience only, "Dative Movement" will mean here a transformation that transforms sentences such as (i) into (ii). It would be possible to reformulate my approach within either of the other two alternate theories. So, when it is stated that "The function of the rule is X," one could equally well say: "The function of choosing (ii) instead of (i) is X." There is, therefore, no conflict between the general approach proposed here and Oehrle's.

It should be mentioned that Dative Movement has been similarly analyzed before by Firbas (1974), Givón (1975), Creider (this volume), and others. These accounts are similar but not identical to the one presented here, and they do not discuss most of the syntactic constraints that will be dealt with in the present chapter.

It is not my intention to deal with all aspects of Dative Movement. Many of the semantic aspects have been discussed in detail by Oehrle (1975). Bolinger (personal communication) also pointed out the significance of the semantics involved and also recommended a diachronic investigation. This chapter is limited to those phenomenon that seem to follow from the pragmatic aspects of the rule.

applied only to what was there called "dominant" constituents. In Erteschik-Shir and Lappin (1977) a definition of dominance was proposed, the extraction phenomena were explicated, and it was also argued that dominance is relevant to a certain interpretive rule. The occurrence of dominant constituents was seen to depend, inter alia, on the main verb and on the determiner system. In Erteschik-Shir and Lappin (1978) it was found that dominance determines sentential stress: In other words, the properties of X listed in (1)–(6) have been found to be interrelated. As for (7), it would be interesting to find out whether there is indeed a correlation between memory and dominance. I believe it has been shown that final constituents are remembered most easily in such tests. I myself have not been able to find detailed accounts of such tests, although I have seen them referred to in the literature; even so, one might hazard a guess that these final constituents are dominant in the sentences tested, and I would like to see an experiment constructed to discover if this is, in fact, the case. Neither do I have any first-hand evidence of (8) or (9); however, it might turn out that the processes discussed in Givon (this volume) and in E. Ochs (this volume) are relevant here. The definition of dominance proposed in Erteschik-Shir and Lappin (1977) that determines its discourse characteristics is as follows:

> DOMINANCE: A constituent C of a sentence S is dominant in S if and only if the speaker intends to direct the attention of his hearers to the intension of C by uttering S.[2]

Thus, it is assumed that a speaker selects a particular constituent of a sentence, intuitively, the most significant one, to which he seeks to direct the speaker's attention. This constituent therefore becomes the natural candidate for the topic of further conversation. One way to test which constituents X of a sentence can be interpreted as being dominant is to set up a discourse situation in which Speaker A utters the sentence being tested and Speaker B responds by means of a sentence in which X is assigned a truth, probability, or even interest value. Let us test the following three sentences as examples:[3]

(1) a. *John said that Mary kissed Bill.*
     b. *John thought that Mary kissed Bill.*
     c. *John mumbled that Mary kissed Bill.*

[2] The concept of intension used is basically the same as that presented in Lewis (1972). Intuitively, the intension of a constituent may be thought of as its semantic content. Thus, what this definition states is that a constituent is dominant in a sentence S when a speaker intends to draw attention to its semantic content by uttering S.

[3] Speakers may differ in their judgments in these tests, reflecting the existence of variation among speakers in the distribution of the possibility of dominance. However, for any given speaker there should be a predictable correlation between the structure of dominance possibilities that he allows and his application of the syntactic rules under discussion.

The discourse test determing whether or not the embedded sentence in each case can be interpreted as being dominant is as follows:

(2)   a.   Speaker A: *John said that Mary kissed Bill.*
             Speaker B: *That's a lie, she didn't.*
                          (or, similarly: *That's amusing, I never thought she would*, etc.)

             Speaker A: *John thought that Mary kissed Bill.*
             Speaker B: *That's true, she did.*

       c.   Speaker A: *John mumbled that Mary kissed Bill.*
             Speaker B: ??*That's a lie, she didn't.*
                          (Note that replacing *is a lie* by *is true, is amusing, is highly probable*, etc., does not improve Speaker B's response.)

The tests show that the embedded clause of (1a) and (1b) can be interpreted as being dominant and that (1c) cannot naturally be used where the context forces a dominant interpretation of the embedded clause.[4] That is, the embedded clauses of (1a) and (1b) [but not (1c)] can function as the so-called "main" or "dominant" part of the sentence. What led me to choose the term "dominance" was the fact that I was able to relate the possibility of extraction out of embedded clauses to their potential for functioning as main clauses (in this sense) in discourse. In the present chapter it will be my concern to determine dominance of NPs. A similar test applies:

(3)   Speaker A: *I saw Picasso's picture of the blue angle yesterday.*
       Speaker B: *Oh yes, I know which one it is.*

Note that *it* can only refer to *Picasso's picture of the blue angel* and not to the *blue angel*. This indicates that it is only the larger NP that can be interpreted as being dominant in the sentence uttered by Speaker A and that *the blue angel* cannot. In other words, the speaker of the sentence is not intending to direct the attention of B to the embedded NP, preventing B from making it the center of conversation in the follow-up sentence. Contrast this case with the following one:

(4)   Speaker A: *I saw a picture of the blue angel yesterday.*
       Speaker B: *Oh yes, I know which one it is.*

---

[4] The test can be modified to apply to different kinds of complement types. See Erteschik-Shir and Lappin (1977) for such cases.

This sentence is ambiguous with respect to dominance, since B could be commenting either on his familiarity with the picture or with the blue angel. (However, when used in context such sentences are disambiguated.)[5]

I would like to show why other, more familiar discourse notions that have been used by others have been rejected here. Following is a selection of such discourse notions (I have chosen the ones that seem to come closest to the concept of dominance): assertion (Creider, this volume); new information Chafe 1975); focus (Chomsky 1971; Garcia, this volume, seems to use focus differently); communicative dynamism (Firbas 1974), comment or rheme (various authors). Although dominance seems to have something in common with all of these notions, this cannot be stated with absolute certainty. A great many of these concepts have never been clearly defined, and, in other cases, no two linguists can agree on a definition. By way of justifying the proposed definition of dominance and the introduction of yet another term

---

[5] Other tests could be devised to determine dominance. Question–answer pairs have been frequently used in the literature for similar purposes (see Chomsky 1971, and Creider, this volume). Thus, the following discourse.

(i)   Speaker A: *Who did you see?*
             Speaker B: *I saw Paul.*

indicates that *Paul* is dominant, since A's question specifies that B must direct A's attention to this NP. The NP that "answers" the wh-question is necessarily dominant. It is, therefore, not possible to wh-question an NP that cannot be interpreted as being dominant. The treatment of wh-questions implied here is part of the theory of extraction presented in Erteschik-Shir and Lappin (1977). Questioning is just one syntactic device for turning an NP into the main point of conversation. The reason I have tried to maintain "pure" discourse tests is that at this stage I am trying to show that these syntactic facts follow from the discourse function of dominance. If syntactic tests were used, such an argument would become circular. So, for example,

(ii)   *Who did you see Picasso's picture of yesterday?*

should not be used to argue that the embedded NP cannot be dominant here, if what one is trying to show is that extraction depends on dominance. Another problem with this sort of test is that the more specific the NP that answers the wh-question, the more natural the answer. This fact has nothing to do with dominance but, rather, with the fact that anyone who asked a question would like as specific an answer as possible. Hence, the answer in (i) is, in some sense, better than the one in (iii).

(iii)   Speaker A: *Who did you see?*
             Speaker B: *I saw someone.*

The test suggested here is, therefore, intended to apply to as broad a set of cases as possible without syntactic or semantic interference. It is, however, possible that in certain cases such interference is inevitable. It is not usually difficult to distinguish such cases in which the test fails for the wrong reasons.

to this rather long list, I would like to show in what way dominance is a different concept. Assertion, new information, and focus are usually defined as that part of the sentence that is not presupposed or given. Pressuposition and givenness, in turn, have been defined in various ways, of which the most relevant is pragmatic presupposition or Chafe's (1975:30) notion of givenness: "Given (or old) information is that knowledge which the speaker assumes to be in the consciousness of the addressee at the time of the utterance." Although a number of clues are given on how to establish what is given in a sentence (low pitch, weak stress, pronominalization), no clear strategy is suggested for determining the division between new and old information. Nonetheless, the distinction here is clearly not that between dominance and nondominance. Specificially, it is possible that information that is not old will not be treated as being dominant by the speaker. For example, in discourse (2b) the embedded clause *that Mary kissed Bill* is dominant and the matrix *John thought* is nondominant, but it does not follow that this part is in any sense part of the hearer's consciousness. In the following analysis of Dative Movement, it will become clear that those constituents that are nondominant are not necessarily "old" in any sense of the term. Similarly, it can be shown that material of recent vintage in a discourse sequence can still be repeated and be dominant.[6]

To the extent that the notions of topic and comment are clear, one might say that the topic of the sentence is necessarily nondominant and that the rest of the sentence, the comment, includes the dominant constituent. Again, however, the pie is not sliced in the way proposed here. Communicative dynamism could probably be correlated with dominance, since it seems that the constituent with the highest CD is the dominant one. Firbas intends CD to be a relative notion, whereas in Erteschik-Shir and Lappin (1977) it was argued that dominance is an absolute property.

We may, therefore, conclude that there is justification for introducing a new term, if for no other reason than to force us to define it clearly instead of relying on the intuitive appeal of notions that may have lingered long in the arena of discussion but over which there has rarely been agreement.

2. DETERMINERS AND DOMINANCE

Before considering dominance relations in double object constructions, let us examine by means of the abovementioned dominance test for NPs the

---

[6] See Lehman (1977) for such examples from real discourse.

behavior of NPs with various determiners and degrees of specificity (read these sentences with nuclear accent on the object NP):

(5)   Speaker A: *John killed a cop.*
       Speaker B: *Oh yes, I know which one it is.*

(6)   Speaker A: *John killed the cop who was a criminal himself.*
       Speaker B: *Oh yes, I know which one it is.*

(7)   Speaker A: *John killed the cop.*
       Speaker B: ?*Oh yes, I know which one it is.*

(8)   Speaker A: *John killed the president.*
       Speaker B: ??*Oh yes, I know which one it is.*

(9)   Speaker A: *John killed Howie.*
       Speaker B: **Oh yes, I know which Howie it is.*

(10)   Speaker A: *John killed him.*
       Speaker B: ***Oh yes, I know who he is.*

This series of tests reveals the well-known principle, that the various determiners form a hierarchy: Indefinites are generally used to indicate that the NP is dominant; definites in general are used as an indication that the NP is nondominant; pronouns cannot possibly be used dominantly.[7]

Individual speakers may not agree with the exact degree of acceptability indicated in (5)–(10). Nevertheless, any speaker of English will have a similar hierarchy, which will very likely progress in the same order. If a speaker should be found who disagrees violently, I would suspect that the same speaker would also disagree—and in a systematic way—with the data in the following sections. The argument here is that, for each speaker, certain strategies exist that are applied consistently. Obviously, speakers of the same community will not be expected to differ greatly, for otherwise the lack of similar strategies used by the speakers would make communication difficult.

---

[7] Chafe (1975) notes that the following combinations are possible: indefinite and new, definite and new, and definite and given. The combination indefinite and given does not occur unless the referent in question is different from the referent that established the givenness. Note, however, that, since the division new–given is not consistently parallel to the distinction dominant–nondominant, we do not derive identical results; indefinities can be both dominant and nondominant.

See also Morgan (1975) for this kind of analysis of the use of the definite article. There, the author calls for linguistic analysis that deals with the function of linguistic items such as articles, complementizers, and the like and also indicates that it is probably the case that transformations can be defined according to the purpose they serve with respect to the speaker's intentions.

If we look at the results of tests (5)–(10) in greater detail, we notice that a definite NP with a relative clause giving additional information about the N [see (6)] is easier to interpret as being dominant than is a simple definite NP [as in (7)]. This makes a good deal of sense. A speaker who uses the NP as in (6) assumes that the hearer would not be able to pick out the referent of the NP if the relative clause were not added. In other words, the referent of *the cop* has not been established sufficiently in the previous discourse to enable the hearer to know which cop is being referred to. The purpose of the relative clause is to enable the hearer to pick out the referent of the NP. In (7), material of this kind is assumed to be known by the hearer, and the NP without the relative clause is, therefore, less easy to interpret as being dominant. In (8), an NP has been chosen where the definite article, due to its idiomatic use in this case, indicates that reference is being made to the current president. The use of this NP only makes sense in case the speaker assumes that the hearer knows who the current president is. The sentence is being used to say something about what happened to the NP, and THAT is the dominant information in the sentence. An identical situation holds when the speaker uses a proper name. When a pronoun is used, it is not only that the speaker assumes that the hearer is able to pick out the referent of the NP; it is also the case that this NP must have been referred to in the immediate discourse context of the sentence. It is, therefore, absurd to place the sentence in a test-context that tries to force a dominant interpretation on the pronoun.

It must be stressed that the use of a definite NP is not always or necessarily to be interpreted nondominantly. I am sure that there are instances in which definite NPs are not interpreted in this way. However, the usual purpose in employing a definite article IS to indicate to the hearer that the speaker takes for granted that the hearer has the referent of the NP in mind and that it is not intended as dominant material. The same holds true with the other kinds of NPs. As far as I know, there is only one NP that cannot possibly be used dominantly, and that is *it*. Other NPs, such as regular pronouns (*him*, *her*), can receive emphatic stress to make it easier to arrive at a dominant interpretation even when it is not the normal one. *It* cannot even receive emphatic stress. This is to be expected, for a speaker can only use *it* in a sentence that immediately follows another sentence in which the referent of *it* has been given. *It* is, thus, the archetype of the nondominant NP.

There is, obviously, much more to be said about the function of using certain kinds of NPs. For example, the position of the NP in the sentence is crucial. Move the same NPs that appear in (5)–(10) into subject position, and the results should be different. Different intonation and stress will also alter the results. Here, it suffices, as a preliminary to examining how these functions interact with Dative Movement, to point to the general functions of the different kinds of NPs in discourse.

3. DOMINANCE AND DATIVE MOVEMENT

The following kinds of sentences have frequently been pointed to as problematic for a transformational analysis of dative sentences.

(11)   a.   *John gave it to Mary.*
              b.   **John gave Mary it.*

(12)   a.   *Who did John give the book to?*
              b.   **Who did John give the book?*

(13)   a.   *Mary was given the book.*
              b.   **Mary was given the book to.*[8]

I will argue here that these data and others are accounted for and explained by the following hypothesis:

A: *In the structure* ... $V NP_1 NP_2$ *(derived from* ... $V NP_2 \begin{Bmatrix} to \\ for \end{Bmatrix}$ NP_1) NP_1 *is nondominant and* NP_2 *is dominant.*[9]

An attempt was made to deal with problem illustrated by (12) and (13) by means of a syntactic constraint described in Culicover and Wexler (1973).

---

[8] If dominance rules this sentence out, then it is possible to have a simpler formulation of the passive rule. However, see Footnote 13.

[9] If an adverb or some other constituent follows the objects, the assignment of dominance might differ. The following sentence, brought to my attention by Richard Oehrle, illustrates this:

(i)   *I don't believe how stupid John is! He's sending me the stuff by régular máil.*

Here the dominant constituent is *by regular mail*. The claim here is that the NP following the V after Dative Movement has occured must be nondominant and that the following NP is dominant except in cases similar to the preceding, where a following stressed constituent is dominant. Note that (ii) is an improvement on (iii).

(ii)   *He's sending me it by régular máil.*
(iii)   *He's sending me it.*

In other words, in (ii) *it* must not be interpreted as being dominant as in (iii), the sort of case that we are trying to rule out by Hypothesis A.

The entire question of sentence-final position as being reserved for dominant material is an important one, but the amount of material relevant to this matter is vast indeed. In this context it would be relevant to examine all transformations that move elements to the right. An extremely likely result of such an investigation would be that all such movement rules function to place dominant material in sentence-final position. In addition, it would be appropriate to examine whether sentence-final position possesses a particular psychological status. (Such studies, I am sure, have been undertaken.) In the present chapter I shall, therefore, limit the discussion to the discourse function of Dative Movement; the fact that sentence-final position is relevant here can then be used in a study of the larger issue.

It was proposed there that the principle of freezing accounts for the unacceptability of (12b). The idea is that, once Dative Movement has occurred,
the VP in which it occurred is frozen to further syntactic movement. From
this approach, it would follow that (13a) should also be unacceptable, which,
of course, it is not. The possibility of passivization in which questioning or
relativization is blocked is, thus, an unresolved issue in this analysis. The
authors try to deal with this difficulty by stating that the data on the passive
is erratic anyway. As we shall see in the section on the interaction of passive
and Dative Movement, the data is, in fact, predicted by the approach given
here. The same approach also explains the data presented in (11). Another
account was proposed by Oehrle (1975), who offers a constraint on variables
that avoids the problem of distinguishing between movement rules over
variables as against passive. However, an independent constraint for this
case is unnecessary within the framework established here, where this data
is an outcome of the function of Dative Movement.

The data to be used to set forth my claim for the role of dominance in
Dative Movement now follows. A rather large number of informants have
been questioned for these data. The preferred order is marked by ✓.

(14)   a.   *John gave a book to Mary.*
              b. ✓ *John gave Mary a book.*

(15)   a.   *John gave a book to the girl.*
              b. ✓ *John gave the girl a book.*

(16)   a.   *John gave a book to her.*
              b. ✓ *John gave her a book.*

(17)   a.   *John gave the book to Mary.*
              b. ✓ *John gave Mary the book.*

(18)   a.   *John gave the book to her.*
              b. ✓ *John gave her the book.*

(19)   a. ✓ *John gave the book to a girl.*
              b.   *John gave a girl the book.*

Sentences (14)–(18) are cases in which the rule places the NP in final position,
which is more easily interpreted as being dominant according to the hierarchy
established above. In each case, the version in which the rule is applied is
preferred by speakers.[10] In (19), the underlying order is already such that

---

[10] Presumably, the data would gain greater strength if one were to take these sentences
from the contexts in which they are actually used. I would predict that speakers would consistently use those sentences that are here indicated as being preferred, unless the context
forced a different interpretation of the NPs with respect to dominance than does the hierarchy.

the more dominant NP follows the less dominant one, and this order is preferred. From this data alone, one could conclude that the rule functions to order object NPs in such a way that the dominant one follows the non-dominant one. In order to see this more clearly, let us test the result of Dative Movement in our dominance test:

(20)   Speaker A: *John gave a book to someone yesterday.*
         Speaker B: *Oh yes, I know who it was.*

(21)   Speaker A: *John gave someone a book yesterday.*
         Speaker B: a.   **Oh yes, I know who it was.*
                   b.   *Oh yes, I know which one it was.*

In (20) the response can be either *someone* or *a book*. In (21), however, the reponse can only be designed to refer to *a book*; that is, *someone* cannot be interpreted as being dominant after Dative Movement has applied. The test thus strengthens the analysis of Dative Movement as a rule that functions to force a dominant interpretation of the NP that ends up in final position (and a nondominant interpretation of the other NP). The validity of the test can be somewhat questionable owing to the fact that, in other cases, the NPs themselves create a more or less dominant interpretation [i.e., if we were to choose both definite and indefinite NPs, as in (14)–(19)], and this interpretation is, therefore, not entailed by the movement rule alone. Nevertheless, the following sentences indicate that choosing two NPs with the same status with respect to dominance could also confuse the issue:

(22)   a.   *John gave a book to a girl.*
         b.   *John gave a girl a book.*

(23)   a.   *John gave the book to the girl.*
         b.   *John gave the girl the book.*

The reaction of most speakers to these sentences is that both (a) and (b) in each case are odd, but the tendency is to prefer the (a) sentences to the (b) versions. The oddness of the (a) sentences arises because it is hard to find a context in which the information they give would contribute to the discourse. A possible context for (22a) would be as a response to:

(24)   *What did John do in the school play?*

Here, it does not matter which book or what girl; the information is that John performed this act on stage. A possible context for (23a) would be:

(25)   *Who did John give the book to?*

Here, it must be clear from the context which book and what girl are being referred to, but *the girl* is dominant in (23a). In each case, it is harder to find an interpretation in which *a book* and *the book*, respectively, is the most dominant in the context; hence, the (b) versions are even worse than the (a) versions. We might wish to apply the dominance test to these sentences, but the results would be skewed due to the fact that the sentences are odd in almost any context. However, the evidence from sentences (14)–(21) seems to be strong enough to argue that the function of Dative Movement is, indeed, that of Hypothesis A. Sentences (22) and (23) support this interpretation of the data in that the (b) versions are less acceptable, since higher dominance is attributed here to one out of two NPs of the same dominance status.

We are now in a position to solve the problem presented by (11), repeated here as (28).

(26)   a.   *John gave it to a girl.*
                 b.   **John gave a girl it.*

(27)   a.   *John gave it to the girl.*
                 b.   **John gave the girl it.*

(28)   a.   *John gave it to Mary.*
                 b.   **John gave Mary it.*

(29)   a.   *John gave it to her.*
                 b.   **John gave her it.*

I have already argued that *it* can never be interpreted as being dominant. I have further argued that the function of Dative Movement is to ensure the dominant interpretation of the NP that ends up in final position—in this case, *it*. What rules out the (b) sentences in (26)–(29) is the fact that dominance is being assigned to an NP that cannot be interpreted dominantly.[11]

---

[11] For some speakers, (29b) is not quite so bad as the rest. It appears that, since the other NP is also a pronoun and is also not a good candidate for a dominant interpretation, the difference between having either NP in final position is not so great, thus somehow improving the sentence for a number of speakers.

Note that adopting Oehrle's approach would enable us to explain the following kinds of cases as well (this was pointed out to me by Oehrle):

(i)   *Does John still have his job?*
                             *No, his last mistake cost him it.

If we assume, with Oehrle, that double-object constructions are lexically rather than transformationally derived whether or not they have related prepositional forms, then we could generalize to say that the choice of such a double object construction determines that the NP following the verb is nondominant and that the following one is dominant. This would explain (i) in the same way that it explains (29b).

Another enigma that may be naturally solved in a problem raised by, among others, Green (1974). She points out that, although one cannot say

(30)   *John gave pneumonia to Mary.,

One does say

(31)   John gave Mary pneumonia.

The following sentence indicates that no condition on Dative Movement that makes the transformation obligatory with "diseases" and the like will suffice:

(32)   John gave Mary pneumonia and **he gave it to Ted** too.

(33)   *John gave Mary pneumonia and **he gave Ted it** too.

Such a condition would rule out (32) as well as (30) unless it were further complicated to take into account cases with pronouns, a rather unsatisfactory solution. Our theory, however, predicts (32) and (33). In the second part of these sentences *pneumonia* is not interpreted as being dominant, since it has been mentioned already in the first part; hence, the pronoun and the non-dominant position that it occupies is the second conjunct of (32). What remains to be explained is why, upon first mention, as in (30), *pneumonia* and other such diseases have to be interpreted dominantly.

To summarize what has been argued so far, let me present the following sets of sentences:

(34)   a.   *Pass the salt to me, please.*
                    b.   *Pass me the salt, please.*

Sentence (34a) is odd unless one imagines a context where the person addressed is seated at the table and is clutching the salt, not knowing what to do with it. In that context, however, (34b) is odd. Most contexts, that is, define the important part of the sentence as the speaker's wanting the salt; sentence (34b), in which this NP must necessarily be interpreted as being dominant, is, therefore, much more natural. In a context where *the salt* need not be dominant, however, (34a) is possible as well. The theory developed here predicts the contexts in which the (34a) and (34b) versions can occur by means of Dative Movement Hypothesis A. Obviously, linguistic theory must include a mechanism to account for the discourse contexts in which the various versions of sentences can occur. My theory is meant to do just that. The fact that it also follows from the theory that (11b) is unacceptable is an argument that the theory can naturally account for certain data that other theories may have difficulty explaining. It indicates, too, that these kinds of data belong to the domain of discourse constraints and not to that of syntactic constraints.[12]

Up to now I have ignored the issue of the interaction of stress placement on the data. This issue is taken up in detail in Erteschik-Shir and Lappin (1978), but a few brief comments would be useful here. We argue in our paper that sentential stress is determined by dominance. Let us examine the stress patterns of the cases under discussion:

(35)   *John gave the book to Máry.*

(36)   *John gave the bóok to Mary.*

(37)   *John gave Mary the bóok.*

(38)   *John gave Máry the book.*

According to our analysis, the stressed NPs of (35), (36), and (37) can be interpreted as being dominant, although (36) should be less natural than (35). However, if stress means dominance, (38) should not be possible. Richard Oehrle (personal communication) noticed that the ONLY possible interpretation here is one in which *Mary* is interpreted contrastively, implying that the speaker believes the hearer has a finite list of persons in mind and the speaker is indicating that, of this list, *Mary* is the relevant one. Since a contrastive NP is not itself dominant [see Erteschik-Shir and Lappin (1978) for an explanation of this point], the fact that we only get a contrastive interpretation here is further evidence for the present analysis.

In what follows, we shall see that the constraints exemplified by (12) and (13) similarly follow from the function of the rule of Dative Movement in discourse. Consider the following sentences in which, as in (12b), the NP that was fronted by Dative Movement has been moved again by another transformation:

[12b]   **Who did John give the book?*

(39)   **The girl that John gave the book is very nice.*

(40)   **It is that girl that John gave the book.*

(41)   **The person who John gave the book is Mary.*

---

[12] For the sake of brevity, I have left out of the discussion examples in which Dative Movement applies to sentential complements. Even so, such cases merely strengthen the analysis. Notice the following distribution:

(i)   **John told that he liked ice cream to Mary.*
(ii)   *John told Mary that he liked ice cream.*

Sentences are always relatively more dominant than NPs, and it is only in the cases in which Dative Movement has applied that we get this interpretation naturally.

In each of these sentences, an NP has been highlighted by means of questioning, relativization, clefting, or pseudo-clefting. It has been argued that, since it is the function of Dative Movement to ensure the dominant interpretation of the NP that ends in final position, it is also the case that the other NP must be assigned nondominance. What causes the unacceptability of sentences (12b) and (39)–(41) is the forced interpretation of a certain NP as simultaneously nondominant (due to the function of Dative Movement) AND as dominant (due to the functions of the transformations that have applied in these sentences that focus on the same NP). Clearly, sentences cannot be processed when two opposite strategies apply to the same NP.

As for the passive, there is no such reason that blocks its applying to this NP, as in (13a). The passive is a process that places NPs and Ss in subject position, which is the usual locus for nondominant material and, thus, does not interfere with the nondominant material of the NP.[13] As mentioned briefly, an attempt was made by Culicover and Wexler (1973) to account for sentences such as (12b). Following their constraint, however, passivization should be blocked as well. But my analysis predicts that the NP that cannot be moved by means of Relativization, Questioning, Clefting, and the like CAN be passivized. One is left with the puzzling fact that passive does not apply with equal ease in all cases. Culicover and Wexler present the following data to illustrate this (their 37):

(42) *John was* *given a book for Christmas.*
                **sent a bomb in the mail.*
                **bought a horse for his birthday.*
                **passed the salt.*
                **thrown a football.*
                **given a birthday party.*
                shown a picture of the Eiffel Tower.
                offered a post in the administration.
                sold the Brooklyn Bridge.
                **written a nice long letter.*
                told a pack of lies.
                **fed some Pablum for breakfast.*
                **read a story about spies.*
                **wished good luck by the President.*
                **lent a good sum of money.*
                **paid a lot of money.*

---

[13] For the purposes of the present argument, it is sufficient to state that passivization is not limited to dominant NPs. A strong hypothesis would be that passivization is restricted to nondominant NPs.

The authors add that very few people will share their judgments, and, indeed, I have found no such speakers. I do agree, however, that speakers differ considerably with respect to this data. Culicover and Wexler believe that the movability of the indirect object depends on the verb. This may be so; on the other hand, the data they present show that with the same verb, *give*, passive is acceptable in one case but not in another. It follows that the whole sentence seems to matter, not just the verb. Let me repeat that the function of Dative Movement as set out in Hypothesis A does not prevent passivization in these cases; in other words, from what has been said so far we should predict that passive will be equally good in all cases.

It has been proposed (Fillmore 1965) that the *for*-Dative rule is distinct from the *to*-Dative rule, since for some speakers passive following *for*-Dative Movement is generally worse than passive following *to*-Dative Movement. Since I have found no speakers who confirm this data, I have not attempted to account for it. The facts are more erratic than that; as Culicover and Wexler state, very few speakers agree with each other on the data, and it seems that there are acceptable and unacceptable passives both among the *to*-Datives and among the *for*-Datives.[14] The question then remains whether the possibility of passivization in these instances depends on the dominance relations in the sentence or on some other aspect of the sentence. I think we can rule out a strictly syntactic cause. Oehrle argues that a thematic hierarchy similar to that of Jackendoff (1972) might account for passivization here, and he also mentions that Fiengo's (1974) idea of "property interpretation" might succeed in doing the same thing. Some process similar to Fiengo's notion of "property interpretation" is probably at work.[15] But, whatever the final analysis, it must necessarily predict the fact that speakers differ so widely in their intuitions.

A further passivization problem is exemplified by the following sentence:

(43)   *A book was given me.*

Oehrle (1975) notes that this kind of passive occurs only when the indirect object is a pronoun. He suggests two alternative analyses, the more preferable one being that cliticization takes place, "which optionally incorporates the first of two noun phrases to the right of the verb (if it is a definite pronoun) in such a way as to make a single constituent of the verb and the pronoun." In the analysis in which Dative Movement precedes this rule of cliticization, the approach taken here may present a problem. If the strong passivization hypothesis, which claims that passive only applies to non-dominant NPs (see Footnote 13), is maintained, then passive could not

---

[14] See Oehrle (1975) for an argument that this is the case.
[15] See Bolinger (1975) for a discussion of this issue.

apply to *a book*, which is dominant after Dative Movement. Sentence (43) would, thus, be ruled out. It seems, then, that the weaker hypothesis of the application of passive must be adhered to, since both dominant and non-dominant NPs can be passivized. Requiring further investigation, however, is the difference between the use of (43) and (44) in discourse.

(44)   *A book was given to me.*

If such a difference exists (and I have not been able to isolate it yet), then this difference should be reflected in the analysis, and it is possible that such an investigation will shed further light on the nature of the restrictions on passives.

It was pointed out by Gundel (1977) that leftward movement of NPs might variously function to topicalize that NP or to contrast it. Note the following sentences:

(45)   *(As for) Mary, I gave her a book.*

(46)   **(As for) a book, I gave her one.*

(47)   *Máry, I gave a book.*

(48)   *Mary, I gave a bóok.*

(49)   *The yellow book, I gave Mary, the blue one, I gave Tom.*

(50)   **The book, I gave Máry.*

According to Gundel, the fronted NPs in (45) and (46) must be interpreted as the topic of the sentence. Sentences (45) and (46) indicate that only the nondominant NP can function as the topic of the sentence, which, of course, is a natural outcome. Sentence (47) provides a case in which the fronted NP is contrasted, and (48) is a case in which it is a topic, as in (45). Sentence (49) is another instance of contrast that is not dependent on dominance, and (50) is a case in which *the book* would be dominant because of Hypothesis A and nondominant as a result of Topicalization (it cannot be interpreted as contrast, since it is not stressed)—it is this conflict that rules the sentence out.

The next problem, which has puzzled a number of linguists, is the interaction of Dative Movement and Particle Shift. It has been pointed out by several linguists, including Ross (1967) and Green (1974), that some constraints on Particle Shift are similar to those on Dative Movement, notably:

(51)   a.   **I pulled out it.*
                       b.   *I pulled it out.*

Note the following sentences as well:

(52)   a. ✓ *John pulled out a present.*
                        b.   *John pulled a present out.*

(53)   a.   *John pulled out the present.*
                        b. ✓ *John pulled the present out.*

(54)   a.   *John pulled out Mary.*
                        b. ✓ *John pulled Mary out.*

These preferences clearly show that when the NP follows the particle it must be interpreted as being dominant. The test supports this:

(55)   Speaker A: *John pulled a present out.*
              Speaker B: *?Oh yes, I know which one it was.*

(56)   Speaker A: *John pulled out a present.*
              Speaker B: *Oh yes, I know which one it was.*

The fact that sequence (56) is more acceptable than (55) indicates that it is easier to interpret *a present* as being dominant in (56) than it is in (55). Having established that the NP following the particle is more naturally interpreted as being dominant, let us examine the interaction of Dative Movement and Particle Shift. Consider these sentences (from Culicover and Wexler 1973):

(57)   a.   *John gave back the money to the bank.*
                        b.   *John gave the money back to the bank.*
                        c. **John gave the money to the bank back.*

(58)   a. **John gave back the bank the money.*
                        b.   *John gave the bank back the money.*
                        c.   *John gave the bank the money back.*

Assume for the sake of argument that (57a) is the base structure. Sentence (57b) is then derived by an optional application of Particle Shift. Both are acceptable sentences. In (57a) both the direct and the indirect object can be dominant (although the latter is the more natural interpretation). In (57b) the position of the particle reinforces the nondominant interpretation of the direct object, and this version is, if anything, an improvement over (57a). Sentence (57c) has no possible derivation unless some other rule in addition to the two rules under discussion exists, and there is, therefore, no reason to explain its nonexistence. Sentence (58b) can be derived from (57a) by means of Dative Movement.[16] The function of Dative Movement

---

[16] Oehrle pointed out to me that the rule could be formulated in this way.

forces a nondominant interpretation of *the bank*, as does the position of the particle. If the Dative Movement rule is written so as to derive (58b) from (57a), (58a) could not be derived. Moreover, (58a) is ruled out for pragmatic reasons as well, since *the bank* would have to be interpreted as both dominant and nondominant, and this conflict makes the sentence unacceptable. Sentence (58c) is derived by Particle Shift that follows Dative Movement. The sentence should be acceptable according to the dominance relations: According to Dative Movement, *the bank* must be interpreted as being nondominant and *the money* as dominant. Our analysis of Particle Shift was that the NP following the particle is dominant and that the natural interpretation of the NP preceding the particle is nondominant, but the latter conclusion is not essential. This permits the acceptability of (58c). Notice, moreover, the following (perhaps fine) distinction:

(59)   *Some student paid the bank his loan back.*

(60)   *?Some student paid the bank a loan back.*

It seems to be the case that, when the final NP is lower on the hierarchy of dominance, it is preferable when it precedes the particle than when it is higher up on the same hierarchy.

If this were the whole story, we could be well satisfied. The data follow from the functions of the rules involved. However, speakers differ widely on whether or not they agree with the data of Culicover and Wexler—and many, in particular, cannot accept (58c) and other sentences with this structure. For example, the following are all unacceptable, according to Emonds (1976:82):

(61)   a.   **The secretary sent the stockholders a schedule out.*
            b.   **Some student paid the bank his loan back.*
            c.   **John read Mary the figures off.*
            d.   **A clerk will type John a permit out.*
            e.   **Bill fixed John a drink up.*
            f.   **He has brought Dad some cigars down.*

As was previously stated, there is a mild pragmatic conflict here. The second object must be interpreted dominantly according to Dative Movement and is most naturally interpreted as being nondominant according to the position of the particle. I have found speakers who agree with Emonds' data in that all the sentences of (61) are rejected equally. My conclusion for those speakers is that, in their grammar, this mild conflict is more significant. However, I have found no speaker who accepts all the sentences of (61), and so a further account remains to be made. (Emonds admits that some people accept sentences with *back* in final position (61b), but he chooses to ignore such sentences, since they seem to him to be unsystematic and limited in number.) Having tried to examine carefully the sentences in (61), I will present the data of one dialect:

(62)   a.   *The secretary sent the stockholders a schedule out.
        b.   Some student paid the bank his loan back.
        c.   *John read Mary the figures off.
        d.   *A clerk will type John a permit out.
        e.   (The speaker didn't **fix up** drinks, but rather **fixed** them.)
        f.   He has brought Dad some cigars down.

For this speaker, Dative Movement did not seem to apply at all with *send out*:

(63)   ??The secretary sent the stockholders out a schedule.

The fact that (62a) was unacceptable is no evidence one way or the other. Given that the source of (62b) is a *to*-Dative and that the source of (62f) is a *for*-Dative, no theory based on that distinction can be valid here. From this set of data it appears that the directional particles are the ones that are allowed in final position. This means that, for these speakers, Particle Shift has different consequences depending on the nature of the particle. Whether or not such is, indeed, the case is a matter for further research. Much more data and many more speakers must be examined. It is clear that the analysis presented here does not preclude the existence of any of the three kinds of dialects mentioned. It must be added that this sort of data has also not been used as evidence for my own theory and that any analysis that does use such erratic data as evidence will be hard pressed to account for any dialect except the authors' own. Emonds admits to different dialects, but he seems to feel that any differences will depend on the *to/for* distinction, and we have shown that this is not always the case.

There are two additional issues that arise in the course of a more careful examination of the data. First, not all cases of verbs with a particle followed by direct and indirect objects allow Dative Movement. Again, speakers may vary as to which verbs they find acceptable and which they do not. I shall refrain from taking a stance on this issue, just as I ignored the question when treating simple verbs.[17]

---

[17] See Oehrle (1975) for a discussion of this problem. It may be that dominance is also relevant to this matter, but I leave that possibility to further research. The purpose of the present chapter is to show that when Dative Movement does apply it has certain consequences for discourse. The question of why it does not apply in certain cases is a separate concern.

The second problem is illustrated by the following sentences from Emonds (1976:46):

(64) a. *?The secretary sent out the stockholders a schedule.*
      b. *?Some student paid back the bank his loan.*
      c. *?John read off Mary the figures.*
      d. *?A clerk will type out John a permit.*
      e. *?Bill fixed up John a drink.*
      f. *?He has brought down Dad some cigars.*

Emonds believes that there are three idiolects. The first, (A), accepts all the sentences in (64) (I have found no such speakers, but this does not mean that they do not exist). The second, (B), rejects them all, but not as firmly as those in (61). In the third idiolect, (C), the sentences derived from *to*-Datives, namely, (64a), (64b), and (64c), are acceptable, and those derived from *for*-Datives, that is, (64d), (64c), and (64f), are not. I have found speakers who accept some of the sentences of (64); again, the distinction is not between *to* and *for* datives.[18] For example, to one speaker, the following data pertained:

(65) a. **The secretary sent out the stockholders a schedule.*
      b. *Some student paid back the bank his loan.*
      c. *John read off Mary the figures.*
      d. *A clerk will type out John a permit.*
      e. **Bill fixed up John a date.*[19]
      f. *?He has brought down Dad some cigars.*

Sentence (65a) is unacceptable because this speaker does not allow Dative Movement to apply at all in this case. Sentence (65d), however, which is a case arising from a *for*-Dative, is perfectly good for this speaker, whereas (65e) and (65f) are not. From this limited set of data, it seems to be that, when the particle does not change the essential meaning of the verb, the speaker analyses the verb—particle as one verb unit, allowing for the acceptability of a sentence, which would otherwise constitute a problem, for the NP following the particle would normally have to be interpreted as being dominant. I would, therefore, suggest that a strategy prevails among some speakers that allows them to "ignore" the particle when it is adjacent to its verb and when it does not change the meaning of the verb essentially, as it does in (65e) and, to a certain extent, in (65f). Another

---

[18] See Oehrle for further arguments against Emonds.
[19] The idiom was changed to one acceptable to the informant.

way of putting it would be to say that, under those circumstances, the particle itself can, be, for some speakers, totally void of dominance. Sentences (65c) and (65d) present no problem for this approach. In (65b), however, one might think that the particle has a separate function. In the context of the sentence in which *a loan to a bank* is in question, *back* is more obviously redundant than in the following.

(66)   ??*Some student paid back his friend $10.*

This is much less acceptable, indicating that this explanation might be correct.[20]

Oehrle (1975) distinguishes two kinds of particles in double object constructions.

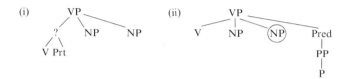

More precisely, he argues that a subset of what has been referred to here as particles are indeed particles and that they occur in structures such as (i). Particle Shift then applies optionally to position the particle between the two NPs. However, another subset actually consists of prepositions that arise from Pred position, as in (ii). Heavy NP shift applies optionally to postpose the encircled NP, and again we get the P positioned between the two NPs. Oehrle emphasizes that there is no exact means of distinguishing the two subsets other than by examining the positions they occur in, although stress factors do play a role. However, he mentions that the Prt in (i) seems to play less of a role with respect to meaning than do the Ps of (ii). If we accept Oehrle's arguments, we can say that *pay back*, *read off*, and *type out* arise from (i) and that *fix up* and *bring down* arise from (ii); hence, (65e)

----

[20] A problem arises due to the unacceptability of the following sentences:

> *Some student paid back me his loan.
> *John read off her the figures.
> *A clerk will type out him a permit.

There is no doubt that these will be rejected in all dialects: That is, here the constraint preventing the particle from being followed by nondominant material holds just as we expected it would hold in *all* the sentences of (65) as well. It seems plausible that the sequence of particle–pronoun here, which is normally ruled out by dominance restrictions in all cases, may not be ignored, thus implying that speakers cannot reanalyze the verb–particle sequence as merely a verb.

and (65f) are ruled out.[21] This also explains the data in (62). Sentences (62c) and (62d) are excluded because these verb-particle pairs cannot occur in (ii), thus permitting no way of deriving them. *Pay back*, however, seems to occur in BOTH constructions. It is possible that Oehrle's theory of particles can be made to account for the data if more criteria for the distinction can be established. If so, we would have to conclude that speakers differ as to which particles can occur in what positions. Some speakers may not allow (ii) at all.

Oehrle (1975) mentions that the positioning of the particle depends on intonational properties and on the existence of "presentational" contexts that "introduce new material into the discourse in which they occur [Part II, Section 5.21]." He rules out conditioning the rule of Particle Shift to take these factors into account and assumes that some independent surface filter will explain these cases. As it turns out, these cases are naturally accounted for by dominance. Take, for example, the following example from Oehrle:

(67) a. *The factory turns out lathes and dies.*
      b. ?**The factory turns lathes and dies out.*
      c. *The factory turns three lathes out per month.*

The point here is that suggested by sentences (52)–(54) above: The natural locus for dominant material is after the particle. Since it is not the purpose of this chapter to examine the function of particles in great detail, I will not continue this discussion. And yet it was necessary to verify that results of the interaction of Dative Movement and Particle Shift do not interfere with the hypothesis of the function of Dative Movement proposed here.

Heavy NP Shift is another transformation that interacts in an interesting way with Dative Movement. Wexler and Culicover (1973) noted the following data:

(68) *John gave the poisoned candy which he received in the mail to the police.*

(69) *John gave to the police the poisoned candy which he received in the mail.*

(70) *Who did John give the poisoned candy which he received in the mail to?*

(71) **Who did John give to the poisoned candy which he received in the mail.*

---

[21] The latter can occur, but less naturally so in (i).

I shall not go into any detail concerning the general function of Heavy NP Shift, although a discourse analysis of this process would have to explain the difference between using (69) and (72):

(72)   *John gave the police the poisoned candy which he received in the mail.*

This I would like to leave for a future work. However, from these cases it seems fairly clear that so-called "heavy" NPs are NPs that, due to their length, must be interpreted as being dominant and are, therefore, preferred in sentence-final position. The unacceptability of (71) then follows from the same principle that explained the unacceptability of the same direct object after Dative Movement: that in this position it cannot be interpreted as the more dominant of the two NPs.

4. CONCLUSION

In this chapter I have tried to show that a discourse analysis of Dative Movement predicts various kinds of data that other analyses find difficult to account for. The arguments against other analyses were either that, since they were purely structural, they could not derive the correct data or that the various problems were dealt with by means of a variety of different constraints. The discourse approach is preferable to these in that a unified analysis of these problems is offered. More importantly, the analysis depends on a definition of the function of Dative Movement (Hypothesis A), which is needed independently to account for the occurrences of either double object form in discourse. Moreover, a new requirement for linguistic "explanation" has been inferred: It seems to be that, when we set up as our goal the understanding of a certain process like Dative Movement and of how it functions in discourse, once we arrive at such an understanding it will explain the facts, including such cases as (11) and (12), the cases I initially set out to account for.

An important issue remains: What repercussions does this approach have on the general theory? Linguists discussing discourse and functional aspects of syntax have often done so outside the framework of transformational grammar. I believe that transformational grammar is a theory of language that easily lends itself to the incorporation of this kind of approach. I would now like to give a rough sketch of how one might go about this. First, however, I would like to mention again that the notion of dominance has been applied to a much wider set of data (Erteschik-Shir and Lappin 1977, 1978) than what we have seen here. Moreover, it appears that a similar analysis of Dative Movement is relevant to a variety of languages.[22] It is, therefore, crucial that the theory incorporate the discourse notion of dominance in a sensible way. It has been shown that dominance relations are relevant in defining the discourse situations in which a certain sentence can occur. It has also been shown that the dominance or nondominance of a specific NP depends on such criteria as which movement rule has applied to it. It follows that dominance cannot be assigned to deep structures. In a theory of syntax that argues for the existence of traces, dominance can be assigned on the surface, for such structures will indicate whether or not Dative Movement, for instance, has occurred in a specific case. It is also possible that dominance is part of the output of the rule; in other words, the rule not only moves an NP but also assigns it a feature, such as +dominant or −dominant. If the latter is the case, then rules such as relativization will have to be defined to apply to NPs that are not marked −dominant. In the former approach, the rules that assign dominance will, in this case, assign

---

[22] I have examined the relevant Danish data carefully and have discovered that Danish seems generally to behave like English. In Hebrew both object positions are possible, but the preposition must be retained. Thus, there is no way to determine whether facts exist similar to those illustrated by (12). However, the following example shows that the pronoun problem arises here as well:

(i)   *Hu natan et hasefer li.*
                     he gave   the book to me

(ii)   *Hu natan li et hasefer.*
                     he gave   to me the book

In order to verify that dominance plays a role with respect to this rule of Hebrew, a separate study would have to be made; still, the unacceptability of (i) is a clear indication that such a study would prove fruitful. The same is true of German, which, again, has different superficial aspects, namely, its case system. Notice the following facts:

(v)   *Peter gab einem Mädchen das Buch.*
                     Peter gave a girl   the book

(vi)   *Peter gab das Buch einem Mädchen.*
                     Peter gave the book a girl

(vii)   *Peter gab einem Mädchen es.*
                     Peter gave a girl   it

(viii)   *Peter gab es einem Mädchen.*
                     Peter gave it   a girl

(ix)   ?*Peter gab ihr es.*
                     Peter gave her it

(x)   *Peter gab es ihr.*
                     Peter gave it   her

Once more, the data are very similar to what we found was true of English, and it is likely that a similar explanation holds.

both + and − dominant to the same NP, and this conflict of features will act as a surface filter that rules out the sentence.

To sum up, I would like to stress that a pragmatic "discourse" approach to certain syntactic problems need not imply an outlook based on ill-defined notions that cannot easily be verified or argued against. I have tried to show how dominance, a well-defined discourse notion applied to a specific rule of grammar, clearly predicts and explains the relevant data. Moreover, it should not be difficult to incorporate a set of rules assigning dominance into a precise theory of grammar. Data such as that illustrated by (14)–(19) is no longer proof that transformational grammar is wrong.

ACKNOWLEDGMENTS

I wish to thank Shoshana Benjamin, Dwight Bolinger, Edward Keenan, Shalom Lappin, and, especially, Dick Oehrle for their many helpful comments.

REFERENCES

Bolinger, D. (1975) "Meaning and Form—Some Fallacies of Asemantic Grammar," in E. F. K. Koerner, ed., *Current Issues in Linguistic Theory, Vol. 1*, (also in *Amsterdam Studies in the Theory and History of Linguistic Science*, IV).

Chafe, W. (1975) "Givenness, Constrastiveness, Definiteness, Subjects, Topics, and Point of View," in C. Li, ed. *Subject and Topic*, Academic Press, New York.

Chomsky, N. (1971) "Deep Structure, Surface Structure and Semantic Representation," in D. Steinberg and L. Jakobovits, eds., *Semantics: An Interdisciplinary Reader in Philosophy, Linguistics, and Psychology*, Cambridge University Press, New York.

Culicover, P. and K. Wexler (1973) "An Application of the Freezing Principle to the Dative in English," *Social Sciences Working Paper* 39, University of California, Irvine.

Emonds, Joseph E. (1976) *A Transformational Approach to English Syntax*, Academic Press, New York.

Erteschik-Shir, N. (1973) *On the Nature of Island Constraints*, Doctoral dissertation, Massachusetts Institute of Technology, Cambridge, Massachusetts (reproduced by the Indiana University Linguistics Club).

Erteschik-Shir, N. and S. Lappin (1977) "Dominance and the Functional Explanation of Island Constraints," to appear in *Theoretical Linguistics*, 1979.

Erteschik-Shir, N. and S. Lappin (1978) "Under Stress: A Functional Explanation of Sentential Stress Patterns," unpublished paper.

Fiengo, Robert (1974) *Semantic Conditions on Surface Structure*, unpublished Doctoral dissertation, Massachusetts Institute of Technology, Cambridge, Massachusetts.

Fillmore, C. (1965) *Indirect Object Constructions in English and the Ordering of Transformations* (*Monographs on Linguistic Analysis I*), Mouton, The Hague.

Firbas, J. (1974) "Some Aspects of the Czechoslovak Approach to Problems of Functional Sentence Perspective," in F. Daneš, ed., *Papers on Functional Sentence Perspective*, Mouton, The Hague.

Givón, T. (1975) "Promotion, Accessibility and Case Marking: Toward Understanding Grammars," *Working Papers on Language Universals, No. 19*, Language Universals Project, Stanford.

Green, G. N. (1974) *Semantics and Syntactic Regularity*, Indiana University Press, Bloomington and London.

Gundel, J. (1977) *The Role of Topic and Comment in Linguistic Theory*, Doctoral dissertation, Ohio State University, Columbus, Ohio (reproduced by the Indiana University Linguistics Club).

Jackendoff, R. S. (1972) *Semantic Interpretation in Generative Grammar*, M.I.T. Press, Cambridge, Mass.

Lehman, Christina (1977) "A Re-analysis of Givenness: Stress in Discourse," in W. Beech, S. Fox, and S. Philosoph, eds., *Papers from the Regional Meeting of the Chicago Linguistic Society*, Chicago Linguistic Society, Chicago, Illinois.

Lewis, D. (1972) "General Semantics," in D. Davidson and G. Harman, eds., *Semantics of Natural Languages*, Reidel, Dordrecht.

Morgan, J. L. (1975) "Some Remarks on the Nature of Sentences," in R. Grossman, J. San, and T. Vence, *Papers from the Parasession on Functionalism*, Chicago Linguistic Society, Chicago, Illinois.

Oehrle, Richard (1975) *Dative in English*, unpublished Doctoral dissertation, Massachusetts Institute of Technology, Cambridge, Massachusetts.

Ross, J. R. (1967) *Constraints on Variables in Syntax*, unpublished Doctoral dissertation, Massachusetts Institute of Technology, Cambridge, Massachusetts.

DISCOURSE FUNCTION OF MORPHOLOGY:
THE FOCUS SYSTEM IN GERMAN

DAVID A. ZUBIN

State University of New York, Buffalo

In order to communicate, you need a code; the design features of that code, if it is to be efficient and useful, will quite naturally depend on the makeup of the code user. A comparison may make this clearer: The makeup of human beings, with respect to language use, stands in sharp contrast to the makeup of computers, which employ artificial languages to communicate with their human users and with each other. The design features of these codes reflect in general ways the makeup of the machines themselves. Computers typically have a large storage capacity and can recall all previously communicated information exactly; their codes, correspondingly, reduce redundancy to a minimum for efficiency. Their ability to infer information or conclusions that have not actually been communicated is, however, extremely poor. The code must provide for maximally precise and harmonious communication in order to make up for this lack of inferential ability, or "intelligence."

Syntax and Semantics, Volume 12:
Discourse and Syntax

Human beings are the opposite: They have extremely poor, short-term verbatim storage capacity and a tendency toward imprecise recall of communicated information. On the other hand, human beings have extensive inferential capacities that can be applied to information processing. Human language correspondingly shows design features[1] different from those of computers: extensively redundant encoding of information and heavy reliance on a sophisticated inferential capacity to decode detailed messages from a relatively vague and abstract encoding mechanism.

A computer can operate indefinitely in one information channel without decrement in processing ability, or, on the other hand, it can switch channels so rapidly that it has, in effect, a large capacity for parallel processing. In addition, as a design characteristic, it has no information bias for particular types of events or entities, unless such is specifically encoded into the program. In contrast, human beings have specific limitations and biases in these respects:

I. **We are subject to the limitations of selective attention.** We tend to focus attention on only one entity or event at a time, and this attention has temporal limitations: It takes time to establish, it tends to be maintained, and then it tends to fade over time.

There is an extremely broad literature on both psychophysical and cognitive characteristics of selective attention. Modern studies of attention have their roots in Titchener's (1908) early experimental and descriptive work. The reader is referred to Woodworth and Marquis (1947), Broadbent (1958), and Neisser (1967) for general discussions of this topic, as well as to a recent review by Carr and Bacharach (1976) expanding the concept of perceptual selectivity to include "perceptual tuning" and "conscious attention" as complementary component functions of selective attention. The various temporal characteristics of selective attention, from orienting behavior through perceptual investigation (maintenance) to satiation and attentional shift, are described by Nunnaly and Lemond (1973) and by J. Zubin (1975). Neisser (1975) is one instance of a study showing the perceptual narrowing of selective attention: Subjects could follow one of two events presented simultaneously (both binocularly and dichotically), but they could not follow both.

E. Schegloff (personal communication) has pointed out that the fabric of the argument connecting cognitive properties of selective attention to the distributional properties of case forms in discourse presented later in the

---

[1] The design features of human language formulated here are different from those listed in Hockett (1966b). They are, however, an attempt to expose the functional relation between characteristics of the code and characteristics of the code user, an enterprise implicit in Section 3 of Hockett's paper.

chapter is quite loose. The experimental work on selective attention was not done in the context of verbal encoding and decoding, so that the psychological literature bears a suggestive rather than a compelling relationship to the distributional linguistic data presented later in this chapter. Ultimately, it must be shown that grammatical encoding is related in a tight sense to the selection, maintenance, and shift of attention. To do so would require research showing behavioral correlations between an individual's attentional (e.g., visual) patterns on the one hand and his behavior in grammatical encoding and decoding on the other. Such research is now in the planning stage.

II. **We are subject to an egocentric bias.** We process information about other human beings more readily than that about nonhumans, and we process information about ourselves most readily. This could be considered a bias of egocentric interest. As William James (1890) put it: "The altogether unique kind of interest which each human mind feels in those parts of creation which it can call *me* or *mine* . . . is a fundamental psychological fact [p. 290]."

The egocentric bias is a specific instance of what Gibson (1950) calls "schematic perception" and Carr and Bacharach (1976) call "perceptual tuning"; that is, the tendency to select stimuli for perceptual investigation on the basis of relatively constant predetermined cognitive biases independent of the immediate stimulus context.

One general paradigm for the investigation of this "schematic" tendency in perception is story-retelling. Gibson (1950) reports that Bartlett (1932) "discovered, as had earlier students of the psychology of testimony, that a story gets retold so as to express the meaning it has for the teller. It is altered in accordance with a schema which is characteristic of the individual, his interests, and his culture [p. 210]." An experiment of specific relevance to the egocentric bias in this paradigm was carried out by Scarlett and Press (1975), who found that a child, in retelling a story about two characters—one of whom has the same name as the child or has that of his best friend—would recall more events performed by the ego (or familiar) character than by the unfamiliar one and would even transfer events to the ego-proximate character that had been performed by the unfamiliar character in the original telling of the story.

Much of the research on skewed attention to certain types of entities in a real-world context has been carried out in connection with the advertising industry (Woodworth and Schlosberg 1954). Burtt (1957) reports several studies showing an attentional preference for people over inanimate objects, as in the following: "When subjects were driven in an automobile past a series of poster boards and then subsequently checked for recall and recognition of the advertisements on those boards, they recalled 39 percent of the ads with pictures of objects and 67 percent of those with pictures of people. The corresponding figures for recognition were 37 and 48 percent [p. 549]." Studies with equivalent results are reported by Nixon (1926) and Lewis (1975), and the editorial application of the egocentric bias to advertising material is reported by Johnson (1966). A useful extension of this research would be to determine people's attentional preferences in viewing scenes in which they themselves are present.

The use of pronominal reference in conversation can be used to shed light on egocentric tendencies in the everyday interests of the average speaker. Guy and Allen (1976), in a test of G. H. Head's concepts of social interaction, show that more pronominal reference in conversation is to the self, less to the conversation partner, and least to the generalized other represented by "they"; this skewing fits a Poisson distribution.

Finally, the advantage of concrete nouns over abstract nouns in cognitive processing has been demonstrated by Paivio (1969) and others in a variety of paired associate learning, free recall, and recognition tasks. James, Thompson, and Baldwin (1973) corroborate these findings and, in addition, show that concrete nouns have an advantage over abstract ones in being recalled as the grammatical subject of an English sentence, even when the voice of the original sentence has to be switched, a finding that establishes a link between concreteness and grammatical encoding.

There is, thus, a good deal of evidence in the psychological and advertising literature supporting the contention that there is an egocentric bias in the cognitive processing behavior of the average person.

Gathering together this evidence seems, at first thought, to be an exercise in bursting through open doors. The egocentric bias seems self-evident. On reflection, however, it may seem that in the course of daily life we pay little conscious attention to ourselves in comparison to the world around us, and it may seem that our thoughts are frequently filled with objects and abstract ideas rather than with people. Carr and Bacharach's (1976) distinction between PERCEPTUAL TUNING, a preconscious selective process, and CONSCIOUS ATTENTION, which is task oriented, is particularly instructive in this context. Following their distinction, our conscious and deliberate attention to tasks (of which we are aware) is functionally distinct from and complementary to a preconscious screening of perceptual input, of which the egocentric bias is a part. Thus, our AWARENESS of what we pay attention to has little to do with the functioning of the egocentric bias, which must, thus, be supported by experimental evidence.

One thesis of this chapter will be that USE of the Focus System in German is at least partly determined by the egocentric bias of the language user. It is already well-established that the STRUCTURE of human language reflects this bias. For example, the linguistic fact that every human language has deictic signals with which the speaker can refer to himself and to his interlocutor (see, e.g., Hockett 1966b) corresponds to the cognitive fact (Stern 1938) that "the personal world has a natural center from which and toward which everything pertaining to it extends [p. 91]," in contrast to the "cosmic world," which is not so centered. This is a basic observation about the phenomenology of perception made by James (1890) and by Stern (1938) and reemphasized by H. Clark (1973) in his attempt to show the cognitive basis of lexical structure.

Ultimately, the link established in this chapter between "egocentric" tendencies in cognition and grammatical encoding in German rests on phenomenological accounts of perception and on experimental evidence applying only to individual links in the scale, such as self–other or human–nonhuman. This evidence remains on a descriptive level and does not confirm the existence of "egocentrism" as a unified function in cognition. K. Salzinger (personal communication) has suggested, for example, that the observed behavior may be the result of the perception of "shared characteristics," whether they lie along an egocentric scale or not. Kuno's (1976) concept of EMPATHY—"the speaker's identification, in varying degrees, with a participant in an event"—suggests another basis for the egocentrism principle, one that does not, however, seem easy to operationalize. In any case, the present argument rests only on the collective observed behaviors motivating the egocentric scale as a DESCRIPTIVE device, and not on a THEORY of "egocentrism" or "empathy."

There are thus at least two properties of human perception—SELECTIVE ATTENTION and THE EGOCENTRIC BIAS—that seem to determine the pattern of an individual's interest in events and entities in the perceived world. They are hypothesized to form a cognitive basis for the semantic substance SPEAKER'S FOCUS OF INTEREST in German.[2] The grammatical system associated with this substance is manipulated by speakers to indicate where the focus of their interest lies at a particular point in discourse. The focus system and its cognitive roots are, thus, of particular importance in investigating how speakers construct their discourse plans.

---

[2] A host of possible relations between the cognitive biases discussed in this paper and the grammatical structure of various languages suggest themselves. What is their relation, for example, to the "great chain of being" (Creamer 1974, Frischberg 1972) affecting the order of nouns in Navajo, to the TOPIC-oriented use of nominal morphology in the Philippine languages (Schachter 1976), to the ROLE-oriented use of case morphology in a language such as Lakhota (Foley and Van Valin 1977), or to the extreme ERGATIVE distribution of nominal and verbal morphology in Dyirbal (Dixon 1972)? Such questions clearly go beyond the scope of this chapter, which deals with the relation between cognitive biases and the grammatical structure of German. Application of these or related principles to other languages will have to proceed by careful analysis of the distribution of morphology in each language on an individual basis.

As a grammatical system, the Focus System consists of a set of morphological signals (case endings) and their meanings.[3]

$$\text{Speaker's Focus of Interest} \begin{cases} \text{FOCUS}_{\text{NOMINATIVE}} \\ \text{NONFOCUS}_{\text{DATIVE}} \\ \text{NONFOCUS}_{\text{ACCUSATIVE}} \end{cases}$$

This system, as a hypothesis about the grammar of German, makes the claim that the speaker uses the nominative case to indicate an entity that is his "focus of interest" in an event and the dative or the accusative cases for entities that are not the focus of his interest.[4] Two features of this system

[3] The nominative, dative, and accusative case forms are simultaneously interlocked in a second grammatical system in which they signal the degree to which individual participants in an event are potent or agent-like relative to one another:

$$\left.\begin{array}{l} \text{NOMINATIVE}\ \text{HIGH} \\ \text{DATIVE}\ \text{MID} \\ \text{ACCUSATIVE}\ \text{LOW} \end{array}\right\} \text{Degree of Contribution}$$

This system is discussed and quantitatively validated in Zubin (1972, 1975, 1976, 1977). For discussions of the theoretical framework in which this approach to grammatical systems is conceived, see Diver (1975), Garcia (1975), Kirsner (1977), and Reid (1977). For applications of this framework to grammatical systems in other languages see Garcia (1975), Gildin (1979), Kirsner (this volume), and Reid (1977).

The reader may have noted that what I call the Focus System corresponds roughly to what others have called the "referentiality" of an NP and what I call the System of Contribution, to "role functions" (Foley and Van Valin 1977). That "referential structure," that is, the Focus System, should be sensitive to discourse phenomena is noncontroversial. It has been supposed, however, that "role functions" pertain only to semantic decisions made within the individual clause (see Footnote 5). But unpublished research (Zubin, forthcoming) on German short stories shows that the opposition between dative and accusative (which are distinguished only in terms of so-called "role functions") is manipulated for stylistic effect on a discourse level.

The reader familiar with German will note that the genitive case, which in traditional grammar and in some recent structural treatments (Firestone 1962, following Jakobson 1936) has been included in the case system because of its morphological similarity to the other case forms, is not included here. This is due to semantic considerations suggesting that the genitive case morphology does not have a meaning related to the semantic substances of Focus or Contribution.

[4] The reader will notice that the term "Focus" is used here with reference to the NOMINATIVE case in German, traditionally known as the case of the "grammatical subject," rather than with reference to the center of "asserted information," a usage of recent popularity in linguistics, and will realize that these usages are frequently in conflict. In light of the fact that the term "Focus" has a long history in the psychological literature in connection with selective attention and interest biases (Neisser 1967:103, Schlesinger 1954:356, Solley and Murphy 1960:183, Woodworth and Marquis 1947:402, J. Zubin 1975:141, and extensively elsewhere), the fact that attention or prominence have been repeatedly associated with the grammatical subject in experiments on English language material (e.g., James et al. 1973, Johnson-Laird

are of crucial importance:

I. THE SYSTEM IS DEFINED WITH RESPECT TO *individual events* IN
    DISCOURSE.

The speaker "decides" which of the several participants in an event is at the center of his interest WITH RESPECT TO THAT EVENT and then puts it in the nominative; other participants not at the center of interest are placed in the dative or in the accusative (or on the basis of semantic decisions not discussed here, in the genitive or, in prepositional phrases). Although the Focus System is, thus, not defined in terms of discourse variables, its use by human speakers is quite naturally subject to discourse influences: The entity that most interests the speaker on a discourse level will, other things being equal, tend to be at the center of his interest in a particular event. This psychological coherence between discourse and single events will be important later, in the quantitative validation of focus meanings.[5]

1968), and the fact that the term "focus" has also appeared in the linguistic literature with respect to grammatical subjects, this writer feels fully justified in using it with reference to the German nominative. Inconvenience to those readers accustomed to the conflicting usage in some recent linguistic literature is regretted.

The terminological conflict may ultimately be resolved by a theoretical distinction between "deictic force," a semantic substance that the speaker uses to deliberately call the HEARER'S attention to some entity, event, or inferential difficulty (García 1975), and "speaker's focus," a semantic substance reflecting preconscious cognitive biases of the speaker.

[5] A popular view among some linguists and psycholinguists is that "subject selection" is a clause-internal process and CANNOT, therefore, be related to discourse variables. Li and Thompson (1976) reflect this position in their distinction between "subject" and "topic." They contend that the subject of a clause is predictable from the lexical information in the verb and from certain other considerations, such as grammatical voice of the verb, from which they conclude that "discourse may play a role in the selection of the topic [p. 463]," but presumably not in the selection of a subject: "The functional role of the subject can be defined within the confines of a sentence as opposed to a discourse [p. 464]." This point of view does accurately reflect a descriptive relationship in a sentence-based grammar: the tight cooccurrence restrictions that exist between the subject and the verb in a variety of languages. But, when this point of view is interpreted as a psycholinguistic encoding strategy, it turns out to be based on the implausible assumption that a speaker, in planning an utterance, MUST decide on the lexical specification of the verb and on its voice BEFORE he decides on the identity of the subject. This assumption is not only intuitively suspect but is also contradicted by experimental evidence.

Lindsley (1975) has shown in a series of experiments with English language material that speakers decide on the subject noun, but only PART of the lexical specification of the verb, before they begin to speak. He had his speakers become familiar with a set of pictures, each depicting two out of a set of four people in which one was touching, kicking, greeting, or standing next to the other. The speaker's experimental task was to state the actor, or the action, or the actor and the action, or the actor, action, and goal of the activity. Lindsley manipulated the order in which pictures were presented so that the speaker either knew in advance or did

II. THE MEANINGS IN THE SYSTEM ARE RELATIONALLY DEFINED.[6]

There is no ABSOLUTE level of attentional focus implied by the nominative and no absolute lack of focus implied by the dative or the accusative. The nominative signals only that MORE interest is directed at an entity in the nominative than is directed at entities in the dative or the accusative in the same event; the degree of interest could still be minimal in an absolute sense.

The affinity between the proposed meanings for the case morphology and the cognitive properties of selective attention and egocentric bias should be apparent. The meanings are formulated in cognitive terms—the speaker's "interest"—and the cognitive properties tend to specify what specific direction this interest will take in individual perceived events. It may not be clear, however, why this psychological specification of a linguistic category is necessary at all, particularly since it irrevocably ties the linguistic analysis, which might stand by itself, to additional claims about human psychology.

The justification for this incursion into psychological reasoning springs from the need for empirical validation. The meaning assigned to the grammatical subject in traditional grammar is generally stated in terms such as "what the sentence is about" or "the center of importance in the sentence," terms that are not overtly psychological (although perhaps they are covertly so). These meanings have been found unsatisfactory by many linguists for a variety of reasons, among them the fact that, in specific

---

not know what each of these elements of the depicted scene was going to be. The speakers hesitated for varying lengths of time before initiating the description of a scene, depending on which elements in the scene they were required to name and on which elements they could anticipate. Through a careful comparison of these reaction times, Lindsley was able to eliminate two hypotheses: that the speaker plans the subject noun only before beginning to speak and that the speaker plans the subject noun and the verb in its entirety. The data support his third hypothesis: that the speaker plans the subject noun, but only part of the lexical specification of the verb, before starting to speak. Lindsley's findings have only limited application to the problem at hand because (a) the speakers had to plan within a highly limited and structured set of choices imposed from the outside; (b) the speakers planned sentences in isolation rather than in discourse context; and (c) the experiment used English rather than German language materials. The findings do nonetheless cast doubt on the assumption that a speaker's choice of subject noun is inevitably determined by his choice of verb.

Thus the assumption that subject selection is determined only by clause-internal choices and cannot be related to the speaker's discourse plans seems unwarranted. It is plausible that the speaker frequently picks his subject FIRST and then decides on an appropriate lexical verb and grammatical voice, rather than the other way around. Chafe (1976), after pondering the same problem, offers the slightly differing conclusion "that normally these two choices are made more or less simultaneously [p. 51]."

[6] The concept of relationally or "negatively" defined meanings is the basis of the Saussaurean notion of system in language (Culler 1975, Reid 1974, de Saussure 1916).

instances, the task of deciding which entity the sentence is "about" seems to be analytically indeterminate.[7] What is lacking is, first, a means for specifying with greater precision the semantic substance of the meanings associated with case morphology and, second, an a priori valid means for applying these meanings to individual utterances.

The grammatical system presented in this chapter, formulated in terms of the "focus of the speaker's interest," is an attempt to provide this greater precision of semantic substance, and the cognitive properties of selective attention and egocentrism are an attempt to provide a basis for empirical validation. The meaning "speaker's focus of interest" does not immediately apply to specific utterances. What kinds of entities interest human beings? What types of entities are they likely to select over others as the focus of their interest and, thus, to place in the nominative case? The cognitive properties of selective attention and egocentric bias suggest that a human speaker is likely to select either (a) the entity most salient to him at a specific point in discourse; or (b) the entity most like himself—namely himself, or another human being—for encoding in the nominative case.

The resort to a cognitive basis for the proposed meanings is, thus, not idle psychologizing. It is an attempt to articulate the specific ways in which speakers of a language will exploit proposed grammatical meanings, a necessary step in predicting the actual distribution of specific morphological forms in utterances; in other words, a necessary step in empirically validating the proposed meanings.

The cognitive properties of selective attention suggest that a speaker will show the following TENDENCIES in the direction of his interest in a narrated scene:

1. To focus interest on entities that are cognitively salient to him
2. To focus interest on relatively few entities in the narrated scene, in comparison to the total range of entities available
3. To focus interest on one entity or on one set of homogeneous entities at a time
4. To persevere in attention on one entity
5. To reach a satiation limit where attention is shifted

[7] The notion of "grammatical subject" as a unified "function" has not been improved upon in modern linguistics. Chafe (1976) concludes that "the best way to characterize the subject function is not very different from the ancient statement that the subject is what we are talking about [p. 43]," although he gives the notion a new psychological twist–reminiscent of paired-associate learning—which he calls a "starting point." Keenan and Comrie (1972) deal with "subject" as a cluster concept in which a "grammatical subject" in any given language will exhibit one or more of a list of universal properties. Thus, their proposal does not even address the question of a unified function in any particular language.

The cognitive properties of the egocentric bias suggest that a speaker will tend to focus interest on that entity in an event that is most like himself, irrespective of the local salience of other entities. This principle can be operationalized with an egocentric scale of the following sort:[8]

speaker > hearer > other > inanimate > abstract
(ego)   person   concrete

The egocentric bias can, then, be restated as follows: Given the choice of focusing interest on one of several entities in an event, the speaker will choose the entity closest to ego on the scale. The particular points chosen for representing the scale are not fixed; for example, the point "nonhuman animate" could be added. The relation of the points to each other is, however, necessarily fixed.

These specific aspects of selective attention and of the egocentric bias lead to specific predictions about the distribution of German case morphology in discourse. The statement of these predictions and their empirical testing form the subject of the body of this chapter.

1. RELATIVE CLAUSES—A DIAGNOSTIC ENVIRONMENT FOR VALIDATING THE FOCUS SYSTEM

As previously discussed, the meaning FOCUS OF INTEREST—interpreted in terms of selective attention—suggests that a speaker will select from among the participants in a particular event the entity that most strongly captures his attention at that point in discourse, that is, that is most SALIENT to him in the immediate context, and will encode that entity in the nominative case. Traditional avenues of linguistic argument cannot be used to substantiate this claim because the determinants of salience are extremely varied and are frequently indiscernible in examples taken in isolation, such as (1a) and (1b):

(1)   a.   *Der Junge stand dem Riesen gegenüber.*
                 'The youth(nom) stood across from the giant.'

            b.   *Der Riese stand dem Jungen gegenüber.*
                 'The giant(nom) stood across from the youth.'

---

[8] This scale, or parts thereof, are contained explicitly or implicitly in the work of Becker (this volume), Clark and Begun (1971), Creamer (1974), Foley and Van Valin (1977), Frishberg (1972), Garcia (1975), Hawkinson and Hyman (1974), Hockett (1966a), Kuno (1976), Silverstein (1976), Zubin (1976), and many others.

In (1a) the speaker seems to have directed his attention to the youth, whereas in (1b) the speaker seems to be attending to the giant. Yet, there is no evidence beyond the nominative itself with which to objectively verify this claim. There are many factors that can guide the speaker's attention, more than can be controlled experimentally at one time, and some of them may not be apparent in the immediate context. What is needed is a diagnostic environment that highlights one factor determining salience and that obviates the rest. Such an environment is provided by relative clauses. In a relative clause it is known—independently of the case forms—which entity has high salience for the speaker: It is the "topic" of the relative clause, the entity about which the relative clause provides identifying or descriptive information.[9] This is, of course, the entity referred to by the relative pronoun. In (2), for example:

(2)   (. . . *Junge* . . .), *der den Riesen ansah.*
             '(. . . youth . . .), who(nom) looked at the giant.'

the speaker gives identifying or descriptive information about the youth, not about the giant; from this we can infer that the youth is most salient to the speaker. The relative clause is, thus, a good diagnostic environment for testing the hypothesis that the nominative, in opposition to the dative and accusative, means "speaker's focus of interest." It is predicted that:

HYPOTHESIS I: IN RELATIVE CLAUSES, THE SPEAKER WILL PUT THE RELATIVE PRONOUN IN THE NOMINATIVE BECAUSE OF THE HIGH SALIENCE OF THE RELATIVIZED ENTITY.

This prediction is illustrated by (2) above. In addition, it is predicted that, because of the egocentric bias:

HYPOTHESIS II: IN RELATIVE CLAUSES, THE SPEAKER WILL PUT THE ENTITY MOST AKIN TO HIMSELF IN THE NOMINATIVE.

For testing this latter part of the hypothesis, the egocentric bias will be operationally defined by the following scale:

speaker > hearer > other   > concrete entity > abstract
(ego)   person   (inanimate)   entity

[9] Kuno (1975) presents evidence showing that it is not possible to construct natural-sounding relative clauses in English that contain information irrelevant to the head noun. He formulates the "Thematic Constraint on Relative Clauses: a relative clause must be A STATEMENT ABOUT its head noun [p. 420]."

It is interesting to note the identity of this statement with traditional definitions of "grammatical subject." It may be that traditional grammarians reacted to the intuitively clear "salience" aspect of the meaning of this morphology but not to the preconscious egocentric aspect. Analysis by intuition seems to have led astray here, as elsewhere.

The hypothesis claims that the entity closest to the speaker at the left hand of the scale will be preferred in the nominative. Example (3) illustrates the application of this scale to a specific utterance:

(3) (. . . *Stein* . . .), *den der Junge warf.*
 '(. . . stone . . .), that(acc) the youth(nom) threw'

 youth > stone
 (animate) (inanimate)

Note that the youth, being animate, is closer than is the stone to the ego end of the scale and that he is in the nominative case, in accordance with the hypothesis. We thus have two valid applications of the Focus Hypothesis in the context of relative clauses: One predicts that the relative pronoun will be in the nominative because of salience, and the other predicts that the entity most resembling ego will be in the nominative. These predictions, it should be emphasized, do not reflect two different meanings for the nominative case but, rather, two different ways in which a human being, given his psychological makeup, is apt to exploit the meaning FOCUS OF INTEREST.

The predictions were tested on a sample of all relative clauses from two texts: a novel and a popular science book. In order to make the test fair, only relative clauses containing at least two candidates for Focus were included. Table 1 gives the results of this test. For clarity, there is a square

TABLE 1

FREQUENCY WITH WHICH THE MORE SALIENT ENTITY (Named by the Relative Pronoun) OR THE MORE EGO-LIKE ENTITY IS IN THE NOMINATIVE CASE IN RELATIVE CLAUSES (A relative pronoun is within a box; a more ego-like entity is circled; and nominatives are in boldface.) [a,b]

	Relative clauses	N	Percentage
A.	(. . . *Stein* . . .), [*der*] (*den Riesen*) *traf.* '(stone . . .), which(nom) hit the giant(acc)'	125	29
B.	(. . . *Stein* . . . , [den] (*der Junge*) *warf.* '(. . . stone . . .), which(acc) the youth(nom) threw'	181	42
C.	(. . . *Junge* . . .), ([*der*]) *den Stein warf.* '(. . . youth . . .), who(nom) threw the stone(acc)'	103	24
D.	(. . . *Riese* . . .), ([*den*]) *der Stein traf.* '(. . . giant . . .), whom(acc) the stone(nom) hit'	19	4
	Total	428	99

[a] The sample is from Heinrich Böll (1972), and Carl Friedrich von Weizsäcker (1957).
[b] The results showed $X^2 = 98.0$ and $p < .001$.

around the relative pronoun and a circle around the more ego-like entity. The nominative is in boldface.

In (A), the relative pronoun, referring to the stone, is in the nominative. There were 125 such clauses in the sample, or 29%. In (B), the youth, who is more ego-like than the stone, is in the nominative. Such clauses made up 42% of the sample. In (C), both these factors coincide. The nominative entity—the youth—is indicated by the relative pronoun and is more ego-like than the stone. Such clauses made up 24% of the sample. Finally, in (D) neither factor correlates with the nominative, which is represented by only a small remainder (4%) of the sample. Note that sentences of type (D) are not unacceptable but that they are extremely low in frequency.

In 96% of the clauses in the sample, a demonstrably focus-deserving entity has been placed in the nominative case.[10] This entity may be focus-deserving because of its momentary salience, as indicated by the relative pronoun, because of its ego-like qualities, or because both these factors

---

[10] A potentially disturbing fact comes to light if the data are combined in another manner: Seventy-one percent of the relative clauses have ego-distant entities (typically inanimate) as their heads, whereas only 29% have ego-proximate (typically human) heads. Here, we have amplifying information (the supposed "function" of relative clauses) being given more often for ego-distant entities than for ego-proximate ones, in apparent contradiction to the egocentric bias.

At the outset it should be pointed out that the relative clause hypothesis makes a claim about which of several entities named WITHIN a clause will be relativized, not about what kind of entity a relative clause will be associated with as its head. Thus, this difficulty can not vitiate the hypothesis at hand.

The strong tendency for relative clauses to have ego-distant, typically inanimate heads can be accounted for as follows. If we investigate the precise notional relation of relative clauses to their heads, we find that they frequently provide information necessary to establish the identity of its referent or to remind the hearer of this. In the discourse samples in question, the number of different inanimate (concrete or abstract) entities referred to far outweighs the number of different animate entities, so that the occasion for providing identifying information for the former arises much more frequently than for the latter. In other terms, animate–human entities are "given" items in discourse much more often than are inanimate entities. The latter are frequently "new" items requiring identification.

A close examination reveals relative clauses to have discourse functions other than that of providing identifying information for an entity; one such "function" is revealed by an examination of the grammatical structure involved. A defining characteristic of relative clauses in German is placement of the finite verb at the end of the clause, a characteristic they have in common with "adverbial" or "dependent" clauses. One apparent discourse function of this verb position is to signal the presence of information that is less important or "subordinate" with respect to the main train of events in the narrative. Thus, relative clauses contain a grammatical signal that backgrounds or defocuses the information contained in them with respect to the narrative. So, the tendency toward inanimate heads of relative clauses is, in fact, a tendency to defocus, with respect to the discourse as a whole, the information in clauses centering on inanimate entities, with a corresponding tendency NOT to do so for clauses centering on animate entities—a finding not at all surprising in light of the egocentric bias.

may coincide. The table reveals a SYSTEMATIC AVOIDANCE in discourse of clauses in which neither of these Focus factors is present. Thus, relative clauses provide a substantial validation for the hypothesis that the nominative means FOCUS OF SPEAKER'S INTEREST, in contrast to the dative and the accusative.[11] But this validation could only be made in relative clauses, representing an extremely limited variety of contexts in which the case forms are used. In order to extend this validation, we must turn to distributional properties of the case morphology in connected discourse. This validation procedure will provide insights into the ways in which speakers manipulate case morphology in organizing their discourse plans.

2.   FREQUENCY OF MENTION IN DISCOURSE

The Focus Index (A Measure of the Discourse Prominence of Entities)

A writer or speaker may reveal in a variety of ways which entities are prominent in his discourse plans: He could explicitly announce a topic (*I'm about to tell you about the blackout in New York*) and then proceed to describe the details without ever mentioning *blackout* again. Or he could achieve dramatic effect by launching right into the confusion in the streets, the heat, the break-ins, and the brave citizens directing traffic and then announce at the end *and that was the blackout in New York*. Both of these are possible, but we recognize them as stylistically extreme effects not typical of normal prose. Usually, we can assume that, if *the blackout* is the topic of the speaker's discourse plans, he will mention it often. Based on

---

[11] A number of alternative explanations for the avoidance of type (D) sentences are eliminated by the frequency of the other sentence types in the table:

1.   The avoidance cannot be ascribed to an accessibility heirarchy of the type found in Keenan and Comrie (1972) because of the high frequency of type (B) sentences, in which an oblique (dative or accusative) participant is relativized over the nominative participant.

2.   Similarly, this avoidance cannot be due to a strong tendency for "agents" (and therefore "subjects") to be animate and for "objects" to be inanimate, because of the high frequency of type (A) sentences.

3.   It cannot be based solely on the tendency, discussed in Footnote 10, for relative clauses to have INANIMATE heads, because of the high frequency of type (C) sentences.

Explanations 1 and 3 could be combined to jointly account for the avoidance of type (D) sentences. A comparison of this possibility with the Focus System Hypothesis presented in this chapter must rest on the explanatory value of the concept of a universal accessibility heirarchy (see Foley and Van Valin 1977 for a critical discussion of this concept) and on its ability to account for the other data presented in this chapter.

this, the assumption can be made that the more prominently an entity figures in the speaker's discourse plans, the more often he will tend to mention it. Thus, the frequency with which a speaker mentions an entity in a given stretch of discourse is a measure of the prominence of this entity in the speaker's discourse plan. Furthermore, it is assumed that, in planning a sentence within the given stretch of discourse, the speaker will tend to associate a discourse-prominent entity with a morphological form that signals his focus of interest (by hypothesis, the nominative case). This leads to the following hypothesis:

HYPOTHESIS III: THE MORE FREQUENTLY AN ENTITY IS MENTIONED IN DISCOURSE, THE MORE FREQUENTLY (IN PERCENTAGES) IT WILL APPEAR IN THE NOMINATIVE CASE AS OPPOSED TO AN OBLIQUE CASE. IN CONTRAST, FREQUENCY OF MENTION IN AN OBLIQUE CASE SHOULD BE INDEPENDENT OF DISCOURSE FREQUENCY.

This hypothesis was tested on a short story by Hans Fallada. The following is a synopsis of the plot:

A group of sisters inherit a farm upon the death of their father. When it becomes clear that they cannot manage by themselves, Uncle Walli arrives to take over. He straightens out the affairs of the farm and concerns himself especially with the care of Malte, the child of one of the women. One day Malte watches Uncle Walli as he goes fishing on the bay. That night Malte disappears, along with the boat. Uncle Walli and neighbors search for him. Malte has drifted across the bay to the other side, where a fisherman and his wife (fishing couple) find him the next morning. Uncle Walli and the sisters come in a wagon to pick him up.

Table 2 gives the frequency with which each of the characters, places, things, and other entities are mentioned in the story. For the quantitative analysis, entities mentioned less than 16 times are grouped together in successively larger groups (by a logarithmic function) so that a meaningful percentage of mentions with each morphological form (nominative, dative, accusative) can be established. The main characters having the highest frequency of mention in the story—Uncle Walli, Malte, and the sisters—are all mentioned a majority of the time in the nominative (67%, 69%, and 75% of the time, respectively). As characters, things, places, and other entities are mentioned less and less, their percentage of mention in the nominative drops; entities mentioned only once each are in the nominative only 15% of the time. This trend does not hold for mentions in the dative

TABLE 2

Focus Index for Nominative, Dative and Accusative Case Morphology without Prepositions (Data from Fallada (1967), pp. 115–126. The first column lists entities mentioned in the story, grouped together according to how often they are mentioned. The following columns show how often each entity or group of entities is mentioned in each morphological category.)

Entity	Total mentions	Nominative		Dative[a]		Accusative[a]		Prepositional phrase		Other[b]	
		N	%	N	%	N	%	N	%	N	%
A. Uncle Walli	97	65	67	3	3	10	10	5	5	14	14
B. Malte	65	45	69	1	2	9	14	6	9	4	9
C. The sisters	28	21	75	0	0	3	11	3	11	1	4
D. Paplow, fishing couple, boat, farm, water. Each mentioned 9–16 times	61	30	49	2	2	7	11	15	25	7	11
E. River bank, farmer, grandmother, town rep. Each mentioned 5–8 times	25	13	52	0	0	5	20	6	24	1	4
F. Daughter, sea, posts, cat, etc. Each mentioned 3–4 times	34	88	25	1	3	5	15	16	47	4	12
G. Suit, beach, fish, sick person, pits, children, etc. Each mentioned 2 times	44	15	34	3	7	8	18	11	26	7	16
H. Rooster, freedom, corner, spray, shed, man, etc. Each mentioned *once*	124	19	15	2	2	26	21	64	52	13	10

[a] These mentions are with case morphology only, that is, without prepositions.
[b] This includes mentions in the genitive and as possessive adjectives.

and accusative cases; mentions in the dative are stable at about 3% and in the accusative at about 15%, regardless of how often or how seldom an entity is mentioned overall in the discourse.

Figure 1 displays these results graphically. The curve for mentions in the nominative case rises from 15% for entities mentioned once in discourse to a peak of 67–75% for the main characters. The curves for the dative and the accusative are nearly flat, showing no interaction between these oblique cases and frequency of mention in discourse. Figure 1 suggests an incongruity: If percentage of mention in the nominative is directly proportional to frequency of mention in discourse and the dative and accusative cases are independent of discourse frequency, then some other morphological form must show an INVERSELY proportional relation to discourse frequency. Figure 2 shows that for prepositions (taken together)

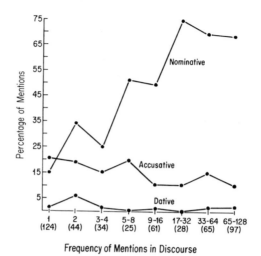

Figure 1 Focus index for nominative, dative, and accusative case morphology without prepositions. In Figures 1–4 the horizontal axis indicates the total number of references to each entity, with entities grouped together so that frequency of mentions at each point is double the previous point. Numbers in parentheses indicate total mentions of all entities in the group. The vertical axis indicates the percentage of mentions that are associated with a specific morphological category. (Data from Fallada 1967:115–126)

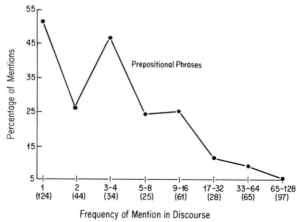

Figure 2 Focus index for prepositional phrases. (Data from Fallada 1967:115–126)

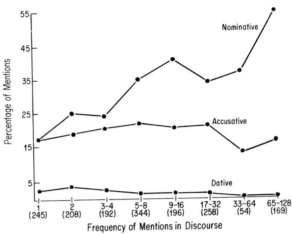

Figure 3 Focus index for nominative, dative, and accusative case morphology without prepositions. (Data from Weizsäcker 1957:74–104)

the more often an entity is mentioned in discourse the LESS likely it is to appear in prepositional phrases.[12] Figures 3 and 4 give data parallel to Figures 1 and 2 for a passage from a popular treatise on atomic energy by Carl Friedrich von Weizsäcker.[13]

[12] An explanation of why mention in prepositional phrases should show an inverse relation to discourse frequency lies beyond the scope of this investigation. The empirical finding is suggestive, however, of the relation between the semantics of prepositions and the semantics of case and of how this relation is worked out in speaker's discourse plans. The abstract, purely relational meanings of the case signals (see p. 474 and Footnote 3) provide no information about the specific roles played by entities in an event. This information is largely specified by the lexical content of the verb, thus semantically tying these entities closely to the verb. Verbs, in addition, provide basic lexical information about the individual events that establish the sequential coherence of discourse. Thus, entities associated with case signals are accorded a relatively high importance in discourse by virtue of their close semantic association with verbs.

The role specification of an entity mentioned in a prepositional phrase, on the other hand, is largely provided by the relatively concrete lexical meaning of the preposition itself and involves the lexical meaning of the verb to a much lesser extent. This semantically isolates the entity from the verb, leading to an inference of relatively more peripheral discourse status than any entity associated with a pure case form.

[13] The data in Table 2 and Figure 1 from the Fallada short story seem to yield to an alternative explanation in terms of animacy; specifically, as a typical story it deals with a relatively small number of human characters, some of whom are frequently mentioned main characters, and a large number of infrequently mentioned nonhuman entities. Since humans, being prototypically agent-like, are especially worthy of being subjects, we could expect frequently mentioned entities to be more often in the nominative as an artifact of the humanness-agency association. This explanation might account for the Fallada data, but it cannot account for the Weizsäcker data in Figure 3, because, in this latter corpus, the most frequently mentioned entities (in the three highest categories) are all inanimate: *reactor, neutron, water, U238*, etc.

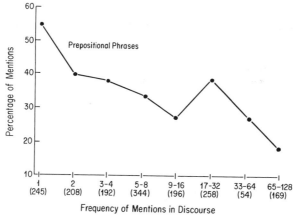

Figure 4 Focus index for prepositional phrases. (Data from Weizsäcker 1957: 74–104)

The Focus Index is based on the assumption that frequency of mention in discourse is a function of prominence to the speaker. If this premise is valid, then Figures 1 and 3 show that speakers do tend to mention an entity in the nominative to the extent that it figures prominently in their discourse plan.

The Focus Index tests the discourse prominence hypothesis as a PRODUCTION strategy; that is, the speaker does something in his discourse plans, and this has an effect on his selection of morphology within sentences. This hypothesis can also be tested as a COMPREHENSION strategy through a questionnaire technique. In a pilot experiment, nine native speakers were given a series of paragraphs such as the two following (translated) and were asked to describe each with a short sentence containing two nouns and a verb. A choice of two or three verbs was given, all of them so-called "reciprocal predicates" for which subject and object have a mirror-image relationship in the state or activity.

Paragraph A: *The central train station in Hamburg is one of the largest stations in Germany. It contains numerous stores and restaurants for various preferences. You can easily reach a number of tourist spots from the train station. For example, you can get to the* **state theater** *simply by crossing the street. The train station is, thus, not only large but also centrally located.*

Paragraph B: *The state theater in Hamburg is one of the historical sights of the city. It is situated downtown, surrounded by nineteenth century commercial buildings. If you want to visit the theater, you should get off at* **the main train station** *and just cross the street. Although the theater is open for tours during the afternoon, the best time to see it is during a performance.*

Because of the reciprocal relationship expressed by the verb *gegenüberliegen* ('to lie across from'), both of these paragraphs can be described with either of the following sentences:

(4)   a. ***Der Hauptbahnhof*** *liegt dem Deutschen Schauspielhaus gegenüber.*
           'the **central train** station is located across from the state theater.'

       b. ***Das Deutsche Schauspielhaus*** *liegt dem Hauptbahnhof gegenüber.*
           'the **state theater** is located across from the main train station.'

But, since the train station and the state theater are mentioned with varying frequency in the two paragraphs, the following hypothesis can be tested:

> HYPOTHESIS IV: IN DESCRIBING THE CONTENT OF A STRETCH OF DIS-
> COURSE, A SPEAKER WILL TEND TO PLACE IN THE NOMINATIVE CASE
> THE ENTITY THAT IS MENTIONED MOST OFTEN.

Table 3 gives the results of the pilot questionnaire. In 72% of their relevant responses, speakers placed the more frequently mentioned entity in the nominative. For example, they tended to formulate a response like (4a) for paragraph A and a response like (4b) for paragraph B. Thus, the question-naire technique leads to the same conclusion that the distributional Focus Index did: The tendency to place an entity in the nominative in a specific sentence is a function of the entity's discourse frequency. The Focus Index and the questionnaire thus both support the Focus hypothesis, that is, that the nominative case, in contrast to the dative and accusative, means FOCUS OF SPEAKER'S INTEREST.

TABLE 3
TENDENCY TO PLACE THE MORE FREQUENTLY MENTIONED
ENTITY IN THE NOMINATIVE, BASED ON THE FOCUS
QUESTIONNAIRE (In the ratio x/y, x = number of
responses in which the more frequently mentioned entity
is chosen for the nominative case, and y = total
responses.)

	Range x/y	Average x/y
By subject (9 subjects)	.5–1.0	.8
By condition (8 paragraphs)	.3–1.0	.8
Subjects × conditions (total responses = 43)[a]		.72

[a] Twenty-nine unscorable responses were eliminated, 23 of them because both nouns were combined together into a coordinate NP. Interestingly, there was a clear tendency to place the more frequently mentioned entity at the beginning of the coordinate NP.

3. RANGE OF REFERENCE IN DISCOURSE

A basic finding in the psychology of attention (James 1890, Neisser 1967) is that a potentially unlimited number of entities can be perceived in the periphery of the attentional field, whereas attention can be focused on only one or a few entities at a time. From this it follows that the speaker will limit his use of the nominative case (if it does signal, by hypothesis, his focus of interest) to comparatively fewer different entities in his discourse plans but will use the dative and the accusative cases to refer to a wide range of different entities. The Token–Type Ratio is a measure of this tendency.

Token-Type Ratio

$$\frac{\text{Frequency of case}_i}{\text{Number of different entities referred to in case}_i} = \frac{\text{Tokens}}{\text{Types}}$$
$$(\text{case}_i = \text{nom, dat, acc})$$

HYPOTHESIS V: RELATIVELY *many* INSTANCES (TOKENS) OF THE NOMINA-
TIVE IN DISCOURSE WILL REFER TO THE SAME ENTITY. RELATIVELY *few*
INSTANCES (TOKENS) OF OBLIQUE CASES WILL REFER TO THE SAME ENTITY.

A low ratio (approaching 1) for a particular case would indicate that the speaker has distributed this form over a wide range of different entities in the discourse. In contrast, a high ratio would indicate that the speaker has limited this form to relatively fewer different entities.

Figure 5 gives the Token–Type Ratio for the short story by Fallada and for the popular treatise on atomic energy by Weizsäcker. The bar graphs for the Fallada text show that, on the average, over 4 instances of nominative

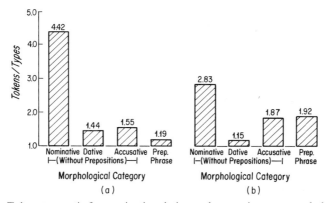

Figure 5   Token–type ratio for nominative, dative, and accusative case morphology without prepositions and for prepositional phrases. The ratio is a measure of the range of different entities over which tokens of a particular morphological category are distributed. [Data from (a) Fallada 1967:115–126; and from (b) Weizsäcker 1957:74–104]

morphology refer to the same entity. In contrast, only about 1.5 instances of dative or accusative morphology refer to the same entity (i.e., 3 instances of morphology for 2 different entities). As for prepositional phrases, practically each one refers to a different entity. This difference between the nominative on the one hand and the dative, accusative, and prepositional phrases on the other is less pronounced for the Weizsäcker text, but it is still apparent.

The Token–Type Ratio thus supports the hypothesis. In the samples studied, the nominative is limited to a relatively smaller number of different entities, whereas the oblique cases are distributed over a wider variety of different entities. This gives credence to the hypothesized meaning for the nominative: SPEAKER'S FOCUS OF INTEREST in contrast with the dative and accusative cases. It also reflects a principle of discourse organization: In order for a sequence of clauses to hang together as connected discourse, they must be thematically centered on a relatively small number of entities. Without this, the discourse would tend to fall apart into a list of unrelated statements.

Number within Noun Phrases

The RANGE OF REFERENCE hypothesis can also be applied to individual noun phrases. A noun phrase may refer to a single entity (singular), an undifferentiated group of like-named entities (plural), or a differentiated series of distinct entities (coordinately conjoined NPs). The tendency of selective attention to pick out one entity or a set of undifferentiated entities at one time (tendency 3) suggests a skewed relation between the nominative and these NP types:

> HYPOTHESIS VI: SINGULAR NPS WILL TEND MOST TO BE IN THE NOMI-
> NATIVE RATHER THAN IN AN OBLIQUE CASE (DAT/ACC). PLURAL NPS
> WILL TEND LESS TO BE IN THE NOMINATIVE, AND NP SERIES WILL TEND
> LEAST TOWARD THE NOMINATIVE.[14]

Figure 6 displays data in support of the hypothesis from a novel by Heinrich Böll and from the treatise on atomic energy by Weizsäcker. Data for the dative and accusative are grouped together because of insufficient data for the dative. In the passage from Böll, 57% of all singular NPs in the sample are nominative, whereas only 21% are oblique. For plural NPs the proportion of nominatives drops (44%) and the proportion of oblique NPs rises (24%). For NP series, the trend is even stronger: 17% in the nominative, 37% oblique. The trend for prepositional phrases parallels that for oblique NPs, with a slightly stronger skewing toward NP series. The data from Weizsäcker parallel the data from Böll.

[14] The idea of using noun phrase number for testing the Focus System Hypothesis comes from Bonny Gildin (1979).

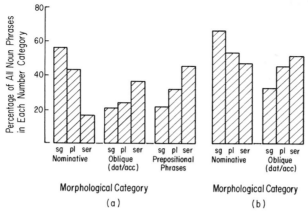

Figure 6   The interaction between case morphology and number. The bars for each number category add up to 100%. Thus, each bar shows the portion (in a percentage) of all mentions in a number category that are associated with a specific type of case morphology. sg = singular; pl = plural; ser = series of noun phrases; dat = dative; acc = accusative. The data represent a random sample of textual occurrences of each number category. [Data from (a) Böll (1972) and from (b) Weizsäcker (1957)]

The data in this section have shown a correspondence between the narrowing of focus in selective attention (tendencies 2 and 3) and the distribution of case morphology, a correspondence motivated by the hypothesized Focus System. The narrowing of focus appears both in the planning of individual clauses (the skewing to singular NPs in the nominative) and in the planning of discourse (the limitation of the nominative to relatively few different entities).[15]

4. SUCCESSIVE REFERENCE IN DISCOURSE: THE CHAINING EFFECT

Tendency 4 of selective attention concerns maintenance. A variety of entities may pass quickly through the periphery of a perceptual field, but it takes time to focus attention on any one of them, and this attention tends to persevere. On this basis, it can be hypothesized that, once a speaker focuses his interest on a particular entity in his discourse plans, he will

[15] The type–token data in Figure 5 and the data in Figure 6 for the Fallada text are susceptible to an alternative explanation parallel to that in Footnote 13. Humanness could account for the Fallada data because of the presence of a small number of frequently mentioned human characters (therefore, a high type–token ratio for the nominative) and of a possible tendency for human beings to be mentioned individually rather than in groups: greater individuation for animates, especially people (therefore, a skewing to the singular for the nominative). But these arguments, again, cannot apply to the Weizsäcker data because of the total domination of the text by inanimate entities.

tend to remain focused on that entity for some subpart of the discourse. A corollary to this hypothesis derives from tendency 5, the phenomenon of "satiation" observed in vigilance experiments: After a point, it becomes more and more difficult through time to maintain attention on one object or task. Thus, the corollary hypothesis claims that a speaker will shift his attention from entity to entity in his discourse plans rather than remain focused on one entity throughout.

HYPOTHESIS VII: A SPEAKER WILL TEND TO APPLY SUCCESSIVE ADJACENT REFERENCES IN THE NOMINATIVE TO THE SAME ENTITY. THE SPEAKER WILL NOT DO SO WITH SUCCESSIVE ADJACENT REFERENCES IN THE DATIVE OR ACCUSATIVE. IN ADDITION, THERE WILL BE A FADING EFFECT.

The number of successive nominatives in running text referring to the same entity—called CHAINING here—will be used as a measure of the extent to which a speaker maintains focus on the same entity. For example, in (5):

(5)   *Der Mann kam in sein Büro. Dann setzte er sich. Als der Student eintrat stand er wieder auf.*

      '**the man**(nom) came into his office. Then **he**(nom) sat down. When
        a   b
      the student(nom) came in **he**(nom) stood up again.'
           c   d

there are two successive nominatives (a, b) referring to the same entity, a nominative chain of length 2. The student in the nominative (c) is surrounded by nominative references to another entity (b, d), so that he is in a chain of length 1, or no chain. In the following, there are two successive ACCUSATIVE references to the same entity, forming an accusative chain of length 2:

(6)   *Der Mann nahm eine Zigarre aus der Tasche und rauchte sie.*
      'the man took **a cigar**(acc) out of his pocket and smoked **it**(acc).'

Data for testing the chaining effect, taken from *Blechtrommel* by Günther Grass, are displayed in Table 4. Overall trends apparent in the table are that (*a*) only a minority of nominative references fail to occur in chains (44%), whereas a majority of dative and accusative references (66% and 81%, respectively) do not occur in chains; and (*b*) nominative references tend to occur in longer chains than do dative and accusative references. These trends are highlighted in the cumulative curves of Figure 7. At each point on the horizontal axis, the values from Table 4 are cumulated over successively longer groups of chains. The figure shows that 56% of nominative references are in chains at least 2 long, whereas only 34% and 18% of datives and accusatives, respectively, are chained. Chains at least 4 units long contain 19% of the nominative references but only 8% and 2% of the dative

TABLE 4

CHAINING: REPEATED MENTION OF AN ENTITY WITH THE SAME CASE FORM (Chain length refers to the number of mentions in a chain. Data from Grass 1963: 315–375)

Chain length	Nominative[a]		Dative		Accusative	
	N	%	N	%	N	%
1 (i.e., no chain)	203	44	213	66	236	81
2	110	24	64	20	32	11
3	60	13	21	7	18	6
4	24	5	4	1	4	2
5	15	3	15	5	—	—
6	12	3	6	2	—	—
7	14	3	—	—	—	—
8	24	5	—	—	—	—
9	—	—	—	—	—	—
Total	462	100	323	100	290	100

[a] This data includes instances of finite verb morphology in the absence of a ("subject") pronoun in the nominative case.

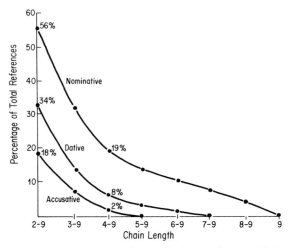

Figure 7 Chaining: repeated mention of an entity in association with the same morphological category. Chain length refers to the number of mentions in a chain and is cumulative 9 → 2 to provide smooth curves. The overall odds ratio for one mention of an entity's being in a chain is: nominative, 1.27; dative, .49; and accusative, .22. (Data from Grass 1963: 315–375)

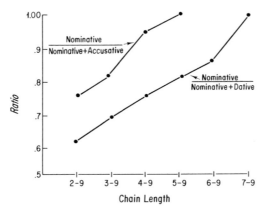

Figure 8 Chaining. Increasing advantage of the nominative case over the dative and accusative cases in longer chains; a ratio of .5 would show no advantage. (Data from Grass 1963: 315–375)

and accusative references, respectively.[16] The nominative thus seems to gain a greater and greater advantage as chains get longer. This trend is clearly depicted in Figure 8, which compares nominative to dative chains and nominative to accusative chains.

The chaining effect thus supports the hypothesis that successive references in the nominative tend to refer to the same entity more so than do successive references in the dative or the accusative. Additional support is gained from the findings that the nominative is involved in longer chains and that the nominative gains over the dative and accusative as chains get longer.[17] A

[16] The category "nominative" in Table 4 and Figure 7 includes instances of finite verb morphology that signal information about the participant in focus, even when there is no overt nominative present. The following utterance would be counted as containing two tokens of the nominative for the purposes of the chaining effect:

> *Der Mann kam in sein Büro und setzte sich.*
> 'The man(nom) came into his office and sat down.'

The reader may wonder why the dative curve lies between the nominative and accusative curves, which suggests a GRADIENT focus affect, nom > dat > acc. But this observation is contradicted by the data in Figure 5, in which the accusative bar is higher than the dative one. Whether these dative–accusative differences are due to individual variations in the data, to the effect of a strong tendency of the dative to be used for animate entities, or to some other variable is a question for further investigation.

[17] An alternative explanation for the chaining data in Figure 7 in terms of the discourse frequency of case morphology is plausible. The nominative occurs much more frequently than does either the dative or the accusative. If we make the ASSUMPTION that repeated references to a particular entity tend to occur in clumps (but with mixed case forms), then there is a greater opportunity for nominative references to fall together just by chance. Suspicion is cast on this account, however, by the fact that the dative curve in Figure 7 lies ABOVE the accusative curve, although the dative occurs much less frequently than does the accusative in discourse.

satiation effect is also observed: There is a relatively smooth decay in chain length, with an abrupt limit at eight successive nominatives; there were no isolated chains of greater length. In other words, the writer shifted focus after dwelling on the same entity for no more than 8 successive nominatives. These results are consonant with the general hypothesis that the nominative, in contrast to the dative and accusative, has the meaning SPEAKER'S FOCUS OF INTEREST.

The chaining effect suggests another discourse-organizing strategy: Speakers provide continuity to discourse by mentioning the same entity repeatedly in the nominative.

5.   EGOCENTRISM IN DISCOURSE

Discourse measures previously discussed have been used in the investigation of "speaker's focus of interest" as a function of attention. Here, we turn to the other psychological correlate of the Focus System that figured strongly in the analysis of relative clauses: The fact that speakers show a preferential interest in themselves or in an entity akin to themselves. In other words, speakers tend to be egocentric in their choice of entities on which to focus.

HYPOTHESIS VIII: IN CONNECTED DISCOURSE, THE PROBABILITY THAT AN ENTITY WILL BE IN THE NOMINATIVE WHEN IT IS MENTIONED WILL BE A FUNCTION OF THAT ENTITY'S "EGO-DISTANCE" FROM THE SPEAKER.

"Ego-distance" will be operationally defined by the egocentric scale used above, with additions made to suit the specific nature of the corpora used:

EGOCENTRIC SCALE:

speaker > hearer > other human >   concrete   > abstract > abstract
                   ⌒   (inanimate)   human
            central > peripheral

The CENTRAL–PERIPHERAL distinction is used for the Böll novel to distinguish main characters from characters peripheral to the plot. The category ABSTRACT–HUMAN refers to abstract concepts such as "thought" or "knowledge," which relate specifically to human beings; ABSTRACT refers to concepts such as "temperature" or "continuity," which do not.

The hypothesis claims that whenever a speaker mentions himself in discourse he will strongly tend to use the nominative case. When he mentions other people, he will tend less to put them in the nominative, and, for entities even more remote from him in kind, he will tend least to put them in the nominative. Figures 9 and 10 display data taken from Weizsäcker and Böll that support the hypothesis. In the discourse sample from Weizsäcker

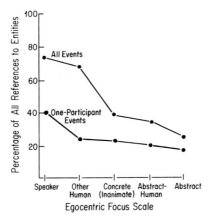

Figure 9 Egocentric focus scale: the tendency for the nominative case to be associated with entities that share characteristics with the speaker. The upper curve refers to the nominative case in all events in running discourse; the lower curve refers to the nominative case in one-participant events only. (Data from Weizsäcker 1957, random sample drawn from pp. 7–164)

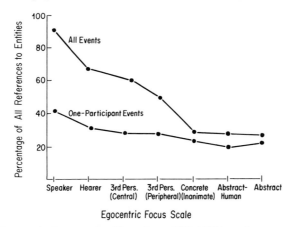

Figure 10 Egocentric focus scale. (Data from Böll 1972, random sample drawn from pp. 5–124)

(Figure 9) the writer has put himself in the nominative about 75% of the time. Concrete inanimate entities are in the nominative less than 40% of the time, and abstract entities only about 25% of the time.

In order to correct for the fact that some of the individual sentences describe events in which the nominative entity is acting on another entity (i.e., potent or agent-like), a subsample of sentences was taken in which an entity participates alone in the event (roughly, sentences with intransitive verbs). The results from this analysis are given in the lower curve of Figure 9.

Even this subsample of nominatives in one-participant events contains about 40% of the speaker's total references to himself but only 20% of his total references to abstract entities. The data in Figure 10 from the Böll novel are parallel to Figure 9.

Thus, as a speaker plans discourse, he does tend to place entities in the nominative just to the extent that they resemble him in kind. This suggests a strategy for maintaining discourse coherence when the speaker has no strong attentional bias in a particular event: Other things being equal, put yourself or the entity most akin to yourself in the nominative.

Soccer Matches

Suitbert Ertel (1976 and 1977) has illustrated an interesting manifestation of the "egocentric bias" principle. He hypothesized that speakers would apply it socially to a distinction between "my group" and "other group." To test this, he analyzed the write-ups of soccer matches in local newspapers. Write-ups were selected in matching pairs, one from each of the home towns of the two teams. From each report he extracted all the sentences in which a player from each team is mentioned, one in the nominative and the other in an oblique case or prepositional phrase. Two such sentences are given below:

(7)   *Overrath verliert den Ball an Müller.*
        'Overrath(nom) loses the ball to Müller(prep. phr).'

(8)   *Diese Bombe von Heinkes konnte Meier nur passieren lassen.*
        'Meier(nom) let this shot(acc) from Heinkes get past.'

Table 5 gives the results of his study. Overall, the writers put a home team player in the nominative more than twice as often as an opposing team player. To check the possibility that the writers were simply putting players from the WINNING team in the nominative, Ertel distinguished between games in which the home team won or lost. Writers showed the same tendency to put home-team players in the nominative even when they lost,

TABLE 5

NEWSPAPER WRITEUPS OF SOCCER MATCHES (Forty Reports)
(The table gives the mean ($\bar{X}$) number of sentences in each report with a home team player or an opposing team player in the nominative. Data adapted from Ertel, 1977)

Total $\bar{X}$	Home team player	Opposing team player
Total $\bar{X}$	2.92	1.21
Home team wins	2.68	1.36
Home team loses	3.13	1.09

that is, were less potent or agent-like. Ertel's study thus supports the general hypotheses that speakers use the nominative for their focus of interest and that this focus tends to be egocentric.

6. ALTERNATIVE EXPLANATIONS FOR EMPIRICAL DATA

The use of quantitative empirical data for the validation of a grammatical analysis, along with the advantage of providing empirical support for the analysis, brings with it the inevitable analytic hiatus between the theoretically derived hypothesis and the data used to support it. Empirical observations are always liable to alternative explanations. One of the most difficult procedures in validating an analysis is the elimination of possible alternative explanations for the data presented; in experimental psychology, it has become standard procedure to raise and to discuss such alternative hypotheses.

A number of possible alternative explanations for individual measures supporting the Focus System hypothesis—explanations based on the association of humanness and agency, on an "accessibility hierarchy," and on possibly confounding distributional properties of human versus inanimate entities in short stories—have been raised and rejected on the basis of conflicting evidence elsewhere in the data (see Footnotes 11, 13, 15, and 17 and the section on "Egocentrism in Discourse"). Ultimately, the weight of the argument in support of the Focus System hypothesis rests not on the continued rejection of alternative explanations for individual measures but on a procedure of empirical TRIANGULATION. A number of independent measures of Focus have been offered. As more and more supporting evidence is brought to bear on the hypothesis through independent empirical measures, the possibility that each measure might be the result of different, unrelated, erroneous variables and that these variables might conspire, by chance, to produce uniform results becomes remote.

One alternative hypothesis potentially covering all the data presented in this chapter is based on the concept of "discourse topic," which has frequently been raised in the literature of linguistics and psycholinguistics as the "function" of the "grammatical subject."[18] Mathesius (1929), a founder

[18] Chafe (1976) warns against confusing the concept of "subject" with that of "topic" and specifically argues against interpreting "topic" as that which is "given." Halliday (personal communication) takes a similar stance. However, in light of the fact that Chafe (1976) must retreat to a traditional definition of "subject" as "what we are talking about," it seems worthwhile to test the possibility that the nominative in German is associated with "given" entities in discourse. It should be noted, however, that an EXTREME version of the topic hypothesis is being tested here.

of the Prague School, was careful to point out the many instances in English where the topic of a sentence is NOT associated with the grammatical subject. This can easily be demonstrated on an anecdotal basis for German, since the relatively free word-order allows a speaker to start with the topic and then to give his focus of interest later on with the nominative:

(9)   *Den Film habe ich schon dreimal gesehen.*
        'The movie(acc) have I(nom) seen three times already.'

It would, nevertheless, be useful to show quantitatively that the nominative does not fit an operationally definable criterion for "topic": that of given versus new information.

The topic hypothesis (in the sense of given versus new information) and the focus-of-speaker's-interest hypothesis lead to the following distinct predictions:

TOPIC PREDICTION: THE FIRST TIME AN ENTITY IS MENTIONED IN DIS-COURSE IT WILL (TEND TO) BE MENTIONED IN AN OBLIQUE CASE. THERE-AFTER, IT WILL (INCREASINGLY TEND TO) BE MENTIONED IN THE NOMINATIVE.

FOCUS PREDICTION: IF AN ENTITY FIGURES PROMINENTLY IN A SPEAKER'S DISCOURSE PLAN, HE WILL TEND TO MENTION IT IN THE NOMINATIVE FROM THE FIRST MENTION ON. IF AN ENTITY DOES NOT FIGURE PRO-MINENTLY IN THE SPEAKER'S PLANS, HE WILL TEND ***not*** TO MENTION IT IN THE NOMINATIVE, WITH NO DIFFERENCE BETWEEN FIRST AND LATER MENTIONS.

Table 6 gives the results of a test of these predictions on a stretch of dis-course taken from Weizsäcker. All entities mentioned at least twice in the discourse (and at least once in the nominative) were scored for whether

TABLE 6

TENDENCY FOR THE FIRST REFERENCE TO AN ENTITY TO BE IN THE NOMINATIVE
(Data from Weizsäcker 1957:74–86)

	In nominative	Not in nominative	Total	Percentage in nominative
First reference to an entity	20	42	62	32.2
Succeeding references to an entity	209	338	547	38.2
Total			609	37.6
			$p > .1$; n.s.	

they occurred in the nominative at FIRST mention and at SUCCEEDING mentions. No statistically significant trend whatsoever ($p > .1$) was found. Thus, in this pilot test the topic hypothesis fails to be supported.

In this chapter I have stated the meaning of the nominative case in German as FOCUS OF SPEAKER'S INTEREST (in contrast to the dative and accusative), avoiding the term ATTENTION as a part of the meaning. This I have done for two reasons:

1. Given a situation in which the speaker himself is involved in an event along with another person, there is a strong trend for the speaker to place himself in the nominative and the other in an oblique case. Thus, (10a) is more probable than (10b):

(10) a. *Ich bin dem Studenten auf dem Universitätsgelände begegnet.*
         'I(nom) met the student(dat) on the campus.'

    b. *Der Student ist mir auf dem Universitätsgelände begegnet.*
        'The student(nom) met me(dat) on the campus.'

Furthermore, passive sentences such as (11a), in which the speaker puts himself in the *by*-PHRASE, are unusual, whereas passives such as (11b), in which the speaker puts himself in the nominative, are not unusual:

(11)   a. *Der Student ist von mir angesprochen worden.*
             'The student(nom) was spoken to by me.'

        b. *Ich bin von dem Studenten angesprochen worden.*
            'I(nom) was spoken to by the student.'

Ertel (1974) discusses a variety of distributional and experimental facts about the tendency for the speaker to place self versus other in the nominative that substantiate this point.

It seems somewhat infelicitous to say that in these instances the speaker is the focus of his own ATTENTION, especially since it is possible for the speaker to overtly direct attention to the other person while keeping himself in the nominative:

(12)   *Mensch, ist der Josef scharf. Dén möchte ich mal besser kennenlernen.*
         'Joseph is really something. Hím(acc) I'd(nom) like to get to know better.'

Here, it seems farfetched to claim that the speaker is focusing ATTENTION on himself. But, given the basic human egocentric relation to the perceived world, it still seems reasonable to say that the speaker remains the focus of his own egocentric INTEREST and thus places himself in the nominative, even while overtly directing attention elsewhere.

2. As sentence (12) suggests, there are other communicative means in German for the speaker to direct the hearer's attention toward a particular entity, namely: (a) Manipulation of pronominal deixis: the distinction between *den* and *ihn* (see Kirsner, this volume, for an equivalent contrast in Dutch); (b) word order (sentence initial); and (c) stress.

We thus find evidence for distinguishing two types of grammatical encoding strategies ultimately based on cognitive properties of ATTENTION. One is based on the "perceptual tuning" (Carr and Bacharach 1976) of the speaker: his preconscious disposition, largely independent of the immediate context, to pay more attention to certain kinds of entities and less to others. This is the Focus System of German. The other is based on the speaker's conscious effort to communicate with the hearer by guiding his attention to informational highlights and comprehension processing difficulties. This is exemplified by the system of deixis and by word-order and intonational strategies.

ACKNOWLEDGMENTS

Major portions of this chapter were written while I was in residence at the University of Illinois at Carbondale. I wish to thank members of the Form–Content Seminar at Columbia University and participants in the Symposium on Discourse and Syntax for their valuable ideas, criticism, and support at various stages of the work.

REFERENCES

Bartlett, F. C. (1932) *Remembering*, Cambridge University Press, London.
Broadbent, D. E. (1958) *Perception and Communication*, Pergamon, Oxford.
Burat, Harold E. (1957) *Applied Psychology*, Prentice Hall, Englewood Cliffs, N.J.
Carr, Thomas, and V. Bacharach (1976) "Perceptual Tuning and Conscious Attention: Systems of Input Regulation in Visual Information Processing," *Cognition* 4, 281–302.
Chafe, Wallace L. (1976) "Givenness, Contrastiveness, definiteness, Subjects and Topics," in C. N. Li, ed., *Subject and Topic*, Academic Press, New York, pp. 25–56.
Clark, Herbert H. (1973) "Space, Time, Semantics, and the Child," in T. E. Moore, ed., *Cognitive Development and the Acquisition of Language*, Academic Press, New York, pp. 27–64.
Clark, Herbert H. and J. S. Begun (1971) "The Semantics of Sentence Subjects," *Language and Speech* 14, 34–46.
Creamer, M. H. (1974) "Ranking in Navajo Nouns," *Navajo Language Review* 1, 29–38.
Culler, Jonathan (1957) *Ferdinand de Saussure*, Penguin, New York.
Diver, William (1975) Introduction to *Columbia University Working Papers in Linguistics* 2, 1–25.
Dixon, R. M. W. (1972) *The Dyirbal Language of North Queensland*, Cambridge University Press, Cambridge.

Ertel, Suitbert (1976) "Der Satz als Handbung," paper delivered at the 30th Congress of the German Psychological Society, Regensberg.

Ertel, Suitbert (1977) "Where do the Subjects of Sentences Come From?" in S. Rosenberg ed., *Sentence Production: Developments in Research and Theory*, Erlbaum, Hillsdale, N.J.

Ertel, Suitbert (1974) "Satzsubjekt und Ich-Perspektive," in L. H. Eckensberger and U. S. Eckensberger, eds., *Bericht über den 28, Kongress der deutschen Gesellschaft für Psychologie* (Bd. 1), Hagrefe, Göttingen, pp. 129–139.

Firestone, R. T. (1962) *The Case System of Modern Standard German*, Doctoral dissertation, Indiana University.

Foley, William A. and R. D. Van Valin (1977) "On the Viability of the Notion of 'Subject' in Universal Grammar," in *Proceedings of the Third Annual Meeting of the Berkeley Linguistics Society*, pp. 293–320.

Frischberg, Nancy (1972) "Navajo Object Markers and the Great Chain of Being," in J. P. Kimball, ed., *Syntax and Semantics, Vol. 1*. Seminar Press, New York.

García, Erica C. (1975) *The Role of Theory in Linguistic Analysis: The Spanish Pronoun System*, North Holland, Amsterdam.

Gibson, James (1950) *The Perception of the Physical World*, Houghton Mifflin, Boston.

Gildin, Bonny L. (1979) "Subject Inversion in French: Natural Word Order or *l'arbitraire du signe?*" in F. Neussel, ed., *Essays in Contemporary Romance Linguistics*, Newbury House, Rawley, Massachusetts (in press).

Guy, Rebecca E. and D. E. Allen (1976) "Pronouns, Proximity, and the Generalized Other," *Language Sciences* 42 (October issue), 10–12.

Hawkinson, Annie K. and L. M. Hyman (1974) "Hierarchies of Natural Topic in Shona," *Studies in African Linguistics* 5, 147–170.

Hockett, Charles (1966a) "What Algonquian is Really Like," *International Journal of American Linguistics* 32, 59–73.

Hockett, Charles F. (1966b) "The Problem of Universals in Language," in J. H. Greenberg ed., *Universals of Language*, MIT Press, Cambridge, Massachusetts, 1–29.

Jakobson, Roman (1936) "Beitrag zur allgemeinen Kasuslehre," *Travaux du Cercle Linguistique de Prague* 6, 240–288 (reprinted in F. W. Householder and R. P. Austerlitz, eds., *Readings in Linguistics II*, University of Chicago Press, Chicago, 1966).

James, Carlton T., J. G. Thompson and J. M. Baldwin (1973) "The Reconstructive Process in Sentence Memory," *Journal of Verbal Learning and Verbal Behavior* 12, 51–63.

James, William (1890) *The Principles of Psychology*, Henry Holt, New York.

Johnson, Robert C. (1966) "Tell your Story with Pictures," in J. W. Schwartz, ed., *The Publicity Process*, Iowa State University Press, Ames, Iowa, pp. 89–122.

Johnson-Laird, Philip N. (1968) "The Interpretation of the Passive Voice," *Quarterly Journal of Experimental Psychology* 20, 69–73.

Keenan, Edward, and B. Comrie (1972) "Noun Phrase Accessibility and Universal Grammar," paper presented at the 47th Annual Meeting, Linguistic Society of America, Atlanta, Georgia.

Kirsner, Robert S. (1977) "The Theory," in W. Diver, ed., *Columbia University Working Papers in Linguistics* 4, 21–58.

Kuno, Susumu (1976) "Subject, Theme, and the Speaker's Empathy," in C. N. Li, ed., *Subject and Topic*, Academic Press, New York, pp. 417–444.

Lewis, Mark S. (1975) "Determinants of Visual Attention in Real World Scenes," *Perceptual and Motor Skills* 41, 411–416.

Li, Charles N. and S. A. Thompson (1976) "Subject and Topic: A New Typology of Language," in C. N. Li, ed., *Subject and Topic*, Academic Press, New York, pp. 457–490.

Lindsley, James R. (1975) "Producing Simple Utterances: How Far Ahead Do We Plan?" *Cognitive Psychology* 7, 1–19.

Mathesius, Villem. (1929) "Zur Satzperspektive im modernen Englisch," *Archiv für das Studium der neueren Sprachen und Literaturen* 155, 202–210.

Neisser, Ulric, (1967) *Cognitive Psychology*, Appleton, New York.

Neisser, Ulric and R. Becklen (1975) "Selective Looking: Attending to Visually Specified Events," *Cognitive Psychology* 7, 480–494.

Nixon, H. K. (1926) *An Investigation of Attention to Advertisements*, Columbia University Press, New York (cited in H. K. Nixon 1937 *Principles of Advertising*, Mcgraw-Hill, New York).

Nunnaly, Jim C. and L. C. Lemond (1973) "Exploratory Behavior and Human Development," in H. W. Reese, ed., *Advances in Child Development and Behavior, Vol. 8*, Academic Press, New York.

Paivio, Allan (1969) "Mental Imagery in Associative Learning and Memory," *Psychological Review* 76, 241–263.

Reid, Wallis (1974) "The Saussurian Sign as a Control in Linguistic Analysis," in *The Two Saussures, Semiotexte* 2, 31–53.

Reid, Wallis (1977) "The Quantitative Validation of a Grammatical Hypothesis: The *passé simple* and the *imparfait*," *Papers from the Seventh Annual Meeting of the Northeastern Linguistic Society*, 5–33.

Saussure, Ferdinand de (1916) *Cours de linguistique générale*, Payot, Paris.

Scarlett, Helaine, and A. Press (1975) "An Experimental Investigation of the Phenomenon of Word-Realism," *Merrill-Palmer Quarterly* 21, 127–137.

Schachter, Paul (1976) "The Subject in Philippine Languages: Topic, Actor, Actor–Topic, or None of the Above?" in C. N. Li, ed., *Subject and Topic*, Academic Press, New York, pp. 491–518.

Schlesinger, Herbert J. (1954) "Cognitive Attitudes in Relation to Susceptibility to Interference," *Journal of Personality* 22, 354–374.

Silverstein, Michael (1976) "Hierarchy of Features and Ergativity," in R. M. W. Dixon, ed., *Grammatical Categories in Australian Languages*, Australian Institute of Aboriginal Studies, Canberra, 112–171.

Solley, Charles M. and Gardner Murphy (1960) *Development of the Perceptual World*, Basic Books, New York.

Stern, William (1938) *General Psychology from the Personalistic Standpoint*, H. D. Spoerl (trans.), Macmillan, New York.

Titchener, Edward B. (1908) *Lectures on the Elementary Psychology of Feeling and Attention*, Macmillan, New York.

Woodworth, Robert S. and D. G. Marquis (1947) *Psychology* (5th ed.), Holt, New York.

Woodworth, Robert S. and H. Schlosberg (1954) *Experimental Psychology*, Chapter 4, "Attention," Holt, New York.

Zubin, David (1972) "The German Case System: Exploitation of the Dative–Accusative Opposition for Comment," Mimeo, Columbia University, New York.

Zubin, David (1975) "On the Distributional Properties of Surface Morphology and Their Consequences for Semantic Analysis," in W. Diver, ed., *Columbia Working Papers in Linguistics* 2, 189–218.

Zubin, David (1976) "The Surface Subject in Relative Clauses in German," Linguistic Society of America Meeting, Oswego, New York, August 1, 1976.

Zubin, David (1977) "The Semantic Basis of Case Alternation in German," in R. W. Fasold and R. Shuy, eds., *Proceedings of the Third Conference on New Ways of Analyzing Variation*, Georgetown University Press, Washington, D.C., pp. 88–99.

Zubin, David. (forthcoming) "Stylistic Exploitation of the Dative/Accusative Opposition in Hesse's 'Augustin': The Continuity of Grammar and Style."

Zubin, Joseph (1975) "Problem of Attention in Schizophrenia," in M. Kietzman, S. Sutton, and J. Zubin, eds., *Experimental Approaches to Psychopathology*, Academic Press, New York, pp. 139–166.

DATA SOURCES

Böll, Heinrich (1972) *Der Zug war Pünktlich*, Deutscher Taschenbuch Verlag, Munich.
Fallada, Hans (1967) *Gesammelte Erzählungen*, Rohwolt, Braunschweig, 1967.
Grass, Günter (1963) *Die Blechtrommel*, Fischer, Frankfurt a. M.
Weizsäcker, Carl F. von (1957) *Atomenergie und Atomzeitalter*, Fischer, Frankfurt a. M.

THE DEVELOPMENT OF THE SWAHILI OBJECT MARKER:
A STUDY OF THE INTERACTION OF
SYNTAX AND DISCOURSE

BENJI WALD
University of California, Los Angeles

1. INTRODUCTION

This chapter is concerned with the use of the Swahili object marker (OM) in actual discourse, as exemplified by speakers from the Mombasa Swahili (MS) speech community. Other dialects of Swahili will be mentioned where relevant, but the focus of attention will remain on the indigenous dialect of Mombasa, Kenya.

The immediate problem confronted in this chapter is: What purpose(s) does the OM serve in discourse? Why do speakers use it when they do? Why is it that some object NPs in discourse induce OM-marking whereas others do not?

Although these questions are directed to the discourse behavior of speakers, it is demonstrated in this chapter that the questions have relevance to the OM as a linguistic category SYNTACTICALLY embedded in the grammatical system of the language. As we might expect for many syntactic

Syntax and Semantics, Volume 12:
Discourse and Syntax

features of any language, the syntactic availability of the OM serves discourse requirements, requirements that might be served by other linguistic means or by none at all in another language.

Discussion takes the following order: Section 2 concerns syntactic constraints on the occurrence of the Swahili OM in the light of reports on other Bantu languages that have the category. Section 3 examines discourse constraints on occurrence of the OM in Swahili according to the discourses analyzed. Section 4 contains conclusions about how syntax and discourse have interacted in the formation of the OM category in Swahili.

2. SYNTACTIC PROPERTIES OF THE SWAHILI OM

The OM as a Bantu Linguistic Category

The OM immediately precedes the V in the most widespread Bantu area. Some Camerounian and Nigerian Bantu languages lack the category altogether. Where the OM is used for pronominal reference to a preceding NP, the latter Bantu languages (non-OM) use a monosyllabic pronoun that may either precede or follow the V, according to the particular language. Givón (1976) and Larry Hyman (personal communication) agree that the OM has its origin in a preverbal pronoun.

$$PRO-V \rightarrow OM-V$$

This proposal for the historical origin of the OM suggests relic status for certain properties of the OM as used in some Bantu languages in which the OM shares the following properties with pronouns: (*a*) possibility of multiple OMs; and (*b*) a single OM slot with freedom of choice among referred-to object NPs.

MULTIPLE OM LANGUAGES

Languages such as Umbundu (Angola: personal observation), KiNyarwanda (Ruanda: Kimenyi 1976), and Haya (Tanzania: Duranti and Byarushengo 1977) allow sequences of OM before V:

$$\ldots OM-OM-V$$

Multiple OM languages are found in both the eastern and the western areas of Bantu. The lack of restriction on the OM to one resembles the freedom allowed pronouns to represent more than one object NP.

$$PRO-PRO-V \quad \text{OR} \quad V-PRO-PRO$$

Swahili and many other Bantu languages, largely East Coastal or Southern, restrict the OM to a single occurrence per VP. These are single-OM languages.

SINGLE OM LANGUAGES

Single OM languages differ in the freedom they allow in the choice among object references in multiobject sentences.

Shona (Zimbabwe: Hawkinson and Hyman 1974) allows either the DO or the IO to be referred to by the OM; the other object may only be referred to by a PRO:

$$OM_1-OM_2-V \quad \begin{array}{l} \rightarrow OM_1-V-PRO_2 \\ \rightarrow OM_2-V-PRO_1 \end{array}$$

Many languages show restrictions on this freedom, usually favoring human objects for OM-marking. For example, Morolong and Hyman (1977) report that in SeSotho (Lesuto) some verbs allow only human objects to be OM-marked, whereas others allow either, as in Shona, previously discussed.

(1) ke-ba- bitselitse   mokete
     *o   bana
     I- OM-call +PREP+PAST feast
                            children
     'I called them (the children) for the feast.'
     '*I called it (the feast) for the children.'

but,

(2) ke-mo- phehetse   lijo
     li   ngoana
     I- him-cook +PREP+PAST food
     it   child
     'I cooked the food for him (the child).'
     'I cooked it (the food) for the child.'

In Swahili, the pattern of (1) is general to all verbs, so that (3), as the Swahili equivalent of Sesotho (2), shows the restricted pattern of Sesotho (1).

(3) ni-li- M- pik- ia   chakula
     *KI   mtoto
     I- PAST-OM-cook-PREP food
                          child
     'I cooked the food for him (the child)'
     '*I cooked it for the child.'

For single-OM languages such as Swahili and SeSotho, in which OM-marking favors human over inanimates, the OM cannot be functioning simply as a form of pronominal reference, since no such constraints hold for independent pronoun objects.

Hawkinson (1976) reports that Langi (Tanzania) allows pattern (1); that is, either the IO or the DO may be OM-marked. However, among several human objects a benefactive is chosen over a causee.

(4)   n-a-   MU-ri-sh-iry-   a   muntumki vasinga
              *VA
         I-Past-her- eat- Caus-Prep woman   children
              *them
         'I fed the children for the woman.'   (Hawkinson, p. 89)

Swahili accords with the pattern in (4), so that only the object of the outermost verb derivational suffix can be OM-marked.

(5)   ni-li-   M- l- iṣh- ia   mwanamke watoto
                      *WA
                  I- Past-her-eat-Caus-Prep woman   children
                      *them

That is, the object of the Prep suffix '(for) the woman' but not the object of the causative '(make) the children (eat)' can be OM-marked.

These studies indicate that the OM has developed constraints where more than one object is present or understood in a sentence. The Swahili pattern is one of the most highly restrictive in that:

1.   Only the human object may be OM-marked if there is more than one object to the V.
2.   In the choice between two human objects, only the one referred to by the outer derivational suffix may be OM-marked.

Even though Swahili shows severe constraints on OM-marking among multiple objects, the syntactic frames that allow embedding of an OM-marked V are relatively free in Swahili, as opposed to many other Bantu languages.

Syntactic Embedding of the OM-Marked V in Swahili

Comparison with other Bantu languages suggests three important frames in which OM-marked Vs may be considered: (a) PR–S (Anaphora and left-dislocation); (b) OR (Object relativization); and (c) POST–V.

The PR–S frame refers to cases in which the OM refers to a NP mentioned preceding the sentence of the OM-marked V.

$$NP_i \ldots {}_S[\ldots OM_i{-}V \ldots]$$

This pattern is general to all Bantu languages having the OM category. It is concluded that it is, historically, the earliest pattern. It requires that the OM refer to OLD information, old information here defined strictly as an NP previously mentioned in the discourse. This accords with the hypothesis that the OM developed from a PRO, since PROs are restricted to old or given information.[1]

For exploratory purposes, PR–S was broken down into two subcategories:

1. PRO–S (anaphora)
2. PRE–S (left dislocation)

In PRO–S the NP referred to does NOT immediately precede the sentence of the OM; for example (see note on p. 253):

(6)   *yule bibi   a-ki-ja   a-ki-MW-angalia*
       that woman she-sub-come she-sub-HIM-look + for
       'the woman came looking for HIM.'   (J 16m, Msa)

The referent of the OM is not found in the sentence.

In PRE–S the NP referred to precedes the V, either in the same sentence or immediately before the sentence. The latter pattern is called TOPIC SHIFT by Givón (1976); for example:

(7)   *yule mwanamke **watoto**   wake h-a-WA-ju-i*
       that woman   children her   neg-she-THEM-know-neg
       'that woman, **her children** she doesn't know THEM.'
       (Ma 50m, Msa)

In (7), the object precedes the verb immediately. There are no clear-cut intonational cues as to whether or not the object NP should be considered in the same sentence as the V.

In the OR frame the OM refers to the antecedent of an Object-Relative clause. This pattern is much less widespread in Bantu than PR–S but is characteristic of all languages having POST–V OM-marking discussed next. This pattern is similar to PRE–S.

$$NP_i[\ldots OM_i-V \ldots]_{Rel\,Cl}$$

Many Bantu languages, including interior Kenyan and Ugandan and interior Eastern Bantu languages, for example, ChiBemba (Zambia: Givón 1972), do not allow an OM referring to the antecedent of an Obj-Rel clause. Swahili, like most of the east and south coastal languages, does; for example:

(8)   *KiSwahili ni   lugha   ambayo watu   wote wa-na-I-jua*
       Swahili   Cop language that   people all they-Tns-IT-know
       'Swahili is a language that everybody knows (IT).'
       (MK 23m, Msa)

---

[1] "Given information" technically includes old information and also information assumed by the speaker to be known from situational context, even if not specified in lexical form. Perhaps the most dramatic form of given information in many languages is the use of pronouns like *it* or other forms, such as the OM, without anaphoric function in order to refer to sexually taboo items.

This appears to be an innovation. Some West Bantu languages show the optional use of the OM in the OR-frame, causing possible structural ambiguity with OM-marking by the PR–S pattern, for example, KiMbundu (Angola, personal observation)

(9)   a.   *diala w-a-sokana   omhatu w-a-zolo*
             man he-Past-marry woman he-Past-love
             'the man married the woman (that) he loved.'

        b.   *diala w-a-sokana omhatu w-a-MU-zolo*
                                         he/she-Past-HER/HIM-love
             same as a. above or 'the man married the woman (who) loved
             HIM.'

In non-OR Bantu languages, (9b) could only have a Subj-Rel interpretation, the OM being marked according to the PR–S pattern. OM-marking with the OR pattern is obligatory in Zulu (South Africa), according to Doke (1955). Such a language is obligatorilly OR.

In the Post–V frame, Swahili is included in a more restricted group of languages that allow an OM to mark the V even when the object NP follows the V in the same clause.[2]

(10)   *pale a-li-M-piga Muhamadi Ali*
        there he-Past-HIM-hit
        'at that point he hit Muhammad Ali.'   (MA 50m, Msa)

The Swahili example in (10) shows the OM referring to a following object NP by the POST–V pattern.

At first glance, the POST–V pattern appears to be a radical departure from the older PR–S pattern. However, languages like Zulu provide a link in restricting the OM to OLD information, also typical of the PR–S pattern. In Zulu, definite and indefinite object NPs are distinguished by the use or nonuse of the OM.

(11)   a.   *ngi-ya-M-bona   umuntu*
                      I-TM-HIM/HER-see person
                      'I see **the** person'

                 b.   *ngi-∅-bona umuntu*
                      I   see   person
                      'I see **a** person.'

Givón (1976) seeks to explain the rise of the POST–V pattern through the medium of a pattern of afterthought, AT (right dislocation). Givón

---

[2] The only language located so far that has OR but not POST-V as a condition for OM-marking is the Zairean language, Dzamba (Bokamba:1975).

defines the AT pattern as one in which the object NP, old information, is separated from the preceding OM-marked V by intonational break signaling a clause or sentence boundary.

OM . . . , NP (*where, means that the object NP is not in the VP*)

This AT pattern is probably common to all OM-languages. Byarushengo, Hyman, and Tenenbaum (1976) report for Haya that the tonal pattern for sentence-final position must precede the object NP if the V is OM-marked. Givón identifies the AT pattern as a performance error in discourse. Following Hyman (1974), he assumes that the AT pattern represents a change of mind on the part of the speaker in producing discourse from identifying the object simply by an anaphoric OM reference to adding parenthetically, as it were, the NP referent of the OM. Implicit in this argument is that the OM is being used to refer to old information but that, after the OM is uttered, the speaker decides that although the object referred to is old information it is not clear which old NP it refers to; so, the speaker supplies the NP as afterthought. Givón then suggests that the AT pattern became grammaticalized in Swahili, etc., so that it no longer is AT but can be used for all definite (old information) object NPs.

The difficulty with the plausibility of the AT origin of the POST–S OM-marking pattern is that a planning error in discourse might somehow become grammaticalized through overuse. Givón's hypothesis focuses attention on the LEXICAL OBJECT as the (originally) unusual element in the construction, rather than the OM. The alternative view given here is that it is the OM and NOT the lexical object that is the originally unusual element in discourse. That is, the innovation is simply the extension of the OM to POST–V in its function as a marker of old information.

Passages such as the following in Swahili are no doubt typical of all languages where old information reappears in lexical form in order to avoid ambiguity and unclarity.

(12)   a.   ***yule mother*** *basi yule akaMWambia*
     b.   *aMWambia*
     c.   *hukuMWua babako*
     d.   *aMWambia*
     e.   *yule si babko*
     f.   *akaMshika **mamake** mkono namna hii . . .*
     a.   So **the mother**, she told HIM (i.e., the son)
     b.   she told HIM
     c.   you didn't kill your father
     d.   she told HIM
     e.   that one isn't your father
     f.   and then he seized **his mother** by the arm.   (J 16m, Msa)

The two people interacting in the described scene are the mother and the son. The mother as subject NP is lexically mentioned in (12a) and then is not mentioned lexically again until (12f), where she is shifted to object position. Without the actually used strategy of lexically specifying the mother again as object or the possible alternative of lexically specifying the son (previously understood object) as subject,

(12)   f.   *a-ka-M-shika*   *mkono*
                        he/she-then-HER/HIM-seize arm
                        'He seized her by the arm.'

might be interpreted as 'SHE seized HIM by the arm', since mother has already been established as the subject over the preceding sentences.

By this account, the innovation is

$$\emptyset \text{ V} \ldots \text{NP } [\textit{old info.}] \rightarrow \textbf{OM–V} \ldots \text{NP } [\textit{old info.}]$$

rather than

$$\textbf{OM–V} \ldots]_s \ldots \text{NP} \rightarrow \textbf{OM–V} \ldots \text{NP}]_s$$

In non-POST-V languages, we expect the equivalent of (12f) to lack the OM. However, addition of the OM by extension from the PR–V pattern marks the following NP object as OLD information, as opposed to cases in which a following NP is new information. This interpretation avoids the implausibility of planning error influencing the development of syntactic constraints.[3]

Swahili has further innovated so that use of the OM in the POST–V frame is not restricted to old information. The following examples show the OM used with indefinite and nonreferential objects.

(13)   INDEFINITE OBJECT.

       a-ka-M-kuta   **mzee mwangine** *ndugu wa yule*
       he-then-OM-meet old   another   sister of that
           a-l-o-ku-wa   *pale*
           she-Past-Rel-Inf-be there
       'then he met **another old woman**, sister of the one who was in the
           first place.'   (SG 19f, Msa)

---

[3] Givon (1976) goes on to propose that the loss of function of the preprefix (PP) to distinguish, first, referential, and, later, definite, NPs gave impetus to the substitution of the OM as an alternative way of signaling old information. Wald (1973) introduces the notion that the PP was an early signal of definiteness in Bantu but was either lost in function or lost in form in much of the Bantu area. Relics of the Bantu PP remain in the Bajuni dialects of Swahili for monosyllabic nouns of class 9, e.g., *i-t'i* 'land' from *i-n-ti*, structure: PP–Class P–N root. MS has totally lost the PP, as has most Swahili; for example, *n-ti* or *n-chi* 'land'.

(14)   NONREFERENTIAL (INDETERMINATE) OBJECT.

> *na-o   mahala wa-na-po-weza   ku-toa lile dukuduku ni*
> and-them way   they-TM-when-can inf-out that frustration Cop
> *ku-M-piga* **mtu**
> inf-OM-hit person
> 'and the only way they can get rid of their frustration is to hit
> **somebody**.'   (JK 23m, DSM)

Givón (1976) suggests that this development is the result of reinterpretation of the OM from DEFINITE to HUMAN on the basis of the high discourse coincidence of human and definite among objects. Givón claims that in texts most definite objects are human and most human objects are definite. This suggestion is supported by the discourse patterns discussed in the second section of this chapter. However, in MS definite objects are NOT obligatorily OM-marked, whether human or inanimate. We will see that this is true of the PR–S pattern as well as of the POST–V. Furthermore, inanimate nonreferential objects may also allow OM-marking; for example:

(15)   *si-   ja-KI- ona cho chote*
        neg + I- Perf-OM-see anything
        'I haven't seen anything'

Givón's scheme for transference of generalization from definite to human is quite speculative if it is required that OM-marking must have been obligatory for definite objects before generalizing to humans. The syntacticization process is not as clear-cut as Givón's proposal suggests.

The data discussed in the following section suggest that reinterpretation as a mechanism of linguistic change does not depend on obligatoriness of OM-marking according to some linguistic dimension such as animacy or definiteness; it is more readily understandable when both definite and human patterning of OM-marking remain variable.

3.   DISCOURSE CONSTRAINTS ON OM-MARKING

Preliminaries to Analysis

In analyzing MS speakers' use of the OM, the following features were taken into consideration.

1.   Whether or not a particular verb could be OM-marked in context. If a verb could take an OM-marked object and that object was identifiable

in the discourse context, then this was considered a case of possible OM-marking. The following are typical examples in which a verb was not OM-marked but might have been.

(16)   *ua   rangi ya zambarau a-I-chukua jus   yake **a-∅-tia**   ndani ya*
         flower color of purple   he-IT-took juice its   he-∅-put inside of
             macho ya T
             eyes   of T
         'He took the juice of a purple flower and **put** (IT) in T's eyes.
         (FY 16f, Msa)

(17)   *yule mama   a-ka-Wa-tukua   watoto . . . **h-a-ku-∅-weka***
         that woman   she-then-THEM-take children . . . neg-she-Past-put
             ndani ya maji
             inside of water
         'The woman took the children . . . she didn't **put** (them) in the water.'
         (SG 19f, Msa)

In these cases, the boldface V can take an object, and the object is under-stood in context, as shown in the glosses. The PR–S pattern of OM-marking could have been used, but was not. It is noteworthy that in both cases the preceding V is OM-marked according to the Post–V pattern, with the lexical object expressed.

Examples (16) and (17) can be contrasted with the following example in which an OM refers to every understood mention of the object NP *kibiriti* 'matchbox'.

(18)   *Basi A a-ka-kasirika a-ka-∅-chukua   kibiriti   **a-ka-KI-tupa**.*
         So   A she-then-mad she-then-∅-take matches she-then-IT-throw

         *yule jamaa a-k-enda   **a-ka-KI-okota***
         that guy   she-then-go she-then-IT-pick+up

         'So A got mad and she took the matches and **threw** THEM. Then the guy went and **picked** THEM up.'   (JK 23m, DSM)

The underlined verbs are OM-marked by the PR–S pattern. However, here it is noteworthy that the verb *chukua* 'take' is not OM-marked by the POST–V pattern, although it could have been.

2.   A distinction was made between the PR–S, OR, and POST–V frames in order to see if there might be any effect of frame in the distribution of the OM.

3.   Human and inanimate object NPs were distinguished, since it is impressionistically observable that human objects tend to be OM-marked more frequently than inanimates.

4. Informational status of the object was distinguished into definite, indefinite, and nonreferential categories, since observers have found that definiteness is involved in OM-marking in many Bantu languages, as was discussed in the preceding section.

DU analysis

Ten discourse units (DUs) were chosen for analysis. The DU is dealt with at length in Wald (1976). Essentially, it is a unit in discourse consisting of more than one sentence and spoken by a single speaker. It has an initial and a terminal boundary, is treated as a unit interactionally by participants to conversation, and has thematic unity and coherence. For present purposes, the DU is a convenient unit in which to distinguish old and new information. Information is old if it has previously been referred to in the DU; otherwise, it is new. Cases of given but not old information were not encountered in the DUs.

The DUs were all extracted from conversations with seven native Swahili speakers born and raised in Mombasa, Kenya. Beyond this, all that the speakers share in common is that they were in the presence of familiars when speaking. Otherwise the DUs and speakers vary according to topic, circumstances of speech (such as who was being addressed), ethnic background, sex, age, and so on. The purpose of the diversification is to investigate what properties the DUs have in common with respect to object NPs, regardless of variety. There are a number of features, not intuitively obvious, that were discovered to be common to all DUs. These will be discussed below.

Briefly, the speakers, DUs, and circumstances of speech are as follows:

SG 19f, Arab-Bajun.   She is telling me a traditional folktale during preparations for a wedding. She is surrounded by other women preparing the bride for the ceremony. She lives in the Kuze section of Old Town, Mombasa.

FY 16f, Omani Arab.   She tells the story of "Midsummer Night's Dream," which she studied in school. The circumstances are the same as for SG above. She has lived in the Inglandi section of Old Town all her life.

B 20m, Barawa.   He is telling me the plot of a story he read in a picture magazine called *Film Tanzania.* Present are some of his friends from his neighborhood, Mkanyageni in Old Town.

J 16m, Arab-Bajun.   He relates two DUs 6 months apart. The first is addressed to me and concerns his activities as a musician and dancer. One of his friends, a Tanzanian native Swahili speaker, is present. The second DU is the story from a movie that he and the other people present had seen. He is addressing the group in general but, in particular, a peer from his neighborhood with whom he was arguing about the details of the plot. He is from the Kibokoni section of Old Town.

AH 53m, Tangana-Swahili.   He tells me two DUs on the same occasion. One is a personal narrative about his life while he lived in Uganda, why he went and why he left. The other is a folktale explaining a poetic verse he had recited earlier. He lives in the Kibokoni section of Old Town.

MK 23m, Kilindini-Swahili.   He is talking at length about the Swahili language, which has a special interest for him as a practicing poet. Also present is one of his younger male cousins, also participating in the conversation.

MA 50m, Digo.   He relates two DUs on two different occasions. On both occasions he is surrounded by his peers and co-workers at the Mwembe Tayari market. One DU is addressed directly to me and concerns the changes he has seen during his life in Mombasa, particularly among women. The second DU is addressed to the group in general and relates to his favorite topic, the boxing exploits of Muhammad Ali. MA was born in the KiSauni suburb of Mombasa and has been bilingual since early childhood in Digo and Swahili. He has lived most of his life in the Majengo section of Mombasa City.

Results of Analysis

OM-marking is invariant for first- and second-person objects. Since it is both human and definite, we might expect this obligatoriness. However, we will see that other definites and human objects are not invariably OM-marked.

The following tables[4] reveal both variation in OM-marking and general properties of discourse into which OM-marked verbs are embedded.

TABLE 1

PERCENTAGE OF OM-MARKING OUT OF POSSIBLE CASES FOR FOUR SYNTACTIC CONTEXTS

	POST–V	PRO–S	PRE–S	OR
Percentage OM (Human)	85	88	79	(100)
N of tokens	161	271	14	(1)
N of DUs	9	9	7	1
Percentage OM (Inanimate)	7	20	25	29
N of tokens	260	44	8	14
N of DUs	10	7	7	3

[4] In the tables on OM-marking, all DUs are summed together before averaging. An alternative method of averaging that gives equal weight to each DU regardless of number of tokens consists of averaging each DU separately and then taking a second average of each individual DU average. It turned out in the present study that the two averages never differed by more than a few percentage points. The unweighted average (average of the individual DU averages) does not appear in the tables.

The most salient points displayed on Table 1 are

1. Human objects are usually OM-marked.
2. Inanimate objects are rarely OM-marked.
3. For humans, no effect of syntactic frame is evident, as if OM-marking operates without regard to syntactic frame.
4. For inanimates, POST–V is more unfavorable to OM-marking than any other frame.
5. The OR pattern is extremely rare in discourse and is largely confined to inanimates.[5]

Although Table 1 does not reveal whether or not all and/or only OM-marked humans are also definite, it is clear that definiteness does not have a decisive effect on OM-marking of inanimates, since all non-POST–V frames necessarily have definite objects; but, OM-marking remains much lower than for humans. Since POST–V is the only frame that allows non-definite objects as well as definite ones, we might assume that definiteness plays some role in promoting OM-marking for inanimates, although certainly not a compulsive one.

The feature "human" appears to have a much greater effect on OM-marking than the feature "definite."

The interplay of human and definite is seen in Table 2, showing the skewing of human and inanimate objects according to syntactic frame.

TABLE 2
PERCENTAGE OF HUMAN TO TOTAL OBJECTS ACCORDING
TO SYNTACTIC FRAME

	POST–V	PRO–S	PRE–S	OR
Percentage	38.2	86.0	63.6	06.7
N of Obj	421	315	22	15

One outstanding result displayed in Table 2 is that, regardless of what might be imagined a priori about discourse, the majority (421) of objects are POST–V and, thus, are lexically specified. It is not the case, as one might naively imagine, that the lexical objects are mentioned once and then go on

[5] Explanation of the OR pattern heavily favoring inanimates will only be treated briefly here, since it involves discussion of subject NPs as well and of passivization. Briefly, underlying human objects tend to be passivized or promoted to subject position if they are coreferential with the antecedent of a relative clause, and, thus, humans tend heavily to exclude OR in favor of Subject-Rel. A similar but less marked trend is evident in Table 1 in the topicalization, front shifting of human objects rather than inanimate objects in PRE–S. The general principle that extends to subject NPs that normally precede the verb is to put an animate NP BEFORE an inanimate one. Needless to say, this is a tendency, not a rule of grammar.

to be anaphorically mentioned such that PRO–S would be a more common pattern than POST–V. However, only a minority (38.2%) of these lexical objects are human. The picture radically changes when PRO–S is taken into account. Although PRO–S objects are less numerous than POST–V, the objects referred to are overwhelmingly (86%) human. Comparing POST–V and PRO–S, it is evident that, although the majority of first-mentioned objects are inanimate, very few survive to a second mention, that is, to definiteness. Human objects, although fewer in number, have DURABILITY in discourse and tend to achieve definite status. Table 2 shows a strong correlation between human and definite. Table 3 shows that this correlation exists within the POST–V frame itself and that informational status has an even greater effect on OM-marking of human objects than of inanimates.

TABLE 3
PERCENTAGE OF OM-MARKING ACCORDING TO INFORMATIONAL STATUS FOR POST–V, THAT IS, LEXICALLY FILLED POSTVERBAL OBJECTS

	Definite	Indefinite	Nonreferential
Percentage OM (human)	90	42	10
N of tokens	132	19	10
N of DUs	8	5	4
Percentage OM (inanimate)	11	03	00
N of tokens	94	103	63
N of DUs	10	9	8

Table 3 shows that humans are almost always OM-marked when definite[6] and less often marked when nondefinite. In spoken discourse, human objects tend overwhelmingly to be definite even when lexically specified [cf. example (12f), given before], whereas the bulk of inanimates are nondefinite. The differential rates of OM-marking of humans and of inanimates indicate that the high discourse correlation between human and definite on the one hand and inanimate and indefinite on the other has led to overgeneralization of

---

[6] In some cases, the absence of OM-marking with definite animates may be due to phonological deletion processes. The phonological problem is that inflectional morphemes tend to be unstressed in spoken Swahili. The vowels are extremely short in duration and are semi-voiced or totally unvoiced. Sometimes only the initial consonant of the OM is audible. The initial consonant of the human OMs are W(A)-plural and M(W)-singular, both weak (non-obstruent) labials. Although they are usually audible with good sound recordings, it is observed that some of the cases coded as ∅ OM-marking have the possible OM immediately followed by a verb beginning with a labial. Possibly, the auditory absence of the human OM in these cases is due to labial assimilation. This line of research has not been further followed up, but Table 3 clearly shows that informational status also has a bearing on the deletion or non-occurrence of the OM.

both patterns: OM-marking has spread to nondefinite humans and has been suppressed in definite as well as in indefinite inanimates. These data substantiate Givon's claim of the association of human and definite among objects but do not support his claim that either feature obligatorily induces OM-marking. There is no evidence that definiteness independent of humanness has a great effect on OM-marking. Moreover, the proposed spread of OM-marking from definite humans to nondefinite ones is far from categorical. One might suspect that there are other features of discourse that promote OM-marking and that tend to occur most often with humans and definites (the latter two linked by DURABILITY of human object referents in discourse) but that may also occur with inanimates and nondefinites.

Further information in Table 3 suggests such a feature, which will be called DISTINCTIVENESS. It is noteworthy that nondefinite human objects are relatively RARE in discourse, occurring in only 5 (indefinite) and 4 (nonreferential) of the 10 DUs analyzed, whereas nondefinite inanimates are more expectable regardless of the specific DU, occurring in 9 (indefinite) and 8 (nonreferential) of the ten DUs analyzed. Nondefinite human objects are DISTINCTIVE in that they are not expectable regardless of the particular DU. Nondefinite inanimate objects are much less distinctive, occurring in most DUs.

Distinctiveness as a Discourse Feature

It has been noted earlier that, in general, the occurrence of animate objects is more distinctive than that of inanimate objects. Inanimate objects are likely to occur regardless of the particular DU. To be sure, it is possible to construct artificially discourses so as to favor human objects and to avoid inanimate objects altogether, but they are hard to find in nature. Speakers are certainly not concerned with such a goal in producing a DU. The OM-marking of a human, even as nondefinite information, automatically calls attention to the following object NP that is less likely to occur than an inanimate object NP. This is a somewhat abstract cue, since it is devoid of immediate discourse context, but it does call attention to the fact that the DU is distinctive, that is, that it has animate as well as inanimate objects. This may have played a role in furthering the development of OM-marking with human objects, especially for nondefinite ones. The distinctiveness principle on a less abstract level may also play a role in the rare marking of inanimates.

This possibility is first suggested by Ashton (1944:45); she writes that "In statements or questions in which attention is directed to the object rather than the action [i.e., the verb—BW], the object prefix is used as well as the noun. The noun in these cases may follow or precede the verb."

Ashton is here restricting comment to the POST–V and PRE–S constructions. Her examples in this and in the section as a whole are restricted to inanimate objects. She does not mention human objects at all, even to observe that they are usually OM-marked. Clearly, she perceives the marking of inanimates as a more difficult problem. Although the above quote is engaging, it is often difficult to evaluate whether or not the speaker wants to draw more attention to the verb or to the object. Therefore, it is not possible to check whether the OM is actually being used for this purpose. Ashton (1944:45) goes on to qualify the statement just given and includes reference to inanimate PRO–S objects:

> As the degree of definiteness to be conveyed is entirely dependent on the context, and is further expressed by tone and gesture, the above principles must be regarded as very general in scope. Beginners should err rather on the side of *omission* [italics mine] in regard to the object prefix, and not imagine that it should be used every time the English translation contains an "it" or a "them."

Thus, in sum, she notes that native speakers rarely use the OM for inanimate objects, so that the English speaking learner will less often use an inappropriate construction by omitting the OM rather than by consistently using it. She ends her discussion with two sentences featuring the PRE–S frame in an attempt to support her contention that special attention is being directed to the object NP.

(19)   a.   *chombo a-me-KI-panza   mwamba*
            vessel   he-Perf-OM-run rock
            'the vessel, he has run it on the rock.'

       b.   *farasi ha-m-WA-wez-i   ndovu*
            horses neg-you-THEM-can-neg elephants

            m-ta-WA-lisha-ni?
            you-Fut-THEM-feed-what

            'the horses, if you can't feed them then the elephants, what will you feed them?"

There is no doubt in the case of PRE–S, that is, topicalization of the object, that special attention is being drawn to it. Table 1 confirms this by showing that PRE–S is a relatively rare type of construction in the DUs; usually, an expressed object follows the verb. However, in the spontaneous speech of the DUs as opposed to the trite and possibly more archaic speech of Ashton's aphorisms, PRE–S does not have any distinctive effect on OM-marking, either for animates or for inanimates.

Nevertheless, her suggestion is attractive, even if for no other reason than the observation that the OM-marking of an inanimate object is so rare in discourse that its very occurrence MUST draw attention to the object. The question then becomes: Why is attention being drawn to the object? If the answer is to be enlightening, it must not be ad hoc for each example.

The following examples show that, though human object NPs may be distinctive in general, inanimate object NPs may be distinctive given the topic of discourse.

(20)   *ukasema kuwa mimi naMwekea na ufunguo huno.* **atalramba** *pesa yako.*

         'and you might say, I'm keeping her with this key, (but) she'll **use up** (literally, **lick up**) all your money.   (MA 50m, Msa)

The theme of this section of MA's DU is that today's women, in his opinion, are no longer motivated to relationships with men by affection or moral values but by the attraction of *pesa* 'money'. The topic of money in relation to women figures heavily in his discourse and, thus, is distinctive as well as durable in the particular discourse.

(21)   *hakuna mmoja ambayo anazungumza lugha yake bila ya kusema lugha ya mwenzake. Yeye* **atalsema** *lugha ya mwenzake kwa maana yake lakini kwa mwenzake ina maana mbali.*

         'there's nobody who speaks his own language without speaking the language of his interlocutor. He may **speak** his companion's language with his own meaning, but to his companion it has a different meaning.'   (MK 23m, Msa)

In this discussion of different dialects of Swahili, MK is making the point that most words in one dialect of Swahili also have a meaning in other dialects but that sometimes the meaning is different; for example, *shoga* means 'female friend' in Zanzibar but 'effeminate homosexual male' in Mombasa. In his extended discussion about different dialects, he often marks the inanimate object *lugha* 'language, dialect' with an OM.

(22)   *yeye manake ndiye alianzisha soul mwanzo. Yeye manake ndiye alianza* **kulfungua** *ile soul. Sasa yeye alipokufa ndio Otis* **akalshika** *jina 'ake.*

         'He (= Sam Cooke) is the one who started soul first. He's the one who started to **open up** (i.e., to the public) the soul (music). Now when he died, then Otis (Redding) **took** his name (i.e., as king of soul music).'   (J 16m, Msa)

In context, J is discussing at length his version of the succession of 'kings of soul music.' His use of OMs may be seen as highlighting the important concepts of his theme, *ile soul* 'that soul (music)' and *jina 'ake* 'his name', that is, the name "King of Soul."

Thus, it is evident with inanimates, as with animates, that the OM is used to mark objects that are distinctive and particular to the topic of the DU.

4. CONCLUSIONS

Several principles are at work in the use of the Mombasa Swahili OM. The most striking principle is the spread of the OM from definite humans to nondefinite humans. In this case, syntacticization is near, if not already arrived. A final example, not previously mentioned in this chapter, of how strong the tendency is for humans to allow OM-marking is the case of OM-marking of humans in the inalienable possession construction, when the human is not an object at all, but merely resembles an object in its position with respect to the verb (cf. Whiteley 1972).

(23)   a.   *mguu wa mtoto u-li-vimba*
                     leg   of child it-Past-swell
                     'The child's leg swelled.'

               b.   *mguu u-li-M-vimba   mtoto*
                     leg   it-Past-OM-swell child
                     'The child's leg swelled.'

               c.   *mtoto a-li-*U-vimba   mguu*
                     child he-Past-*OM-swell leg
                     'The child swelled (in) the leg.'

The verb *vimba* 'swell' does not normally take an object. However, the human possessor of a body part presented in subject position may be placed after the verb and may induce OM-marking. This is a purely syntactic fact. On the other hand, the inalienable possessor may remain in subject position, as in (23c), and the body part may be placed after the verb. In this case, the body part, being inanimate, cannot induce OM-marking on the verb.

It has been argued previously that the OM began in Bantu as an anaphoric pronoun. In Pre-Swahili it was reduced to a single occurrence immediately before the verb, and restrictions were placed on which of several possible objects it could refer to. It was extended to Post–V position as a marker of old information, that is, definiteness. Because of the high correlation between humanness and definiteness, a purely discourse feature, and the high correlation of inanimacy with nondefiniteness, the extension of the OM to indefinite human objects and the suppression of the OM with definite inanimate objects causes a qualitative change in the distribution of the OM in Swahili, without having much quantitative effect on its overall use in discourse. Durability of the object in discourse, that is, repeated reference, favors OM-marking for both humans and inanimates (although at highly differential rates) so that the feature "human" is much more influential in promoting OM-marking than is either definiteness or durability (a subtype of definiteness). Finally, the additional feature of DISCOURSE DISTINCTIVE-NESS has been proposed, through which OM-marking may achieve complete syntacticization for human objects on the grounds that human nondefinite objects are not independent of the topic of discourse and are not to be expected in a randomly selected discourse. Inanimate indefinites, on the other hand, appear to be much more expectable independently of the topic of the DU and are generally only OM-marked when they satisfy the criteria of definiteness, durability, and discourse distinctiveness by being topical to the particular DU under consideration. In sum, the OM is nearing syntacticization with human objects under the influence of generalizations about discourse at the same time as it remains a discourse marker for inanimate objects.

NOTE

The parenthesized material following the English gloss of speech example (6) and all subsequent quotes of MS speakers identifies the speaker of the quote by the initial or initials of the speaker's first name followed by age at the time of speaking, then sex, and, following the comma, the city of the speaker's preadolescence as well as current dwelling [Msa = Mombasa, DSM = Dar es Salaam].

ACKNOWLEDGMENTS

I would like to express my appreciation to Annie Hawkinson, Sukari Salone, Sara Mirzah, Talmy Givón, and Larry Hyman for work and discussions that stimulated my interest in pursuing this topic.

REFERENCES

Ashton, E. O. (1944) *Swahili Grammar (Including Intonation)*, Longmans, London.
Bokamba, E. G. (1975) "Observations on the Immediate Dominance Constraint, Topicalization, and Relativization," *Studies in African Linguistics* 6, 1–22.
Byarushengo, E., L. M. Hyman, and Sarah Tenenbaum (1976) "Tone, Accent and Assertion in Haya, in L. M. Hyman, ed., *Studies in Bantu Tonology*, SCOPIL 3.
Doke, C. M. (1955) *Zulu Syntax and Idiom*, Longmans, London.
Duranti, Alessandro and E. R. Byarushengo (1977) "On the Notion of Direct Object," in E. Byarushengo, A. Duranti, and L. Hyman, eds., *Haya Grammatical Structure*, SCOPIL 6.
Givón, T. (1972) "Studies in ChiBemba and Bantu Grammar," *Studies in African Linguistics*, Supplement 3.
Givón, T. (1976) "Topic, Pronoun and Grammatical Agreement," in C. Li, ed., *Subject and Topic*, Academic Press, New York.
Hawkinson, Ann K. (1976) *A Semantic Characterization of Verbal Agreement and Word Order in Several Bantu Languages*, masters thesis, University of Dar es Salaam.

Hawkinson, A. K. and L. M. Hyman (1974) "Hierarchies of Natural Topic in Shona," *Studies in African Linguistics* 5, 147–170.

Hyman, Larry M. (1974) "On the Change from SOV to SVO: Evidence from Niger–Congo," in C. N. Li, ed., *Word Order and Word Order Change*, University of Texas, Austin, Texas.

Kimenyi, Alexandre (1976) *A Relational Grammar of KiNyarwanda*, Doctoral dissertation, University of California, Los Angeles, California.

Morolong, Malillo and L. M. Hyman (1977) "Animacy, Objects and Clitics in SeSotho," *Studies in African Linguistics* 8, 199–218.

Wald, Benji (1973) "Syntactic Change in the Lake Languages of Northeast Bantu," *Studies in African Linguistics* 4, 237–268.

Wald, Benji (1976) "The Discourse Unit: A Study in the Segmentation and Form of Spoken Discourse," manuscript, University of California, Los Angeles, California.

Whiteley, W. H. (1972) "Case Complexes in Swahili," *Studies in African Linguistics* 3, 1–46.

SUBJECT INDEX

CONTENTS OF PREVIOUS VOLUMES

Contents of Previous Volumes

Contents of Previous Volumes